THE
GOSPEL
OF
MARK

An Expositional Commentary

A revised edition of *Mark: A Portrait of the Servant*

D. Edmond Hiebert

BOB JONES UNIVERSITY PRESS
Greenville, South Carolina 29614

Library of Congress Cataloging-in-Publication Data
Hiebert, D. Edmond, (David Edmond), 1910-
    The Gospel of Mark : an expositional commentary / D. Edmond Hiebert.
        p.   cm.
    Rev. ed. of: Mark, a portrait of the servant. c1979.
    Includes bibliographical references and indexes.
    ISBN 0-89084-768-1
    1. Bible.   N.T.   Mark—Commentaries.   I. Hiebert, D. Edmond (David Ed-
mond), 1910-   Mark, a portrait of the servant.   II. Title.
BS2585.3.H5   1994
226.3'07—dc20   94-22793
                                                                                        CIP

NOTE:
The fact that materials produced by other publishers are referred to in this volume does not
constitute an endorsement by Bob Jones University Press of the content or theological position
of materials produced by such publishers. The position of Bob Jones University Press, and the
University itself, is well known. Any references and ancillary materials are listed as an aid to the
reader and in an attempt to maintain the accepted academic standards of the publishing industry.

The Gospel of Mark: An Expositional Commentary
D. Edmond Hiebert

This book is a revised edition of *Mark: A Portrait of the Servant* (© 1974, 1979),
published by Moody Press.

Edited by Greg Kuzmic

Cover by Doug Young

© 1994 Bob Jones University Press
Greenville, South Carolina 29614

ISBN 0-89084-768-1

15   14   13   12   11   10   9   8   7   6   5   4   3   2   1

Contents

Preface

This interpretation of the Gospel According to Mark presents the force and meaning of the original in a nontechnical manner for the careful student who may not be proficient in the use of the Greek. Greek terms and technical matters have been sparingly introduced. While attention has been given to important theological concepts, this undertaking is not intended as a contribution to contemporary studies in Marcan theology. No attempt has been made to read this Gospel in the light of the doctrinal assumptions underlying its treatment in recent redaction criticism. Rather, it is an attempt to interpret the Gospel According to Mark simply as it stands.

The introduction, dealing with the usual introductory matters, is simply intended to offer sufficient orientation for a fruitful study of the Gospel itself. A fairly detailed outline of Mark provides the reader with an analytical view of the contents of the Gospel. This outline is used in the discussion to indicate the progression of Mark's narrative and to identify the contents of the individual sections. The interpretation is built around a clause-by-clause consideration of the Gospel, and nearly the entire Gospel is thus quoted. But since the continuous Gospel text is not reproduced, the student will find it helpful to have a copy of Mark continually before him.

Anyone who attempts to provide an interpretation of one of the Gospels cannot escape a deep awareness of how much he owes to the diligent labors of others before him. The notes and bibliography will indicate something of my heavy indebtedness to many different sources.

Abbreviations

For the full publishing information on these versions, see pp. 491-92 of the bibliography.

ASV	American Standard Version (1901)
Beck	William F. Beck, *The New Testament in the Language of Today* (1964)
Darby	J. N. Darby, *The "Holy Scriptures": A New Translation from the Original Languages* (1949)
Goodspeed	Edgar J. Goodspeed, *The New Testament, An American Translation* (1923)
KJV	King James Version (1611)
Luther	*Die Bibel, oder die ganze Heilige Schrift des Alten and Neuen Testaments* (1897)
LXX	Septuagint
Moffatt	James Moffatt, *The New Testament: A New Translation*
NASB	*New American Standard Bible* (1971)
NEB	*New English Bible* (2nd ed. 1979)
Norlie	Olaf M. Norlie, *Norlie's Simplified New Testament in Plain English—For Today's Reader* (1961)
Rotherham	Joseph Bryant Rotherham, *The Emphasized New Testament* (1878)
RSV	Revised Standard Version (1946)
TEV	Today's English Version (1966)
T.R.	Textus Receptus
Weymouth	Richard Francis Weymouth, *The New Testament in Modern Speech* (5th ed. 1929)
Williams	Charles B. Williams, *The New Testament: A Private Translation in the Language of the People*

Wuest   Kenneth S. Wuest, *Wuest's Expanded Translation of the Greek New Testatment* (1956)

Introduction

In the ancient church, the Gospel of Mark, the shortest and simplest of the four Gospels, did not command the attention received by the other three. Since it was commonly regarded as a mere abbreviation of the First Gospel, Mark did not elicit the popularity enjoyed by the more comprehensive Matthew. But the views of modern critical scholarship have terminated this comparative neglect of the Second Gospel and have catapulted it into the limelight of scholarly interest and critical study. It is no longer held to be an abridgment of a fuller account but is accepted as an independent work, complete in itself, written with a specific purpose, and eminently suited for an initial study of the gospel story.

Attestation

The Second Gospel, like its companions, contains no statement of authorship. But the uniform tradition of the early church attributes it to Mark, the attendant of the Apostle Peter.

The earliest direct witness to the Gospel of Mark and its origin is Papias (ca. 70-150), bishop of Hierapolis, who wrote about A.D. 140.[1] Eusebius quoted his testimony as follows:

> And the elder [i.e., the elder John] used to say this: Mark, having become Peter's interpreter, wrote accurately as many things as he remembered, not, indeed, in order, of the things spoken and done by the Lord. For he neither heard the Lord nor did he follow Him, but afterwards, as I said, he followed Peter, who used to give his teachings according to the needs [i.e., of his hearers], but not as though he were

---

[1] Some scholars accept slightly earlier dates. D. F. Wright, "Papias," in J. B. Douglas, *The New International Dictionary of the Christian Church,* p. 746, gives the dates for Papias as "(c. 60–c. 130)." James A. Brooks, *Mark,* The New American Commentary, p. 18, dates the writings of Papias as "about A.D. 120-130."

making a connected account of the Lord's oracles. So then Mark made no mistake in thus recording some things as he remembered them, for he made it his one concern not to omit anything of the things he heard nor to falsify anything in them.[2]

This ancient testimony, coming from the province of Asia, contains several significant assertions concerning our Gospel and its author. First, Mark was not a personal follower of Jesus. Second, Mark was a companion of Peter and attendant upon his preaching. Third, Mark recorded accurately, but the things he heard from Peter were recorded "not, indeed, in order." And fourth, Mark was the "interpreter" of Peter's preaching.

The intended meaning of *interpreter* is not clear. It may mean translator, and some scholars favor this meaning.[3] Then, Mark must be thought of as translating the messages of Peter, given in Aramaic, for his Greek audiences. But Peter, like Mark, was bilingual. More probable is the meaning that "Mark became the interpreter of Peter to the church at large by putting Peter's words into writing in his Gospel."[4] Thus, as Peter had treasured up and proclaimed the words of Jesus, "so Mark in his turn did the same for the treasured words of his venerated Rabbi, Peter."[5]

It seems that the direct testimony of John "the elder" is confined to the first sentence quoted by Eusebius and that the remainder of the quotation records the personal comment of Papias. But Papias represented himself as transmitting the Johannine tradition. The content of the testimony reaches back to apostolic times.

The Elder obviously gave this testimony in defense of Mark's Gospel as an answer to detractors. Many men raised questions about this Gospel, its omissions, its failure to record things "in order," as well as the reliability of some of its contents. This defense implies that at the time these criticisms were being voiced there were other gospels with which it was being compared.

The answer of the Elder and of Papias to these criticisms was that the character of Mark's Gospel and its limitations were due to its origin. It recorded the public testimony of the aged Peter, who had not always presented his material in chronological order but had shaped it according to the needs of his hearers. This circumstance accounted for its

---

[2] Eusebius *Ecclesiastical History* 3. 39.

[3] W. W. Sloan, *A Survey of the New Testament*, p. 15; Alfred Wikenhauser, *New Testament Introduction*, pp. 160-61.

[4] R.C.H. Lenski, *The Interpretation of St. Mark's and St. Luke's Gospels*, p. 9.

[5] R. A. Cole, *The Gospel According to St. Mark*, p. 36.

omissions as well as its order. Mark had faithfully reproduced Peter's testimony. The Papias tradition thus asserts that the true source of the Gospel of Mark was Peter himself.

The fact that Eusebius, writing in A.D. 326, quoted this explanation of the origin of Mark's Gospel indicates that it commended itself to the judgment of the church. He apparently knew of no other explanation, nor did he feel the need for further explanation. Yet Eusebius did not accept Papias's explanation simply because of its antiquity. This is evident from his scornful rejection of Papias's millennial views. Eusebius accepted the explanation for its authenticity.

Papias's statement finds support in other early witnesses. In his *Dialogue with Trypho* (chap. 106), Justin Martyr, about A.D. 150, quoted Mark 3:17 as found in the "Memoirs of Peter." A fragmentary Latin prologue to Mark's Gospel, known as the *Anti-Marcionite Prologue* and dated by scholars at A.D. 160-80, says "Mark . . . was the interpreter of Peter. After the death of Peter himself, he wrote down this same Gospel in the regions of Italy." Thus while agreeing with the testimony of Papias, this document adds the further assertion that Mark's Gospel was composed in Italy after Peter's death.

Irenaeus (ca. 140-203), bishop of Lyons in Gaul, in his famous work *Against Heresies* (3. 1. 1), written about A.D. 185, said in a passage naming the writers of our four Gospels: "Now after the death [Gr. *exodus*] of these [i.e., Peter and Paul], Mark, the disciple and interpreter of Peter, himself also transmitted to us in writing the things preached by Peter."

The remark of Irenaeus that Mark wrote his Gospel after the *exodus* of Peter and Paul has been differently understood. Manson,[6] who favors a date for Mark's Gospel before the death of Peter takes *exodus* to mean their "departure" from Rome. But the context seems to favor the meaning "death." Wenham in his recent volume *Redating Matthew, Mark & Luke* accepts that the rendering of *exodus* as " 'death' makes admirable sense in the context." He insists that the point of Irenaeus's statement "is the continuity of the apostles' witness before and after their deaths: Mark has handed on in writing the things proclaimed orally by Peter." But he stresses that "Irenaeus does *not* say that after the death of Peter and Paul, Mark *wrote* his gospel, but that he has *handed on* the preaching of Peter to us in writing."[7] Thus Wenham holds that Mark wrote his Gospel before Peter's death but

---

[6] T. W. Manson, *Studies in the Gospels and Epistles,* pp. 38-39.

[7] John Wenham, *Redating Matthew, Mark & Luke,* p. 139. Wenham's italics.

that his Gospel continued to "transmit" or "hand on" Peter's preaching after the apostle's death.

Clement of Alexandria (ca. A.D. 195) gave a somewhat different account in two statements preserved by Eusebius. Clement is quoted as saying that many of those who heard Peter's preaching in Rome requested "Mark, as one who for a long time had followed him and remembered the things said, to write down his words. Having done this, he delivered the Gospel to those who made the request of him. When Peter knew of it, he neither actively hindered nor encouraged it" (*Ecclesiastical History,* 6. 14). But in another place, Clement is quoted as saying that when Peter learned by a revelation from the Spirit what Mark had done, "He was pleased with the zeal of the men and ratified the writing for use in the churches" (*Ecclesiastical History,* 2. 15). It is very probable that Mark should undertake the task at the urging of others; that he completed the task during Peter's lifetime is less probable. It is contrary to the testimony of Irenaeus and the *Anti-Marcionite Prologue,* as well as the early testimony of Papias, if his words "as he remembered them" are taken to mean Mark rather than Peter, as seems most natural.

Eusebius (*Ecclesiastical History,* 6. 25) also quoted the testimony of Origen (ca. 230) that Mark wrote the Gospel "as Peter guided him." This assertion that Peter was personally connected with the actual production of the Gospel seems a natural heightening of the early tradition to underscore the apostolic sanction of our Gospel.

Thus the tradition that the Second Gospel was written by Mark, "the interpreter of Peter," goes back to the beginning of the second century and is derived from the three centers of early Christianity, Asia, Rome (with Gaul), and Alexandria. The validity of this tradition is strengthened by the fact that there is no reason that it should have been assigned to a minor like Mark if he did not write it. The ancient caption to this Gospel, *Kata Markon* ("according to Mark"), supports this uniform tradition. The title clearly was meant to indicate authorship, not merely source of information; otherwise it would have been *Kata Petron* ("according to Peter").

Author

The identification of the Mark of Papias with the John Mark of the New Testament has been commonly assumed. Taylor remarks, "To-day this view is held almost with complete unanimity."[8] Those

---

[8] Vincent Taylor, *The Gospel According to St. Mark,* p. 15.

objections which have been raised have succeeded in winning but little support.[9]

There is no evidence for another Marcus in the Roman church who had the same close connection with Peter that Papias and the New Testament assert. Nor is it easy to see why the church at Rome would be willing to sanction such a work by an unknown Christian named Marcus when it was well known that Mark, the cousin of Barnabas, had the necessary close relationship with Peter to produce this Gospel. The picture of the New Testament Mark is in full agreement with the Papias tradition.[10]

The assertion of Papias that Mark was not a follower of Jesus agrees with the fact that his name never occurs in the Gospels, although it is clear from Acts that John Mark did reside in Jerusalem. The fact that he was not personally associated with Jesus' ministry may have been due to his age at the time or to a lack of personal commitment to Christ. It seems a natural assumption that the "young man" in Gethsemane mentioned in Mark 14:51-52 was Mark himself, although this has been stamped as a "completely improbable conjecture."[11] It seems the most natural explanation for the insertion of this trifling incident, otherwise quite irrelevant to the circumstances. Surely it is best understood as "a bit of autobiography embodied in his Gospel"[12] to indicate the author's own brief connection with these stirring, nocturnal events.

The traditional author of the Second Gospel is first introduced in Acts as "John, whose surname was Mark" (Acts 12:12). Since the two names are alternatives, there is some inaccuracy in calling him "John Mark"; the New Testament never uses the combination. *John* was a common Hebrew name, while *Mark,* or *Marcus,* was Latin. The use of such a Latin (or Greek) second name was quite common among Greek-speaking Jews.

---

[9] Among these objections are: (1) *Marcus* is too common a name to allow the identification. (Admittedly the name does not establish the identification.) (2) The identification is not explicitly mentioned until the time of Jerome. (Earlier writers apparently took it for granted and did not feel that the identification needed to be stressed.) (3) The writer cannot have been from Jerusalem, since he apparently was unfamiliar with Palestinian geography. (This claim has not been established and has found little acceptance. The Gospel contains nothing that is demonstrably inconsistent with the knowledge of one who lived in Jerusalem during his youth.)

[10] For a fuller treatment of Mark see D. Edmond Hiebert, *In Paul's Shadow: Friends & Foes of the Great Apostle,* pp. 67-78.

[11] Werner Georg Kümmel, *Introduction to the New Testament,* p. 69.

[12] Manson, p. 35.

In Acts, he is three times identified as bearing both names (12:12, 25; 15:37), twice as John (13:5, 13), and once as Mark (15:39). In the Epistles he is always simply called "Mark." Clearly, the Mark of the Epistles is the same as the John Mark of Acts from the fact that the epistolary references (Col. 4:10; 2 Tim. 4:11; Philem. 24; 1 Pet. 5:13) always link him with the same people (Paul, Barnabas, Peter) as in Acts. Either name might be used according to circumstances. In Jewish circles, he would appropriately be known as John; but in a Gentile environment, he would use his Latin name. The complete disappearance of his Jewish name in the Epistles shows that Mark had moved out into the Gentile world as the sphere of his activities.

Mark was the son of a Jerusalem widow whose spacious home was a meeting place for the believers during the early days of the church. Rhoda's reaction to Peter's voice proves that Peter was a familiar visitor there (Acts 12:12-17). Mark thus was familiar with the person and preaching of Peter from early days.

When Barnabas and Saul returned to Antioch after the famine visit to Jerusalem, they took Mark along with them (Acts 12:25). Mark apparently remained in Antioch until the time of the launching of the first missionary journey, when he accompanied Barnabas and Saul as "their minister [attendant, ASV]" (13:5).

For some unstated reason, Mark left the missionary party at Perga and returned to Jerusalem (13:13). Paul regarded Mark's action as unjustified. He vigorously rejected Barnabas's proposal to have Mark accompany them on the second journey. The resultant sharp disagreement over Mark led to the separation of Paul and Barnabas. Barnabas took his cousin (Col. 4:10) and sailed to Cyprus, while Paul found a new coworker in Silas (Acts 15:36-40).

Nothing further is heard of Mark until the time of Paul's first imprisonment in Rome. In his letters to the Colossians (4:10) and to Philemon (v. 24), Paul sent greetings from Mark. In Philemon, Paul included Mark among those whom he called "my fellowlabourers." These references indicate that full reconciliation had taken place between Paul and Mark and that Mark was actively laboring with Paul.

When Paul left Rome upon his release, Mark apparently remained there; and upon Peter's arrival in Rome, Mark joined his work. In 1 Peter 5:13 Peter sent greetings to the churches in Asia Minor from the church "at Babylon," apparently a cryptic designation for Rome, and added greetings from "Marcus my son." This letter seems to have been written shortly before Peter's martyrdom in Rome.[13]

In 2 Timothy 4:11, written shortly before his death in Rome, Paul requested Timothy to come to him and added the illuminating instruction, "Take Mark, and bring him with thee: for he is profitable to me for the ministry." This last biblical glimpse of Mark leaves us with the picture of a valued servant who has overcome his initial failure and has proved himself a true servant of the servants of the Lord.

The uniform tradition that Mark, "the interpreter of Peter," was the author of the Second Gospel has generally commended itself as consistent with the internal features of the book. The general outline of this Gospel conforms to the outline of the gospel story as given by Peter in Acts 10:34-43. Thus there may be some ground for regarding the Gospel as a catechetical expansion of the preaching of the Apostle Peter. Harrisville indeed asserts, "The best way by which to describe the Gospel of Mark is to call it a *sermon,* the kind of sermon which audiences in the first century of our era customarily heard from Christian evangelists and orators."[14] But there is no need to assume that when Mark commenced the writing of his Gospel he deliberately restricted himself to a reproduction of Peter's preaching. It must be remembered that Mark was acquainted with the preaching of the apostles in Jerusalem from early days. Peter's preaching indeed was the main source upon which he drew, but before Mark became Peter's assistant, he already knew a great deal about Jesus.

Mark no doubt sought to arrange his material in some chronological or logical order when he began to compose his book. While the material in Mark's Gospel appears generally to be arranged in chronological order, there seems to be some ground for the comment of Papias that Mark did not write "in order" in recording "the things spoken and done by the Lord." At times Mark's arrangement seems to be topical, as in 2:1–3:6, where he seems to group together a series of events setting forth opposition to Jesus. It may also be that Papias, familiar with the carefully constructed sequences in the Fourth Gospel, felt that Mark's narrative was somewhat irregular in its arrangement.

The acceptance of the traditional connection of Peter with this Gospel is not necessary for its interpretation, but certain features in it

---

[13] On the place and date of 1 Peter, see Charles Brigg, *A Critical and Exegetical Commentary on the Epistles of St. Peter and St. Jude,* International Critical Commentary, pp. 67-80; D. Edmond Hiebert, *An Introduction to the New Testament,* vol. 3, *An Introduction to the Non-Pauline Epistles,* pp. 122-27; J.N.D. Kelly, *A Commentary on the Epistles of Peter and of Jude,* Harper's New Testament Commentaries, pp. 26-34.

[14] Roy A. Harrisville, *The Miracle of Mark,* p. 14. Harrisville's italics.

take on added interest if that connection is given credence.[15] The addition of the two little words *and Peter* (16:7), found only in Mark, becomes freighted with additional emotional overtones. Also, the eyewitness vividness of many of Mark's episodes is thus naturally accounted for. In a number of instances, Mark's use of *they* introducing a story concerning Jesus seems most naturally to represent Peter's *we* in his recital of the event as the experience of one who was a disciple of Jesus. (See 1:21, 29; 5:1, 38; 6:53-54; 8:22; 9:14, 30, 33; 10:32, 46; 11:1, 12, 15, 20, 27; 14:18, 22, 26, 32.)

Place and Date

Place

The early witnesses to Mark's Gospel almost uniformly agree that Mark penned it in Rome. The one exception is Chrysostom, who associated its composition with Egypt.[16] But it is incredible that on this point his view should be more reliable than that of the earlier witnesses. Taylor suggests that his view was due to "a misunderstanding of an ambiguous statement of Eusebius" (*Ecclesiastical History,* 2. 16).[17]

The contents of the Gospel are consistent with the tradition. Mark used a number of Latin terms in preference to their Greek equivalents, apparently because they would be more familiar to his readers. (See 6:27; 7:4; 12:14; 15:15, 16, 39.) Consistent with a Roman origin is also the fact that Mark carefully explained Jewish customs and terms (cf. 7:3-4; 12:42; 14:12) and regularly translated Aramaic words and sentences whenever they were introduced (cf. 3:17; 5:41; 7:11, 34; 14:36; 15:22, 34). While these observations prove only that the Gospel was intended for Gentile readers, they agree with the testimony concerning its Roman origin.

More substantial evidence for a Roman origin comes from Mark's reference to Simon of Cyrene as "the father of Alexander and Rufus" (15:21). This is most naturally to be understood as meaning that these men were personally known to Mark's readers. Romans 16:13 indicates that Rufus was a member of the church at Rome.

There is nothing in the Gospel which militates against the tradition concerning its Roman origin. We agree with the conclusion of Brooks: "Rome remains the most likely place for the origin and original readership of this work."[18]

---

[15] A. T. Robertson, *Studies in Mark's Gospel,* rev. ed., pp. 38-43.

[16] Chrysostom, *Homily on Matt.* 1.

[17] Taylor, p. 32.

[18] Brooks, p. 28.

Date

The traditional testimony concerning the date of the Gospel raises a conflict. Irenaeus, according to the more natural meaning of his testimony, placed it after the death of Peter and Paul. This dating is supported by the *Anti-Marcionite Prologue.* The testimony of Papias does not explicitly touch the point, but he is generally held to support the position of Irenaeus, since Irenaeus seems to have drawn his testimony directly from Papias.

Clement of Alexandria and Origen, on the other hand, placed the composition of the Gospel during Peter's lifetime. This view makes possible a much wider range in the proposed dating of the Gospel. Guthrie suggests that the conflicting views may be brought into harmony under the assumption that "Mark began his Gospel before and completed it after Peter's death; a suggestion which merits more consideration than it generally receives."[19] Less probable is Martindale's view that it was completed before Peter's death but not officially published until after Peter's death in A.D. 64.[20]

If we accept the view of Irenaeus that Mark wrote after the death of Peter, then the earliest date would be A.D. 64, the generally accepted date for the martyrdom of Peter during the Neronian persecution. Thus the Gospel has generally been dated between A.D. 65 and 68. Taylor holds that "there is most to be said for the date 65-67." Cranfield agrees.[21]

Those scholars who accept that Mark's Gospel was written during Peter's lifetime variously suggest a date between A.D. 45 and 60. This view assumes that the reference by Irenaeus to Peter's "exodus" meant not his death but his departure from the place where Peter and Mark worked together. This view brings the testimony of Irenaeus into agreement with that of Clement. But it rejects the testimony of the *Anti-Marcionite Prologue.*

Since it is generally assumed that Peter did not come to Rome until around A.D. 63, any prior date thus seems to imply a non-Roman origin for the Gospel. But this is inconsistent with the generally accepted tradition which points to Rome as the place of origin.

As a strong advocate of a Roman origin as well as an early date for the Gospel of Mark, Wenham insists that Peter and Mark actually first worked together in Rome from A.D. 42 to 44. He suggests an

---

[19] Donald Guthrie, *New Testament Introduction,* 3rd ed., p. 73.

[20] C. C. Martindale, *The Gospel According to Saint Mark,* p. xiii.

[21] Taylor, p. 32; C.E.B. Cranfield, *The Gospel According to Saint Mark,* Cambridge Greek Testament Commentary, p. 8.

appropriate setting for this early trip to Rome in Acts 12, when after Peter's miraculous escape from death at the hands of King Herod, and his night visit to the home of Mark, Peter went "into another place" (v. 17). He suggests that Mark may have gone with Peter on this journey, or "if not, he was presumably summoned to join him soon after."[22] The work of Peter stimulated the development of an active church in Rome. But the development of a highly successful work among Gentiles at Antioch "created enormous tensions between Jerusalem and Antioch, and these may well have been the cause of Peter's leaving Rome. Agrippa was dead, and with the church involved in the greatest crisis of its history, the chief of the apostles may have seen it as his duty to leave his own important work in order to tackle the situation. In any case we find Peter in Jerusalem in 46, when Saul and Barnabas brought the famine relief."[23] Wenham concludes his study with the assertion that Mark "was probably written before the apostle's death, quite possibly after a stay in Rome by Peter from 42 to 44 and before Mark started on his missions with Paul and Barnabas."[24]

If the "discovery" of the identity of the "place" where Peter hid from the wrath of Herod Agrippa as Rome is accepted as authentic, an early date for Mark is quite acceptable. Wenham dates the Gospel of Mark about A.D. 45.[25]

On the other hand, some scholars advocate a date after A.D. 70.[26] It is held that such a date is necessary to allow time for the development of the gospel tradition in the church which was embodied in this Gospel.[27] Such an argument will have weight only for those who hold that the writer of this Gospel was simply a collector of the developing traditions of the early church concerning Jesus. In support of a date after A.D. 70, it has been urged that the reference to "the abomination of desolation" in 13:14 was studiously vague because the author wrote after the destruction of Jerusalem. But it is more plausible to argue that he would have been less vague had he written after the prophecy of Christ was fulfilled. No argument concerning the date of the Gospel can be drawn from Christ's eschatological discourse given in chapter 13, unless we deny Christ's ability to predict the future.

---

[22] Wenham, p. 169.

[23] Ibid., p. 169.

[24] Ibid., p. 182.

[25] Ibid., pp. 238, 243.

[26] B. Harvie Branscomb, *The Gospel of Mark,* Moffatt New Testament Commentary, p. xxxi; Ernest Findley Scott, *The Literature of the New Testament,* pp. 56-57.

[27] D. E. Nineham, *The Gospel of St. Mark,* p. 42.

We do not possess the data needed to establish a specific date for Mark's Gospel. While an earlier date is possible, a date between A.D. 64 and 67 for the publication of the Gospel seems most probable.

Purpose

The Gospel of Mark, unlike the Fourth Gospel, contains no statement of purpose. Our understanding of its purpose must be drawn from our evaluation of its contents.

The opening statement of the Gospel suggests that it was Mark's purpose to present the story of Jesus Christ as the "good news," the unique message of Christianity. Mark at once introduced Him in His official and public career as the busy worker for Jehovah. But his initial identification of Jesus as "the Son of God" (1:1) at once underlined the basic truth that the service He rendered must be viewed in the light of His unique personality. He was not only God's Messiah but also the Son of God. The busy worker pictured in this Gospel was the mighty Servant of Jehovah who, as the Son of God, revealed His power over the visible and the invisible world. In recounting the story of His amazing deeds and arresting teaching, Mark let the record produce its own witness to His unique and striking personality. His mighty and beneficent ministry proclaimed the fact that in Him "the kingdom of God is at hand" (1:15). Mark's purpose was not merely to tell the story of a great religious teacher but to proclaim the coming of Jesus Christ as the saving event announced in the Hebrew prophets and expected in Judaism. His basic purpose was evangelistic, to win converts to the Christian faith.

Mark's account portrays Jesus Christ as the suffering Servant of the Lord. He made it clear that the mighty ministry of Jesus soon fell under the shadow of unbelief and open hostility. He was misunderstood, attacked, and rejected by the very people He came to serve and to save, because He did not fulfill their preconceived expectations concerning the Messiah. Suffering was the inevitable lot of the Messiah. The picture of Jesus' suffering and death looms large in the story. As in all of the Gospels, the cross and resurrection are central to Mark's picture of the Christ. The key to the understanding of Mark's portrayal is his deliberate contrast between the personal dignity of Jesus as the Son of God and the stark experiences of suffering and rejection which He voluntarily accepted. The portrait contains a remarkable blend of matchless strength and amazing submission, of the achievement of glorious victory through apparent defeat. Brooks observes, "Such a balanced Christology as Mark's weighs against the theory that he was battling a heresy. Mark was especially concerned to emphasize the suffering and death of Jesus as a ransom for sinners.''[28]

The Gospel of Mark is not a biography of Jesus but rather a delineation of the ''good news'' of salvation made available through the suffering Servant of Jehovah. The picture presented is in harmony with the declared purpose of Jesus that ''the Son of man came not to be ministered unto, but to minister, and to give his life a ransom for many'' (10:45).

Contents

Mark's Gospel is familiarly known as the shortest of the four Gospels, being less than two-thirds the length of the Gospel of Luke. Its comparative brevity is partly due to Mark's omission of the nativity account as well as the genealogy. The story of the Servant of the Lord required no space allotment for His birth or ancestry. Not the pedigree but the performance of this Servant was the primary concern. But the brevity of the Gospel is largely due to the fact that Mark eliminated all but two of the long discourses of Jesus (4:1-34; 13:3-37). And the two discourses included are considerably shorter than the corresponding sections in Matthew.

This Gospel is characteristically a book of action. It moves with breathless activity and, not without reason, has been dubbed the ''go Gospel.''[29] Mark used the Greek adverb *euthus,* translated ''immediately, straightway,'' more often than the other three Gospel authors together. He also made frequent use of *and* to tie one event to another.

The primary stress is upon the deeds of Jesus. It vividly portrays the fact that Christ's work was continuous, persistent, and strenuous. He was incessantly busy. Mark alone recorded that Jesus was so busy that there was no time even to eat (3:20; 6:31). Repeatedly the crowds intruded upon Jesus with their demands. It has been observed that ''to read this Gospel at a single sitting is to feel hemmed in by crowds, wearied by their demands, besieged by the attacks of demons.''[30]

The miracles of Jesus occupy a prominent place in the record. Proportionate to its length, Mark's Gospel gives more space to Christ's miracles than do the other Gospels.

---

[28] Brooks, p. 30.

[29] Manford George Gutzke, *Go Gospel: Daily Devotions and Bible Studies in the Gospel of Mark.*

[30] Gerard S. Sloyan, ''The Gospel of St. Mark,'' in *New Testament Reading Guide,* p. 7.

Mark recorded comparatively little of the systematic teaching of Jesus. He repeatedly mentioned the fact that Jesus taught but without recording what He taught (1:21, 39; 2:2, 13; 6:2, 6, 34; 10:1; 12:35). The numerous fragments of discourses included by Mark sprang out of Jesus' controversies with the Jewish leaders (cf. 2:8-11, 17, 19-22, 25-28; 3:23-30; 7:6-23; 10:2-13; 12:1-11, 38-40). They have their natural setting in the narratives of which they form a part. Jesus' teaching ministry, as presented by Mark, was part of His work as the Servant of Jehovah.

The Second Gospel is characterized by the vividness and detail of many of its accounts. While some events are recorded with brevity, events related in common with the other synoptics frequently are recorded in greatest detail by Mark. His episodes often leave the impression of being given by an eyewitness; they contain those extra touches which suggest the oral reminiscences of a personal observer. Mark's abundant use of the historical present tense has the effect of making the story unfold before the reader's eyes. His presentation of events is vigorous and popular, characterized at times by a looseness of structure and roughness of expression. Several times, Mark uses two expressions where one would suffice (cf. 1:35; 2:4; 4:5; 9:2; 11:1; 13:1, 19, 35; 14:61).

Mark recorded his story with remarkable candor. He threw no halo over the disciples but frankly recorded their obvious dullness in numerous instances (4:13; 6:52; 8:17, 21; 9:10, 32). He did not withhold the fact that, on occasion, they even dared to criticize Jesus (4:38; 5:31). The unfavorable attitude of Jesus' family toward Him is also told with undisguised frankness (3:21, 31-35).

Mark's Gospel gives prominence to the human reactions and emotions of Jesus. It mentions His compassion (1:41; 6:34; 8:2), His sighing (7:34; 8:12), His indignation (3:5; 10:14), His distress and sorrow (14:33-34). It takes notice of His sweeping gaze (3:5, 34; 5:32; 10:23), the touch of His hand (1:31, 41; 7:33; 9:27), His warm interest in little children (9:36; 10:14-16). It alone records how Jesus on the last journey to Jerusalem resolutely went before His disciples amidst a prevailing feeling of apprehension (10:32). If Mark portrayed Jesus as the Son of God, he also pictured Him as a sympathetic man who freely mingled with men and shared their feelings and their sufferings. The common people were drawn to Him and heard Him gladly (12:37). Mark was attentive to the varied reactions of different people to Jesus. They reacted toward Him in amazement (1:27), criticism (2:7), fear (4:41), and astonishment (7:37), as well as bitter hatred (14:1).

The basic theological concepts of the Gospel are those which characterized the faith of the Christian community from the very first. Its high Christology is literally thrust upon the attention of the reader with the opening identification of Jesus Christ as "the Son of God" (1:1). This assertion of His unique nature was confirmed by the testimony of the Father (1:11; 9:7), by demons (3:11; 5:7), by Jesus Himself (13:32; 14:61-62), and by the centurion who supervised the crucifixion (15:39). This supernatural element in His being manifested itself in His authoritative teaching as well as in His miraculous deeds, which were almost always performed to meet some definite human need. Mark's account suggests that Jesus personally preferred not to use the title "the Messiah" in speaking of Himself because in the thinking of the people, the term had become overlaid with connotations that were inimical to His saving mission. Jesus preferred for Himself the title "the Son of man," found fourteen times in this Gospel, and joined it to the concept of the suffering Servant in the prophet Isaiah. Because of who He was, He had the right to forgive sins (2:10), to exercise authority as the Lord of the Sabbath (2:28), to announce that with His appearing the kingdom of God was at hand (1:15) and that He would ultimately return in power and glory (8:38; 13:26; 14:62). But all of this demanded that He must first suffer all things the prophets foretold concerning Him (8:31; 9:31; 10:33, 45).

The contents of Mark's Gospel make it eminently suited for Gentiles. It does not have the strong Jewish-Christian coloring which characterizes Matthew. It does not presuppose a comprehensive knowledge of the Old Testament on the part of its readers. Mark himself quoted only once from the Old Testament (1:2-3), although he frequently indicated that Jesus quoted it. Mark's account of the sending out the Twelve contains no mention of the prohibition concerning preaching to Samarians and Gentiles (6:7-11; cf. Matt. 10:5-6). In Christ's eschatological discourse, Mark recorded that the gospel was to be preached to all nations (13:10) and noted that Jesus cleansed the temple to preserve it as "a house of prayer for all the nations" (11:17, ASV). The author of this Gospel had well learned the lesson that the gospel of Jesus Christ was for all mankind. Mark's was a Gospel well suited to the practical Romans, for whom, evidently, it was originally written.

Outline

Mark does not lend itself easily to a satisfactory outline. Its contents are largely composed of a succession of events which do not readily fall into a climactic sequence. However, a roughly geographical organization of its contents is clear; therefore, after the introductory section, the material is geographically grouped—Galilee, Galilee and surrounding areas, journey to Jerusalem, and Jerusalem.

The theme may be stated as "The Servant of Jehovah."

           1) Plea of Jairus (vv. 21-24)
           2) Woman with the flow of blood (vv. 25-34)
           3) Raising of Jairus's daughter (vv. 35-43)
        d. Rejection of Jesus at Nazareth (6:1-6)
        e. Mission of the Twelve (6:7-13)
        f. Reaction of Antipas to the reports about Jesus (6:14-29)
           1) Excited reaction of Herod Antipas (vv. 14-16)
           2) Explanatory account of John's death (vv. 17-29)
  2. Second withdrawal and return (6:30–7:23)
        a. Feeding of the five thousand (6:30-44)
        b. Walking on the water (6:45-52)
        c. Ministry of healing among the people (6:53-56)
        d. Controversy concerning defilement (7:1-23)
           1) Condemnation of human tradition (vv. 1-13)
           2) Source of true defilement (vv. 14-23)
  3. Third withdrawal and return (7:24–8:13)
        a. Appeal of the Syrophoenician woman (7:24-30)
        b. Cure of the deaf stammerer (7:31-37)
        c. Feeding of the four thousand (8:1-10)
        d. Request for a sign from heaven (8:11-13)
  4. Fourth withdrawal and return (8:14–9:50)
        a. Warning concerning leaven (8:14-21)
        b. Blind man at Bethsaida (8:22-26)
        c. Confession of Peter (8:27-30)
        d. Announcement concerning the cross (8:31–9:1)
           1) Coming passion foretold (8:31-32*a*)
           2) Rebuke to Peter (8:32*b*-33)
           3) Teaching about cross bearing (8:34–9:1)
        e. Transfiguration on the mount (9:2-8)
        f. Discussion concerning Elijah (9:9-13)
        g. Cure of the demoniac boy (9:14-29)
        h. Renewed teaching about the cross (9:30-32)
        i. Teaching in Capernaum to the disciples (9:33-50)
           1) Question of greatness (vv. 33-37)
           2) Mistaken zeal of John (vv. 38-41)
           3) Seriousness of sin (vv. 42-50)
C. Journey to Jerusalem (10:1-52)
  1. Departure from Galilee (v. 1)
  2. Teaching concerning divorce (vv. 2-12)
  3. Blessing of little children (vv. 13-16)
  4. Question concerning eternal life (vv. 17-22)

Part 1
The Coming of the Servant

1
The Coming of the Servant (1:1-13)

In this brief opening section, Mark skillfully prepares the stage for his portrayal of the official ministry of Jesus Christ, the unique Servant of Jehovah. Beginning with the title, which comprises verse 1, the introductory section naturally falls into three paragraphs, standing in logical sequence: verses 2-8 describe the preparatory ministry of John the Baptist; verses 9-11 concisely relate the Servant's entry upon His public ministry; and verses 12-13 summarily record the Spirit-arranged testing of the Servant by Satan to prove His fitness for the work He had assumed.

A. Title of the Book (1:1)

Verse 1 is best regarded as a title for the whole book and may well be punctuated with a period. It aptly summarizes the contents of the entire Gospel. One cannot confine it to the ministry of John, since it goes far beyond his preparatory work. Neither is it closely connected grammatically with the verses immediately following. Some would join it with verses 2-3, while others would connect it directly with verse 4, putting verses 2-3 into a parenthesis. Such connections are unnecessarily involved, and obscure the character of verse 1 as a title. It is improbable that Mark would begin with such a complicated sentence.

"The beginning of the gospel"—not of the book but of the message, the good news of salvation through Jesus Christ. *Beginning* implies a continuation (cf. Acts 1:1). In Galatians 4:4-6, Paul viewed the gospel story as in two parts, God's sending "his Son" and the sending of "the Spirit of his Son." The full apostolic message thus included the sending of the Holy Spirit. Mark covers the first of these two sendings. The story of the sending of the Son of God had its historical beginning with the coming of John the forerunner. The word translated "gospel" meant originally a reward for good news, then simply the good news itself. In the New Testament, it always has this meaning, namely, the good news of salvation in Christ. It implies that "there is an essential historicity to the Christian message."[1] The word *gospel* here does not mean a book; it never has that meaning in the New Testament. But Mark's use of "Gospel" in the title of his account doubtless contributed to the fact that by A.D. 150 the term was applied to the first four books in our New Testament.

"Of Jesus Christ"—not here as the herald of the good news but as the subject of the good news. The message of the gospel centers in a person whom Mark identified with a threefold designation. *Jesus* is the Greek form of the Hebrew *Joshua,* meaning "Jehovah is salvation"; that is, the one through whom Jehovah effects His salvation. It is the Savior's human name, given by the angel before His birth (Matt. 1:21; Luke 1:31). *Christ* is the Greek equivalent of the Hebrew "Messiah,"[2] both meaning anointed. In its original significance, it denoted office, one inducted into office by anointing, hence, the anointed one. This designation points to the office of the Savior, God's agent upon earth for the establishment of God's kingdom. The divine anointing qualified and equipped Him to fulfill His messianic office. Its use here without the article indicates that it is now employed as a proper name.

"The Son of God"—to be interpreted in the full sense of the New Testament meaning. Going beyond the previous designations, this title expresses His peculiar relation to God. He had in Him a nature higher than man's. The original has no article with *Son,* indicating that He was Son of God by nature. Only one who had this nature could perform the mighty ministry of service depicted in this Gospel. The Father's voice bore testimony to this relationship at the baptism (1:11) and reaffirmed it at the transfiguration (9:7). The Jewish leaders condemned Jesus to death because of His insistence that He was the Son of God (Matt. 26:63-66; Mark 14:61-64). His resurrection gloriously vindicated His claim.

Mark's use of the designation *Son of God*[3] in the very title of his book serves to draw immediate attention to his high Christology. It is

---

[1] Donald English, *The Message of Mark,* The Bible Speaks Today, p. 25.

[2] It "is actually translated 'Messiah' in some passages by the NRSV, NEB, REB, and GNB" (James A. Brooks, *Mark,* The New American Commentary, p. 38).

[3] The words *Son of God* are omitted by a few important biblical manuscripts, but the evidence for their genuineness is too strong to justify discarding these important words. Cranfield advances five reasons for accepting them as genuine here: (1) the manuscript evidence for them is very strong; (2) the evidence for omission from the patristic writers is weakened by their practice of omitting words that were not relevant to the point being made; (3) the similarity of ending to that of the preceding terms would easily explain their omission; (4) the designation strikes the theme of this Gospel

his testimony to the unique nature of the subject of his story and is the counterpart in Mark to the nativity story in Matthew and Luke.

B. Ministry of John the Baptist (1:2-8)

Verses 2-8 of chapter 1 form a closely knit unit setting forth the ministry of Christ's forerunner. His ministry fulfilled prophecy (vv. 2-4) and made a profound impact on the hearers (v. 5). His appearance is described in verse 6, while verses 7-8 give the essence of his messianic messages.

Verses 2-4 are best construed as one complete sentence. The prophetic citation (vv. 2-3) forms the introduction, while the historical statement (v. 4) completes the sentence. This joining of prophecy and history underlines the character of the forerunner of Christ and constitutes a confirmation of the messiahship of Jesus. This is the only place where Mark introduced such a quotation from the Old Testament into his own narrative, not counting the quotation in 15:28, which lacks manuscript authority.

"As it is written"—the standard formula for introducing a quotation. *As* (also translated "even as" or "just as") marks the exact fulfillment of that which was prophetically announced. The perfect tense of *written* denotes that the prophetic utterance stands as a permanent record.

"In Isaiah the prophet" (ASV)—Mark's quotation comes from two different prophetic books, verse 2 from Malachi 3:1, and verse 3 from Isaiah 40:3. Jerome (on Matt. 3:3) records that Porphyry, the early enemy of Christianity, seized upon this "mistake" by Mark and hurled it into the face of the Christians. Some ancient scribes sought to remove the difficulty by substituting "in the prophets" (KJV), but the manuscripts are decidedly in favor of "in Isaiah the prophet" as the original reading.

The suggestion of some that the quotation from Malachi was a later addition has no textual evidence to support it. Others hold that Mark quoted from an early Christian "testimony book," a collection of proof texts from the Old Testament used in the churches to undergird the teaching concerning Jesus Christ, and that Mark mistakenly regarded the entire quotation as from Isaiah. Still others attribute it to an understandable lapse of memory on Mark's part. But as Brooks remarks,

---

(1:11; 3:11; 8:38; 9:7; 12:6; 13:32; 14:36, 61; 15:39) and is therefore to be expected in the opening verse; (5) the words may have been omitted on stylistic grounds to eliminate so many genitives in a row. These are strong reasons for accepting them as authentic. (C.E.B. Cranfield, *The Gospel According to Saint Mark,* in Cambridge Greek Testament Commentary, p. 38.)

"Mark and other biblical writers simply did not employ the technical precision of modern research. It was not necessary for their purpose."[4]

Some inexactness is obviously involved, but it need not be attributed to carelessness or ignorance. Mark's wording at once indicates that his real interest centered in the Isaiah prophecy. The quotation from Malachi served as the passageway through which his mind rapidly passed, to fix attention on the more specific prediction in Isaiah. Bruce remarks that "it is something analogous to attraction in grammar."[5] The point of the whole quotation is that John's preparatory ministry, in fulfillment of prophecy, authenticated Jesus' messiahship and prepared for the beginning of His official ministry as the Messiah.

"Behold, I send my messenger"—the speaker is Jehovah Himself. *Behold* bids the hearer or reader give full attention to the important announcement being made. *I send,* present tense, marks the imminence of the promised sending. *Messenger* is the Greek word commonly translated "angel." It denotes a messenger, whether supernatural or human, who is sent with a message. *My* marks him as God's envoy. This divine promise to the coming Messiah found historical fulfillment in John the Baptist, as verse 4 indicates.

"Before thy face"—a change from the original "before me," marking the quotation as interpretative. The Old Testament statement pictured the coming messenger as preparing the way for the coming of "the Lord" Himself. The New Testament rephrasing makes prominent the truth that the coming Lord, "the messenger of the covenant" (Mal. 3:1), was the historical person Jesus Christ. It interprets the divine promise made to the people of Israel as addressed to the Messiah Himself. It is another instance of the New Testament practice of applying to Jesus what in the Old Testament related to Jehovah.

"Before thy face"—intimates the close connection between John and the Messiah. John's ministry would be performed in the personal presence of the coming Lord. The climax of John's ministry was his personal identification of Jesus as the promised Messiah, "the Son of God" (John 1:30-34).

"Which shall prepare thy way"—the divine promise to the Messiah concerning the forerunner's work. He would prepare and make fully ready the road before Him, putting it into a fit condition for the Lord to travel over. Roads in the East were generally poorly maintained. A coming king would send ahead of him a representative to assure that

[4] Brooks, p. 40.

[5] Alexander Balmain Bruce, "The Synoptic Gospels," in *The Expositor's Greek Testament,* 1:342.

the roads had been adequately prepared. Spiritually, this was John's advance task. He was to remove hindrances in the hearts of the people so that they would be ready to receive "the coming one."

Verse 3 quotes the dramatic words of Isaiah 40:3, upon which Mark's thought had been focused. The function assigned the forerunner in Malachi was more vividly set forth in this older prophecy.

"The voice of one crying"—more literally, "a voice of one shouting." *Crying* denotes a loud cry or shout, heard from a distance. John's cry was marked by intensity and emotion. He was eager to arrest attention and gain an effective hearing for his message.

"In the wilderness"—may be connected either with what precedes or with what follows. The Hebrew poetic parallelism connects it with the following summons; the Greek quotation more naturally connects the words with the voice of the crier. Either connection is appropriate: both the one crying and the needed preparation were in the wilderness. Mark's connection effectively prepares for John's appearance in the wilderness.

"Prepare ye the way of the Lord"—a summary command, setting forth the essential demand and requiring immediate compliance. *Ye* directs the command to the people of Israel; the duty to prepare for the coming Messiah rested on them. The aorist imperative, *prepare*, has the force of a curt military command. It conveys the picture of leveling the roads and making them safe for the coach of the Lord before His arrival. "Lord" is the common Septuagint rendering of the name Jehovah, or *Yahweh*. It is clear that Mark understood "Lord" as a reference to Jesus, who was commonly called by that title.

"Make his paths straight"—an elaboration of the continuing duty. The plural verb *make* calls for the continued cooperation of the people. *Paths* denotes "beaten ways, worn paths," while *straight*, the opposite of crooked, requires that the winding and twisting footpaths be straightened. John's task was to get the people to remove the obstacles and to smooth the road. He called for moral and spiritual rectification in the hearts and lives of the people. The coming of the expected Messiah made its moral demands upon them.

All the synoptics here agree against both the Hebrew and the Septuagint in the rendering "his paths." The Hebrew reads "a highway for our God"; the Septuagint has "the paths of our God." The rendering "his paths" again distinctly brings out the reference to the Messiah.

Verse 4 records the historical fulfillment of the prophecy just quoted.

"John"—a common name among the Jews, meaning, "to whom Jehovah is gracious." The angel Gabriel gave the name to John's father when announcing John's birth (Luke 1:13). Mark omits all reference to John's birth and ancestry and at once begins with his preparatory ministry. Luke's Gospel shows that John was six months older than Jesus (1:26-56).

"Came" (ASV)—appeared on the scene as a definite event in history. Mark, unlike Luke (3:1-2), made no attempt to date that appearing.

"Did baptize"—marking his distinctive activity. Mark's use of the present tense underlines John's administration of baptism as the characteristic feature of his ministry.[6] It became the one permanent note of identification for him. The RSV rendering "John the baptizer" is based on a slightly different reading; it is an appositional construction, "the one baptizing" (*ho baptizōn*), and stresses his personal identity as marked by his characteristic activity. Mark alone uses this precise form; it is the accepted reading in 6:14 and 24 and has good textual support here. Mark also uses the common noun form "the Baptist" (*ho baptistēs,* 6:25; 8:28). The two terms are quite synonymous, but the former places more stress upon his characteristic activity.

"In the wilderness"—the phrase designates the place of John's ministry. Mark adds no further description. Matthew identified it as "the wilderness of Judaea" (3:1), the rugged area west of the Jordan and the Dead Sea, extending upward toward Jerusalem. Useful as pastureland, it remained uninhabited except by hermits and ascetics. It was a broken, rugged, barren, treeless, arid, and forbidding region. John deliberately avoided the large centers of civilization, thereby indicating his consciousness of, and stern denunciation of the corruption of human society. The Gospels make it clear that John carried on his baptizing ministry in different locations.

"Preach"—better, "proclaim, announce as a herald." This was another characteristic feature of his ministry. The verb pictures John as a herald who has been given a message to announce by his lord and whose responsibility it is to convey that message clearly, accurately, and authoritatively. John's assignment was to make a public proclamation of the good news of the advent of the Messiah in a forceful manner.

"The baptism of repentance"—a baptism characterized by repentance. His baptism was not intended to induce repentance but rather was administered to those who were repentant (cf. Matt. 3:7-10). Repentance is more than grief or regret for sin; it is a deep change of

---

[6] For a study of the N.T. usages of "baptism" see Kenneth S. Wuest, *Studies in the Vocabulary of the Greek New Testament for the English Reader,* pp. 70-76.

mind, an altered attitude toward sin which has its proper fruit in a deliberate change of conduct for the better. Their failure to manifest such a change in their conduct disqualified the Jewish leaders for John's baptism.

"For the remission of sins"—the spiritual end in view in submitting to John's repentance-baptism. The physical rite itself did not produce this spiritual result. But submission to the baptism as the outward testimony of personal repentance was the condition for receiving the divine forgiveness. Repentance is the normal, scriptural condition for the forgiveness of sins (Isa. 1:16-18; Ezek. 18:30-32; Luke 16:30-31; 2 Cor. 7:10). The root meaning of *remission,* or forgiveness, is a sending away, a dismissal. It speaks of the cancellation of sin without demanding the deserved punishment. *Sins,* used without an article, does not denote specific sins or the sins of certain offenders, but of sins in general. Such forgiveness of sins is based on the vicarious sacrifice of Christ on the cross.

Verse 5 vividly pictures the effect of John's ministry. The recorded sphere of impact was the province of Judea where he began his work.

"Went out unto him"—the imperfect tense pictures the steady stream of those proceeding to the place of baptism. *Unto him* denotes not only movement toward but a personal, face-to-face encounter with John.

"All the land of Judaea"—*the land,* used figuratively, means its inhabitants.

"And all they of Jerusalem" (ASV)—more literally, "and the Jerusalemites all." Although located in Judea, Jerusalem is distinguished from the province. This is a common practice in the Gospels. The twofold *all* is rhetorical, stressing the deep and widespread interest aroused by John's ministry. After centuries of silence, the prophetic voice of John created a tremendous stirring among the Jews, resulting in a massive outpouring to attend his preaching.

"Were all baptized of him in the river of Jordan"—the common response on the part of the multitudes who came to hear John's preaching. The imperfect tense, *were baptized,* pictures the continuing procession of candidates, one after the other, being baptized. *Of him,* denoting agent, means that John himself administered the baptism. (Some suggest that the verb, being middle rather than passive, indicates that the candidates immersed themselves under John's direction rather than that he baptized them personally.[7] But this is unlikely. Others

---

[7] Sherman E. Johnson, *A Commentary on the Gospel According to St. Mark,* p. 36.

maintain that it was "not an act of self-baptism."[8]) There is no evidence that John ever delegated this task to any of his followers.

In the river of Jordan connects John's baptism with this one notable river of Palestine, rich with sacred associations in Jewish history. Tradition marks the Jericho ford as the site where John began his ministry.

"Confessing their sins"—confession of sins at the time of their baptism marked the reality of their repentance. The original, "confessing out," indicates the openness and fullness of the confession. It was a public acknowledgment of sins, although certainly not in full, colorful detail. *Confessing* basically means "speaking the same thing." They openly agreed with the divine verdict concerning their deeds. True confession implies our willingness to call our sins by the name that God gives them.

Verse 6 describes John's dress and diet. Both were plain and simple, consistent with his ascetic character as a lifelong Nazarite (Luke 1:15). The very appearance and personal life of John undergirded his demand for repentance by a sinful, self-indulgent people.

"Was clothed with camel's hair"—wore habitually, not just when preaching, a long, loose robe woven of camel's hair. Such a rough, hairy garment was worn by the poor and the ascetic.

"A girdle of a skin about his loins"—needed to keep the loose robe in place. As an important part of a man's attire, girdles were often made of costly materials and were richly adorned as a sign of wealth. John simply used a piece of untanned leather, corresponding to his coarse coat.

Both parts of his dress gave John a likeness to Elijah (2 Kings 1:8), which could hardly be accidental. His very appearance reminded the people of that ancient prophet who would, according to the teaching of the scribes, return as the forerunner of the Messiah (Mal. 4:5-6). John has aptly been called "a modern edition of the ancient Elijah."[9]

No corresponding description of what Jesus wore is found in any of the Gospels. Jesus' appearance conformed to the conventional standards set by the rabbis for a Jewish teacher and required no comment,[10] but John's appearance was unusual and distinctive. Such a rough attire had come to be associated with a prophet (Zech. 13:4). Thus John's dress served to enhance his position as God's prophet.

---

[8] V. Taylor, *The Gospel According to St. Mark*, p. 155.

[9] James Morison, *A Practical Commentary on the Gospel According to St. Mark*, p. 7.

[10] See Ethelbert Stauffer, *Jesus and His Story*, pp. 58-61, for a discussion of Jesus' clothing and physical appearance.

"Locusts and wild honey"—the customary diet of a dweller in the wilderness. John's food likewise spoke of rigor and austerity, preaching a stern sermon of protest against the prevailing habits of luxury and self-indulgence of his contemporaries.

Four kinds of locusts were allowed as food in Leviticus 11:22. Prepared in various ways, they were eaten by the poor, especially in times of famine. Some scholars think that the wild honey referred to a vegetable product, the sweet gum that exuded from the leaves of certain trees. More probably, the reference is to honey produced by wild bees and deposited not in hives under human care but in hollow trees and rocky recesses of the wilderness (cf. Deut. 32:13; 1 Sam. 14:25). Such honey, abundant in wilder regions, was often collected and sold by bee hunters.

Verses 7 and 8 are Mark's brief record of John's message. He mentions only that part which related directly to the coming Messiah. Matthew and Luke inserted here John's severe denunciation of the Jewish leaders (Matt. 3:7-10; Luke 3:7-9), and Luke further recorded John's instructions to various groups that came to him for baptism (Luke 3:10-14). John, like Jesus Himself, apparently avoided the term *Messiah,* probably because of the political connotations that the term had acquired among the Jews. He continued to herald his message concerning the person (v. 7) and work (v. 8) of the one whose way he was preparing.

"There cometh one mightier than I after me"—the use of the definite article, "There cometh the one mightier than I after me," points to the coming one as outstanding, distinctive, and unique. John was firmly convinced of the personal superiority of the coming Prince whose harbinger he was. *Cometh* conveys a note of immediacy. John eagerly anticipated His manifestation. *Mightier than I* bears witness to John's personal consciousness of divine strengthening, experienced in connection with his obedience to his commission. Luke records that the multitudes were so strongly impressed with John that they entertained the thought that he himself might be the Messiah (3:15). But John emphatically pointed them to the one coming after him, who was vastly superior. Verse 8 of Mark 1 suggests that the superiority of the coming one lay in His superior baptism, the baptism of the Holy Spirit.

"The latchet of whose shoes I am not worthy to stoop down and unloose"—a strong statement of John's personal feeling of unworthiness to perform the most menial service for the coming one. The shoes, protecting the soles of the feet, were tied on by a thong or strap. To remove the master's sandals was considered the most menial task of the slave. The words *to stoop down,* found only in Mark, add to John's picture of self-depreciation and humility. Matthew speaks of the slave's carrying the master's sandals (3:11), but Mark mentions the duty of stooping and untying the sandal strings, which was, if possible, an even more menial task. John's attitude enhanced the dignity of the coming Lord.

John further exalted the coming one by his emphatic contrast between his baptism and that of the Messiah (v. 8). This unmistakable contrast is underlined by his use of the emphatic pronouns *I* and *he*. It proved the superiority of the coming one.

"I indeed have baptized you with water"—the aorist tense[11] views John as addressing those whom he has baptized. His baptism was with water, speaking of repentance and purification. But he could not personally bestow the inner reality to which it pointed. His was a limited, preparatory work.

"But he shall baptize you"—introduces the contrast. *You* is unemphatic; the prospect was not limited to those whom John was addressing.

"With the Holy Ghost"—marking the superior character of the coming baptism. None but the eternal Son of God, after completing the work of redemption, could send the Spirit (John 16:7). The Spirit would bestow the grace that only God could give, working that inner, transforming reality which would make believers in Christ new creatures. This promise of the Spirit was a well-known feature of the prophecies concerning the messianic age (Isa. 44:3; Joel 2:28-29). Visibly fulfilled at Pentecost, it was cited by Peter in his Pentecostal sermon as proof that Jesus was the promised Messiah (Acts 2:32-33).

John's baptism had a present as well as future significance. Those who received his repentance-baptism bore open witness that a change was taking place in their lives. In receiving baptism at the hands of the forerunner of the Messiah, they pledged to receive the Messiah when He came. Thus, John prepared the way for the Messiah.

C. Baptism of Jesus (1:9-11)

Having skillfully pictured the preparatory work for Messiah's coming, Mark briefly records His arrival and induction into office (vv. 9-11). In his eagerness to press on to the story of the actions of the messianic Servant, Mark sketches these preliminary events in the barest detail. He simply records the fact of Jesus' baptism by John (v. 9) and

---

[11] The Greek tense called "aorist," which means undefined, in the indicative mood, denotes action in past time. While the aorist tense is usually used to denote point action, it may be employed to refer to a process or to repeated action which is simply presented as an undefined whole. The aorist tense here does not indicate how long or how many John had already baptized.

relates two attendant events which confirmed His identity as the Messiah (vv. 10-11).

"And it came to pass"—an introductory formula comparatively rare in Mark's Gospel. It lends dignity to the event to be described and marks the baptism now to be recorded as distinct from, and more significant than, those already mentioned.

"In those days"—this rather indefinite time indication links this event with the preceding announcement by John of the coming Messiah. At the time, John was at the height of his ministry.

"Jesus came from Nazareth of Galilee"—thus Mark informally introduces the central character of his story. *Jesus,* used without any further identification, implies that He was already well known to the readers. *Came* indicates that He took this step of His own volition; He voluntarily entered upon His messianic office. His baptism marked the dividing line between His private and His public life. Being "about thirty years of age" (Luke 3:23), He had waited until His powers were fully developed and at their best before He offered Himself to God in self-sacrificing service. *From Nazareth* implies that Nazareth had been Jesus' place of residence until that time. This obscure village is never mentioned in the Old Testament, Josephus, or the Talmud. *Of Galilee* indicates that Mark's readers would not readily know where Nazareth was located, although it was well known among the early Christians that Jesus came from Nazareth. This is further evidence that Mark wrote for non-Palestinian readers.

"And was baptized of John in Jordan"—a simple statement of the historic fact without any further explanation. *In Jordan* is literally "into the Jordan" and together with the verb *baptizō,* which basically means "to dip, immerse," most naturally conveys the thought of immersion.[12]

Mark leaves untouched the problem of why Jesus desired baptism from John. Receiving John's baptism was not an open acknowledgment of His sinfulness. Although He was baptized with a baptism that called for confession of sin, the early church firmly held to the sinlessness of Jesus. Jesus regarded it as the proper way to enter upon His work: "to fulfill all righteousness" (Matt. 3:15). He thus deliberately identified Himself with sinners, taking His place with them in order that, as their

---

[12] The construction here is not identical to that used in v. 5. There the preposition *en,* "in," with the locative case denotes the place where John performed his baptizings; here the preposition *eis,* "into," with the accusative case carries the thought of motion into. "The prep. here coincides with the proper meaning of the verb, indicating that the form of the rite was immersion into the stream" (Ezra P. Gould, *A Critical and Exegetical Commentary on the Gospel According to St. Mark,* International Critical Commentary, p. 11).

representative, He might redeem them. In entering upon His redemptive mission by this symbolic act, Jesus committed Himself to a program of death and resurrection which would in due course consummate in the reality of His death and resurrection on behalf of sinners. Jesus clearly seems to have associated His baptism with death (Mark 10:38; Luke 12:50). The baptism pictured His acceptance of His role as the suffering Servant of the Lord.

"And straightway"—the first occurrence of Mark's favorite adverb (*euthus*). Mark uses it more often than authors of the other three Gospels combined.[13] Mark's frequent use of this adverb, together with the conjunction *and,* gives his narrative a tone of ceaseless activity. It here stresses that Jesus did not tarry in the Jordan but walked out at once. What followed took place at once; no interval occurred.

"Coming up out of the water"—giving the time and situation for the two significant events which followed Jesus' baptism. The first event was visible (v. 10), the second audible (v. 11).

"He saw"—the subject of the verb is Jesus, not John. John also saw it (John 1:32-34); it was the sign given him whereby he would positively know the identity of the Messiah. *Saw* implies an objective phenomenon, not just a subjective vision.

"The heavens opened"—the first of two things seen by Jesus. Mark's use of the present tense pictures the heavens—the sky—in the very act of being torn apart. The passive voice of the verb suggests that this was an act of God. The ASV "rent assunder" reflects the strength of the term. In 15:38 the same verb was used to describe the veil in the temple ripped in two at the time of Jesus' death. This strong term is an instance of Mark's love for picturesque language. Our word *schism* is derived from the verb for "opened." The event implies the start of a new era of open communication between heaven and earth. What, if anything, Jesus saw beyond the rending heavens is not indicated.

"The Spirit like a dove descending upon him"—Mark assumes that his readers would know that the Holy Spirit was meant; Matthew made the identification specific (3:16). *Like a dove* stressed the objective fact of the Spirit's coming in the physical form of a dove. The significance of the Spirit's dovelike appearance has been variously

---

[13] In the Nestle Greek text, the figures are as follows: Mark, 41 times; Matthew, 18; Luke, 7; and John, 6. The Textus Receptus has some variation: Mark, 42; Matthew, 18; Luke, 8; and John, 7. In the Gospels, the KJV variously uses "straightway," "immediately," "forthwith," "as soon as," "by and by," and "anon." The ASV renders it "straightway," except three times when it has "immediately." The RSV uses "immediately" or "at once."

understood. Some would connect it with Genesis 1:2, where the Spirit is seen brooding creatively over the primeval waters. Others think of the dovelike qualities of gentleness which characterized Jesus' ministry. But more probably, the assumed form indicates that Jesus was being empowered by the spirit of humble self-sacrifice. The dove was preeminently the bird of sacrifice for the Jews. Jesus was empowered for that self-emptying service as the Servant of the Lord to whom He had committed Himself.

Upon him, literally, "into him," indicates the Spirit's entrance into Him in full empowerment for His messianic ministry. The expression does not mean that the Spirit had not been present in His life before.

"And there came a voice from heaven"—the speaker is made clear by what the voice says. *From heaven,* more literally, "out of the heavens," underlines its supernatural character. On two other occasions, at the transfiguration (9:7) and during Passion Week (John 12:28), such an audible voice spoke of Jesus from heaven. All came at great turning points in His life. That others besides Jesus heard this voice is not certain. Luke 3:21 implies that Jesus received baptism after John had completed his work with the other candidates that day. The declaration of John the Baptist, "This is the Son of God," implies that he heard it (John 1:31-34).

"Thou art my beloved Son"—the Father's confirmation to the incarnate Son, as He stood upon the bank of the Jordan. *Thou* is emphatic: "you yourself, in contradistinction to all others." *Thou art,* not "Thou hast become," acknowledged His unique sonship, not as a newly established relationship but as an abiding reality. *Beloved* stands emphatically at the end with the article—"Thou art my Son, the beloved"—stressing the love relationship. It was the Father's love-response to Jesus' dedication to His mission as the Servant of Jehovah. Wuest remarks that in the Greek construction "equal emphasis is laid upon the fact that Messiah is the Son of God, and that He is the beloved Son."[14] The verbal *beloved* is used at times with the sense of "only." That would be doubly appropriate here. The heavenly voice confirmed the already existing filial consciousness of Jesus. No shadow of doubt ever obscured that glorious consciousness during His ministry.

"In whom I am well pleased"—more literally, "in thee I was well pleased." The aorist tense used naturally denotes a past historical fact. Some interpret the verb form as referring to Jesus' preexistent life with the Father, others to His perfect life upon earth until the time of the

---

[14] Kenneth S. Wuest, *Mark in the Greek New Testament for the English Reader,* p. 24.

baptism, still others even to the fact that He had voluntarily accepted baptism. It seems best to take the aorist here as timeless and render it as present, indicating that the Father had always been pleased with the Son and was still pleased with Him. In Him the Father found perfect satisfaction and delight. "It is a delight that never had a beginning and will never have an end."[15]

The verb *well pleased,* when used with persons, may also mean "to select, choose," with the implication of the emotional good will of the one selecting. Thus Schrenk interprets this baptismal declaration as indicating "the election of the Son, which included His mission and His appointment to the kingly office of Messiah."[16] The Father's good pleasure in the Son expressed itself in the choice of Him for the work of human redemption. That program would require more of Him than just His enthronement as the royal Son. The double assertion in the divine voice of approval seems to suggest that the Son thus approved was the suffering Servant of the Lord as well as the Davidic Messiah. The first phrase in the divine word of approval identified Him as the royal Son of David, as announced in Psalm 2:7; but the added words, *In whom I am well pleased,* recall the divine assertion to the suffering Servant in Isaiah 53:11. F. F. Bruce concludes that this indicates "that His Messiahship was to be realized in terms of the portrayal of the Servant, humble, obedient, suffering, accomplishing His mission by passing through death, and committing His vindication confidently to God."[17] The Father now expressed His supreme delight in the Son as He assumed His redemptive mission to which He had just committed Himself.

In the baptismal scene, we have a clear manifestation of the Trinity. The Father spoke His approval from heaven; the incarnate Son stood ready to begin His mission; the Spirit descended to empower Him. All three persons of the Trinity were involved in the accomplishment of human redemption.

D. Temptation by Satan (1:12-13)

Mark briefly records in verses 12-13 the temptation as another historical event preparatory to Jesus' ministry. His account makes no mention of the inner reactions of Jesus, yet it makes clear that a great spiritual crisis was involved.

---

[15] Ibid., p. 25.

[16] Gottlob Schrenk, *"eudokein,"* in *Theological Dictionary of the New Testament,* ed. Gerhard Kittel, 2:740.

[17] F. F. Bruce, "Messiah," in *The New Bible Dictionary,* ed. J. D. Douglas, p. 818.

"And immediately the spirit driveth him"—the temptation followed immediately upon the baptism and was arranged for by the Spirit. *And immediately* forcefully brings the two events into immediate juxtaposition. The Spirit, having come upon Jesus, at once took control. Matthew 4:1 specifically asserts that the Spirit led Jesus "into the wilderness to be tempted of the devil." Jesus did not enter the scene of temptation at His own fancy. He did so under the strong, conscious leading of the Spirit.

Driveth is a stronger term than the terms used by Matthew and Luke; it quite literally means "to throw or cast out, to force out," more or less under compulsion. Mark used it of the expulsion of demons. The expression here does not mean that Jesus was forced out into the wilderness against His will but indicates that He went with a strong sense of the Spirit's compulsion upon Him. Since the object of His messianic mission was to "destroy the works of the devil" (1 John 3:8), Jesus recognized that His acceptance of the Servant vocation made the encounter essential. It was the initiation of His mission to overthrow the devil. His miracle-working ministry of authority over the demons was based on the victory won in this encounter.

The present tense *driveth* marks the first occurrence of the historical present in this Gospel, a characteristic feature of Mark's style.[18] It vividly depicts the action as though taking place before the reader's very eyes.

"Into the wilderness"—the actual place is unknown. The Gospels indicate that Jesus went there directly from the Jordan. Tradition dating from the time of the Crusades locates the place in the rugged limestone heights west of the city of Jericho, at the precipitous place commonly called *Mons Quarantania* (a reference to the forty days). Some would place the location some miles further south, while others suggest a place in Transjordan, somewhere in the great wilderness of Arabia. Jewish thought associated the wilderness with danger and gloom and the abode of demons (Matt. 12:43; Luke 8:29; 11:24). If Mark had such scenes and associations in mind, Jesus was pictured as taken into the very domain of Satan for the encounter.

"Forty days"—all the synoptics mention this time period, but Mark makes no reference to the fasting of Jesus. The number forty may have recalled the forty years of Israel in the wilderness when God tested the people in the matter of their obedience (Deut. 8:2). Jesus

---

[18] All the Gospels use the historical present tense: Matthew, 93; Mark, 151; Luke, 9; John, 164 (Taylor, p. 46).

experienced the temptations of the enemy as the victorious representative of God's people.

"Tempted of Satan"—the present-tense participle indicates that Jesus was repeatedly subjected to temptation during the entire period. Luke's account agrees with this inference, whereas Matthew speaks of only the three temptations at the end of the period. The three temptations, described in Matthew and Luke, came when Jesus was exhausted and at His weakest as the mighty climax in Satan's assaults against Jesus. *Tempted* basically means "tried, tested," and may be used to denote any testing or trying. Generally, as here, it has the sinister connotation of solicitation to evil. Satan definitely sought to bring Jesus to a fall. But Mark's account offers no hint concerning the precise nature of the temptations.

Satan identifies the agent of the temptation and clearly states the personal existence of the tempter. The temptation was not the result of Jesus' own conflicting thoughts and emotions; it was an attack from without by a personal antagonist. The name Satan is derived from a Hebrew word meaning "adversary." When used in the Old Testament with the definite article (Job 1:6; 2:1; Zech. 3:1-2), "the adversary" denotes the supernatural opponent of God and His work. It is the personal name of that mighty spiritual being who is the head of the kingdom of evil and is engaged in constant warfare against God's kingdom. The name is used about thirty-five times in the New Testament. With almost equal frequency, he is designated as the Devil, which means "the slanderer," but this term does not occur in Mark. Matthew also used the participial designation "the tempter," describing him by his characteristic activity.

"Was with the wild beasts"—a touch to the picture which appears only in Mark. "The region," Wuest observes, "abounded with boars, jackals, wolves, foxes, leopards, and hyenas."[19] It apparently was intended to accentuate Jesus' utter loneliness. He was far from human habitation, in a place where the wild beasts prowled at liberty. Their precise identity can only be surmised. Some have conjectured that Mark intended to picture Jesus as happily surrounded by these wild animals, rendered harmless by His presence as the restorer of paradise (Gen. 1:26; 2:19-20). But the desolate scene, as well as the satanic assaults, make any thoughts of paradise very remote. More likely, the presence of these wild animals was an added element of terror for Jesus. The first Adam succumbed in an environment that was beautiful and friendly; the last Adam maintained His purity in an environment that was desolate and hostile.

---

[19] Wuest, *Mark,* p. 26.

"The angels ministered unto him"—in structure this statement is parallel to the preceding remark about the wild beasts. It seems to place the angels in contrast to the wild beasts and agrees with the suggestion that the beasts were dangerous but that God gave His protecting care through the angels. Mark's imperfect tense suggests that their ministry was rendered to Jesus on repeated occasions during the entire temptation period. Matthew speaks only of the angels' coming to minister to Him at the close of the temptation (4:11). The two statements are complementary. Mark thinks of the angels as ministering to Jesus in connection with His various victories during the entire period, while Matthew notes only their ministry at the conclusion of the temptations. *Ministered* denotes a service freely and voluntarily given for the benefit of another. The precise nature of the angelic service is not certain; it may include the supply of physical as well as spiritual needs. If the ministries took place during the entire period, they apparently were of the nature of spiritual assurances to Jesus of the divine presence. This angelic ministry attests the human weakness of the incarnate Christ, but it also bears witness to His sonship.

Part 2
The Ministry of the Servant

2
Ministry in Galilee
(Part 1; 1:14-45)

Mark devoted the bulk of his book (1:14–13:37) to a description of the mighty ministry of the Servant of the Lord. Following the rough geographical arrangement of the material, we may divide his account into four sections: (1) the expanding ministry in Galilee and the resultant reactions (1:14–4:34), (2) the four separate withdrawals of Jesus from Galilee with His disciples (4:35–9:50), (3) the journey to Jerusalem for the final Passover (10:1-52), and (4) the ministry in Jerusalem during Passover Week (11:1–13:37).

A. Ministry in Galilee (1:14–4:34)

Mark, like Matthew and Luke, began his account of Christ's ministry with His work in Galilee. He thus passed over in silence the earlier ministry of Jesus recorded in John 1:15–4:42, which covered a period of perhaps a year, often called "the year of obscurity." None of the synoptics assert that the work in Galilee marked the actual commencement of the public ministry of Jesus.

1. Summary of the Preaching (1:14-15)

This brief paragraph gives the keynote of the work of Jesus in Galilee as a whole. It identifies the time of its beginning, notes that Galilee was the chief scene of the work, and gives a summary of His message.

"Now after that John was put in prison"—this introductory chronological note implies that John's arrest was already known to the readers. The details of his arrest and execution are given later (6:17-29). The verb (literally, "delivered up") in papyrus usage had become a technical term meaning to deliver up as a prisoner. Translated "betrayed" in Mark 3:19, it is used of Judas's "delivering up" Jesus (ASV marg.). But no evidence exists indicating that some traitor betrayed John into the hands of Herod Antipas. "The use of the passive voice," Brooks remarks, "implies that what was done was in accordance with God's purpose."[1]

"Jesus came into Galilee"—the northernmost of the three divisions of Palestine. It was also the most fruitful and populous. Mark passes directly from the temptation to the Galilean ministry (v. 9), but that does not prove he knew of no interval. Matthew's designation of the journey as a withdrawal into Galilee (4:12) fits in with John's account (4:1-3) of Christ's reason for leaving Judea. Galilee was not as priest-ridden and Pharisee-dominated as Judea and would offer Jesus a freer environment for His work.

"Preaching the gospel of God" (ASV)—a summary designation of the central message of Jesus.[2] *Preaching,* better "proclaiming, heralding," pictures this as His characteristic activity in Galilee. In this first chapter, Mark employs the terms *preaching* and *teaching* to describe the oral ministry of Jesus; in the following chapters, Mark restricts himself to the word *teaching. The gospel of God* may mean the good news *from* God, or the good news *about* God. Both meanings may be included, but the former is probably intended. Jesus proclaimed a message of hope and mercy, not of accusation and condemnation.

Verse 15 is the summary statement of Jesus' message. He had a momentous announcement to deliver and an urgent summons to make. Both receive a double statement in this verse.

"The time is fulfilled"—the forward position of the verb makes it emphatic; and the perfect tense, "has been fulfilled," indicates that the time which God had appointed for the Messiah's arrival had now fully come. *Time,* denoting a favorable season for a particular undertaking, stressed that it was the opportune moment for the establishment of God's kingdom in the acceptance of the messianic Servant. It was "a time heavy with eternal significance."[3]

"The kingdom of God is at hand"—the perfect-tense verb is again emphatic by position. The announcement is that the kingdom, whose coming had long been anticipated, was now in a state of being near—so near, in fact, that the hearers were urged to enter into it by meeting the conditions which immediately followed. Jesus' announcement was a continuation and development of the previous proclamation of John the Baptist (Matt. 3:2).

---

[1] James A. Brooks, *Mark,* The New American Commentary, p. 47.

[2] The KJV reading, "the gospel of the kingdom of God," a variant reading in some Greek texts, is an elaboration. The good news of God that Jesus as Messiah proclaimed was inseparably connected with the kingdom of God.

[3] Donald English, *The Message of Mark,* p. 49.

The kingdom of God, an expression occurring fourteen times in Mark's Gospel,[4] is a comprehensive biblical term. The concept it conveys has been variously understood.[5] The primary meaning of *kingdom* is the sovereign's actual rule, the reign itself; but the idea of the people or realm over which he rules is necessarily involved. McClain points out that *kingdom* involves "at least three essential elements; first, a *ruler* with adequate authority and power; second, a *realm* of subjects to be ruled; and third, the actual exercise of the function of *rulership*."[6]

Of God identifies the kingdom announced and describes it as belonging to God; it is the kingdom which He establishes and rules over. It "is essentially God's Kingdom and not ours. It is something which God gives, and not something which men 'build.' "[7] In its widest sense, the kingdom of God denotes His sovereign rule over all moral, intelligent beings, the angels included (1 Chron. 29:12; Ps. 103:19-20). But the kingdom announced here by Jesus would naturally be understood by His hearers as denoting the eagerly expected messianic kingdom.

The kingdom of God was a familiar concept to Jesus' hearers. It was a common theme in the Old Testament and was widely discussed by the rabbinical teachers. Jesus could assume that His hearers would have at least a basic understanding of the kingdom He announced. Therefore no formal definition of its nature was added in making this initial announcement of the kingdom of God.

Jesus presented the kingdom as being *at hand* in Himself. The messianic kingdom, which in the Old Testament was in the future, had now come close to mankind in His own person and work. In Him, it was now "in the midst of" them (Luke 17:21, ASV marg.). He Himself was the center and substance of the good news concerning the kingdom. Thus, Ridderbos observes, "Jesus' self-revelation as the Messiah, the Son of man and Servant of the Lord, constitutes both the mystery and the unfolding of the whole gospel."[8]

---

[4] Mark 1:15; 4:11, 26, 30; 9:1, 47; 10:14, 15, 23, 24, 25; 12:34; 14:25; 15:43.

[5] George E. Ladd, "Kingdom of God," in *Zondervan Pictorial Bible Dictionary,* ed. Merrill C. Tenney; Alva J. McClain, *The Greatness of the Kingdom,* pp. 7-15. This important volume presents a full, inductive study of the kingdom in both testaments from a premillennial viewpoint.

[6] Ibid., p. 17.

[7] Alan Richardson, "Kingdom of God," in *A Theological Word Book of the Bible,* ed. Alan Richardson, p. 120.

[8] H. Ridderbos, "Kingdom of God, Kingdom of Heaven," in *The New Bible Dictionary,* ed. J. D. Douglas, p. 694.

His presence as the personal embodiment of the kingdom produced an unavoidable crisis. Men's response to Him determined their relationship to the kingdom. His presence also precipitated the conflict of righteousness with evil. His miracles and His power over the demonic world established the presence and triumph of God's kingdom over the kingdom of Satan. In Him the kingdom of God invaded this present evil world and has established a present, spiritual reign in those who accept Him as their Sovereign.

However, the presence of the kingdom in Him did not result in the immediate abolition of the existing world order. The result is a present conflict between good and evil, but "the children of the kingdom" and "the children of the wicked one" continue to grow side by side until the time of the coming harvest (Matt. 13:37-43). The presence of the kingdom in the world is now veiled: its coming is "not with observation" (Luke 17:20-21); it is not observed as a visible, cataclysmic event.

Jesus also spoke of the kingdom as still future (Matt. 6:10; 7:21-23; Mark 9:47-48; Luke 22:18). The kingdom will yet come "with observation" (Luke 17:22-24), as a critical visible event beheld everywhere, when the King will return to establish His authority over all the world. The triumphant cataclysmic establishment of the divine kingdom over the earth which the Old Testament revelation portrayed (Dan. 2:31-45; 7:13-14) is still future. Those who have given their allegiance to Christ as their King now eagerly await His return in glory. This future, visible phase of the kingdom also centers in Christ Himself. What His people now await "is not something more complete than Christ himself, but rather Christ manifest and in glory."[9]

"Repent ye, and believe the gospel"—the twofold call to the hearers in view of His great announcement. Jesus continued the call to repentance which John had made (v. 4; see p. 27). The call to repentance will never become obsolete until human sin has been completely vanquished. The hearers must also put their continuing trust in the gospel.

To believe means more than to give credence to the message; it involves a personal commitment to, and reliance upon, that which is believed. The call to believe *the gospel,* the only clear example of the expression in the New Testament, points to the good news as the basis of faith. "Faith in the message was the first step; a creed of some kind

---

[9] C.E.B. Cranfield, *The Gospel According to Saint Mark,* Cambridge Greek Testament Commentary, p. 66.

lies at the basis of confidence in the Person of Christ.''[10] Faith in the gospel message becomes the medium for faith in the Christ proclaimed by the gospel. The demands for repentance and faith run parallel. Genuine repentance prepares the heart for true faith in the gospel; faith in the gospel makes the repentance evangelical. Repentance without faith leads to despair; faith without repentance from sin becomes presumption.

2. Call to Four Fishermen (1:16-20)

Mark begins his narrative of the public ministry of Jesus with a vivid account of Jesus' call to four fishermen, two pairs of brothers, to be His intimate followers. The vividness of the details suggests the reminiscences of Peter behind the account.

"As he walked by the sea of Galilee''—Mark gives the occasion and setting of the call. It was early morning as Jesus walked along close to the edge of the water. The Sea of Galilee, which had such a prominent place in Jesus' Galilean ministry, is an inland lake, about $12\frac{1}{2}$ miles long and $7\frac{1}{2}$ miles wide. This warm-water lake, located some 680 feet below sea level, was the scene of a thriving fishing industry. The designation of it as "sea" is Semitic. Luke always called it a lake.

Verses 16-18 describe the call to the first pair of brothers.

"Simon and Andrew his brother''—*Simon* was the Greek form of the Hebrew *Shimeon,* a common name among the Jews, popularized apparently by Simon Maccabeus. *Andrew* was an old Greek name, an instance of Jewish families adopting Gentile names for their children. Of the two, Simon, later "surnamed Peter" (3:16), is decidedly the more prominent personality in the Gospels.

"Casting a net''—the verb, not used elsewhere in the New Testament, implies the use of the circular throw net, which Matthew specifically mentioned (4:18). It consisted of a circular rope with a tent-shaped net attached. The skillful fisherman threw this net over his shoulder while standing on the shore or in a boat so that it spread out in a circle as it fell into the water. Weights caused it to sink rapidly. It was pulled back by the cord attached. Others, however, prefer to explain *casting* as meaning that the net was "thrown about," first on one side of the boat, then on the other.

"For they were fishers''—their habitual employment. It was a humble vocation, but success called for skill, alertness, and patient persistence, qualities whose development was a valuable preparatory training for their evangelistic commission. Wuest remarks, "When God

---

[10] Henry Barclay Swete, *The Gospel According to Saint Mark,* p. 14.

looks for someone to use in a special mission, He looks for the person who is already busy, the energetic individual."[11]

"Come ye after me"—a majestic invitation having the force of a command, asking them to join Him as He continued on. This common New Testament figure for discipleship is based on the respectful practice of disciples' allowing their master to walk ahead as they passed along. The thought of discipleship is prominent in Mark.

"I will make you to become fishers of men"—the purpose for which He called them. It is still Christ's central purpose for His followers. This first instance in Mark of His use of figurative language obviously comes from the occupation of the brothers. Jesus asked them to leave their work catching fish in order that He might train them to become fishers of men. The call implied the need for intensive training for the new task, which was analogous to, but of a higher order than, their old employment. *Men* makes the scope worldwide; it transcends all national or social lines. "These men," Williamson notes, "are not called to save the world by their heroic performance, but rather in their subordination to Jesus to bear witness to him."[12]

"And straightway"—their acceptance of the call was instant and complete.

"Forsook their nets"—a definite act which terminated their old fishing business. It does not imply abandonment of property; proper arrangements certainly were made.

"Followed him"—associated themselves with Jesus as their accepted Leader and Teacher. "He embodied the divine initiative: they embodied appropriate human response."[13] Mark's Gospel gives no indication of any previous acquaintance with Jesus, but from John 1:35-42 and 3:22-30, it is clear that they had already accepted Him as Messiah and even assisted Him in His work. The call now given them was a call to intensive training as His disciples.

Verses 19-20 give the parallel call to the second pair of brothers.

"When he had gone a little farther"—indicates the relationship in time and place between the two calls. The second pair of brothers were busy a short distance farther along the shore.

"James the *son* of Zebedee, and John his brother"—*James* is the English form, from Wycliffe onward (coming through the Italian), for the familiar Old Testament name *Jacob*. The common order of their

---

[11] Kenneth S. Wuest, *Mark in the Greek New Testament,* p. 28.

[12] Lamar Williamson, Jr., *Mark,* Interpretation: A Bible Commentary for Teaching and Preaching, p. 46.

[13] English, p. 53.

names[14] and the fact that John is identified as his brother indicates that James was the older of the two. This is the only place where Zebedee appears personally in the Gospel story. He is always mentioned in connection with his sons. Some have conjectured that Zebedee did not live long after this call to his sons. From a comparison of Matthew 27:55-56 with Mark 15:40, it may be assumed that his wife's name was Salome, and further comparison with John 19:25 indicates that she was the sister of the mother of Jesus. So, James and John were Jesus' cousins.

"In the ship mending their nets"—no longer fishing but still busily putting their nets in order for their next fishing expedition. This included not only repairing broken places but also cleaning and folding the nets after the night's work. The ship was not a little rowboat but a regular fishing vessel, equipped with sails as well as oars.

"Straightway he called them"—the call given them was identical with that to the first pair. Again Jesus initiated the relationship that made them His disciples. The calls followed in quick succession.

"They left their father Zebedee"—their response likewise was a definite break with their past work. The Scripture gives no indication that Zebedee opposed the action of his sons, but clearly it involved a sacrifice for him.

"With the hired servants"—a note peculiar to Mark. Its intended significance is not clear. Perhaps it was a point of comfort to the two sons that they did not need to leave their father without help. Or it may indicate that, for Zebedee, the sacrifice was not so drastic as it might otherwise seem. Clearly, Zebedee was conducting a prosperous fishing business. The business seemingly had far-reaching contacts, since his son John was known to the high priest in Jerusalem (John 18:15). Zebedee was a man of some position in Capernaum, financially able to employ others.

3. Ministry in Capernaum (1:21-34)

"And they went into Capernaum"—marking the transition from the seashore to the city that became the center for the Galilean ministry. *They* reveals Jesus and the four disciples as now forming one company with a common interest. Verse 21 contains three features characteristic of Mark's style: the historical present (literally, "they go"), the repeated *and,* and the adverb *straightway.* They all serve to underline the ceaseless activity of Jesus.

---

[14] "James and John" occurs fifteen times in the Gospels and "John and James" twice (Luke 8:51; 9:28) in the critical text; the Textus Receptus has it only in Luke 9:28.

Capernaum, or Capharnahum ("village of Nahum"), is one of the few specific places named in Mark's Gospel. Jesus made this strategic town His headquarters after His rejection at Nazareth (Luke 4:16-31). It became known as "his own city" (Matt. 9:1) and was the scene of many of His mighty works (Matt. 11:20). It was at the heart of the most populous district of Palestine, being an important road center and a station for a detachment of soldiers. Jesus' prediction of its overthrow (Matt. 11:23-24) was so thoroughly fulfilled that for centuries its very location was uncertain. It is now generally located at Tell Hum, an archaeological site on the northwestern shore of the lake, about two miles west of the Jordan entrance.

The account of the ministry in Capernaum illustrates Jesus' authority. His authority, felt by the four when He called them, was further demonstrated in the synagogue by word and deed (vv. 21-28), privately in the home of Peter (vv. 29-31), and extensively by the mass healings that evening (vv. 32-34).

a. Excitement in the Synagogue (vv. 21-28).

The unique authority of Jesus was revealed in the synagogue by His teaching (vv. 21-22) and His expulsion of a demon (vv. 23-26). Both made a profound impact and gave wings to His fame (vv. 27-28). A parallel account appears in Luke 4:31-37.

"Straightway on the sabbath day he entered into the synagogue"— on the first Sabbath after the call of the four disciples, which may have been on the preceding Friday. Jesus lost no time in beginning His public ministry in Capernaum and logically began in the synagogue, apparently the only one in Capernaum. Derived from a Greek word meaning "a bringing together, an assembly," the word *synagogue* might mean the people assembled for worship or the place where they assembled, as here. The synagogue building was put to a threefold use: the place of worship on the Sabbath, the schoolhouse during the week, and a courtroom to try minor cases (Mark 13:9; Luke 12:11). The services on the Sabbath day consisted of prayers, the reading of the Old Testament, and teaching. The reading of the Scriptures and the teaching were open to any qualified individual selected by the ruler of the synagogue. It was a lay institution and did not require a priest, or even a rabbi, although customarily some rabbi present was invited to address the audience. The democratic character of its services made the synagogue readily available to Jesus. His teaching there was a prominent feature of His early ministry, as long as it remained open to Him.

"And taught"—a feature of Jesus' ministry Mark made prominent (2:13; 4:1-2; 6:2, 6*b*, 34; 8:31; 10:1; 11:17; 12:35; 14:49), although he recorded little of *what* the Master taught. The imperfect tense underlines the teaching session. The demoniac apparently cried out as He was teaching.

"They were astonished at his doctrine"—Mark recorded only the profound impact produced, nothing of what was taught. *Were astonished,* a strong verb, indicates that Jesus' teaching[15] struck the people like a blow, knocking them out of their normal state of mind. Their prolonged amazement was produced by the manner and contents of the teaching.

"For he taught them as one that had authority"—spoke with the consciousness of divinely given power and authorization to teach. His authority came from the inner assurance of knowing eternal truth. He knew that His message was directly from God. This consciousness also pervaded His conduct (1:27; 2:10; 8:38).

"Not as the scribes"—Jesus' teaching was in striking contrast to what the people were familiar with from the scribes, the professional interpreters of their Scriptures. Their teaching was characteristically based on secondhand authority. They habitually established their views by long, learned quotations from other rabbis. At best, they could claim only an authority derived from their understanding of the law. Their teaching was generally pedantic and dull, occupied with minute distinctions concerning Levitical regulations and petty legalistic requirements.

The synagogue audience that Sabbath soon received another surprise because of the authoritative word of Jesus (vv. 23-26). His authoritative deeds authenticated His authoritative message.

"And there was in their synagogue a man with an unclean spirit"—the teaching of Jesus also evoked demoniac disturbance. *Their synagogue* points to the regular attendants there and implies that the man was not one of their usual number. *With an unclean spirit* is literally "in a spirit unclean" and views the man as moving in the sphere of the spirit's power, under its control. The adjective *unclean* made unmistakable for Mark's readers the nature of the spirit.[16] The term may imply the thought of estrangement from God, but it certainly depicts the moral nature of the spirit. All moral purity had been lost; the spirit was utterly impure and foul by nature.

---

[15] The word for "teaching" (*didachē*) is usually translated "doctrine" in the KJV.

[16] Mark used "demon" and "unclean spirit" as interchangeable terms, but he used the latter designation more often (eleven times) than Matthew and Luke together. Neither term occurs in the Fourth Gospel.

This is the first instance in Mark's Gospel of demon possession.[17] The Scriptures accept the existence of demons as an unquestioned reality but do not indicate the origin of these evil beings. They clearly distinguish this phenomenon from mental disorders. The demons recognized Jesus' messianic identity long before the people were aware of it. His presence invariably evoked their terrified acknowledgement of His power, but Jesus always silenced their testimony. Their unfailing obedience to His word demonstrated Christ's victory over Satan and his kingdom.

"He cried out"—gave notice of his presence without being addressed, thus calling attention to himself. Ordinarily this demoniac was not so violent as to be excluded from society; but the unclean spirit felt a tension in the presence of Jesus which forced a violent outcry of protest, creating a disturbance in the synagogue. *Cried out* denotes a strong emotional outcry: "shrieked."

In the KJV, following the Textus Receptus, the first word of the demon-possessed man is a fierce command, "Let us alone," but it is generally accepted that this command is not a true part of the Greek text. If accepted as original, his command is a fear-prompted effort to thwart any adverse action by Jesus. His two questions are an effort to put Jesus on the defensive before the people and force Him to justify His action.

"What have we to do with thee"—literally, "What to us and to you?" The idiom means, "What do we have in common?" or probably, "Why do you meddle with us?" The spirit felt a strong incongruity between Jesus and himself. Belonging to opposite realms, they could only repel each other. In saying *us,* this spirit was speaking for the entire class of demons.

"Jesus of Nazareth"—literally, "Jesus Nazarene," declaring His personal identity as well as his place of origin, "coming from Nazareth." In the New Testament, the designation of Jesus as Nazarene is never used apart from His human name. This is the first of four occurrences of this designation in Mark's Gospel (10:47; 14:67; 16:6).[18] It

---

[17] William Menzies Alexander, *Demonic Possession in the New Testament;* Werner Foerster, *"daimōn, daimonion,"* in *Theological Dictionary of the New Testament,* ed. Gerhard Kittel, 2:1-19; J. S. Wright, "Possession," in *The New Bible Dictionary,* ed. J. D. Douglas; John L. Nevius, *Demon Possession and Allied Themes;* Merrill F. Unger, *Biblical Demonology,* chap. 6; Unger, *Demons in the World Today,* chap. 6.

[18] Concerning the variants for this designation in the original and the meaning, see H. H. Schaeder, "Nazarēnos, Nazōraios," *Theological Dictionary of the New Testament,* ed. Gerhard Kittel, 4:874-79; V. Taylor, *The Gospel According to St. Mark,* pp. 177-78.

was a common Jewish practice to identify a man by his place of origin. Since they knew that Jesus had resided several years at Nazareth, the people of Capernaum would identify Him as the Nazarene.

"Art thou come to destroy us"—this clause may be punctuated either as a question or a positive assertion. If taken as a question, it was an instinctive expression of dread. Knowing the power of Jesus, all the demons stood in dread of what His mission would mean for them. They feared not only expulsion but also being remanded to torment in the abyss (Matt. 8:29; Luke 8:31). Perhaps it was a positive assertion of hopeless certainty. Jesus' presence could only mean destruction. *Destroy* means not annihilation but ruination; Messiah would ruin their power and activity. *Us* again makes the demon the representative of the infernal kingdom of which he was a part.

"I know thee who thou art, the Holy One of God"—the spirit's testimony to the true character of his enemy. He knew Jesus to be not only personally sinless and pure but also wholly consecrated to God and sent by the Father to destroy the works of the Devil. The designation, *the Holy One of God,* was evoked by the consciousness of his own unholy nature. It acknowledged Christ's supernatural character as true deity. The demon's recognition and confession of the deity of Jesus Christ stands in amazing contrast to the dullness of the people to that fact.

"Jesus rebuked him"—rejected and silenced the testimony. *Him* refers to the unclean spirit as the following commands show.

"Hold thy peace"—literally, "be muzzled," conveying the thought of an enforced silence. The command demanded prompt compliance. The audacious testimony was instantly refused by Jesus. To have accepted it would at once have exposed Him to the charge of being in league with Satan. Jesus at once rejected any thought of compromise the demon might offer and emphatically commanded him to come out of the man.

"And come out of him"—a command equally sharp, demanding instant obedience. *Him* here denotes the possessed man; Jesus recognized the spirit as a real personality, distinct from that of the man himself.

Verse 26 describes the immediate response by the unclean spirit to Jesus' command. Yielding to His authority, the spirit displayed a final burst of demonic rage. The participle rendered "had torn him" here more probably means "had convulsed him." Luke added that the spasm left the man unharmed (4:35). It demonstrated the degraded, vicious nature of the spirit.

"Came out of him"—the text states simply the decisive victory of Jesus in this encounter with the demoniac world, the first one recorded in Mark's Gospel.

Verses 27-28 record the excited reaction to the events both in the synagogue and beyond.

"They were all amazed"—were all swayed by the same strong, emotional reaction. This strong verb, used only by Mark, conveys the thought of great astonishment passing into awe. The amazement evoked rational reflection and inquiry, "insomuch that they questioned among themselves." Instinctively, each turned to his astonished neighbor to ask his opinion. The present tense pictures prolonged, animated discussion.

"What thing is this?"—refers both to the teaching and the exorcism. "One surprise following close on another provoked wondering inquiry as to the whole phenomenon."[19] Two things excited their astonishment: the nature of His teaching and His ability to expel a demon with a word.

"What new doctrine *is* this? for with authority commandeth he even the unclean spirits"—the punctuation is uncertain. *With authority* may be taken with what precedes or follows. The KJV and others accept the latter connection, leaving the words *What new doctrine is this?* ("A new teaching!" ASV) as an independent phrase. But in view of verse 22, the connection with what precedes is preferable. They were surprised not only because His teaching was *new,* fresh in its quality; the real cause for surprise was the note of authority. And that authority extended even to the demonic world! Exorcism among the Jews was bound up with the use of elaborate magical formulas, but they had just witnessed an expulsion with a simple command. The plural *unclean spirits* generalizes. If He could cast out one demon, He could also cast out others.

How pathetic it is that they were occupied with the effect and failed to inquire further about the person before them.

Verse 28 heightens the impact of the occurrence by noting its effect far beyond Capernaum. The amazing report of the synagogue events at once spread as if the wind carried it. All Galilee soon heard of it.

b. Healing of Peter's Mother-in-Law (vv. 29-31).

This condensed but graphic account displays the authority of Jesus in another area. Peter's vivid recital of the occurrence apparently lies

---

[19] Alexander Balmain Bruce, "The Synoptic Gospels," *The Expositor's Greek New Testament,* 1:346.

behind Mark's story. Parallel accounts are given in Matthew 8:14-15 and Luke 4:38-39.

"And forthwith"—the characteristic adverb (*euthus*, "immediately, straightway") stresses that this happening occurred in close sequence with the casting out of the demon. Miracle followed miracle in quick succession.

"When they were come out of the synagogue"—the clause indicates a continuation in the exciting experiences of the four disciples. An alternative reading, *he was,* has strong support; it centers the attention on Jesus as the central figure in the story.

"The house of Simon and Andrew"—the two brothers shared the home. The expression may mean that it was the joint possession of the two. Perhaps Andrew simply resided with his married brother. When they first met Jesus along the banks of the Jordan, Andrew and Peter were identified as being from Bethsaida (John 1:44). But they had moved to Capernaum, perhaps on learning that Jesus was establishing headquarters there.

"With James and John"—a touch given only by Mark. It affords an interesting glimpse of the pleasant social life maintained by these friends. It also indicates that these four witnessed the miracle performed in the privacy of Peter's home.

"But Simon's wife's mother"—apparently her husband had died before the mother came to live with her married daughter.

It cannot be assumed that Peter was a widower, since in later years Peter's wife accompanied him on his preaching tours (1 Cor. 9:5). Her name is not given in the New Testament. Tradition relates that she suffered martyrdom.

"Lay sick of a fever"—more literally, "was lying prostrate, burning with fever." She was lying thus when the group returned from the synagogue. *Of a fever* translates a present-active participle built on the word for fire and suggests the burning fever which held her in its grip. Luke more specifically called it "a great fever" (4:38), apparently a reflection of his own medical interests.

"And anon they tell him of her"—their motive in telling Jesus is not indicated. Some suggest that it was to explain why the meal was not ready, forgetting the presence of Peter's wife. Apparently it was an implied invitation to Jesus to use His marvelous powers on her behalf. Luke stated that "they made request to him concerning her" (4:38, Rotherham).

"He came and took her by the hand, and lifted her up"—His response was prompt and gracious, marked by calm confidence. Approaching her couch and facing her, He grasped her hand and raised up the prostrate sufferer. The physical contact served to establish rapport with the sufferer and made it obvious that the healing was an expression of His own volition.

"Immediately the fever left her, and she ministered unto them"—a simple statement of the fact of the healing, followed by the unmistakable demonstration of its reality and completeness. There was no lingering weakness or lassitude, such as accompanies ordinary convalescence. Her strength fully restored, she at once resumed her normal domestic functions, rendering beneficial ministries to the guests. Brooks well comments: "The Mother-in-law is presented simply as a model of discipleship, which requires lowly service from all, male and female. By including accounts of the healing of women as well as men, Mark implies that Jesus was concerned about all people, including those who have a lowly place in society."[20]

c. Healing Ministry at Sundown (vv. 32-34).

The intense excitement in Capernaum, created by events in the synagogue and fed by reports of the miraculous healing in the home of Peter, exploded into action at sundown. Verses 32-33 record the city-wide activity, while verse 34 reports Jesus' complete competence to deal with the demanding situation. Parallel accounts occur in Matthew 8:16-17 and Luke 4:40-41.

"At even, when the sun did set"—a curious double time designation. But it is not just needless repetition. *At even* might mean "later afternoon," since the Jews distinguished two evenings, the first beginning at 3:00 P.M. The second designation made it unmistakable that the time was at the close of the Sabbath day. The excited inhabitants held themselves in check until the close of the Sabbath day in order not to infringe upon Sabbath regulations. The law prohibited any work on the Sabbath (Exod. 20:10), and rabbinical regulations stressed that no burdens should be carried on that day. Hence sunset, marking the close of the Sabbath day, was the signal for action.

"They brought unto him"—the indefinite *they* denotes the people of Capernaum. *Brought* means "to carry, bear as a burden," and the imperfect tense pictures the steady stream of people coming with their sick. Case after case was being brought *unto him,* to put them into personal touch with Jesus.

"All that were diseased, and them that were possessed with devils"[21]—two distinct classes correspond to the two miracles performed

---

[20] Brooks, p. 52.

[21] The KJV rendering "devils" should be changed to "demons." There is only one Devil (Rev. 12:9), but there are many demons.

that day. The first class included all those suffering from various human afflictions, but the second class could not strictly be included in that category. All the synoptics make this distinction.

"All the city was gathered together at the door"—a comment found only in Mark. The reference is apparently to Peter's house. The scene made an indelible impression on Peter. *Was gathered* is in the perfect tense and pictures the crowd, having previously flocked to the door, now forming a dense mass as they waited for the Healer to get to them.

Verse 34 graphically summarizes Jesus' compassionate ministry to the needy that evening. This general statement refutes any idea that all the miracles of Jesus have been recorded in detail.

"Many that were sick of divers diseases"—the sufferers were many, and their sicknesses presented a wide variety of human afflictions. *Many* does not mean that there were some who were not healed, either because of inability or lack of time; those who were brought to Jesus were not a few but a large number. Matthew clearly asserted that Jesus "healed all that were sick" (8:16). Luke noted that they were healed by the method of individual treatment (4:40).

"Cast out many devils"—The passage clearly distinguishes between healing and exorcism. They were brought to Jesus because the exorcism in the synagogue had aroused new hope for many such sufferers in the city.

"Suffered not the devils to speak"—Jesus recognized the demons as intelligent personalities distinct from the personalities of the people possessed. *Suffered not* is in the imperfect tense, indicating that again and again, Jesus refused to let these demons speak out as they desired to do. This was contrary to the usual technique of exorcism, which sought to force the demons to speak out and reveal themselves.

"Because they knew him"—the demons always revealed an accurate knowledge of the true identity of Jesus. "This knowledge is one of the arguments for the supernaturalism of these cases."[22] Jesus did not want any testimony that was given grudgingly and in fear. His messianic identity was a revelation that God must work in human hearts.

4. Tour of Galilee (1:35-45)

Jesus combined concentrated efforts in Capernaum and vicinity (Matt. 11:20-23) with extensive preaching tours throughout the province. Mark gives a brief summary of the first tour (vv. 35-39) and then describes one striking event during that tour (vv. 40-45).

---

[22] Ezra P. Gould, *A Critical and Exegetical Commentary on the Gospel According to St. Mark,* International Critical Commentary, p. 27.

a. Departure from Capernaum (vv. 35-39).

"In the morning, rising up a great while before day"—another odd but vivid time designation. The adverb rendered "in the morning" means early, and was an elastic term for the last watch of the night, from 3:00 to 6:00 A.M. The second designation, composed of two adverbs, is literally "at night very much." It was still very definitely during nocturnal darkness. The double designation seems to reflect the reaction of those in the house the next morning, upon discovering that Jesus had already slipped out.

"A solitary place"—a quiet and uninhabited spot somewhere in the vicinity of Capernaum. Since the land around Capernaum was cultivated, it need not denote a barren and desolate place, unless Jesus withdrew to one of the ravines in the surrounding mountain range.

"And there prayed"—this protracted prayer session is mentioned only in Mark. The verb does not denote intercession for others, but rather the conscious outgoing of the soul toward God in desire for Him. After a busy day of service, Jesus felt the need for inner refreshment through renewed fellowship with the Father. His example is a standing challenge to us. Barnhouse comments: "If Jesus in His great power and oneness with God could feel the urgent necessity of communion with the Father, how much more you and I need to go to the Father for the strength that fills our weakness and the knowledge that fills our ignorance. . . . Prayer brings us into a fellowship with God that nothing else can provide."[23]

"Simon and they that were with him"—the language suggests the personal narrative of Peter. He assumed the leadership. It is the first instance of that impulsive leadership which distinguishes Peter in the Gospels. The others with him are not identified.

"Followed after him"—the verb stands emphatically at the beginning of the sentence and is in the singular: "And he followed after him, Simon and those with him." The strong compound verb occurs only here in the New Testament and quite literally means "to pursue, to hunt down." It implies a strenuous and determined search. It reflects a recollection of the anxiety of the disciples before they succeeded in locating Jesus.

"All *men* seek for thee"—the continuing excitement at Capernaum justified their search for Him. The seeking crowds did not want Him to leave. Luke explicitly said that the people came to Jesus and asked Him not to leave (4:42). The disciples implied that Jesus must return

---

[23] Donald Grey Barnhouse, *Mark: The Servant Gospel,* p. 32.

with them and follow up the tremendous popularity. They felt that Jesus must regulate His movements by the desires of the masses.

Mark 1:38 states the counterplan advanced by Jesus. Instead of feeding the miracle-inspired popularity, He proposed a preaching tour elsewhere.

"Let us go [elsewhere, Gr.] into the next towns"—the present tense implies a tour of some duration. The plural invites the disciples to join Him in this tour to the surrounding places. Instead of returning to Capernaum, Jesus suggested that they go in a different direction, into the next towns. *Towns,* a compound form found only here in the New Testament, means village-cities. It denotes places having a considerable population unified by the presence of a synagogue but in organization ranking only as villages. Perhaps the chief distinction was that they were without walls. Galilee had numerous villages.

"That I may preach there also"—an implied rebuke to the efforts of Capernaum to monopolize His ministry. Jesus was eager to continue His primary mission of preaching, heralding the good news of the kingdom. *There also,* emphatic by position, urges that these other places too must hear His message. The preaching was central; the miracles were the appended seal authenticating the message. Jesus was determined not to allow preoccupation with the miracles to obscure the message. He refused to embark on a career as a mere wonder worker.

An interesting cycle may be traced. The miracles accompanying His preaching spread His fame. The reported miracles caused the crowds to flock to Him, the people seeking Him because of His healings. When simply sought as a miracle-worker, Jesus deliberately departed to teach elsewhere.

"For therefore came I forth"—*therefore* ("to this end," ASV) looks to the proposed preaching tour; Jesus' express purpose was to begin work in a larger field. *Came forth* does not have primary reference to the departure from Capernaum. He had left the city not to preach but to pray. It is a veiled reference to His coming forth from God. Thus Luke worded it "for therefore am I sent" (4:43). The divine mission was not made more explicit, since it was a truth that would dawn gradually upon the disciples.

Verse 39 summarizes the itinerant ministry through Galilee. It must have required a number of weeks, perhaps even months. Matthew 4:23-25 elaborates on the nature and scope of this tour. Mark summarizes the work in two participles. Christ's main activity was *preaching.* Jesus centered His work in the synagogue, not in the marketplaces, indicating that His was a religious rather than a political or economic ministry. The other activity mentioned is *exorcising,* the only type of miracle referred to in this summary. The next paragraph makes it clear that healings did occur, but the casting out of demons was the outstanding feature of the work. Jesus' work always brought Him into victorious conflict with these evil powers and demonstrated that the establishment of the kingdom of God meant the overthrow of the kingdom of Satan.

b. Cleansing of a Leper (vv. 40-45).

The cleansing of a leper, the only miracle on this tour described by Mark, offers one of the most striking evidences of Jesus' supernatural power. Only two instances of the healing of leprosy, one a multiple healing (Luke 17:12-19), are given in the Gospels. But other instances did occur. Some time before the second recorded instance, Jesus pointed to the cleansing of lepers as assurance to John the Baptist of His own messianic identity (Matt. 11:5; Luke 7:22). Mark records the cleansing of the leper (vv. 40-42) and Jesus' stern order to the man, which was promptly disobeyed (vv. 43-45). Matthew 8:2-4 and Luke 5:12-16 give parallel accounts.

"There cometh to him a leper" (ASV)—Mark gives no indication of place, but Luke noted that it was "in a certain city" (5:12). Since under the law a leper was ritually unclean and excluded from society, his coming to Jesus boldly was remarkable. This horrible affliction was regarded as distinct from other physical maladies. Leprosy had a religious significance as a type of sin, the outward and visible sign of inward spiritual corruption. The leper was considered unclean, the very embodiment of impurity. The Old Testament term (Lev. 13-14) included some other inflammatory skin diseases, but this man's affliction undoubtedly was true leprosy. The cure for a minor skin disorder would not have produced the excitement of this case. True leprosy, known today as Hansen's disease, was a loathsome and progressively disfiguring disease, for which no cure was known. The rabbis scrupulously avoided any contact with lepers in order not to incur ceremonial defilement.

"Beseeching him, and kneeling down to him"—he made an urgent plea with deep humility. Kneeling was the accepted posture of the supplicant. His request proves that he had faith in the supernatural power of Jesus to heal him. Reports of Jesus' miracles had awakened this faith in him.

"If thou wilt, thou canst make me clean"—here is no imposition on the will of Jesus, no doubt of His ability. The leper humbly submitted his case to Jesus and let Him determine how He would react. Jesus apparently had not previously dealt with a leper; his case would demonstrate Jesus' response to such sufferers. Since leprosy was considered a symbol of defilement, its cure is naturally referred to as a cleansing.

"Moved with compassion"—Mark alone recorded this emotional reaction of Jesus to the pitiable man before Him. The verb denotes not only a pained feeling at the sight of suffering but also a yearning to relieve it. In the New Testament, only the synoptic Gospels use the term, and, except in His parables, always of Jesus.

"Put forth *his* hand, and touched him, and saith unto him"—His tender feeling found immediate expression in act and word. "The point of mentioning this," Hurtado suggests, "seems to be to show that Jesus not only healed the man but also established immediate social contact with him."[24] Doubtless deeply conscious of the social ostracism that his leprosy had brought upon him, Jesus' warm touch moved the man's heart and assured him of the true love of Jesus for an outcast like himself. Unlike the rabbis, Jesus did not hesitate to touch a leper for fear of ceremonial defilement. Divine holiness is not defiled by touching human uncleanness but rather imparts cleansing. Jesus' symbolic touch and assuring word formed a unit, indicating that the healing was an act of His own will.

"I will; be thou clean"—a sublime command, calmly spoken in the consciousness of His perfect power to cure the leper. *I will* is present indicative, expressing His standing will for the man; *be thou clean* is an aorist imperative, commanding the man's cleansing as a definite act. The passive voice indicates that the man is the passive recipient of cleansing ("be thou made clean," ASV).

"Immediately"—the cure was instantaneous, hence miraculous. The leprosy vanished, leaving him free of the disease and its ravages.

"He was cleansed"—a definite act, corresponding to the definite command of Jesus. It marked an exact fulfillment of Jesus' word.

"And he straitly charged him"—Mark's term, stronger than that used by the other synoptics, denotes strong emotion and marks a swift change from tender pity to stern command. The verb usually indicates indignant displeasure but may signify deep emotion expressed in tone and manner. An element of real displeasure seems implied here. Jesus feared that the man would be too demonstrative in his gratitude, thus arousing a veritable hurricane of unwanted popularity for Jesus as a miracle-worker. Jesus sought to keep the man from doing what he later did do.

"And forthwith sent him away"—"at once thrust him out," indicating a prompt and peremptory dismissal. It may imply that the miracle took place in a house or synagogue. But the verb may simply

---

[24] Larry W. Hurtado, *Mark, A Good News Commentary,* p. 16.

mean that Jesus was urgent to have the man leave His presence and the circle of people with Him.

"See thou say nothing to any man"—a strong prohibition. The cured leper must see to it that not a word be spoken to anyone about what had happened to him. The prohibition was temporal, in force until the following command had been carried out.

"But go thy way, show thyself to the priest"—"be going and, as a definite act, show thyself to the priest" for his inspection. *Thyself,* emphatic by position, stressed this act as his personal duty. He must observe the requirements of the Mosaic law concerning one who had been cleansed of leprosy (Lev. 14). *The priest* meant not just any priest but the one on duty in the temple at Jerusalem. The offering for his cleansing must be received by the inspecting priest.

"Those things which Moses commanded"—until the legal offerings had been made, the man was still ceremonially unclean. They were necessary for his official reinstatement in society. Jesus' insistence upon their fulfillment revealed that He was not antagonistic to the law.

"For a testimony unto them"—the priest's acceptance of the man's offering for his cleansing would be an authoritative public testimony to the reality of his cure. Some would interpret the indefinite *them* to mean "the people" (RSV), making his offering a proof to the Jewish people in general of the reality of the healing. But Mark makes no mention of the people, and the nearest antecedent, *the priest,* naturally means that the offering made at the priest's direction would be a testimony or proof to the priestly class of the reality of the miracles wrought by Jesus. It would be an undeniable messianic sign to them.

Verse 45 records the man's disobedience and the result for Jesus.

"But he went out"—some would interpret the indefinite *he* as meaning Jesus rather than the cured leper, holding that no change of subject is indicated. But the context indicates that Mark meant the cleansed leper.

"Began to publish *it* much"—Mark alone specifically recorded the man's disobedience. *Much* indicates that he heralded forth the matter at length and did so repeatedly. Swete remarks, "An oriental with a tale not only tells it at great length, but repeats it with unwearied energy."[25] His aggressive action is psychologically understandable, and no doubt the man acted in gratitude, but he failed to consider that he was violating the express command of the one who had given him the desire of his heart.

---

[25] Swete, p. 31.

"Insomuch that Jesus could no more openly enter into the city"—literally, "a city." This was the result of the man's disobedience. Mark used the indefinite *he*, but the rendering "Jesus" removes the ambiguity. The reports of the cure produced a rush to Jesus as a miracle-worker so that He could no longer publicly enter a city without causing a tumultuous gathering. It brought His synagogue ministry on this tour to an abrupt halt. Jesus deliberately avoided the cities to let the excitement die down.

"Was without in desert places"—remained in uninhabited areas, moving from place to place. Luke added that He withdrew to pray (5:16).

"They came to him from every quarter"—the imperfect tense pictures the people as continuing to come to Him from all sides. Jesus did not hide from people, nor did He cease to preach, but His purpose to spread His message through the synagogues throughout Galilee was frustrated.

3
Ministry in Galilee
(Part 2; 2:1–3:6)

5. Conflicts with the Scribes (2:1–3:6)

The beneficent ministry of Jesus had resulted in tremendous popular enthusiasm and curiosity. But upon the religious leaders among the Jews, the Servant of the Lord made an entirely different impression. They found many things in His words and deeds which aroused their hostility. Mark now depicts the causes and early display of that hostility. The opposition manifested itself in a series of charges against Jesus, coming with mounting intensity. The scribes were offended by His claim to forgive sins (2:2-12), His fellowship with publicans (2:13-17), His supposed neglect of ascetic duties (2:18-22), and His violations of their Sabbath regulations (2:23–3:6).

a. Paralytic Forgiven and Healed (2:1-12).

All the synoptics record this initial conflict with the scribes (Matt. 9:1-8; Luke 5:17-26), but Matthew placed it at a later date than Mark and Luke. The Gospel writers did not always adhere to a strict chronological order in their narratives but grouped their material according to their own design and purpose.

Verses 1-2 provide the general setting for this first indication of scribal hostility toward Jesus.

"And again he entered into Capernaum"—*again* looks back to 1:21, marking a return to the scene of the opening ministry as recorded by Mark. Mark often notes the recurrences of scenes and places in his account. Matthew here identifies Capernaum as "his own city" (9:1).

"After *some* days"—a vague time designation. The length of the first tour of Galilee is thus left indefinite.

"It was noised that he was in the house"—the return to Capernaum had been quiet, but the report of Jesus' return at once stirred excitement. "It was noised," more literally, "it was heard," indicates the simple news which prompted this mass assembly. In the original, *house* is without an article and the verb is present tense, so that the probable meaning is "He is at home!" This suggests the eager interest of the people of Capernaum in the movements of Jesus. The house may have been Peter's, although some think that the reference is to the house where Jesus lived with His mother in Capernaum.

The report caused the people to flock to the house in great numbers (v. 2). Using the freedom which Oriental custom allowed, they entered without previous invitation. They soon packed the place, leaving no longer any room for others. But the people kept coming and soon there was no room even about the door, which seems to have opened directly onto the street. Apparently the house was an unpretentious one, without an inner open courtyard.

"He preached the word unto them"—Jesus readily used the opportunity thus thrust upon Him. The verb *preached* is not the term denoting the public proclamation of an authoritative message, but a term pointing out the conversational tone of the speaker. Wuest remarks, "The beauty of His voice, the charm of His manner, and the tenderness and love of His countenance, must have come to this weary, sick group of people as a breath from heaven."[1] *The word* is the good news of the gospel, the word par excellence. Jesus was still speaking when the interrupting action, vividly described in verses 3-5, occurred.

"And they come unto him"—the historical present pictures the past occurrences with the vividness of present reality. *Unto him* does not mean into His immediate presence but rather toward Him.

"Bringing one sick of the palsy"—an unusual faith-prompted response to the report that Jesus had returned. They were carrying as a burden a helpless paralytic, a man who had lost the power of bodily movement.

"Borne of four"—Mark alone mentions their number. How he was being brought is made clear by the mention of the bed in verse 4. It was a poor man's bed, or pallet, a thickly padded quilt or flexible mattress.

The efforts of the four to push their way through the dense crowd proved futile. They recognized that the attempt was hopeless. But they refused to be frustrated in their purpose. As Maclaren notes, their faith developed a "sanctified ingenuity" to overcome the difficulty.[2]

---

[1] Kenneth S. Wuest, *Mark in the Greek New Testament for the English Reader,* p. 45.

[2] Alexander Maclaren, "St. Mark," in *Expositions of Holy Scripture,* 8:50.

"They uncovered the roof where he was"—marking the extraordinary procedure they adopted to get the man to Jesus. They ascended to the flat roof of the house, either by means of an outside stairway or from the roof of an adjoining house. The flat housetop was generally used for various purposes. The house apparently was a modest one-story building.

"When they had broken *it* up"—literally, "having dug out," indicating that the roof was made of clay or marl. Luke recorded that the man was let down "through the tiling" (5:19). It need not follow that Luke thought of a different kind of house. The flat roof for an ordinary house would be constructed by laying beams about three feet apart from wall to wall. Short sticks were laid closely together across the beams and covered with a thick matting of thorn bushes. At other times, as seems the case here, stone slabs or plates of burnt clay were laid across the beams. A coat of clay was spread on top of this and rolled hard to keep out the rain. They would be readily able to dig out a hole large enough for the purpose without damaging the rest of the roof. Having cleared away the clay, they lifted the tiles to make the opening.

Admittedly, the precise situation is not too clear from the brief references. Because of the unconventional character of the action and the supposed danger involved, some critics have stamped the story as fictitious. Plummer replies, "To treat the whole narrative as fiction, because we have no certain explanation of this interesting detail, is not sane criticism."[3] The entire procedure is so unique that the invention of the whole account is highly implausible.

"They let down the bed"—the successful culmination of their amazing course of action. Probably ropes, which may have been borrowed from some of Peter's fishing tackle lying on the roof, were fastened to the four corners of the pallet on which the prostrate sufferer lay.

"When Jesus saw their faith"—the extraordinary, ardent, persistent action of the four in getting the man to Jesus was visible evidence of their faith in His ability to heal. It proved the living nature of their faith. Although their bold action interrupted His teaching activity, Jesus did not rebuke the intrusion but approvingly noted the expression of their faith. He indirectly commended their faith by turning at once to their suffering friend. That the paralytic also had faith need not be questioned. We concur with English, "In view of the circumstances it

---

[3] Alfred Plummer, *The Gospel According to St. Mark,* Cambridge Greek Testament, p. 81.

seems more likely that the ill man also had faith, bearing in mind all that he went through simply to be where he was."[4]

"Son"—an affectionate address aimed at encouraging the faith of the unfortunate man (cf. Matt. 9:2). *Son,* literally, "child," implies a parental attitude. The term does not prove that he was a youth.

"Thy sins be forgiven thee"—a positive declaration of fact, meeting the man's deepest need. The verb stands emphatically before the subject. The manuscripts are divided between the perfect and the present tense, but it is now generally accepted that the present is the original, "are here-and-now being forgiven." Jesus thus first spoke peace to the man's conscience. Seemingly, his affliction had caused the man deep searching of heart, leaving a troubled conscience because of his keen sense of personal sinfulness. That personal sins had caused his affliction is neither asserted nor expressly ruled out. Christ's word assured the removal of guilt in real forgiveness. The procedure of Jesus was in harmony with the currently Jewish view that the forgiveness of sins must precede physical recovery. The rabbis said, "There is no sick man healed of his sickness until all his sins have been forgiven him."[5]

Verses 6-7 describe the source and nature of the opposition aroused.

"Certain of the scribes sitting there"—the first mention of the presence of the scribes in Mark (cf. 1:22). Luke identified them as "Pharisees and doctors of the law" and added that they had "come out of every town of Galilee, and Judaea, and Jerusalem" (5:17). They were men of importance in Jewish affairs. The scribes devoted themselves to the study and teaching of the laws and traditions which governed all of Jewish life. Obviously, their concern about the growing popularity of Jesus had caused them to gather in order to keep a close watch on Him. *Sitting,* although the room was so crowded that most of the people stood, suggests the honor that had been accorded the scribes.

"Reasoning in their hearts"—their reaction was not openly expressed, but it produced a hostile atmosphere which Jesus immediately sensed. They began a dialogue with themselves, advancing thoughts and considerations concerning the objectionable nature of Jesus' words. It was a deliberate process of reasoning and mental debate, not just excited emotional response.

"Why doth this *man* thus speak"—*this man* is contemptuous, "this fellow." *Thus* looks back to the words of Jesus and expresses their disdain.

---

[4] Donald English, *The Message of Mark,* p. 66.

[5] Henry Barclay Swete, *The Gospel According to St. Mark,* p. 35.

"Blasphemies"—As theologians, they saw the blasphemous implications. They immediately concluded that Jesus' pronouncement to the paralytic was irreverent and blasphemous.

"Who can forgive sins but God only?"—the irrefutable proof for their indictment. Jesus was deliberately arrogating to Himself the prerogative of God to forgive sins. The passive verb in Jesus' pronouncement of forgiveness did not state who forgave and could mean either God or Himself. The suspicious scribes at once took it that Jesus personally claimed to forgive the man. Their conclusion of blasphemy was a flawless logical deduction from their premises:

> Major premise: Only God can forgive sins.
> Minor premise: This man claims to forgive sins.
> Conclusion: He blasphemes, being a mere man.

Verses 8-11 record Jesus' response to the reasoning of the scribes. He would not allow this challenge to His right to forgive sins to go unanswered.

"And immediately when Jesus perceived in his spirit"—He instantly detected their hostile reaction without prior visible or audible indications. Inwardly and intuitively, He perceived their hostile reasonings. *In his spirit* may also be rendered "by his spirit"; it indicates that it was by His spirit, rather than by eye or ear, that He knew their thoughts. *His spirit* does not refer to the Holy Spirit. Neither need it be pressed to denote His divine nature in contrast to the spiritual element of His human nature. Swete well remarks: "His spirit, while it belonged to the human nature of Christ, was that part of His human nature which was the immediate sphere of the Holy Spirit's operations, and through which, we may reverently believe, the Sacred Humanity was united to the Divine Word."[6]

"So reasoned within themselves"—Jesus recognized the nature of their hostile thoughts. It was their bias toward Him that evoked their negative reaction.

"Why reason ye these things in your hearts?"—His counter-question corresponded in form to their question and implied censure. Had they been willing to acknowledge the true significance of the supernatural in His ministry, they would have been kept from such hostile reactions. They had expected Him to say a word of healing, operating in the realm of the physical. Instead, He had made a declaration of forgiveness, reaching into the realm of the divine. To this they objected. But Jesus at once proposed a test that could verify His

---

[6] Ibid., p. 36.

authority to meet the inner moral need of the man. It would establish the fact that He had the right to exercise the divine prerogative.

Verse 9 states the test as a challenge to His critics. His question does not merely contrast the performance of the two acts but stresses the authoritative nature of the pronouncements. Jesus implied that neither is to be said without authority to do so. The scribes might insist that His claimed right to forgive sins was easier to declare since it was an inner matter which could not be verified by outward observation. But His authority to say "Arise, and take up thy bed, and walk" could at once be validated by the visible test of success or failure. If, when He spoke these words to the man, the obvious result proved His authority to give the helpless man such an order, then they could have no reason to question His authority to forgive the man's sins.

"That ye may know that the Son of man hath power on earth to forgive sins"—the point to be proved by the test. It was a question not merely of His ability to forgive sins but also of His authority or moral right to do so. The forgiveness of sins is a moral issue; its exercise has to do with moral rights and liabilities. To claim that right falsely would indeed make Jesus guilty of blasphemy. But if the proposed test will establish that right, it will prove that He is no mere man. The test was intended to show that their premise concerning His human nature was wrong. The test centered in His authority as the Son of man. The expression cannot mean simply that He was a real man, since the authority He was going to establish does not belong to any mere man.

The title *the Son of man* occurs fourteen times in Mark's Gospel.[7] This is chronologically its first occurrence in the synoptic narrative. The Fourth Gospel reports Jesus' using it of Himself from the very beginning of His public work (John 1:51; 3:13-14). The occurrences of this title throughout the four Gospels show that Jesus used it of Himself during all parts of His ministry and before any company.[8] Clearly it was one of His favorite designations of Himself. In every instance, except in John 12:34 (in which Jesus is quoted) and Acts

---

[7] Mark 2:10, 28; 8:31, 38; 9:9, 12, 31; 10:33, 45; 13:26; 14:21 (twice), 41, 62.

[8] Its other New Testament occurrences are Matthew 8:20; 9:6; 10:23; 11:19; 12:8, 32, 40; 13:37, 41; 16:13, 27, 28; 17:9, 12, 22; 19:28; 20:18, 28; 24:27, 30 (twice), 37, 39, 44; 25:31; 26:2, 24 (twice), 45, 64—T.R. also in 18:11 and 25:13. Luke 5:24; 6:5, 22; 7:34; 9:22, 26, 44, 58; 11:30; 12:8, 10, 40; 17:22, 24, 26, 30; 18:8, 31; 19:10; 21:27, 36; 22:22, 48, 69; 24:7—T.R. also in 9:56. John 1:51; 3:13, 14; 5:27; 6:27, 53, 62; 8:28; 12:23, 34 (twice); 13:31. Acts 7:56. Revelation 1:13. The expression in Revelation 14:14 is akin but different, being a precise reproduction of Daniel 7:13 in the Greek.

7:56, the title is used by Jesus of Himself. It obviously was not a designation that the early church was in the habit of applying to Jesus.

The precise intended significance of this title has been much discussed.[9] Varied views about its significance have been advanced.[10] Most expositors accept that it has a messianic significance. This view, as Warfield points out, "is apparent not only from its obvious origin in the vision of Daniel 7:13, to which reference is repeatedly made (8:38; 13:26; 14:62), but also from the easy passage which is made, in the course of the conversations reported, from one of the other designations to this, whereby they are evinced as its synonyms."[11] The title apparently was not in popular usage as a messianic designation, but the Gospels give no hint that either Jesus' disciples or the common people entertained any doubts about its messianic connotation. John 12:34 proves that the crowd understood it as a messianic designation. They had heard the term from the lips of Jesus and accepted it as a reference to the Messiah, but their difficulty lay in their inability to reconcile their conception of the Messiah as abiding forever with His reference to exaltation through death.

Jesus apparently chose this title for Himself because its use would not immediately associate Him in the thinking of the people with the undesirable connotations which had developed around the common term *Messiah*. Thus, His use of the term half concealed and half revealed His self-identification as the personal Messiah. While the term was recognized to have messianic connections, the title *Son of man* would not force the people to make a premature decision concerning His identity in terms of their usual messianic expectations. It would enable Him to connect His messianic self-presentation with views more in harmony with His own person and teaching.

It seems clear that Jesus took the term from and understood it in the light of Daniel 7:13-14. That His understanding of the term was

---

[9] George P. Gould, "Son of Man" in *Dictionary of Christ and the Gospels,* ed. James Hastings, 2:659-65; James Stalker, "The Son of Man," in *International Standard Bible Encyclopedia,* ed. James Orr, 5:2828-30; C.E.B. Cranfield, *The Gospel According to St. Mark,* Cambridge Greek Testament Commentary, pp. 272-77.

[10] V. Taylor summarizes the different views as follows: (1) that Jesus was speaking of "man" in general; (2) that Jesus was thinking of the elect messianic community of which He is head; (3) that He was referring to Himself as the Messiah, or as the representative man; (4) that He used the term of Himself without expressly claiming to be the Messiah; (5) that the designation represents the theology of the primitive Christian community. Vincent holds that the most is to be said for the third view. *The Gospel According to St. Mark,* pp. 197-98.

[11] Benjamin B. Warfield, *The Lord of Glory,* p. 24.

associated with the prophetic picture given there seems clearly established from Jesus' words in Mark 14:62 and Matthew 26:64. Understood in the light of its prophetic origin, the title *Son of man* expressed
the thought of a personal, transcendental majesty which the common
term *Messiah* failed to convey to the people of His day. Tillman states
that "Jesus adopted this designation because it corresponded best to
His nature and His purposes, and gave least occasion for the political,
national hopes which His people connected with the person of the
Messiah."[12]

A survey of the passages in which Jesus used the title indicates that
He employed it in connection with two predominant concepts, His
suffering and death (8:31; 9:9-13, 31; 10:33, 45; 14:21, 41) and His
future return in glory (8:38; 13:26, 32; 14:62). His use of the title
permitted Him to blend the concept of the suffering Servant with that
of the messianic King. While the prophetic picture in Daniel 7:13-14
did not explicitly indicate His prior suffering and death, the designation
Daniel employed did not exclude the suffering which Jesus knew lay
ahead for Him. Thus this title was more suitable for His purpose than
the term *Messiah,* which conveyed the concept of the messianic King
in His capacity as ruler and was commonly felt to be inconsistent with
the thought of His death (cf. 8:31-32). Perhaps Jesus also favored the
title *Son of man* because it was capable of being understood in a general
or indefinite sense as connecting Him with the entire human race.

"Power on earth"—or literally, "authority, right." To forgive sin
was God's acknowledged prerogative in heaven. Jesus' claim to the
right to exercise that authority implied that He possessed it as God's
representative on earth. The hostility of the scribes stemmed from their
refusal to accept His claim to exercise the divine prerogative.

"(He saith to the sick of the palsy)"—the parenthesis marks the
turning from the scribes to apply the test to the man. Jesus well knew
that the credibility of His whole ministry and mission rested on the
outcome of His command to the man. Conscious of His authorization,
He spoke with calm, sublime certainty.

Verse 11 records the emphatic utterance of His crucial command.

"I say unto thee"—a threefold command was directed to the paralytic personally.

"Arise"—testing the man's faith. His faith would be shown by his
cooperation with the command, believing that he could do as told.

"Take up thy bed"—demanding his prompt obedience as a definite act.

---

[12] F. Tillman, quoted in Warfield, p. 31, n. 44.

"Go thy way into thine house"—ordering him to be on his way home. The command implies that he was a resident of Capernaum. He would be a standing witness there to Jesus' authority to forgive sins.

Verse 12 records three instantaneous acts on the part of the man, corresponding to the three commands given him. His response was undeniable evidence of his complete healing at the word of Jesus; it proved the supernatural power of His utterance, whether in the realm of physical healing or in the realm of the forgiveness of sins.

"Before them all"—a public attestation of Jesus' authority. It made the scribal unbelief inexcusable.

"They were all amazed, and glorified God"—the miracle taking place before their very eyes filled them with intense amazement and awe. It was an acknowledged operation of supernatural power. *They* refers to the bystanders; nothing is said about the reaction of the scribes.

"We never saw it on this fashion"—they were impressed by what they saw with their eyes: the visible, physical restoration. But no comment was made about the forgiveness of sins which the healing established. Matthew noted that they saw Jesus only as the agent of God's amazing power (9:8).

b. Call of Levi and His Feast (2:13-17).

This brief paragraph records a second ground for the adverse reaction of the scribes toward Jesus. The two brief narratives, the calling of Levi (vv. 13-14) and the feast in his house (vv. 15-17), portray what the scribes regarded as Jesus' too intimate associations with the religious outcasts of the day. Parallel accounts occur in Matthew 9:9-13 and Luke 5:27-32.

"He went forth again by the sea side"—perhaps as soon as the crowd dispersed after the healing of the paralytic. Jesus went forth both from the house and the city of Capernaum. *Again* looks back to 1:16, the scene in which Jesus began His ministry at Capernaum. *By the sea side* suggests that He walked along the seashore, probably for refreshment and quiet communion with the Father. Clearly, Jesus was a lover of nature and enjoyed being out in the open.

"All the multitude resorted unto him, and he taught them"—this statement may be rendered, "All the crowd kept on coming to him, and he kept on teaching them." The imperfect tenses picture successive groups coming out to Jesus, and each group received His teaching. Mark alone noted this fact here. While noting the fact, Mark gave no indication of the contents of the teaching. No doubt many publicans were among those who came to hear Him.

"As he passed by"—Jesus had moved from place to place along the seashore; now a specific event is recorded that took place as He traveled. Levi's office evidently was located on the great caravan route which ran through Capernaum from Damascus to the Mediterranean, probably near the wharf at Capernaum.

"He saw Levi"—no previous acquaintance between Jesus and Levi is indicated, but Levi must have known a good deal about Jesus. The excitement produced by His teaching and miracles must have been well known to him. Mark and Luke called him Levi, but in Matthew 9:9 he is identified as "a man called Matthew." Apparently, Levi was his original name, and Matthew, meaning "gift of the Lord," a second name, either given him by Jesus or self-assumed to commemorate his call to be a disciple. It was not uncommon for a man to receive or assume a new name upon entering a new career. The name Levi is not used again in Mark.

The identification of Levi with Matthew is strengthened by the fact that in the various lists of the Twelve, Matthew is always named but never Levi. Mark called him Levi here, yet in his list of the Twelve, Mark names Matthew, suggesting that he accepted the identification as well known. But this identification is not without some difficulty and has not always been accepted, either in the past or now.

"The *son* of Alphaeus"—mentioned only by Mark. James the Less was also identified as "the *son* of Alphaeus" (Matt. 10:3; Mark 3:18; Luke 6:15; Acts 1:13), but that does not prove that the two disciples were brothers, as is sometimes asserted. The name *Alphaeus* was quite common; their fathers easily could have had the same name. The lists of the Twelve never name these two disciples together, as they do the two known pairs of brothers in the apostolic body.

"Sitting at the receipt of custom"—the place where customs or dues were collected. Levi was presumably in the employment of Herod Antipas, the ruler of Galilee. He would collect dues on exports from Capernaum and import taxes on goods passing through. To hold this office required that he know Greek and possess a fair measure of education. Levi sitting *at* (*epi*) may mean that he was sitting outside and leaning against the building, but more probably the preposition, meaning "upon," pictures him as seated cross-legged on the elevated platform or bench which formed the central and essential part of the tax-collecting station.

"Follow me"—the present imperative called him to a continuing relationship of personal attendance upon Jesus as His regular disciple. Wuest notes that "me" is in the associative-instrumental case and marks that Jesus "welcomed him to a participation in His companionship."[13] Jesus took the initiative in establishing the relationship. It

---

[13] Wuest, *Mark,* p. 52.

marked a crisis for Levi. Unlike a fisherman, a publican who abandoned his position could not later return to it.

"He arose and followed him"—the aorist tenses record Levi's decisive response. He made a definite break with his past in accepting the call. The call seemed abrupt, but Jesus knew that Levi's heart was hungry and ready to accept something higher. His effective call to Levi is another illustration of the winsome authority of Jesus. That Jesus would call a despised tax collector to be His disciple no doubt created a stir in Capernaum and further scandalized the Pharisees.

"And it came to pass"—this transitional formula implies an interval between the call of Levi and the feast in his house. Mark here used the present tense, "It comes to pass," as though viewing the scene as a spectator.

"He was sitting at meat in his house" (ASV)—the personal identity of the two pronouns has been much discussed; it is best to accept that *he* refers to Jesus and *his house* means the house of Levi. The construction is somewhat loose, but this view is in harmony with Luke's assertion that "Levi made him a great feast in his own house" (5:29). This should solve the problem, except for critics who persist in finding perpetual war between the Gospel writers.

Was sitting is quite literally "was lying prostrate" and pictures the practice of reclining at a table. Jews did not always recline while eating, but it was common practice at feasts with guests present. The guests, whose unsandled feet extended toward the outer edge of the couch, leaned upon their left elbow and used the right hand for eating. The Gospels use no less than six different verbs to denote this posture, five of them by Mark.

"Many publicans and sinners"—Levi's house must have had a spacious hall or a large open court to accommodate the crowd. These publicans and sinners represented a section of Jewish society which Jesus could not contact in the synagogues. The feast obviously was Levi's method of introducing his former associates to his newfound Master. *Many* had accepted this opportunity for close association with Jesus, pointing to a widespread interest in Him among them.

These *publicans* were local Jewish tax collectors, many of them apparently in the service of Herod Antipas, who used the common tax-farming system to raise his revenues. These guests of Levi's feast were obviously not of the well-known *publicani,* wealthy persons who bought from the Roman government for a set sum the right to collect the taxes of a certain province. They generally employed natives of the provinces to do the actual work of collecting and pledged to pay their employers a certain sum. The money these local publicans collected flowed into the coffers of Herod Antipas. These collectors were hated in all the provinces. In Palestine they were regarded as especially odious because of their continual contacts with unclean Gentiles; their cooperation with the hated, oppressive Roman government; and their frequent unjust demands upon the taxpayers.[14] The common double designation "publicans and sinners," used three times in vv. 15-16, underlines the prevailing feeling toward them. They were classed with sinners. *Sinners* may denote those of questionable morals (cf. Luke 7:37), but many of those so branded were guilty of no greater offense than neglecting the observance of the ceremonial regulations insisted upon by the Pharisees.

"With Jesus and his disciples"—the first of 44 references to His disciples as a distinct group in Mark's Gospel. Disciples joined themselves to a teacher to acquire his teaching. The distinctive feature of the disciples of Jesus was their deep personal devotion to the teacher Himself. They were attached to His person, not just to His teaching. This relationship is of vital importance in this Gospel.

"For there were many, and they followed him"—a reference either to the number of Jesus' disciples or to the publicans who now followed Him. The latter seems preferable. It accounted for their presence at this feast.

"The scribes and Pharisees"—literally, "the scribes of the Pharisees," the scribes belonging to the Pharisee party (cf. Acts 23:9). The expression, found only here in the Gospels, indicates that not all scribes were Pharisees, although most of the scribes did uphold the position of the Pharisees, who are here first mentioned by Mark. Only a few Pharisees were scribes by profession. The Pharisees were separatists in the sense that they stressed separation from all they considered impure on the basis of the Mosaic law and their traditions. The Pharisee party is first mentioned in connection with the reign of John Hyrcanus (135-105 B.C.). Apparently they were the spiritual descendants of the Hasidim, the "pious ones," of Maccabean times. They were opposed to the Sadducees, who were more lax in their interpretation of the law. The Pharisees accepted as binding not only the written law but also a growing body of oral tradition, professedly dating back to Moses, which increasingly came to regulate every area of life. (See further comments under Mark 7:1-13; especially vv. 3-4).

"Saw him eat with publicans and sinners"—as arch-inquisitors, they kept a close watch on Jesus' social movements. They probably

---

[14] A.W.F. Blunt, *The Gospel According to St. Mark,* pp. 155-56; J. H. Harrop, "Publican" in *The New Bible Dictionary,* ed. J. D. Douglas, pp. 1064-65; Otto Michel, "*telōnēs,*" in *Theological Dictionary of the New Testament,* 8:88-105.

did not actually enter Levi's house; they would have felt that to do so would be contaminating. Since table fellowship was regarded as a sign and pledge of real intimacy, they regarded Jesus' action as a scandal. The unusual order (in the original), *sinners and publicans,* may imply the Pharisees felt that Jesus' eating with open sinners was a clear violation of the Old Testament standard for the godly man (cf. Ps. 1:1).

"Said unto his disciples"—apparently the scribes did not yet dare to charge Jesus directly. Since the disciples shared the meal, they too were guilty, but perhaps the aim was to shake their faith in a Master who set them such an example.

"How is it that he eateth and drinketh with publicans and sinners?"—His censurable act discredited Jesus in their eyes. In view of the absence of the words *how is it* in the original, the quotation may be rendered as an amazed exclamation, "With the publicans and sinners he eats!" But the interrogative is more probable, implying that His act was incomprehensible.

"When Jesus heard *it,* he saith unto them"—He may have overheard their words; more probably they were reported to Him. In His reply, Jesus took the responsibility for what had been done and made His answer directly to the critics. His quotation of a well-known proverb and His statement of His own mission provided a full vindication of His conduct. It was axiomatic that the *whole,* "those who are strong," do not need a doctor but those who *are sick*—literally, "having it badly," that is, physically. Jesus' sense of sin was not less acute than that of His critics. As the Physician of souls, He was deeply conscious of the disease gripping those with whom He ate, but He was seeking to carry out His mission as their healer. In the words of Brooks, "For Jesus to refuse to associate with sinners would have been as foolish as for a doctor not to associate with the sick."[15]

"I came not to call the righteous, but sinners"—a statement of His special mission. His mission meant that His work was not with the righteous, those who had no admitted need of restoration, but with acknowledged sinners. The healthy should not condemn the doctor for going to the sick. Jesus did not associate with sinners as their boon companion, but His purpose was to call them, turn them from their sinful ways. It is an indication of the blindness of sinners that the ordinary relationship between the doctor and the sick is here reversed. The doctor is calling the sick instead of the sick calling the doctor. It was an act of divine compassion.

---

[15] James A. Brooks, *Mark,* The New American Commentary, p. 63.

c. Question About Fasting (2:18-22).

A third ground of complaint against Jesus was the failure of His disciples to keep the fast days which pious Jews observed. His free association with sinners seemed to lead to the neglect of devout practices. In Matthew 9:14-17 and Luke 5:33-39, the problem is also raised immediately after the feast in the house of Levi.

"John's disciples and the Pharisees were fasting" (ASV)—appearing only in Mark, the comment is another explanatory note for his non-Jewish readers. The imperfect tense may point to their observance of regular times of fasting, or it may mean that they were fasting at the time their question was presented to Jesus. The latter is apparently meant.

The Mosaic law prescribed only one fast day a year, on the Day of Atonement (Lev. 16:29), but fast days were often proclaimed in times of crisis. During and after the Babylonian captivity, the practice of fasting received increasing emphasis and came to be regarded as meritorious. During the time of Jesus, the pious Pharisees fasted twice a week (Luke 18:12), on the second and fifth day. If the feast of Levi fell on the evening beginning either of their weekly fast days, the disciples of Jesus were feasting at the very time the pious Pharisees were fasting. Since Jesus and His disciples formed an earnest religious group, it was regarded as astonishing that they did not adhere to the pious practice.

Fasting was also practiced by John's disciples, who kept together as a group after John's imprisonment. The Gospels contain several references to them as a distinct group (Matt. 11:2; Mark 6:29; Luke 7:18; 11:1; John 1:35-37). In thus remaining a distinct group, they did not follow out John's aim of preparing them to receive the Messiah when He came. The Gospels make no reference to John teaching about fasting; it seems clear that he must have approved of it as a means of deepening the consciousness of sin and inducing repentance. The practice of fasting by John's disciples would be in keeping with the ascetic spirit of their master. But the addition of the phrase "and make supplications" in Luke 5:33 makes it possible that the fasting mentioned here was their expression of mourning for John's imprisonment.

"They come and say unto him"—*they* seems to denote representatives of the two groups just mentioned. It is remarkable that the disciples of John should thus be associated with the Pharisees, but obviously both groups were concerned with the problem raised by the conduct of Jesus and His disciples. The Pharisees may well have used the perplexity of John's disciples to push them into raising the problem with Jesus. Matthew 9:14 says that John's disciples asked the question. The answer of Jesus seems clearly to be directed to John's disciples.

In asking why, they indicated their desire to know the reason for the difference between their practice and that of Jesus' disciples. The question may imply censure, but no open charge was made. Clearly the disciples of Jesus were not violating the law in not fasting. Whether the question by John's disciples to Jesus was motivated by hostility or perplexity is not indicated.

The reply of Jesus was given in two parts. Verses 19-20 record His explanation, while verses 21-22 set forth a larger justifying principle.

"Can the children [sons, Gr.] of the bridechamber fast, while the bridegroom is with them?"—an explanatory counterquestion to their question. The original indicates that a negative answer was expected. The suggested course of action would be incongruous with the spirit of the occasion. Jesus thus indicates that there is no spiritual value "in performing outward religious rituals that bear no relation to what is in the heart. That principle," Barnhouse notes, "cuts religious formalism at the very roots."[16] "The sons of the bridechamber," a Hebrew idiom, were the groom's attendants who accompanied him to the house of the bride to bring her to the groom's house, which was now hers. They had the responsibility of providing what was necessary for the nuptials. They shared in the joy of the bridegroom. Jewish custom exempted them from certain religious observances, including the weekly fasts. Weddings were occasions of laughter, merriment, and song.

"As long as they have the bridegroom with them, they cannot fast"—Jesus' answer to His own question, given only in Mark. *As long as* introduces the condition which made fasting an incongruity for His disciples and indicates that it would not last. Now they cannot fast as an honest expression of their true feelings. For them it was a time of joy, since they had the bridegroom with them. Jesus' picture of the bridegroom was a veiled reference to Himself. He seems intentionally to be referring John's disciples back to John's own statement about Him given in John 3:29. They had forgotten John's witness to His true identity. His position on the problem of fasting was bound up with His identity as the bridegroom rejoicing with His bride.

"The days will come, when the bridegroom shall be taken away from them"—a clear intimation that Jesus knew what awaited Him. *Days* is without an article in the original and stresses the nature of the days as a time of deprivation by the removal of the bridegroom. The statement indicates that He, rather than the disciples, will be removed. The verb *taken away,* here used by all the synoptics but nowhere else in the New Testament, means "to lift off, to take away

---

[16] Donald Grey Barnhouse, *Mark: The Servant Gospel,* p. 40.

from someone,'' and implies a violent removal. It is the first intimation of the coming ordeal of the cross in Mark's Gospel. *When,* used with a verb in the subjunctive mood, means "whenever" and leaves the time undetermined.

"Then shall they fast in those days"—when His removal has become a sad reality. Their resultant sorrow will provide a proper occasion for fasting as the appropriate expression of their true feelings. The added *in those days* (literally, "in that day") emphatically points to that coming day. The primary reference is to the time of the crucifixion. Matthew 6:16-18 shows that Jesus did not oppose fasting. He condemned fasting as a matter of outward form and show, not when it was a genuine expression of inner sorrow. His words do not establish fasting as a prescribed institution in the church. Christ's account here does not strictly apply to this age. Nowhere does Scripture picture the church as a widow who bewails her bereavement with recurrent periods of fasting and tears. The picture of Jesus indicates that "it is not fasting to which objection is taken but fasting according to rule, instead of its inherent principle. As a piece of legalism, or asceticism, in which fasting per se becomes of moral obligation, it is incongruous with the free spirit of Christianity.''[17]

In verses 21-22, Jesus makes a twofold appeal to a recognized principle in life, adding a reminder of the results of its nonobservance. The principle confirmed His position concerning fasting. The teaching is parabolic in that it employs a familiar practice of everyday life to convey spiritual truth. It is the first instance of the use of the parabolic method by Jesus in Mark's Gospel. Luke specifically called His words a parable (5:36). The parabolic pictures indicated that the question of fasting was only a part of a far greater truth. The new life in union with Him could not simply be confined to the old forms of Judaism.

In both verses, a negative principle is illustrated, with an added reminder of the result of its violation. No one who was wise would attempt to patch an old, worn garment by sewing a piece of yet unshrunk cloth over a hole in it. If he foolishly ignored this wise negative practice, the result would be that the unshrunk patch, when it became wet, would shrink and tear away from the old garment at the sewn edges, leaving a larger hole than before. To seek to preserve the old by patching it up with what is new is worse than useless.

Verse 22 gives another common-sense observation. The skins of goats, stripped off as nearly whole as possible and partly tanned, were

---

[17] Ezra P. Gould, *Critical and Exegetical Commentary on the Gospel According to St. Mark,* International Critical Commentary, p. 47.

commonly used in the Orient as containers for liquids. With age, such skins became hard and lost their elasticity. To put new wine (fresh from the wine vat) into them would mean that inevitably the fermenting wine would burst the old skins. A double loss would result: the wine would be lost, and the skins would be ruined. The common-sense thing was to put new wine into fresh or unused wineskins. Because of the elasticity and strength, they would safely contain the fermenting wine.

The teaching of both parables is that the new life of redemption in Christ cannot be confined to the old legalistic forms of Judaism. In the first, the new patch proved useless and the old was made worse; in the second parable the new was wholly lost and the old was ruined. The first figure seems specially applicable to the mistake of John's disciples, while the second seems to picture "the utter impossibility of containing young Christianity as a mere 'Reformed Sect' within Judaism."[18] Judaistic Christianity and its forms perished, but the freedom of the gospel, for which Paul contended, remained and developed as it found expression in new forms of life harmonious with its new nature.

d. Controversies About Sabbath Observance (2:23–3:6).

Jesus' opponents found a fourth ground for antagonism in His failure to adhere to their rigid Sabbath regulations. All the synoptics record two successive incidents of conflict between Jesus and the Pharisees on this point. Matthew (12:1-14) places these incidents much later in his account than Mark and Luke (6:1-11). In the first event, the enemies charged Jesus with permitting His disciples to do what they regarded as a Sabbath violation; in the second, He performed a healing in open disregard of their Sabbath regulations.

1) Plucking of grain on the Sabbath (2:23-28). Verses 23-24 describe the occasion for the controversy, and verses 25-28 record the two-part answer of Jesus to the charge made.

"And it came to pass"—this phrase, a familiar formula in Mark, marks the recorded event as a further example of the attacks of the critics. It suggests a topical connection.

"He went through the corn fields on the sabbath day"—the ideas of *alongside* and *through* are combined in Mark's statement. Jesus was proceeding along a footpath with standing grain[19] on both sides. The place must have been close to some town, for no charge was made of

---

[18] R. A. Cole, *The Gospel According to St. Mark,* p. 72.

[19] "Corn" in the KJV rendering "corn fields" is the British term for grain. In the American sense "corn" denotes "Indian maize" which was unknown in the Orient until after the discovery of the New World.

exceeding a Sabbath day's journey of two thousand cubits (Acts 1:12). These grain fields, literally "sown lands," were fields of barley or wheat, probably the latter, ready to be cut. It was somewhere between mid-April and mid-June, perhaps the latter part of May.

"His disciples began, as they went, to pluck the ears"—a statement found only in Mark. The statement is somewhat puzzling. Literally it reads, "The disciples began to make a way, plucking the heads of grain." "To make a way" has been taken to mean that the disciples saw that the path was overgrown and began to clear a way for Jesus by plucking off the heads that stood in the way. This view is improbable. As their Teacher, Jesus naturally walked ahead of the disciples. Plucking a few heads would not make a road unless they also trampled down the stalks, which would have been an act of destruction, wrong on any day. This view also puts Mark into conflict with the other synoptics. They say that the disciples plucked to eat, while Mark is held to picture them as making a road through the grain. Mark contented himself with a statement that they plucked, for the charge of the Pharisees centered on that act. It is simplest to render the statement, "The disciples began to make their way, plucking the head of grain."[20] As they advanced along the narrow path through the grain field, the disciples plucked some of the heads, rubbed out the grain with their hands (Luke 6:1), and ate it.

"The Pharisees said unto him"—another indication that Jesus was seldom free from the presence of others, either friends or foes. The watchful Pharisees, noting the act of the disciples, raised immediate objection to it. *Said* is in the imperfect tense; they continued to press their objection, turning first to the guilty disciples (Luke 6:2) and then to their Master for permitting the act.

"Behold"—excitedly drawing Jesus' attention to the objectionable act.

"Why do they on the sabbath day that which is not lawful?"—they demanded an explanation from Jesus for permitting such an unlawful activity. The law forbade any work on the Sabbath day (Exod. 20:10). Deuteronomy 23:25 permitted such plucking of grain from a neighbor's field, but the Pharisees' objection was that it was done on the Sabbath. To ensure observance of the Sabbath law, the scribes had enumerated "the main classes of work: forty save one,"[21] among them reaping, threshing, and winnowing. But in their eagerness to "fence"

---

[20] This rendering accepts that the classical distinction between the active and middle voices was not observed in Koine Greek. Cf. Judges 17:8 (LXX).

[21] Herbert Danby, trans., *The Mishnah,* p. 106.

the law against violation, they had gone to extremes in stipulating acts that were regarded as work. Thus the pedantic Pharisees regarded the plucking of the heads as reaping, the rubbing out of the grain as threshing, and perhaps the blowing away of the chaff as winnowing. The disciples were guilty of working on the Sabbath!

In His reply, Jesus referred the critics to an incident in their own Scriptures (vv. 25-26) and then stated an underlying principle (vv. 27-28).

"Have ye never read what David did"—His counterquestion indicated that in reading their Scriptures, they had failed to see the significance of David's act in the case before them. They were so occupied with their minute rabbinical regulations that they missed the deeper meaning of the divine record. Jesus turned them back to their own Scriptures.

"When he had need, and was an hungred, he, and they that were with him"—the account is given in 1 Samuel 21:1-6. In citing that incident, Jesus gave recognition to the reason for the action of His disciples. David had *need,* a general term, and *was an hungred,* a specific need. Matthew 12:1 states that the disciples were hungry. There was thus a parallel between David and his followers and the Son of David and His disciples.

"How he went into the house of God"—the tabernacle, the place where God dwelt among His people. It was located at Nob, the old priestly town near Jerusalem (Isa. 10:32). David entered the court of the tabernacle, not the tabernacle itself.

"In the days of Abiathar the high priest"—a clause peculiar to Mark, a well-known difficulty. First Samuel 21 says Ahimelech was the priest who gave David the bread. His son Abiathar, the only priest at Nob who escaped slaughter at the hand of Saul (1 Sam. 22:19-20), later was well known as high priest during David's reign. The critics usually charge Mark with a historical blunder. To this, Ralph Earle replies, "To label this as a clear mistake on Mark's part is not only a denial of divine inspiration but also a reflection on the intelligence of the evangelist, who certainly knew his Old Testament well enough to have avoided any such confusion."[22] A variety of solutions have been proposed, none of which are wholly free from difficulty.[23] Some propose that the names of Ahimelech and Abiathar were borne by both

---

[22] Ralph Earle, *The Gospel According to St. Mark,* The Evangelical Commentary on the Bible, p. 49.

[23] J. Morison, *Practical Commentary on the Gospel According to St. Mark,* pp. 60-63, discusses some ten different suggestions.

father and son; ground for this view is seen in the strange variation found in the use of the names in the Old Testament (cf. 1 Sam. 22:20 with 2 Sam. 8:17; 1 Chron. 18:16; 24:3, 6). This suggestion has some merit but seems unlikely. Others hold that Mark's clause is an erroneous scribal addition which should be omitted. While a few old manuscripts do not have it, it is strongly supported. The omission is more readily explained as a scribal effort to relieve the historical difficulty. Most probable is the suggestion that the phrase simply means "during the lifetime of Abiathar the high priest." If the article with *high priest* had stronger manuscript support, this would be the obvious reconciliation. Without the article, the expression, strictly taken, means that the event took place "when Abiathar was high priest" (ASV). Mark may simply have added the designation to denote the well-known companion of David who later became high priest. Since the father soon perished after the incident, the son who escaped later recorded the event, and thus the facts might be said to have taken place during his priesthood.

"Did eat the shewbread"—the twelve loaves of unleavened bread, placed in two rows upon the golden table in the holy place and renewed every Sabbath (Lev. 24:5-9). *Shewbread* is literally, "the bread of the setting forth, or presentation," corresponding to the Hebrew "the bread of the face." The loaves apparently denoted God's presence with His people as Sustainer. The law restricted to the priests the eating of the showbread after it had been removed.

"Which is not lawful"—a deliberate echo of the charge of the Pharisees. The eating of the holy bread by David and his men was a violation of the Mosaic law, yet that act was nowhere condemned in Scripture. Human need overruled the ceremonial regulation. David's uncondemned act was a reminder to the Pharisees that their rigid demands concerning their traditional observance of the Sabbath were inconsistent with the case of David.

Matthew added another illustration and a second scriptural quotation (12:5-7).

"And he said unto them"—apparently Mark intended the repeated phrase (cf. v. 25) to denote a new stage in the argument. The case of David answered the criticism of the Pharisees. But Jesus seized the occasion to support His position by announcing a basic principle.

"The sabbath was made for man, and not man for the sabbath"— the fundamental principle underlying the institution of the Sabbath. Mark alone recorded this basic assertion. The Sabbath was instituted for the benefit of man (the word *man* is generic, "mankind," the human race); hence the application of the Sabbath law must be elastic to assure that man's welfare is promoted. The minute, arbitrary regulations of the Pharisees made man the slave of the Sabbath, making its observance a burden rather than a blessing. Their binding traditions tended to nullify God's gracious purpose in giving the Sabbath to man. The institution of the Sabbath, requiring a periodic day of rest, has been an inestimable boon to mankind. It was a gift that afforded man not only physical rest but also refreshment in spirit in raising his thoughts above his daily labors.

"Therefore the Son of man is Lord also of the sabbath"—a deduction from the Sabbath principle just stated. The words may be taken as Mark's own comment, but more probably they are the words of Jesus Himself. Because of His identity as the Son of man (cf. v. 10), His authority extended also to the Sabbath. As its lord, He asserted His authority over the Sabbath to regulate its beneficent observance. The claim does not mean that Jesus was now abolishing the Sabbath or was permitting His disciples to violate the Mosaic law concerning the Sabbath at will. But He was using His authority to set aside the restrictive regulations of the Pharisees which perverted the divine intention for the Sabbath. In the Old Testament, the Sabbath is the Lord's day; Jesus' claim to be lord of the Sabbath was an implied claim to equality with Jehovah. "As a human figure, he best knows human needs; as a divine figure, he has the authority to say how the Lord's day should be used."[24]

2) Healing of man with the withered hand (3:1-6). The opening *and* marks a topical connection with what precedes. As the last of five conflict stories, this incident forms the climax to these accounts of growing antagonism to Jesus.

"He entered again into the synagogue"—the setting for this further collision between Jesus and the Pharisees. The singular "he," with no reference to any companions, marks Jesus as central in this series of conflicts. *Again,* after Mark's manner, seems to refer to 1:21, where the place was Capernaum. Mark gave no indication of chronological sequence; Luke noted that it was "on another sabbath" (6:6).

"There was a man there which had a withered hand"—the condition of his hand became the occasion for the controversy. It is the only detail given about the man. *Withered* describes an abiding condition and implies that the affliction was due not to a congenital defect but to an accidental injury or some disease. Apparently just his hand was affected, not the whole arm. Luke noted that it was his "right

---

[24] Lamar Williamson, Jr., *Mark,* Interpretation: A Bible Commentary for Teaching and Preaching, p. 74.

hand'' (6:6). Tradition says that the man was a stone mason and that the condition of his hand had forced him to beg for a living.

"And they watched him"—no subject of the verb is expressed, but the previous account and verse 6 make it clear that the Pharisees are meant. The verb is a compound form with the root meaning to keep alongside of. The imperfect tense pictures them as continuing to watch Jesus closely and intently as eager observers.

"Whether he would heal him on the sabbath day"—more literally, "if on the sabbath he will heal him." They suspected that He would do so. The Gospels speak of other Sabbath healings by Jesus (Luke 13:10-17; 14:1-6; John 5:2-18; 9:1-17). Mark's future tense placed the readers at the time of the watching of the Pharisees; they were intently watching to see what He would do. They well knew His ability to heal and had learned that the sight of suffering could be expected to elicit the exercise of His healing power. But, according to their Sabbath regulations, to perform such a work of healing on the Sabbath would be unlawful. Healing measures might be taken on the Sabbath only when there was danger of death. They were concerned not with the man's need but with their legalistic proscriptions.

"That they might accuse him"—the malicious intention of the watchers. Their attentive observance was motivated by personal animosity. They were looking for an occasion that would enable them to make formal charges against Jesus before the Sanhedrin. They were motivated by "the true spirit of ecclesiastical bloodhounds."[25]

"He saith unto the man"—apparently after He had finished teaching (Luke 6:6). Luke stated that Jesus knew the thoughts of the critical observers (6:8), while Matthew related that the enemies asked Jesus, "Is it lawful to heal on the sabbath days?" (12:10). Apparently when Jesus gave an indication that He intended to heal the man, they raised the legal question challenging the propriety of the act.

"Stand forth"—he was not asked to come and stand beside Jesus but rather commanded to stand "into the midst," in a place where all could see him and his pathetic hand. Jesus' opponents need not spy on Him; Jesus indicated that He would act openly. He intended to use the man to give a public demonstration of His attitude toward the perverted Sabbath rules of the scribes and Pharisees.

In verse 4, Jesus directed a counterquestion to His opponents. His question elevated the matter from a legal to a moral problem.

"Is it lawful to do good on the sabbath days, or to do evil?"—the question sets two types of doing in contrast. Which of the two was

---

[25] Morison, p. 66.

consistent with the Mosaic law to which they acknowledged obedience? The healing of the man was related to the larger question about which of the two alternatives was in harmony with the purpose of the Sabbath. His question implied that failure to do good was to harm. An act humane and beneficial certainly was in harmony with the divine intention for the Sabbath (2:27). Jesus' illustration, given in Matthew 12:11, concerning an owner's retrieving his sheep which had fallen into a pit on the Sabbath, proved that they recognized the principle in practice. For them to object to the good deed of relieving the man of his wretched condition on the Sabbath implied that they advocated the doing of what was harmful on the Sabbath.

"To save life, or to kill"—the extension of the contrast carried the alternatives to their logical conclusion. If, as they admitted, the use of healing means was lawful on the Sabbath to save a life, then surely an act of restoration to wholeness was also praiseworthy. That which is morally good does not become morally evil just because it is done on the Sabbath. To place their religiously held scruples above any concern for human need was inconsistent with God's beneficent concerns for humanity in instituting the Sabbath. Eric Bishop asserts that Jesus' statement of the startling extremes was "reminiscent of Palestinian psychology. The Semitic mind demands clear-cut decisions. There are no middle terms between 'doing good' and 'doing evil,' between 'saving a life' and 'destroying.' The choice is absolute."[26]

"But they held their peace"—recorded only by Mark. They sullenly refused to be drawn into a discussion which viewed the matter from an ethical rather than a legal standpoint. The obvious answer could only stamp their pious Sabbath practices as false.

Verse 5 records three particulars, one external and two internal. References to the emotions of Jesus are peculiar to Mark.

"When he had looked round about on them"—Luke also mentioned this look. Elsewhere the references to Jesus "looking around" are confined to Mark's Gospel (3:34; 5:32; 10:23; 11:11). Only once did Mark use the expression as describing someone other than Jesus (9:8). Mark seems to preserve faithfully Peter's recollections of these frequent looks of Jesus. Jesus' eyes swept the whole group of Pharisees before Him (Luke 6:10). Vainly, He looked for a man who would respond to His question.

"With anger"—the inner feeling accompanying the sweeping look. Here only is anger ascribed to Jesus. It is not mentioned in the parallel accounts in Matthew 12:12-13 and Luke 6:8-10. His holy

---

[26] Eric F.F. Bishop, *Jesus of Palestine,* p. 111.

indignation against evil was unalloyed by that feeling of malignity and vindictiveness which renders human anger almost always sinful. Anger against sin is an essential part of a healthy moral nature. Jesus' reaction was perfectly consistent with His love and mercy. As a true man, Jesus experienced normal human emotions, among them anger as well as grief at obstinate sin. Thus Mark notes that Jesus "is 'grieved' at men's hardness of heart (3:5); he marvels at their unbelief (6:6); he has 'compassion' on the hungry crowd (6:34; 8:2); he 'sighs deeply in his spirit' when Pharisees seek a sign from him (8:12); he is 'indignant' at the disciples' treatment of children (10:14); he betrays his love for the rich man (10:21); he is 'greatly distressed and troubled,' his soul is 'very sorrowful' at Gethsemane (14:33-34).''[27] In His reaction to the sullen refusal of the Pharisees to respond to the truth, the incarnate Christ revealed the character of our holy God.

"Being grieved for the hardness of their hearts"—His anger was mingled with grief at the sinful attitude of the opponents. The aorist tense implies that the look in anger was momentary, but *grieved* is present tense, picturing a prolonged feeling of grief or distress at such men. The verb is a compound form, denoting His deep grief. He felt intense grief at the hardening of their heart, denoting a process. Their obstinate and willful resistance to the truth indicated that a process of hardening was taking place, rendering their heart, their inner moral being, more and more unresponsive. The singular *heart* (in the original) indicates the unity of the reaction; they were all alike in the matter.

"He saith unto the man"—the historical present vividly pictures the dramatic scene. From the sullen Pharisees, Jesus turned to the needy man.

"Stretch forth thine hand"—a command demanding prompt obedience. It was a command the man could obey, but his response would show that he believed that his hand would be restored. By holding out his hand, all could see its withered condition and observe what would take place.

"He stretched *it* out: and his hand was restored"—both verbs denote specific occurrences. All eyes in the synagogue were fixed on that extended hand; as they watched, the hand was instantly, completely restored. The healing was an act of Jesus' own volition, wrought without a touch or the use of external means. Jesus thus did nothing that violated their trivial Sabbath regulations. The healing did not even have the appearance of work. It was unmistakably an act of supernatural

---

[27] Roy A. Harrisville, *The Miracle of Mark,* pp. 34-35.

power. His ability to heal the man's hand by the exercise of His will was proof that Jesus was more than a mere man.

"The Pharisees went forth"—that is, exited from the synagogue and the presence of the people. They had suffered another humiliating defeat in their conflict with Jesus. Luke noted that "they were filled with madness" (6:11).

"Straightway took counsel with the Herodians against him"—the event sent the furious Pharisees immediately into hot activity against Jesus. Mark alone recorded the consultation initiated with the Herodians, who here first appear in the Gospel story.[28] Their only other appearance in the Gospels is during Passion Week, when they joined with the Pharisees in asking Jesus about paying tribute to Caesar (Matt. 22:15-16; Mark 12:13). The name, which does not occur in the New Testament outside the Gospels, is built on the name *Herod* with a Latin suffix *-ians* (*ianoi*), denoting party adherents. It indicates that they were adherents of a Herod or the Herodian dynasty; more specific identification is uncertain. They probably were the political supporters of Herod Antipas and were a political rather than a religious party among the Jews. Although the two parties had little in common, they were willing to submerge their own differences in their battle with a common enemy.

"How they might destroy him"—first explicit mention in Mark of the intention of the enemies to kill Jesus. Their vicious reaction cast a dark cloud over the further ministry of Jesus. That He must be destroyed was assumed. The only question was how, by what method and means, that end was to be achieved. They regarded as a terrible crime Jesus' healing on the Sabbath, but they had no qualms about plotting murder on the Sabbath!

With this remark Mark gave his readers a sobering hint of how the ministry of Jesus would end.

---

[28] H. H. Rowley, "The Herodians in the Gospels," *Journal of Theological Studies,* 41 (1940): 14-27; Alfred Edersheim, *The Life and Times of Jesus the Messiah,* 1:237.

4
Ministry in Galilee
(Part 3; 3:7–4:34)

6. Ministry to the Multitude (3:7-12)

The conflicts with the Pharisees did not diminish Jesus' popularity with the masses. They seemed to draw the common people to Him in even larger numbers. The parallel passage in Matthew 12:15-21 lacks most of the details given by Mark, but characteristically, Matthew saw in this ministry a fulfillment of prophecy.

"Jesus withdrew himself with his disciples to the sea"—Matthew noted that He withdrew because He knew of the plotting of His enemies. *Withdrew* does not assert but may imply retreat from danger (cf. Matt. 2:12-14; 14:13). Moulton and Milligan remark, "The connotation of 'taking refuge' from some peril will suit most of the NT passages remarkably well."[1] The withdrawal to the Sea of Galilee was an act of prudence. On the open beach, surrounded by crowds of followers, Jesus would be safer from treachery than in the narrow streets of Capernaum. But it was primarily prompted by His desire to avoid a head-on collision with the Jewish leaders and to make Himself freely accessible to the masses.

With his disciples, placed emphatically before the singular verb in the original, suggests that they intimately shared His alienation from the Jewish leaders. Their association with Him in the withdrawal seems to have prepared them for a larger position in the work soon to be assigned them.

"A great multitude from Galilee followed him"—*Great* is emphatic by position and draws attention to the exceptional size of the multitude that flocked to Jesus. The ASV punctuation of verses 7-8 (". . . from Galilee followed; and from Judaea, and from Jerusalem . . . a great

---

[1] James Hope Moulton and George Milligan, *The Vocabulary of the Greek Testament,* p. 40.

multitude . . . came unto him'') makes clear that Mark is thinking of two multitudes. The Galilean crowd, from districts near at hand, *followed* Jesus, while the second multitude, from various remoter districts, *came* to Him. Both verbs are aorist, simply stating the historical fact without indicating the time element involved. Only Mark on this occasion noted that the people came from all parts of Palestine.

''Judaea''—the southern area, where, according to John 3:22, Jesus had earlier engaged in a public ministry. Many of the common people, as well as the watchful Pharisees (Luke 5:17), were drawn to Jesus' ministry.

''Jerusalem''—the city again distinguished from the province (cf. 1:5).

''Idumaea''—a region named only here in the New Testament. It was the area to the south of Judea, inhabited by many of Edomite descent (1 Mac. 4:29; 5:65). The area had become largely Jewish and in Roman times was considered a part of the land of Judea.

''Beyond the Jordan''—the territory east of the Jordan, called Perea by Josephus (*Wars of the Jews* 3. 3. 3). Its inhabitants were mixed but contained a large Jewish element. It was under the rule of Herod Antipas.

''About Tyre and Sidon''—the territory around these two Phoenician cities. Phoenicia is often designated by the joint names of these two cities (Jer. 47:4; Joel 3:4; Matt. 11:21; Acts 12:20). Many Jews lived in that area. Phoenicia maintained close connection with Galilee.

No representatives from Samaria are mentioned. The Samaritans remained aloof from the religious interests of the Jews.

''When they had heard what great things he did, came unto him''— the repeated reports of Jesus' miracles drew vast crowds. Such running after a famous leader or prophet has always been an Oriental characteristic. The ready gathering of such crowds was facilitated by the network of Roman roads which extended throughout the land.[2]

''He spake to his disciples''—He instructed them how to deal with the danger created for Him by this vast multitude. The vivid picture in verses 9-10 is found only in Mark, suggesting the memory of an eyewitness.

''That a little boat should wait on him'' (ASV)—the diminutive, *little boat,* suggests a rowboat, not a regular fishing vessel. The verb *wait* means ''to be in constant readiness for one's use.'' The disciples were asked to keep the boat available for Him at any moment, wherever He was along the shore.

''Because of the multitude''—a large but confused and unorganized throng.

---

[2] Michael Avi-Yonah, *The Holy Land,* pp. 181-87.

"Lest they should throng him"—the boat may on occasion have been used as a pulpit for preaching, but the order was to have it available as a means of escape from the pressure of the undisciplined crowd. It is not said that it was ever thus used.

"For he had healed many"—an explanation for the arrangement just mentioned. This ministry by the seashore seems to have been essentially a healing ministry. *Many* stresses its scope.

"They pressed upon him for to touch him, as many as had plagues"—the excited impact produced by the healings. The original is very vivid: "So that as a result they are falling upon him in order to touch him, as many as were having scourges." The subject stands emphatically at the end. *Plagues,* literally, "a whip, lash," figuratively denotes painful bodily illnesses, torturing maladies. The afflicted eagerly and excitedly thrust themselves forward to touch Jesus, so that those next to Jesus were jostling Him and falling upon Him. In their excitement, the afflicted were determined to secure healing by a touch, however rude the collision. From the manner of Jesus' healings, the crowd had concluded that if they could but touch Him they would be healed (cf. the story of the woman with an issue of blood in 5:25-34). The little boat would enable Jesus to escape such impetuous efforts. He was willing to heal these sufferers, but He wanted to do it in an orderly manner. Hurtado notes, "The crowd is portrayed as more interested in satisfying their curiosity and physical needs than in becoming true followers."[3]

"The unclean spirits, whensoever they beheld him" (ASV)—a second type of suffering, again clearly distinguished from ordinary physical sickness (cf. 1:34). In the original the definite article is used with both the noun and the adjective, "the spirits, the unclean ones," thus stressing the true character of these spirits. *Beheld* indicates that these unclean spirits (cf. 1:23) were looking at Jesus with critical interest to measure His true character and identity. They openly revealed their presence whenever they came into the presence of Jesus. The imperfect tense denotes repeated instances.

"Fell down before him"—the demoniacs are identified with the demons controlling them. Falling prostrate, they acknowledged His authority.

"Cried"—"shouted," or "screamed." Mark uses the verb of the wild cry of demoniacs (1:23; 5:5; 9:26).

"Thou art the Son of God"—this full Christological title was their unwavering affirmation of His true identity. *Thou* is emphatic. They

---

[3] Larry W. Hurtado, *Mark,* Good News Commentary, p. 42.

recognized His unique nature. Mark clearly regarded this confession as an acknowledgment of Jesus' superhuman nature. Swete comments, "The earliest confession of the Sonship seems to have come from evil spirits, who knew Jesus better than he was known by His own disciples."[4] Brooks remarks, "Mark probably intended to contrast what the demons acknowledged as a fact with what the religious leaders were not willing to consider as a possibility."[5]

Jesus invariably silenced the testimony of demons. He did not want the recognition of His true nature to be associated with the impure and malevolent testimony of demons. He wanted men to realize His true identity through His words and works.

7. Appointment of the Twelve (3:13-19a)

The appointment of the Twelve marked an important turning point in the Lord's ministry. They formed an official body of adherents closely related to Him whom He would train to help in the work and equip to carry on the work after His death. Their participation was demanded by the growth of the work and the deepening hostility of the religious leaders. Luke 6:12-16 gives a parallel account.

"And he goeth up into a mountain"—*and* introduces a further significant event but need not imply close chronological sequence. "The mountain" (Gr.) may denote some specific mountain in the vicinity of the lake, one familiar to Jesus. The traditional Horns of Hattin, the most prominent height on the western side of the lake, would well suit the occasion. Others take the expression as indefinite ("the hills," RSV), denoting the hill country of central Galilee in contrast to the lowlands around the lake. The mountain setting for the act by Jesus now recorded clearly implies that the event is distinct from everyday life and work. Since a mountain is often associated with God's specific dealings with His people, the scene here "may carry with it certain nuances of revelation and authority."[6]

Luke (6:12) recorded that Jesus ascended the mountain for an all-night prayer session. He took counsel with His heavenly Father concerning the selection of the Twelve, making each an object of prayer and careful thought.

"Calleth unto him whom he would"—the choosing occurred early the next morning after His prayer vigil. *Calleth* is middle voice and indicates that Jesus was acting in His own interest. He took the initiative

---

[4] Henry Barclay Swete, *The Gospel According to St. Mark,* p. 57

[5] James A. Brooks, *Mark,* The New American Commentary, p. 70.

[6] Lamar Williamson, Jr., *Mark,* Interpretation: A Bible Commentary for Teaching and Preaching, p. 80.

in the call, and His will determined those called. It was not a call for volunteers.

"They came unto him"—the compound verb, "they went off," implies separation. It was a definite call to them to leave the uncommitted crowd and take their stand with Him as His disciples. This they did voluntarily. Luke 6:13 expressly asserts that Jesus first called "his disciples," those who were His recognized followers. From them He selected the Twelve.

"And he ordained twelve"—literally, "made twelve." By a definite act, He created or constituted them a distinct group composed of twelve men. Previously there had been no such distinct group. *The Twelve* soon became a technical term for this select body. Their number was no doubt intentional, corresponding to the twelve patriarchs and the twelve tribes. They formed the foundation for Christ's spiritual kingdom. But the call of the Twelve does not imply that His coworkers were now limited to them; in Luke 10:1 He appointed "seventy others" and sent them out on a preaching mission. Each group served in response to Christ's own call.

Some ancient manuscripts here add, "whom also he named apostles," but it is probably a scribal insertion from Luke 6:13. Mark first employs the term *apostle,* meaning "one sent forth," after the Twelve were sent out on a preaching mission (Mark 6:30).

"That they should be with him, and that he might send them forth to preach"—the double purpose in the appointment of the Twelve, one relating to the present, the other to the future. The two parts correspond to the two official titles, "disciples" and "apostles." Only the first part of this double program was fully carried out during the lifetime of Jesus.

Jesus' immediate purpose for the Twelve was that they should be constantly with Him as His personal associates. This constant companionship with their Master would qualify them for their future work as His personal witnesses. "Fellowship with Him must precede preaching about Him."[7]

Their future mission is given a double statement. Their primary duty would be *to preach,* "to act as a herald," in accurately and authoritatively proclaiming the message committed to them. The commission included their limited preaching during Jesus' ministry (6:7-12) as well as their entire ministry after Christ's resurrection.

---

[7] George Williams, *The Student's Commentary on the Holy Scripture,* 5th ed., p. 734.

"And to have authority to cast out demons" (ASV)—a second aspect of their mission, to be exercised in connection with their primary duty of preaching. *To have authority* implies that they were given both the power and the right to expel demons. But it was so different from preaching that it required special authorization. Exorcism is mentioned as representative of the miracles they were to perform as evidence that the kingdom of God was present in Jesus Christ.

Verses 16-19 give the names of the chosen twelve. Each of the synoptics and Acts give a list. The Fourth Gospel gives no list, does not even name all of the Twelve. Mark's list gives no indication of any grouping of the Twelve, but a study of the parallel lists is revealing.

Matthew 10:2-4	Mark 3:16-19	Luke 6:14-16	Acts 1:13
1. Simon Peter	Simon Peter	Simon Peter	Peter
2. Andrew	James	Andrew	John
3. James	John	James	James
4. John	Andrew	John	Andrew
5. Philip	Philip	Philip	Philip
6. Bartholomew	Bartholomew	Bartholomew	Thomas
7. Thomas	Matthew	Matthew	Bartholomew
8. Matthew	Thomas	Thomas	Matthew
9. James of Alphaeus	James of Alphaeus	James of Alphaeus	James of Alphaeus
10. Thaddaeus	Thaddaeus	Simon the Zealot	Simon the Zealot
11. Simon the Canaanite	Simon the Canaanite	Judas of James	Judas of James
12. Judas Iscariot	Judas Iscariot	Judas Iscariot	———

These lists show three groups of four each, with the same names in each group. The same name heads each group, but there is variation within each group. Mark has already named five of those listed as having received a previous call from Jesus. John 1 shows that some of the others also had had previous associations with Jesus.

"Simon he surnamed Peter"—He "imposed a name on Simon—Peter" (Rotherham). Mark's statement need not mean that the name was now first bestowed.[8] Up to this point, Mark called him Simon; throughout the remainder of the book, except in 14:37, he is always called Peter. Mark never used the familiar double name, Simon Peter. The new name did not wholly supersede the use of the old (Acts 15:14). *Peter,* meaning a rock or stone, was not used as a proper name in Aramaic or Greek and was clearly meant as a descriptive designation.

---

[8] It was first given to him when Peter met Jesus at the scene of John's baptism (John 1:42), but it was prophetic. Matthew 16:18 records the fulfillment of the designation.

But interpreters are not agreed about whether the reference is to his personal character, picturing a rocklike firmness, or to his official function as a foundation rock in the building of the church. The latter seems more probable in view of Matthew 16:18 and Ephesians 2:20.

Peter is named first in all four lists. Matthew's list begins, "The first, Simon, who is called Peter" (10:2). This does not mean that Peter was given an official position of primacy. His eminence was due to his native aggressiveness as well as to the fact that he was among the first chosen. He inevitably assumed a position of leadership due to the dynamic force of his personality.

"James the *son* of Zebedee, and John the brother of James"— identified in the same way when Jesus first called them (1:19).

"Boanerges, which is, The sons of thunder"—the designation is mentioned only by Mark. The translation, "sons of thunder," has no known parallel and may be a secondary meaning current in Galilee. The difficulty concerning the vowels, not yet solved, may be due to the strange pronunciation of the word in Galilee. The intended significance of the title is variously viewed: (1) a commendation of their mighty eloquence; this is improbable since at this time the disciples had not yet done any preaching to call attention to their thundering eloquence; (2) a rebuke for some fiery emotional outburst (cf. Luke 9:54; Mark 9:38); if Luke 9:54 was the occasion, Jesus might well have called them "sons of lightning"; (3) a recognition of their impetuous, ardent nature; this is most probable. The fiery words of James may have contributed to his becoming one of the first martyrs (Acts 12:2). Christ's love mellowed John's character, but his writings ring with thundering condemnation of sin.

"Andrew"—an old Greek name meaning "manly." While always listed in the first group, only in 13:3 does Andrew appear with the inner circle composed of the other three. Although Andrew personally introduced his brother to Jesus (John 1:40-42), in the Gospel accounts he played "second fiddle" to his brother.

"Philip"—always named at the head of the second group. It is also a common Greek name. John 1:43-44 records an earlier call Jesus gave him.

"Bartholomew"—a patronymic, meaning "son of Tolmai" (Ptolemy). His personal name apparently was Nathanael, suggested on the basis of John 1:45-51. The name *Nathanael* is never used in the synoptics, but the fact that *Bartholomew* always stands next to *Philip* in the lists in the synoptics seems to point to the close association between the two, seen in John's Gospel.

"Matthew"—in view of the account in 2:14, one wonders why Mark did not write "Levi, whom he surnamed Matthew." In Matthew's list, he is identified as "Matthew the publican." His name is a shortened form of the Old Testament name "Mattathias" (1 Macc. 2:1 ff.; 2 Macc. 14:19; Luke 3:25-26).

"Thomas"—in the synoptics, a mere name in the lists. In the Fourth Gospel, he emerges as a living person (John 11:16; 14:5; 20:24-28; 21:2). He was also called Didymus, "the twin." Both of his names have the same meaning.

"James the *son* of Alphaeus"—always named first in the third group. *Of Alphaeus* served to distinguish him from the more prominent James, the son of Zebedee. He is probably the same as "James the less" (15:40).

"Thaddaeus"—the only name that does not appear uniformly in all the lists. Mark and Matthew have *Thaddaeus,* with "Lebbaeus" as an alternative reading in some old manuscripts. Luke and Acts have "Judas the son of James." He apparently had three names. He is "Judas (not Iscariot)" in John 14:22.

"Simon the Cananaean" (ASV)—the identification does not mean that he was a Canaanite or from the village of Cana. It is a transcription of the Aramaic term meaning the Zealot (Luke 6:15). It may mean that he was a former member of the Zealot party among the Jews, or it may indicate the zealous personal disposition of the man. Paul's use of the term in Galatians 1:14 favors the latter meaning, but the former view is generally accepted. Both meanings may apply.

"Judas Iscariot"—the son of one Simon, himself called Iscariot (John 6:71; 13:26). *Iscariot* is apparently a Hebrew term meaning man of Kerioth, either Kerioth-Hezron (Josh. 15:25), south of Hebron, or Kerioth in Moab (Jer. 48:24). It suggests that Judas was not a Galilean. If the family had moved to Galilee, the designation would naturally be applied to both father and son.

"Which also betrayed him"—*also* frankly identified the betrayer as one of the Twelve. The appalling identification is rarely absent from his name in the Gospels. *Betrayed,* more literally "handed over," points to his performance of the dastardly deed of handing Jesus over to His enemies.[9]

Clearly the Twelve whom Jesus chose to carry on His work represented various types of character and different grades of ability, but

---

[9] See William Barclay, *The Master's Men,* for a study of the biblical and traditional information concerning the Twelve. See also William S. McBirnie, *The Search for the Twelve Apostles.*

all had made a personal decision to follow Jesus. It has been pointed out that the list begins with Peter, who denied Jesus, and ends with Judas, who betrayed Him; it was not a list of the immediately perfect.

Luke's Gospel makes it clear that the Sermon on the Mount was delivered following the appointment of the Twelve. Mark does not mention it.

8. Mounting Opposition to Jesus (3:19b-35)

Two types of opposition to Jesus' popular ministry manifested themselves. There was the malicious opposition from the hostile Jewish leaders but also a well-meant but misguided interference on the part of His family. Mark introduces the two types of opposition. Jesus' family decided to put Him under restraint (vv. 19b-21), but before their arrival the religious leaders maliciously raised a slanderous charge against Him (vv. 22-30). The evident lack of sympathy with His ministry on the part of His family led Jesus to point out the identity of His spiritual kindred (vv. 31-35). "In this passage," Williamson notes, "the two groups who should have recognized Jesus first, his own family and the teachers of the law, are both blind to his true identity."[10]

a. Anxiety of His Friends (vv. 19b-21).

These verses, unique to Mark, suggest the recollection of an eyewitness.

"He cometh into a house" (ASV)—rightly connected with verse 20 as beginning a new paragraph.[11] More probably the meaning is "He comes home," marking a return to Capernaum. (cf. 2:1).

"The multitude cometh together again"—*again* looks back to a similar occurrence in 2:2. The historical present vividly conceives the scene. As soon as Jesus returned, the people flocked to the house and filled it. In spite of official hostility, He was popular with the people.

"So that they could not so much as eat bread"—they had no time for eating, much less for needed relaxation. Evidently they had traveled a distance and were hungry. The similar comment in 6:31 shows that it was no solitary occurrence. It is an added touch in Mark's picture of the ceaseless activity of the Servant of the Lord. The persistent pressure of the clamoring crowds formed one of the burdens of His strenuous ministry.

"And when his friends heard *of it*"—heard reports of His incessant ministry to the crowds without apparent consideration for His own

---

[10] Williamson, p. 83.

[11] When in 1551 Robert Stephens introduced verse divisions, he rightly included the phrase in verse 20, but unhappily, later editors, with poorer judgment, attached it to verse 19.

needs. A report of the situation at Capernaum reached *his friends,* a term denoting those closely connected with Him. In the papyruses, the term was used of a man's "agents," his "friends or associates," and in the narrow sense of "family."[12] "His family" seems the best rendering here. Verse 31 seems naturally to be a resumption of the narrative concerning them.

"They went out to lay hold on him"—they were spurred into action by the report. Apparently they left Nazareth for Capernaum intending to take Him into their control and restrain Him for His own good. Mark several times uses the term with the sense of arresting a person (6:17; 12:12; 14:1, 44, 46, 51). They were deeply concerned for Jesus but lacked an understanding of His aims and activities. Hurtado remarks, "In recent years we have heard stories of other families who have attempted to dissuade family members (usually young adults) from fervent religious or political associations, sometimes forcibly in what is popularly called deprogramming, usually in the belief that their loved ones have been 'brain-washed' and are not in control of their minds. Seen in this light, the passage before us has a familiar human ring in it."[13]

"They said, He is beside himself"—they were asserting, "He has lost His mind!" They felt that Jesus was not acting rationally, that He was unbalanced. They could not explain His willingness to be constantly imposed on by people except as an abnormality in Him. Taylor well notes, "Deep personal concern for Jesus is combined with a want of sympathy for His aims and purposes."[14]

Some interpreters suggest that *they said* must be impersonal, "It was being said," giving the rumored opinion of others. But the plural can hardly be viewed as impersonal, nor does the context suggest such a switch. Nor does this suggestion free the family of blame; even if they did not originate the opinion, they gave credence to it and acted on it. Mark frankly recorded it as an example of unexpected opposition to Jesus.

b. Charge of Collusion with Beelzebub (vv. 22-30).

In the meantime, Jesus encountered opposition that was deliberately malicious. The slanderous charge was evoked by favorable public reaction to the healing of a blind and mute demoniac (Matt. 12:22-23). Mark did not record the miracle, concentrating on the nature of the

---

[12] Moulton and Milligan, pp. 478-79.

[13] Hurtado, *Mark,* Good News Commentary, p. 50.

[14] Vincent Taylor, *The Gospel According to St. Mark,* p. 236.

mounting opposition. The controversy is given at greater length in Matthew 12:22-37.

"The scribes which came down from Jerusalem"—the phrasing of the original, "The scribes, those from Jerusalem," indicates the prestige of this embassy from the capital. Their aim was to neutralize Jesus' influence. This reference to Jerusalem may well indicate where this hostility against Jesus will reach its consummation in His death.

"Said"—imperfect tense, denoting repeated expression of the opposition. Two distinct charges are quoted, relating to His person and to His work.

"He hath Beelzebub"—as an abiding condition. Their verdict may mean that Jesus controlled Beelzebub, operated in his power, but more probably they meant that Beelzebub used Jesus as his agent. In the Greek, the name is always *Beelzeboul;* the familiar "Beelzebub" is from the Vulgate. Some view the name as a derisive corruption of the title of the god of Ekron, *Baal-zebub,* "the lord of flies," to make it mean the lord of dung. More probably it means lord of the dwelling, that is, the dwelling of the evil spirits. This agrees with the reference to "the strong man's house" in verse 27, as well as Christ's comment in Matthew 10:25 that as "the master of the house" He has been called Beelzebub. Instead of recognizing Jesus as the Son of God, the scribes charged that He was the permanent tool of Satan. It was a vicious attack upon His person.

"By the prince of the devils casteth he out devils"—this second charge admitted the reality of the expulsion but sought to discredit His work by attributing it to a satanic source. *Prince* means ruler. It denotes him as first in importance as ruler of the demons, regarded as Satan's subjects and part of his kingdom. The preposition rendered *by* (*en*) may denote instrumentality: by means of his power. More probably it was intended to convey the thought of Jesus' intimate union with Satan as the explanation of His power. He was in alliance with Satan as Satan's subordinate.

"He called them *unto him*"—the charges were made behind His back in an effort to discredit Him with the crowd. Aware of their thoughts (Matt. 12:25), Jesus acted to counteract the slander. His answer to the scribes consisted of refutation (vv. 23-27) and warning (vv. 28-30).

"In parables"—His picturesque and proverb-like manner of reply. His answer was parabolic in that He used the principle of likeness between well-known facts and the truths to be conveyed.

"How can Satan cast out Satan?"—the counterquestion, recorded only by Mark, assumes that the title used by the scribes meant Satan. Jesus thus openly stated their bitter implication. With the scribes He accepted the personal existence of Satan and of the demons as his subjects. *How* pointed to the absurdity of their suggestion, for it assumed the suicidal action of Satan casting out himself. No rational, intelligent being would act thus.

Verses 24-25 give two illustrations of the absurd assumption underlying their charge. Both are hypothetical examples, suggesting the unreality of the principle illustrated. Their suggestion is self-destructive for the large, complex affairs of a kingdom as well as the intimate, local relations of an individual household. In each instance, if the unit were divided against itself and one part rose up against the other to subdue and dominate it, the result would be inevitable downfall for the kingdom or household.

"If Satan rise up against himself, and be divided"—the climax of the refuting illustrations. The two verbs, in the aorist tense ("rose up" and "was divided"), are viewed as asserting past realities. On the basis of their logic, Satan had actually risen up against himself, and he and his kingdom had become a divided force.

"He cannot stand, but hath an end"—their assumption means that Satan is under a standing inability to be the head of the kingdom of evil. The added assertion *hath an end* found only in Mark, solemnly announces Satan's doom. The reference is not to his personal existence but to his position as prince of the demonic world.

"[But, Gr.] no man can enter into a strong man's house, and spoil his goods, except he will first bind the strong man"—against the absurdity of their claim (vv. 24-26) stands the fact of His true relation to Satan in His work of casting out demons. *But* is a strong adversative, setting forth the contrasted truth. The contrast is stated in the form of an analogy, picturing Satan as a powerful brigand who has filled his house with his plunder. The strong man is Satan; his house is the kingdom over which he rules, with the demons as members of his household doing his bidding. His *goods,* or "vessels," apparently are the hapless human victims whom Satan holds in his power through his demonic agents. Only one who is stronger than Satan can deliver them from his grasp. In expelling the demon, Jesus had done exactly this, thus proving that He was acting in opposition to Satan, not as his cooperating agent. It proved that He had entered Satan's house, had overpowered him, and had bound him. In Him, the master of the demons had found *his* master.

"Then he will spoil his house"—Jesus established His mastery over the Devil by His victory in the wilderness temptation, but the future tense *will spoil,* "will plunder," looks forward to the coming full overthrow of Satan and his kingdom. Satan is already a defeated foe, but his final immobilization awaits the open establishment of Christ's kingdom in visible manifestation at His return.

From calm reasoning to show the absurdity of their claim, Jesus turned to solemn warning (vv. 28-30). Their charge revealed their inner moral condition.

"Verily I say unto you"—the first occurrence in Mark of this solemn formula of affirmation. It is found only in the Gospels, always on the lips of Jesus.[15] It always introduces a statement of solemn import. *Verily,* literally "amen," is a Hebrew word meaning truth or verity. It thus means "surely," "of a truth," and "truly." It is always followed by *I say unto you,* indicating that Jesus is speaking from His own authority. The formula thus conveys the thoughts of truthfulness and authority, the equivalent of the Old Testament "As I live, saith the Lord." By its use here Jesus solemnly guaranteed His antagonists of the truth of the profound assertion He was about to make.

"All sins shall be forgiven unto the sons of men"—a magnificent assertion of the wideness of God's forgiving mercy. It is not an assertion of universal forgiveness but a declaration that *all* classes and kinds of sins may be forgiven (with the one exception subsequently stated). *The sons of men,* an Aramaism found only here in the Gospels, means human beings. Men's sins, their acts of disobedience producing a barrier between them and God, may all be forgiven and removed.

"And blasphemies"—a specific class of sins. To blaspheme is to speak reproachfully, to utter malicious, injurious things. When directed against God, it denotes hostile speech that is derogatory of God's honor and power. God's willingness to forgive is amazing indeed!

"But he that shall blaspheme against the Holy Ghost"—the original order, "the Spirit, the holy," stresses the holy nature of the Spirit. *Against* is literally "into" (*eis*), going out to malign Him. It is the Spirit's office to convict men of sin and to reveal to them the propitiatory provision in the atonement. When men deliberately dishonor the Spirit, misrepresenting His nature and work, they commit a crime which closes the door to the possibility of forgiveness. English asserts, "There is no forgiveness here because such an attitude is incapable of seeking it."[16]

"Hath never forgiveness"—an absolute negation of the possibility, either here or hereafter. (Cf. the fuller statement in Matt. 12:32.)

---

[15] It occurs thirteen times in Mark, thirty in Matthew, six in Luke, and twenty-five in John, where the "verily" is always double.

[16] Donald English, *The Message of Mark,* p. 89.

"But is guilty of an eternal sin" (ASV)—the positive assertion of the abiding consequence of the sin. The sin is *eternal,* remaining unforgiven forever. He remains under the guilt of its unending consequences.

"Because they said, He hath an unclean spirit"—a Marcan explanatory comment giving the reason for Christ's solemn assertion. *Said,* looking back to the charge in verse 23, is imperfect tense, marking their persistence in the malicious charge. By persistently attributing Jesus' act of exorcism, wrought in the power of the Holy Spirit, to the agency of the Devil, the scribes were consciously maligning the Spirit's work. Motivated by their hatred for Jesus, they were willing to stamp as satanic the holy power in which He worked. It was a perversion of moral distinctions, ascribing the manifest work of the Spirit of God to Satan. The tense indicates that it was not so much a single act as an attitude of heart which persisted in rejecting the light by calling good evil and evil good. In such a state, the Holy Spirit can no longer work to produce conviction of sin. Many serious souls have been deeply agitated with the thought that they may have committed this sin. Ryle well observed, "Those who are troubled with fears that they have sinned the unpardonable sin, are the very people who have not sinned it."[17] After noting that Jesus' warning was made to the duly accredited theological leaders of the day, Cranfield remarks, "Those who most particularly should heed the warning of this verse today are the theological teachers and the official leaders of the churches."[18]

c. Identity of His True Kindred (vv. 31-35).

This brief paragraph is apparently a resumption of the narrative in verse 21. The unsympathetic attitude of His family toward His ministry prompted, and gave force to, Jesus' words about the true identity of His kindred. The pronouncement is basic for a true conception of the nature of His church.

"[And, Gr.] there came then his brethren and his mother"—*and* simply joins the narrative without indicating chronological sequence; Matthew explicitly noted the close chronological connection (12:46). Only here does the mother of Jesus appear personally in Mark's Gospel. In 6:3 she is mentioned as the mother of Jesus. Joseph's absence in all the Gospels during the ministry of Jesus is commonly assumed to mean that he had died. His last appearance in the Gospels is in Luke 2:51.

---

[17] J. C. Ryle, "Mark" in *Expository Thoughts on the Gospels,* pp. 58-59.

[18] C.E.B. Cranfield, *The Gospel According to Saint Mark,* Cambridge Greek Testament Commentary, p. 143.

Four *brethren* are named in 6:3. The precise relationship of these brothers to Jesus has been disputed for ages. Three views are still advocated, conveniently named after their chief proponents in a discussion late in the fourth century: (1) the Helvidian (after Helvidius, A.D. 380), that they are the sons of Joseph and Mary, hence all younger than Jesus; (2) the Epiphanian (after Epiphanius, A.D. 382), that they are the sons of Joseph by a former marriage, hence all older than Jesus; (3) the Hieronymian (after Jerome, A.D. 383), that they were the cousins of Jesus, the sons of Mary's sister, the wife of Cleopas. The first view is the simplest and the most natural, although the thorny problem will probably never be settled to the full satisfaction of everyone.[19]

"Standing without"—either outside the house filled with listeners or beyond the assembled circle of people around Jesus in the open air. The former is the more natural meaning.

"Sent unto him, calling him"—the size and density of the crowd made immediate access to Jesus impossible. Reluctant to declare their intention to others, the family sent in a message asking Jesus to come out for a consultation.

"The multitude sat about him"—the crowd apparently consisted mostly of those friendly to Jesus, many of them His disciples. *About* indicates that the people were seated in a circle around Jesus (cf. v. 34). The people were seated cross-legged on the floor or ground in concentric circles around Jesus. His most intimate disciples would be nearest Him.

"They said unto him"—the message for Jesus, given to someone on the edge of the crowd, had been passed on from person to person until someone near Him (Matt. 12:47), perhaps during a pause, informed Jesus.

"Behold, thy mother and thy brethren without seek for thee"—the speaker prefaced his announcement with the exclamation *Behold* to call attention to the strange fact of their presence and request.[20] It was indeed a strange and unusual occurrence.

"He answered them"—not His family but those informing Him.

"Who is my mother, or my brethren?"—not intended as a repudiation of them. The words do imply His disappointment at their lack

---

[19] On the problem, see James Hardy Ropes, *A Critical and Exegetical Commentary on the Epistle of St. James,* International Critical Commentary, pp. 54-59; V. Taylor, *The Gospel According to St. Mark,* pp. 247-49; D. Edmond Hiebert, *An Introduction to the New Testament,* vol. 3, *An Introduction to the Non-Pauline Epistles,* pp. 46-50.

[20] Some manuscripts add "and your sisters," but it is clearly a scribal addition, an inference drawn from verse 35. His sisters lived in Nazareth (6:3) and would hardly have taken part in a public mission aimed at restraining Jesus in His work.

of sympathy for His work and suggest that they were not qualified to direct His activities. The question was intended to call attention to the fact that, in His work, there were ties that were higher than those of flesh and blood.

"And he looked round about on them which sat about him"— another reference to the characteristic "looks" of Jesus preserved by Mark. Matthew 12:48-50 makes clear that these words of Jesus were addressed directly to "his disciples" before Him. It apparently was a look of affectionate recognition as His eye swept over the circle of disciples around Him. Matthew added that He also stretched out His hand toward His disciples as He spoke (12:49).

"Behold my mother and my brethren!"—His interjection, *Behold,* likewise called attention to His startling assertion. The kinship which He acknowledged goes beyond natural ties, for it is based on spiritual relationships. This has aptly been called "the adoption of the obedient."[21]

"For whosoever shall do the will of God"—the decisive point in the kinship being recognized. *Shall do* sums up the individual's entire life as united in doing God's will. Not a profession of discipleship but active obedience establishes the relationship. *Whosoever* indicates that the relationship is not limited to natural ties but is open to all alike. All who are His kin are characterized by their obedience to the Father's will. Such "a ministry of servanthood produces offspring for the 'family of God' far beyond the number of our blood relatives."[22]

"The same is my brother, and my sister, and mother"—*the same* is resumptive, the one characterized as doing God's will. Such a one is a member of the family of God. "Kinship is now lifted to a new plane and put on a new basis: obedience to God, as exemplified by the total ministry of Jesus."[23] The three terms, *brother, sister, mother,* used without the articles, are figurative, denoting the spiritual family. All true believers constitute the household of God. Jesus did not add "and father," for in the realm of the spiritual, that term marked a position which no human being could fill. Jesus always used the term *Father* of the heavenly Father.

9. Parabolic Teaching to the Crowd (4:1-34)

Mark chapter 4 forms the first of two lengthy passages devoted to the teaching of Jesus. Here the theme of His teaching is "the kingdom

---

[21] W. N. Clarke, *Commentary on the Gospel of Mark,* in An American Commentary, p. 56.

[22] David L. McKenna, *Mark,* The Communicator's Commentary, p. 86.

[23] M. Robert Mansfield, *"Spirit and Gospel" in Mark,* p. 70.

of God'' (vv. 11, 26, 30) presented in parables; in chapter 13 His theme is the eschatological future. Matthew 13 contains a fuller record of this parabolic teaching; Luke 8:4-18 recorded only the first parable of Jesus on this occasion. Mark noted the setting (vv. 1-2) and contents of the parabolic teaching (vv. 3-32) and added a summary statement concerning the method employed (vv. 33-34).

a. Setting for the Teaching (vv. 1-2).

Mark gives no indication of time in introducing this parabolic teaching ministry, but Matthew 13:1 expressly asserts that it was ''the same day'' when Jesus was charged with working in the power of Beelzebub. The teaching was given amidst growing hostility to, and sad misunderstanding of, His ministry. It was part of Christ's ''busy day at Capernaum.'' (This ''busy day'' included the events narrated in Matt. 12:22–13:53; Mark 3:19–4:41; Luke 8:4-25.)

''And he began again to teach by the sea side''—*and* introduces a further phase of Christ's incessant activity. *Again* looks back to 3:7, perhaps also to 2:13; such seaside teaching was nothing new. But *began* points to a new departure in the *nature* of the teaching now given. Morally rejected by the Jewish leaders, Jesus adopted a new method.

''There was gathered unto him a great multitude''—the scribal accusations no doubt affected the attitude of many but did not destroy the common people's interest in Jesus. His seaside teaching drew a very great multitude, a vast but promiscuous assemblage. The superlative (rendered ''very great'' in the ASV) may literally mean that the crowd size was the greatest, for the occasion formed the climax of Christ's great Galilean ministry.

''So that he entered into a ship, and sat in the sea''—*ship* here is not diminutive, as in 3:9, and suggests a vessel larger than a rowboat. *Sat in the sea* pictures Him as encircled by the sea, since the boat had been rowed a little way from shore. His sitting posture indicated that a teaching session was to begin.

''The whole multitude was by the sea on the land''—the vast crowd stood on the rising beach in a circle, all facing the speaker seated in the boat. A cove between Capernaum and the mouth of the Jordan, where the beach rises rather rapidly from the water, which is quite deep within a few yards from shore, may have provided the needed natural amphitheater with acoustics adequate for the occasion.

''He taught them many things by parables''—in this teaching session, Jesus taught the multitude many things, but they were all conveyed in parables, several of which Mark recorded. It marked a new stage in His didactic ministry. Previously, His teaching had been more direct and in less pictorial terms, but now His teaching concerning the kingdom of God was exclusively parabolic.

Parable, a transliteration of the Greek term *parabolē,* "something thrown alongside of," has the basic meaning of a comparison or an analogy. The parable places the truth to be taught alongside of that which is known and familiar by way of comparison and illustration. Mark's previous use of the term (3:23) indicates that it need not be a narrative. The Hebrew word *māshāl,* which *parable* translates, was used for a variety of materials, including ethical maxims, proverbial sayings, riddles, oracles, as well as the familiar narrative form. Thus Mark applied it to a pithy saying (7:17), a mere comparison without narrative (13:28), as well as to the parabolic narrative (here). Christ's parables always teach some moral and spiritual truth by illustrations drawn from familiar occurrences in human experience. Some of His parables seem to be based on known historical events, but clearly He molded their form to convey the intended truth adequately.

Jewish audiences were familiar with the use of parables. Jesus did not invent the parable, for the rabbis often employed parables in their teaching. But His teaching skill brought the use of the parable to its highest level of perfection. He knew how to use the common things of everyday life to set forth profound truths in an unforgettable manner. When interpreting the parables, one must view and evaluate the details according to the central thrust of the parable.

b. Content of the Teaching (vv. 3-32).

Of the various parables uttered by Jesus during this day, Mark recorded only three, all of them drawn from familiar agricultural pursuits. Mark's account makes it clear that there were intervals between Christ's presentation of the different parables.

1) Parable of the sower (vv. 3-20). This is the only parable spoken during this day which was recorded by all the synoptics. It served as a pattern parable (v. 13), forming the basis for the parabolic teaching during the day. Mark's account gives it the most space. He recorded the parable (vv. 3-9) and the interpretation of it as given by Jesus (vv. 10-20).

"Hearken"—a call for careful attention to the teaching to be given. Mark alone recorded this introductory summons. The present imperative calls for the continuing attention of the hearers. It was probably intended to introduce the whole parabolic discourse. The method would make serious demands upon the attention and thought of the hearers.

"Behold, there went out a sower to sow"—the introductory *Behold* draws attention to the common picture of the sower as something that deserves careful consideration. There is a deep spiritual lesson in the familiar scene. The sower literally *went out* from his home in the village to his field in the open country. He worked with a leather bag containing the seed, either wheat or barley, tied to his waist while he scattered the seed by hand. The field would be neither extensive nor fenced. The scattered grain was plowed in by means of a wooden plow, generally drawn by a pair of oxen.

"It came to pass, as he sowed"—the formula *it came to pass* calls attention to the fact that during the process of sowing, something happened, which, while quite common, was not part of the sower's purpose.

"Some fell by the way side"—the seed sown was all the same kind, but its productiveness was determined by the place where it fell. The wayside was either a road at the edge of the field or a footpath crossing the open field. In his efforts to cover the whole field, some of the grain being broadcast fell along the trampled wayside. These seed kernels, lying openly on the hardened pathway, invited the self-seeking activities of the birds.

"Stony ground"—not a place with rocks strewn over its surface, but an area with only a thin layer of soil covering a solid ledge of limestone a few inches below the surface. This thin soil caused two effects. It caused quick germination of the seed. The warm, moist soil induced immediate sprouting and rapid growth of the plant which pushed prematurely upward under the "hot-bed" conditions.

Verse 6 states the second effect of the underlying rock ledge. Unable to put down deep roots, when the hot sun began to beat down on it, the young plant was scorched, succumbing to the burning heat. Unable to draw moisture from below, it quickly dried up.

"Among thorns"—not among thorn bushes, but into ground infested with their uncut roots. The thorn bushes had been burned down but their roots not eradicated. In the productive soil, both the seed and the thorns sprang up, but the rapid and luxurious growth of the thorns soon topped the grain plant and choked it, stifling its life by depriving it of needed light and moisture.

"It yielded no fruit"—it was able to form a green head; but, robbed of the needed energies, it produced no grain.

"Other fell on good ground"—the plural "others" (Gr.), contrasting with the three separate instances of failure of a part of the seed sown, looks to the three classes into which the remaining seed was distributed. *Good ground* stresses the nature of the ground as attractive to contemplate for the intended result.

"Did yield fruit that sprang up and increased"—Unlike the preceding instances, here the seed yielded fruit, fulfilling the intention of the sower. The Greek participles "growing up" and "increasing," peculiar to Mark, picture the steady growth after the sowing.

"Some thirty, and some sixty, and some an hundred"—the numbers indicate the increase in grain harvested over the amount of grain sown. The yield, arranged by Mark in an order of climax, varied according to the fertility of the soil. The soil of the plain of Genesaret, on the northwestern shore of the lake, was prodigiously productive. Josephus enthusiastically called it "the ambition of nature" (*Wars* 3. 10. 8).

While much of the sower's work seemed to be in vain, the picture presented by the parable was not pessimistic, but realistic. The larger part of the field consisted of good soil where the seed sown produced amazing results.

"He that hath ears to hear, let him hear"—a call found here in all the synoptics, marking the special importance of the parable. It was more than a pleasant story; it set forth truth that required serious consideration. It called for attention as well as discernment. The present imperative pressed upon the hearers their continuing duty to hear and heed what was taught. Jesus placed serious responsibility upon the hearer of the Word of God. Effective communication makes its demands upon the hearer as well as the speaker.

"And when he was alone"—indicating a chronological break in the account of the parables taught during this day. Before recording further parables, Mark pauses to record Jesus' discussion with the disciples concerning the parabolic teaching. *Alone* denotes comparative seclusion, free from the pressure of the crowd. It was apparently after the termination of the public ministry from the boat (cf. Matt. 13:36).

"They that were about him with the twelve"—the wider circle of His disciples. As committed disciples, they shared the intimacy of the Lord's fellowship with the Twelve. These followers are here distinguished from the larger crowd of uncommitted hearers as well as the Twelve.

"Asked of him the parable"—the plural ("parables," Gr.) shows that more than one parable had been given when they presented their inquiry. The parables obviously dealt with a common subject that aroused their interest. Mark's concise statement of their inquiry includes the reason for the parabolic method (cf. Matt. 13:10) as well as the meaning of the parable (cf. Luke 8:9). In reply, Jesus gave His explanation for the parabolic method (vv. 11-12) as well as the interpretation of the parable of the sower (vv. 13-20).

"Unto you is given the mystery of the kingdom of God" (ASV)—the emphatic *unto you* distinguished the disciples from those without. As Jesus' disciples, they have been given *the mystery,* a term occurring in the Gospels only in connection with this parabolic ministry, but common in Paul's letters.[24] In the New Testament it denotes not something mysterious and inscrutable but something formerly hidden which cannot be known by man apart from divine revelation but which is now revealed and imparted to those spiritually qualified to receive it. In its ultimate development, this mystery is the fully unfolded message of the gospel (cf. Rom. 16:25-26).

The parables Jesus spoke this day revealed the nature and development of *the kingdom of God*. The essence of the revelation was that the kingdom was embodied in the Person, words, and work of Jesus. Their faith qualified the disciples to understand that the lowly Jesus is the very revelation of God to men. *Is given* asserts that they had received the mystery as a permanent gift, given them by God. As yet, they understood but little of the full import of the kingdom of God as embodied in Christ, but the reality that had been sown in their hearts would produce a glorious harvest in the future. But the fact that they had been given this mystery carried with it a sacred responsibility.

"But unto them that are without"—a designation used here only by Mark. It points to those outside the circle of discipleship. The use of the parabolic method has instituted a sifting process among Jesus' hearers, producing a separation between disciples and those uncommitted to Him.

"All *these* things are done in parables"—*parables* may here have the sense of "riddles." Minus the key to their interpretation, the message the stories conveyed was not apparent to those without. Christ's parables served to veil the truth concerning the kingdom as well as to *un*veil it, depending upon the attitude of the hearer toward Him. The attitude of unbelief on the part of those without rendered them unqualified to understand and receive the revelation; the unexplained parables remained to them a veiled mystery. But faith penetrated the veil and grasped the revelation. This parabolic ministry thus served to reveal the inner heart condition of the hearers. Unbelief nullified the divine effort to give them the revelation.

"That seeing they may see, and not perceive"—if the Greek conjunction *hina* is here given its ordinary meaning—"in order that," instead of "that"—Jesus seems to be saying that He used parables deliberately to veil the truth from the hearers. This presents a difficulty, and Mark has been charged with misrepresenting Jesus. More probably *hina* here means "so that," as expressing simple consequence. Mark's statement should be interpreted by Matthew 13:13, which indicates that

---

[24] *Mystery* (*mustērion*) occurs twenty-seven times in the New Testament: once in each of the synoptics, twenty times in Paul's letters, four times in Revelation.

Jesus used parables because of the spiritual blindness of the people. Matthew follows his explanation with a long quotation from Isaiah 6:9-10. Mark notes no quotation but presented Jesus as giving the substance of Isaiah's words. These words of Isaiah appear several times in the New Testament (cf. John 12:40; Acts 28:26) to denote a judicial blindness that comes to people as the penalty for hardening their hearts against the light. Jesus implied that the parables did serve as a judgment on those who deliberately rejected Him and His revelation. His desire was not to hide the truth from them. In view of their unbelieving attitude, He used parables in an effort to win attention and to stimulate reflection upon the truth contained in the parables. But the scribes' persistent rejection of Him concealed the message from them and turned the parables into an instrument of judgment upon the self-blinded enemies. Plummer well remarks, "This judgment is a merciful one. The parable which the cold-hearted multitudes hear without understanding they remember, because of its penetrating and impressive form; and when their hearts become able to receive its meaning, the meaning will become clear to them. Meanwhile they are saved from the guilt of rejecting plain truth."[25]

"And hearing they may hear, and not understand"—the form preserves the Hebrew parallelism. The statement is in terms of hearing rather than seeing.

"Lest haply they should turn again" (ASV)—an implication that there is in their unbelief an aversion to this turning as something to be avoided. By their persistent rejection of His message, they were acting as though their turning from sin must follow as an undesirable result if they see and hear. *Turn again* conveys the sinner's personal responsibility as a definite act to turn from his sins. All Scripture makes it clear that it is never God's intention to keep people from turning away from sin.

"And *their* sins should be forgiven them"—the sin of their willful rejection of the truth is apparently in view. But forgiveness is assured if only they would turn away from it.

"He said unto them"—the formula marks the transition to another phase of the discussion, namely, the interpretation of the parable of the sower (vv. 14-20). This verse is peculiar to Mark.

"Know ye not this parable?"—either a statement or a question in the original. If a question, Jesus conceded that the disciples did not have the intuitive insight into the meaning; if a statement, He expressed

---

[25] Alfred Plummer, "The Gospel According to St. Mark," in *Cambridge Greek Testament*, p. 124.

surprise that they did not perceive the meaning. The question is preferable.

"How then will ye know all parables?"—implying that in some sense, this parable is the key to all those given or yet to be given in connection with this parabolic teaching concerning the kingdom of God. The future, *will ye know,* or understand, suggests an intended order in the parables and implies that the disciples' lack of perception in this case will extend to all the others. To meet their need, Jesus gave them not general rules of interpretation but an example of interpretation. The illustration was to give them guidance in the interpretation of the other parables.

"The sower soweth the word"—the sower is not identified; stress is placed on the fact that he sows *the word,* "the word of God" (Luke 8:11), or more specifically, "the word of the kingdom" (Matt. 13:19). This is central to the whole picture. In the interpretation of the four soils, the attitude toward the Word on the part of those represented determines the result. The analogy between sowing and teaching was well known. Jesus' explanation makes clear that the message heard and the response to it are the two inseparable sides of the same reality.

Verse 15 refers to those alongside the way—the hard.

"These are they by the way side"—the demonstrative *these,* used for each of the first three classes, centers attention on the people represented. The brief descriptive phrase "the ones alongside the road" points forward to the type of hearers represented in the parable.

"Where the word is sown"—the location, along the road, pictures their unresponsive ears. The important point is their contact with the divine Word. McKenna comments that their characterization as soil repeatedly trampled suggests "the hardening of minds from the constant tramp of life-long habits. A hardened shell of emotional and intellectual defenses will not let the Word of God penetrate through to the point where they consciously change their minds, turn around and go the other way."[26]

"When they have heard, Satan cometh immediately"—whenever as a definite event they hear the Word proclaimed, Satan's activity is immediately aroused. The activity of the birds in the parable has its corresponding reality in the action of "the Satan," the well-known adversary standing at the head of the kingdom of evil. The fact that Jesus did not explain the birds as impersonal temptations is evidence that He accepted the actual existence of a personal Devil. In the parable, *the birds* suggests the varied means operating to remove the Word; in

---

[26] McKenna, p. 94.

the interpretation, the reference to Satan indicates the unity of the power directing the opposition to the Word. This activity of the satanic kingdom must be recognized in any explanation of the varied obstructions encountered by God's Word.

"Taketh away the word that was sown in their hearts"—the hardened hearts of the hearers do not give the Word a chance to penetrate below the surface of their thoughts. It lies exposed until Satan arrives, and then he works to remove it by the power of suggestion or persuasion.

Verses 16-17 mention those on rocky ground—the shallow.

"Likewise"—this identity of the second group is established by the same principles of interpretation as that of the first. There is consistency of interpretation.

"Which are sown on stony ground"—the plural ("stony places," Gr.) pictures several places in the field where there was an unbroken, underlying rock ledge. The present tense, "are being sown," leaves open the result of the sowing.

"When they have heard the word, immediately receive it with gladness"—these hearers respond immediately, readily accepting the Word proclaimed with enthusiasm. The message, seen as something desirable and attractive, evokes a hasty response without due consideration of its implications. Stirred by the personal advantage it offers, they fail to count the cost. *With gladness* denotes their enthusiastic but shallow acquiescence in the gospel.

"Have no root in themselves"—the Word is unable to penetrate into their inner life and fasten a transforming hold on their nature. The influence of the Word is speedily arrested because their old nature remains unbroken. "Shallow growth," McKenna notes, "is the result of a spiritual experience that is emotionally exhilarating, but intellectually rootless."[27]

"Endure but for a time"—"for a season," temporarily. They maintain their professed acceptance of the Word as long as the results are acceptable. Their shallow, superficial nature easily becomes enthusiastic, but it cools off just as readily.

"Afterward, when affliction or persecution ariseth"—*afterward* introduces the logical result of their lack of rootage. Their hasty profession is inevitably tested by tribulation, crushing trials, or persecution, a specific form of affliction. *Affliction* basically denotes the exertion of pressure and includes varied providential experiences, while *persecution* is specific harassment at the hand of enemies.

---

[27] Ibid., p. 95.

"For the word's sake"—because of their professed acceptance of the Word. In this world of moral conflict, such acceptance cannot remain untested.

"Immediately they are offended"—just as there was an immediate joyous response, so there is an immediate adverse reaction. When the glad prospect gives way to the demand for suffering, they do not stop to consider if the affliction is worth enduring for the sake of the Word. The verb *skandalizō,* also translated "stumble" (ASV), is formed from the noun *skandalon,* which means "the trigger stick that springs the trap or snare." It is used here figuratively and has the basic meaning of to entrap, ensare. It was generally used to mean "to cause to sin, to lead to sin." The meaning seems to be that, when persecution because of the Word arises, these of the shallow soil are caused to sin in giving up their profession. They take mortal offense at the suffering demanded because of the Word. Luke here used a word which means to apostatize.

Verses 18-19 concern those among the thorns—the divided.

"These [others, Gr.] are they which are sown among thorns"— "others" draws attention to the third class. They go further than those already portrayed. *Sown* in the present tense again leaves the outcome open.

"The cares of this world"—more literally, "the distractions of the age," the present evil age in which we live in contrast to the world to come. These distracting *cares,* drawing the mind in different directions, leave little time for spiritual and eternal concerns. Jesus clearly saw how worries distract the mind from things which are important and of lasting value.

"The deceitfulness of riches"—riches present themselves as the great good, enticing men to strive for the delights which they promise. But the promises to those that trust in wealth are deceptive; they are never realized. The devotees of wealth, who count its possession their true welfare, fall ready victims to its deceptions, blinding them to spiritual values, which do give abiding satisfaction.

"The lusts of other things"—Luke adds "the pleasures of life"; Mark's statement is more comprehensive. It denotes the various other things of the same character as wealth, for which men crave in this life. These lusts, or strong cravings, would include sensuality.

"Entering in, choke the word"—these three competitive influences are seen as intrusive strangers, forcing their way into the heart after the Word has found lodgment there. Because they are not shut out, they produce a divided heart, choking or smothering the Word by their overwhelming power as competitive forces. *Choke,* a compound form, denotes the completeness of the process.

"It becometh unfruitful"—no seed is produced. The ultimate purpose of the sowing is never realized; it contributes nothing toward the propagation of the Word in the world. "The test of genuine appropriation of the truth is, that it produces effects of life and character corresponding to itself."[28] Believers are born in order to reproduce.

The picture of these first three soils offers a serious reminder that the message of the Kingdom of God is "no easy pill to swallow and no mild word of spiritual uplift but a declaration of war upon the powers of evil and thus, as is true of any war, demands preparation for opposition and sacrifice."[29]

Verse 20 finally comes to those on the good soil—the fruitful.

"[Those, Gr.] are they which are sown on good ground"—*those,* instead of "these," marks the contrast to all the preceding classes. *Sown* here is aorist, indicating a successful sowing, accomplishing the sower's purpose.

"Such as hear the word, and receive *it,* and bring forth fruit"—three present participles, denoting continuing action, characterize them. They continue to have a listening attitude which welcomes the Word, allowing it to work out its purpose in their lives. Their lives are characterized by their productiveness. These three features distinguish them from all the preceding soils.

"Some thirtyfold, some sixty, and some an hundred"—the different degrees are not further identified. Thompson remarks that the differences may be due either to capacity or consecration. "Jesus may mean that some bear more fruit than others because their capacity is greater. But He may also mean, and probably does, that in many lives the seed bears only a fraction of what it might bear because the truth is only partially assimilated."[30] The life that continually takes in God's Word, assimilates it, and is submissive to its demands will be characterized by personal goodness and power for continued service to God's glory.

The parable of the sower, which might better be called the parable of the soils, reflects the immediate situation in which Jesus found Himself as He confronted the people with His message of the kingdom. The varied soils exposed the different attitudes of the people toward Him and explained the indifference and opposition being encountered.

---

[28] Ezra P. Gould, *A Critical and Exegetical Commentary on the Gospel According to St. Mark,* International Critical Commentary, p. 76.

[29] Hurtado, p. 61.

[30] Ernest Trice Thompson, *The Gospel According to Mark and Its Meaning for Today,* pp. 88-89.

The parable also enunciates abiding principles which are operative during this present age, the period of Christendom, whenever the message of Christ the King is proclaimed.

2) *Responsibility of the hearers (vv. 21-25).* This paragraph of proverbial sayings has a parallel in Luke 8:16-18 but none in Matthew. But almost the entire paragraph reappears in Luke as well as Matthew, scattered in different places with different applications.[31] These brief proverbial utterances are pithy seed thoughts which might be used on numerous occasions with different applications. The evidence shows that Jesus did use them on several occasions, and the appropriateness of the paragraph here strongly implies that Jesus also used them here as recorded by Mark. The paragraph forms an important appendix to the recorded explanation for the use of the parabolic method.

"And he said unto them"—in harmony with Mark's previous usage (cf. vv. 9, 11, 13), the formula seems simply to denote a change of subject. The sayings are especially suitable to the circle mentioned in verse 10.

The two negatives in the original indicate that verse 21 contains two separate questions. Rotherham renders quite literally, "Doth the lamp come that under the measure it should be put, or under the couch? Is it not that upon the lampstand it may be put?" The first question expects a no answer, the second, yes. The definite articles with each item mentioned denotes that they were all well known as essential furnishings in every Galilean household. The lamp[32] was a small terra-cotta vessel with a lighted wick. In Jesus' day, it was generally a closed bowl with a hole on top to pour in the oil, a spout for the wick, and usually a handle for carrying. It generally held only a spoonful or two of oil. Mark's expression that the lighted lamp "comes" is a colloquial personification, just as we speak about a message coming, or the mail coming.

Bushel denotes a common household vessel containing somewhat more than a peck. Taken over from the Latin, the term indicated a standard dry measure. The bed, "a place for reclining," may be the common Palestinian bed, which was a matting spread on the floor for the night and rolled up during the day. More probably, this refers to the dining couch, the Roman *triclinium,* used in the more refined homes

---

[31] Verse 21 in Matthew 5:15, Luke 11:33; verse 22 in Matthew 10:26, Luke 12:2; verse 24 in Matthew 7:2, Luke 6:38; verse 25 in Matthew 13:12, 25:29, and Luke 19:26.

[32] "The KJV translation 'Candle' is an anachronism because candles were not invented until the Middle Ages" (Brooks, p. 84, footnote 30).

of Palestine (cf. 2:15). The expected negative answer indicates that no one in his right mind would bring a lighted lamp into the room only to hide it. Rather, it was the natural and expected thing to place the lamp on the stand, usually simply a projection from the wall. Wealthier homes might use separate lampstands.

The "light" which Jesus entrusted to His followers by giving them the explanation of the parables was not intended to be kept hidden from those outside. His teaching was not intended to be esoteric, restricted to an inner circle of enlightened followers. Just as it is the function of light to shine, so it is the duty of His disciples to let their light shine that others too may come to know the truth.

The opening *for* of verse 22 indicates a close connection with what precedes. What had just been said in figurative language is now elucidated in literal terms: "For there is nothing hid, which shall not be manifested; neither was anything kept secret, but that it should come abroad." The double statement stresses the idea of purpose. The underlying law is that when things are hidden, the intention is that in due time they will be revealed. Things that are precious are hidden in order that they may not be abused or misappropriated by those who do not recognize their true nature or function. But they are hidden in order that at the proper time they may be brought forth; for things that are never seen again are lost, not hidden. Prudently the parabolic method now hid the mystery of the kingdom from those without, but the intention was that it was to be made known by His enlightened disciples. They must not think that He intended the revelation to them to remain secret. The kingdom of God, as embodied in Jesus' Person and ministry, was now a veiled revelation to those without, but He intended that later it should receive a glorious manifestation through the ministry of His followers. The full content of this revelation could only be known and understood after His death and resurrection.

"If any man have ears to hear, let him hear"—the conditional sentence assumes the possession of *ears,* the ability to hear; therefore the man must go on hearing. In verse 9, the duty was laid on the entire assembled multitude; here the duty is repeated to the disciples. Jesus said it three times during this session of parabolic teaching (vv. 9, 23; Matt. 13:43). It is recorded as having been used by Jesus on two other occasions (Matt. 11:15; Luke 14:35).[33]

---

[33] The call does not occur in the Fourth Gospel but appears in each of the seven letters in Revelation 2-3 and in Revelation 13:9. In the Gospels, *ears* is always plural, but in Revelation the singular is always used.

"And he said unto them"—this may point to a different occasion, but more probably verses 24-25 were uttered on the same occasion as the preceding teaching. The introductory phrase may imply that there was a pause in the teaching before these words were uttered with impressive solemnity. These maxims have abiding value, whatever the occasion may have been for their utterance.

"Take heed what ye hear"—an appeal for spiritual perception. The Lord made it their standing duty to give careful attention to what they heard in order that they might truly understand it. Superficial hearing must be avoided, especially in spiritual matters.

"With what measure ye mete, it shall be measured to you"—in Matthew 7:2, Jesus used this maxim to underline the result of censorious judgment. Here it is applied to the reward for diligent effort. It is a universal law that the measure of their diligent attention to the teaching will be the measure of the profit they derive from it. The principle operates in the moral and spiritual as well as the intellectual realm.

"Unto you that hear shall more be given"—a gracious promise that the benefit will be even greater than the effort required. God, in His generosity, will give the diligent hearer a blessing that is disproportionately large, more than could justly be expected. The promise is peculiar to Mark.

"For"—introducing an explanation of the preceding by another proverbial saying, also found in other connections (Matt. 25:29; Luke 19:26).

"He that hath, to him shall be given"—to one who possesses something good, because he has acquired it by the diligent use of his powers, more will assuredly be given. Truth received and carefully assimilated enlarges one's capacity to receive more truth. The maxim is not to be applied to material property; its application is spiritual.

The principle also works the other way. The man who does not use his ability to understand the truth thereby blunts his ability to understand it. Disuse of spiritual ability results in spiritual atrophy. The disciples must use their knowledge of the mystery of the kingdom, or their grip on it will diminish until they lose even that which they now possess. This two-sided reality is a challenge to His disciples to comprehend more completely His message about the kingdom of God.

3) Parable of the seed growing (vv. 26-29). This parable is peculiar to Mark, the only one which he alone recorded. It supplements the parable of the sower in elaborating the law of spiritual growth as seen in the good soil.

"And he said"—apparently marking the resumption of the account of the public teaching (cf. vv. 33-34). Verses 10-25 are then, in effect, a parenthesis, recording the private teaching to the group named in verse 10. This may account for the omission here of "to them."

"So is the kingdom of God, as if"—each of these kingdom parables portrays one aspect of the kingdom. The emphatic *so* stresses the likeness which is set forth with *as* in the picture of the entire parable. This parable may point to the analogous growth of the kingdom in the world at large or to its development in the life of the individual.

"A man should cast seed into the ground"—the sower is left unidentified, the main point being the growth of the seed. *Cast* does not imply carelessness but points to the usual method of sowing the seed broadcast by hand. The aorist tense denotes a definite act that needed not to be repeated. The subjunctive mood presents the whole scene as hypothetical, although it was a common scene of rural life.

"And should sleep, and rise night and day"—having sown his seed, the farmer leaves the field and makes no further efforts to assist the germination of the seed sown. He continues his ordinary routine of life, leaving the seed alone. The verbs *sleep* and *rise* denote recurrent actions which go on night and day. The order "night and day," rather than "day and night," "reflects the oriental understanding of a 'day' beginning at sundown."[34]

"The seed should spring and grow up"—present tenses again mark the continuous process. *Grow up* is literally "should be lengthening itself," and pictures the mysterious power of growth in the plant.

"He knoweth not how"—the process of growth is quite independent of the sower, and he may not even understand it. The farmer well knows the conditions that aid or hinder that growth, but the growth process itself is part of the mystery of life in the seed, which even today challenges man's ability to explain fully. "How could the essence of life lay dormant for 4000 years in the seeds found in an Egyptian tomb and still spring to full life when planted?"[35] Even so today, the process of spiritual growth, while "natural" to the kingdom, remains a mystery to the unsaved.

"The earth bringeth forth fruit of herself"—*of herself* (our English word *automatically*) is emphatic and denotes that the growth is produced by a self-acting, spontaneous power within the seed which acts independently of man's agency. The earth itself does not produce the growth but is the medium for the germinating power in the seed. What is produced depends upon the nature of the seed sown. So the human heart responds to the seed of the Word sown into it, but it also responds

---

[34] Robert A. Guelich, *Mark 1–8:26*, Word Biblical Commentary, p. 241.

[35] McKenna, p. 101.

to tares sown in it. The need for suitable weather conditions is not denied but simply assumed. The point is that the seed does not require cultivation during the period of growth. The continued growth is independent of man's action. But as Thompson remarks, "Our duty is to prepare and clean the soil and sow the right kind of seed, confident that fruit will appear in time."[36]

"First the blade, then the ear, after that the full corn in the ear"— the successive stages in the production of the fruit. The repeated *then* stresses the progressive development from stage to stage; the grasslike, green, leaf-equipped stalk; the green, unfilled head; and finally the soft, pulpy kernels swelling to full size and hardening as ripening grain. Any effort on the part of the farmer to hasten the process would only result in damage. Even so, spiritual development cannot be prematurely forced.

"But when the fruit is brought forth"—*when,* literally "whenever," indicates that the time of reaping is not predetermined by the wish of the farmer but dependent upon the condition of the grain. *Is brought forth* is literally "may give alongside" and here has the unusual meaning of allow or permit, that is, when the condition of the grain permits it to be harvested (thus, "is ripe," ASV).

"Immediately he putteth in the sickle, because the harvest is come"—*he* looks back to the man who sowed the grain. During the entire growth season, the farmer has remained inactive, but *immediately* vividly marks the termination of his inactivity as soon as the grain is ripe. At once, he sends forth the sickle, the familiar harvesting instrument, in the hand of the reaper. The farmer has not produced the grain, but his action is needed to preserve the result achieved by the seed he has sown.

Some view the parable as giving a picture of the kingdom as a whole, from the time of Christ's sowing until the eschatological harvest. According to this view, Jesus recognized that His sowing had not yet produced a harvest, but a sowing was being accomplished in His disciples which He confidently trusted God would bring to its future fruitful consummation. This view seems in keeping with the broad scope of the parabolic teaching during this day.

Others see in the parable a picture of the work of the gospel in the life of an individual. The development of spiritual character follows a slow but orderly process and cannot be forced prematurely by human means. Then the harvest is viewed as denoting the ingathering of the results of evangelistic endeavors (cf. John 4:35-36). The duty of the

---

[36] Thompson, p. 93.

Christian worker is to sow the seed and wisely conserve the God-wrought results, while allowing the Word of God to do its work in the individual according to the laws of development which God has established in human nature.

4) Parable of the mustard seed (vv. 30-32). Matthew places this parable immediately after that of the tares (13:24-30), but Luke has it in an entirely different setting (13:18-19).

"And he said"—directed to the assembled multitude (v. 1), as explicitly asserted by Matthew (13:31, 36). Mark's formula implies an interval.

The challenging double question of verse 30, given only by Mark, appealed to the hearers to join in the search for appropriate similes to set forth the kingdom of God. This is the only instance in the recorded teaching of Jesus in which He used *we* to associate Himself with His hearers. Jesus skillfully sought to stimulate His hearers to develop an alertness to perceive such comparisons to the kingdom in the natural world. His disciples would better understand the nature of the spiritual kingdom if they were alert to illustrative comparisons with it in the material world. Any such efforts by those outside (v. 11) would soon show them that they did not understand the nature of the kingdom. But Jesus had a parable ready for the contemplation of His hearers.

"*It is* like a grain of mustard seed"—the parable would answer His questions *how* and *in what*. One important aspect of the kingdom could be illustrated by the tiny mustard seed and its great growth. The reference is apparently to the common black mustard, *Sinapis nigra,* a thick-stemmed plant grown in Palestine for its leaves and seed.[37] Jesus mentioned it several times,[38] each time referring to the smallness of the mustard seed. Its small size was proverbial. The tiny seed, about the size of a grain of sand, produced a plant which often attained a height of ten to twelve feet.

"Less than all the seeds that be in the earth"—not the smallest known to botanists but the smallest of the different kinds of seeds Jews were accustomed to sow in their fields. The smallness of the seed is one of the central features of the parable.

"Groweth up, and becometh greater than all herbs"—a vivid picture of the great result from a small beginning. *Herbs* denotes edible garden plants, vegetables. The leaves of the mustard plant were used as a vegetable and its seed as a condiment. *Greater than* stresses its

---

[37] Harold N. and Alma L. Moldenke, *Plants of the Bible,* pp. 59-62.

[38] Christ apparently referred to it on four different occasions: (1) Matthew 13:31; Mark 4:31; (2) Matthew 17:20; (3) Luke 13:19; (4) Luke 17:6.

stupendous size in relation to all the other plants of its class. Its size at maturity was out of all proportion to the smallness of the seed.

"The fowls of the air may lodge under the shadow of it"—its branches were substantial and sturdy, offering a welcome haunt to numerous birds. They feasted on the seed, but the branches also enabled them to lodge there. The verb is literally "are tenting down, are pitching their tents." It implies more than perching on the branches. These birds made their nests there.

Jesus' interpretation of this parable is not recorded (cf. v. 34*b*). It pictures the smallness of the beginning of the kingdom and its subsequent stupendous growth. Its small beginning does not doom it to insignificance; it will yet reveal an amazing development.

The stupendous growth has been evaluated in two different ways. The traditional view sees in the parables the successful growth of the Christian church from a tiny beginning to a mighty movement of God. The potent and pungent mustard seed pictures the tremendous inner vitality of the gospel and the results achieved by it in human history. This view assumes that the kingdom and the church are identical. It offers no interpretation for the birds and confines itself to the single thought of the growth displayed.

Others see in the great growth an indication of the abnormal development of the kingdom. Beginning as a small, insignificant movement, Christendom developed into a mighty imperial power in the world. That it "becometh a tree" (Matt. 13:32) is held to indicate that the mustard plant developed into something foreign to its very nature. The tree, the biblical symbol of a kingdom, denotes that Christendom will depart from its original nature to become a mighty kingdom exercising imperial powers, a worldly-minded organization. This view sees the birds as representing evil forces which for various reasons embrace Christianity and find shelter in its branches. It finds support in the actual development of the church in history, when under Constantine it gained world recognition and power, with the result that corrupting forces invaded the professing church and altered its original spiritual nature and outlook. This seems the more probable view.

c. Summary of the Parabolic Section (vv. 33-34).

These two verses close the account of this parabolic ministry. Mark records no further parables from the lips of Jesus until Passion Week.

"Many such parables"—the three recorded were representative selections. Exactly how many parables Jesus spoke during this day is not known. *Many* clearly implies more than have been preserved. *Such* indicates that all the parables spoken that day were similar in nature and aim, all setting forth some aspect of the kingdom of God.

"Spake he the word unto them"—the *word* spoken in parables was "the mystery of the kingdom of God" (v. 11). *Spake* is in the imperfect tense, picturing the protracted teaching session.

"As they were able to hear *it*"—Jesus carefully fitted His message to the condition of His audience, intuitively reading their hearts to see what they could receive. *As,* more exactly "even as," marks the exact correspondence between His teaching and the capacity of the hearers. Because of their prejudices and misunderstandings of His person, He spoke the message in a form they were morally qualified to accept.

"Without a parable spake he not unto them"—on this occasion, in seeking to present to them the mystery of the kingdom. The reaction to Him that very day had made it clear how little those who were not His disciples were prepared to understand the message of the kingdom of which He was the very embodiment. His veiled presentation of that message did not force them at once to decide for or against Him as the personal embodiment of the kingdom. "The parabolic teaching was at once a judgment pronounced upon their unpreparedness for the kingdom of God and also the expression of divine mercy that desires to spare and save."[39]

"But privately to his own disciples" (ASV)—in contrast to "those without." *His own disciples* indicates their unique relationship of intimacy with Jesus as followers belonging to Him. They received further instruction because of this relationship. Their need for this additional instruction is obvious from the Gospel accounts.

"He expounded all things"—a statement unique to Mark. The verb means "to loosen, to untie, to solve," and was used of solving or interpreting knotty problems, riddles, or dreams. The disciples needed such help in order to understand the parabolic message. Theirs was a high privilege, but believers today are equally privileged to receive the teaching ministry of the indwelling Spirit, who takes the things of Christ and reveals them to receptive hearts (cf. John 16:14).

---

[39] Cranfield, p. 171.

5
Withdrawals from Galilee
(Part 1; 4:35–6:29)

B. Withdrawals from Galilee (4:35–9:50)

Four separate withdrawals from Galilee by Jesus and His disciples marked the latter part of the great Galilean ministry. Prompted by His desire for relief from the pressure of the crowds, Jesus' first withdrawal was of short duration and was followed by further aggressive work in Galilee (4:35–6:29). The second withdrawal, an effort to get some time alone with His disciples for rest and discussion, also was brief; and His return marked further ministry and controversy (6:30–7:23). During the third withdrawal, of considerable duration, Jesus deliberately took His disciples out of Galilee in order to be able to devote time to their special training (7:24–8:13). Immediate opposition from the Pharisees upon His return prompted the fourth withdrawal, marking the termination of His public ministry in Galilee (8:14–9:50).

1. First Withdrawal and Return (4:35–6:29)

This first withdrawal and return were marked by a series of miracles which demonstrated the lordship of Jesus in different areas (4:35–5:43). The further ministry in Galilee was marked by rejection, intensified work, and growing agitation (6:1-29).

a. Stilling of the Tempest (4:35-41).

This stirring event, demonstrating Christ's lordship over nature, is found in all of the synoptics (Matt. 8:18, 23-27; Luke 8:22-25). Mark's account, vivid and forthright, contains several details not included by the others.

"The same day"—this specific chronological designation reaches back to 3:20 and includes all the subsequent events. It had been a busy day of teaching for Jesus. Such precise time designations are not characteristic of Mark. The other synoptics do not note this strict chronology, but clearly, Mark intended to indicate close chronological sequence in giving this event.

"When the even was come"—a further chronological note, indicating the time of day. *Even* may be either the Jewish first evening, from midafternoon to sundown, or the second evening, from sundown to dark. Perhaps the latter is meant here. Mark's account does not give Jesus' further private teaching in the house (Matt. 13:36-52), but verse 34 does mention a time alone with the disciples. The trip apparently started at sundown, and the storm arose during the evening.

"He saith unto them"—to His personal attendants, the Twelve.

"Let us pass over unto the other side"—Jesus took the initiative and united the disciples with Himself in this suggested withdrawal. The aorist verb *pass over* carries a note of urgency. The verb is commonly used of a journey by land, but here of crossing a body of water. The "other side" was the eastern side of the Sea of Galilee, which, in contrast to the western shore, had no large cities along the shore of the lake. The obvious purpose of the withdrawal was to get away from the pressure of the crowds after an exhausting day. Alexander Jones's suggestion that "our Lord's intention is probably to open up a new mission field" is unlikely.[1]

"When they had sent away the multitude"—weary and worn from the work of the day, Jesus gave no further teaching to the crowd which still lingered. The plural *they* may suggest that, in response to the directive by Jesus, the Twelve acted directly to dismiss the crowd. More probably, the aorist participle in the original may mean "having left the multitude" and records the departure by ship in keeping with the order of Jesus. Yet the reference to *other little ships* indicates that the intended departure was announced.

"They took him"—as the owners and navigators of the boat, the disciples took Jesus. They acted to depart in obedience to His wish.

"Even as he was in the ship"—the Twelve left with Jesus in the one boat *as he was,* without any further preparation for the trip. Since the verb *he was* can also be rendered "it was," Williamson holds that the reference is not to Jesus "but to the boat, first held in readiness (3:9), then used as a pulpit from which to teach (4:1-34), and now about to figure importantly in the action."[2]

---

[1] Alexander Jones, *The Gospel According to St. Mark,* p. 103.

[2] Lamar Williamson, Jr., *Mark,* Interpretation: A Bible Commentary for Teaching and Preaching, p. 100.

"And there were also with him other little ships"—mentioned only by Mark. They were apparently filled with friends eager to remain with Jesus. This seemingly purposeless comment, as well as the "pillow" in verse 38, suggests that the account was derived from Peter's vivid recollections.

"There arose a great storm of wind"—such sudden, furious storms of hurricane proportions were characteristic of the lake, which lies 682 feet below sea level. These storms often swept down on the sea through the deep gaps in the highlands surrounding the lake. The deep ravines served as gigantic funnels to draw the wind down upon the waters. For a boat to capsize in such a storm meant sure death.

"The waves beat into the ship"—lashed by the howling wind, the gigantic waves hurled themselves against the boat and were actually breaking into it. *Beat,* in the imperfect tense, pictures the waves as repeatedly throwing themselves into the boat.

"The boat was now filling" (ASV)—not filled, but in the process of gradually filling up. As wave after wave crashed into the boat, the water began to accumulate dangerously.

"He was in the hinder part of the ship, asleep on a pillow"—*he* is emphatic, marking the contrast between Jesus and the anxious crew. Leaving all navigation to the disciples, Jesus had found a place to relax in the stern, the back part of the boat, and had fallen asleep on the cushion, probably the leathern cushion of the steerman's seat. He slept calmly amidst the howling storm and dashing waves. All the synoptics mentioned the sleep of Jesus, but only Mark noted His position. His sound sleep points to the fact of His utter exhaustion from the work of the busy day. His human nature needed rest as other men's, and found refreshment in sleep. Only here do the Gospels directly mention Jesus sleeping.

"They awake him, and say"—aroused Him, breaking in on His sound sleep with their cries. Each Gospel records their appeal somewhat differently.

"Master" (*didaskalē,* "Teacher")—the Greek equivalent for the Hebrew word *rabbi.*[3] They appealed to Jesus as a religious teacher. Several of the disciples were experienced fishermen, men acquainted with such storms, yet in their extremity, they instinctively turned to Jesus for help in the critical situation.

---

[3] In the Synoptics, both terms are used in addressing or referring to Jesus. Mark has *Teacher (didaskalos)* twelve times, *rabbi* three times; Matthew has *Teacher* nine, *rabbi* twice; Luke has *Teacher* thirteen times, *rabbi,* none.

"Carest thou not that we perish?"—*perish,* the present tense, denotes that the disciples saw themselves as already going down to destruction. Their cry, as given in Mark, implies a feeling of resentment at Jesus' apparent indifference to their peril. The formulation in Mark, not found in the other synoptics, may be drawn from Peter himself. He seems to have been the only disciple who dared to reprove Jesus openly on other occasions. It was a cry of distrust, but one often matched by believers today in difficult circumstances when they feel that the Lord has forsaken them. Gutzke remarks, "How common this is with all of us: we know God can and we are inclined to be pathetically petulant when He doesn't take action we can see. In this instance the disciples forgot they had not asked before."[4]

"He arose"—more literally, "having been thoroughly aroused." Their cries fully aroused Jesus, but their panic did not excite Him.

"Rebuked the wind, and said unto the sea"—the two elements producing the dangerous situation were directly addressed as though they were rational agents. A peremptory rebuke was given them, as though they had transgressed their legitimate bounds.

"Peace, be still"—only Mark recorded the very words of the command. *Peace,* literally, "Be silent," was addressed to the howling wind; *be still,* literally, "be muzzled" (cf. 1:25), was an apt command to the raging waves. "The simplicity and brevity of his command to wind and waves express the assurance of one who is in control."[5] The dramatic form of the command to inanimate objects may suggest that Jesus recognized demonic powers behind the raging of the elements. It is noteworthy that "rebuked" and "be still" were used in 1:25 with reference to an exorcism. The conjecture of certain critics that the words were addressed to the disciples, not the natural elements, is baseless and out of harmony with the context.

"The wind ceased, and there was a great calm"—*ceased,* in the aorist tense, denotes that the wind stopped suddenly. *There was a great calm* records the effect upon the dashing waves. The furiously heaving sea became perfectly still. Such raging winds were known to die down suddenly, but the sudden dying down of the dashing waves was most extraordinary. The simplicity of the narrative recounting the amazing effect of Christ's command is itself striking; the amazing results spoke for themselves.

"He said unto them"—Jesus found it necessary to rebuke the disciples as well as the wind and waves.

---

[4] Manford George Gutzke, *Plain Talk on Mark,* p. 70.

[5] Williamson, p. 101.

"Why are ye so fearful? how is it that ye have no faith?"—the double question, peculiar to Mark, rebuked their feeling and probed the cause. The textual evidence for the exact wording of these two questions is beset with diversity. Metzger indeed suggests that the variations seem to "have arisen from a desire to soften somewhat Jesus' reproach spoken to the disciples."[6] The text supported in the United Bible Societies text, third edition,[7] underlies the ASV rendering, "Why are ye so fearful? have ye not yet faith?"

In the first question the term "fearful" renders an adjective basically denoting "cowardly, timid." It carries an implied rebuke for their timidity in the face of danger confronted. It was unworthy of them in view of what they had seen and heard in association with Him. The second question does not imply that they were devoid of all faith; "not yet" probes the amazing failure that they had not yet apprehended the true significance of the fact that the kingdom was present in the Person and work of Jesus. Their fear implied lack of faith in Him and His power.

"They feared exceedingly"—a different kind of fear from that engendered by the storm. It was deep reverential awe in the presence of the supernatural. This fear did not draw the rebuke of Jesus.

"And said one to another"—deeply awed in His presence, they kept silent toward Jesus, speaking about their feeling of awe only to one another. Even Peter was awed into silence.

"What manner of man is this"—more literally, "Who then is this?" The *then* implies a logical deduction from what they have just experienced. In hushed tones, they pondered Jesus' true identity. They realized that they did not yet really know Him.

"That even the wind and the sea obey him"—the cause for their awe. The verb is in the singular and indicates that wind and sea acted in unity in their obedience to the command of Jesus. The disciples were profoundly impressed that wind and waves, not known to yield obedience to human command, thus readily obeyed the word of Jesus. Surely only one who was more than human could thus make the wind and sea obey Him. Their perplexity shows that they still did not understand who Jesus really was. "In Mark," Brooks notes, "the mystery of who Jesus is continues until his death and resurrection and even beyond."[8]

---

[6] Bruce M. Metzger, *A Textual Commentary on the Greek New Testament*, p. 84.

[7] Kurt Aland, Matthew Black, Carlo M. Martini, Bruce M. Metzger, and Allen Wikgren, *The Greek New Testament*, United Bible Societies, 3rd ed., p. 137.

[8] James A. Brooks, *Mark*, The New American Commentary, p. 88.

This nature miracle, so contrary to ordinary human experience, has been the object of much skeptical scoffing. Unquestionably the disciples accepted the conclusion on the spot that the wind and waves had miraculously responded to the command of Jesus. The Gospel writers obviously intended their account to be understood literally. Men's evaluation of the credibility of the account will be determined by their attitude toward the supernatural. No one who accepts the scriptural portrait of the supernatural nature of Jesus Christ will have much difficulty in accepting this picture of His authority over the material creation. Rawlinson aptly remarks, "The broad truth of the Christian doctrine of the Incarnation once assumed, no wise person will proceed rashly to draw the limits between what is and what is not possible."[9]

b. Cure of the Gerasene Demoniac (5:1-20).

This event, which all the synoptics place immediately after the stilling of the storm, gave dramatic proof that Jesus was Lord over demons. Although Jesus had previously cast out demons, this was an extraordinary case, one that had frustrated all human efforts. Mark's vivid and detailed account seems to have been drawn from the rugged report of an eyewitness. Taylor remarks that there is "good reason to classify the narrative as Petrine in origin."[10]

"They came over unto the other side of the sea"—marking the completion of the boat trip Jesus ordered in 4:35. *They,* denoting Jesus and His disciples, contains the only reference to the disciples in this whole paragraph. Throughout, Jesus speaks and acts alone. Luke identified *the other side* as being "over against Galilee" (8:26), the eastern shore.

"The country of the Gerasenes" (ASV)—variant names for the place have caused much discussion. It is now generally accepted that the original reading in Mark and Luke was "the Gerasenes," while Matthew wrote "the Gadarenes." *Gerasenes* has been taken to refer to the important city of Gerasa (Jarash), located thirty-seven miles southeast of the Sea of Galilee. Then the designation was used very loosely to connect the area with the one well-known city in the general area with which non-Palestinian readers would be familiar. More probably the reference is to the small town called Kersa, or Gersa, located near the sea about midway on the eastern shore. There are steep hills and cave-tombs about a mile south of Kersa.[11] Matthew called it "the country of the Gadarenes" (8:28, ASV) with reference to the city of

---

[9] A.E.J. Rawlinson, *St. Mark,* p. 60.

[10] V. Taylor, *The Gospel According to St. Mark,* p. 278.

[11] Brooks, p. 89.

Gadara, located six miles southeast of the southern end of the sea. The jurisdiction of the city of Gadara may have extended to the sea to include the small town of Kersa on the shore. Obviously the story took place on the eastern shore of the lake. The area near the village of Kersa meets the topographical requirements for the story.

"Immediately"—Mark's characteristic term indicates that there was no long interval between the disembarking and the encounter which followed.

"There met him out of the tombs a man"—*met* simply states the encounter as an historical event. The details are given in verses 6-7. Matthew (8:28) mentions two demoniacs; Mark and Luke, while they speak of only one, do not assert that he was alone. The one man apparently was the leader and such an alarming case that the other remained almost unnoticed. As Jesus stepped ashore, the man emerged from the tombs, either burial places built above ground or, more probably, natural caves or rock-hewn chambers in the side of the hill. Such tombs were common haunts for demented men.

"With an unclean spirit"—literally, "in a spirit unclean" (cf. 1:23).

The realistic account of this history of the demoniac in verses 3-5 is largely unique with Mark. It seems to be a faithful reproduction of the recital given to the disciples by the neighbors who knew the case.

"Who had *his* dwelling among the tombs"—the plural implies that he found shelter first in one, and then in another tomb. Such places were considered unclean and were located in remote areas outside the city. His residence there marked his abnormal condition, a voluntary outcast from society.

"No man could bind him, no, not with chains"—literally, "not even with a chain no longer could no one bind him." This accumulation of negatives, peculiar to Mark, stresses the great strength of the man. "No longer" indicates that his case had grown steadily worse. Now his herculean strength rendered all such attempts futile. It recalls the ancient practice of restraining demented people. Mental hospitals were unknown.

Because (v. 4) introduces the evidence that the man was now untamable. Repeated efforts to confine him "with fetters and chains" had proved useless. *Fetters* denotes bonds for the feet, whether of cords or chains. *Chains* may mean metal bonds for other parts of the body, but the term underlines the strength of the materials used. With abnormal strength, he had rent asunder the chains placed on him; and the fetters he had "broken in pieces," crushed or shattered them like pottery. *Broken* has the root meaning "to rub together" and may imply that the fetters were shattered by being violently rubbed together. The perfect tenses picture the past circumstances which explain his present untamable condition.

"Neither could any *man* tame him"—the verb *tame* was used of subjugating lower animals to the control of man. His indomitable fierceness made him the despair of human efforts.

Verse 5 describes the utter misery of the unfortunate sufferer. *Always* indicates how his time was spent, *night and day* being more specific. His restlessness spurred him to action during the night as well as during the day, leaving no long intervals between his frenzied actions. At times, he would sit moodily in the tombs, but soon he would be excitedly roving around in the mountains of that area. *Crying,* in the imperfect tense, denotes that repeatedly his cries were heard among the hills. The verb means an unearthly yell or scream under strong emotional excitement. *Cutting himself,* also imperfect tense, indicates that repeatedly the man lacerated his body with stones, sharp flints. Apparently his whole body was covered with the scars.

"[And, Gr.] when he saw Jesus afar off"—*and* connects the description of the man's past with his conduct on this occasion. The account now picks up the summary *met* of verse 2 and records the details of the encounter. That he could see Jesus from afar indicates that it was now daylight, the morning after the storm.

"He ran and worshipped him"—Matthew (8:28) records that the demoniacs were so fierce it was unsafe for anyone to pass that way. Luke (8:27) notes that the demoniac habitually went naked. Any spectators would regard the sight as another instance of a violent attack upon travelers. The sight of this naked maniac rushing down upon them must have been a terrifying experience for the disciples, but Jesus calmly awaited his arrival and ordered the demon to come out of the man (v. 8). If he started toward Jesus with hostile intent, it was not carried out. Probably he felt himself irresistibly drawn toward Jesus. In view of the demoniac's confession of the true identity of Jesus, it seems that his approach and act of worship were prompted by the demons possessing him. The worship was not willing worship but rather a forced confession of Jesus' true nature and of demonic impotence before Him.

"And cried with a loud voice"—the aorist tense of the participle (literally "having cried") indicates the man's scream before he entered into conversation with Jesus. The shriek was evidence of his demon possession (v. 5).

"What have I to do with thee"—an idiom of protest (cf. 1:23-24).

"Jesus, *thou* Son of the most high God"—the man had never met Jesus before and certainly would have no personal knowledge of Him, but the indwelling demon immediately displayed his knowledge of the supernatural nature of Jesus. *Son of God* asserts His identity of essence with God. *Most high God* distinguishes the true God from all false gods. The title goes back to the earliest stages of Hebrew faith and worship. In the Septuagint non-Israelites used the term for the God of Israel (Gen. 14:18-20; Num. 24:16; Isa. 14:14; Dan. 3:26; 4:2), and it was also used in Jewish circles (Deut. 32:8; Pss. 18:13; 21:7; Luke 1:32; Heb. 7:1). So use of the title here does not prove that this man was a pagan rather than a Jew.

"I adjure thee by God"—Mark alone put this formula of exorcism into the mouth of the demoniac here. The demon apparently resorted to this adjuration in an effort to influence Jesus. While capitulating to His divine authority, the demon sought to soften the fate awaiting him at the word of Jesus.

"Torment me not"—a frantic appeal based on the knowledge of his certain fate. The other synoptics make it clear that the torment of the final judgment was in view. According to Matthew (8:29), the demon appealed not to be tormented "before the time," while Luke gave it as a request not to be sent "into the abyss" (8:31, Gr.). Brown comments, "Behold the *tormentor* anticipating, dreading, and entreating exemption from *torment!*"[12]

"For he said unto him"—introducing the reason for the demon's adjuration. *Said,* in the imperfect tense, may mean that Jesus was repeatedly ordering the demon out of the man, but more probably the open-ended imperfect was used to intimate that something was to follow. Having been ordered to leave, the demon delayed to parley for more favorable treatment.

"Come out of the man, *thou* unclean spirit"—a firm command to the spirit to leave the man as a definite act. Jesus used no formula of exorcism; His simple command was sufficient. The original order, "Thou spirit, the unclean one," again stresses the nature of the spirit.

"And he asked him"—a resumption of the conversation after Mark's explanatory comment in verse 8. *Asked,* in the imperfect tense, may denote that the question was repeatedly put to the demon who was reluctant to give his name. The tense, however, may be due to Mark's practice of viewing a conversation as a process.

"What *is* thy name?"—addressed either to the unfortunate man or to the indwelling spirit. If the question was addressed to the man, Jesus was seeking to get the man to recall his own identity and thus to

---

[12] Robert Jamieson, A. R. Fausset, and David Brown, *A Commentary Critical and Explanatory on the Old and New Testaments,* vol. 2, *New Testament,* p. 70.

distinguish himself from the demons that were dominating his personality. But in view of the appeal just made not to be tormented, the question probably was addressed to the spirit. Clearly, Jesus did not ask the question for His own information. In the ancient world, the view prevailed that it was essential to know the name of the demon for success in exorcism. But Jesus' power to expel the demon obviously did not depend on the demon's revelation of his name. Some suggest that the question was intended to bring into the open the complexity of this unusual case.

"My name *is* Legion: for we are many"—*legion,* a Latin term which had become common in Greek and Jewish circles, denoted the Roman military organization consisting of about six thousand infantrymen. As the representative of the foreign power that dominated them, the term had impressed itself upon the Jewish mind as signifying vast numbers, complex organization, invincible strength, and relentless oppression. The man was possessed by a veritable army of militant spirits. Hurtado notes that the term *Legion* "has the effect of making the scene like a battle between the powers of evil and Jesus, who comes in the name of the Kingdom of God."[13] *My name* implies that this was the name of the spirit who acted as spokesman. Others, less probably, suggest that it was a ruse by the demons to avoid revealing their true names. *For we are many* at once revealed the significance of the demon's name. He was the leader of a vast host of demons associated with him. The number of the swine (v. 13) may imply that there were at least two thousand, but Brooks insists that "no attempt should be made to equate the number of pigs with the number of demons."[14]

"He besought him much"—*he* may mean either the man or the spokesman of the demonic host, but the latter seems clearly meant, in view of the request made (Luke 8:31). The leading demon, calling himself Legion, was begging on behalf of the other demons as well. *Besought* is a strong term of entreaty, aimed at producing a particular effect upon the one addressed. *Much* underlines the intensity behind the repeated request.

"That he would not send them away out of the country"—Mark's phrase "away out of the country" is apparently parallel to Luke's "into the abyss." But *country* seems naturally to mean the country of the Gerasenes (v. 1). They desired to remain in the area where they had long exercised their tormenting powers on their victim. Gould remarks, "What preference they should have for one country over

---

[13] Larry W. Hurtado, *Mark,* Good News Commentary, p. 71.

[14] Brooks, p. 91.

another is one of the mysteries connected with these stories of demoniacal possession."[15] Grotius made the ingenious suggestion that the demons loved the area of the Decapolis because it was "full of Hellenizing apostate Jews."[16]

"Now there was there"—*now,* transitional, introduces a parenthetical remark which turns the center of attention in a new direction. Verses 11-13 form the next stage of the story.

"Nigh unto the mountains"—literally, "in a place facing the mountain." The place was apparently a sloping plateau stretching toward the particular mountain towering in the background in that vicinity.

"A great herd of swine feeding"—Matthew noted that the herd was "a good way off from them" (8:30), but it was in plain sight from where Jesus stood. Such a herd of swine, considered unclean, would not have been found on the western shores of the lake. It is generally assumed that the owners were non-Jewish, but it is possible that hellenizing Jews, lured by the good market for swine flesh in the cities of the Decapolis, may have engaged in raising pigs for financial gain. This herd of swine was feeding under the supervision of swineherds.

"All the devils besought him"—after the revelation in verse 9, the demons are always referred to in the plural. Swete comments, "The Spirits at length dissociate themselves from the man, for they know that their hold over him is at an end."[17] *Besought* is aorist, implying that Jesus at once responded to their request.

"Send us into the swine, that we may enter into them"—they urged that Jesus at once order them into the swine. The second clause gives a fuller statement of their request. They acknowledged that they could do so only subject to His will. Perhaps it was a frantic appeal aimed at avoiding a worse fate. Others suggest that their aim was malicious, hoping to turn the people against Jesus because of the loss of their pigs.

"Jesus gave them leave"—permitted them to carry out their suggestion. We are not told why Jesus consented to the demonic request. The distinction between permitting and sending them admittedly does not help much in freeing Jesus from responsibility for the resultant

---

[15] Ezra P. Gould, *A Critical and Exegetical Commentary on the Gospel According to St. Mark,* International Critical Commentary, p. 91.

[16] Grotius, quoted in Alexander Balmain Bruce, "The Synoptic Gospels," in *The Expositor's Greek Testament,* 1:372.

[17] Henry Barclay Swete, *The Gospel According to Saint Mark,* p. 96.

destruction of property. The claim that He did not foresee the consequences is unacceptable. Jesus may have regarded it as necessary for
the man's highest welfare. The sight of the whole herd rushing into
the sea would give the newly delivered man an unforgettable demonstration of the fearful strength of the evil from which he had been
delivered.

If the pig's owners were Gentiles, for whom the business was not
illegal, Christ's permission presents something of a moral problem.
But if the owners were indifferent Jews who engaged in this unclean
business for the profit in it,[18] the loss would well serve to jar their
conscience.

"The unclean spirits went out, and entered into the swine"—all
the synoptics assert that the demons actually entered the swine. Ra-
tionalists have claimed the assertion is absurd, but Plummer replies,
"Of the marvellous power of mind over matter our knowledge is
increasing rapidly."[19] And English well remarks, "Mark, as elsewhere,
plainly tells the story as something that happened, from start to finish.
If we trust his account as guided by God's spirit, we will accept this
story too."[20]

"The herd ran violently down a steep place into the sea"—the
plateau where the pigs were feeding terminated in a steep, not necessarily high, bank at the edge of the water. The whole herd stampeded
down the slope and plunged into the sea, which here was quite deep
near the shore. Riddle remarked, "Few animals are so individually
stubborn as swine, yet the rush was simultaneous."[21]

The demons' leaving the man and entering into the swine were
invisible events, but the frenzied action of the herd was visible evidence
of the reality of the transition. Rationalistic explanations have suggested that the exorcism threw the man into a paroxysm and that the
screaming man violently hurled himself upon the pigs, throwing them
into a panic, thus causing their terror-stricken rush to the sea. But such
rationalizing is quite unnecessary in the light of the New Testament
teaching concerning the reality of demonic powers.

---

[18] Eric F.F. Bishop relates, "During the war there was a boom in pig-raising in
order to provide the British Army with bacon. Muslims and Jews, unable to do it
themselves, employed Christians for looking after their swine. Thus did history repeat
itself" (*Jesus of Palestine,* p. 135).

[19] Alfred Plummer, "The Gospel According to St. Mark," in *Cambridge Greek
Testament,* p. 144.

[20] Donald English, *The Message of Mark,* The Bible Speaks Today, p. 110.

[21] Matthew B. Riddle, "The Gospel According to St. Mark," in *International
Revision Commentary on the New Testament,* p. 60.

"About two thousand"—a detail given only in Mark. The number may have been obtained from the owners, but the disciples may well have made the estimate themselves. The number indicates that the owners had gone into the pig-raising business in a big way. The size of the herd was also too large to permit the total destruction to be explained as due to some natural external influence.

"Were choked in the sea"—the imperfect tense describes the sinking of the pigs as one after the other they plunged into the water and were suffocated.

Verses 14-17, recording the effect of the drowning, form a further stage in the narrative.

"They that fed the swine fled"—fled panic-stricken to report the loss. They had observed all that had taken place.

"Told *it* in the city, and in the country"—reported the startling events in the city and the surrounding fields. The city, left unidentified, probably means the small town of Kersa (cf. v. 1). *The country,* literally, "the fields," denotes the open fields where the people were working. The news spread rapidly.

"They went out to see what it was that was done"—the people from the city and the country round about came to see with their own eyes. Not quite able to credit the astonishing report, they came to find out for themselves what really had taken place.

"They come to Jesus"—the natural center of interest in this incredible affair. He had remained where the demoniac had been encountered.

"And see him that was possessed with the devil"—literally, "and are beholding the one demonized," the one they knew as belonging to that class. *See* in the present tense pictures them staring at the man, intently contemplating him as a spectacle. The historical present tenses vividly stress the continuing action.

"And had the legion"—an addition heightening the contrast between his past state and his present condition. The perfect participle looks back to the time when he was characterized as dominated by the legion.

"Sitting, and clothed, and in his right mind"—three features about him arrested their attention. The present participle *sitting* marks the contrast between his present restful condition and his former state as a roving, raving maniac. The present participle *clothed* underscores the continuing contrast between his present condition and former practice of going naked. Perhaps one of the disciples had fetched an extra robe for the man from the boat. *In his right mind,* while declaring his restored sanity, has the basic meaning of "self-controlled." He was now a rational, self-controlled being, no longer yelling in frenzy under the domination of demons.

"They were afraid"—"became afraid," were seized with a strong sense of fear. They were keenly conscious that they were in the presence of the supernatural. "This 'fear' reflects their perception of Jesus' awesome power rather than any feeling of 'reverential awe', as their request for Jesus to leave the area indicates."[22]

"They that saw *it*"—the primary reference seems to be to the Twelve, but the swineherds would be included.

"Told them how it befell to him that was possessed with the devil, and *also* concerning the swine"—readily and fully rehearsed what had happened on both points and set forth the relationship between the two events. The verb *told* (*diēgeomai*) "well expresses the voluminousness of the Eastern storyteller."[23]

"They began to pray him"—*they* no doubt included the owners who had come out to Jesus. The rendering "pray" implies that they "requested" or "appealed" with the fervency of an earnest prayer. When they understood the relationship between the two events, they "drew a natural inference: cure cause of catastrophe."[24] English notes, "Mark could hardly spell out more clearly his conviction that even the most powerful of healing miracles cannot, do not, of themselves induce faith or provide a foundation for it. Everything hangs on the openness of the observers to see beyond the miracle to the person at its heart."[25]

"To depart out of their coasts"—they feared further material losses if one with such powers should remain within their borders. They were more concerned to protect their financial interests than to rejoice in the deliverance of the neighborhood demoniac. Luke recorded that it was the unanimous request of the inhabitants (8:37).

Verses 18-20 again center attention on the man with whom the story began. They mark the closing phase of the dramatic narrative.

"When he was come into the ship"—immediately granting the inhospitable request. Jesus would not force Himself on those who did not want Him.

"He that had been possessed with the devil"—literally, "he that was demonized." The aorist tense used here denotes a past fact no longer true.

---

[22] Robert A. Guelich, *Word Biblical Commentary, Mark 1–8:26,* p. 284.

[23] Swete, p. 98.

[24] Bruce, 1:373.

[25] Donald English, p. 111.

"Prayed him that he might be with him"—repeatedly requested to be permitted to remain in His company (cf. the verb in v. 17). Gratitude would naturally cause the man to cling to his benefactor. Perhaps he was trying to dissociate himself from the reaction of his countrymen. The suggestion that he feared a relapse if he were left behind seems improbable.

"Jesus suffered him not, but saith unto him"—of the three requests made of Jesus in this story (vv. 10, 17-18), only the delivered demoniac's request for continued personal fellowship with Jesus was denied! The reason for the refusal is indicated in the contrasted command which followed.

"Go home to thy friends"—*Go* bids him be on his way back to his house, long deserted in favor of residence among the tombs. *Thy friends* denotes a circle larger than his immediate family. These friends, who had given him up as hopeless, were now to be the recipients of his message and be blessed by his restored presence with them. "The man was free to be his own person and reenter normal human relations. He had been delivered."[26]

"Tell them how great things the Lord hath done for thee"—make a definite report to them of the deliverance he has experienced. *The Lord* may be an indirect reference to Jesus Himself, but the more natural reference seems to be to the God of the Old Testament, as Luke has it (8:39). *Hath done* underlines the abiding nature of the blessing bestowed upon him.

"And hath had compassion on thee"—this additional assertion reminded the man that the deliverance freely given him was an undeserved expression of God's favor. Divine compassion, as a definite act, had granted deliverance.

The reasons for the silence usually asked of recipients of Jesus' miraculous benefits (cf. 1:44; 5:43; 7:36) did not apply in this case. The man would be spreading the message in an area where Jesus would not Himself be working; the publicity would not hinder His ministry in Galilee. The order left behind a message of His grace in a place where Jesus had been asked to leave.

"He departed"—acted in prompt obedience to the injunction laid on him by his benefactor.

"Began to publish in Decapolis"—marking the commencement of a new and important activity by the man. He was privileged to be a missionary in a new area. The Decapolis was a league of ten Greek

---

[26] Guelich, p. 285.

cities, all of which, except one, were located east of the Jordan River.[27] Although the area formed a working unity because of the common military, political, commercial, and religious interests of these cities, it apparently never was a distinct geographical unit. Mark alone here mentioned the Decapolis. In this predominantly Gentile area, the man's report would not immediately arouse excited messianic speculations as it would in distinctly Jewish areas. How much of the area the man covered is not certain. Luke simply said that he proclaimed the news "throughout the whole city" (8:39).

"How great things Jesus had done for him"—he naturally connected his deliverance with Jesus. In exalting Jesus as his deliverer, the man rightly felt that he was glorifying the Lord.

"All *men* did marvel"—only Mark mentions this result. The man's story produced astonishment, but the response fell short of actual faith in Jesus.

c. Two Miracles upon Returning (5:21-43).

Two further miracles portray the unique nature of Jesus as Lord over disease and death. Both were humanly hopeless cases, but human despair and helplessness served only to reveal the greatness of God's salvation through Christ.

All three synoptics have the same arrangement of the two miracles, obviously due to a vivid recollection of actual historical sequence.[28] Mark and Luke placed these miracles immediately after the cure of the Gerasene demoniac, but Matthew placed several occurrences between them and expressly connected these two miracles with Jesus' teaching concerning fasting (9:18). Mark placed all of Matthew's intervening events earlier. It is another clear instance of the fact that the Gospel writers did not record all of their material in strict chronological sequence.

These interlocking miracles illustrate the pressure under which Jesus often worked. Mark's narrative is the fullest of the three and bears traces of being based on an eyewitness account. The narrative vividly portrays the appeal of Jairus (vv. 21-24), the interruption caused by

---

[27] The cities usually listed as belonging to the Decapolis were Damascus, Kanatha, Scythopolis, Hippos, Raphana, Pella, Philadelphia, and Gerasa. For a fuller description of the Decapolis, see J. McKee Adams, *Biblical Backgrounds,* (rev. ed. 1965), pp. 150-60.

[28] The suggestion, on the basis of supposed differences in syntax and vocabulary, that the two stories were originally unrelated but were "artistically combined" by Mark, is unconvincing. See Sherman E. Johnson, *A Commentary on the Gospel According to St. Mark,* pp. 104-5.

the woman with the flow of blood (vv. 25-34), and the raising of the daughter of Jairus from the dead (vv. 35-43).

1) Plea of Jairus (vv. 21-24). "Was passed over again by ship unto the other side"—*the other side* here denotes the western or northwestern shore of the lake. The crossing was made in the boat in which they had left (4:36).

"Much people gathered unto him"—the approaching boat had been recognized, and the crowd swarmed down to the beach upon its arrival. Luke says that they "*gladly* received him" (8:40). Jones suggests that "very likely that enthusiasm had been intensified by the news of what had happened on the lake the previous evening" by those in the "other little ships" (4:36) which had returned and "told the story of how Jesus at a word had stilled the tempest and rescued them out of deadly peril."[29] Unlike the reaction to Jesus on the eastern shore, interest in Him was still running high in Galilee. *Gathered* renders the aorist passive verb, "was gathered," and indicates that what they knew and had heard, as an irresistible urge, drew them out. *Unto him* implies that the crowd pressed closely upon His person.

"He was nigh unto the sea"—apparently at or near Capernaum. Finding a large crowd waiting for Him, Jesus remained out beside the sea. Apparently He had not yet begun teaching them when Jairus arrived.

"There cometh one of the rulers of the synagogue"—the designation indicates an individual of importance. The ruler of the synagogue was the president of the board of elders—"the rulers"—who were over the affairs of the local synagogue. He was a lay official, not a priest, responsible for the arrangement for the various parts of the synagogue worship service. Matthew simply calls him "a ruler," while Luke uses the two terms interchangeably of him since he would be a member of the body of rulers over the synagogue. *One of the rulers* seems simply to mean that he belonged to that important class, but it is possible that large synagogues had more than one ruler (cf. Acts 13:15). Cranfield suggests that the term was sometimes applied to distinguished members as an honorary title.[30]

"Jairus by name"—the Greek form of the Hebrew name Jair, meaning "he will give light." The suggestion that the name was later added because of its symbolic significance is groundless, for it was Jesus, not Jairus, that gave the enlightenment. As a leading individual

---

[29] J. D. Jones, *Commentary on Mark,* p. 144.

[30] C.E.B. Cranfield, *The Gospel According to Saint Mark,* Cambridge Greek Testament Commentary, p. 38.

in the community, his name would readily be remembered. Nothing is known of him beyond this passage. He probably was among the Jewish elders who came to Jesus to intercede on behalf of the centurion's sick servant (Luke 7:3). Whether his attitude toward Jesus had been sympathetic or hostile, when sudden catastrophe struck in his own family, he turned to Jesus in his desperation. What he knew and had heard about Him prompted his action.

"When he saw him"—upon catching sight of Jesus personally in the crowd.

"He fell at his feet"—in Oriental demonstrativeness to emphasize the fervency of his plea. In his distress, he publicly prostrated himself before Jesus in recognition of His superiority.

"Besought him greatly"—made an intense, fervent plea from a full heart. *Greatly* stresses his fervor and earnestness.

"My little daughter"—the diminutive form, used only by Mark, heightened the pathos. *My* underlines the personal relationship and reveals the father's deep affection for his little loved one. "For her sake," McKenna notes, "he is willing to risk religious ridicule and public embarrassment by kneeling at Jesus' feet and begging Him to come to his home and heal his daughter."[31] Luke noted that she was "an only daughter," about twelve years old (8:42).

"Lieth at the point of death"—now lying "at the last gasp," at the point of dying. Matthew's statement that she "is even now dead" (9:18) is due to his abbreviated account, which leaves out all reference to the further communication coming from the ruler's house.

"*I pray thee,* come and lay thy hands on her"—the original, beginning with *hina,* usually translated "that" or "in order that," indicates that the construction is broken, reflecting the deep emotion of the speaker. The construction may be taken as a substitute for the imperative, "Come and lay your hands on her" (RSV). The added *I pray thee* implies that with a choking voice, Jairus explained that his prostration and plea were "in order that" Jesus might come and lay hands on the dying daughter. His request indicated his faith in Jesus' power to heal, but erroneously assumed that His personal presence was necessary. Neither in the Old Testament nor in rabbinic literature was the laying on of hands associated with physical healing. Jesus' frequent symbolic use of the practice apparently had caused the popular association of it with His healings.

"That she may be healed; and she shall live"—more literally, "in order that she may be saved," that is, from death, "and live" as a

---

[31] David L. McKenna, *Mark,* The Communicator's Commentary, p. 118.

result of His action. ''Be saved'' implies the father's recognition that her death was inevitable unless Christ intervene.

''And *Jesus* went with him''—He went from the seashore toward the house of Jairus. No reply by Jesus is recorded; His prompt action was His answer.

''Much people followed him''—sensing an opportunity to see another miracle, a large, assorted crowd eagerly joined in the movement toward the house.

''And thronged him''—the curious, thoughtless people kept crowding in on Jesus from every side. *Thronged,* a strong term used by Mark alone and only in connection with this story (vv. 24, 31), pictures the crowd as exerting a suffocating pressure on Jesus which impeded His rapid movements. The remark prepares for the next stage in the narrative.

*2) **Woman with the flow of blood** (vv. 25-34).* These verses center the attention on one individual in that dense crowd. Her action resulted in a miracle within the account of a miracle.

''And a certain woman''—the woman, as usual, is left unnamed. Tradition has not remained silent about her, giving her name as Bernice or Veronica. Eusebius (*Ecclesiastical History* 7. 18) related the tradition that she was a native of Caesarea Philippi and that at the gates of her house she had erected a bronze statue, still extant in his day, depicting the scene of her healing. But the identification of the statue with the woman of this story is undoubtedly erroneous. Others have made her a princess of Edessa and even Martha, the sister of Lazarus. Mark's elaborate description of the woman, consisting of seven participial clauses (vv. 25-27), forms the longest single sentence in his Gospel.

''Had an issue of blood twelve years''—probably a chronic uterine hemorrhage. *Had an issue,* literally,''being in a flow,'' denotes that she was continuously in its grip. This made her ceremonially unclean (Lev. 15:25-27), barring her from normal social relations. *Twelve years,* mentioned by all the synoptics, speaks of the long duration of her agony and distress. It accounts for the remainder of the description.

''Had suffered many things of many physicians''—suffered not only from her malady but also from the doctors. Numerous physicians had treated her and their varied remedies, often severe and loathsome, had resulted only in added suffering for her. It was a common practice in such cases to call in as many different doctors as possible, and frequently their conflicting remedies only made the malady worse.

''Had spent all that she had''—no expense had been spared, and she had wasted her whole fortune. *All that she had* does not indicate the amount spent but implies that all she owned had passed from her possession into the possession of the doctors. Medical services were not cheap in that day either!

"Was nothing bettered"—doctor after doctor had proved a disappointment to her expectations of recovery.

"But rather grew worse"—her health had actually deteriorated under their treatment. They had bungled her case. McKenna notes, "Mark's mildly caustic comment is more than an aside to his argument. As a part of his case to prove that Jesus has authority over incurable illness, he is saying the best and most expensive of medical science has joined with the woman in a confession of human futility."[32] Luke, who was himself a doctor (Col. 4:14), protected the dignity of his profession by remarking that she "neither could be healed of any" (Luke 8:43). Her problem extended beyond the reach of medical skills!

"When she had heard of Jesus"—the description now turns from her past to her connection with Jesus. Mark here used the definite article with the name *Jesus* which was very common in Palestine. "The use of the definite article here points to the fact that our Lord's fame had spread so that He was known as The Jesus."[33] The reports of His healing powers aroused faith in her that He could also heal her. Her faith spurred her into action, and she was in the waiting crowd when Jesus returned.

"Came in the press behind"—The KJV rendering "the press" stressed the condition of the people closely thronged or pressed together.[34] The woman approached from behind because she desired to remain unobserved. She desired secrecy, because an open appeal to Jesus for healing, involving a public disclosure of her condition, would be too embarrassing. She must not have been a resident of Capernaum, since her condition apparently was not general knowledge to the people in the crowd. When Jesus started for the house of Jairus, the woman persistently pushed herself through the jostling crowd until she was directly behind Him.

"Touched his garment"—a deliberate act, prompted by faith. *Garment* denotes the outer cloak worn over the inner robe next to the body. Matthew and Luke note that she touched "the border of his garment." The word rendered "border" may mean fringe, implying that Jesus

---

[32] Ibid., p. 121.

[33] Kenneth S. Wuest, *Mark in the Greek New Testament for the English Reader,* p. 110.

[34] The Greek noun *ho ochlos,* "the multitude," occurs 82 times in the New Testament; in the KJV it is rendered "the press" only in Mark 2:4; 5:27, 30; Luke 8:19; 19:3. This archaic rendering is entirely devoid of the modern usage to denote a throng of newspaper reporters.

wore an outer garment, a large square cloth, to the four corners of which tassels were attached (cf. Num. 15:37-40; Deut. 22:12), so that two tassels hung down behind. The term, however, may simply mean the outer edge of His outer garment. In either case, she could touch Him only lightly, not enough to be felt.

"For she said"—introducing the reason for her action. *Said,* in the imperfect tense, indicates that she continued to hold this prospect before herself as she moved with difficulty into a position behind Jesus. She spoke "within herself" (Matt. 9:21), for she did not want to inform others of her condition or intention.

"If I may touch but his clothes"—the unrealized hope that spurred her on. The plural *clothes* indicates she felt that contact with any part of His garments would be sufficient for her healing. It reveals her great faith in His healing powers. She did touch Him in faith, though it was flawed.

"I shall be whole"—she believed that she could be healed without the knowledge or consent of Jesus. Jesus did not allow her to retain this false conception. He wanted to show her that there was a better way to receive her healing than through secrecy and stealth. She did not yet know His tender heart. Jesus responded to her timid but faith-prompted persistence.

"And straightway"—*and* connects the touch with the result, while *straightway* stresses the instantaneous effect.

"The fountain of her blood was dried up"—the inner source of her continual bleeding was dried up, like a spring drying up. The passive voice implies that it was wrought by an outside agent.

"She felt in *her* body that she was healed of that plague"—the instantaneous healing produced a definite physical sensation within, which thrilled her with the assurance that she had been healed. The perfect tense denotes her consciousness that the healing was complete and permanent. *Plague,* "whip, scourge" (cf. 3:10), points to the painful affliction she had endured.

"Immediately"—Mark's favorite adverb, standing emphatically at the beginning of the verse, notes that Jesus' response was immediate.

"Jesus . . . knowing in himself that virtue had gone out of him"— "virtue" is more literally "power," the first occurrence of this term in Mark's Gospel, and denotes the inherent power in Him which effected the healing. This does not mean that the power went forth independently of His own knowledge or will. His healing power did not work automatically, like a battery discharging its power when accidentally short-circuited. Jesus perceived in Himself, without any external suggestion, the significance of the woman's touch, and, actively willing to honor her faith, He was immediately conscious of His healing power going toward her. His power, the inherent ability to perform, was always under the control of His conscious volition. His consciousness of that power going forth from Him suggests that His healing ministries cost Jesus much spiritual energy. It would explain why He found it necessary at times to escape the crowds to find time for refreshing through fellowship with the Father.

"Turned him about in the press"—the touch had come from behind. This remark, peculiar to Mark, is apparently due to an eye-witness who remembered Jesus suddenly turning around to face those behind Him.

"And said"—the imperfect tense implies that the question was repeated. When the woman failed to respond, Jesus repeated His question. His insistence brought a general denial from the crowd (Luke 8:45).

"Who touched my clothes?"—the individual who had touched His clothes as a definite act was asked to reveal his identity. He asked not because of ignorance but to bring the one that touched into personal communion with the one touched. He wanted to give more than just physical healing.

"His disciples said"—apparently the Twelve. Luke (8:45) notes that Peter acted as their spokesman. In view of the jostling crowd, Peter regarded the question as unreasonable. With a certain tone of assumed superiority, he impulsively proceeded to correct Jesus.

"Thou seest the multitude thronging thee"—under the circumstances, Jesus ought to realize that numerous people would inadvertently press against Him. Mark records no reply by Jesus to the criticism, but Luke (8:46) records Jesus' insistence that someone had touched Him, not in an accidental way, but in a way to draw forth power from Him. Nineham comments, "The common sense of what they say only serves to emphasize the wonder of Jesus' ability to distinguish the healing-touching from any ordinary touch."[35]

"He looked round about"—His characteristic look is an essential feature of the story here. The imperfect tense portrays a long, searching gaze. His eyes passed from one to another as He searched the faces before Him.

"To see her that had done this thing"—the aorist *to see* implies that He continued to look around until He spotted the individual. *Her* naturally implies that Jesus knew her identity and searched to locate her. She had apparently shrunk back in the crowd in an effort to conceal herself.

---

[35] D. E. Nineham, *The Gospel of St. Mark*, p. 161.

"But the woman"—the only individual in the crowd who fully understood the meaning of Jesus' question. When His eyes rested on her, she realized that she could not remain hidden (Luke 8:47). She knew that the truth would have to be told before all.

"Fearing and trembling"—the inner feeling which gripped her and its outward manifestation. Upon being detected, she was seized with a feeling of fear (aorist tense); the resultant trembling continued to show itself visibly (present tense). She feared His displeasure because the healing had been secured without His permission. She may also have dreaded His anger because her touch had made Him ceremonially unclean until the evening (Lev. 15:19).

"Knowing what was done in her"—fully conscious that the healing was permanent. It was this consciousness, as well as the realization that she could not be hidden, that produced her emotions.

"Fell down before him"—an expression of humility and reverence toward her benefactor. It acknowledged the unworthiness of her stealthy way in securing the healing from Him.

"Told him all the truth"—made a full confession of her condition, the reason for her action, and the immediate result (Luke 8:47). The details given in verses 25-27 were probably based on her own testimony. Her account of her hopeless condition brought into striking display what had just been done to her. The whole ordeal naturally was embarrassing to her, but Jesus knew that it was necessary to give her the assurance that she needed. However, He made it as easy as possible for her by waiting until she was healed.

"Daughter"—the only recorded instance where Jesus addressed a woman by this title. It affectionately assured her of the spiritual relationship with Him into which she had entered. Her faith had not only resulted in physical healing but also brought her into a relationship with Him as His own spiritual child (Isa. 53:10).

"Thy faith hath made thee whole"—His public acknowledgment of her faith and its result. He required her confession to perfect that faith and to give her its full reward. Her faith had been somewhat marred by her belief that she must touch His garment to be healed and still more by the fact that she had approached Him in a timid and secretive manner. But her faith in His ability had brought her rich blessings. *Hath made thee whole,* the perfect tense of the common verb "to save," acknowledged that her healing was permanent. It added His assurance to her inner conviction.

"Go in peace"—literally, "go into peace," somewhat stronger than "go in peace." *In peace* would imply that the peace was a reality at the time of her departure; *into peace* connects her sense of rest and well-being with the life that lay before her. This assurance of future peace stands in contrast to the disquiet and suffering she had experienced to this moment. The benediction of her Healer also freed her conscience from the guilty feeling that she had stolen the healing without His consent.

"Be whole of thy plague"—the present imperative, "be continually whole," assured her that she was to continue in the state of being whole, having sound health.

3) Raising of Jairus's daughter (vv. 35-43). The interruption caused by the woman further served to bring into display the fact that, as Jehovah's Servant, Jesus was also the Lord of life. This is the only instance of a resurrection by Jesus in this Gospel.

"While he yet spake"—marking the close chronological sequence of the two miracles. This turn of events diverted the unwelcome gaze of the crowd from the woman and again made Jairus the center of attention. The interruption must have proved very trying to Jairus and greatly increased his anxiety, but the record says nothing of his feeling or action during the delay.

"There came from the ruler of the synagogue's *house*"—more literally, "they came from . . ."; *they* leaves these messengers unidentified. Since they felt free to tell Jairus what he should do, they probably were not servants but friends or relatives who had come to be with the family during this crisis. Those in the home knew that Jairus had gone to call Jesus. The move had been discussed and agreed upon, apparently as a last resort, perhaps when the news reached them that Jesus had been observed returning to the western shore (v. 21).

"Thy daughter is dead"—the aorist tense simply states the historical fact that she died. What had been feared had actually transpired.

"Why troublest thou the Master any further?"—the verb *troublest* implies that, under the circumstances, still to desire the busy Teacher to come to the house would be an annoyance and an irksome imposition on Jesus. Their suggestion to Jairus, politely expressed in the form of a question, shows that they felt that the girl's death had ended all hope that Jesus could help. Why bother Him any further? *The Master*, or "Teacher," indicates that Jesus was currently known among the people as the noted Teacher, or rabbi. It had not occurred to them that this Teacher could restore her to life. Their suggestion apparently was intended to spare Jairus the added trouble of having to care for the noted rabbi if He entered his home when nothing could be gained through the visit. The suggestion that the messengers spoke in bitter vexation because Jesus had stopped to deal with the chronic invalid and had thus let the child die seems wholly due to Western views. Bishop points out that it was characteristically Palestinian for Jesus to deal with things as they came. He says, "There is no hint of anyone taking it amiss that Jesus did not proceed as fast as He could to Jairus' house; or that He could have dealt with the haemorrhage after the more serious case of the child at death's door. . . . It is quite Palestinian still to do the things that need doing at the psychological juncture."[36]

"As soon as Jesus heard the word that was spoken"—the participle *heard* may be rendered either "overhearing" or "hearing carelessly, ignoring." Both meanings have been advocated here. The latter is favored by the common usage of the verb in the New Testament,[37] the Septuagint, and the papyruses (thus, the ASV "But Jesus, not heeding the word spoken"). But the parallel statement in Luke 8:50, "But when Jesus heard it," supports the view that the meaning here is "overhearing" what was said. Jesus did overhear the words spoken to Jairus. He spoke in response to that message, which seemed to make His going useless. But he also ignored the suggestion made to Jairus and refused to be deterred by it. He promptly spoke to encourage the father who was in danger of being overwhelmed with grief at the news.

"Be not afraid, only believe"—both imperatives are present tense, denoting continuing action. The first, with the negative, prohibits the continuation of fear. Jairus had been seized with the fear that now everything was too late. Jesus urged him, "Cease fearing, continue to believe." The faith which he had shown in coming to Jesus for help he must steadily maintain; it was the only fitting response in his help-lessness. Luke noted that Jesus added a word of assurance, "Believe only, and she shall be made whole" (8:50). Jesus spoke with perfect self-assurance about the outcome.

"He suffered no man to follow him"—Jesus now summarily acted to rid Himself of the crowd that had been surging about Him. He refused to permit anyone in the crowd to approach the house of Jairus in His company. Luke's account seems to imply that the crowd was dismissed when they reached the house, but this apparent difference seems due to the fact that his compressed account relates to those permitted to enter the death chamber with Jesus (8:51).

"Save Peter, and James, and John"—the first instance of special privileges accorded these three disciples. They formed an inner circle in the apostolic band. Their names are united under one article in the original, suggesting that they formed a group. In each instance where these three were favored (9:2; 14:33), they were selected as witnesses. Jesus thoughtfully limited the number admitted into the death chamber

---

[36] Eric F.F. Bishop, *Jesus of Palestine,* p. 137.

[37] It occurs elsewhere only in Matthew 18:17, where it appears twice and is rendered "neglect to hear."

to three, the number which legally established the validity of a witness (Deut. 17:6).

"John the brother of James"—the identification seems to imply that James was better known than John and gave greater promise of eminence than his brother, who was probably younger.

"[They, Gr.] come to the house"—the messengers to Jairus had met him some distance from his home. *They* denotes Jesus and the three disciples with Jairus. A noisy, confused scene greeted them upon arrival.

"Seeth the tumult"—a noisy, clamorous uproar, shrill and piercing cries filling the air. The word rendered *seeth* pictures Jesus as standing for some moments and viewing the scene as a spectator, carefully noting the details.

"And them that wept and wailed greatly"—the sure signal in an Oriental home that a death had taken place. Mark's participial construction leaves the agents unnamed and stresses the action. While members of the household and relatives surely joined in the mourning, Matthew's reference to "the minstrels and the people making a noise" (9:23) clearly indicates that those making the tumult were principally paid mourners.

When Jairus left the house, he knew that death was imminent. The hired mourners, who were alerted, would not have taken long to arrive on the scene. The use of such hired mourners was expected as evidence of esteem for the one who had died.

The *Mishnah* stipulated that even the poorest husband "in Israel should hire not less than two flutes and one wailing woman" when his wife dies (*Ketuboth* 4. 4).[38] The custom of hiring such mourners went back to ancient times (Jer. 9:17; Amos 5:16). So much was such wailing an assumed part of a scene of sorrow that even the children in their games reproduced it (Matt. 11:17; cf. John 11:33; Acts 9:39).

The wailing of these professional mourners was made to order and carried on according to approved patterns. "Wailing greatly" indicates the shrill, monotonous cries of the mourners, uttered with great volume. Interspersed could be heard the pensive tones of the flute players. Travelers have often observed the practice of using such professional mourners in various parts of the Orient when death comes.

"When he was come in, he saith unto them"—having watched the scene from the door, Jesus, upon entering, at once spoke to those making the din. He acted to control the situation.

---

[38] Herbert Danby, trans., *The Mishnah*, p. 250.

"Why make ye this ado, and weep?"—the exaggerated noise and ostentatious mourning were inconsistent with the fact that He had been called. His question indicated that He had no patience with their superficial mourning. Before silencing them, He sought to reason with them.

"The damsel is not dead, but sleepeth"—explaining why the tumult was unwarranted. The startling assertion, given by all the synoptics, is capable of two different interpretations. Some hold that Jesus was speaking literally: this was merely a case of apparent death, the girl had not actually died but was in a coma. This view eliminates an actual resurrection, holding that Jesus spoke under the assurance that she would recover. But Lenski retorts, "What is gained by the rationalistic assumption of a coma? Can human power with a grasp and a word abolish a coma?"[39] Furthermore, the coma explanation runs counter to the natural implications of the entire account. It makes Jesus pronounce a keen medical diagnosis before He has even seen the child. Luke asserts that the mourners knew she was dead (8:53).

The second view recognizes that Jesus was speaking figuratively. He meant that she was not dead in the ordinary sense of the word in that her condition was not final and irreversible. In describing her condition as "sleeping," He implied that her death was like a sleep which would soon be terminated. She would soon be reawakened to the realities of this life. The same terminology was used by Him in connection with Lazarus's death.[40] Thompson remarks, "What He wished especially to do was to put a meaning upon death more worthy of those who believe in God than that suggested by such unbridled expressions of hopeless grief."[41]

"They laughed him to scorn"—derisively laughed in His face. They understood Jesus literally, and regarded His assertion as absurd. Knowing that she was dead, they derided His claim with a burst of mocking laughter. The sudden transition demonstrated the shallowness of their professional mourning. Their mockery also proves that they were certain the girl had died and confirms the reality of the miracle of her resurrection.

"When he had put them all out"—*He* is emphatic, "he on his part" in contrast to the mocking mourners whom He promptly expelled. Their forceful exclusion was another remarkable display of the

---

[39] R.C.H. Lenski, *The Interpretation of St. Mark's and St. Luke's Gospels,* p. 143.

[40] John 11:11-14. See also Acts 7:60; 13:36; 1 Corinthians 11:30; 15:6, 18, 20, 51; 1 Thessalonians 4:13-14.

[41] Ernest Trice Thompson, *The Gospel According to Mark and Its Meaning for Today,* p. 106.

authority of Jesus. Their irreverence made them unfit to share in the miracle to be performed.

"Taketh the father and the mother of the damsel, and them that were with him"—five people were taken with Him into the death chamber. The mother had no doubt been with the girl when she died but had come out to await the return of her husband. Jairus seems simply to have followed the leading of Jesus in all that transpired following the news of his daughter's death; that news seemingly left him numb. Unlike Elijah and Elisha (1 Kings 17:19-20; 2 Kings 4:33), Jesus, knowing the outcome, chose to raise the girl in the presence of sympathetic witnesses.

"Where the damsel was lying"—the death chamber would be an inner apartment.

"Took the damsel by the hand"—took a firm grip on her hand. By this act, He established a visible contact between Himself and the one toward whom His power was to be exercised. It was not necessary for her raising but was apparently done for the benefit of the witnesses. The act again shows that Jesus did not fear ceremonial defilement.

"And said unto her, Talitha cumi"—with His act went His word, addressed directly to the personality of the girl, not merely to her dead body.[42] Mark alone recorded the very words of Jesus in the original Aramaic, best explained as due to Peter's vivid recollection of the exact words uttered. *Talitha* is the feminine form of a word meaning "lamb" or "youth," and *cumi* (or *koum*) is a feminine imperative meaning "arise." Jesus commonly spoke in Aramaic, but Greek was also used. Galilee was bilingual.

"Which is, being interpreted"—Mark at once added the Greek translation for the benefit of his non-Jewish readers.

"Damsel, I say unto thee, arise"—Mark's addition, *I say unto thee,* serves to bring out the spirit of the original. *Damsel,* or "little girl," suggests tenderness in the voice of Jesus. "Jesus' authority, tough with wild winds and raging demons, becomes as tender as a shepherd lifting the littlest of lambs."[43] *Arise* may also mean "wake up." It has been suggested that His very words were those used by the mother each morning to arouse her daughter from sleep.

In recording the effect of Jesus' simple command (v. 42), Mark used his favorite adverb, *straightway*. The impact, both for the girl and

---

[42] In each instance in the Gospels in which Jesus raised the dead, His words commanding their resurrection were addressed explicitly to the person being raised (Luke 7:14; John 11:43).

[43] McKenna, p. 121.

the witnesses, was immediate. For the Lord of life, there was no struggle to overcome death such as the prophets of old experienced.

"The damsel arose, and walked"—the first verb is in the aorist, marking the special act; the second is imperfect, denoting the continuing act of walking. Having risen from her deathbed, the girl continued to walk around the room, demonstrating the completeness of her restoration.

"They were astonished with a great astonishment"—*they* includes the parents and the three disciples. The repetition of the fact of amazement in both verb and noun stresses the greatness of their astonishment. This strong expression underlines the fact that the girl had actually been dead.

"He charged them straitly"—two explicit orders were given, one relating to the future conduct of the parents, the second to the immediate needs of the girl. *Straitly* underlines Jesus' earnestness.

"That no man should know it"—it would be impossible to conceal the miracle, since many had known of her death; her subsequent appearing as alive and well would have to be explained. Apparently Jesus intended to keep the news from spreading until He had left the area. But surely Jesus also laid the injunction on the parents for the sake of the girl herself. For the sake of her normal development, she was not to be made the center of curiosity and excited talk.

"Commanded that something should be given her to eat"—an instance of Jesus' thoughtfulness that was long remembered. While the spectators were lost in amazement, Jesus concerned Himself with the needs of the girl. The passive *be given* does not indicate who was to supply the food, but obviously the mother would act at once to provide the needed nourishment. "Life restored by a miracle must be supported by ordinary means; the miracle has no place where human care and labor will suffice."[44]

d. Rejection of Jesus at Nazareth (6:1-6).

This paragraph again throws the shadow of stark unbelief over the triumphant ministry of Jesus. It reveals that the rejection of Christ has no basis, except in men's blindness and sin.

This account of Jesus' visit to Nazareth has a clear parallel in the somewhat shorter account in Matthew 13:54-58. Some scholars hold that this visit is also recorded in Luke 4:16-31. Favoring the identification is the improbability of two such similar rejections at the same place; yet notable differences strongly support the view of two separate visits. The visit in Luke came at the beginning of the great Galilean

---

[44] Quoted in Thompson, p. 107.

ministry, that in Mark sometime later. In Luke's account, Jesus appeared alone and announced the beginning of His messianic mission; in the second visit, He came as a well-known teacher accompanied by disciples. In the first visit, Jesus evoked their violent, uncontrollable rage; in the second, they responded with cool indifference and personal insult. The violent rejection during the first visit did not keep the yearning heart of Jesus from giving His townsmen another opportunity to receive Him. The distinctness of the two visits seems established by the fact that Matthew clearly notes two separate visits to Nazareth. The rejection recorded by Luke coincides with the visit mentioned in Matthew 4:13 when Jesus left Nazareth to establish headquarters in Capernaum. The visit recorded in Matthew 13:54-58 came later, agreeing with Mark's account. After the second visit, He began another tour of Galilee. Clearly, this visit seems later than that in Luke 4:16-31.

"He went out from thence"—Jesus deliberately left *from thence,* apparently Capernaum, the place where the preceding double miracle occurred.

"Came into his own country"—*country* may mean fatherland, homeland, or hometown, one's own part of the country. Here it denotes the place of His family residence, Nazareth, although neither Mark nor Matthew name it here. Having twice before indicated that Jesus came from Nazareth (1:9, 24), Mark did not feel a need to name the place here.

"His disciples follow him"—the presence of the disciples indicates that this was not a private visit to His family. As a noted teacher accompanied by an organized band of disciples, He came to do public work. The presence of the disciples plays no role in the story, but it did prepare them for the mission Jesus gave them in 6:7-13.

"When the sabbath day was come"—the time reference suggests that no public teaching was done until the Sabbath. The inhabitants of Nazareth did not flock to Him as soon as He arrived. They did not give their returning townsman an excited welcome.

"He began to teach in the synagogue"—*began* looks back to the commencement of His address but intimates that the reaction of the audience did not encourage Him to continue. In keeping with the democratic character of the synagogue services (see comments under 1:21), as a recognized visiting rabbi He had been given opportunity to speak. This is Mark's last mention of Jesus teaching in a synagogue, or even His presence there. "The synagogue had become a place of rejection. Later in the narrative the emphasis is placed on teaching in houses (7:17, 24; 9:33; 10:10; cf. 6:10)."[45]

---

[45] Brooks, p. 98.

"Many hearing *him* were astonished"—*many* has the definite article, "the many," indicating that this was the effect produced upon the majority of the hearers, but not all. *Astonished* is the same strong verb used in 1:22, but here the conclusion drawn from the impact is quite different. Their feeling of astonishment, upon further reflection, gave way to a different attitude. The questions they asked themselves indicate their mounting agitation as they thought about the identity of the speaker. They knew that as "a home town boy" He had not studied under any rabbi, hence lacked the proper credentials for such a ministry. Three of their questions aimed at His ministry and two at Him personally.

"From whence hath this *man* these things?"—a more literal rendering will serve to reflect their feeling of agitation, "Whence to this fellow these things?" They felt a sharp contrast between the man, long known to them, and the things He said. Compelled to admit His obvious authority, they asked themselves concerning the source of the change. They seemed unwilling to entertain the thought that He had been divinely commissioned.

"And what wisdom *is* this which is given unto him"—a second and separate critical question, voiced by a second critic. He was perplexed about the nature and source of the remarkable wisdom displayed by Jesus. The passive *is given* recognizes it as a gift, not as the result of long rabbinic study, but leaves the giver undetermined. The questioner was not ready to accept that the wisdom was from God, leaving available the lurking suspicion that it was demonic. *Unto him,* more literally, "to this fellow," again is contemptuous.

"And *what mean* such mighty works wrought by his hands?" (ASV)—*and* is best taken as introducing a third distinct comment. Omitting the italics, the words are best understood as an exclamation of amazement: "Such mighty works as these through his hands are coming to pass!" (Rotherham). They had not known Him to possess such miraculous powers during His years at Nazareth, nor were other members of His family possessed of them. They could not account for such powers in Him without raising suspicion concerning His integrity. The very powers which caused the fame of Jesus to spread elsewhere became a stumbling block to His own townsmen. His stirring "teaching" and His "mighty works" challenged His audience "to recognize that God was at work in him in a new way inaugurating God's sovereign reign in the lives of those who would respond (cf. 6:6a). But the townspeople reject this claim because they knew who Jesus 'really' was."[46]

---

[46] Guelich, p. 309.

"Is not this the carpenter"—only here is Jesus expressly called the carpenter. Their designation of Him by trade placed Him on a level with themselves. They rejected any thought that He was better than they.

As "the carpenter's son" (Matt. 13:55), Jesus had carried on the family trade as the village carpenter, and His townsmen still thought of Him in that light. *Carpenter* means a craftsman making things out of hard material, but papyrus usage indicates that the word properly means a worker in wood. Had He been a builder of houses, the skill of a stonemason would also have been required, since Palestinian buildings were primarily erected of stone. Justin Martyr (in the middle of the second century) said that Jesus made "plows and yokes." Whether his statement was based on actual knowledge or was an inference from conditions in Palestine is not certain. Justin commented that Jesus thereby "taught the symbols of righteousness and an active life."[47] Christians have generally accepted the view that by working as a carpenter, Jesus established the dignity and sanctity of daily labor. But some members of the early church felt that the statement that Jesus engaged in manual toil was something of a reproach, since manual labor was often regarded as below the dignity of a free man. Some scribes here wrote "the son of the carpenter," assimilating the reading to that in Matthew. And Origen asserted that no Gospel described Jesus as a carpenter.[48] But the reading "the carpenter" has strong manuscript support here and is unquestionably original. It is more probable that the scribes changed the reading here to agree with Matthew than vice versa. In the New Testament the word *carpenter* occurs only here and in the parallel account in Matthew 13:55.

If Mark had intended to say whose son Jesus was, he would more naturally have given the father's name than have given his occupation; the other members of the family are all mentioned by name. Origen either forgot this passage in Mark or had copies that assimilated the reading to that in Matthew.

"The son of Mary"—only here is Jesus expressly so called. It was the common practice among the Jews to use the father's name, whether he were alive or dead. A man was called the son of his mother only when his father was unknown. During His former visit to Nazareth, the people spoke of Him as "Joseph's son" (Luke 4:22). Stauffer holds that "the son of Mary" was now used as a deliberate insult, stamping Jesus as a bastard. He points out that custom required that so long as

---

[47] Justin Martyr *Dialogue with Trypho the Jew* chap. 88.

[48] Origen *Contra Celsus* 1. 28.

the son of an adulteress lives "a life pleasing to God, nothing insulting shall be said about his birth"; but if he becomes an apostate, "his illegitimate birth shall be spoken of publicly and unsparingly."[49] Consequently, the people of Nazareth now recalled the rumors concerning His birth and openly threw the fact at Him as an insult. Later, rabbis bluntly called Jesus the son of an adulteress and even claimed to know the name of His illegitimate father. Cranfield accepts the view that John 8:41 and 9:29 imply that rumors of Jesus' illegitimate birth did circulate during His ministry and holds that Mark's account here "reflects those rumors and accusations." It therefore "is an important piece of evidence in support of the Virgin Birth, though of a sort that the Church would naturally tend to avoid."[50]

"Brother of James, and Joses, and of Juda, and Simon"—only here and in Matthew 13:55 are the names of these four brothers given.[51]

James is a variant English form of the name "Jacob." Apparently the oldest of the four, James was the most famous among them, having a leading part in the early church at Jerusalem (Acts 12:17; 15:13; 21:18; 1 Cor. 15:7; Gal. 1:19; 2:9, 12). He is generally held to be the author of the Epistle of James (James 1:1; Jude 1). Josephus gave an account of his violent death under the high priest, Annus the younger. Eusebius preserved an extract from Hegesippus, a second-century Christian historian, describing his devout life and martyrdom.[52]

Joses is a variant form for "Joseph" (Matt. 13:55). Nothing further is known of Joses. His identification with the Joses of Mark 15:40 is improbable.

Juda, or Judas, is the Old Testament name "Judah." Jude wrote our brief Epistle of Jude. Eusebius quoted Hegesippus as relating that the grandsons of "Judas, called the brother of our Lord," were brought before the emperor Domitian for questioning, but were dismissed as harmless simpletons when they explained that they were poor farmers and that the kingdom for which they looked would be set up by Christ at His return.[53]

Simon is another common Jewish name. Simon is entirely unknown.

"Are not his sisters here with us?"—their names are never given. Matthew's "all" (13:56) implies that there were three or more. "Here with us" indicates that they lived in Nazareth as accepted members of

---

[49] E. Stauffer, *Jesus and His Story,* pp. 207-8; see also pp. 16-17.

[50] Cranfield, p. 195.

[51] For the much disputed meaning of *brothers* see comments under 3:31.

[52] Josephus *Antiquities* 20. 9. 1; Eusebius *Ecclesiastical History* 2. 23.

[53] Eusebius *Ecclesiastical History* 3. 20.

the community. No mention is made of them in Acts 1:14. It is not even known whether they became Christians like the rest of the family.

"They were offended at him"—the strong verb (cf. 4:17) denotes that the people of Nazareth took mortal offense at Jesus, became fatally ensnared because of their unbelief. Brooks suggests that "Mark's choice of the word is further evidence that he saw in the event a typical Jewish rejection of Jesus."[54] Unable to explain Him, they rejected Him. "Shut out His Divinity, and Jesus becomes a stumblingblock."[55]

"Jesus said unto them"—the imperfect tense of *said* suggests that whenever unbelieving criticism was expressed, Jesus responded with His aphorism. Their reaction illustrated a general principle which was so common as to be proverbial.

"A prophet is not without honor"—Jesus compared Himself to a prophet, a role commonly accorded Him (Matt. 21:11, 46; Mark 6:15; 8:28; Luke 7:16; 24:19; John 6:14; 7:40; 9:17). As such, He sustained a unique relationship to them. He did not evoke further opposition by claiming to be the Messiah.

"But in his own country, and among his own kin, and in his own house"—three decreasing circles of persons to whom the prophet is related. Their rejection of Him was explained by the commonly observed fact that those who know the prophet best think least of him. Their intimate acquaintance with His private life led them to fear that there was something unreal about His public position.

"He could there do no mighty work"—He felt it morally impossible to exercise His beneficent power in their behalf in the face of their unbelief (Matt. 13:58). It closed the door against the operation of His power. He refused to force Himself upon those who did not want Him. "God and his Son could do anything, but they have chosen to limit themselves in accordance with human response. . . . The statement clarifies that Jesus was not the kind of miracle worker whose primary purpose was to impress his viewers."[56]

"Laid his hands upon a few sick folk, and healed *them*"—only a few opportunities for the exercise of His healing power were offered Him. Those healed were apparently inconspicuous individuals who did not share the prevailing attitude of their neighbors. The laying on of His hands gave visible evidence that the healings came directly from Him.

[54] Brooks, p. 99.

[55] J. D. Jones, *Commentary on Mark*, p. 164.

[56] Brooks, p. 100.

"He marvelled because of their unbelief"—not at the fact but at the cause of their unbelief, because they thought they knew all about Him. He saw its paralyzing effect. It was an astonishing reaction. Even the rejection at Kersa (5:17) had not prepared Him to expect such unreceptiveness in His native town. The inhabitants' unbelief caused Him to leave Nazareth, apparently never to return.

Only on two occasions do the Gospels record that Jesus marvelled. Here at Nazareth, among His own people Jesus "marvelled because of their unbelief" (v. 6). It offers a striking contrast to the other occasion when Jesus marvelled. In Matthew 8:5-10 we have the account of a Roman centurion who came to Jesus and told Him that his servant at home lay grievously ill; when Jesus offered to go with him and heal him, the centurion replied that Jesus need not come but "speak the word only, and my servant shall be healed," assuring Jesus that he understood the power of true authority. At this expression of faith in the power of His word, Jesus marvelled and said to those with Him, "I have not found so great faith, no, not in Israel." What a sad contrast!

"He went round about the villages, teaching"—a transitional statement, well set off as a separate paragraph. It marked the outcome of the visit to Nazareth but also set the background for the mission of the Twelve. Mark's statement is literally, "He was going round the villages in a circle," indicating that the tour of Galilee started at Nazareth and ended near the place where He began. His primary activity was teaching. Matthew 9:35 gives a fuller picture of this tour.

e. Mission of the Twelve (6:7-13).

Both Luke (9:1-6) and Matthew (9:35–11:1) have parallel accounts, but the commission to the Twelve is given at greater length in Matthew. The future work of the apostles was foreshadowed in this mission, and the address of Jesus given in Matthew goes beyond this preliminary mission and also covers their mission to the world. The time was the beginning of His third tour of Galilee.[57] Jesus sent forth the Twelve in response to the great need to extend the outreach of His message (Matt. 9:36-37). In keeping with His purpose in calling them, the Twelve were now sent out to share in His mission by words and works. Up to now they had been faithful students in Christ's peripatetic school; now they are being sent forth to practice what they had learned.

"He called *unto him* the twelve"—*called* indicates a formal, authoritative act, while *unto him* denotes face-to-face relations in the

---

[57] Three different tours are mentioned: (1) Matthew 4:23-25; Mark 1:35-39; Luke 4:42-44; (2) Luke 8:1-3; (3) Matthew 9:35–11:1; Mark 6:6-13; Luke 9:1-6

receiving of their commission. The Twelve were now a recognizable group.

"Began to send them forth by two and two"—*began* implies the beginning of a new method; they had not thus previously been sent forth to preach. *To send* is present tense and may indicate that each pair was individually commissioned to go forth as His authoritative representatives. *By two and two* is stated only by Mark, but it is an indication of the independence and trustworthiness of the Gospels that Matthew, who here introduces the names of the Twelve, names them in pairs. It was a wise Jewish practice (cf. Eccles. 4:9-12) observed by the Jewish collectors of alms. It was also employed by John the Baptist (Luke 7:19) and the early Christian church (Acts 13:2-3; 15:39-41; 19:22). Jesus likewise seems always to have sent out His disciples in pairs (Mark 11:1; 14:13; Luke 10:1). Their work in pairs provided mutual help and fulfilled the legal requirement for an authentic testimony (Deut. 19:15). Brooks remarks that "it may also tone down individualism and suggest the necessity of team work."[58] Apparently specific areas were assigned.

"Gave them power over unclean spirits"—the only phase of their work mentioned by Mark in the commission given them. *Gave* is imperfect tense and again seems to denote the separate bestowal of authority upon each pair. If the gift was conveyed by some specific act, no mention is made of it. *Power* denotes delegated authority, giving them the right as well as the ability to exercise authority over the unclean spirits, spirits morally unclean by nature. The disciples' ability to exorcise demons in the name of their Master would authenticate their message.

"Commanded them"—verses 8-9 contain His directives concerning their preparation for the trip.[59] The major point in these instructions is that they were to go forth without elaborate preparations. Jesus intended the mission to be a lesson in trust to His disciples. They were to learn that in His service their needs would be supplied (Matt. 10:10). When during Passion Week Jesus asked them about their experience, they testified that they had lacked nothing (Luke 22:35).

"That they should take nothing for *their* journey"—*take* means to pick up and carry; no luggage was to be taken along. They were to go into the land unencumbered by ordinary provisions. They were to

---

[58] Brooks, p. 101.

[59] The Greek of verses 8-9, forming one sentence, presents a curious instance of the blending of three different grammatical constructions: *hina* with the subjunctive after "charged" (v. 8); the accusative "shod" implying an unexpected infinitive "to go" (v. 9); and finally a change to direct discourse with "put *ye* on."

operate by the principle of functional simplicity, a principle that is still valid in Christian service.

"Save a staff only"—the one concession in the sweeping prohibition. The staff was the common walking stick, the universal companion of travelers. The disciples were already using one. According to Matthew 10:9-10, the disciples were not to get, or "acquire," a staff, not to go to the trouble of providing a *new* one. This explanation, which is strictly grammatical, removes the supposed contradiction between Mark and the other synoptics. This pertains also to the sandals; no new ones were to be procured.

"No bread, no wallet, no money in their purse" (ASV)—the three items form a climax: no food, no bag for carrying any provisions for the trip, no money to buy necessities on the trip. The wallet was the common leather traveler's bag, generally thrown over the shoulder while walking. It has been suggested that the term here denotes the beggar's bag, used for collecting alms. Such a bag was a part of the equipment of an itinerant Cynic preacher. This would mean that they were not to go around collecting money, either for their own support or for their Master. But there is no evidence that Jesus or His disciples ever traveled as mendicants. "No money in their purse" is literally "no copper into the girdle," implying no previous insertion even of small copper coins. They were the only kinds of coins these missionary travelers would be likely to handle on the trip. The folds of the girdle were the common receptacle for the money travelers carried along.

"But *be* shod with sandals"—*sandals,* the ordinary footwear of the common people, would provide needed protection for their feet on the rough roads. These sandals usually consisted of a sole made of leather or wood, and were bound on by straps around the instep and ankle. *But* indicates a concession, in case any of them might be barefooted at the time. According to Matthew, they were instructed not to procure a new or extra pair of shoes. Some would harmonize Matthew and Mark by distinguishing between sandals and shoes, but from the usage of the two terms in the Septuagint and the New Testament, there seems to be no warrant for distinguishing between them here.[60] The italics properly indicates the change in construction.

"And not put on two coats"—literally, "and *ye* may not put on two tunics." Here is a further grammatical change, a sudden switch to the direct discourse in the original. The coat or tunic was the inner

---

[60] H. B. Swete suggests that here and in Acts 12:8 *sandal* (*sandalion*) rather than *shoe* (*hupodēma*) was used in order to avoid writing *hupodedesthai hupodēmata,* literally, "to have bound under the things bound under" (*The Gospel According to St. Mark,* p. 117).

garment worn next to the body. Persons of distinction customarily wore two tunics, the evidence of comparative wealth. According to Matthew and Luke, the disciples were not to obtain or possess two coats for this trip. "They were to encumber themselves with nothing that would be unsuitable for plain men going about among ordinary folks."[61]

"And he said unto them"—Mark's favorite formula marking a transition to another aspect of the instructions (cf. 4:13, 21, 24). Verses 10-11 deal with the conduct of the disciples while on their trip. The condition of expectancy used by Jesus put them on guard that they could expect both acceptance and rejection.

"In what place soever ye enter into an house"—as invited guests. It was the accepted duty and practice to offer hospitality to strangers arriving in a village. But the selection of a house was not to be made carelessly; they were to make careful inquiry about the fitness of the place they entered (Matt. 10:11), for they came not as ordinary travelers but as heralds.

"There abide till ye depart from that place"—the invitation from a worthy home was to be accepted in good faith. This requirement would guard them against any temptation to be self-indulgent by seeking more luxurious quarters. It would also keep them from unnecessarily lingering in one location, since they would not wish to become burdensome to their host.

"Whosoever shall not receive you"—they could also expect definite rejection as His messengers. Mark's statement (literally "whatever place shall not receive you") views this as the reaction of a whole town, but Matthew noted that this might also be the reaction of an individual household (10:14). Jesus' directions to them would apply to both situations.

"Nor [will they, Gr.] hear you"—with the plural *they,* the thought passes from the place to the inhabitants of that place. The rejection would be shown in a definite refusal to listen to their message, the message of Christ and His kingdom. It implies that the disciples had made a sincere effort to get a hearing. Whenever their gentle persistence was rebuffed, they were not to treat it lightly because of the tremendous consequences. Swete remarks, "It was a visible sign of acceptance or rejection of the Master and the Father who sent Him (Matt. x. 40, Luke x. 16), and therefore an index of the relation in which the inhabitants as a whole stood to the eternal order."[62]

---

[61] S.D.F. Salmond, "St. Mark," in *The Century Bible,* p. 183.

[62] Swete, p. 118.

"When ye depart thence"—from the house or city rejecting them. Having been rejected, they were to leave. While in the act of leaving, they were to demonstrate their reaction to the rejection.

"Shake off the dust under your feet"—as a definite act, they were to shake off the dust, or soil, which stuck to their sandals as they walked. This symbolic act denoted a complete disavowal of further fellowship with them because of their rejection and a renunciation of all further responsibility for those who refused their message. Perhaps it was also intended to imply that the inhabitants by their rejection had rendered themselves unclean.

"For a testimony against them"—the moral purpose behind the act. The act was not to be motivated by a vindictive spirit or a feeling of insult; it was rather to be a testimony to the rejecters themselves, a witness inviting them to further reflection. It was in effect "a testimony against them" (cf. Luke 9:5) in reminding them of the greatness of their guilt in rejecting the message of the King and His kingdom.[63]

"They went out"—from the presence of the commissioning Master, or the place where the commission was received. The extent or exact area of their work is not indicated; undoubtedly, it covered most of the towns and villages of Galilee not previously reached directly by Jesus.

"Preached that men should repent"—the only direct reference in Mark to the content of their message. Repentance as the fundamental preparation for the kingdom was the central duty urged upon the hearers. *Preached,* in the aorist tense, summarizes their activity as heralds of the message. *Repent* is present tense and stresses not the act of repentance upon hearing the message but the resultant changed attitude. It was the message they had heard their Master preach (cf. 1:15).

"They cast out many devils"—the first of two types of activity accompanying their message. *Cast out,* in the imperfect tense, pictures the repeated instances of their success in exorcism. Mark's order makes this feature prominent, being accounted a greater work than physical healing. Unbelief may question the ability of Jesus to transfer His power over demons to His disciples. Branscomb makes the skeptical comment, "That Jesus could thus transfer His power to His disciples is not borne out by other evidence, and smacks of the magical."[64] But the disciples found that the bestowal did not fail to function under

---

[63] On the basis of textual evidence, the latter half of v. 11, comparing the guilt of the rejectors to the guilt of Sodom and Gomorrah, stands unquestioned in Matthew 10:15, but forms no part of the best text in Mark.

[64] B. Harvie Branscomb, *The Gospel of Mark,* Moffatt New Testament Commentary, p. 104.

testing. Jesus' ability to pass on His power to others marked His unique nature as the Servant of the Lord.

"Anointed with oil many that were sick, and healed *them*"— mentioned only by Mark, and the only reference to the practice in the Gospels. The use of oil, olive oil, for medicinal purposes was common in that day, but here the mention of anointing in connection with the supernatural healing indicates that its use was symbolic rather than medical in intention. The healing power lay not in the oil but in the Lord in whose name and authority the apostles acted. Still, their use of oil, as a well-known healing agent, was a fitting material and visible medium through which the divine power wrought the healing of the sick, those feeble and without strength.

Matthew noted that after the Twelve were sent out, Jesus continued His own work of teaching and preaching (11:1). This multiplied teaching and healing ministry, as a deliberate effort on the part of Jesus to stir the people, made a strong impact. The length of the disciples' preaching tour is not indicated; perhaps it lasted several weeks or longer.

f. Reaction of Antipas to the Reports About Jesus (6:14-29).

This paragraph forms an interlude between the sending out of the Twelve and their return. It consists of two parts: the excited reaction of Herod to the stir caused by preaching (vv. 14-16) and the explanatory account of the death of John the Baptist (vv. 17-29). Matthew 14:1-3 and Luke 9:7-9 run parallel to the first part, but only Matthew (14:4-12) gives a parallel account of John's martyrdom. Luke earlier mentioned John's imprisonment (3:19-20), but he omitted an account of his death.

1) Excited reaction of Herod Antipas (vv. 14-16). "King Herod heard"—Herod Antipas, the son of Herod the Great and Malthace, a Samaritan, was the ruler of Galilee and Perea (4 B.C.–A.D. 39). Mark did not use his official title, *tetrarch* (Matt. 14:1; Luke 3:19; 9:7), but called him king, using the common parlance of his subjects. In his account, Matthew also called him king (14:9). Bruce points out that "it was natural for Mark writing for the Roman world to use this title, as it was applied freely in Rome to all eastern rulers."[65] Antipas's ambition to secure for himself the official title of "king" resulted in his downfall under Caligula.

What Antipas heard is left undefined, but the context points to the stirring events flowing from the augmented preaching activity in Galilee. It is in keeping with the materialistic interests of Antipas that the

---

[65] Bruce, 1:380.

palace was late in hearing the spiritual news. The king's reaction indicates that the exciting news reaching him centered on Jesus Himself rather than on the Twelve. The Twelve exalted their Master in their preaching and miracle-working ministry.

"For his name was spread abroad"—*for* introduces an explanatory clause, a characteristic of Mark's style.[66] *His* refers to Jesus, but Mark did not feel it necessary to declare the identity. His *name,* in the sense of fame, had become public knowledge, so that even the king heard about Him. Jesus was the center and hero of the whole stirring movement; His notoriety had placed His name on all lips. We need not assume that Antipas had never previously heard the name of Jesus, but the stir He was creating drew the king's attention to Him.

"And he said"—some manuscripts read "they said," but the singular is much better attested. The reading, "they said," would refer "the estimate of Jesus to the court talk, not alone to Herod."[67] Mark's account stresses the strange conviction which Herod reached concerning Jesus. Verse 16 makes it clear that it was prompted by his troubled conscience rather than by the rumors which he had heard about Jesus. The rumors heard initially stirred perplexity and doubt in Herod (Luke 9:7-9), but Mark's statement records his settled conviction. *Said* is imperfect tense, suggesting that this was Herod's reply whenever the subject was mentioned to him.

"John the Baptist was risen from the dead"—the participial construction, "the one baptizing," identifies John by his characteristic activity, even after that activity had been terminated (cf. 1:4). His baptizing work had become inseparably associated with his person. *Was risen* is perfect tense, "was raised and is now alive and active."

"And therefore mighty works do shew forth themselves in him"—*therefore* indicates that Herod was making a deduction. His explanation of these powers, the supernatural phenomena being reported, reveals that "the guilty monarch's conscience was haunted by ghastly reminiscences and weird forebodings."[68] If Herod was a Sadducee, his fears broke through his doctrinal unbelief concerning a resurrection. Although John's ministry had not been marked by miracles (John 10:41), one who had returned from the dead could be expected to bring supernatural powers back with him. Herod felt that this explained the supernatural powers now operating through the resuscitated John.

---

[66] Cf. 1:22; 2:15; 3:10; 5:8, 28; 6:17, 18, 20; 7:3; 11:13; 16:8.

[67] Wuest, p. 126.

[68] James Morison, *A Practical Commentary on the Gospel According to St. Mark,* p. 149.

"Others said, That it is Elias"[69]—*said,* in the imperfect tense, suggests that this identification was being offered repeatedly in discussion concerning Jesus. The identification was based on the prevailing Jewish expectation that the return of Elijah would precede the coming of the Messiah (cf. Mal. 4:5). This explanation also was meant to account for the supernatural powers operating in Jesus.

"Others said, That it is a prophet, or as one of the prophets"— another explanation, content to be less specific. These people were willing to accept Jesus as belonging to the category of prophets in general, but not as exceptional and exalted as Elijah. They were willing to accept Jesus as one in whom the long-suspended line of prophets was being resumed. According to Luke 9:8, this opinion also involved the idea of a resurrection. These opinions reveal that the people could not escape the impression of something definitely supernatural about Jesus. But their high estimates of Him were not high enough. None suggested that He was the Messiah. English remarks that it shows "how men are willing to believe anything but the truth."[70]

"But when Herod heard *thereof,* he said"—the italics indicate that the verb *heard* has no expressed object. It may be regarded as marking a resumption of the verb in verse 14, but more probably the reference is to the views expressed in verse 15. *Said,* in the imperfect, implies that whenever Herod heard one of these opinions expressed, he gave his own view about the identity of the miracle worker.

"It is John, whom I beheaded: he is risen"—more literally, "He whom *I* beheaded, John, this one was raised." The jerky construction reveals the excitement of the speaker. Herod's emphatic *I* is a self-tortured confession of his personal guilt in the death of John. He could not forget the horrible sight of that head dripping with blood on a platter in the banquet hall. He himself had beheaded John, for he had ordered John's decapitation. But his troubled conscience led him to the strange conclusion that John "was raised" as an actual occurrence. "This one" stresses the identity between the martyred John and the present miracle worker.

2) Explanatory account of John's death (vv. 17-29). This paragraph explains Herod's remark that he had beheaded John. The narrative falls into two parts: the events leading up to his death (vv. 17-20) and the plot resulting in John's death (vv. 21-29). Vincent Taylor

---

[69] The rendering "Elias" in the KJV is a transliteration of the Greek spelling of the name, since the Greek can have an *h* only at the beginning of a word. "Elijah" comes from the Hebrew form.

[70] E. Schuyler English, *Studies in the Gospel According to Mark,* p. 176.

points out that this is the only narrative in Mark "not in some sense or other a story about Jesus."[71] But the story is relevant to Mark's purpose as showing what happened to Messiah's forerunner as well as foreshadowing Jesus' own violent end. Mark recorded the story with complete objectivity; the events were allowed to speak for themselves.

"For Herod himself had sent forth and laid hold upon John"—*for* introduces the story of John's death in retrospect. *Herod himself* stresses John's arrest as emphatically Herod's own act. Where John was arrested is not indicated; it may have been at Aenon (John 3:23). Herod had sent forth soldiers with orders to arrest John. Josephus relates that Antipas imprisoned and executed John to prevent him from fomenting political trouble.[72] The account of Josephus is wholly independent of the biblical story, but the differences in the accounts offer no valid grounds for discrediting the trustworthiness of the Gospel narratives.[73] Josephus, writing some sixty years after the event, was interested in its public and political aspects, while the Gospel writers pointed out the sinister, private activities that led to John's death. Taylor well remarks that "political ends and the anger of an insulted woman cannot be regarded as mutually exclusive."[74]

"And bound him in prison"—kept him fettered while in prison. Josephus said that the place of imprisonment was Machaerus, near the northeastern shore of the Dead Sea. Located near the southern end of Perea, it was a fortress, a palace, and a prison all in one. John's disciples had access to him while he was confined there (Luke 7:18).

"For Herodias' sake, his brother Philip's wife"—Herodias was the daughter of Aristobulus, a half-brother to Antipas, thus his niece. She had married her uncle, here called Philip,[75] and they had had a daughter named Salome. Philip had been disinherited by his father, Herod the Great, and lived with Herodias in Rome as a private citizen. While visiting his brother in Rome, Antipas became enamored with Herodias, who, as an ambitious woman, agreed to marry Antipas on

---

[71] Taylor, p. 310.

[72] Josephus *Antiquities* 18. 2.

[73] For a summary of the arguments against the historical accuracy of the biblical accounts, see Cranfield, pp. 208-9.

[74] Taylor, p. 311.

[75] The charge that Mark erroneously confused this Philip with Philip the Tetrarch remains unsubstantiated. Josephus simply called him Herod, and he may well have had the personal name Philip. In the family of Herod the Great, who had ten different wives, it is not impossible that two half-brothers should have the common name of Philip.

the condition that he would divorce his wife, a daughter of the Nabataean king Aretas IV. Upon learning of the treacherous intentions of her husband, his wife of many years fled to her father at whose hands Antipas later suffered a humiliating military defeat.

"For he had married her"—the evil plan was carried out. Ambitious to be the wife of a ruler, Herodias deserted her husband, or got a Roman divorce, and as the wife of Antipas became the mistress of the palace at Tiberias. It further tangled the marriage web of the Herodian dynasty.[76] This independent causal statement, already implied in the previous expression, stresses the fact of the marriage as the basis for John's rebuke.

"For John had said unto Herod"—another explanatory note. *Had said,* in the imperfect tense, apparently means that on more than one occasion John had spoken in rebuke to Herod. Mark's words imply a private confrontation between John and Herod. Where such meetings took place is not indicated. If they occurred at the time John was working at Aenon, Tiberias would not be far away, and he could easily have visited Antipas there. But others think it unlikely that John, who kept to the open country, would go to Tiberias voluntarily. It may be that the rebuking messages were sent to Herod by John's disciples, or given publicly during John's preaching.

"It is not lawful for thee to have thy brother's wife"—John's denunciation was based on the fact that it was not lawful, was contrary to the Mosaic law to which Antipas, a professed convert to Judaism, was subject (Lev. 18:16; 20:21). His marriage to Herodias was a crime against his brother as well as against his own wife. This bold denunciation of sin wherever he found it was characteristic of John (cf. Matt. 3:7-10).

"Herodias had a quarrel against him"—an idiomatic expression which literally rendered is "was having [it] in for him." Like our English expression, it denotes the feelings of animosity and hatred which Herodias nursed in her heart against John. She regarded John's bold rebuke of the marriage as a gross insult to herself and Herod. The imperfect tense pictures the protracted feeling; she harbored an undying hatred against John. But the open-ended imperfect also prepares for something to happen because of that hatred.

"Would have killed him"—she was not satisfied with John's imprisonment but craved a revenge which would be satisfied with nothing

---

[76] Herodias, the *niece* of Antipas, by her marriage to her uncle Philip became the *sister-in-law* of Antipas, and then became his *wife.* Through the later marriage of her daughter Salome to Philip the Tetrarch, Herodias, his *niece* and *sister-in-law,* became Philip's *mother-in-law.*

less than his death. The parallel to the Old Testament story of Jezebel is obvious.

"But she could not"—her unflagging desire to kill John was thwarted, as the next verse explains. The imperfect tense again may imply that she would persist until she found a way to overcome the hindrance.

"For Herod feared John"—continued to have a mixed feeling of awed respect and superstitious dread for John. Morison remarks, "Kingliness changed places: the subject did not fear the sovereign; the sovereign feared the subject."[77]

"Knowing that he was a just man and an holy"—Herod's reaction was inspired by his instinctive recognition of John's moral excellence. The two terms seem to stand in an ascensive order: the first describes his blameless relations toward his fellow men; the second portrays his character of total separation unto God.

"And observed [protected, Gr.] him"—continued to preserve John from the murderous intentions of Herodias. He kept John in prison as the best protection against the plottings of Herodias. Antipas, then, was aware of the hostile intentions of his wife. Matthew indicates that Herod himself had felt a desire to kill John but was restrained because "he feared the multitude," dreaded the political consequences of John's execution, since the people regarded John as a prophet (Matt. 14:5). Without this political motive, Herod would not have had the strength to oppose the will of Herodias.

"And when he heard him"—on various occasions, Herod had John brought into his presence to talk with him. These interviews must have taken place whenever Herod visited Machaerus. That John was brought all the way to Tiberias seems improbable.

"He was much perplexed" (ASV)—the interviews evoked tangled, conflicting feelings in Herod, leaving him at a loss as to what to do. He was torn with indecision between the voice of conscience and his passion for Herodias. The statement pictures his moral weakness. Many manuscripts here have a different reading, "He did many things" (KJV). The textual evidence for this reading is strong but the other reading has good quality of textual support and is decidedly preferable on internal grounds. This alternative reading seems due to a scribal change made in view of the word *gladly* in the following clause.

"Heard him gladly"—"with pleasure." He found the message of John bracing and refreshing to his jaded mind. He could appreciate the unpretentious grandeur of John's character, while the vigor and purity

---

[77] Morison, p. 152.

of his mind, which moved on quite a different level from that which Herod daily encountered in his court, appealed to his better nature.

"When a convenient day was come"—Herodias's malicious purpose was frustrated until the opportune day came to carry out the cunning plot she had concocted.

"That Herod on his birthday made a supper"—the Jews generally disapproved of such birthday festivals as being pagan, but the Herods followed the Romans in the practice. *Supper,* the main meal of the day, eaten at evening, here denotes a luxurious banquet. Herod put on a grand celebration. The suggestion of some that *birthday* denotes the anniversary of Herod's accession lacks adequate support.

"To his lords, high captains, and chief *estates* of Galilee"—three groups of distinguished guests. The lords, "the great ones," were the dignitaries holding high civil offices under Antipas. The high captains (*chiliarchs*), commanders over a thousand men, here denote the military officials of high rank. Their presence may imply that Antipas at this time was consulting with them concerning his collection of forces to meet Aretas, the father of his repudiated wife. The chief men of Galilee were the important social leaders of the province. The mention of the third group would seem to suggest that the gathering was at Tiberias, but to hold it at the fortress of Machaerus would give it a distinctive image. Futher, it seems doubtful that Herod could have gathered "the chief men of Galilee" (ASV) for this birthday party if it was held in Tiberias since Josephus tells us that pious Jews avoided that city because it had been built on a cemetery (*Antiquities* 18. 2. 3).

"When the daughter of the said Herodias came in, and danced"— the aorist tenses simply state the historical facts. The climax of the entertainment was a solo dance by the daughter of Herodias herself.[78] The expression indicates the unusual fact. Such solo dances were grossly suggestive pantomimic representations, comparable to a striptease act in a modern nightclub. They were regularly performed by professional entertainers of low moral character, and it was an almost unprecedented thing for Salome to perform such a dance before Herod's

---

[78] A textual variant reads, "his daughter Herodias." It is supported by some important manuscripts and was adopted by Westcott and Hort, but it is highly improbable. It would make her the daughter of Antipas himself, but verse 24 asserts that she was the daughter of Herodias. The marriage of Antipas and Herodias was a comparatively recent event, and they could not have a daughter old enough to perform this dance. The variant reading puts Mark in error concerning the girl's name; her name, according to Josephus, was Salome, the daughter of Herodias by her former husband. Salome was about twenty years old at this time. That Herod would allow his own daughter thus to be degraded to please his guests is highly incredible, but it is entirely consistent with Herodias's fierce hatred for John thus to prostitute her own daughter.

guests. Some have indeed questioned the accuracy of the biblical account, but Rawlinson replies that the occurrence is "not wholly incredible, however outrageous, to those who know anything of the morals of Oriental courts, or of Herod's family in particular."[79]

"And pleased Herod"—the aorist verb, which simply states the fact, may be regarded as impersonal: "it pleased Herod," that is, the dance. But it is equally possible to supply the personal reference from the preceding clause and render "she," stressing that he was pleased with her personally. This seems more in keeping with the immediate context. Salome probably showed extraordinary skill in her dancing. Herod must have regarded Salome's willingness to dance for them as a special favor conferred on him.

"And them that sat with him"—those reclining with him on the *triclinia* around the banquet table (cf. 2:15). All the guests shared the king's delight in the voluptuous dance.

"Ask of me whatsoever thou wilt"—*ask* is aorist imperative, urging her at once to make her request concerning what her reward was to be. *Whatsoever* left the selection entirely open to her own desires.

"And I will give *it* thee"—in making this unlimited, "blank check" promise, Herod was ostentatiously aping the style of Oriental monarchs (cf. Esther 5:6; 7:2), seeking to impress his guests with his generosity. He had no realization of the trap into which he was falling.

"And he sware unto her"—when Salome apparently hesitated to express her request, Herod confirmed his rash promise with an oath, making it irrevocable. It was a further attempt to display his royal grandeur.

"Unto the half of my kingdom"—the oath appears to limit the previous promise, but in effect it was intended to enhance the appearance of his generosity. "That Herod was a vassal of Rome only makes this oath the more brash."[80] As a tetrarch under the aegis of Rome, Antipas actually had no "kingdom" to dispose of, but to read his offer literally is entirely too prosaic. All those who heard it understood it as an absurd exaggeration to indicate his generous mood.

"And she went forth"—from the banquet hall to rejoin her mother in the women's quarters. Women were not present at the banquet.

"Said unto her mother"—implying that no advance agreement had been made between mother and daughter. Herodias shrewdly counted on the vanity of Herod to elicit just such a response, but she could not be sure what Herod would offer as a reward for Salome.

---

[79] Rawlinson, p. 82.

[80] Guelich, p. 332.

"What shall I ask?"—more literally, "What should I ask for myself?" The aorist subjunctive indicates that the girl was undecided in her own mind what the request should be. Her use of the middle voice naturally denotes that her own advantage in the request to be made was uppermost in her mind. The middle voice of this verb was used for requests in business transactions and may here mean, "What should I claim?"

"And she said"—the aorist tense implies a prompt, premeditated reply.

"The head of John the Baptist"—more specific than a request for the death of John. She demanded the head of John as tangible evidence of the unmistakable reality of his death. The request shows the vicious temper and iron determination of Herodias.

"She came in straightway with haste"—Salome promptly entered into the spirit of her mother's request and without any delay returned to the banquet hall to present her request with haste, with eagerness in her step. Her heart was in the business. She seemingly shared her mother's hatred of John. Realizing that Herod might refuse the request upon sober reflection, she rushed in to press her claim.

"I will that thou give me by and by"—her *I will* takes Herod at his word (v. 22). She had been asked to determine the gift, and now she was indicating her decision. *By and by* (rather, "at once" or "immediately") stresses that she demanded her ghastly reward without delay. Her manner betrays a callous brashness that equals that of her mother.

"In a charger"—indicating that the head was to be severed from the body. Alexander comments that this gruesome request for service on a platter was "probably added by the daughter of her own accord, as a hideous jest implying an intention to devour it."[81]

"The king was exceeding sorry"—*exceeding sorry,* a strong term used by Mark again only in 14:34, pictures Herod as surrounded on all sides, engulfed, with grief. His sorrow, although genuine, was shallow and not sufficiently strong to arouse him to break out of the trap into which he had foolishly fallen. Neither Mark nor Matthew said that he was sorry for John. The context clearly indicates that he was sorry to be forced to act against John contrary to his own desires. Herodias had skillfully outmaneuvered him to gain her own purpose.

"*Yet* for his oath's sake, and for their sakes which sat with him"—the two grounds on which Herod felt forced to act contrary to his better wishes. The plural "oaths" (Gr.) may mean that Herod had repeated

---

[81] Joseph Addison Alexander, *The Gospel According to Mark,* p. 159.

his oath to Salome, but Bruce remarks that "the plural was sometimes used for a single oath."[82] The king foolishly felt that honor did not permit him to escape from his rash oath.[83] Moral cowardice made him afraid to break his word in the presence of those reclining with him. But Herod would certainly have stood taller, even in the eyes of his fellow revelers when they regained their full sobriety, had he refused to go through with his promise. "Timidity, which takes the form of false pride, is accountable for the moral failure of thousands."[84]

"He would not reject her"—did not have the strength of will to do so. *Reject,* which literally means to displace what had been placed, when used with a person means to break faith with, to disappoint. Herod did not have the courage to repudiate her request and thus disappoint her.

"And immediately the king sent"—allowed himself no time for further reflection. *Immediately* underlines the fact that the king ordered done what Salome requested while she waited in the banquet hall.

"An executioner"—The designation is a loan-word from the Latin. The word originally meant a spy, or scout, and came to be used of a member of the staff of a legionary commander; they acted as couriers and, at times, as executioners. Roman tribunes customarily surrounded themselves with such bodyguards, and Herod adopted the custom.

"He went and beheaded him in the prison"—a prompt and exact performance of the command given him. No glimpse is given of the scene in the prison. Apparently John was alone at the time.

"And brought his head in a charger, and gave it to the damsel"— The prompt return clearly indicates that John was in a prison near the scene of the banquet. This places the banquet at Machaerus, unless we accept the unlikely assumption that John had been transferred to Tiberias. Machaerus, located on a ridge about a mile long and overlooking a deep ravine, had a palace at one end and a prison at the other.

"The damsel gave it to her mother"—"a fit presentation for cannibals."[85] Salome thus acknowledged her mother as the instigator of the heinous act. The Gospel writers throw a veil over the treatment accorded the severed head.

---

[82] Bruce, 1:382.

[83] A missionary teacher in Africa related that his students, when studying this story, found it almost unbelievable that Herod did not talk himself out of the trap. When asked what they would have said, the reply was, "I would have said, 'The head of John the Baptist is not that half of the kingdom which I promised you.'"

[84] J. D. Jones, *Commentary on Mark,* p. 185.

[85] Morison, p. 158.

"When his disciples heard *of it*"—evidently none of John's disciples were with him at the time.

"They came and took up his corpse"—*took up* implies that the headless body lay on the floor where it had fallen. Corpse, literally, "a thing fallen," designates the remains of what was left of the noble martyr. It was not the real man himself. Herod apparently gave the disciples free access to the body in an effort to mitigate his own remorse.

"Laid it in a tomb"—its location is not indicated, perhaps somewhere near Machaerus. Later tradition held that the body was buried at Sebaste, in Samaria. Matthew added that the disciples went and told Jesus (14:12). Whether this means that John's disciples were now willing to throw in their lot with Jesus is not clear. We do know that beyond Palestine they continued as a separate group for many years (Acts 19:1-7). Where Jesus was when John's disciples came with their shocking report is not indicated. Apparently He had just returned to Capernaum.

6
Withdrawals from Galilee
(Part 2; 6:30–7:23)

2. Second Withdrawal and Return (6:30–7:23)

The second withdrawal from Galilee, of brief duration, was marked by two miracles which strikingly set forth the unique nature of Jesus (6:30-52). The return to Galilee resulted in further ministry to the needy multitudes (6:53-56) and sharp controversy with the Jewish leaders (7:1-23).

a. Feeding of the Five Thousand (6:30-44).

Here for the first time, all four Gospels record the same event (Matt. 14:13-21; Luke 9:10-17; John 6:1-13). The Fourth Gospel makes valuable contributions to the fuller understanding of the event. All the Gospel writers recognized that this miracle formed the climax of the great Galilean ministry. Mark's account contains some vivid touches which suggest the reminiscences of an eyewitness.

"The apostles gathered themselves together unto Jesus"—marking the termination of their preaching tour (6:7-13). *Gathered themselves together* pictures the Twelve's reassembling in pairs from the various areas where they had been working. *Unto Jesus* clearly implies that "the Jesus" who had sent them out had arranged for them to rejoin Him at a certain time and place. This is Mark's only use of the term *apostles* for the Twelve, although some manuscripts also have it at 3:14. (See remarks under 3:14.) It is fitting here, because they were returning from their first official mission as His commissioned representatives. Perhaps Mark intended the term here not as an official title but in the general sense of missionary; yet he probably did have in mind also the official connotation of the word, which it certainly had by the time he was writing. But as English points out, "The stress as far as the apostle is concerned is on function, not status. Indeed the commission relates to the task itself. The Twelve had a particular function, as companions, eye-witnesses and authorities on his ministry."[1]

"Told him all things"—having worked as His representatives, they freely gave Him a complete report of the trip. Although no indication of their mood is given, eagerness and enthusiasm seem a fair inference. Jones comments, "Their preaching tour had cost them nothing in money, but it had made vast demands upon their emotions and sympathies and spiritual energies."[2]

"What they had done, and what they had taught"—the repeated *what* points to two distinct phases of their report: the things done in the nature of miracles and the things taught in the proclamation of the kingdom. The order suggests that their ability to perform miracles created their chief excitement and received the major stress in their reports.

Verse 31 is peculiar to Mark. Both parts of it, Jesus' consideration for the disciples and the pressing circumstances, are characteristic interests of his Gospel.

"Come ye yourselves apart into a desert place"—Jesus' evaluation of their work is not indicated, but His consideration for the workers is stressed. He realized that after their strenuous activities and novel experiences, they needed privacy and rest. "Ye yourselves" restricted the invitation to the Twelve. The phrase rendered *apart* (*kat' idian*) need not suggest concealment in withdrawal, but rather a withdrawal so that they could be in private, could arrange their own affairs. *Desert place* denotes not a sandy, waterless place but a lonely place, uninhabited and unsuitable for cultivation. The rocky shores around the Sea of Galilee, especially the eastern side, offered many such places.

"And rest a while"—the aorist tense with the adverb *a while* (better, "a little") indicates that Jesus recognized the rest would be of short duration. He envisioned a short period of relaxation, not a cessation of activities. For continued effectiveness, every worker must now and then stop to take a breath and relax a little.

Matthew's account makes it clear that there was a further motive for this invitation to withdraw. The coming of John's disciples with their report of John's death coincided with the return of the Twelve (Matt. 14:12-13). The shocking news was just becoming known in Galilee, adding to the religious excitement that had been aroused by the preaching tour of the Twelve. The crowds would be eager to learn how Jesus had reacted to the sad affair. He could have easily stimulated

---

[1] Donald English, *The Message of Mark: The Mystery of Faith,* p. 133.

[2] J. D. Jones, *Commentary on Mark,* p. 195.

a popular movement against Antipas because of John's martyrdom. Aware of the tense situation, Jesus deliberately withdrew from the territory of Antipas.

"For there were many coming and going"—the articles in the original, "the ones coming and the ones going," distinctly picture two streams of people. As soon as one group left, another group arrived, leaving no interval for privacy and rest. These visitors were drawn by the growing fame of Jesus, and no doubt their number increased because of the approaching Passover (John 6:4). Some may have been politically motivated (cf. John 6:14-15).

"They had no leisure so much as to eat"—had no opportune time to take their regular meals. The imperfect tense indicates that this was no isolated experience (cf. 3:20).

"They departed into a desert place by ship privately"—this restatement of the thought of verse 31 in the third person indicates that the proposal of Jesus was being carried out. The boat was the same boat they had used before (5:1-2). It shows that they assembled by the seashore, and Capernaum, as Jesus' headquarters, would be the natural place. *Into a desert place* states their destination, not their arrival there, which is given in verse 34. According to Luke 9:10, they withdrew "to a city called Bethsaida," that is, Bethsaida-Julius, which was located on the eastern bank of the Jordan, just above its entry into the Sea of Galilee. But they apparently did not touch the city at all, since Luke mentioned that the feeding of the multitudes took place in a desert area. The time of their departure was apparently early morning.

"The people saw them departing"—they got away alone but they did not escape notice. In the original the verb is impersonal, "they saw." It does not identify the witnesses or indicate their number. Those who saw them going speedily reported the fact to the eager inhabitants of Capernaum. Now that Jesus had returned home, they kept His movements under close observation.

"And many knew him"—in the original no object is expressed, but many manuscripts insert either *him* or *them* as the object of the verb. Recognizing the occupants of the boat, they perceived what was taking place.

"And ran afoot thither out of all cities"—the crowd watched the course of the boat until it became apparent that it was headed toward the northeastern shore. The direction and speed of the boat stimulated the decision to follow by land. According to John 6:2, their following Jesus was motivated by the signs they saw Him perform. The verb ("ran together," Gr.) pictures the multitude that joined those who began the race around the head of the lake. The young and strong headed the race, while others hurried along as fast as they could. *Thither* points to the place toward which they saw the boat was headed. *Out of all cities* reveals that the people from the various neighboring cities through which the excited crowd was running joined them in the excited movement toward the place where Jesus was expected to land. This vivid picture of the eager crowd is peculiar to Mark.

"And outwent them"—a detail preserved only by Mark. The young and the strong in the crowd outran the larger part of the multitude, and they were already at hand when the boat landed. The distance across the water would be about four miles, while the distance by land would be nearly twice that far. This accomplishment would be possible if the boat sailed slowly because of little wind or a contrary wind.

"He came out"—from the boat. From John's Gospel we learn that, upon landing, Jesus and His disciples ascended the hillside and sat there, apparently waiting until the whole multitude had assembled. His seated position would indicate His willingness to teach them when they had all arrived.

"Saw much people"—an unorganized mass of people approaching along the shore must have been visible even before they left the boat. Apparently from the hillside the extent of the crowd was more clearly visible. John's Gospel records that while Jesus watched the approaching crowd, He asked Philip where they were to get bread to feed them (6:5).

"Was moved with compassion toward them"—was touched by the eagerness of the people and their obvious needs. In spite of the unbelief He was encountering and His desire to be alone with His disciples, the sight of the people stirred His shepherd heart with a feeling of compassion, a feeling of pity which made Him yearn to help them. The aorist tense may be rendered, "He was gripped with compassion." It is an "illustration of that wonderful love that never sought its own, but always forgot its own needs and worries and sorrows in sympathy and care for the burdens and sorrows of other people."[3] English notes that "this verb is used only to describe Jesus himself (Mk. 8:2; Mt. 9:36; 14:14; 15:32), or to explain the actions of people in his parables who resemble him (Mt. 18:27; Lk. 10:33; 15:20)."[4]

"Because they were as sheep not having a shepherd"—Mark alone records the reason for His compassion. Jesus viewed them not as a group but as individuals, "as sheep not having a shepherd." The picture, drawn from the Old Testament (Num. 27:17; 1 Kings 22:17;

---

[3] Ibid., p. 198.

[4] English, p. 134.

2 Chron. 18:16; Ezek. 34:5), portrays them as helpless, lacking nourishment, guidance, and protection, exposed to the perils of dispersion and destruction. He saw that the religious leaders did not meet the spiritual needs of the people.

"He began to teach them many things"—began at once to shepherd them. The central point of His work was to teach them, for this was their greatest need. "Many things" (*polla*) is here best taken as adverbial, "at length." His teaching ministry was continued until the day was far advanced. Luke indicates that He taught of "the kingdom of God" and that He also healed "them that had need of healing" (9:11). The presence of sick people indicates that others joined the crowd during the course of the day. Certainly they were not among those who outran the boat.

"When the day was now far spent"—the ministry to the crowd was continued until the hour had become late. Matthew noted that "it was evening" (14:15), that is, the first evening which began at 3 P.M. (Matt. 14:23 mentions the second evening, beginning with sunset.) Hour after hour, He continued to deal with the multitude, appearing to be unmindful of their physical need for food.

"His disciples came unto him"—the longer Jesus continued to speak, the more tense the disciples became. The question that Jesus had asked Philip concerning food for the crowd (John 6:5) had led to discussion on the matter among the disciples. They arrived at no solution other than that the crowd must be dismissed. They therefore approached Jesus, apparently while He was still teaching, with their well-meaning suggestion.

"This is a desert place, and now the time *is* far passed"—their anxious reminder to Jesus of the pressing circumstances. He seemed to them to have forgotten that the hastily assembled multitude had failed to bring along any food, and the place offered them no convenient way to get it. The late hour demanded that immediate attention be given to the matter.

"Send them away"—prudence demanded that He at once release the crowd and bid them go their way. The disciples too were motivated by concern for the people, but it was prompted by natural considerations, not faith.

"Go into the country round about, and into the villages, and buy themselves bread"—their proposed plan of action for the people to meet their own need. The crowd must be directed to go out into the surrounding country, fields or cultivated spots, villages or hamlets, to purchase food for themselves. If they waited any longer, some might not be able to procure food because of the late hour.

"He answered and said unto them"—Jesus calmly put further pressure on the disciples with His startling countermand.

"Give ye them to eat"—all the synoptics record the identical command, indicating that the startling order was unforgettably registered on the disciples' memories. In Matthew, the command is introduced with the assertion, "They need not depart" (14:16), thus firmly overruling their proposal. In rejecting their plan, Jesus gave the disciples an astonishing countermand. His emphatic *ye* laid the duty to feed the crowd squarely on the disciples. Instead of sending them away, they must feed them.

"They say unto him"—the historical present, *they say,* takes the reader into the very presence of the bewildered disciples, as one after the other they express astonishment. The command of Jesus turned their anxiety into frustrated amazement.

"Shall we go and buy"—His order had thrown them back upon their own resources, but they knew that they had nothing adequate to meet the need. Did He therefore mean that they should go and buy the needed bread? Their question suggests that He was demanding the impossible.

"Two hundred pennyworth of bread"—literally, "loaves for two hundred denarii." Mark alone of the synoptics mentioned this figure, and that without comment, but John's account (6:5-7) makes clear their use of the figure. In response to the question Jesus put to him, Philip had made a mental calculation and concluded that it would require 200 denarii worth of bread to give all a moderate amount of food. Philip was easily able to determine how much was needed, but he had no suggestion about how the need was to be met. The other disciples agreed that they needed *two hundred pennyworth* of bread. This rendering fails to convey the picture adequately to the modern reader. The denarius was the ordinary pay for a day's work in the vineyard (Matt. 20:2). Thus the amount suggested would be about eight month's wages for a common workingman. It would be a sum quite beyond the means of the disciples.[5]

"How many loaves have ye?"—He met their incredulous question with a practical counterquestion. They must take stock of what resources were actually available.

"Go and see"—the two commands, only in Mark, order them into action. The first is present tense, "Be going"; the second is aorist,

---

[5] Figuring a minimum wage of $34 today, the amount would be $6,800; but when used to buy food for 5,000 people the cost per person would be only $1.36. Philip's calculation was very conservative!

"See definitely." From John's Gospel it is clear that the disciples went among the people to inquire, "Does any one here have any food?" With this question, the people, who had been absorbed in the teaching of Jesus, were brought to a sudden consciousness of their physical needs. They suddenly realized that they had not eaten anything during that day.

"When they knew"—literally, "having come to know" by inquiry.

"Five, and two fishes"—all the synoptics report the amount available, but the Fourth Gospel records that Andrew brought the report that a lad in the crowd had the food with him. Matthew notes that Jesus asked that the food be brought to Him. Jesus' willingness to start feeding the crowd with this scant supply at once suggested that something extraordinary was to occur.

"He commanded them"—the command was given to the Twelve to be conveyed to the people. In view of the inadequacy of the supply of food, it was a test of their faith, when they were directed to request the people to sit down for a meal.

"To make all sit down by companies"—more literally, "that all recline company by company." The order to have all "recline" was in accord with the customary posture while eating and was especially appropriate for an open-air meal without the usual tables. Had they remained standing, they would have crowded around the distributors of the food and hindered orderly distribution. "By companies" (literally, "company, company") indicates that they were to be arranged in regular groups. The term meant originally "a drinking party," then any group of people eating together.

"Upon the green grass"—the phrase suggests springtime. After May, the grass, which had sprung up with the rainy season, would become dry and brown. Its greenness harmonizes with John's remark that Passover was near (6:4). While Matthew and John both mention the grass, only Mark notes that it was green, an optical detail apparently derived from Peter.[6]

"They sat down in ranks"—*sat down,* more literally, "dropped down," is aorist tense and may suggest the simultaneous action of the crowd. It was an act of faith on their part, in view of the infinitesimal supply of food available. *In ranks* is literally "garden bed, garden bed," another picturesque touch found only in Mark. It suggests the

---

[6] The rejection of this implication by D. E. Nineham is due to his form-critical presuppositions which lead him to reject the view of a close connection between Peter and the writer of this Gospel (*The Gospel of St. Mark,* p. 183).

visual impression upon a spectator observing the rows of people on the green hillside; they looked like well-arranged garden plots. The expression implies the rectangular shape of the groups. It may also reflect the bright variegated garments of the people. Bruce holds that this unique description bespeaks "an eyewitness of an impressionable nature like Peter."[7]

"By hundreds, and by fifties"—Luke says that they reclined "by fifties in a company" (9:14). Symmetrical arrangement is clearly indicated, but just how the groups are arranged is not so clear. English suggests that "there were fifty semi-circles, one behind the other, of one hundred each; thus they would be seated "by hundred if counted across the ranks, by fifties if counted from front to back."[8] Such group arrangements would not be strange to the people, in view of the way they ate their sacred meals in Jerusalem during the great festivals. The arrangement made distribution of the food convenient and made it simple to determine the number fed.

"When he had taken the five loaves and the two fishes"—Jesus acted as host to the people assembled for the meal. The loaves and fishes could easily be held in His hands as He spoke the blessing. John notes that the loaves, secured from a lad in the crowd, were "barley loaves," the coarse food of the poor people. In form these loaves were flat cakes or biscuits, not like our modern loaves of bread. The two fishes were either dried or salted fish and were commonly eaten with the bread as a relish.

"He looked up to heaven"—a characteristic prayer posture of Jesus (cf. 7:34; John 11:41; 17:1). Luke 24:35 seems to indicate that Jesus had a characteristic way of speaking the blessing for the bread. The posture suitably portrayed the elevation of His thoughts above the present world to "the heaven," which all men instinctively regard as the dwelling place of God.

"And blessed"—"He spoke a blessing," apparently the common Jewish blessing before a meal.[9] The word literally means "to speak well of" and was appropriately used to denote the expression of gratitude to God. All the synoptics use the same word, but John says that

[7] Alexander Balmain Bruce, "The Synoptic Gospels," in *The Expositor's Greek Testament,* 1:384.

[8] E. Schuyler English, *Studies in the Gospel According to Mark,* p. 176.

[9] The common Jewish blessing before meals was, "Blessed art thou, O Lord our God, King of the world, who bringest forth bread from the earth" (quoted in V. Taylor, *The Gospel According to Mark,* p. 324).

Jesus "gave thanks." The two words were used as practical synonyms; the blessing spoken was in fact a form of thanksgiving.

"Brake the loaves"—literally, "broke down the loaves"; that is, broke them into pieces. As a definite act, Jesus broke the flat barley loaves into several pieces in preparation for the distribution.

"Gave *them* to his disciples"—the imperfect tense denotes the continued action of giving the broken pieces to the disciples. While none of the Gospels explicitly assert where the multiplication of the bread took place, the tense seems to indicate that the bread multiplied in the hands of Jesus. He continued to give out the broken pieces; yet always there was more to give out.

"To set before them"—the ordinary term used of servants placing the food on the table before the guests. The disciples, serving as waiters, thus had a close connection with the miracle being wrought.

"The two fishes divided he among them all"—here Mark was content to use the aorist tense simply to state the fact that the two fishes in like manner were shared with all, the entire multitude. *All* stresses the greatness of the miracle in asserting that two small fishes were multiplied so that all received a part of them.

"They did all eat"—the order of the original, "they ate all," emphasizes both verb and subject. The aorist stated the historical fact, while *all* stressed that none were excluded from the meal.

"And were filled"—the hunger of all was fully satisfied. All had "as much as they would" (John 6:11). The verb suggests that all ate as much as they could hold, having no desire for any more. It was not the scanty meal that Philip had envisioned (John 6:7). Jones aptly points out, "It was not with five loaves and two fishes that the disciples fed the crowd, but with five loaves and two fishes blessed and multiplied by Jesus."[10]

"They took up twelve baskets full of the fragments"—taken up by the disciples in response to the order of Jesus (John 6:12). *The fragments,* or the broken pieces, may refer to what was left uneaten by the multitude after it was distributed, but more likely, they were the broken pieces still left after Jesus ceased to break the bread. The supply of food was more than enough for the entire crowd. The original is literally "fillings of twelve baskets" and indicates that pieces equivalent to the amount contained in twelve baskets were left over. The word rendered "baskets" (*kophinoi*) is uniformly used in the Gospels in connection with the feeding of the five thousand. It denotes a small wicker basket such as the Jews used when traveling to carry their

---

[10] Jones, p. 202.

provisions in order to avoid eating Gentile food. They were apparently the baskets the disciples used in taking the food to the people. "The twelve baskets full," Donald English remarks, "as a leftover more than they began with, can be both physically true and therefore reflective of God's gracious ways with the kingdom."[11] While the amount supplied was more than needed, Jesus directed that none of it should be wasted. It was not His purpose that the superabundant supply should displace human prudence.

"And of the fishes"—a comment found only in Mark. The broken pieces gathered up consisted of fish as well as of the loaves.

"They that did eat of the loaves were about five thousand men"—one little loaf for each one thousand men! The word *men* (*andres*) means men literally, not people in general. Matthew added that this number was "besides women and children." The women and children, according to Jewish custom, were apparently grouped separately from the men for the meal. There probably were not many of them in the crowd, but the reference proves that the crowd fed was not strictly composed of those who had run around the head of the lake that morning. Others had joined the vast gathering during the day.

John alone recorded the reaction of the crowd to the miracle (6:14-15, 22-71). The reaction showed unmistakably that the crowd recognized a miracle had taken place. It is equally obvious that all the Gospel writers understood the event as miraculous. Rationalistic attempts to explain away the miraculous are based not upon the Gospel accounts but upon the alleged incredibility of the story. Plummer remarks, "The attempts to explain away the miracle as a myth, or a parable, or a gross exaggeration, are very unsatisfactory."[12] The miracles of Jesus form an inseparable part of the gospel itself, and any attempt to remove the supernatural from the ministry of Jesus is an effort to undermine the reliability of the Gospels as a whole. To those who accept the gospel portrait of Jesus as God incarnate, this story offers no insuperable difficulty.

b. Walking on the Water (6:45-52).

This miracle, following closely upon the feeding of the five thousand, is the only other miracle which the Fourth Gospel (John 6:16-21) records in common with the synoptics. But we do not have a fourfold account, because Luke omits it. Matthew alone records the further episode of Peter walking on the water (14:24-33).

---

[11] Donald English, p. 136.

[12] Alfred Plummer, "The Gospel According to St. Mark," in *Cambridge Greek Testament,* p. 174.

"And straightway he constrained his disciples"—*and straightway* stresses the close connection between this action of Jesus and the miraculous feeding. *Constrained,* carrying a sense of urgency and pressure, indicates that Jesus found it necessary to use gentle but firm insistence that the disciples leave at once. Clearly, they were reluctant to go, and His demand must have seemed strange and unreasonable to them. Only that morning He had asked them to go to that area, and now He was abruptly sending them away. The synoptics give no explanation, but the key to the action by Jesus is found in John's statement (6:15) that the crowd intended to make Jesus king by force. The Twelve would have been delighted to see this proposal carried out. Jesus acted decisively to get the disciples away from the scene lest they should get involved in the plot.

"To get into the ship, and to go to the other side before unto Bethsaida"—the two infinitives state the course of action which Jesus insisted upon for His disciples. *To get into* is aorist, denoting the act of embarking, while *to go before* is present tense, picturing the journey they must undertake. The implication is that Jesus would rejoin them later. How was not indicated. *The other side* simply denotes the shore beyond the intervening stretch of water and is indefinite regarding the location, but *unto Bethsaida* names the exact destination. The location of this Bethsaida has been much discussed. That morning, according to Luke 9:10, Jesus and the Twelve had sailed toward Bethsaida, near which the feeding of the five thousand took place. This was Bethsaida-Julius, east of Jordan. But since John noted that the boat that night was headed toward Capernaum (6:17), and the boat actually landed on the western shore, where was this Bethsaida located? Two different answers have been given.

Those who hold that there was only one Bethsaida understand the order to the disciples to mean that they were to cross the narrow bay to Bethsaida-Julius, where Jesus was expected to meet them, but that a strong northeastern wind suddenly came up and forced the boat toward the western shore. Others hold that there was another city named Bethsaida, called "Bethsaida of Galilee" (John 12:21), located near Capernaum, so that the direction could be spoken of as being either toward Bethsaida or Capernaum. It is not improbable that there should be two places named Bethsaida (Fishing House) on the shores of the lake, one in Galilee and the other in the tetrarchy of Philip. It must be admitted that we have no such direct evidence for a western Bethsaida as we have for Bethsaida-Julius, and the view of two Bethsaidas is now abandoned by many scholars. These scholars hold that the designation "Bethsaida of Galilee" is due to the fact that the city had spread across the Jordan. But other scholars insist that "the various

Gospel narratives require, in the movements recorded, a western as well as an eastern Bethsaida, otherwise all is confused and unintelligible.''[13] Bethsaida clearly seems to be a town close to Capernaum. According to Matthew 11:20-24, Jesus upbraided Chorazin, Bethsaida, and Capernaum for their failure to repent although ''most of his mighty works were done'' in them. This Bethsaida is clearly a Jewish city, not a Gentile place like Bethsaida-Julius. Since all the disciples, except Judas Iscariot, seem to have been Galileans (Acts 1:11), it seems improbable that Peter, Andrew, and Philip were all natives of the Bethsaida of Gaulanitis (John 1:44). Ruins of other towns near Capernaum make a western Bethsaida very probable. Christie argues that a western Bethsaida is supported by the fact that tradition in the early Christian centuries mistakenly located the place of the feeding of the five thousand on the western side, holding that the similarity of the place names was the connecting link.[14] The existence of two Bethsaidas seems best to harmonize all the data.

''While he sent away the people''—the emphatic ''he himself'' (Gr.), setting a contrast between Jesus and His disciples, indicates that it was a task He would not leave to anyone else. The people were in an excited condition, and prudence would be necessary.

''When he had sent them away''—the crowd, not the disciples. Matthew simply states that Jesus dismissed the crowd, but Mark's expression denotes that the dismissal was a friendly and courteous exercise of His authority to induce them to disperse. Bishop comments, ''He must have sent them off in a manner consonant with the best tradition of the Near East.''[15] Swete suggests that ''nothing in His manner betrayed anxiety or consciousness of their intentions.''[16] This double reference to the dismissal of the crowd indicates that it was an important concern for Jesus.

''He departed into a mountain to pray''—the mountain in that area, on the slopes of which the feeding had taken place. The whole region east of the lake is mountainous. Jesus withdrew up the mountain to escape the crowd (John 6:15), but chiefly to pray. *Pray,* a general term for prayer, is not restricted to petition, and indicates that Jesus withdrew to a solitary place for a time of communion with the Father (1:35). His actions indicate His consciousness that He was facing a serious turn of

---

[13] W. M. Christie, *Palestine Calling,* p. 61.

[14] Ibid., pp. 62-63.

[15] Eric F.F. Bishop, *Jesus of Palestine,* p. 144.

[16] Henry Barclay Swete, *The Gospel According to Saint Mark,* p. 136.

events. He needed strength and counsel for what lay ahead. He recognized in the offer of the crowd a repetition of the wilderness temptation to bypass the cross. By His prompt actions, He had forestalled any parleying with the temptation, but He needed fellowship and communion with the Father for strength on the following day to face the consequences of His decision. He most likely also voiced His petitions for the Twelve, that they might not succumb to false messianic expectations. This reference gives us another glimpse of the vital place that prayer had in the life of Jesus.

"When even was come"—the second evening, extending from sunset to dark. The feeding of the five thousand had begun after the beginning of the first evening (cf. Matt. 14:15; Mark 6:35).

"The ship was in the midst of the sea"—John's account suggests that the disciples were slow to cross the lake without Jesus and lingered in starting out. When darkness fell, their boat was in the midst of the sea, not necessarily in its geographical center, or halfway across, but out to sea, well away from the land.

"And he alone on the land"—peculiar to Mark, stressing the contrast between Jesus and the disciples. They had been loath to leave without Him.

"He saw them toiling in rowing"—this mention of Jesus seeing the disciples out on the stormy lake is peculiar to Mark. They were the definite objects of His consideration. It is generally held that no supernatural powers of sight are implied, since from His position on the mountain the boat would be visible to Him in the light of the paschal moon. But others, like Clarke, assert, "Even the full moon of the passover season is not sufficient to account for such seeing, and it certainly appears as if Mark meant to tell of a supernatural seeing from afar."[17] I accept the latter view as being more in keeping with Mark's portrayal of the uniqueness of Jesus. Guelich points out that "limited visibility is assumed by the story, since the disciples mistook Jesus for a ghost when they saw him."[18] Whatever the intended meaning, it stresses that Jesus was not unmindful of the needs of the Twelve who were distressed in rowing. *Toiling*—more literally, "tortured"—suggests the grievous physical pains and mental distress to which the Twelve were subjected in their efforts to reach the western shore as directed. Efforts almost beyond their strength were demanded to keep the boat facing the wind and waves. *In rowing*—literally, "in the

---

[17] W. N. Clarke, "Commentary on the Gospel of Mark," in *An American Commentary,* p. 95.

[18] Robert A. Guelich, *Mark 1:1–8:26,* Word Biblical Commentary, p. 350.

driving''—pictures them as propelling the boat against the adverse wind and waves by means of oars. It was hard work, and they were making little headway.

''For the wind was contrary''—the explanation for their difficulty. The adverse wind, apparently from the northwest, had sprung up after they had set sail.

''About the fourth watch of the night''—the Jews originally divided the night into three watches (Judges 7:19), but with the Roman supremacy in Palestine the four watches of the Romans were generally used. It was sometime after 3 A.M. when Jesus drew near to the boat. Apparently, He had continued His prayer session well past midnight.

''He cometh unto them, walking upon the sea''—the historical present *cometh* vividly presents His approach. *Unto them* indicates that the object of His course was the boat with the distressed disciples. *Walking upon the sea* can mean only that Jesus was walking, not *by* the sea but actually *upon* its stormy surface, in direct contact with the water. The present tense pictures His progress, as He moved steadily over the waters, unhampered by the wind and waves. Denials that Jesus actually walked on the water are not due to the obscurity of the language but rather spring from rationalistic assumptions that such an act is impossible. In reply to such skeptical assertions, Plummer remarks, ''It is rash to be positive as to what would be possible or impossible for a unique Personality such as that of Jesus Christ.''[19]

''And would have passed by them''—reported only by Mark. *Would* is more literally ''wished'' or ''desired,'' while *have passed by* is ''to come alongside of.'' As Jesus approached the boat, He deliberately changed His course so that He would come alongside the boat, following a parallel course with it. Obviously, His intention was that the disciples should recognize Him and ask Him to come into the boat with them. He seemed intent on testing their faith. Knowing His miraculous powers, would they have enough faith to recognize Him in this unique manner of coming to them?

''When they saw him''—the form that they saw approaching on the waters looked like Jesus, but under the circumstances they just could not believe that it really was Jesus Himself.

''They supposed it had been a spirit''—they readily adopted the opinion that what they saw was a ghost, the term from which our word *phantom* is derived. They could not believe that what they were seeing had physical reality.

---

[19] Plummer, p. 176.

"Cried out"—screamed in terror. It is the term used elsewhere by Mark of the unearthly shrieks of the demoniacs.

"For they all saw him, and were troubled"—*for* at once introduces the explanation for their fright. *All saw him* stresses that the object on the water was seen by the whole group. It was no subjective delusion conjured up by a few overwrought minds among them. *Were troubled* gives their emotional response to what they saw. The aorist tense indicates that they were suddenly gripped by a feeling of confused terror and agitation. There was no thought on their part that it was Jesus Himself coming to them.

"Immediately he talked with them"—because of His sympathetic heart, He at once spoke to them to abolish their superstitious fears. *Talked* (*laleō*) suggests that He spoke to them in a familiar way so that they would at once recognize His voice.

"Be of good cheer: it is I; be not afraid"—all three accounts have the same words, except that John omitted the words *be of good cheer.* This command occurs seven times in the Gospels, always from the lips of Jesus, except in Mark 10:49 where it is a word of encouragement spoken by the crowd to the blind beggar. The call to cheer always implies some previous condition of alarm or apprehension. The present tense calls upon them to adopt a continuing attitude of courage and good cheer. *It is I* gives the reason for the command to take courage. What they saw was not a specter but their own Lord and Master. The words, literally "I am," may simply be self-identification, but an echo of the Old Testament self-revelation of God may well be latent in the words. Such mastery of the sea is a divine attribute, and it clearly demonstrates His superhuman nature. *Be not afraid*—better, "Stop being afraid"—demanded a permanent end to their fears. Between His two commands, the first positive, the second negative, stood the fact of His personal presence with them. The fact that He was present should serve to calm their fears. McKenna remarks, "These are presumptuous words for anyone other than Jesus Christ during the middle of a storm. . . . He has the power to back up His words with action."[20]

Matthew here inserted the further episode of Peter walking upon the water (14:28-31). The reason for Mark's failure to include it can only be conjectured. The omission is not inconsistent with the assumed closeness between Peter and the writer of this Gospel. Probably Peter passed over it in his preaching because he was reluctant to picture himself in such a unique and spectacular incident.

---

[20] David L. McKenna, *Mark,* Communicator's Commentary, p. 146.

"He went up unto them into the ship"—the unusual term *went up* may imply that the side of the boat stood quite high above the level of the water where Jesus stood. A large ship is not implied.

"The wind ceased"—stopped blowing, as though it had grown tired. Mark did not assert that the cessation was supernatural, but he did feel it significant that the wind fell at the very time that Jesus entered the boat. The cessation as the response to the will of Jesus is consistent with the narrative. John's remark that "immediately the ship was at the land" (6:21) clearly suggests something supernatural in the event.

"They were sore amazed in themselves"—"Exceedingly within themselves were they astonished" (Rotherham). The remark, only in Mark, records their strong, inward reaction to the experiences. This strong verb is in the imperfect tense and pictures the disciples as thrown into a continuing astonishment which carried them quite beyond their normal selves. *Sore,* or exceedingly, indicates that their amazement was greater than there was just reason for. Many manuscripts strengthen the statement by the use of a double superlative, "exceedingly beyond measure." *In themselves* stresses the inward feeling but does not deny an outward expression. Matthew explicitly recorded an outward reaction in that the disciples reverently acknowledged Jesus' claim to deity: "Of a truth thou art the Son of God" (14:33).

"For they considered not *the miracle* of the loaves"—a negative assertion in explanation of their utter astonishment. Because of their failure to understand the true significance of the multiplication of the loaves, they had no basis for an intelligent understanding of this demonstration of His power over the waters. They had not grasped the significance of the miracle that afternoon as a pointer preparing them to understand the true character of Christ. Their failure to understand was due not to willful obstinacy but to mental sluggishness.

"For their heart was hardened"—a positive description of their condition. *Heart* here includes their intellectual nature in its relationship to the spiritual. *Hardened* denotes a state of being hardened. They were in a state of being spiritually unperceptive. Their reaction was unworthy of those to whom it had been given to know "the mystery of the kingdom of God" (Mark 4:11). Brooks comments, "This verse contains one of the harshest statements about the disciples' lack of understanding. Even so they were still followers of Jesus and not enemies. This is Markan irony at its boldest."[21]

---

[21] James A. Brooks, *Mark,* New American Commentary, p. 112.

The two miracles just recorded were clearly intended by Jesus to be part of His training of the Twelve. They were well suited to lead the disciples into a fuller and truer understanding of His own unique person. His firm rejection of the desire of the crowd that afternoon to make Him king (John 6:15) must have deeply perplexed the Twelve and been the object of serious discussion among themselves in the boat. It threatened to cloud their confidence in Him and aroused confusion in them concerning His intentions. The supernatural way in which Jesus revealed Himself to them that night was obviously intended to bolster their faith. Even if they could not understand His ways, it let them maintain their confidence in Him because of what they knew Him to be. This strange nocturnal experience must strengthen their faith for the further testing that lay ahead the next day (John 6:22-71).

c. Ministry of Healing Among the People (6:53-56).

This intensely vivid paragraph of the healing ministry of Jesus has a brief parallel in Matthew 14:34-36. Mark's summary picture apparently relates to the work of more than one day. No teaching is mentioned, but Jesus is pictured as moving rapidly from place to place.

"When they had passed over"—the welcome termination of a laborious and perilous crossing. The crossing was from east to west.

"They came into the land of Gennesaret"—the place of landing was apparently due to the adverse wind during the night. Some suggest that Gennesaret was the name of a town or village, but the probable reference is to the famous plain on the northwestern shore which gave its name to the lake, "the Lake of Gennesaret" (Luke 5:1; 1 Macc. 11:67). It was about three miles long and a mile wide and was densely populated. Josephus described its fertility, climate, and beauty in glowing terms.[22]

"And drew to the shore"—the verb, found only here in the New Testament, means that the boat was secured on the shore either by dropping anchor or by fastening to an anchorage.

"When they were come out of the ship"—it must have been early morning, shortly after daybreak.

"Straightway they knew him"—the indefinite "they" denotes the inhabitants of Gennesaret. Their immediate recognition of Jesus shows that He was now well known to the masses of Galilee.

"Ran through that whole region round about"—the realization that Jesus was in their area immediately stimulated excited activity. The news was spread with haste and zeal. The aorist verb *ran round about,*

---

[22] Josephus *Wars of the Jews* 3. 10. 8.

occurring only here in the New Testament, summarily pictures the hurried circulation of the news throughout the plain.

"Began to carry about in beds those that were sick"—the intended result in spreading the news. *Began* indicates that the procession of sick people being brought on their beds or pallets began at once and continued afterward. *To carry about* is present tense and vividly pictures the sick being carried in various directions, suggesting that when they did not find Jesus in one place they carried their sick to another place where they were likely to find Him. The "beds" here used were pallets or cots upon which the sick might readily be brought to Jesus.

"Where they heard he was"—the imperfect tense, "were hearing," denotes that those carrying the sick were repeatedly making inquiries about where Jesus was and were being informed that He was in such and such a place.

"Whithersoever he entered"—whatever the place, Jesus always found a crowd awaiting Him. The imperfect tense pictures the repeated occurrences. The scope in this verse seems wider than the plain of Gennesaret.

"Into villages, or cities, or country"—the repeated *into* (in the original) marks the various kinds of places Jesus entered. The enumeration suggests that Jesus was moving around rather rapidly without any protracted teaching ministries. *Country* here apparently denotes open fields where people would be at work in large numbers. Swete remarks that "the combination of the three covers every collection of dwellings large and small."[23]

"Laid the sick in the streets"—or literally the "marketplaces" (*agorais*), open spaces, either just inside the city walls or near the center of the city, where the people gathered for various purposes. Usually only cities had such marketplaces, but the term here may have as its original meaning a place where people assemble. The sick were brought to the places where Jesus would be most likely to pass.

"Besought him"—the imperfect tense indicates that the appeal was made again and again. Faith in His healing ability was general.

"That they might touch if it were but the border of his garment"— they simply desired that the sick might be permitted as a definite act to touch the border of His garment (cf. 5:27). This suggests that the story of the healing of the woman with the flow of blood through just such a simple touch (5:25-34) had become widely known. Swete thinks that "so simple a means of obtaining a cure appealed to the popular

---

[23] Swete, pp. 141-42.

imagination.''[24] However, the healings were effected not by the touch but by the will of Jesus, who consented to honor the faith in Him thus expressed. Alexander points out that such a procedure would make it possible for Jesus ''to reach greater numbers in a given time without destroying all perceptible connection between the subject and the worker of the miracle.''[25]

''As many as touched him were made whole''—*touched,* an aorist tense, points to the momentary act of touching. *Were made whole* is imperfect, denoting the rapid succession of cases healed. The verb is literally ''were being saved,'' were rescued from their affliction and restored to physical wholeness.

This scene makes clear that ''out of all the facets of Jesus' ministry—preaching, teaching, healing the sick, casting out demons, raising the dead, feeding the multitudes—the people identified Him first as a healer.''[26] Although many of them did not understand or receive the spiritual truths He taught, they were eager to profit personally from the physical and material blessings He bestowed. But the love and compassion of Jesus made Him willing and ready to minister to their conscious needs.

d. Controversy Concerning Defilement (7:1-23).

Mark's ''and'' (Gr.) connects this paragraph with what has gone before by way of contrast. The phenomenal popularity of Jesus with the masses (6:53-56) stood in striking contrast to the hostility of the Jewish leaders. No close chronological sequence is indicated. This controversy evidently took place after the Passover that was near when Jesus fed the five thousand (John 6:4). The mention of the scribes coming from Jerusalem indicates that it took place in Galilee, but the exact place is uncertain. It was apparently in or near Capernaum. Only Matthew gives a parallel account (15:1-20). Luke records a similar controversy later in Perea (11:37-52). The coming of these Jewish leaders from Jerusalem clearly marks the focal point of the opposition to Jesus. In this controversy with the Jewish leaders, Jesus struck at their perverted traditions, which raised the controversy (vv. 1-13), and then dealt with the problem of the nature of true defilement, which underlay the controversy (vv. 14-23).

1) Condemnation of human tradition (vv. 1-13). ''Then came together unto him the Pharisees''—the historical present tense again

---

[24] Ibid., p. 142.

[25] Joseph Addison Alexander, *The Gospel According to Mark,* p. 178.

[26] McKenna, pp. 147-48.

vividly conceives this gathering. The Pharisees have not been mentioned in Mark since 3:6, where they were last seen plotting the death of Jesus. The use of the definite article marks them as a class distinct from other groups. The passive voice[27] ("are gathered together," Gr.) does not imply external compulsion but indicates that they were motivated by their own inner concern to counter the popularity of Jesus. They voluntarily came to face Jesus personally. *Unto him* denotes that the Person of Jesus was the rallying point for this assembling of Pharisees.

"And certain of the scribes, which came from Jerusalem"—implying that the scribes were not as well represented as the Pharisees. Their coming meant the arrival in Galilee of another "fact-finding commission" for the Jerusalem authorities (cf. 3:22). Mark's wording might mean that only the scribes came from Jerusalem and that the Pharisees were residents of Galilee, but Matthew 15:1 indicates that this entire delegation came from Jerusalem. The use of the definite article serves to distinguish the scribes from the Pharisees as a distinct group. They were the official interpreters of the Mosaic law and the guardians of its sanctity. Their interpretations formed the basis for the practices of the Pharisees. These scribes had apparently been selected for their known skill in dealing with violations of the law, of which Jesus was suspected.

"Saw some of his disciples"—*disciples* need not be limited to the Twelve, but that is the probable meaning. Members of this delegation had actually seen some of them, not all twelve, in the very act of committing a flagrant violation of the tradition which the scribes zealously promoted. No formal meal is indicated. Apparently amidst the pressing demands on their time, some of the Twelve had stopped to take some food. Alexander remarks that "this incident naturally brings to view the constant and intrusive *surveillance* to which our Lord and his disciples were subjected."[28]

"Eat bread with defiled, that is to say, with unwashen, hands"—this states the essence of the report of those who had witnessed the act. The word rendered "defiled" means "common" and in classical Greek was used of that which was "common" as contrasted to "private." The scribal charge was that the disciples were eating with hands that were ceremonially "common," had not been separated from the defilement resulting from contact with profane things. They held that such unclean hands must be purified by an act of ceremonial washing

---

[27] The voice may be middle, "are gathering themselves together."

[28] Alexander, p. 178.

to remove the defilement. The charge was not that the disciples were eating with grimy hands but that they had not cleansed their hands with the proper rite of purification. This scribal insistence upon ceremonial washing before eating was a comparatively recent traditional development. The full development of these scribal regulations concerning ceremonial purity were later embodied in the Mishnah. The last and longest of the six divisions of the Mishnah is given over to this matter of "cleanness."[29]

The verb "they found fault" at the end of verse 2 in the King James Version follows the Textus Receptus; it is not found in the oldest manuscripts and is best omitted. If a full stop is made at the end of verse 1, this verse is thus left incomplete, or has its verb in verse 5. The American Standard Version regards verse 2 as the direct continuation of verse 1. In either case, verses 3-4 are a parenthetical explanation inserted by Mark for the benefit of his non-Jewish readers. Verses 3-4 have no parallel in Matthew.

"For the Pharisees, and all the Jews"—*for* indicates that the brief explanation in verse 2, "that is, unwashen," is now to be set in its larger context. The controversy arose out of the common practice of *the Pharisees, and all the Jews*. The order implies that the practices began with the Pharisees, the strictest sect among the Jews (Acts 26:5), and by now was commonly observed by all the Jews. The expression is not to be pressed too literally, for there were many Jewish people, scorned by the scribes as "the people of the land," who did not rigidly observe all these ceremonial regulations. The meaning apparently is that all the Jews who wished to be known as righteous adhered to these ritualistic washings.[30] The expression is popularly used to denote the widespread adherence to this Pharisaic practice.

"Except they wash *their* hands oft, eat not"—no eating without prior purification. The present tenses denote this as the standing practice. The manuscripts show that the scribes in copying Mark found the word *pugnē* ("diligently," ASV; "carefully," NASV) difficult. A few omitted it, while others have *pukna* ("oft," KJV). The preferred word *pugnē* literally means "with [the] fist," but the precise meaning intended is still a puzzle.[31] It describes the manner of washing, but the

---

[29] Herbert Danby, trans., *The Mishnah,* pp. 603-789.

[30] The suggestion of Lyman Abbott that it means "the Judeans, the inhabitants of Judea, the southern province of the Holy Land, where the influence of the ecclesiastics was very considerably greater than in Galilee," is less probable ("The Gospel According to Mark," in *An Illustrated Commentary on the Gospels* [1906]).

[31] In despair, the translators of the RSV left it untranslated.

exact procedure has been differently conceived. "With the fist" may be viewed figuratively or literally. The ASV "diligently" is a figurative rendering, in accord with the Hebrew idiom of the fist as denoting strength or vigor. But Mark's non-Jewish readers probably were not familiar with this expression. It seems best to take "with the fist" literally, but the exact procedure is not clear. It has been taken to mean a washing (1) in which one clenched fist was turned about in the hollow of the other hand; (2) up to the elbow, or to the wrists; (3) with a handful of water; or (4) by rubbing the hand with the dry fist.

"Holding the tradition of the elders"—the Pharisees held firmly to these ceremonial washings as part of "the tradition of the elders," an expression occurring in the Gospels only in this passage and the Matthew parallel. *Tradition* designates the teaching that is passed on from teacher to pupil. *Elders* denotes not the elders of the synagogue or the members of the Sanhedrin as the upholders of this teaching, but rather the noted Jewish teachers of the law of the past whose judgments were regarded as binding and their interpretations diligently passed on to others by the scribes. To enhance the binding character of the oral tradition, the claim was sometimes advanced that God had delivered these teachings to Moses, who passed them on orally to the elders. During the day of Jesus, this tradition was orally transmitted, but it was later codified and embodied in the Mishnah. The development of these traditions was motivated by the commendable purpose to preserve the integrity of the Mosaic law by guarding against any violations thereof. The tradition was built up as "a fence around the Law."[32] The intention was to keep the actual law from being broken by adding many minute stipulations around it which must be observed. All these additional requirements made the religious life a grievous burden. The problem was tradition alienated from the law.

"And *when they come* from the market"—as shown by the italics, the original is "and from the market." It may refer to that which is brought from the market or to the people coming from the marketplace. The former view is represented in the version of Moffatt, which reads, "they decline to eat what comes from the market till they have washed it."[33] But it is more natural to take the phrase as referring to the conduct of the scrupulous Jews concerning their own purification upon coming from the crowded marketplace where the possibility of contracting

---

[32] Danby, p. 452.

[33] The view is as old as the Arabic version of Tatian's *Diatessaron,* the oldest known harmony of the Gospels, ca. A.D. 160. The versions of Goodspeed, Norlie, Williams, and TEV are similar.

personal defilement was very great. Under either view, the washing was not for sanitary purposes but was ceremonial.

"Except they wash, they eat not"—as involving more serious chances of personal defilement, the return from the marketplace was followed with a bath. "Bathe" is the reading of most manuscripts, but two important manuscripts read "sprinkle"[34] This reading probably arose from the fact that the scribes felt a practical difficulty with "bathe."[35] The reading "bathe" forms a natural climax. Before any eating, the Pharisees always washed their hands; when returning from the marketplace, they always took a bath. Others, less probably, think that only the immersion of the hands is meant. Having been jostled in the marketplace, the scrupulous Pharisees would feel the need to purify their entire person. The Levitical law required such bathing only of ministering priests (Lev. 16:4, 24, 26; 22:6) and of others on specific occasions (Lev. 14:8-9; 15:5-27).

"Many other things there be, which they have received to hold"— scribal concern for ceremonial purity extended also to the dishes used. *Received,* in the aorist tense, looks back to their actual acceptance, while *to hold,* present tense, denotes their continued efforts to maintain the traditions. Hurtado feels that "*many other things* seems intended as a criticism of what Mark regarded as a complicated mass of regulations and procedures."[36]

"Washing of cups, and pots, brasen vessels"—to assure their ceremonial cleanness. Cups were the ordinary drinking vessels. Pots were larger jugs or pitchers from which the cups were filled. They were household vessels in which water for drinking or purifying was kept. Such vessels might be made either of wood or earthenware. Brazen vessels were larger vessels of brass or copper used for cooking. The Mishnah devotes thirty chapters to the matter of the purification of vessels.[37]

"[And, Gr.] the Pharisees and scribes asked him"—the *and,* Mark's favorite conjunction, shows the continuation of the narrative from verse 2. The articles with both *Pharisees* and *scribes* marks them as two distinct yet allied parties. *Asked,* the vivid historical present,

---

[34] Sinaiticus and Vaticanus, both from the fourth century, read "sprinkle." It is the reading adopted in the Westcott and Hort and the Nestle texts.

[35] This is specially true if "and tables" (KJV)—better, "couches"—is read at the end of v. 4. The genuineness of the addition is doubtful and is omitted by the critical editors.

[36] Larry W. Hurtado, *Mark,* Good News Commentary, p. 100.

[37] Danby, pp. 604-49.

suggests a formal and dignified inquiry which they feel they have every right to make. Although the question was ostensibly about His disciples, it was addressed to Jesus and was really a direct challenge to Jesus Himself.

"Why walk not thy disciples according to the tradition of the elders"—*why* asks the reason for the conduct of the disciples. As their Master, He was held responsible for the reprehensible conduct. *Walk* is a common Hebrew figure to denote habitual conduct. Only on this occasion is it used in the synoptics with this figurative connotation. (The figurative meaning is common in the Fourth Gospel and in the Pauline Epistles.) *According to* points to the standard for measuring conduct, which for the questioners was the tradition of the elders. Their seeing Jesus' disciples eating with "defiled hands" is now used to confront Jesus with the larger question of "the tradition of the elders."

"But eat bread with unwashen hands"—*but* marks the contrast between the indicated standard and the conduct of the disciples. It implies that they had no right to act as they did. *Bread,* literally "the bread," seems specifically to point to the bread they had before them.

"And said unto them"—in His reply, Jesus made no reference to the conduct of the disciples but dealt directly with the basic issue underlying the question. The time had come to deal openly and firmly with this issue which lay at the very heart of the controversy between Jesus and the Jewish leaders. In verses 6-8 He condemned their position on the basis of the Scriptures which they professed to accept as authoritative, and in verses 9-13 He exposed the results of their position.

"Well hath Esaias prophesied of you hypocrites"—the quotation of Isaiah 29:13 is from the Septuagint almost verbatim. *Well* (*kalos,* "beautifully, excellently, appropriately") stresses that the words of Isaiah, speaking as God's prophet, admirably fitted the Pharisees and scribes. *Prophesied* does not mean that the people to whom Jesus spoke were the special objects of Isaiah's prophecy; it means they were a perfect fulfillment of the picture Isaiah drew of his contemporaries. *You hypocrites,* literally "you, the hypocrites," marks them as conspicuous examples of hypocrites in all ages. Here for the first time is this charge explicitly made against the Pharisees and scribes. The term, which appears only in the synoptics,[38] carried the basic picture of a man giving off a judgment under the cover of a mask; it is the picture of a man assuming an identity and character different from what he really is. Perhaps the charge is not so much that they were consciously

---

[38] *Hypocrite* occurs twenty times: fifteen in Matthew, once in Mark, four times in Luke.

acting an unreal part as that there was a radical inconsistency between what they claimed to be and really were. They professed to be followers of God but were in reality followers of men. "Religion had been smothered beneath ritual. Washing the hands counted for more than the devotion of the heart. They were careful of petty rules, and careless of the great commands of God."[39]

"As it is written"—better, "as it stands written," indicating that the scriptural portrait stands permanently on record.

"This people honoureth me with *their* lips"—their continued verbal profession was that they were honoring Jehovah.

"But their heart is far from me"—exposing the contrast between their outward profession and their inner condition. *Is far from me* pictures them as actively holding their heart at a great distance from God. They were more concerned with their rituals than with their own inner heart relationship with God.

In verse 7, the quotation from the Septuagint differs from the Hebrew which the ASV renders, "Their fear of me is a commandment of men which hath been taught them" (Isa. 29:13). The Septuagint is a free but effective paraphrase of the Hebrew text, the fundamental meaning being the same. Jesus used the Septuagint as more explicitly stating the charge. Isaiah charged that the fear of Jehovah expressed by the Israelites was learned by rote from men without a conscious experience of its inner reality. *In vain do they worship me* admitted that they had a form of devout piety, but it was in vain, void of constructive results.

"Teaching *for* doctrines the commandments of men"—the reason for the futility of their worship. *Teaching,* a present participle, denotes their continued activity in setting forth as their doctrines the precepts of men. That which they taught as doctrines, authoritative teachings, were in reality nothing but commandments originated by mere men. Swete suggested that the plural *commandments* "perhaps points to the multiplicity of the details, and the absence of an underlying principle."[40] Worship acceptable to God must be based on His own requirements, not human arrangements which replace the divine requirements.

With the quotation completed, Jesus made a direct attack upon His opponents with a double charge.

---

[39] Jones, p. 214.

[40] Swete, p. 147.

"Laying aside[41] the commandment of God"—their guilt was not merely adding to but deserting *the commandment of God,* referring to the aggregate of the divine commandments as a whole. *Of God* underlines the source and nature of what they are deserting.

"Ye hold the tradition of men"—*hold* indicates that they had taken a firm hold on these traditions and continued to cling faithfully to them. What they adhered to was simply humanly devised tradition. By placing the humanly devised fence around the divine law and assigning binding authority to their human additions, they were in reality displacing the law of God. Whenever any human interpretation is substituted for the Word of God itself as the authoritative standard, the same evil reappears. Jesus categorically rejected the binding character of their tradition.

"And he said unto them"—a favorite formula with Mark, best taken as indicating a new phase of the discussion (cf. 4:13, 21, 24, 26, 30). Verses 9-13 show the evil consequences of their tradition.

"Full well"—the identical adverb rendered "well" in verse 6. There it was used seriously; here it conveys a note of stinging sarcasm: "This is the beautiful result of your practice of fencing the law with your traditions!"

"Ye reject the commandment of God"—the present tense asserts this as their continual practice. To *reject* means "to set aside, to declare invalid that which had been authoritatively laid down by regarding it as no longer in force." This was the way they were treating God's commandment.

"That ye may keep your own tradition"—their overruling purpose. *Keep* is aorist tense, setting forth as their deliberate intention to adhere effectively to their tradition. *Your own tradition* indicates that they had accepted and were advocating it; hence, they shared in the guilt of thereby nullifying the commandment of God. Christ dissociated Himself from any share in that guilt.

To translate this verse as a question, as some propose—"Are ye doing well to reject the commandment of God in order to keep your tradition?"—is to seriously weaken its import. It was not a searching question addressed to the conscience of His opponents but a shattering verdict on their practice. It succinctly asserts the true effect of their tradition.

---

[41] Many manuscripts have the participle *leaving* rather than the finite verb "ye leave" (ASV). The participle would set forth the reprehensible condition under which they were clinging to their manmade tradition.

"For Moses said"—assumes the Mosaic authorship of the quotations. Both passages are quoted as by Moses, but in verse 13 they also are equated with the Word of God. Moses was not the giver of the law, only the agent through whom God gave it. Since both Jesus and His opponents accepted the law as binding, Jesus laid down a firm basis for His condemnation of their tradition. Jesus built His case around the divine command that parents must be honored. His quotations establish this positively and negatively.

"Honour thy father and thy mother"—quotes the Septuagint of Exodus 20:12, the fifth commandment. God stipulates this as the abiding duty of a man toward his parents. To honor a person implies bestowing the proper esteem due that person.

The second quotation, from Exodus 21:17, shows how seriously God regards this matter of honoring parents. "Speaketh evil of" (ASV) does not mean "curse" (KJV) but "to speak ill of, revile, insult." Such action toward parents was clearly a violation of the fifth commandment. *Let him die the death* means to come to an end; the life of the offender is to end by the infliction of death in judicial punishment.

"But ye say"—the emphatic *ye* stresses the contradiction between God's demand and their teaching, as shown in the illustration which Jesus placed in their mouth. The case is hypothetically stated ("suppose a man should say"), but Taylor correctly remarks that the supposition "is pointless unless there were actual cases of the kind."[42] Rotherham renders the supposed words of this son to his parents, "Korban! that is, A gift, whatsoever out of me thou mightest be profited." *Corban* is a Hebrew term which Mark again translates for his readers, meaning "given to God." It denotes money or goods which have been dedicated to God by a vow and which, as consecrated to God, could be used only for sacred purposes. In an argument or fit of anger, the son might declare, "that wherewith thou mightest have been profited from me is Corban!" When the son had once pronounced this vow concerning that from which the parents had rightly expected support, it was henceforth to be regarded as consecrated and not used for the support of the parents. This view was based on the proposition that what has been devoted to God is holy and cannot be used for secular purposes.

In the ASV, the if-clause is left unfinished. The translators of the KJV completed it by adding, "he shall be free." But the words are not in the original, either here or in Matthew. Lindsay remarks, "Our Lord

---

[42] Taylor, p. 340.

seems to have stopped short, allowing the words to be filled up by the indignation of the hearers."[43]

Verse 12 gives Christ's condemnation of the evil result of their tradition. Although the regulation concerning *Corban* had not been invented for this purpose, the eagerness of the scribes to safeguard the validity of vows, especially when temple interests were involved, led them to sanction this conclusion. The Mishnah shows that later rabbinical authorities modified this ruling (Nedarim 9:1).[44]

"Making the word of God of none effect through your tradition, which ye have delivered"—pressing home their guilt. *Making of none effect* is stronger than *reject* in verse 9 and means "to deprive of authority, to cancel." In the papyruses it is used of annulling contracts. The Pharisees and scribes were thus cancelling out the divine Word by means of "your tradition, which ye have delivered." The original contains a word play which the English cannot reproduce. Both the terms *tradition* and *delivered* have a common root.[45] *Have delivered* is aorist tense; they had not only received the tradition but also passed it on as a definite act; thus they were inescapably involved in the guilt.

"Many such like things do ye"—the illustration of *Corban* was not an isolated instance. *Do* is present tense and charges them with repeatedly doing "many such like things," many things that had the same reprehensible character.[46]

2) Source of true defilement (vv. 14-23). The controversy concerning the tradition of the elders had raised the deeper question of the nature and source of true defilement. It was a matter of fundamental importance, and Jesus did not leave the question untouched. Verse 15 gives His concise, somewhat enigmatical statement of the basic principle, while verses 17-23 give His full statement to the disciples.

"When he had called all the people unto him [again, Gr.]"— suggests that the common people lingered a short distance away. Apparently they had respectfully withdrawn a little when the dignified delegation from Jerusalem approached Jesus. *Again* implies that the people had previously been close about Him. *Called unto him* indicates that He invited them to a close face-to-face relationship.

---

[43] Thomas M. Lindsay, "The Gospel According to St. Mark," in *Handbooks for Bible Classes,* p. 139.

[44] Danby, p. 275.

[45] We might crudely convey the word play by rendering "your deliverance, which ye delivered," or "your tradition, which ye tradition," that is, pass on as tradition.

[46] The words here are a genuine part of the text, but not in v. 8, where the Textus Receptus also inserts them.

"Hearken unto me every one *of you,* and understand"—the authoritative call indicated that He was about to enunciate a principle of far-reaching importance. *Every one,* peculiar to Mark, stresses its universal nature. The aorist tenses urge careful attention to, and intelligent perception of, what was to be said. They may imply that, by contrast, the Pharisees and scribes, as zealous expounders of their human traditions, were unable to understand its real sense.

His basic canon concerning defilement is stated both negatively and positively in verse 15. Jesus spoke as a moralist, not as a physiologist. Jones aptly characterizes His pronouncement as "one of those great sweeping truths that Christ delighted to utter."[47]

"There is nothing from without [the, Gr.] man"—the statement is formulated in the most comprehensive terms; in Matthew, it is more restricted, indicating that foods are in view. *The man* is generic, individualizing him as a representative of the class, "the human being."

"That entering into him can defile him"—food entering the man's body is unable to make him morally unclean. *Can,* "is able," states this as a standing fact. It cannot make the man "common" (cf. v. 2), impart that moral impurity which characterizes the unsanctified world.

"But the things which come out of him"—the things that have their origin in the inner moral nature of man himself. Their nature is here left undefined. The double use of the preposition *ek,* "out," prefixed to the verb as well as the noun, strengthens the emphasis that these things that defile are not "an import, but an export."[48]

Christ's solemn affirmation gave utterance to a moral truth which is today recognized as commonplace, but was startlingly original when uttered. The view of Rawlinson, that Jesus was simply contrasting two types of pollution—namely, "that pollutions from within are more serious than pollutions from without"[49]—is inadequate in view of verse 19. His utterance placed Him in direct opposition to the scribal view concerning ceremonial defilement. Literally understood, it also placed Him in opposition to the regulations concerning clean and unclean food in the Mosaic law (Lev. 11; Deut. 14). To the extent that His words involve a real opposition to these ceremonial stipulations of the law, they demonstrate His function not to destroy the law but to fulfill it, revealing the principle that these stipulations illustrated. The Pharisees

---

[47] Jones, p. 216.

[48] James Morison, *A Practical Commentary on the Gospel According to St. Mark,* p. 188.

[49] A.E.J. Rawlinson, *St. Mark,* p. 96.

recognized the radical implications of His statement and were deeply offended (Matt. 15:12).

Verse 16 is of doubtful manuscript authority and is omitted in the ASV. It does not occur in the parallel passage in Matthew. However, it has considerable manuscript support, and its appropriateness here may support its genuineness. More probably its appropriateness here suggests its scribal introduction from 4:9.

"When he was entered into the house from the people"—*house* does not have the definite article here and may simply mean indoors, where He would be away from the crowd, or His own home, His place of residence at Capernaum (cf. 2:1)—probably the former.

"His disciples asked him concerning the parable"—Matthew noted that Peter was the spokesman for the disciples (15:15). It is another instance where a public utterance by Jesus became the subject of further discussion with the disciples in private. *The parable* refers to verse 15 and indicates that the disciples felt it was a dark saying or riddle which they did not understand.

"Are ye so without understanding also?"—*so,* or "thus," standing at the beginning, looks back to their inquiry. It shows that they "also," like the uninstructed multitude, were still without understanding, without that discernment of the meaning which the proper use of their intellectual ability would have given them. The words may be taken as a question or as an exclamation of surprise. The question seems preferable. In either case, the words carry a note of rebuke. After all the instruction given them, He should be able to expect more of them.

"Do ye not perceive"—implying that He rightly expected that they should apprehend. What they failed to understand was not a mystery which required a revelation but an obvious truth which they could have understood by attentive thought. What they had failed to apprehend He restated in the form of a question. It restates verse 15 with a reason appended (v. 19).

"Because it entereth not into his heart, but into the belly"—explaining why food which is eaten cannot defile. It does not enter into one's heart, the inner personality, and does not change one's moral nature. Food enters only one's belly, the abdominal cavity with its digestive organs, and these are not moral agents. They simply extract the nourishment from the food eaten for the maintenance of the body, and that which has no nutritive value they expel "into the draught," the "privy" or the "latrine." All this is a physiological process which does not require any moral reactions of the inner spiritual man, hence cannot morally defile.

"Purging all meats"—The phrase may be taken as a part of the words of Jesus or as an added comment by Mark. Under the former view, it is to be closely connected with the statement of the expulsion of the excrement, thus purifying the food eaten by the removal of the useless portion of it from the body. This connection would call for the participle to be neuter gender, but it is textually certain that it is masculine. The masculine participle is best regarded as grammatically going back to the subject of the verb *Saith* in verse 18. This connection may be made clear by the use of quotation marks:

> And he says unto them—''Thus are you also without discernment? Perceived you not that nothing entering into the man from without is able to defile him, because it enters not into the heart but into the belly and goes out into the privy?''—purifying all foods.

It seems best to follow this interpretation, which goes back to Origen. This makes the appended phrase a comment by Mark himself and indicates that the words were not actually spoken by Jesus at the time. In the light of subsequent events, it became clear that this was the logical implication of His words. This elimination of the distinction between clean and unclean food became vividly clear to Peter in connection with his vision at Joppa (Acts 10:15), where this same verb, *purifying,* is employed. Christ's abolition of these ceremonial distinctions was part of His purpose to fulfill the law. These ceremonial regulations in the law had a function, teaching symbolically the reality and importance of *moral* purity. They demanded an external separation which pointed to the need for an inner heart condition of separation unto God. But these external regulations in themselves did not convey the purity of heart to which they pointed. They were the shadow and not the substance (Heb. 10:1). When they found their fulfillment in Christ, these ceremonial foreshadowings became obsolete. It was a truth that the early church was slow to grasp. This comment, found only in Mark's Gospel, may well reflect Peter's acknowledgment of the true implications of Christ's words as he later recounted the teaching given here.

"And he said"—marking the resumption of the words of Jesus after the interpolated comment by Mark. In verses 20-23, Jesus gave an expanded statement of the true nature of defilement. The positive fact that moral defilement arises from within the man is introduced by a restatement of the latter part of verse 15.

"For from within, out of the heart of men"—*for* introduces the justification for the preceding statement, while the two phrases "from within" and "out of the heart" emphasize the nature of that which proceeds out of the man. *From within* underlines the contrast with that which is from without. The defiling things proceed out of the heart of

men, out of the inner moral nature of human beings. Thus, "to concentrate on issues of ritual cleanliness for eating, while neglecting the
source of evil in human life, is truly to be imprisoned."[50]

"Proceed evil thoughts"—*thoughts,* occurring almost always with
an evil connotation in the New Testament, denotes well-considered
thoughts, deliberations, reasonings. The repeated article with the adjective, "the thoughts, the evil ones," stresses their nature as morally
bad. They are thoughts that unite with the will to evoke action. Thus
Guelich holds that "evil divisings" more nearly captures the thrust of
the term.[51] Standing before the verb in the original, they are viewed as
the root of the varied evils enumerated. Mark's list contains twelve
items, six in the plural and six in the singular. Matthew's list (Matt.
15:19) contains only six items; it includes "false witness," not found
in Mark's list. Both lists agree in indicating that all these sins begin in
the region of the heart, the inner man. The manuscripts do not fully
agree in their order for these sins. Mark's list reveals no logical order
in the different items given. The list bears impressive witness to the
unorganized diversity of sin.

"Adulteries, fornications, murders, thefts"—the plurals indicate
successive acts of these different evils, all well known in the tragic
history of fallen mankind. They are placed first, as they set forth the
worst offenses against morality and justice. *Fornications* is a broad
term used to cover every kind of unlawful sexual intercourse, but it is
distinguished here from *adulteries*, which denotes the unlawful sexual
relations of the married person.

"Covetousness, wickedness"—coveting is the inner craving for
more of that to which one has no right; the plural ("covetings," ASV)
indicates the various ways in which this spirit expresses itself in acts
of selfish grasping for self-gratification. Since the word is often associated with other terms denoting sexual sins, it may perhaps here denote
deeds of lust. *Wickedness,* the last in the series of plurals, denotes the
various ways in which the spirit of maliciousness or evil-mindedness
expresses itself in action.

"Deceit, lasciviousness, an evil eye, blasphemy, pride, foolishness"—these six singular nouns denote moral evils. *Deceit,* containing
the underlying thought of a lure or bait, signifies trickery, cunning,
guile. It thus denotes that vice which cunningly devises varied means
of entrapping others for personal advantage. This term covers the

---

[50] Donald English, p. 146.

[51] Guelich, p. 379.

thought of false witness in Matthew's list. *Lasciviousness* is unrestrained licentiousness which unblushingly plunges into moral debauchery in open defiance of public opinion. It is a wantonness which shocks public decency. *An evil eye* is a Hebrew expression denoting a jealous or grudging attitude (Deut. 28:54; Prov. 23:6; Matt. 20:15). The term does not mean a witch's casting a spell upon someone. *Blasphemy* means injurious speech which may be against either God or men; the context suggests the meaning of slander or defamation, rather than religious blasphemy. *Pride,* a common Greek word found only here in the New Testament, has the root meaning "to show oneself above others" and pictures an individual who has a swollen opinion of himself, exalting himself above others, whom he regards with scornful contempt. "It is the sin of the 'superior' person, who loves to make himself conspicuous and 'sets all others at nought' (Luke xviii. 9)."[52] *Foolishness* denotes not an intellectual but a moral quality and may be translated "folly." It is that moral senselessness which lacks ethical perception and ignores religious responsibilities. It includes all forms of moral senselessness, in thought, word, or deed. Standing at the end of the list, it pictures the character of the fool, one who does not know God and has no desire to serve Him.

"All these evil things come from within"—summarizing all the moral viciousness that has its origin within man's evil nature.

"And defile the man"—again asserting the true source of defilement. Man is the fountain of his own uncleanness. Since this and the preceding verb are both present tense, Wuest suggestively renders, "are constantly proceeding and are constantly defiling the man."[53] Jesus released His followers from the fear of defilement from things coming to them from without but uncovered a vastly more serious defilement springing out of man's own nature.

---

[52] Plummer, p. 187.

[53] Kenneth S. Wuest, *Mark in the Greek New Testament for the English Reader,* p. 150.

7
Withdrawals from Galilee
(Part 3; 7:24–8:13)

3. Third Withdrawal and Return (7:24–8:13)

From the route of travel implied in Mark's account, Jesus' third withdrawal from Galilee must have extended over a period of considerable time. Yet Mark records only three events during the withdrawal and one immediately upon His return to Galilee. The appeal by the Syrophoenician woman (7:24-30) came at the beginning of the withdrawal, whereas the cure of the deaf stammerer (7:31-37) and the feeding of the four thousand (8:1-10) occurred near the close of the withdrawal. His return to Galilee was immediately marked by another confrontation with the Pharisees (8:11-13). Only Matthew includes a parallel account of this withdrawal (15:21–16:4).

a. Appeal of the Syrophoenician Woman (7:24-30).

A new turn in Mark's narrative is indicated by the geographical reference as well as his rare use of the particle *de* to open the paragraph. Mark commonly employs *and* (*kai*) to begin a new paragraph, but here he uses *de,* perhaps best rendered *now.*[1] It serves to introduce an additional fact. Not only did Jesus take a firm stand against the Jewish leaders' regard for their traditions, but He also left for non-Jewish territory, thus symbolically breaking down the barriers which kept the gospel from the Gentiles.

"From thence he arose, and went"—*arose* simply marks the preparatory action for the departure. *From thence* naturally relates to the place, not named, where the controversy with the Jewish leaders took place, apparently Capernaum. *Went* merely records the fact of the

---

[1] Only six of the eighty-eight sections in Mark, according to the Westcott and Hort text, begin with the particle *de,* while eighty begin with *kai.*

departure, but Matthew 15:21 designates it as a withdrawal. It was a prudent withdrawal from the hostility of the Jewish leaders, but there is no indication that Jesus withdrew from Galilee because of danger of arrest.

"Into the borders of Tyre and Sidon"—the word rendered "borders" in the singular means a boundary, but in the plural, as here, it means the region or the district of Tyre and Sidon.[2] The territory around these two great cities on the Mediterranean constituted what was known as the land of Phoenicia. It lay north and west of Galilee. Since the days of the Roman general Pompey, Phoenicia was politically a part of Syria, but geographically and culturally it remained distinct. *Into* implies that Jesus did cross the border of this area and went deep into the country. This trip marked the first time during His ministry that Jesus actually penetrated recognized pagan territory. It foreshadowed the extension of the gospel to the Gentile world.

"Entered into an house"—whether of a Gentile stranger or of a Jewish friend is not indicated. Mark's concern was not with the householder but with the woman whose story follows.

"Would have no man know *it*"—clearly, His purpose was not to carry on a public ministry in that area. He desired to keep His presence unknown. He needed relief from the pressure of the crowds as well as privacy in order to have uninterrupted time to instruct the disciples, a work which had been much hindered by the crowds. There is no mention of His work in any town during this withdrawal.

"But he could not be hid"—the comment is peculiar to Mark. His fame had preceded Him across the border. People from the area had previously attended His ministry in Galilee (3:8), and He would be readily recognized.

"For a *certain* woman"—the strong adversative, "but" (*all'*), introduces the contrast between the indicated desire of Jesus and what actually happened. The intrusion on His privacy came from an unnamed woman. In this account Mark, unlike Matthew (15:23), makes no mention of the disciples, thus underlining the direct encounter between Jesus and the woman. The adverb "immediately" (not translated in the KJV) stresses that she acted at once upon learning of His presence. Mark first stated the reason for her intruding activity (v. 25) and then paused to establish her identity (v. 26).

---

[2] Some important manuscripts omit "and Sidon," and the reading is textually uncertain. Perhaps the words were omitted to avoid a supposed difficulty with the reading in v. 31.

"Whose young daughter had an unclean spirit"—the massive demonic activity during the day of Jesus was not limited to the Jews and affected children as well as adults. The diminutive, "little daughter," is a term of endearment and does not establish the age of the daughter. She could be old enough to be married.[3]

"Heard of him, and came"—*heard,* aorist tense, points to the specific report that had reached her that Jesus was in the vicinity. This implies that she had previously heard of His power to expel demons. She at once hurried to the house, lest the opportunity be lost.

"Fell at his feet"—with typical Oriental gracefulness, she threw herself toward His feet as an expression of her deep respect for Him and her crushing personal grief. Mark uses "fell at his feet" only one other time, with reference to Jairus, who requested help for his daughter (5:22). "The contrast in types between a gentile woman and a president of the synagogue could not be more exaggerated."[4]

"A Greek, a Syrophenician by nation"—a double identification of the woman. The second term makes it clear that she was not a Greek by nationality. *Greek* is here used in a general sense to note that she was a Gentile and not a Jew. It apparently also indicates that she was Greek in language and religion. Undoubtedly, her conversation with Jesus was carried on in the Greek language. Concerning nationality, she was a Syrophoenician, a modern term at that time which denoted that she was a native of Phoenicia, then a part of the province of Syria. Matthew identifies her as "a woman of Canaan" (15:22), indicating that she was a descendant of the old Canaanite people whom God had ordered the Israelites to exterminate.

"She besought him"—the verb implies that her request was made with dignity and respect, while the imperfect tense indicates that she continued to press her petition that Jesus would cast the demon out of her daughter. Mark is here more abbreviated than Matthew, who presents her as making three separate appeals. Mark omits her first appeal for mercy to Jesus as the Son of David, the silence of Jesus to her cry, the response of the disciples to the situation, and the reply of Jesus concerning the extent of His mission (Matt. 15:22-24). In persistent faith, the woman followed Jesus, dropped the messianic title, and appealed to Him for help on the basis of her crushing need. Her deep love for her needy daughter turned her into a persistent intercessor.

---

[3] William F. Arndt and F. Wilbur Gingrich, *Greek-English Lexicon of the New Testament,* p. 365.

[4] Robert A. Guelich, *Mark 1:1–8:26,* Word Biblical Commentary, p. 385.

"Let the children first be filled"—Christ's reply, in proverbial form, was meant for the woman as well as the disciples. Jesus wanted the disciples to understand that His withdrawal from Jewish territory did not mean abandoning His ministry to the Jews, designated as "the children" of God's family. Jesus firmly held to the distinctive position of the Jews in God's purpose. His first responsibility as "a minister of the circumcision for the truth of God" (Rom. 15:8) was to them. Although the children were rejecting Him, His love and faithfulness insisted that they have the first claim on His ministry. But His *first* carried a note of hope for the woman. It implied that the time of the Gentiles was coming.

"For it is not meet"—*for* introduces the reason for His refusal. His words pointed out the woman's true position to her. *Meet* means beautiful or excellent and indicates that the suggested action would not be proper.

"To take the children's bread, and to cast *it* unto the dogs"—*the children's bread* denotes the blessings His ministry offered the Jews. He could not take that food from them and cast it to the dogs. *Dogs* was a common Jewish term of abuse and contempt for Gentiles. The Scriptures commonly use the term as a reproach (1 Sam. 17:43; 24:14; 2 Sam. 16:9; 2 Kings 8:13; Matt. 7:6; Phil. 3:2; Rev. 22:15). Oriental dogs were ownerless, fierce, and filthy marauders; they were scavengers, eating the refuse that was thrown out into the streets. Jesus' use of the term does not mean that He approved of it or accepted it as accurate.[5] His purpose apparently was to test the woman to see if she would be willing to accept the lowly position that it assigned to her. Jesus softened the force of the expression with His use of the diminutive, "little dogs." Plummer comments, "The Gentiles are not called 'dogs' but 'doggies,' not outside scavengers, but household companions."[6] Clearly His reference is to the little household pets, which, while not children in the house, yet had a place in the affairs of the household.

"Yes, Lord"—*Lord* may here be rendered "sir." She acknowledged Jesus as the Master who had the power to decide the situation. She readily agreed to the humble position assigned her. Skillfully, she

---

[5] "The fact that the statement is unexpected is an argument for its authenticity. It is unlikely that the early church would have invented and attributed to Jesus a saying that could reflect adversely upon him" (James A. Brooks, *Mark*, New American Commentary, p. 121, note 66).

[6] Alfred Plummer, "The Gospel According to St. Mark," in *Cambridge Greek Testament*, p. 189.

accepted His word and used it to press her plea. Her reply showed not just a quick wit but a deep faith in His generosity.

"Yet the dogs under the table eat of the children's crumbs"—she urged her request from the fact that the "doggies" down under the table waited for the crumbs, the small bits that the children, "their masters" (Matt. 15:27), surreptitiously dropped. She argued for the granting of her request from the fact that it did not affect the Jews' abundance.

"For this saying go thy way"—better, "because of this saying." Matthew notes that Jesus praised the woman's faith (15:28); Mark notes that He granted her request as a reward of her faith. Her words were clear evidence of her remarkable faith, which showed itself not only in her persistence and humility but in her intelligent understanding and acceptance of what Jesus insisted on concerning His messianic mission. *Go thy way* bids her to be on her way, since her mission had been accomplished.

"The devil is gone out of thy daughter"—assurance that her request had been granted.[7] *Is gone out* renders the perfect tense, indicating that the cure was complete. This is the only case recorded in Mark where Jesus performed a cure at a distance.

"She went away" (ASV)—an act of faith in response to Jesus' word. The statement is peculiar to Mark. Perhaps one of the disciples went with her.

"Laid upon the bed"—the perfect tense indicates that the daughter was in a state of peaceful repose on the bed. She was in a condition free from the demons as Jesus had said.

b. Cure of the Deaf Stammerer (7:31-37).

This story of healing has no parallel in the other Gospels. But the generalized account in Matthew 15:30-31 seems to coincide with the concluding verse of this paragraph. Mark briefly noted the long journey by Jesus (v. 31) and gave a vivid account of a healing east of the Sea of Galilee (vv. 32-37).

"And again, departing from the coasts of Tyre"—*again* looks back to the journey mentioned in verse 24. Since the miracle just recorded no longer made privacy possible in the borders of Tyre, the area associated with that city, Jesus again moved on. That He entered Tyre is not said.

---

[7] The suggestion of V. Taylor that the words of Jesus are simply a statement of fact, thus reducing the case to "a telepathic awareness of what is happening at a distance," is unacceptable. It does not account for the departure of the demon and stands in contradiction to Matthew's account (15:28) (*The Gospel According to St. Mark,* p. 351).

"And came through Sidon" (ASV)—this reading, which is now accepted as textually established,[8] makes it unmistakable that Jesus penetrated deeply into Gentile territory. Leaving the region of Tyre, He followed the coastline north some twenty miles and passed through Sidon. The phrase implies that He passed through the city as a traveler, and in that busy Gentile city He would have no difficulty in remaining unrecognized.

"Unto the sea of Galilee, through the midst of the borders of Decapolis" (ASV)—Jesus did not return directly to the Sea of Galilee from Sidon but made a long detour and approached the lake from the east. The exact route He took is not certain. Swete pictures it thus: "A road led from Sidon across the hills; it crossed the Leontes near the modern Belfort, and climbing the ranges of the Lebanon, passed through the tetrarchy of Abilene, and eventually reached Damascus. The Lord probably left it where it skirted Hermon, and striking south kept on the east bank of the Jordan till He reached the Lake."[9] But He seemingly did not approach the lake at the northeastern edge, near Bethsaida-Julius, where the feeding of the five thousand took place (6:30-44). *Through the midst of the borders of Decapolis* clearly implies that He penetrated some distance into the area of the Decapolis, east and southeast of the lake. No mention is made of visiting any of the cities of the Decapolis (cf. 5:20). Mark gave no explanation for the circuitous journey. Concerning it, Blunt declared, "The geography is impossible. . . . The journey here described must have taken months."[10] We may agree that the journey did take several months, but the impossible geography which Blunt asserts arises out of his unwillingness to believe that Jesus made such a journey. Cranfield realistically remarks that it "is certainly roundabout, but there is no particular reason why Jesus should not have made it."[11] In keeping with Mark's statement in verse 24, it seems clear that Jesus deliberately kept to areas where He would not be recognized so that He could give His full time to the disciples. Describing this long, circuitous trip with His disciples as "their walking seminar," McKenna remarks, "During this uninterrupted period, Jesus can intensify His teaching with the disciples in

---

[8] The reading of the Textus Receptus, "out from the borders of Tyre *and Sidon,*" (cf. v. 24), makes no mention of any northward movement.

[9] Henry Barclay Swete, *The Gospel According to St. Mark,* p. 159.

[10] A.W.F. Blunt, *The Gospel According to St. Mark,* p. 192.

[11] C.E.B. Cranfield, *The Gospel According to St. Mark,* Cambridge Greek Testament Commentary, p. 250.

order to prepare them for leadership after His death.''[12] Mark gave no hint of any public teaching or miracles during this long trip.

"And they bring unto him"—*they* is impersonal but clearly refers to some people in the Decapolis. Jesus had briefly touched the area before and had sent the delivered Gadarene demoniac back into the area as His witness (5:1-20). Jesus was now in an area where people knew about Him, and when His presence became known, these individuals took advantage of it to bring their needy friend to Him for help. *Bring* vividly pictures the man being conducted into the presence of Jesus by concerned friends. Except for their active concern, this deaf man with limited speaking ability might never have been healed. The active interest of others in seeking to meet our needs is a God-approved blessing.

"One that was deaf, and had an impediment in his speech"—a double description of the needy individual. Both his hearing and his speech were impaired. *Deaf* translates an adjective meaning "blunt, dull" and suggests that the affected organ had been dulled, its loss of sensitivity depriving it of its power. The term might be used also of other bodily functions such as sight or speech, but here it denotes the loss of hearing. *Had an impediment in his speech* is the rendering of a single word in the original. This rare adjective literally means "speaking with difficulty." It occurs in the New Testament only here, but the Septuagint uses it in Isaiah 35:6 to render the Hebrew word meaning "dumb." While the meaning "dumb" finds some support in verse 37, the statement in verse 35 suggests that the man was not a deaf-mute but had lost his ability to speak plainly because of his deafness. Moffatt renders it "a deaf man who stammered." The strict meaning of the term, represented in our version, seems best here.

"They beseech him to put his hand upon him"—since the man could not speak for himself, those bringing him presented their request in his behalf. They assumed that the great Healer must lay His hand on the man to cure his double ailment. They apparently knew that He commonly used this method.

Verses 33-34 describe the miracle with extraordinary vividness. Jesus dealt with the man in His own unique way, suiting His actions to the needs of the man. His method was never stereotyped. Mark did not interpret the actions of Jesus, and they have been variously understood. But clearly, Jesus used the method of sign language in dealing with the deaf man.

---

[12] David L. McKenna, *Mark,* The Communicator's Commentary, p. 159.

"He took him aside from the multitude privately" (ASV)—*privately* stresses that Jesus sought to avoid open publicity. He did not wish to encourage a wide healing ministry now. But He also acted to remove the man from the excitement and distraction of the crowd in order to gain his full attention. "Took him aside" renders an aorist middle participle, setting forth the preparatory action. The middle voice indicates that Jesus wished to bring the man into a personal relationship with Himself. The man needed to understand His kindly intentions and personal interest in his case.

"Put his fingers into his ears"—*put,* better "thrust," indicates that He pushed His fingers into the man's deaf ears to convey to him the thought that something was to be done for his deafness. No doubt the sign language was intended to stimulate the man's faith. By His actions "He quickened expectation and faith, which was an indispensable condition of His every act of power."[13]

"He spit, and touched his tongue"—Mark does not say that Jesus spat on the man's tongue, nor yet that He spat on His own hand and applied the saliva to the man's tongue. His acts of spitting and touching the man's tongue with His finger were further symbolic actions to call the man's attention to his tongue and mouth, which were in need of His aid. They conveyed the thought that the power to deal with them came from Jesus.

"Looking up to heaven, he sighed"—the upward look conveyed to the man the message about the source and nature of the power needed to heal him. *Sighed,* better "groaned," reveals Jesus' own strong feeling. He felt deep emotional sympathy for the unfortunate man. Cranfield thinks "it indicates the strong emotion of Jesus as he wages war against the power of Satan."[14]

"Saith unto him, Ephphatha, that is, Be opened"—with the man's eyes fixed on Him, Jesus uttered the command *Ephphatha,* an Aramaic word which Mark again translates for his readers. The man would need little lip reading ability to catch the meaning. "Be opened," a peremptory command, was addressed to the man's organs of hearing and speech. The compound form means, "be thoroughly, or completely, opened." But others, like English, hold that the command "is not limited to the opening of ears and the loosening of a tongue. It is the whole person who is opened up, set free, in relation to God's kingly rule."[15]

---

[13] J. D. Jones, *Commentary on Mark,* p. 239.

[14] Cranfield, p. 252.

[15] Donald English, *The Message of Mark,* p. 152.

"His ears were opened"—the aorist indicative records the historical fact. His ears were completely opened as commanded. *Ears* is literally "hearing" and figuratively applies the action to the organs.

"The string of his tongue was loosed, and he spake plain"—*string* does not mean that he had been tongue-tied, but that the restraint to clear speech had been removed. *Loosed,* aorist tense, again records the definite occurrence, while *spake* is imperfect, "began to speak." He was now able to speak *plain,* "rightly, correctly." Evidently he was one who had suffered from defective speech because of a loss of hearing rather than having been a deaf-mute.

The power of healing lay not in the actions of Jesus, as though they conveyed some magical power, but in the explicit, divinely empowered command of Christ.

"He charged them that they should tell no man"—gave strict orders that the miracle should not be publicized. *Them* was directed to the man and his friends but would include others who learned of the cure. Brooks asserts, "Jesus did not want to be known as a Hellenistic miracle worker, and Mark reiterated that Jesus' true identity could not be understood until after the passion and resurrection."[16]

"The more he charged them"—*charged* here is imperfect tense and apparently indicates that when the initial command was not heeded, Jesus repeated it on different occasions.

"The more a great deal they published *it*"—His insistence only inflamed their zeal. *The more a great deal* is a double comparative, "to a greater degree beyond measure." *Published* means "heralded," proclaimed the cure as a public announcement. Gould aptly remarks, "The conduct of the multitude is a good example of the way in which men treat Jesus, yielding him all homage, except obedience."[17]

"Were beyond measure astonished"—the imperfect verb *astonished* indicates that the miracle left them in a continuing feeling of being struck out of their usual self-possession. *Beyond measure* stresses the super-abundant measure of the astonishment. Nowhere else is such a great astonishment depicted because of a miracle.

"Saying, He hath done all things well"—repeatedly, they expressed their amazement by exclaiming, "Excellently all things hath he done." *Well,* standing emphatically forward, stresses that what He had done was not only good in a moral sense but also admirable and noble. *All things* seems to require more than one miracle, while the

---

[16] Brooks, p. 123.

[17] Ezra P. Gould, *A Critical and Exegetical Commentary on the Gospel According to St. Mark,* International Critical Commentary, p. 139.

perfect verb *hath done* implies a reflection on the past as well as the present. They apparently thought also of the deliverance of the Gadarene demoniac. His story as well as this miracle deeply impressed them with the admirable nature of the deeds of Jesus.

"He maketh both the deaf to hear, and the dumb to speak"—an admiring generalizing statement of the deeds of Jesus. The statement does not stress the deaf more than the dumb, "the speechless." Both terms are plural, representing them as two distinct classes. The present tense *maketh* denotes repeated occurrences.

English well points out that behind this scene of excited people lies a needed message for the church of Christ. "Crowds being impressed by the things Jesus did, even if they tell others excitedly about them, do not necessarily become disciples. There is need for a perception of the meaning behind the things Jesus did. Without this, true faith is likely to be lacking."[18]

c. Feeding of the Four Thousand (8:1-10).

The feeding of the five thousand was recorded in all four Gospels; this miracle was recorded only by Mark and Matthew (15:32-38). Nineham asserts, "It is now generally accepted that we are dealing with alternative, and somewhat divergent accounts of a single incident."[19] This critical conclusion of the liberal scholars is urged from the general similarities of the two accounts but especially from the dullness of the disciples as seen in verse 4. The latter argument has some weight but is not insuperable. The obvious similarities are more than outweighed by the striking differences between the two events.[20] The fact that both Mark and Matthew record both miracles in close juxtaposition and note that Jesus referred to the two as distinct events (Mark 8:19-20; Matthew 16:9-10) strongly argues for the historical reality of the two accounts. Brooks aptly comments, "One might think that Mark and Matthew were in a better position than modern interpreters to know whether there was one or two."[21] The critical assumption is the concomitant of a low view of inspiration.

"In those days"—the reference is chronologically indefinite but points back to the visit to Decapolis (7:31-37). It implies that Mark

---

[18] Donald English, p. 152.

[19] D. E. Nineham, *The Gospel of St. Mark,* p. 206.

[20] Note the differences in place, the time of the multitude with Jesus, the number fed, the number of loaves, the amount left over, the different kinds of baskets used. See E. Schuyler English, *Studies in the Gospel According to Mark,* pp. 231-32, for a list of seven similarities and seven differences.

[21] Brooks, p. 124.

regarded the miracle as taking place in predominantly Gentile territory. *Those days* are further described by means of three clauses setting forth the circumstances for the feeding of the four thousand.

"[Again, Gr.] the multitude being very great"—Mark's reference to the zealous publicizing of the healing of the deaf stammerer (7:36) offers an adequate explanation for this great multitude. *Again* draws special attention to the fact that this is another instance of a similar event. It seems to look back to the feeding of the five thousand (6:34-44).

"They had nothing to eat" (ASV)—the basic fact behind the feeding to be recorded. *They* individualizes the members of the great multitude. The subjunctive in the original, "may eat," suggests that the question of what they might eat demanded serious deliberation.

"Called his disciples *unto him*"—another circumstantial construction in the original. In view of the urgent situation, Jesus took the initiative and called His disciples to discuss with them the need. Since Jesus was intent on training the Twelve, He would not perform such a miracle of feeding without first calling the attention of the disciples to the need and getting their reaction. Such miracles were not performed by Him as a matter of course, whether needed or not.

"I have compassion on the multitude"—only on this occasion is Jesus recorded as using this verb of Himself (Matt. 15:32). Mark elsewhere used it three times of Jesus (1:41; 6:34; 9:22). In Mark 6:34, Jesus was pictured as having compassion on the multitude because of their spiritual destitution; here, His compassion was evoked by their bodily needs. He who had Himself felt the pangs of hunger (Matt. 4:2) empathized deeply with the hungry and was constrained to meet their need.

"Because they have now been with me three days"—the people were in an eager, receptive mood and had continued to maintain a close, face-to-face relationship with Him for three days. This time indication, found also in Matthew, distinguishes this occurrence from the feeding of the five thousand where the multitude was with Jesus less than a whole day.

"And have nothing to eat"—because of their deep interest in Jesus, the people had stayed longer than anticipated, and their provisions were now completely exhausted. Their very eagerness to remain with Him had brought about the condition of need, and it deeply touched His heart.

"If I send them away fasting to their own houses"—the course of action is stated hypothetically, "Suppose I send them away fasting." Jesus apparently had in mind the suggestion made by the disciples on the previous occasion (6:36). He indicated that such action would be unadvisable. The people would be sent home fasting: hungry because they had not eaten anything, fasting because of their lack of food.

"They will faint by the way"—indicating the sure result if the suggested action were carried out. *Faint,* "become weary, give out," is an expressive term. It literally means to be completely unloosed; it suggests that the strength of the hungry people will relax, like an unstrung bow, and they will be unable to continue homeward. They would collapse physically before reaching their homes.

"Divers of them came from far"—the words of Jesus, not a comment by the writer. Jesus knew that some in the crowd had come from a great distance. In the Decapolis, the distances between the cities were greater than in thickly populated Galilee.

"From whence can a man satisfy these *men* with bread here in the wilderness?"—the bewildered counterquestion of the disciples indicated that they recognized the need as utterly beyond any ordinary means available. *Here in the wilderness* notes that in that area any thought of going out to buy the needed food was out of the question. Mark's *a man,* or "any one," is indefinite, but Matthew's use of *we* shows that the disciples were thinking of themselves in their bewildered question. They realized that the people would need a good meal before leaving; a meager supply of food would not fill them to satisfaction.

This reply by the disciples is admittedly the main problem when this incident is accepted as a separate occurrence of the feeding of the multitude. That the disciples showed themselves dull of apprehension is obvious. But even more so is their dullness manifested in 8:14-21. The Gospels do not conceal the deficiencies of the disciples. Nevertheless, some feel that the reply here is incredible. Gould asserts, "The stupid repetition of the question is psychologically impossible."[22] In reply, Swete points out that "the question is not repeated exactly"; in the first instance, it was a matter of the lack of means to buy the needed bread, but here it is a question of the scarcity of food in this thinly populated area. He adds, "Such stupidity as it shews is in accordance with all that we know of the condition of the Apostles at this time."[23] Alexander observed, "Even those who now reject the statement as incredible would probably have done the same if similarly situated."[24] It is a common observation that believers frequently forget God's amazing dealings with them in the past when confronted with some new crisis. To view their reply simply as an expression of hopelessness

---

[22] Gould, p. 142.

[23] Swete, p. 164.

[24] Joseph Addison Alexander, *The Gospel According to Mark,* p. 208.

seems to misread the situation. Plummer suggests that in their reply the disciples simply "confess their own powerlessness and leave the solution to Him."[25] McKenna insists that "there is a world of difference between this question and the one they asked at the first feeding. Now, with faith in Jesus, they ask, '*How* can we feed them?' "[26] It may be noted that when the amount of bread available was indicated, none of the disciples now said, "But what are these among so many?" (John 6:9). We conclude that the difficulty found in the disciples' reply is best viewed not as placing the accuracy of the record in question but as vindicating the faithlessness of the reporters.

"How many loaves have ye?"—Jesus' practical question turned the attention of the disciples to their own resources. It implied that they must become involved with what they did have.

"They said, Seven"—they were all that the disciples had left of their own supplies. According to Matthew, they also mentioned that they had "a few little fishes" (15:34).

"He commanded the people to sit down on the ground"—Jesus issued an authoritative order to the people "to recline," as a definite act, on the ground. No mention is now made of "the green grass" (6:39); months had passed since the feeding of the five thousand, and the dry, hot season had left the hills bare. Although it was probably done, no mention is now made of seating the people in orderly groups.

"He took the seven loaves, and gave thanks"—Matthew mentions that Jesus took both the loaves and fishes in giving thanks; Mark mentions them separately (vv. 6-7). Mark's account suggests that the loaves were passed out first, with the fish as a separate serving. Mark notes that Jesus gave thanks for the bread and blessed the fishes, but the two terms are quite synonymous as indicating the usual prayer before meals (cf. 6:41).

"Brake, and gave to his disciples"—*brake* is aorist tense, denoting the definite act, while *gave* is imperfect, "kept on giving."

"They did set *them* before the people"—the Twelve served as deacons.

"They had a few small fishes"—dried fish, commonly eaten with the bread. *Few* indicates that they had more than two (6:38), but *small* stresses their diminutive size.

"They did eat, and were filled: and they took up"—the aorist verbs simply record the momentous historical facts with greatest brevity. *Were filled* records that the abundant meal which the disciples had

---

[25] Plummer, p. 195.

[26] McKenna, p. 165.

envisioned as impossible had been provided. *Took up* indicates that again more than sufficient had been provided. Whether Jesus directed the disciples to gather up what was left over is not indicated.

"Broken *meat*[27] that was left seven baskets"—more literally, "remainders of broken pieces, seven hampers." *That was left* indicates the superfluous amount provided, the pieces which Jesus had broken but which remained undistributed. "When God is in it, you will notice, there is always a surplus," McGee comments.[28] This food filled seven baskets, standing in contrast to the twelve baskets at the feeding of the five thousand. The word *baskets* (*spuridas*) is a different word from that used in 6:43 (*kophinon*). The two terms are always kept distinct in reference to the two miracles, evidence that different kinds of baskets were used. Both were woven wicker baskets and might be of various sizes. The baskets here evidently were larger than those used at the feeding of the five thousand, which were traveler's baskets used to carry a day's food supply. These baskets, apparently borrowed from the crowd, were likely hampers. The word for them is the term used in Acts 9:25, where it refers to a basket big enough to carry a man. Moulton and Milligan cite the use of this word in the papyruses for "a basket in which were fifty loaves."[29] The size implied would suggest that the food now left over was actually more than that remaining after the feeding of the five thousand. What was done with the food is not indicated. That the disciples did not take it with them seems clear from Mark 8:14. It may have been given to those people in the crowd who had a long journey before they reached their homes.

"They that had eaten were about four thousand"—Matthew adds, "beside women and children" (15:38). The number was probably ascertained from the arrangement of the people in definite groups as on the former occasion.

"He sent them away"—only the act of dismissal is recorded. No hint of the effect of the miracle on the crowd is given. Obviously, there was now no plot to crown Jesus as King as before (John 6:14-15). This crowd, apparently largely Gentile, simply acted in mute astonishment.

---

[27] The italics indicate that "the word is not in the Greek text, but is supplied by the translators to complete the meaning for the English reader. The word *meat* meant food of any kind when the A.V. was translated. Today its use is limited to edible animal flesh." Kenneth A. Wuest, *Mark in the Greek New Testament for the English Reader*, p. 158.

[28] J. Vernon McGee, *Mark*, p. 94.

[29] James Hope Moulton and George Milligan, *The Vocabulary of the Greek Testament*, p. 618.

"Straightway he entered into a ship with his disciples"—at once departing from the place where the crowd had been fed. Now Jesus did not send the disciples off ahead of Him but went with them. The boat used was apparently the boat Jesus and the disciples were accustomed to using. This boat apparently had been left at Capernaum when the trip north was begun. Perhaps it had been brought over to the eastern shore by friends on hearing that Jesus was working there.

"Came into the parts of Dalmanutha"—Matthew (15:39) identifies the place as "the borders of Magadan" (ASV). Neither designation occurs elsewhere.[30] The relationship of the two localities to each other is not clear; they may have been two different names for the same place, or Dalmanutha may have been within "the borders of Magadan." Their location on the lake is uncertain. Some have proposed a location on the southeastern shore, but this is improbable from the mention of the Pharisees in the next verse, since they would not be found in a Gentile neighborhood. The location apparently was on the northwestern shore, perhaps at the southern end of the plain of Gennesaret.

d. Request for a Sign from Heaven (8:11-13).

The parallel account in Matthew 16:1-4 is fuller than that given in Mark.

"And the Pharisees came forth"—either from the multitude that had gathered when the boat landed or from their homes upon hearing of His arrival. The latter seems preferable, but Mark does not tell where these Pharisees resided. They may have come from Capernaum, where they had waited for Jesus' return to Galilee. No time sequence is indicated, and it is not certain that the confrontation took place in Dalmanutha. Jesus may have gone on to Capernaum. Matthew added that there were Sadducees in the group. As Jones remarks, "Pharisees and Sadducees were, as a rule, at daggers drawn. They were separated from one another by deep religious and political differences."[31] Undoubtedly the Pharisees were dominant in the party, but the fact that Sadducees now united with the Pharisees in their opposition to Jesus boded ill for Him. "Extremes of error combined from hatred of the truth."[32] It marks the first appearance of Sadducees in Galilee in opposition to Jesus.

---

[30] Variant readings in the manuscripts in both Gospels indicate that these unfamiliar names puzzled the scribes.

[31] J. D. Jones, p. 249.

[32] Matthew B. Riddle, "The Gospel According to St. Mark," in *International Revision Commentary on the New Testament,* p. 99.

"Began to question with him"—*began* stresses their initiation of the dispute which they intended to carry on with Jesus. *To question* basically means "to seek together, to investigate," hence "to carry on a discussion." When the seeking is conducted in a challenging and demanding manner, it denotes a dispute.

"Seeking of him a sign from heaven"—a *sign,* whether a miracle or some other deed, points beyond itself as authenticating the authority of the doer. They desired a sign *from heaven,* coming from the realm of the sky, as distinguished from His healings, which were confined to things here on earth. The source of His miracles, they implied, was dubious, and they wanted a sign that would unmistakably establish His messianic authority. "They do not specify what precise sign they want; 'that He should stop the sun or rein in the moon, or hurl down thunder or the like.' says Chrysostom."[33] They wanted some startling celestial phenomenon, some audible or visible sign in the sky, which would incontrovertibly establish His claims. But for Jesus to have yielded to this passion for sensational display would have made faith impossible; it would have precluded a free, personal acceptance of His messianic character.[34] Their demand was demonstration of their spiritual blindness. They failed to recognize the messianic signs already being given, while demanding a sign of their own choosing.

"Tempting him"—they aimed to put His power to perform such a sign to an open test. It was an attempt to catch Jesus in a dilemma: if He tried to perform such a miracle, they were confident He would fail, stamping Him as an imposter; if He refused, it would be regarded as an admission that He was not the Messiah, causing Him to lose popular support, since there was an expectation that the Messiah would perform such celestial signs. Jesus referred to such signs in the eschatological discourse in chapter 13.

"He sighed deeply in his spirit"—*sighed deeply* is an intensive compound form occurring only here in the New Testament; in 7:34 Mark used the simple verb. This intensive form literally means "groaned upwardly," indicating that the groan welled up from the very depths of His inner being. Jesus was deeply distressed by the moral perversity of these Jewish leaders. He groaned sympathetically in the presence of physical suffering (7:34), but obstinate sin evoked a deeper

---

[33] J. D. Jones, p. 250.

[34] "A belief into which a man is bludgeoned by some ocular demonstrations which leaves him no course but to submit, has none of the moral quality of that faith which avails to the saving of the soul" (W. F. Howard, *Christianity According to St. John,* p. 160).

reaction from Him. This reference to the emotional reaction of Jesus is peculiar to Mark, apparently derived from Peter's vivid memory.

"Why doth this generation seek after a sign?"—addressed meditatively to Himself. *Why* asks "With what right?" or "On what grounds?" It implies that such persistent seeking was unjustified. His questioners had deliberately rejected the evidence already given. *This generation* denotes His contemporaries as represented by these questioners. Guelich notes that Jesus "uses a designation applied to the 'generation' of Noah's day (Gen. 7:1) and the stubborn, disobedient wilderness wanderers in Ps. 95:10-11 (cf. Deut. 32:5, 20)."[35]

"Verily I say unto you"—emphatically sealing the truth and authority of the declaration being made (cf. 3:28).

"There shall no sign be given unto this generation"—literally, "If shall be given unto this generation a sign—!" In form it is the if-clause of a conditional sentence, with the conclusion left unstated, which might be "may God punish me," or "may I die." Its force is a categorical rejection of the demand.[36] *No sign* means a sign of the kind asked for. Matthew recorded a fuller response (16:2-4), and noted that Jesus indicated an exception, "the sign of the prophet Jonas." Jesus' resurrection would be the supreme sign to them that He was Messiah.

"And he left them"—Jesus deliberately left these unbelieving Jewish leaders, abandoning any further discussion with them now. He would not cast His pearls before the swine (Matt. 7:6)!

"Departed to the other side"—again embarking, Jesus and His disciples sailed to the other side, the northeastern shore (cf. 8:22). The return to Galilee was abruptly terminated. The crossing to the other side leaves unsolved the problem of the location of Dalmanutha.

---

[35] Guelich, p. 414.

[36] The construction is a characteristic Hebrew idiom, used in oaths, but the construction is not exclusively Hebrew since it occurs also in the papyruses. (A. T. Robertson, *A Grammar of the Greek New Testament in the Light of Historical Research* [1923], p. 94.)

8
Withdrawals from Galilee
(Part 4; 8:14–9:50)

4. Fourth Withdrawal and Return (8:14–9:50)

The fourth withdrawal from Galilee, following immediately after the return from the third withdrawal, was devoted almost entirely to the private training of the Twelve. It marked the termination of Jesus' public ministry in Galilee. Only two of the events during this withdrawal, as recorded by Mark, did not specifically center on Christ's personal dealings with His disciples. The occasion prompting the withdrawal led Jesus to warn the disciples against the leaven of the Pharisees and Herod (8:14-21). Following the healing of a blind man at Bethsaida (8:22-26), Jesus tested the faith of His disciples at Caesarea Philippi (8:27-30) and began His explicit instruction concerning the coming crucifixion (8:31–9:1). The transfiguration on the mount (9:2-8) evoked a discussion concerning Elijah (9:9-13) and was followed by the cure of a demoniac boy (9:14-29). On the way home, after further teaching about the cross (9:30-32), Jesus continued His private instructions to the disciples in Capernaum (9:33-50).

a. Warning Concerning Leaven (8:14-21).

Mark's "and" (Gr.) indicates continuation and implies that this paragraph stands in close connection with the scene just described (vv. 11-13). The warning Jesus gave the disciples was prompted by His contemplation of that encounter with the Pharisees. Only Matthew has a parallel account (16:5-12).

"*The disciples* had forgotten to take bread"—an understandable result of their haste in setting out on another journey. The implied subject of the verb is *the disciples* as distinguished from Jesus, who had indirectly occasioned it by hurrying them away. Matthew's account suggests that the oversight was discovered upon arrival at the northeastern shore.

"Neither had they in the ship with them more than one loaf"—an unimportant exact reminiscence that suggests the vivid memory of a personal witness. The one loaf, a thin, hard bread cake which kept well, was the sole remainder of their previous store of food.

"He charged them"—apparently when they realized that they had forgotten to secure the necessary provisions before leaving. He used the occasion to give them some needed teaching. The verb denotes a strict order. The imperfect tense may indicate that the charge was repeated, or more probably, it looks forward to the resultant conversation as a process.

"Take heed, beware of"—the utterance of a double caution. Both verbs are present imperatives, stressing attitudes that ought to continue. The first verb calls for mental alertness, while the second demands that one look attentively at the object called to one's attention in order to avoid the danger that it presents. The two verbs underscore the intensity of the warning.

"The leaven of the Pharisees, and *of* the leaven of Herod"—the repeated definite noun, *the leaven,* views the two leavens as distinct yet closely related as a common moral danger because both were allied against Christ. Since leaven was strictly forbidden with certain offerings (Lev. 2:11) and had to be removed during the Passover, it readily became a figure of evil or corruption. This was the meaning given it in rabbinical teaching and seems to be its uniform meaning in the New Testament.[1] As producing a process of fermentation, leaven or yeast pictures a pervasive corrupting tendency that works invisibly. Christ's warning was thus "a pithy one-word parable for unseen pervasive influence."[2] Mark did not give an interpretation of Christ's meaning, but Matthew (16:12) noted that His reference was to "the teaching" of those warned against. Clearly Christ was thinking of the penetrating and corrupting influence of the teachings of His opponents. His warning against the leaven of the Pharisees is to be understood in the light of what had just occurred (vv. 11-13). Their perverted views concerning moral goodness and moral evil (cf. 7:1-23) left them morally blind and unable to discern the mission and character of the Messiah.

The mention of the leaven of Herod, Herod Antipas, is unexpected, but the union of his supporters with the Pharisees against Jesus was noted previously by Mark (3:6). The reference seems to be to the

---

[1] The one possible exception is the parable of the leaven. But it may be doubted that Christ would use the figure in the parable with the meaning the very opposite of what it was commonly taken to mean.

[2] R. A. Cole, *The Gospel According to St. Mark,* p. 130.

corrupting influence of Herod's irreligious conduct, self-seeking political views, and corrupt practices. His examples set the policy for the Herodians. Matthew did not mention the leaven of Herod but spoke of the leaven of the Pharisees "and the Sadducees." The Sadducees, who were strongest in Judea, as a whole fell in with the worldly policy of the Herodians. The rationalistic worldliness of the Sadducees was essentially the same as that of the Herodians. It blinded them to the true character of our Lord.

"They reasoned among themselves"—discussed the meaning of Christ's warning in animated conversation. "Here," Guelich notes, "we find the climax of the repeated Markan theme about the disciples' lack of understanding (8:17b, 21; cf. 4:13, 41; 6:37, 52; 7:18; 8:4)."[3]

"Saying, *It is* because we have no bread"—occupied with their failure to procure the needed bread, their minds readily adopted the view that He was warning them against buying ordinary bread from these enemies. By putting such a grossly material interpretation on His spiritual warning, they revealed an amazing blindness to spiritual truth. They were, in effect, attributing to Jesus the very spirit He had condemned in the Pharisees.

"When Jesus knew *it,* he saith unto them"—His prompt perception of their unwarranted view of His intended meaning caused Jesus to speak out in sharp rebuke. His rebuke was directed not so much at their failure to understand His meaning as at the low and spiritually dull meaning they had given to His warning. The entire rebuke is formulated in a series of questions (vv. 17-20) that convey surprise and indignation. In no other place does Jesus direct such a series of rebuking questions to His disciples.

"Why reason ye, because ye have no bread?"—what justification could they have for connecting His warning with such a natural trifle as lack of some bread? Matthew noted that, in addressing them, Jesus said, "O ye of little faith" (16:8). Their trouble was little faith in Him. They still failed to perceive who He really is.

"Perceive ye not yet, neither understand?"—*not yet* indicates that after all the teaching given them, He had expected more of them. Could they not understand by using their minds?

"Have ye your heart yet hardened?"—instead of becoming spiritually enlightened, have they allowed their heart, their inner moral being, to reach a state of being hardened? The perfect tense denotes a present state of insensitivity as the result of a past process.

---

[3] Robert A. Guelich, "Mark 1:1–8:26," *Word Biblical Commentary,* p. 419.

Verse 18 states three further questions probing the extent and cause of the hardness of their heart. Is their heart really so dull and unperceptive that they cannot use their eyes, their ears, and their memory to penetrate into the meaning of His word? Have they become like those "outside" (4:11-12) to whom the mysteries of the kingdom could not be revealed? Has their memory failed them concerning the things they had seen Him do?

Verses 19-20 record His questions concerning the two miraculous feedings, aimed at arousing their memory. *I brake* reminded them that His own act had twice created material abundance in a time of crisis. Would they then need to worry about their material needs when they had one loaf with them? The memory of the disciples was clear and accurate concerning the historical facts, but they had failed to deduce the appropriate spiritual truth from those facts. They yet failed to grasp the true significance of His Person. The reference to the distinctive features of the two miracles "cannot possibly be removed from the passage without utterly destroying one of the most vivid and self-witnessing scenes in the whole Gospel narrative."[4] Those who deny that there were two separate miraculous feedings must conclude that Mark has given "a debased form of the words of Jesus."[5] We hold a higher view of the accuracy of the inspired record.

"And he said unto them"—implying a pause in the words of Jesus. He had paused to let the force of His questions shake them up.

"How is it that ye do not [yet, Gr.] understand?"—this question is best taken not as a continuation of the rebuke but as a searching appeal to the disciples. After what He has just said, do they not yet have a better understanding? Here His use of "not yet" holds out "the real possibility that they, to whom the 'mystery of the Kingdom' has been given, will know and understand."[6] Mark stops with this question, indicating that Christ allowed the disciples to find their own answer. Matthew added that they realized Jesus was talking not about bread but about the teaching of the Pharisees and Sadducees. They realized that the concern of Jesus was not about material bread but about the permeating effects of the designated false teaching.

b. Blind Man at Bethsaida (8:22-26).

This vivid account has no parallel in any of the other Gospels. This healing and the one in 7:31-37 are the only miracles recorded in Mark

---

[4] W. N. Clarke, "Commentary on the Gospel of Mark," in *An American Commentary,* p. 115.

[5] V. Taylor, *The Gospel According to St. Mark,* p. 368.

[6] Guelich, p. 425.

alone. Both were performed outside of Galilee during the period of Christ's ministry when He was attempting to be alone with His disciples. This healing has the unique distinction of being the only recorded miracle which Jesus performed in distinct stages. This is remarkable, since it occurs in a Gospel that repeatedly stressed the immediacy of Christ's miracles (cf. 1:42; 2:12; 5:29, 42; 10:52).

"[They come, Gr.] to Bethsaida"—probably to procure the needed provisions. The place seems to be Bethsaida-Julius, located on the eastern bank of the Jordan above its entrance into the lake.[7] This seems evident from the fact that the town lay on the natural route to Caesarea Philippi (v. 27).[8] *Unto,* better "into," indicates that they were on one of the streets of the city, or in an open space where the crowds gathered, when the appeal on behalf of the blind man was made to Jesus.

"They bring a blind man unto him"—*they* were some unidentified relatives, friends, or neighbors of the blind man. They recognized Jesus and took advantage of His presence to procure healing for the blind man. This is the first instance in Mark's Gospel of a blind man being brought to Jesus for healing. (A second case is noted at 10:46.) Blindness was a common affliction among the people. Each of the Gospels records one or more of such healings in detail. They were included among the messianic signs which Jesus mentioned in His reply to the question of John the Baptist (Matt. 11:5; Luke 7:22).

"Besought him to touch him"—the usual request for His help. The appeal assumes that personal contact was necessary for a cure.

"He took the blind man by the hand"—responded to the appeal in friendly, personal action. Although someone had conducted the man to Jesus, He now acted as guide to the man personally. Only here is this graphic action used in any of His miracles. The blind man confidently accepted the leadership of Jesus.

"Led him out of the town"—Jesus acted to avoid publicity as well as to secure the undisturbed attention of the blind man. *Town* is apparently a popular designation reflecting local usage. Philip the tetrarch had rebuilt the old city of Bethsaida and raised it to the dignity of a town. It was now a considerable place, but the development of the place had occurred quite recently. The original stresses the departure

---

[7] See comments under 6:45 on the question of whether there were two places named Bethsaida.

[8] Some hold that the reference must be to "Bethsaida of Galilee," which may have been a suburb of Capernaum, since Bethsaida-Julius was not properly a "village" (v. 23) but a "town." But this would place Jesus in the very area He had left because of the Pharisees (v. 13) and was seeking to avoid during this period of retirement.

from the town by the use of *ek* (''out'') both in the verb and as an adverb, ''brought him out, out of the village.''

''When he had spit on his eyes, and put his hands upon him''— the aorist participles in the original are not connected with *and*, indicating that the second act followed immediately upon the first. Both acts prepared the man for the question Jesus asked him. The spitting on his sightless eyes was a symbolic act which the man could feel, assuring him that Jesus would deal with those eyes. The accompanying touch of His hands gave the man further assurance. For a blind man, touch means more than sound.

''He asked him if he saw ought''—*asked* is imperfect tense, implying that the question was part of the process of restoration underway. The question indicates Jesus knew that the recovery of sight at this stage would be only partial. It is unwarranted to assume that Jesus did not have the power to heal the man completely at once.

''He looked up''—the man had been standing with his eyes closed; now, as a definite act, he looked up in response to the question.

''I see men; for I behold *them* as trees, walking'' (ASV)—looking up, his eyes caught sight of what he knew were men, and he excitedly exclaimed, ''I see men.'' *Men* has the definite article, *the* men, whom he knew to be around him, probably the Twelve. *For,* or ''because,'' gives his reason for identifying them as men, the fact that they were walking, moving about. He was no longer totally blind, but he recognized that his sight was still imperfect and qualified his statement. To him, the men looked like trees, large and indistinct objects. The comparison indicates that he knew what trees look like.[9] It supports the view that he had not been born blind.

''After that he put *his* hands again upon his eyes''—the particle rendered *after that,* used to enumerate separate items, makes clear that this act marked the second stage in the process of restoration. *Again,* best connected with the verb, states that the second touch was also on his eyes.

''He looked stedfastly, and was restored'' (ASV)—two aorist verbs state the historical facts. *Looked stedfastly* is literally ''looked through,'' and recalls the penetrating gaze which the man gave, enabling him to ''see through'' or clearly distinguish the things he looked at. This intensive look would be remembered by the eyewitnesses of

---

[9] The suggestion that he was comparing men to the trunks of trees which he had felt seems unlikely. Eric F.F. Bishop suggests that the reference may be to ''men and women who can be seen almost enveloped in the brushwood they are carrying for the fire, so that they do resemble 'trees walking' '' (*Jesus of Palestine,* p. 151).

the event. *Restored* denotes that normal vision had returned, showing that his blindness was not congenital.

"Saw every man clearly"—the imperfect verb *saw* means either "began to see" or "continued to see," probably the latter. The adverb *clearly,* a compound form of two terms meaning afar and radiance, far shining, or far beaming, means that the man now saw with clarity *every man,* or more likely "all things," even those far off. The restoration of his sight was perfect.[10]

Why Jesus chose to heal the man in stages can only be conjectured. From the standpoint of the man himself, it has been suggested that "Christ was accommodating the pace of His power to the slowness of the man's faith."[11] Others have suggested that it was intended as a parabolic lesson to the Twelve to teach them that they too needed a further touch to clarify their understanding of the Person of Christ. The fact that this miracle occurs following clear instances of the spiritual dullness of the disciples (vv. 4, 18) is suggestive of an intended lesson for them. "Their obtuseness," Guelich notes, "only becomes more pronounced in the following sections of 8:27–10:52 and 11:1–16:8. They are in need of a 'second touch' which ultimately comes after Easter."[12]

"He sent him away to his house"—apparently the man did not reside in Bethsaida. He should go home to reflect on the healing.

"Neither go into the town"—the aorist tense indicates that this was a temporary injunction. Having received restoration of sight, the man must avoid the temptation to enter the village, apparently Bethsaida, to publish what had happened to him. Jesus was seeking retirement with His disciples and acted "to avoid creating a run on Him for cures."[13] Unlike the response in 7:36, this order apparently was obeyed, for there is no indication that the healing aroused popular enthusiasm in the area.

c. Confession of Peter (8:27-30).

All of the remaining events concerning this fourth withdrawal recorded by Mark have parallel accounts in Matthew (16:13–17:23) as

---

[10] Three compound forms of the verb *blepō,* "to see," occur in this passage. *Anablepō,* "look up" (v. 24), is used of the blind man tentatively glancing up when asked if he saw anything. *Diablepō,* "look stedfastly" (v. 25), pictures the man looking through the haze to see distinctly or clearly. *Emblepō,* "see clearly," stresses the man's ability "to look in," to concentrate attention on a specific object.

[11] Alexander Maclaren, "St. Mark," in *Expositions of Holy Scripture,* 8:326.

[12] Guelich, p. 434.

[13] Alexander Balmain Bruce, "The Synoptic Gospels," *The Expositor's Greek New Testament,* 1:395.

well as Luke (9:18-45). Mark's condensed account of Peter's confession forms a watershed for the contents of this Gospel. From this point on, the teaching of Jesus to His disciples concerning the cross looms large (8:31-34; 9:12, 31-32; 10:32-34).

"And Jesus went out, and his disciples"—*and* connects loosely, but the natural assumption is that the reference is to the departure from Bethsaida. *Went out* is singular, with *Jesus* as the expressed subject, centering the attention on Him. *And his disciples* is added to complete the picture, since what follows involved them closely.

"Into the towns of Caesarea Philippi"—accompanied by His disciples, Jesus moved northward, following the course of the Jordan, until they came into the neighborhood of Caesarea Philippi, some twenty-five miles north of Bethsaida. Located in an area of great natural beauty, this city was situated at the easternmost of the four sources of the Jordan, where a big spring gushes from a wide and lofty cavern at the foot of Mt. Hermon. The place had long been associated with the worship of the Greek god Pan, whence it was known as Paneas. Herod the Great had erected there a magnificent temple in honor of the Roman emperor Augustus. Philip the tetrarch, as ruler of the area, had recently enlarged the city and renamed it Caesarea in honor of the emperor; but to distinguish it from the Caesarea on the coast, he attached his own name to it, Caesarea Philippi, literally, "Caesarea, the one of Philip." It was a Roman city, dominated by the spirit of paganism. But it is not said that Jesus entered the city. He remained in the villages of Caesarea Philippi, the different villages which clustered around the principal city. The area was predominantly Gentile, although not exclusively so in the villages. Here, "far from the crowds and critics of Galilee,"[14] He could give His time to the disciples.

"By the way he asked his disciples"—in the district of Caesarea Philippi but still traveling northward, or perhaps on a journey while in that area. Thus, while on the road, Jesus put the Twelve to the test to determine the result of His work with them. Luke indicates that Jesus gave Himself to a period of prayer before examining the disciples (9:18). Jesus was keenly conscious that this testing of His disciples was an event of crucial importance for His work. The open-ended imperfect verb *asked* looks forward to the answers of the disciples.

"Whom do men say that I am?"—this first question asked for the views concerning His identity held by men, literally, "the men," the common masses as distinguished from the Jewish leaders. The answers

---

[14] Alexander Jones, *The Gospel According to St. Mark*, p. 137.

would help them to see the inadequacy of these views when they were called upon to state their own conviction.

"And they answered"—perhaps different disciples voiced the different opinions which they had heard the people express. These opinions are, in effect, the same as those mentioned in 6:14-15. Matthew notes that in viewing Jesus as "one of the prophets" some people made a specific identification, asserting that He was "Jeremiah." All these views were favorable toward Jesus, and all acknowledged something supernatural about Him. They were impressed with His prophetic character, but His messiahship was concealed from them.

"And he saith unto them"—without comment, Jesus turned directly to His disciples for their own answer to His second question. The emphatic *he* stresses that Jesus Himself was the questioner. "Here as elsewhere in Mark it is Jesus who initiates dialogue and does all he can to lead men on to the truth about himself."[15] The repetition of the imperfect *asked* again looks forward to the expected answer. That answer was the crucial point in the examination under way.

"But whom say ye that I am?"—*but* is adversative and passes to the point of supreme concern for Jesus. *Ye* stresses the contrast between the disciples and the people. They are personally asked to crystallize their own faith in an open declaration. *Say* is present tense and implies that He is asking for what they are already saying among themselves or in conversation with others. *Whom . . . I am* asks them to identify His Person, not what He did but who He was. Jesus had not previously demanded that they give a direct answer to this question concerning His identity. His method had been to impress upon them the truth concerning Himself through what they heard and saw. He had left them to arrive at the truth concerning Him through personal reflection. But now the time had come to lead them to a positive declaration of faith.

"Peter answereth and saith"[16]—all the synoptics indicate that Peter responded as the spokesman for the Twelve. His ready reply was in harmony with that impulsive quickness which characterized Peter. He uttered his own conviction, but the rest readily accepted his answer as their own. This is the first time that Peter appears as the spokesman for the Twelve in Mark's Gospel.[17] Only twice before has Peter been

---

[15] Hugh Anderson, *The Gospel of Mark,* p. 214.

[16] *Answereth* translates an aorist participle and looks back to the historical fact that it was Peter who replied; *saith* is a present-tense verb and transports the reader to the very scene as Peter speaks. This strange combination of aorist participle with the present-tense verb is frequent in Mark (3:33; 9:5; 10:24; 11:22, 33; 15:2).

[17] Only twice before do the Gospels present Peter as acting as the spokesman for the other disciples (Luke 8:45; John 6:68).

named in this Gospel (3:16; 5:37), but from this point on, his name becomes prominent.[18]

"Thou art the Christ"—*thou* is emphatic, giving weight to the whole assertion. Peter categorically identified Jesus as *the Christ,* "the Anointed One." It is the equivalent of the Hebrew term from which we derive our word *Messiah.* It is the first occurrence of the term in Mark's Gospel as a specific messianic title (cf. 1:1). In the time of Jesus, it was the current Jewish designation for the promised greater Son of David who would restore the kingdom of David and reign in worldwide power.[19] The occurrences of the title in the Gospels show that Jesus was reluctant to use the term of Himself, apparently because of the limited and inadequate nature of the current messianic hopes. In popular thought, the Messiah had largely become a nationalistic figure; and, if used of Jesus, the title would at once have inflamed the political aspirations of the people (cf. John 6:14-15). But Jesus did not reject the title whenever it was applied to Him. He understood and fulfilled His messianic mission in a way different from and larger than the current messianic expectations. In His own understanding of His Person and mission, Jesus fused the Old Testament pictures of the Messiah, the suffering Servant, and the Son of man. Thus, His own presentation of Himself was not at once fully understood. The present discussion with His disciples was intended by Jesus to lead them into a fuller understanding of His messianic identity and function.

In his confession, Peter asserted his firm conviction that Jesus Himself was the expected Messiah. As recorded in Matthew (16:16), Peter confessed not only Jesus' messianic office but also His supernatural character. This open acknowledgment of Jesus as Messiah does not mean that the disciples had not previously accepted or confessed Him as such. The Fourth Gospel makes it clear that they had accepted Him as Messiah from the very first (John 1:41, 51). But now that the masses were obviously failing to perceive His true identity and the religious leaders were openly hostile to Him, it was essential that they solemnly and formally express their adherence to Him as indeed the promised Messiah. That confession was essential for the further revelation concerning Himself which Jesus was about to make.

Mark omitted all reference to the joyous response of Jesus to the reply of Peter, given at length in Matthew (16:17-19). If Peter himself

---

[18] This is true in all four Gospels. Counting the use of his name in this incident with the following occurrences, the figures are: Matthew—5 before, 18 after; Mark—2 before, 16 after; Luke—4 before, 16 after; John—4 before, 29 after.

[19] David H. Wallace, "Messiah," in *Baker's Dictionary of Theology,* ed. Everett F. Harrison, pp. 349-51.

was the main wellspring of Mark's information, the omission can be attributed to Peter's modesty. The omission of any commendation to the reply by Jesus indicates that Mark's chief concern was not Peter's confession as such but its opening the way for the Lord's direct teaching concerning the coming cross.

"And he charged them"—a strong term generally implying censure and rebuke (cf. 1:25; 3:12). It occurs twenty-nine times in the New Testament, and all but five times is translated "rebuke" in the King James. Here it indicates a prohibition that would receive His strong censure if it were violated.

"That they should tell no man of him"—*of him,* as just confessed, "that he was the Christ" (Matt. 16:20). For them to go out and broadcast the fact that He was the Messiah would simply raise false hopes among the people who were expecting an earthly Messiah who would fulfill their political hopes. Furthermore, the disciples themselves were not yet qualified to proclaim the whole truth concerning Him as Messiah. "The disciples now clearly see 'who' Jesus is, but they do not yet see afar enough to understand 'how' He will fulfill His mission as the Christ."[20] His messianic mission could not be rightly understood apart from the work of the cross. Only when they understood the relationship between His suffering and His glory would they be qualified to proclaim Him adequately as the Messiah.

d. Announcement Concerning the Cross (8:31–9:1).

The close connection with the preceding prohibition is evident from the fact that Luke did not even begin with a new sentence here (9:22). The teaching about the coming cross was the direct sequel to Peter's confession. Mark recorded Christ's explicit announcement of His passion (vv. 31-32a), His reaction to Peter's objection (vv. 32b-33), and His teaching concerning cross-bearing for His followers (8:34–9:1).

1) Coming passion foretold (8:31-32a). "And he began to teach them"—marking a definite turning point in His teaching. The aorist verb *began* asserts the actual commencement of this new teaching, while *to teach,* present tense, indicates the continuation of the instruction. Instead of talking about His eventual reign, Jesus talked about His imminent suffering and death. The disciples had not associated the thought of suffering and death with Him as the Messiah. "All their lives they had thought of Messiah in terms of irresistible conquest, and they were now being presented with an idea which staggered them."[21]

---

[20] David L. McKenna, *Mark,* The Communicator's Commentary, p. 179.

[21] William Barclay, *The Gospel of Mark,* p. 199.

"That[22] the Son of man must suffer many things"—Peter had just identified Him as the Christ, but Jesus used His own favorite designation, the Son of man. That He used the term of Himself is undeniable from Peter's reaction. On the basis of Daniel 7:13, it was a recognized messianic title in rabbinical literature. Jesus preferred it probably because it was free of political connotations and enabling Him to associate with it the thought of the suffering Servant. In Mark 10:45, Jesus clearly connected the thought of His redemptive suffering with this title. *Must* asserts the inevitability of those sufferings. From the divine standpoint, they were God's will for Him, for only thus could man's redemption be realized. From a purely human standpoint, His sufferings would be the inevitable result of His rejection by the Jewish leaders. *Many things* implies the greatness and diversity of the sufferings but throws a veil over the details.

"Be rejected of the elders, and *of* the chief priests, and scribes"—*be rejected* means that He would be subjected to an official examination and, like a spurious coin, be disapproved. Because He did not meet its standards for the Messiah, the Sanhedrin as a definite act would reject Him. The three groups composing the Sanhedrin are made distinct by the definite article before each; each group would equally share the guilt. The elders were influential lay leaders of the nation who were members of the court. Only in this enumeration of its constituent elements are they named first. The chief priests included the official high priest, any ex–high priest, and the leaders of the twenty-four courses. They were Sadducees and the most influential element in the court. The scribes, mostly Pharisees, were the professional interpreters of the Mosaic law and the guardians of the rabbinical tradition. Had the Sanhedrin not persisted in its absolute rejection of Jesus, Pilate would not have crucified Jesus.

"And be killed"—Jesus clearly foresaw a violent death. The time was left indefinite, nor was its mediatorial purpose now indicated.

"And after three days rise again"—this fact, always included in His announcements of His coming death, was so incomprehensible to the disciples that it never registered with them. They accepted the teaching of a resurrection "at the last day," but the thought of Messiah's death and resurrection was inexplicable to them. The evidence of the Septuagint and later Greek writers shows that *after three days*

---

[22] *That* (*hoti*) may be taken as introducing direct discourse: "The Son of man must needs suffer many things" (Rotherham). It reads similarly in Weymouth, Beck, and TEV. Direct discourse, giving the very words of Jesus, would be more dramatic.

and "on the third day" (Matt. and Luke) could be used with identical meaning.

"And he spake that saying openly"—in Mark only. *That saying* points back to verse 31. *Spake,* the imperfect tense, indicates that the thought of that verse was repeated or enlarged upon. He tried to impress the truth upon the minds of the disciples. *Openly,* occurring only here in the synoptics, is a noun with the basic meaning of freedom of speech, liberty to speak out. Here it means that Jesus spoke in clear and unambiguous language to the disciples, not in veiled allusions as he had done before.[23] Jones observes, "If Christ had allowed His death to come upon Him without a word of warning to His disciples, it would have shattered their faith completely."[24]

2) Rebuke to Peter (8:32b-33). "Peter took him, and began to rebuke him"—Peter was scandalized by Jesus' announcement of His coming death. The whole idea was abhorrent, inconsistent with the confession Jesus had just warmly approved. Like his countrymen after the crucifixion, Peter reacted to "the offense of the cross." Motivated by his affection for Jesus, Peter felt it was essential to pressure Him to eliminate these gloomy forebodings from His mind. *Took him* renders an aorist middle participle, "having taken him to himself," and pictures Peter confidently drawing Jesus aside a little in order to remonstrate with Him for His own good. Peter acted with "an air of conscious superiority."[25] Matthew gave his very words, "Mercy on thee, Lord! In nowise shall this befall thee" (16:22, Rotherham). *Began to rebuke* implies that he was cut short by the severe response of Jesus.

"When he had turned about and looked on his disciples"—Jesus whirled around to face Peter, and in doing so, observed that the other disciples knew and approved of what Peter was saying. His reply was for their benefit as well.

"Rebuked Peter"—Peter's intended censure was turned back on him. While Mark did not record Christ's commendation of Peter, he did record the censure. Luke recorded neither the commendation nor the censure.

---

[23] Previous obscure intimations of His death were given in (1) His statement to the Jews at the first Passover, John 2:19; (2) His words to Nicodemus in John 3:14; (3) His remark about the bridegroom's being taken away, Matt. 9:15, Mark 2:20; (4) His words about giving His flesh for the life of the world in John 6:51; and (5) His reference to the sign of Jonah, Matt. 16:4.

[24] J. D. Jones, *Commentary on Mark,* p. 271.

[25] Henry Barclay Swete, *The Gospel According to St. Mark,* p. 180.

"Get thee behind me, Satan"—the peremptory command is similar to that given Satan in the wilderness (Matt. 4:10). However, Peter was not commanded to leave Him but to get out of His way, for he was a stumbling block (Matt. 16:23). In Peter's effort to dissuade Him from the cross, Jesus recognized a repetition of the wilderness temptation; Peter had made himself an unwitting agent of Satan. *Satan* does not identify Peter with the Devil but names Peter as a real adversary. Jesus banished Peter's suggestion with the finality used against Satan in the wilderness.

"For thou savourest not the things that be of God, but the things that be of men"—an explanation of Peter's error. *Savourest* denotes what dominated and swayed Peter's thoughts. He was motivated not by the things of God, things related to God's purposes, but by the things of men, the concerns of fallible human beings. His human desire to spare his Master such sufferings prompted Peter to urge Jesus to avoid the very suffering to which Jesus had committed Himself as the messianic Servant.

3) Teaching about cross-bearing (8:34–9:1). Peter's objection to the necessity of the cross for his Master led Jesus to make the further revelation that the cross was necessary also for the disciples. A suffering Messiah requires also a suffering messianic community.

"And when he had called the people *unto him* with his disciples"—evidently Jewish residents in the villages of Caesarea Philippi who had learned of Jesus' presence and were expectantly remaining near by. His utterance to them implies that those called had some knowledge of Him. Only Mark here mentions the multitude, but Luke's *all* (9:23) implies their presence. In the Orient it was always easy for some outstanding individual to gather a crowd. The calling of the multitude with His disciples indicated that the teaching to be given was important for all who had any interest in Him as Messiah.

"If any man would come after me" (ASV)—the conditional sentence assumes that there were those who had the desire to come after Him, to follow Him in the way as His disciples. *Any man* makes the challenge individual but unrestricted and open to all. The demands of discipleship now set forth were not only for the Twelve but for all of His disciples. They were not for the first Christians only, but for Christians of every age. *Would,* better "wills" or "desires," is present tense and denotes a continuing desire to be His genuine disciple. The emphasis is placed on the conscious willing to be a disciple. Such a one must accept the conditions for discipleship. The reference is not to the way of salvation but to the path of discipleship. Three conditions are laid down. The first two are decisive acts; the third is a continuing relationship.

"Let him deny himself"—as a definite act renounce the claims of self as no longer the supreme object of regard. The aorist imperative stipulates this act as a crisis duty. The disciple must no longer make his own interests and desires the supreme concern of his life. He must "turn away from the idolatry of self-centeredness."[26]

"And take up his cross"—aorist imperative again demands the acceptance of the cross as a definite act. Execution by crucifixion was well known in Palestine, and Jesus' figure must have carried startling implications for His hearers. The Romans compelled the condemned criminal to bear the cross-beam to the place of execution; to *take up his cross* meant that such a one was going out to die. Like his Lord, each disciple must bear *his* own cross. The reference is not to the common sufferings experienced in life but to that shame and suffering which the disciple assumes because of his relationship to Jesus and which can be escaped by denying that relationship. Luke's statement "Take up his cross daily" does not mean that a new cross must be taken up each day but that this willingness to accept his cross must characterize the disciple every day. Brooks aptly remarks, "The concept should never be cheapened by applying it to enduring some irritation or even a major burden. . . . It is a willingness to suffer for Jesus and for others. Such a concept of discipleship is so radical that many contemporary Christians in the West have difficulty relating to it."[27]

"And follow me"—the present tense denotes a continuing relationship. Christian discipleship centers in this personal relationship to Christ, expressed in persevering obedience to His leadership. He heads the procession as it goes to His death, and all who follow Him must also face death to self.

Verses 8:35–9:1 justify the stringent conditions for discipleship just announced. This is underlined by the repeated use of *for.*

In verse 35, *for* introduces a statement of the personal consequences of rejecting or accepting the conditions. *Whosoever will,* or "wills," again stresses that the choice is a matter of the individual will. A man may decide "to save his life," to preserve his personal interests by keeping aloof from Christ and His self-sacrificing demands. The sure result will be that he will "lose his life," more literally, "destroy" it. His self-preserving action will result in the destruction of his higher welfare.

---

[26] C.E.B. Cranfield, *The Gospel According to St. Mark,* Cambridge Greek Testament Commentary, p. 281.

[27] James A. Brooks, *Mark,* The New American Commentary, p. 137.

The alternative statement assumed the matter of the will and stresses the higher objects for which the disciple sacrifices himself, "for my sake and the gospel's." The calm assertion "for my sake" reflects Christ's consciousness of His unique supremacy, which justly claims the absolute allegiance of His disciples. *And the gospel's,* added only in Mark (cf. 10:29), points to the message which the disciple accepts and propagates at the cost of himself. The two form two sides of one great reality. Christ is known to us only through the gospel, and our adherence to the gospel means our loyalty to Him.

The paradoxical statement derives its force from the two meanings of the word *life (psuchē),* often translated "soul," the self-conscious life. The term here has a lower and higher meaning. In both statements it first means the outward, earthly life with its pleasures and aims and then the inward, spiritual life which begins here and reaches into eternity. The one who refuses to become a disciple to preserve the lower thereby destroys the higher; the present self-sacrifice of the interests of the lower life will result in true and ultimate self-preservation.

In verse 36, *for* elucidates by contrasting the higher life with the world, all that it stands for as estranged from God. The thought is presented under a commercial metaphor, and the question implies that there is not profit in the suggested transaction. The present gain is pictured in its highest form, "gain the whole world," a clear impossibility for any individual. But granting the impossible, if a man should accomplish it and thereby forfeit his life, what is the profit in it? The argument is valid whether *life* be taken in its lower or higher meaning.

In verse 37, *for,* omitted in the KJV, again confirms the declaration, setting forth the finality of the unprofitable transaction. The question suggests that no exchange will be possible. The loss is irrevocable. The question underlines the incomputable value of the human soul.

In verse 38, the final *for* vindicates the demands of discipleship by relating them to the eschatological messianic victory (8:38–9:1). In that day the crucial point will be man's relation to the one now making the demands.

"Whosoever therefore shall be ashamed of me and of my words"—the relationship is presented as undetermined, but it will be decided by the reaction of each individual to the claims of Christ. By refusing the demands of discipleship, he shows himself ashamed of Christ, fearing the shame and suffering involved. *Of me and of my words* again unites the Person of Christ with His truth as determining ultimate destiny.

"In this adulterous and sinful generation"—describes the governing environment of one who is ashamed of Him. He lives amidst and has his ties with a generation of people characterized as adulterous and sinful. *Adulterous* is best taken figuratively as denoting the spiritual unfaithfulness of the people to their covenant relationship with God. Their refusal to accept the Messiah revealed their apostate condition. *Sinful* denotes their moral state.

"Of him also shall the Son of man be ashamed''—the one who now disowns Him in shame shall then be disowned in shame. "The supreme paradox is that this lowly One, who confronts men with the choice between the authentic life of discipleship and the inauthentic existence of self-concern, will occupy the place of power and glory with God in God's final judgment of the world.''[28] Christ will find it morally impossible to own such a one as His disciple.

"When he cometh in the glory of his Father''—the first explicit reference in Mark to Christ's future return in glory. Then the way of the cross will be seen to have been the way to glory. He will return in the glory of his Father, invested with the glory belonging to the Father as the unmistakable Ruler of the world. *With the holy angels* underlines the dignity and power of the returning Lord.

"And he said unto them''—Mark's use of his favorite formula makes the statement of 9:1 stand by itself.[29] It may well indicate a brief time break and was probably uttered to the Twelve as a solemn conclusion to the preceding discussion after the multitude had dispersed.

"Verily I say unto you''—marking the solemnity and importance of His announcement. Jesus' announcement in 9:1 has been called one of the most puzzling statements in the Gospels. (See comments on this formula of assurance and authority in 3:28.)

"There be some of them that stand here''—wholly indefinite except that it concerns some of those standing around Jesus.

"Shall not taste of death''—a Hebrew idiom for physical death. The figure regards death as a bitter poison which all, sooner or later, must taste. The emphatic *not* stresses that those in view will assuredly not drink the potion until after the indicated event.

"Till they have seen the kingdom of God come with power''— *come* renders a perfect participle, "having come,'' hence "present.'' *With power* is an addition here peculiar to Mark, in keeping with his emphasis upon the power of Christ. The arrival of the kingdom mentioned will be associated with visible power. Varied have been the views concerning what event in the lifetime of certain of the disciples

---

[28] Anderson, p. 220.

[29] It is generally agreed that this verse should go with chapter 8. In Matthew it concludes the chapter. The chapter division here apparently was due to the following account of the transfiguration, with which it seems to have an intended connection.

was meant. Among those advocated are (1) the transfiguration; (2) the resurrection and ascension; (3) Pentecost; (4) the destruction of Jerusalem in A.D. 70; (5) the manifestation of the kingdom in the church.

In my judgment, the most probable view is that the primary reference was to the transfiguration serving as a visible type of the eschatological coming of the kingdom. This interpretation was accepted by most of the church fathers. In supporting this view, Cranfield points out that it agrees with the context; Mark's precise dating for the transfiguration indicated a definite connection between that event and what had gone before.[30] The assertion that certain ones would see the event announced agrees with the narrative in 9:2-8. Cranfield feels that the expression "the kingdom of God come with power" is a fair description of what the three saw on the mount as a type of the future kingdom in manifestation. Second Peter 1:16-18 indicates that the early church saw an eschatological significance in the transfiguration. The glory of the Lord which the disciples saw there was in essence the very glory which will receive an open manifestation when Christ returns to establish His visible kingdom. The argument that the reference cannot be to the transfiguration since Jesus' words imply that most of the disciples will have died before the predicted event is unwarranted. In reality, nothing is said about the rest, and it is unnecessary to assume that they must have died before the event. This argument would also eliminate almost all of the other views advocated.

e. Transfiguration on the Mount (9:2-8).

The epochal event of the transfiguration is recorded in all three of the synoptics (Matt. 17:1-8; Luke 9:28-36), each adding some features not found in the others. Its absence from the Fourth Gospel is in harmony with John's practice of not repeating events that had already been sufficiently recorded. Also, the Fourth Gospel in its entirety sets forth the glory of Christ.

"And after six days"—the most precise dating of any event in Mark's Gospel before the Passion story. All the synoptics specifically date this event, thus firmly situating it in historical time and place. Matthew gives the same dating, while Luke says, "about an eight days after these sayings." This may be taken as an inclusive count; *about* indicates that Luke apparently intended it as an approximate designation of the interval, about a week. Nothing is recorded of what was said or done during this interval, but apparently Jesus used the time to seek to instill in His disciples a conception of the fact of His coming

---

[30] Cranfield, pp. 287-88.

sufferings. Luke's "after these sayings" refers to the previous discussion about the cross, as recorded in 8:31–9:1.

"Jesus taketh *with him* Peter, and James, and John"—at the initiative of Jesus, the three disciples accompanied Him as His companions.[31] It is the second time these three were accorded a special privilege (cf. 5:37). They were chosen to be the select witnesses of the transfiguration.

"Leadeth them up into an high mountain"—*leadeth up* seems to suggest a steep and difficult ascent as they climbed the high mountain. The mountain is nowhere identified, but apparently it was in the vicinity of Caesarea Philippi. Not until verse 30 do we read that Jesus went through Galilee, and in verse 33, we are told of the return to Capernaum. The traditional identification of the place with Mt. Tabor is improbable since it is too far south, was not a high mountain, and apparently had a fortification on it at the time.[32] A southern spur of Mt. Hermon, which is truly a high mountain, is now generally accepted, but one of the three different mountains, each over four thousand feet high, southeast of Caesarea Philippi, is also possible. Any of these would provide the solitude which Jesus desired. Brooks remarks, "The exact site, however, is unknown and unimportant. What is significant is that a high mountain in the Bible was often the place of revelation."[33] Luke stated that He went there "to pray" (9:28).

"Apart by themselves"—"privately, alone." Only Mark here has this characteristic fullness of statement. It stresses that the transfiguration occurred when no other human being was around. Luke's account suggests that it took place at night (9:37).

Luke 9:29 indicates that the transfiguration took place "as he prayed." What He was praying for is not indicated, but doubtless He was praying for His disciples who had been deeply shaken by His clear announcement of His approaching crucifixion. Clearly He was praying "for His disciples, that when the dreaded blow actually fell, their faith might not utterly fail. But," Jones feels, "also He went up this mountain that by communion with God He might be strengthened to face and bear it." The transfiguration "strengthened Him to bear the cross, and by the grace of God to taste death for every man."[34]

---

[31] Mark's use of two definite articles, one with Peter and one with James and John, groups the two brothers together in contrast to Peter.

[32] Josephus *Wars of the Jews* 4. 1. 8; 2. 20. 6.

[33] Brooks, p. 141.

[34] J. D. Jones, p. 287.

"He was transfigured before them"—*transfigured* is our word *metamorphosed* and means changed into another form. It denotes a visible change of the outward form as expressive of the true inner nature. The aorist tense simply records the historical fact, while the passive voice indicates that the change was wrought by the Father.[35] Matthew employed the same verb, but Luke used the expression "was altered," literally, "became different." It was the glorification of the physical body of His humiliation, the divine crowning of His perfect humanity. As McGee remarks, "The transfiguration teaches the perfect humanity of Jesus and not His deity."[36] The change was wrought before them, in the actual presence of the three disciples. They were "eyewitnesses of his majesty" (2 Pet. 1:16), seeing a foregleam of His future glory as the exalted Messiah.

"His raiment became shining, exceeding white"—the effect of the transformation of Jesus extended even to His garments. It is remarkable that Mark, unlike Matthew and Luke, said nothing about the brilliance of His face but confined his description to His clothing. *Shining* was used of the reflection of polished metal surfaces or of the flashing of lightning. Luke noted that His raiment became "white *and* glistering."

"So as no fuller on earth can white them"—a homely comment, found only in Mark, to stress the superearthly whiteness of the garments. This is the only New Testament reference to the occupation of the fuller, one who cleaned and dyed woolen clothes. The translucent whiteness of the garments was beyond the ability of any earthly fuller to produce.

"There appeared unto them Elias with Moses"—*Elias* transliterates the Greek spelling for *Elijah* (cf. p. 164, note 69). The verb *appeared,* occurring only here in Mark, is generally used of the sudden appearance of a heavenly form and implies the objective presence of the form. *Them* denotes the three disciples; they saw the actual presence of the heavenly visitors. Luke (9:32) relates that the disciples had been very sleepy, but they were thoroughly aroused by the occurrence and saw the glory of Christ and of the two talking with Him. The order, "Elias with Moses," occurs only here. (In v. 5, Moses is named first).[37] Not only is Elijah named first, but he alone is the subject of the singular

---

[35] In Rom. 12:2 and 2 Cor. 3:18, this verb is used of believers in reference to the spiritual change in their inner nature.

[36] J. Vernon McGee, *Mark,* Thru the Bible, p. 103.

[37] Eric F.F. Bishop asserts, "It is Palestinianly natural that Elijah should be mentioned as accompanied by Moses. The other evangelists have reversed the order, possibly in the interests of history. . . . Elijah has always meant more in Palestine than the great lawgiver" (*Jesus of Palestine,* pp. 156-57).

verb *appeared*. Elijah appeared with Moses, accompanied by him. This stress on Elijah may be due to the fact that the scribes expected his return as the preeminent harbinger of the Messiah (Mal. 3:1; 4:5). Of the return of Moses the prophets said nothing; his appearing came as a surprise. The disciples probably recognized them by intuition. Moses and Elijah are commonly accepted as the illustrious representatives of "the law and the prophets," which bore witness to Jesus. Their presence with Jesus testified to Him as the true Messiah.

"They were talking with Jesus"—the paraphrastic construction, *were talking,* stresses linear action. Their conversation was a protracted one. Luke alone notes that the subject of their conversation was "his decease [exodus] which he should accomplish at Jerusalem" (9:31). Even on the mount of transfiguration, the accomplishment of the messianic sufferings was the central consideration. The coming Passion, to which Peter had so strongly objected, was an object of supreme interest to these heavenly visitors in conversation with Jesus. Their work had been preparatory to the culminating redemptive work of the Messiah. "At that moment," Barclay comments, "Jesus was assured that he was on the right way because all history has been leading up to the Cross."[38]

"Peter answered and said to Jesus"—Peter listened to the conversation. He had not been addressed, but impulsively he felt that the situation demanded a response from him. He replied to the occasion. Luke records that Peter spoke as Moses and Elijah were about to depart. Peter aimed to prolong the glorious experience by detaining the two heavenly visitors. He directed his suggestion to Jesus as at once the most exalted and most familiar of the three glorious personages.

"Master, it is good for us to be here"—Peter's address to his beloved and now glorious Lord as *Master* (*rabbi,* properly "my great one") indicates that this Aramaic title was commonly used by the disciples in addressing their Lord.[39] *Good* denotes that which is intrinsically good, hence attractive, commendable, excellent. It may mean that the experience was "good" and one which he wished to prolong or that it was "good" as offering them an excellent opportunity to serve Jesus and His honorable visitors. The former is probably the intended meaning.

---

[38] Barclay, p. 211.

[39] Matthew translated *rabbi* with the Greek equivalent *Lord* (*kurios*), while Luke used the term *epistata,* a term peculiar to his Gospel, meaning "chief, commander, overseer."

"Let us make three tabernacles"—if Jesus consented (Matt. 17:4), Peter proposed to construct three tabernacles, "tents" or "booths," temporary shelters made of the branches of trees, such as the Israelites used during the Feast of Tabernacles. As the leader of the disciples, Peter was eager to render this service for the three to make their protracted stay more comfortable. No thought was given to the disciples' own need for shelter. His primary concern was to prolong the glorious situation. That would be better than the sufferings of which Jesus had spoken. "He wanted the mount without the valley, the prize without the cost."[40]

"For he wist not what to say"—*for* introduces Mark's explanatory comment on Peter's words. *What to say,* better "what he should answer," suggests the perplexity that Peter felt about an appropriate reply. According to Luke, Peter spoke "not knowing what he said." He was so dazzled by the glory that he neither knew what to say or what he actually did say. Peter spoke foolishly, for crude earthly tabernacles are not fitting to glorified persons. Jones comments: "I see no reason whatever for doubting the old tradition that Mark got his material from St. Peter. Here is his apology."[41]

"For they were sore afraid"—*for* explains Peter's condition. The whole glorious scene caused the three disciples to become terrified, seized with extreme alarm. The feeling accounted for Peter's ill-advised words. The adjective rendered "sore afraid" elsewhere in the New Testament occurs only in Hebrews 12:21.

"There was a cloud that overshadowed them"—Peter's proposal received no answer from Jesus. Instead, a sudden, remarkable change in the scene occurred, while Peter was yet speaking (Matt. 17:5). A luminous cloud (Matt. 17:5) suddenly hung over them and enveloped them. *Them* may be restricted to Jesus and His two visitors, since the voice came out of the cloud, but Luke's statement that the disciples "feared as they entered into the cloud" most naturally means that the cloud enveloped all of them. This was the Shekinah, the glory cloud, symbolizing the presence of God, which led the Israelites and rested on the tabernacle.

"A voice came out of the cloud"—the same voice that spoke at the baptism. We have four reports of what the voice said. Each of the synoptics and 2 Peter 1:17 quote it.

"This is my beloved Son"—the identification is similar to that given Jesus at His baptism. (See comments regarding 1:11.) There the

---

[40] W. Graham Scroggie, *The Gospel of Mark,* p. 156.

[41] J. D. Jones, pp. 293-94.

commendation was spoken to Jesus; here it was addressed to the three disciples. As given in Matthew, "The full text of the Father's witness is,—'This is my beloved Son, in whom I am well pleased; hear ye him.' " Scroggie notes that "it is taken from the three divisions of the Old Testament Scriptures, the Psalms, the Prophets, the Law, (1) Ps. ii. 7; (2) Isa. xlii. 1; (3) Deut. xviii. 15."[42]

"Hear him"—the present imperative sets forth the continuing duty. *Hear,* in the sense of hear and obey, indicates that the person of Jesus must be obediently heard. He, rather than Moses or Elijah, is now God's authorized spokesman. Matthew recorded that when the disciples heard this voice, they fell prostrate in fear (17:6). The fear kindled by the scene generally (Mark 9:6) and enhanced by their entry into the cloud (Luke 9:34) was brought to its height by the voice addressing the disciples (Matt. 17:6).

"Suddenly, when they had looked round about, they saw no man any more"—the transfiguration scene ended abruptly as things suddenly again appeared to the disciples in their natural condition. Matthew recorded that Jesus came and touched the prostrate disciples and told them to arise without fear. When the disciples dared to lift their faces and look around, they suddenly realized that the glory was gone.

"Jesus only with themselves"—the heavenly visitors had disappeared, and Jesus only—in His natural state—was with them. *With themselves,* peculiar to Mark, suggests the self-consciousness of an eyewitness.

The natural simplicity of the synoptic accounts and their sober insistence upon the detailed features powerfully testify to the historical reality of the event. Second Peter 1:16-18 asserts the historicity of the occurrence. But the accounts of the event have evoked much critical discussion.[43] In accepting the scriptural accounts as factual, we readily recognize that nowhere in the Gospels are we led further into that which is beyond ordinary human experience than in this singular occurrence. Beyond the confirmatory assertion in 2 Peter, Scripture makes no comment on the significance of the event. It obviously had a value for Jesus Himself, encouraging Him and assuring Him of the divine approval of His fitness to be our sinbearer on the cross. To the disciples, it confirmed the necessity of the coming cross and impressed them with the divine endorsement of Christ's teaching concerning His impending sufferings. But it also inseparably linked the teaching of His

---

[42] Scroggie, p. 157.

[43] For a summary of the various critical evaluations of the transfiguration account, see Taylor, pp. 386-88; see also Cranfield, pp. 292-96.

suffering with His glory and gave them a vision of the future glory of the reigning Messiah.

f. Discussion Concerning Elijah (9:9-13).

This brief paragraph preserves a discussion which arose naturally out of the transfiguration scene. Only Matthew gave a parallel account (17:9-13), but Luke's comment in 9:36 indicates that he probably knew of it.

"As they came down from the mountain"—the descent "on the next day" (Luke 9:37) would take some time. The conversation occurred during the descent from the mountain, literally, "out of the mountain," implying that "they come out of some secluded spot on the mountain"[44] (cf. v. 2, "apart by themselves").

"That they should tell no man what things they had seen"—the three disciples were ordered not to recount or narrate the things they had seen with their own eyes. They did not yet understand the true significance of what they had seen; under the circumstances, they would not be able to lead others to a true understanding. The injunction applied also to the other disciples, assuming that they also would learn of the events on the mount. Reports to a wider circle of what they had seen would fan into flames the materialistic expectations of a glorious reigning Messiah among the masses and do much harm.

"Till the Son of man were risen from the dead"—the time limitation upon the injunction to silence. Only after the resurrection of Jesus would the event be understood in this true perspective. *Till,* better "whenever," left the time quite indefinite. "It is only in the light of the crucifixion and resurrection that Jesus' true person can be understood, for he is not just a wonderful visitor from heaven or an especially favored man given mystic glory but one called to 'give his life to redeem many people' (10:45)."[45]

"They kept that saying with themselves, questioning one with another"—*kept* may mean that they strictly obeyed the saying, the injunction to silence. But the strong verb, meaning "to take hold of, to seize," more probably means that the three disciples fastened their thoughts on the saying about His resurrection. This they did by questioning among themselves, discussing its possible meaning. The discussion was confined to the three; they did not ask Jesus about His meaning.

---

[44] Alfred Plummer, "The Gospel According to St. Mark," in *Cambridge Greek Testament,* p. 216.

[45] Larry W. Hurtado, *Mark,* p. 132.

"What the rising from the dead should mean"—more literally, "the rising from among the dead." The doctrine of the future resurrection was familiar to them, being one of the central tenets of the Pharisees and a teaching commonly accepted among the Jews. Their perplexity concerned Jesus' strange reference to His own resurrection from among the dead as something to take place soon. It conveyed the unwelcome implication of His coming death. This confused them, because they associated the idea of reigning, rather than dying, with the Messiah. They still had no conception of the fact that the death and resurrection of Christ would constitute the center of the gospel.

"They asked him"—their reflection on the transfiguration scene raised a fresh point of perplexity for the disciples, which they presented to Jesus. The imperfect *asked* looks to the resultant discussion.

"Why say the scribes"—it seems simpler to take their words as a statement of fact, "The scribes are saying that Elias must first come."[46] Their quotation of what the scribes were teaching was an invitation to Jesus to give His interpretation. The scribes, basing their view on Malachi 4:5, taught that Elijah's return must precede the coming of the Messiah. The disciples had already recognized Jesus as the coming Messiah. How did the appearing of Elijah, whom they had just seen on the mount, accord with the scribal teaching?

"Elias verily cometh first, and restoreth all things"—Jesus replied that the scribal teaching was correct. Elijah must come first, before the Messiah. And "having come," he "restoreth all things." The present tense *restoreth* states the doctrinal fact and does not carry a present time reference. Elijah's work of restoration is spiritual, bringing the hearts of the people in repentance and faith to the scriptural principles and practices of the fathers (Mal. 4:5-6).

"And how it is written of the Son of man"—*and* indicates that Jesus now advanced a complementary problem. *How* introduces a question, but how far does the question extend? The ASV places the question mark at the end of the verse. Then Jesus asked them, "What about the scriptural teaching concerning the suffering Messiah?" Others suggest, quite probably, that the question mark should be placed at the close of the first clause, "And how is it written of the Son of man?" Accordingly, Jesus asked the disciples to think about the scriptural record concerning the Son of man, and He added the essence of the teaching, namely, "That he must suffer many things, and be set at

---

[46] This reading accepts the first occurrence of *hoti* in the original as having the force of our quotation marks. Those who hold that their words are a question give the first *hoti* an interrogative force.

nought." This was the important point. The treatment awaiting Him explained His assertion about His coming resurrection. His many sufferings would result in His being set at nought, ignored, treated with contempt as though He were nothing. That evaluation of Him would lead to His death. Thus the Old Testament predictions of His suffering (Isa. 53; Ps. 22) would be fulfilled.

Further (v. 13), His coming sufferings also helped to explain the realities concerning Elijah's coming.

"But I say unto you"—a solemn formula underlining the importance of the utterance to be made. Jesus confirmed the teaching of the scribes concerning Elijah's coming, but He went a step further, asserting its fulfillment.

"Elias is indeed come"—more literally, "Also Elijah has come," he as well as the Messiah. He actually came, and his career is now a completed fact.

"And they have done unto him whatsoever they listed"—the aorist verb *have done* states the historical fact concerning Elijah. *They* leaves the persons unidentified, since the disciples would recognize who was meant. *Whatsoever they would* veils their deed, but the expression indicates the arbitrary action of absolute power. Jesus' *and* (better, "also") indicated that what was done to the forerunner pointed to the sufferings awaiting the Messiah Himself.

"As it is written of him"—added only in Mark. *Of him* makes clear that the case of Elijah is in view. *It is written* recalls the permanent record. By regarding the preceding clause as parenthetical, some hold that the reference is to the fact of Elijah's coming. More probably it refers to the treatment he received. If so, where are the predictions? Swete offers a probable solution: "In this case Scripture had foretold the future not by prophecy but by a type. The fate intended for Elijah (1 Kings xix. 2, 10) had overtaken John"[47] *As* (better, "even as") points to the exact fulfillment of the parallel. Matthew (17:13) adds that the disciples understood that Jesus was talking about John the Baptist. Mark let his readers draw that conclusion themselves.

Clearly, John the Baptist was the spiritual fulfillment of the Elijah prophecy for the first advent. Will it also have a literal fulfillment in connection with the Second Coming? Many reply with a categorical no. Others admit that the view of a double fulfillment is possible but decline to commit themselves. Still others insist that when all the Elijah references are taken together (Mal. 3:1; 4:5-6; Matt. 11:11-14; 17:10-13; Mark 9:11-13; Luke 1:17; John 1:19-23), a consistent explanation

---

[47] Swete, p. 194.

points to two comings: John was the typical fulfillment of the prophecy for the first advent, but there will be a literal, personal return of Elijah in connection with the second advent. This view recognizes John's unique moral position in relation to Christ's first coming (Mal. 3:1; Matt. 11:11-14; Mark 9:11-13; Luke 1:17) but maintains that the prophecy in Malachi 4:5-6 relates to Elijah personally and will have its true fulfillment at the eschatological Day of the Lord. Therefore John categorically denied that he was Elijah (John 1:21). This view of a double fulfillment was accepted by important church fathers.[48] We regard it as the most probable view.

g. Cure of the Demoniac Boy (9:14-29).

All the synoptics place this event immediately after the transfiguration, but Mark's account is longer than the combined accounts of Matthew (17:14-21) and Luke (9:37-43). Cranfield remarks, "The wealth of detail and great vividness of the section strongly suggest that it is based directly on personal reminiscence—probably Peter's."[49]

"When they came to the disciples" (ASV)—the reference is to Jesus and the three disciples returning from the mount of transfiguration. The story is told from the standpoint of the three disciples returning with Jesus. Where the nine disciples had been left is not indicated.

"They saw a great multitude about them" (ASV)—a large but confused crowd gathered closely around the nine.

"And the scribes questioning with them"—*scribes,* used without the Greek definite article only here in Mark, does not denote a representative committee but certain individual scribes who had seized upon the failure of the disciples as an opportunity to taunt and shame them before the crowd. That they were from Jerusalem, or even Galilee, need not be assumed; they probably were from the Jewish communities around Caesarea Philippi (cf. 8:34). The subject of their questioning, or disputing, is not indicated but may be surmised; it related to the failure of the nine to exorcise the demon and was apparently aimed at discrediting Jesus because of it. That made the situation so delicate. The events of verses 14b-16 are peculiar to Mark.

"Straightway all the people"—the entire crowd which had flocked around the frustrated disciples had been so intent on what was taking place that the approach of Jesus had been unobserved. The sudden realization of His presence evoked an immediate strong reaction.

---

[48] See J. C. Ryle, "John" in *Expository Thoughts on the Gospels,* pp. 49-51. For a modified view, see J. Dwight Pentecost, *Things to Come,* pp. 309-13.

[49] Cranfield, p. 299.

"Were greatly amazed"—a strong compound verb, used in the New Testament only by Mark (14:33; 16:5-6), suggesting a certain emotional shock. The qualifying adverb *greatly* is used to bring out the force of the preposition (*ek*) in the compound; it suggests that the amazement was so intense that it was exhausting, reaching the full limit. Some suggest that this strong amazement, bordering on alarm, was due to the afterglow of the transfiguration still lingering on Jesus' face. But Mark's account gives no hint of this in His appearance, and it seems contrary to the implication of verse 8. It is inconsistent with His command to keep the transfiguration event a secret, since such a glow on His face now would naturally invite inquiry about what had taken place on the mount. The strong reaction is adequately accounted for by Jesus' sudden, unexpected, and opportune appearance at the very time He was the center of unsympathetic discussion. "They had been so engrossed in their argument that they had not seen him come, and now, just when the moment was right, here he was in the midst of them."[50]

"Running to *him* saluted him"—the next impulse of the crowd was to run to Jesus and gladly welcome Him who, they had thought, was far away. They welcomed the fact that He who was the subject of critical discussion was now present Himself.

"And he asked [them, Gr.]"—*them* may refer to the crowd generally or to the scribes specifically. The former view would imply that the crowd had joined in the critical reaction to the failure of the nine, being sympathetic with the father. If it is restricted to "the scribes," as the KJV rendering assumes, it would indicate that Jesus had taken in the true situation at a glance, and understanding the motives of the malicious scribes, turned upon them directly with His rebuking question. This view makes His question more penetrating. In either case, His question transferred the scribal hostility from the nine disciples to Himself. "What question ye with them?" may also be rendered, "Why question ye with them?" This rendering would stress His awareness of the hostile motive behind the questioning.

"One of the multitude answered"—the crowd generally, as well as the scribes, preserved a discreet silence. Reply was made by one of the multitude, who, as the central occasion for the scene, felt himself obligated to relate to Jesus the true situation. Matthew (17:14) indicates that he approached Jesus and knelt before Him in giving his story.

"Master, I have brought unto thee my son"—*master,* or "teacher," indicates reverence and respect and denotes that he regarded Jesus

---

[50] Barclay, p. 215.

as a miracle-working rabbi. *Have brought unto thee* states what his intention had been. He had brought his son who was his "only child" (Luke 9:38).

"Which hath a dumb spirit"—identifying the son's condition as explaining his action. *Dumb,* or "speechless," may mean that the spirit itself was speechless, refusing to speak or reveal its identity. There is no indication that the spirit made a verbal protest on being expelled (cf. 1:23-24). But more probably the meaning is that the spirit made the one possessed dumb, depriving him of his power of speech, since the father's description relates not to the moral character of the spirit but rather to its effect upon his son.

"Wheresoever he taketh him"—*wheresoever* indicates that the seizures might occur at any place. Verse 22 reveals that they occurred frequently. *Taketh* conveys the picture of seizing something and pulling it down. The seizures prostrated the boy and were accompanied by his sudden screams (Luke 9:39). Four finite verbs follow to describe the symptoms; the tenses are all present as describing the effects in operation. They are the symptoms of epilepsy; Matthew states that "he is epileptic" (17:15, ASV). Rationalism would reduce this to a case of simple epilepsy, but the scriptural record asserts that the symptoms were produced by the demon and that Jesus dealt with the case as being caused by demon possession.

"He teareth him"—the verb, depending upon its accepted derivation, may mean "convulses him" or "dashes him down." Either meaning aptly brings out the violence of the seizures. Luke used another term which means "tearing" or "convulsing."

"He foameth, and gnasheth with his teeth, and pineth away"—here the personal subject of the verbs changes; it is no longer the demon but the demoniac. The change, natural in passing from the demonic action to its effects, points to the close connection between the demon and the one possessed. The first two verbs occur only here in the New Testament. (*Foameth* appears also as a participle in v. 20.) *Pineth away* means "to dry up, to wither." It here describes the haggard and rigid condition of the boy's body which resulted. It apparently is a picture of dehydration and exhaustion. The father vividly described the son's case to impress Jesus with its seriousness.

"I spake to thy disciples that they should cast him out"—finding Jesus gone, the desperate father had appealed to His disciples to exorcise the demon. Apparently, the father had heard reports that the disciples as well as Jesus were casting out demons. Having previously been able to cast out demons (6:13), the disciples accepted the father's request, but their attempt to cast out this demon had proved tragically futile.

"And they could not"—the lack of power to expel the demon was no doubt a surprise to the disciples and a keen disappointment to the father.

"He answereth [them, Gr.] and saith, O faithless generation"—the aorist participle here rendered *answereth* indicates that Jesus spoke in response to the father's story of heartbreak and disappointment, but *them* makes clear that the words were not directed specifically to the father. *Them* seems to embrace the crowd as a whole, including all the faithless elements represented. But the nine disciples seem to be specifically in view, since it was their lack of faith that had caused the painful situation. It showed that they too must be ranked as belonging to that faithless generation among which He found Himself. The historical present *saith* takes the reader to the very scene as Jesus uttered His lament. In Greek the *O* is seldom used with direct addresses; its use here points to His deep emotion.

"How long shall I be with you? how long shall I suffer you?"—the repeated *how long,* "until when," indicates His disappointment and weariness. He questions until what time it will be necessary for Him to remain "with you" in a relationship of intimacy and fellowship before His mission is realized. *Suffer you,* or "bear with you," gives the picture of holding one's self up under a load to support another; it indicates that their spiritual dullness was a heavy load to the Lord.

"Bring him unto me"—the command was a promise. Fully conscious of His power, He indicated that He would act where weakness had failed. The present imperative *bring,* "be bringing," has a plural subject; it was directed to the crowd generally. The boy was now not with the father; he had been taken to a place of safekeeping not far away.

"They brought him unto him"—the people promptly responded with their aid. *Brought* implies that the lad was assisted in his walk, if not carried, to Jesus.

"When he saw him"—the participle rendered "when he saw" is masculine gender. Grammatically, it seems to refer to the boy, since *spirit* is a neuter noun. But probably the reference is to the spirit regarded as a person.

"Straightway the spirit tare him"—the demon, knowing that he would soon lose his control over his victim, upon seeing Jesus, immediately vented his rage on the boy, throwing him into a complete convulsion. *Tare him* is a compound verb indicating the intensity of the tearing effect of the convulsion (thus the ASV rendering, "tare him grievously"). Prostrated, the lad wallowed foaming. The imperfect-tense verb *wallowed* describes the continued twisting and rolling of the victim, while his mouth was foaming. The affliction of the boy was displayed before the very eyes of Jesus in all its intensity.

"He asked his father"—introducing a second conversation between Jesus and the boy's father. Verses 21-24 are also peculiar to Mark.

"How long is it ago since this came unto him?"—the inquiry, having no special bearing on the cure, is a tender touch showing the compassionate interest of Jesus. But the question led the father to confess the natural hopelessness of the boy's condition. *This* tactfully refers to the pathetic scene before their eyes. The perfect tense "hath come" indicates that Jesus recognized it as an abiding condition.

"Of a child"—"from childhood." The answer does not establish the age of the victim but indicates that the condition has characterized most of his life. Verse 24 indicates that he was still a youth.

"Ofttimes it hath cast him into the fire, and into the waters"— after indicating that it was a long-standing case, the father added further particulars to show its critical nature. Occurring often, the seizures were frequent and unpredictable. They might occur while the boy was near the fire or near the waters. Neither term has the definite article in the original—near "fire" or different "bodies of water." To be thrown into either might prove fatal.

"To destroy him"—the father recognized that these dangerous occurrences were not accidental. Behind them he saw demonic malice.

"But if thou canst do any thing"—with *but,* the father placed the possible power of Jesus over against the need. The failure of the disciples reflected on the Master, and the father was no longer sure that the Master Himself had power sufficient for this special case. In verse 24 the father confessed his unbelief.

"Have compassion on us, and help us"—the original order is, "Help us, having had compassion on us." *Help* was a desperate cry for immediate aid. His *us* instinctively identified the father with the misery of his son. Deliverance for the son would be deliverance for the father. His help given would be evidence of Jesus' compassion. Of that compassion he had no doubt.

"If thou canst!" (ASV)—some manuscripts read, "If thou canst believe" (KJV), but the oldest manuscripts and versions omit "believe." The words *if thou canst* have the neuter article before them, making them a noun and the specific object of attention. The exclamation point effectively reveals their exclamatory force. Jesus indicated that it was not a question of His ability but of the father's doubt. Lack of faith lay at the bottom of the pathetic situation. Jesus first of all challenged the father's lack of faith.

"All things *are* possible to him that believeth"—perhaps an exclamation point should also be placed here to enforce the striking nature of the assertion. The mighty power of faith was placed over against the father's doubt. "To him that believeth" is not a reference to Jesus Himself but a challenge to the father to have faith. He was assured that all things can be done for the one who is characterized by faith. "One who has faith will set no limits to the power of God."[51] But the faith that has such mighty results will submit to the will of God in making its petitions. Faith-prompted prayer asks in harmony with the will of God.

"Straightway the father of the child cried out"—the father immediately recognized the demand that the words of Jesus made on him. *Cried out* indicates that he responded with deep emotion as he sought to rise to the demand for faith made on him.

"I believe; help thou mine unbelief"—"I do believe!" was his exclamation of faith. He did have faith as required, but his second exclamation frankly acknowledged his consciousness of its weakness. *Help* calls for the Lord's continued help in rising to a stronger faith. *Mine unbelief* is his designation of his half faith that needed strengthening by the removal of the remaining unbelief to bring it to effectiveness. A faith which declares itself openly and at the same time recognizes its weakness and pleads for help is a growing faith. "Both are the frequent experience of disciples of all times."[52] The father realized that in order to secure help for his son, he must have help himself.

"[And, Gr.] when Jesus saw that the people came running together"—*and* serves to add a further point to the total picture. The historical present, rendered "came running together," vividly views the multitude as in the act of running together, converging on the place where Jesus was. The people, realizing that something exciting was about to take place, hurried together to observe it. Either this multitude is in addition to that mentioned in verse 14, or we must assume that the crowd had withdrawn while Jesus talked with the father and now hurried back to witness what would take place. Desiring to avoid any greater publicity, Jesus acted at once. He did not desire to perform miracles for gaping sightseers.

"He rebuked the foul spirit"—Jesus recognized the boy's affliction as demonically caused. All the synoptics recorded the fact of His rebuke to the demon, but only Mark preserved His very words.

"*Thou* dumb and deaf spirit, I charge thee"—the spirit was addressed directly as a conscious personality subject to His authority. *Deaf* is a new detail, found only here, and apparently means "causing

---

[51] A.E.J. Rawlinson, *St. Mark,* p. 124.

[52] Brooks, p. 147.

deafness." His emphatic *I*, in "I command thee," stressed His authority; it was the Master Himself, not one of His weak disciples, now commanding the demon.

"Come out of him, and enter no more into him"—the two commands met the needs of the case for the present and the future. The second command, recorded in Mark alone, mercifully assured that the demon would not return at some future time (cf. Matt. 12:43-45).

"And *the spirit* cried, and rent him sore, and came out of him"—the spirit screamed in rage and wreaked final fierce vengence on his victim before coming out. The convulsion was violent and prolonged.

"He was as one dead"—the terrible effect of the final struggle. The lad lay limp and motionless, pallid as a corpse.

"Many said, He is dead"—the verdict of the majority in the crowd was "He died."

"But Jesus took him by the hand, and lifted him up"—*but* indicates the contrast between the common verdict and the restoring act of Jesus. The expulsion of the demon was followed by the infusion of reviving energy into the prostrate body of the boy. It was another remarkable instance of the supernatural power of the Servant of Jehovah. Anderson remarks, "One may suppose that to the first Christian hearers this part of the account would have suggested the power of the risen Christ to awaken the dead."[53]

"And he arose"—the active response of the boy indicated the instantaneous restoration to normal strength and health. Mark said nothing of the effect of the miracle on the crowd, but Luke noted that all the people were "amazed at the mighty power of God" (9:43).

"When he was come into the house"—*house* is without an article and means that Jesus and His disciples went indoors. They withdrew to the privacy of some home to escape the excited crowd.

"His disciples asked him privately"—Luke omitted this scene, but Matthew (17:19-20) and Mark both recorded that the nine were deeply concerned about their ignominious failure and presented the problem to Jesus.

"Why could not we cast him out?"—*we* is emphatic, contrasting themselves to Jesus. Their effort had not been an unauthorized act (cf. 6:7); they had been able to do so on previous occasions (6:13). We have here the same elliptical expression found in verse 11. Their spoken words were a statement of fact, "We could not cast it out," inviting the comment of Jesus.

---

[53] Anderson, p. 231.

"This kind can come forth by nothing, but by prayer"—*this kind* may be taken generally to denote the genus evil spirit, but more probably the meaning is "this class or sort of demon." Jesus elsewhere taught that there are differences between the demons (Matt. 12:45) and here indicated that this kind was particularly difficult to expel. It could successfully be driven out only through prayer. Rather than castigating them for their failure, Jesus pointed them to the true source of power to meet such a condition. They had failed to realize that there was no hope to dislodge it except through a believing appeal to the power of God. They had failed to maintain their continued sense of dependence upon God's power through continued communion with Him. Having known the power to cast out demons, they had taken it for granted. This demon's stubborn refusal to obey their command resulted from their failure to resort to prayer for God's power to overcome the demon.[54]

The answer recorded by Matthew differs from Mark's account in attributing the failure to the "little faith" of the disciples. When they attempted to exorcise the demon in the name of Jesus and the demon refused to yield, their faith in the power of that name sagged. Their loss of faith must be understood in the light of their lack of sympathy with Jesus concerning His teaching about the coming cross. Their inability to follow Him in that announcement brought a sense of estrangement between Him and them and cut their power to use His name effectively.

h. Renewed Teaching about the Cross (9:30-32).

Verses 30-32 record the second explicit endeavor of Jesus to lead the Twelve into an acceptance of the fact of His coming death (cf. 8:31-32). All the synoptics record the endeavor and give varied statements of the reaction of the disciples (Matt. 17:22-23; Luke 9:43-45).

"They departed thence"—*thence* refers to either the house of verse 28 or more generally the neighborhood of the mount of transfiguration. The publicity created by the healing of the epileptic boy had ended the possibility of seclusion there.

"Passed through Galilee"—the imperfect verb denotes their progress through Galilee over byways without any prolonged stay at any place. They were on the way back to Capernaum (v. 33) and were traveling through northeastern Galilee. The statement is found only in Mark.

---

[54] Many manuscripts add "and fasting," but the addition is not found in the oldest and best manuscripts. It may have been added in the interest of asceticism. If genuine, it points to the further matter of the need for self-discipline.

"He would not that any man should know *it*"—In Galilee His appearance would readily draw a crowd, and Jesus desired to keep His presence from becoming known. It was a continuation of His policy to seek seclusion with His disciples, begun with His departure for Tyre (7:24).

"For he taught his disciples"—*for* introduces the reason for His desire to remain unrecognized. He was seeking time for uninterrupted teaching of the Twelve concerning His coming Passion. *Taught,* imperfect tense, underlines His continued effort to impress this truth on their minds. His heart was set on getting the thought across to them. His public ministry in Galilee was ended, and Jesus was devoting His efforts to preparing the disciples for the future. There is no evidence for the suggestion of Blunt that Jesus was seeking to remain incognito "because of the danger from Antipas."[55] Taylor well says, "There is no need to assume this purpose."[56]

"And said unto them"—*said,* again imperfect, stresses the reiterated teaching. Mark's brief statement may well be regarded as "the text of Christ's whole talk with His disciples as they went along."[57]

"The Son of man is delivered into the hands of men"—a new element to the teaching given in 8:31. *Is delivered* is a futuristic present and carries a note of the certainty of the thing announced. The passive voice hints at an agent of betrayal. The verb is used of the act of betrayal by Judas as well as of God's delivering up Jesus for our redemption (Acts 2:23; Rom. 8:32). Both thoughts are latent in the expression, but the latter seems to be the primary meaning, since *into the hands of men* is almost superfluous if restricted to Judas. "By a conscious act of will, man may perpetrate betrayal, but only as the will of God permits it in order to fulfill the divine purpose."[58] Scripture clearly teaches that the Passion of Christ had its ultimate ground in God's initiative and plan for our salvation. The reference to men is less precise than the teaching in 8:31, but it is wider in its scope and opens the picture for the part that Gentiles would have.

"They shall kill him; and after that he is killed"—the double reference underlines the fact and reality of His being put to death violently.

"He shall rise the third day"—as in 8:31, Mark again uses the active voice, indicating that Jesus would rise in His own power and

---

[55] A.W.F. Blunt, *The Gospel According to St. Mark,* p. 209.

[56] Taylor, p. 403.

[57] Bruce, 1:404.

[58] McKenna, p. 193.

might. Matthew uses the passive, pointing to God as the agent of the resurrection. In His teaching Jesus kept His death and resurrection together. They are the foci around which the whole Gospel story moves.

"But they understood not that saying"—remained ignorant and uncomprehending of the true import of His solemn utterance. Their views of a reigning Messiah made His words utterly enigmatical to them. What He appeared to be saying just did not make sense. "By this time," Barclay notes, "they were aware of the atmosphere of tragedy, but to the end of the day they never grasped the certainty of the Resurrection. That was a wonder that was too great for them, a wonder that they grasped only when it became an accomplished fact."[59] Luke said that "it was hid from them, that they perceived it not" (9:45). In the providence of God their failure to understand was allowed in order to spare them the agony of the prospect of the Passion.

Skeptics assert that Jesus could not have made such explicit predictions concerning His future and hold that these predictions were created by the early church after His death. Such predictions are held to be improbable from the lips of Jesus since men cannot thus foresee their future in detail. But even on the human level, the keen mind of Jesus could have seen that some such fate awaited Him. To deny His ability to foretell the future is inconsistent with the portrait of the person of Jesus found in the Gospels. "Purely human categories are quite insufficient to explain this Person and we cannot set arbitrary limits to what He may or may not have said."[60]

"Were afraid to ask him"—they remembered the rebuke that Peter had received (8:33); in view of His obvious seriousness about the teaching, they feared that critical inquiry would certainly draw another sharp reprimand. Their natural reluctance to discuss the whole unpleasant idea made them unwilling to ask for further information. They were more interested in their future status in the kingdom (cf. v. 34) than in the thought of coming suffering. Matthew noted that the teaching caused them to be "exceeding sorry" (17:23). They understood enough of what He meant to make them very uneasy about their hopes for the future.

i. Teaching in Capernaum to the Disciples (9:33-50).

This section, containing occasion-inspired teaching to the Twelve, has a partial parallel in Luke 9:46-50. Matthew 18:1-35 gives a more extended account of the teaching, but omits reference to John's confession. All three of the synoptics record similar teaching given on

---

[59] Barclay, p. 221.

[60] I. H. Marshall, *St. Mark,* Scripture Union Bible Study Books, p. 35.

other occasions. In this paragraph Jesus gave the disciples needed teaching about greatness in the kingdom (Mark 9:33-37), answered John's report of his zealous action (vv. 38-41), and showed the seriousness of causing offense (vv. 42-50).

1) Question of greatness (vv. 33-37).

"Came to Capernaum"—after an absence of probably five months. The third withdrawal from Galilee (7:24–8:13) had been of considerable duration, and there is no evidence that Jesus had returned to Capernaum before the fourth withdrawal (8:14–9:32). This is the last event in the Gospels connected directly with Capernaum. The great Galilean ministry began (1:21) and ended in Capernaum. Before reporting this teaching, Matthew records the incident of the inquiry concerning the temple tax (17:24-27).

"Being in the house"—*the house* seems to point to the particular house in Capernaum where Jesus usually resided when in that city. Some hold that the reference is to Peter's house, others to a house of His own. The event occurred indoors in contrast to what had taken place on the road.

"What was it that ye disputed among yourselves by the way?"—Jesus asked, not to gain information, but to give needed teaching. *Disputed* indicates that the disciples had been vigorously discussing, or arguing, a disputed point. The imperfect implies that it continued for some time. Mark does not indicate whether Jesus knew because He had overheard them or knew intuitively; Luke (9:47) implies the latter.

"They held their peace"—the unexpected question brought conviction; confusion and shame sealed their lips. "Faced with the question posed by the one prepared to surrender himself to the lowliness and obscurity of the cross, they whose thoughts are all of their own status and prestige can have nothing to say."[61] Matthew recorded that the disciples asked Jesus, "Who then is greatest in the kingdom of heaven?" (18:1, ASV). Their "then" indicates that something had preceded, namely, the question recorded by Mark. The question was probably presented after Jesus had assembled them for His teaching session (Mark 9:35). Until then, they maintained their silence.

"For by the way they had disputed among themselves"—*among themselves* is emphatic by its position at the beginning of the clause in the original and indicates that the argument had been carried on in a close face-to-face relationship. They had argued on the way back to Capernaum. At times on this trip, Jesus apparently walked ahead alone

---

[61] Anderson, p. 233.

while the disciples followed at a distance. His thoughts turned to His approaching death while they argued about future positions in glory.

"Who *should be* the greatest"—*greatest* is comparative in form, "the greater." But here, as often in Hellenistic Greek, the comparative is used for the superlative. The argument apparently was stimulated by the privileges which had been given to Peter, James, and John. Supposing that obtaining rank *now* among them would assure rank in the future kingdom, they argued about who would have the chief place under Jesus in the messianic kingdom. Questions of rank were important to the Jews and arose repeatedly among them (cf. Luke 14:7-11). "Pride and ambition are temptations in every age."[62] The dispute shows that the disciples did not regard Peter as having been assigned a position of primacy among them at Caesarea Philippi (Matt. 16:17-19).

"And he sat down, and called the twelve"—indications that an important lesson was to be taught. Rawlinson suggests that Jesus sat down "to rest after His journey,"[63] but more probably the action was His deliberate assumption of the recognized position of the Jewish teacher (Matt. 5:1; 13:1; Luke 5:3; John 8:2). *Called the twelve* implies a formal summons. It indicates His concern that those called should learn the lesson. Only Mark preserved these picturesque details.

"If any man desire to be first"—the condition assumes the reality of the desire. *Desire,* or "will," indicates his continuing resolve or determination to occupy the position of being first, not absolutely but in relation to those around him. *Any man* stresses that this is a general principle; it applies to all in the kingdom, not just to the Twelve. "Jesus does not despise the desire to be first, but his definition of greatness stands the world's ordering of priorities on its head and radically challenges a fundamental assumption about achievement."[64]

"Shall be last of all, and servant of all"—it is possible to view Jesus' words as a condemnation of the desire to be first and to take this as an assertion of the degrading result of such ambition. But it is more natural to take His words as a highly paradoxical statement of the true way to achieve the position of being first. The innate ambition to excel need not be unspiritual (cf. 1 Tim. 3:1). Jesus now guided His disciples into a wise application of that desire. *Shall be last* is best taken as a volitive future; "he will be last" by his own deliberate choice. He will voluntarily humble himself to assume the position of

---

[62] Brooks, p. 150.

[63] Rawlinson, p. 127.

[64] Lamar Williamson, Jr., *Mark,* p. 170.

being last of all in his own circle. *Servant of all* asserts that his attitude of humility will express itself in voluntary services to others. The word *servant* denotes not a slave but an attendant who renders a free service to others. As a technical term, the word is translated "deacon" (Phil. 1:1; 1 Tim. 3:8). The term has reference to the service being rendered rather than to the servile status of the one rendering it. True humility is not self-depreciation and humiliation, but an attitude of unselfishness and self-forgetfulness which seeks the welfare of others. Humility and service are not only the passport to greatness in Christ's kingdom but also the very essence of greatness in His kingdom.

"And he took a child"—*and* connects the paradoxical statement with an emblematic action. Matthew said that "Jesus called a little child unto him," implying he was nearby and readily responded to His call (18:2).

"Set him in the midst of them"—Jesus had the child stand beside Him, facing the half circle of men seated before Him.

"When he had taken him in his arms"—derived from a noun meaning the bent arm, the verb pictures Jesus holding the little child in the crook of His arm and embracing him. The whole scene demonstrated the submission and trustfulness of the child. It was a touching picture of Jesus' tenderness and love for children. That it was Peter's child is not impossible, nor even improbable.

"Whosoever shall receive one of such children in my name, receiveth me"—an oral lesson based on His action. *Whosoever* again leaves the pictured blessing available to anyone. The child is representative of his class, a type of the simple, trusting, unassuming disciple. *Receive,* or "welcome," speaks of a definite, kindly reception given such an individual "in my name," as the basis for the action. The name of Christ embodies the revelation made concerning Him. The individual is received in, literally "upon," the basis of that name, which provides an inner connection between them. "They are to be 'welcomed,' not because they seem to be 'great' by worldly standards, but because they are Christ's."[65] Such a kindly reception of even one of these young, insignificant disciples means that he "receiveth me." *Me* is emphatic by position, "me he receives." Christ regards the act as done to Himself. "As a servant loses his identity by serving others, he takes on the identity of his master."[66]

---

[65] Hurtado, p. 140.

[66] McKenna, p. 196.

"Receiveth not me, but him that sent me"—*not me* means "not only me." The action passes into the region of the invisible. It terminates not with Christ but also involves reception of the heavenly Father, who sent Him and whose representative He is. There is a spiritual unity between the humble believer, Christ the sent one, and the Father who commissioned Him.

2) Mistaken zeal of John (vv. 38-41). "John answered him"— the absence of a connecting participle in the original, unusual for Mark, probably indicates that John's remark was an integral part of the scene in the house. It was drawn out by what Jesus had just said (cf. Luke 9:49, "answered and said"). Only here in the synoptics did John speak out alone. (He is pictured as joining with others in Mark 10:35 and 13:3.) His words gave a factual report and invited the response of Jesus. They create "an impression of candour and conscientiousness."[67] His conscience was stirred, and he wondered whether they had done right in the case which he recalled.

"We saw one casting out devils in thy name"—if *we* means the disciples as a group, the incident may have occurred on the way back from Caesarea Philippi; more probably James and John encountered the man while they were on their preaching mission in Galilee (6:7-13; Matt. 10). *Casting out* implies that the man was effective in his efforts to exorcise demons "in thy name," using the authority of that name to expel them. By faith he had grasped the power of that name, and his concern for the unfortunate demoniacs had stirred him to use it for their deliverance. All attempts to identify the man are speculative. *One* renders an indefinite pronoun, "someone," "implying that his name was unknown or forgotten or of no importance to the end for which the fact was stated."[68] But this passage clearly shows "how powerfully the word and work of Jesus had awakened in individuals even beyond the circle of His constant followers a higher power, which even performed miracles."[69]

"We forbad him"—"we were hindering him" The imperfect may mean that they repeatedly insisted that he must stop the practice, but it is better to take it as denoting intention, "We tried to prevent him."

"Because he followeth not us"—*us*, not "Thee," indicates that they acted because he did not belong to their party, was not one of the

---

[67] Swete, p. 207.

[68] Joseph Addison Alexander, *The Gospel According to Mark,* p. 261.

[69] Heinrich August Wilhelm Meyer, *Critical and Exegetical Handbook to the Gospels of Mark and Luke,* p. 119.

openly acknowledged followers of Jesus. Obviously they had not ascertained the man's inner convictions concerning the person of Jesus
Christ. They were jealous for the honor of Jesus, holding that no one
had the right to use His name without being openly allied to Him.
"The practical result was an act of exclusiveness, narrowness and
intolerance."[70]

"Jesus said, Forbid him not"—the negative with the imperative
means, "Stop forbidding him." The prohibition not only rebuked their
past act but also provided direction for the future. Such action was
prohibited. Jesus had no sympathy with the exclusive spirit they had
displayed. McGee comments: "That which is done in the name of
Jesus cannot be denied by any follower. However, the label of 'Jesus'
is put on much today that actually is not 'in His name.' "[71]

"For there is no man which shall do a miracle in my name"—
giving the reason for the order not to oppose the man. Jesus accepted
the possibility that one who did not follow Him might actually perform
a mighty work, revealing the operation of supernatural power, "in my
name," literally, "upon," as the basis for its performance. It implied
a friendly attitude toward Him.

"Can lightly speak evil of me"—*speak evil of,* "vilify," denotes
an action arising out of a hostile attitude toward Him. Such an action
would be incongruous with the preceding and would require a serious
change of mind which could not occur quickly, or suddenly. While the
man was not of their company, this action showed that his attitude was
friendly. Their attitude toward such a man must be one of neutrality,
one of openness rather than positive repudiation. Jesus was not speaking of a man who had determined that he would not be known as a
disciple of Jesus.

"For he that is not against us is on our part"—the absence of a
hostile attitude indicated that the individual was basically friendly toward them. His *us* graciously associated Himself with His disciples. A
man's attitude toward Jesus would determine his attitude toward His
disciples. On another occasion, Jesus reversed the statement, "He that
is not with me is against me" (Matt. 12:30). The two statements are
complementary, excluding the possibility of neutrality toward Him.
"One cannot be against Christ if he has faith, however imperfect, in
his name. One cannot be the friend of Christ if he has so little faith in
him as to think that his works are works of Satan."[72] In the case of a

---

[70] J. D. Jones, p. 319.

[71] J. Vernon McGee, *Mark,* p. 109.

[72] S.D.F. Salmond, "St. Mark," in *The Century Bible,* p. 238.

man who was basically friendly, Jesus desired to avoid a situation where such an individual would be forced to make a premature declaration of his decision.

"For whosoever shall give you a cup of water to drink"—*For* again confirms. To give a cup of water was a small service that might soon be forgotten, but such a trifle might be the true indication of a man's inner attitude toward them as disciples. (Others hold that the connection is with v. 37, resuming the line of teaching broken off by John's interruption.)

"In my name, because ye belong to Christ"—indicating the motive which gave the act its significance. This rendering brings out the force of the unusual phrase used here, which may be literally rendered, "in connection with a name that ye are Christ's." The recognition that they were Christ's prompted the kind deed. *Christ* here is a proper name, but it retains its basic significance of *Messiah;* it is a rare instance where Jesus used the term instead of His favorite expression, "the Son of man." Salmond observes, "The time is coming when the Messianic claims of Jesus are to be made openly and definitely."[73]

"He shall not lose his reward"—though small, the action is commendable, and God will certainly reward it. God recognizes and rewards whatever is done to His people for His own sake. The reward will be given not because the trifling deed merited it but because God's grace values it as a token of faith and obedience.

This brief incident stands as a firm rebuke to the spirit of sectarianism. It condemns that exclusive attitude which insists that only those who carry on their work in harmony with one's own views and practices can be accepted as really doing God's work. If they demonstrate that they are on God's side in the war with Satan, even though their views may be imperfect, they must not be condemned for such work or regarded with abhorrence.

3) *Seriousness of sin (vv. 42-50).* Verse 42 is a solemn statement of an opposite reaction, whether taken as a direct contrast to verse 41 or referred to verse 37. *Shall offend,* or "shall cause . . . to stumble" (ASV) denotes a serious offense. It is viewed as hypothetical but probable. The verb basically means "to entrap, ensnare" and is commonly used to mean "to cause to sin, lead into sin" (cf. 4:17), either by bad example or direct seduction. It denotes the causing of a moral fall resulting in serious damage. The one injured is "one of *these* little ones that believe in me." The appositional designation *that believe in me,* that are characterized by faith in Him, makes clear that Jesus was

---

[73] Ibid.

thinking of weak and obscure believers, not just children. *One of these* stresses that not even the lowliest among them may thus be willfully injured without the incurring of terrible guilt. The enormity of the sin is measured by the fact that the one thus injured is Christ's (v. 41).

"It is better for him"—the remainder of the sentence vividly portrays the awful fate that would be preferable for one thus guilty.

"That a great millstone were hanged about his neck"—the Greek *if*-clause here assumes the reality of the fearful fate being meted out. A *great millstone,* literally, "millstone of a donkey," denotes the upper millstone of a mill so large that a donkey was used to turn it. "The mills used to grind grain in ancient Palestine were composed of two circular stones mounted on a pivot. The upperstone turned on the other, and grain poured in between them was ground into meal and flour."[74] Such a big mill stands in contrast to a small handmill which the women turned by hand when grinding grain. *Were hanged* is present tense and vividly pictures the millstone being securely fastened to his neck.

"Were cast into the sea"—the perfect tense, "has been cast," pictures the completed act. He has been hurled into the sea with the enormous weight around his neck and is now somewhere at the bottom. This stern, severe pronouncement from the lips of Jesus bears eloquent testimony to the heinousness of leading weak and unstable believers into sin.

In verses 43-48, the warning, by an easy transition, passes from the danger of ensnaring others to that of allowing oneself to be ensnared. Plummer remarks, "Seducing simple souls is disastrously easy work; but still more easy is seducing oneself, by letting the body lead the spirit astray."[75] The warning is given a solemn threefold reiteration.

"If thy hand offend thee"—the statement is hypothetical but viewed as probable. The hand is symbolic of the things that we do. But deeds, good and useful in themselves, may be directed to a bad use. Since the hand does not act independently of the will, the hand is but the instrument for the gratification of the evil desires of the heart.

"Cut it off"—the aorist imperative demands prompt, decisive action. "Use unsparingly spiritual surgery."[76] The command, of course, is figurative. Merely to cut off the hand would not cut out the lustful heart that caused the hand to act. As a surgeon does not hesitate to cut off a gangrenous hand to save a life, so evil and destructive practices,

---

[74] Hurtado, p. 143.

[75] Plummer, p. 226.

[76] James Morison, *A Practical Commentary on the Gospel According to St. Mark,* p. 264.

though precious to us as a very part of our lives, must be sacrificed to save the soul.

"It is better for thee to enter into life maimed"—good or excellent in view of the alternative. *Maimed,* emphatic by position, denotes the "crippled" or mutilated condition resulting from the requirement. "Better to live under a sense of partial mutilation and incompleteness than to perish in the enjoyment of all one's senses."[77] The drastic action is necessary in order to enter into life. *Life* has the definite article, "the life" rightly so called, the eternal life as the opposite of eternal death. The aorist tense *to enter* looks to the future, final entry into eternal life. "The surpassing value of entering the Kingdom of God makes every other good expendable."[78]

"Having two hands to go into hell"—this is the terrible alternative. The aorist *to go,* "to go off," looks to the future, fatal entry into hell, literally, "the Gehenna," the final place of punishment of the lost. The word is a loose transliteration of *Ge-Hinnom,* "the valley of Hinnom," which lay just south of Jerusalem. Under Ahaz and Manasseh, children were sacrificed there to the god Molech (2 Chron. 28:3; 33:6; Jer. 7:31), but the good king Josiah defiled the place by making it the dumping ground for the offal and rubbish of the city (2 Kings 23:10). Worms were at work, and fires were kindled to consume the mass of corruption. The valley came to be regarded as a fitting picture of the place of the future punishment of the wicked. *Gehenna* occurs twelve times in the New Testament, always with this significance—eleven times from the lips of Jesus Himself.[79]

"Into the fire that never shall be quenched"—an appositional description of hell. The original, "the fire, the unquenchable," stresses the character of the fire. Unlike the fires in the valley of Hinnom, this fire is inextinguishable. Such fire is unknown in this world. Lenski well says, "A fire that is 'unquenchable' is by that very fact eternal. It is useless to dispute about the kind of fire that this is. . . . Let no man quibble about the kind of fire, let him make sure that he will escape that fire."[80]

Verses 44 and 46 do not appear in the oldest and best manuscripts and apparently were added by a later hand from verse 48, where the words are unquestionably authentic. It is certainly more probable that

---

[77] Swete, p. 210.

[78] Martinson, p. 172.

[79] It occurs in Matt. 5:22, 29, 30; 10:28; 18:9; 23:15, 33; Mark 9:43, 45, 47; Luke 12:5; James 3:6.

[80] R.C.H. Lenski, *The Interpretation of St. Mark's and St. Luke's Gospels,* p. 252.

some scribe deliberately added them in some manuscripts to heighten the solemn effect than that they were purposefully omitted in others. Morison points out that such an addition was in harmony with "a tendency to give peculiar emphasis to the dreadful effects, within the sphere of sensibility, of persisted-in wickedness."[81]

Verse 45 gives the same solemn warning concerning the foot. In contrast to the hand, the foot may be taken to denote the improper places the individual allows himself to go. *Be cast into hell* is a stronger term than that used in verse 43. It indicates a forced entrance into *Gehenna.*

Verse 47 gives a third statement of the solemn warning, this time relating it to "thine eye." The *eye* may denote here the lusts which are stimulated from without, aroused by the sight of things forbidden. The separate mention of the hand, the foot, and the eye points to the fact that dangers come to different individuals from different directions. The various God-given human abilities and functions can be perverted to become instruments of sin and Satan.

"To enter into the kingdom of God"—the equivalent of "enter into life" (v. 43). The contrast with Gehenna shows that it is the future, rather than the strictly present, form of the kingdom that is in view.

"Where their worm dieth not, and the fire is not quenched"— asserting the continuous operation of two destructive forces in Gehenna. The forces symbolized by *their worm* and *the fire* are spiritual realities belonging to the world of the lost. "It is the permanence of the retribution that is expressed in these material figures."[82] *Their worm* seems to suggest a destructive force that is inherent, while *the fire* seems to denote a punitive force applied from without. This terrible picture of the extremely painful and unending punishment in Gehenna is part of what some superficially designate as "the simple teachings of the Master."

Verse 49 has no scriptural parallel. It is commonly acknowledged to be one of the most difficult verses in the New Testament to interpret, and varied views have been given to it.[83] The textual variants reveal that the verse was perplexing to the scribes.[84]

---

[81] Morison, p. 265.

[82] Ezra P. Gould, *A Critical and Exegetical Commentary on the Gospel According to St. Mark,* International Critical Commentary, p. 180.

[83] Meyer, pp. 120-23, lists fourteen interpretations besides his own.

[84] For the textual problem, see Taylor, pp. 412-13, and Cranfield, pp. 314-15. The Textus Receptus seems clearly the result of conflation of variants.

"For every one shall be salted with fire"—the connection indicated by *for* is best taken as being with verses 43-48 as a whole, rather than with verse 48 alone. This verse sets forth the demand that assures escape from the fire of Gehenna. This view implies that "every one" is to be limited to the disciples; it does not include the lost. Jesus informed the disciples that the way to escape the fire of Gehenna was to be salted with fire. It is the combination of salt and fire that makes the statement so startling and difficult. Salt was a recognized preservative, and "to be salted" meant to receive the application of that which has a preserving and purifying effect. Thus Thompson notes, "Salt was used in Jesus' day, when there was no artificial ice and no refrigeration, as a preservative against corruption in things apt to putrefy."[85] That purifying element here is asserted to be fire. The effect of fire is to purify that which is not consumed. The disciples must be acted upon by a power that is both preserving and purifying. This seems clearly to point to the work of the Holy Spirit through the Word. The Spirit and the Word have a burning, purifying effect upon the life of the believer. Others think that the purifying elements in view are persecution and suffering.

"Salt *is* good"—the definite article *the salt* points to the particular salt just spoken of. It is good, or excellent, because of its wholesome, sanctifying effect.

"But if the salt have lost his saltness"—a warning pointing to a serious danger, although hypothetically stated. It is now well known that pure salt is a stable element and cannot lose its saltiness. "The stability of sodium chloride as a chemical compound has raised a problem about salt being said to be liable to lose its quality of saltiness. Jesus is referring to one of the impure salts of Palestine in everyday usage which can and does lose its savour through physical disintegration or through being mixed with wind blown gypsum dust (Pliny 3, 3, 34)."[86] Since salt turns liquid when in contact with moisture, it is possible for salt to lose its true saltiness when, for example, it is in too close contact with a damp earthen floor. "Salt becomes saltless" speaks of the loss of its intrinsic nature. The warning is against losing that precious preserving power which must characterize Christ's disciples.

"Wherewith will ye season it?"—once lost, how will its preserving power be restored? The question implies the impossibility. There is no

---

[85] Thompson, p. 160.

[86] Norman Hillyer, "Salt" in *The New International Dictionary of New Testament Theology,* 3:446.

salt for salt. The salt of true Christian character is an excellent thing, but when it becomes corrupted, it is worse than useless.

"Have salt in yourselves, and have peace one with another"—two timely commands rounding out the discussion. The present imperatives denote continuing duties. "Have salt in yourselves" is a character demand on the disciples (cf. Matt. 5:13). They must possess the purifying power in themselves and not depend on outside forces for their restraint on corruption. The second duty, "have peace one with another," is linked with the first by *and*. It will follow as a result of the first. If they have the purging salt in themselves, their selfish ambitions, which are destroying the peace of the group, will be eliminated. As Anderson remarks, "When the followers of Christ were ready to sacrifice themselves for his sake and the kingdom's, all arguments about status would be silenced and the peace that stems from a genuine community of purpose would be assured."[87]

---

[87] Anderson, p. 239.

9

The Servant Goes Up to Jerusalem

C. Journey to Jerusalem (10:1-52)

Chapter 10 constitutes a distinct section in Mark's Gospel. It consists of a series of events during Jesus' last journey to Jerusalem, the only one mentioned in Mark.[1] While on this journey, Jesus dealt with the problem of divorce (vv. 2-12), blessed little children brought to Him (vv. 13-16), answered a rich inquirer's question concerning eternal life (vv. 17-22) and discussed with His disciples the problem of wealth and reward raised by the inquiry (vv. 23-31), made another announcement to the Twelve of His coming Passion (vv. 32-34), dealt with the problem of position among the disciples (vv. 35-45), and healed a blind beggar at Jericho (vv. 46-52). Thus, representatives of various segments of society—married people, children, rich men, future leaders in the kingdom, and the physically handicapped—are all dealt with during this final journey to Jerusalem.

1. Departure from Galilee (v. 1)

"He arose from thence"—a reference to Capernaum (9:33), the last geographical location mentioned. It had been the center of His activity during His whole Galilean ministry; all further work there was terminated with this departure. Matthew 19:1, which is parallel, says that Jesus "departed from Galilee." Swete notes that the expression "arose from thence" implies "the commencement of a considerable journey."[2] In 7:24 it was used of the long journey into Phoenicia. It

---

[1] The lack of references to previous visits to Jerusalem by Jesus does not mean that Mark was ignorant of such visits. He unquestionably accepted the position that, as a Jew, Jesus would have attended the national feasts at Jerusalem. The Fourth Gospel establishes that Jesus made several visits to Jerusalem during His ministry.

[2] Henry Barclay Swete, *The Gospel According to Saint Mark,* p. 214.

marks a departure into a new territory. Here it denotes the commencement of His last official journey.

"Cometh into the borders of Judaea and beyond the Jordan"
(ASV)—*borders* in the plural, as here, means not the boundary but
rather the "district," or "region." Because of variant readings in the
manuscripts, it is somewhat uncertain whether two regions or only one
locality is meant.[3] The *and,* which may be accepted as the original
reading, connects two regions. The phrase "beyond the Jordan" had
acquired the force of a proper name, equivalent to the noun *Perea,* the
territory east of the Jordan. The double designation may be viewed as
an intentional summary statement relating to the ministry which Jesus
carried on in Judea and Perea following the close of the work in Galilee.
The order would suggest that Jesus went to Perea from Judea, but this
is not conclusive from Mark's usage. Judea may have been mentioned
first as the goal of the journey (cf. 11:1, where Jerusalem is mentioned
before Bethphage and Bethany). Less probable is the view that Mark
meant the area in Perea over against Judea. Then the journey of Jesus
would have been east of the Jordan until He came opposite to Jericho.
Most probable is the view that the expression is a summary statement
of this final journey to Jerusalem. Judea was His goal. In either case,
it is evident that Mark omitted any account of the later Judean and the
Perean ministries, as recorded in Luke 9:51–18:34 and John 7:1–11:54.

"Multitudes come together unto him again" (ASV)—the plural
multitudes, used only here in Mark, although it appears frequently in
Matthew and Luke, is without an article, making it indeterminate. The
reference is to the different crowds that flocked to Jesus in different
places. It clearly implies that Jesus was famous in Judea and Perea, as
well as in Galilee. *Come,* the historical present tense, portrays the
repeated occurrence. *Again* suggests that for some time, Jesus had been
deliberately avoiding such crowds in order to be alone with His
disciples.

"As he was wont, he taught them again"—following an interval
devoted to the training of the Twelve, Jesus resumed His practice of
public teaching. Mark's double use of *again* underlines this return to
public teaching. The imperfect *taught* stresses the fact of His teaching

---

[3] Three variants occur: (1) some omit the "and" (*kai*), giving the reading "Judea
beyond the Jordan," "the territory of Judea over the Jordan" (Moffatt); this reading
is unparalleled and linguistically improbable; Judea did not extend beyond the Jordan;
(2) some read "through" (*dia*) instead of *kai;* this is the reading of the KJV; this
seems clearly a scribal correction to indicate that Jesus went to Judea by way of Perea;
(3) the reading "and" between the two place designations has good manuscript support
and agrees with the view that v. 1 is a summary statement.

on different occasions. Mark, the Gospel of action, mentions here the teaching of Jesus, while Matthew, the Gospel of the words of Jesus, noted that Jesus "healed them there" (19:1). Bruce observes that each Gospel writer thus "is careful to make prominent, in general notices, what he comparatively neglects in detail."[4]

2. Teaching Concerning Divorce (vv. 2-12)

This paragraph has a parallel only in Matthew 19:3-12. The accounts in Matthew and Mark vary considerably in arrangement and detail, but they present the same essential message. Then, as now, divorce was a prevailing evil, and it was inevitable that Jesus would be confronted with the problem.

"Pharisees came to him"—came forward from among the crowd to face Jesus with their inquiry. *Pharisees,* used without the article, points not to an official party but to certain individual members of the party in Perea. They showed the same hostile attitude toward Jesus displayed by the Pharisees encountered in Galilee and Jerusalem. As soon as Jesus resumed His public teaching, they renewed their attacks on Him. Just where in Perea the encounter took place is not indicated.

"Is it lawful for a man to put away *his* wife?"[5]—this absolute formulation of the question implies that they suspected Jesus was opposed to divorce under all circumstances; their question invited Jesus to commit Himself with a categorical yes or no. Either answer would be sure to arouse opposition and diminish His influence. The question was a test of His orthodoxy: if He opposed divorce, He would prove Himself to be in collision with the Mosaic legislation in Deuteronomy 24:1-4. But the interpretation of this Mosaic regulation had already evoked strong differences of views among the Jewish teachers about the grounds for divorce. The meaning of the vague expression "some uncleanness" (Deut. 24:1), literally "a thing of nakedness, or shame," was not agreed upon. The strict school of Shammai allowed divorce only if the wife was guilty of unchastity, whereas the liberal school of Hillel permitted divorce for other reasons, even the most trivial.[6] As Barclay notes, "Human nature being as it is, it was the laxer view

---

[4] Alexander Balmain Bruce, "The Synoptic Gospels," *The Expositor's Greek New Testament,* 1:408.

[5] The original is literally, "if it is lawful for a husband to put away a wife." It may be rendered either as a direct question, as above, or as an indirect question, "whether a man should be allowed to divorce his wife" (C. B. Williams; similarly Moffatt). The difference is immaterial.

[6] The school of Hillel held that a valid ground for divorce was "if she spoiled a dish for him." Rabbi Akiba said, "Even if he found another fairer than she" (Henry Danby, trans., *The Mishnah,* p. 321).

which prevailed. The result was that divorce for the most trivial reasons, or for no reason at all, was tragically common."[7] The Pharisees probably did not intend their question to be taken in the strictest technical sense, for according to Matthew they presented their question in terms of the teaching of Hillel, "for every cause" (19:3). Assuming that divorce was lawful, they desired Jesus to state under what conditions He accepted its legality.

"Tempting him"—putting Him to the test to see where He stood as a rabbi on this much disputed matter. The participle, rendered according to its common secondary meaning, denotes "tempting, soliciting a person to do evil"; but here it carries its primary meaning, "to test, to prove a person's ability." The question of divorce was a knotty problem well fitted to test, and hopefully to discredit, Jesus as a qualified teacher. The question was asked not for the purpose of obtaining guidance but to test His ability as a teacher. It is possible that they hoped His open declaration concerning divorce would embroil Him with Antipas, who had beheaded John the Baptist for his bold condemnation of his adulterous marriage to Herodias (cf. 6:14-29).

"He answered and said"—the aorist tenses point to His prompt reply to the cunning question. He did not fear to deal with the problem.

"What did Moses command you?"—this counterquestion was legitimate as at once pointing to the proper basis for any discussion of divorce. Not their hair-splitting rabbinical distinctions but the divine law must decide the answer. *Command you* reminded the questioners that they too must turn to the true authority for the answer. Jesus agreed with them in accepting the authority of the law, but He claimed the right to interpret its true meaning and to free it from rabbinical abuse.

In verse 4, the questioners readily replied with a summary reference to Deuteronomy 24:1-4, which formed the basis for their divorce practices. In saying "Moses suffered"—that is, "allowed, permitted"—they implied that he had "turned over to" them the right of divorce. They pointed out the law's procedure for divorce: that if they wanted to put away a wife, repudiate her, and terminate the marriage, they were to write a bill of divorcement, prepare a written divorce certificate as the formal instrument for her dismissal. Their statement emphasized the privilege of divorce but did not mention the legal restrictions Moses had stipulated. They were interested in the legal aspect of the issue— the law's provision for the practice of divorce—but not in its deeper moral aspect. They were more concerned with their own rights within the limits of the law than with the matter of God's will when facing

---

[7] William Barclay, *The Gospel of Mark,* revised ed., p. 239.

the problem of divorce. The Mosaic legislation did not establish or sanction divorce but simply recognized the husband's right to put away his wife under certain conditions. It was intended to put a restraint upon an evil practice to prevent worse situations from arising. The requirement to write a bill of divorce made it necessary for the husband to state a formal reason for the action. Matthew noted that he had "to give" the wife the written divorce.[8] For a valid divorce, the bill of divorcement must be written and delivered to the repudiated wife. The requirement restrained the rash and heartless dismissal of a wife and served to give the wife so treated at least some character and protection.

"For the hardness of your heart he wrote you this precept"—*this precept,* emphatic by its position at the end, does not mean a commandment to divorce the wife, for there was no such commandment; it refers to the restrictions Moses laid down in permitting a divorce. The concession made was required by their low moral condition. For the questioners to hide behind the concession was an exposure of their own moral nature, their hardness of heart. *For (pros)* asserts that the concession was made "with reference to" their hardness of heart, their stubborn and obstinate nature. The phrase, standing first with emphasis, charged them with being insensitive to the need for unselfish love as well as to the call of God to a higher view of marriage.

"But from the beginning of the creation"—*but* introduces a contrast between their view of marriage and the higher intention of God. The divine intention went back to the very beginning of things, *creation,* of which man was the crown and climax. Brooks remarks, "Just as God is inseparably one being, so he intended for a male and a female in marriage to become one being who would not be divided."[9] But the divine intention in marriage, dating back to the beginning of the human race, was not being carried out because of the presence of sin.

"God made them male and female"—a quotation of Genesis 1:27 from the Septuagint. The distinction of the sexes, established at creation, underlies the institution of marriage and is the foundation of the human family. *Male* and *female* are without an article and singular, "a male and a female," indicating that the reference is to a single pair, Adam and Eve. Their distinctive physical constitution made each the complement of the other, fitted for each other. Our Lord's quotation assumes the historical truth of the first two chapters of Genesis.

---

[8] *The Mishnah* has a section of nine chapters on *Gittin* (Bills of Divorce), treating both the problem of what constitutes a legal bill of divorce and the legal requirements concerning its delivery to the wife being divorced (Danby, pp. 307-21).

[9] James A. Brooks, *Mark,* The New American Commentary, p. 157.

"For this cause"—another quotation, nearly verbatim, from Genesis 2:24 in the Septuagint. It introduces a natural and necessary consequence of the unity between husband and wife. In the original, these are the words of Adam, prompted by his realization of Eve's complementary relationship to him. Jesus adapted these words to apply to the marriage relationship as such.

"Shall a man leave his father and mother"—because the marriage relationship is closer than the relationship between child and parents. It is based on a supreme reciprocal affection between husband and wife. *Leave* is a strong term, the compound form meaning "to leave behind, to abandon." Many a marriage has floundered because the young husband or wife was not willing to accept the responsibility of independence from the parental home.

"Cleave to his wife"—the necessary complement of the preceding. *Cleave* literally means "be glued to" and serves to stress the closest possible relationship of adherence.[10]

"And they twain shall be one flesh"—continuing the quotation from Genesis 2:24, Septuagint. The words *they twain,* the man and the woman, are not in the Hebrew, but they were inserted in the Septuagint to bring out the force of the original and are retained in all New Testament quotations of the verse (Matt. 19:5; 1 Cor. 6:16). *Shall become one flesh* asserts the intimate union established between them. Created as biologically complementary beings, in the sexual union in marriage their duality gives place to a structural unity. The two form one complete whole, one flesh. Accordingly, their marriage is not a business partnership that may be dissolved at will, but a union of two lives fused into one. They now form a unit, each forming part of the very existence of the other.

"So then they are no more twain, but one flesh"—*so then* states the actual result. The words are Jesus' own deduction, stating the factual consequence. Their oneness demands that they remain together.

"What therefore God hath joined together"—*therefore* points to the logical conclusion concerning the permanency of marriage that must be drawn from the divine, creative arrangement. The neuter *what* makes the statement abstract, asserting the abiding principle. *Hath joined* is the aorist tense, not the perfect; it does not refer to special cases where two individuals have been joined in marriage, but rather looks back to the union instituted by God Himself in the creative

---

[10] Some important ancient manuscripts omit this phrase, but it is found in the majority of the manuscripts and versions. It may have been inserted here from Matt. 19:5, where it is unquestionably genuine.

arrangement. He arranged the abiding union when as yet there were only one man and one woman. *Joined* is literally "yoked together" and gives a beautiful and appropriate picture of the marriage relationship. Husband and wife are united under a common yoke and must work cooperatively in love as true yokefellows. Jones remarks, "Here our Lord appears as the defender of woman and the lifter up of her head. Woman, according to our Lord's teaching, is not man's slave or toy, to be dismissed and cast off at the merest whim and caprice; she is man's complement and counterpart; and matrimony is a holy estate, in which woman has equal rights with man."[11]

"Let not man put asunder"—an abiding prohibition against man's disruption of the union which God has established. The statement marks the contrast between God's action and man's. *Man* may be general to denote any mere human authority, but probably the reference is to the husband acting to divorce his wife. Jesus asserted the indissoluble nature of marriage as the divine intention. Under certain circumstances, human sinfulness may make relief through divorce necessary as a lesser evil, but it is still an evil, because it is contrary to the divine intention. The phrase "saving for the cause of fornication" (Matt. 5:32; 19:9) shows that Jesus recognized *one* ground for divorce. But even then Jesus did not command divorce. Forgiveness and restoration are open and desirable for those who have thus failed in the marriage relationship. Yet Jesus recognized that the fornication of the wife had in reality already broken the marriage tie; the husband in sending away his wife only accepted the disruption that she had caused. Jesus was concerned with the sin that caused the disruption of the marriage relationship, whatever its nature. Clarke has observed, "Separation for other causes than adultery there may be, but dissolution of marriage, never. If it is said that such a law works hardship in many cases, the answer is that all laws that are for the general good sometimes work hardship while sin continues."[12]

"And in the house"—the particular house where Jesus and the disciples found lodging at the time. The encounter with the Pharisees was over, but His teaching given them evoked further discussion in private on the part of the disciples.

"Asked him again"—looks back to verse 2. After the answer was given the Pharisees, the disciples still had questions about divorce. His strict position on divorce greatly surprised them (cf. Matt. 19:10-12).

---

[11] J. D. Jones, *Commentary on Mark*, p. 339.

[12] W. N. Clarke, *Commentary on the Gospel of Mark*, in An American Commentary, p. 146.

"Whosoever shall put away his wife, and marry another"—the statement is indefinite: *whosoever,* anyone thus guilty. The two verbs *put away* and *marry* are aorists, picturing the actual release of the wife and the entrance into marriage with another woman. *Put away* is the basic sin, for it unjustly disrupts a union which God intended to be indissoluble. His marriage to another adds to his sin in that it establishes an adulterous relationship. (Jesus is here stating the basic rule, and the exception clause is not brought in.) Among the Jews the prevailing reason for divorce was for the very purpose of marrying another.

"Committeth adultery against her"—to divorce the wife was a sin, but not adultery; the guilt of adultery came with marrying another. *Against her* has been understood in two ways: it refers to either the first or the second wife. Under the latter view, the man is guilty of bringing adultery upon the woman with whom he now lives. More probably, the reference is to the first wife. He thus makes himself guilty of committing adultery against her. Brooks asserts that, contrary to prevailing Jewish views, "by insisting that a husband could commit adultery against his own wife, Jesus greatly elevated the status of wives and women in general."[13] In either case, "The marriage with the second is a crime against the first, as well as adultery with the second."[14]

Verse 12, restating the acts of divorce and remarriage as initiated by the woman, is found in Mark alone. Matthew omitted it, since Jewish practice did not permit the wife to procure a divorce from her husband.[15] But it is clear that a Jewish woman could induce her husband to give her a divorce. The words of Jesus were significant for Mark's readers since the divorcing of the husband by the wife was legally possible and practiced under Roman law. But this does not warrant the assumption that the words were not spoken by Jesus. In preparing His disciples for their future world mission, Jesus, in this private lesson, completed His instructions on divorce by including the situation as it

---

[13] Brooks, p. 158.

[14] Matthew B. Riddle, "The Gospel According to St. Mark," in *International Revision Commentary on the New Testament,* p. 128.

[15] Josephus recorded that Salome, the sister of Herod the Great, sent her husband a bill of divorce, thus dissolving her marriage with him; and then he added, "Though this was not according to the Jewish laws; for with us it is lawful for a husband to do so; but a wife, if she departs from her husband cannot of herself be married to another, unless her former husband put her away" (*Antiquities* 15. 7. 10). A Jewish woman might *claim* divorce, but if her husband refused to give her a bill of divorcement, the claim could not be enforced. "In the last resort, divorce among the Jews was always the man's act" (D. E. Nineham, *The Gospel of St. Mark,* p. 266, note).

existed among the Greeks and Romans. The pagan practice of women's initiation of divorce was known to the Twelve and the inhabitants of Palestine generally. The fact that Herodias had forsaken her first husband to live with Antipas was common knowledge.

"And if a woman shall put away her husband"—Jesus held the sexes equally accountable in this matter of disrupting the marriage tie. The hardness of heart with which Jesus charged the Pharisees might be equally true of the wife.

"And marry another" (ASV)—the active voice pictures the woman also as taking the initiative in getting married again.[16]

In summary Brooks comments: "The effect of Jesus' teaching is to condemn all divorce as contrary to God's will and to set forth the highest standards of marriage for his disciples. Christians of all eras have often fallen short of the ideal just as ancient Jews did. . . . God can forgive divorce as well as other sins. Divorce may sometimes be the lesser of two evils, but it is never pleasing to God or good in itself. It should not be looked upon by conscientious Christians as the preferred option."[17]

3. Blessing of Little Children (vv. 13-16)

The beautiful little paragraph of verses 13-16 has parallels in Matthew 19:13-15 and Luke 18:15-17. Both Matthew and Mark appropriately placed it immediately after the discussion on divorce. It balances the opposition just encountered with an incident of simple trust. This lovely picture of the affection of Jesus for children and His tenderness toward them was treasured in the early church. It later came to be used in connection with the baptism of infants, but it contains no reference to baptism as such.

"And they brought young children to him"—the impersonal *they* most probably included some fathers or older sisters with the mothers. The word rendered "young children" was used in 5:39 of a girl twelve years old, but it generally denoted young children. The ages of the children no doubt varied, including some babes in their mother's arms (Luke 18:15). *Brought* does not necessitate the view that the children were carried. Their number can only be conjectured. Mark's *and* gives no chronological connection, but Matthew's "then" implies a close connection with the preceding. Apparently, the children were being brought to Him personally while Jesus was in the house (v. 10), before the commencement of the journey mentioned in verse 17.

---

[16] While some manuscripts here read the passive "and be married to another," the best manuscripts read the active.

[17] Brooks, p. 158.

"That he should touch them"—Matthew's fuller statement interprets the character of this desired touch: "that he should put *his* hands on them, and pray" (19:13). Jesus had just championed the sanctity of marriage and the home. Now those bringing their children yearned that this great Teacher should pronounce His benediction upon their children. Clearly His demeanor had strengthened this desire. There is no warrant for assuming any superstitious idea that His wonder-working touch would convey magical benefits.

"*His* disciples rebuked those that brought *them*"—the disciples, who were outside the house, were intent on protecting Jesus from what they considered an unnecessary and perhaps undignified intrusion upon His time and energy. Clearly the disciples did not make access to Jesus, whenever He was in retirement, an easy matter. They acted with an officious sense of their own importance as His protectors. *Rebuked* indicates that they reproved or censured the action with the intention of bringing it to an end. *Those* is masculine and indicates that those bringing the children were not exclusively mothers. The disciples felt that Jesus had weightier matters to deal with and to spend His time on than blessing little children. Had they remembered His teaching concerning children in Capernaum (9:36-37; Matt. 18:2-14), they could hardly have objected now.

"When Jesus saw *it*"—noticed from within what was going on outside the house. His sharp response was prompted by what He observed.

"He was much displeased"—another reference by Mark to the emotions of Jesus. The verb *much displeased,* used only here of Jesus, is a term of strong emotion and denotes His pained, angry reaction to what was going on. He was deeply displeased that the very men whom He had so explicitly taught misunderstood so grievously the basic principles of His ministry.

"Suffer the little children to come unto me, and forbid them not"— His double command put an end to the interference of the disciples. The aorist imperative *suffer,* better "permit, allow," was a peremptory command, demanding that they permit the children at once "to come unto me," to have continued access to Him. The command views the children as themselves being hindered; they had eagerly started toward Jesus on their own feet. *Forbid them not* is more literally, "Stop hindering them." The disciples had put out restraining hands, but they were told to cease their interference.

"For of such is the kingdom of God"—the explanation for His orders. *Such* denotes those who have certain definite qualities or characteristics. Jesus was not thinking of children per se but of the qualities they typify: the spirit of receptivity, dependence, and trustfulness. "It is simple character that counts and not tender years."[18] The genitive rendered "of such" may be possessive, "to such belongeth" (ASV), meaning that they possess the kingdom; but it can mean "of such is," that the kingdom is composed of those who possess these childlike characteristics. Gould remarks, "The kingdom of God in the world consists of those who substitute for self-will and independence the will of God, and trust in his wisdom and goodness. And this is the attitude of childhood. What children feel towards their parents man should feel towards God."[19] On the contrary, "The person who imagines that he or she is somehow worthy of God's favor and that participation in the Kingdom of God depends upon social or religious rank will never really enter the Kingdom that Jesus announces."[20] *The Kingdom of God* here clearly relates to the present rule of God in the lives of men. (See comments under 1:15.)

"Whosoever shall not receive the kingdom of God as a little child"—not *while* a child but with the attitude of a child. The point of comparison is not the innocence of children (for they too have a sinful nature and are not innocent) but their attitude of receptiveness and willingness to be dependent upon others for what they need. *Receive* stresses that, as a definite act, the kingdom must be accepted as a gift; it is not a human achievement, is never gained on the basis of human merit. Just as a child receives a gift from a loved one in guileless trustfulness, so the kingdom of God must be received as God's gift in simple trusting faith. Here is the essence of the doctrine of justification by faith.

"He shall not enter therein"—the strong double negative (*ou mē*, "no, not") here simply rendered "not" categorically excludes any other way of entry. *Enter therein* now pictures the kingdom of God as a society under His sovereign rule, whereof an individual becomes a member by subjecting himself to the divine authority. Refusing to receive the kingdom as a gift excludes one from a share in its blessings and responsibilities. Brooks aptly remarks, "Note that the kingdom is both to be received and entered—two ideas that stand side by side throughout the Bible. The blessings of the kingdom are to be received as a gift, yet we enter the kingdom through responsive faith and obedience."[21]

---

[18] Alfred Plummer, *The Gospel According to St. Mark,* in Cambridge Greek Testament, p. 236.

[19] Ezra P. Gould, *A Critical and Exegetical Commentary on the Gospel According to St. Mark,* International Critical Commentary, p. 188.

[20] Larry W. Hurtado, *Mark,* p. 149.

[21] Brooks, p. 160.

"He took them up in his arms"—Luke notes that Jesus called the children unto Him (18:16). Mark alone fully describes His actions in receiving them, going beyond the desired touch (v. 13). What He had already done with one child (9:36) He now did on a larger scale. As the children successively came up to Him, He took each of them in His arms and embraced them. Each repetition of the action was a rebuke to the attitude of the disciples.

"Put *his* hands upon them, and blessed them"—as each child was folded to His breast, Jesus disengaged one hand to lay it upon the little head while He pronounced His blessing upon the child, content to yield to His embrace. The compound verb *blessed,* occurring only here in the New Testament, is best viewed as intensive, "fervently blessed." The bestowal of His benediction was not a formal, perfunctory act. He blessed each child with fervent heart, for they refreshed His spirit. The benediction bestowed on these children did not confer upon them any special magical or spiritual virtue or quality. In keeping with Jewish rabbinical practice, Jesus was fervently invoking God's blessing upon them.

Barclay observes that this event "tells us a great deal about Jesus. It tells us that he was the kind of person who cared for children and for whom children cared. He could not have been a stern and gloomy and joyless man. There must have been a kindly sunshine on him."[22]

4. Question Concerning Eternal Life (vv. 17-22)

The vividness of Mark's account in verses 17-22 is evident from a comparison with the parallel passage in Matthew 19:16-22 and Luke 18:18-23. Yet each account supplies some particular additions. All the synoptics place it immediately after the blessing of the children as a striking illustration of the failure to attain a childlike spirit.

"When he was gone forth into the way"—the setting for the story, added only in Mark. The present tense participle suggests that Jesus was in the act of leaving the house where He had blessed the children. He was ready to resume His journey toward Jerusalem when He was met by the unnamed inquirer.

"There came one running, and kneeled to him"—the numeral *one* pictures the man as coming alone. Mark did not further characterize him, but Matthew described him as a "young man" (19:20, 22), while Luke called him "a certain ruler" (18:18). *Ruler* may mean that he was a ruler in a local synagogue, but his youth is somewhat against that view. Possibly the term means no more than that he was an influential man. His wealth and exemplary conduct would make him a

---

[22] Barclay, p. 241.

prominent individual in his community. The compiled designation, "The rich young ruler," is often used. He possessed admirable qualities. *Running* reveals his earnestness and eagerness to meet Jesus. Having heard of His presence, he hurried to reach Jesus before He left the community. *Kneeled to him* depicts an act of profound respect. It was not customary to kneel to a rabbi. It was the posture of the petitioner, acknowledging the superiority and authority of the one being approached.

"Good Master"—a very formal form of address to a Jewish teacher. It expressed great admiration for Jesus as one who would be able to give him the spiritual guidance he desired. His use of *good* was certainly sincere but betrayed a superficial concept of moral goodness. He regarded Jesus as a good rabbi who had mastered the secret of spiritual perfection, and he desired to learn that secret from Him.

"What shall I do that I may inherit eternal life?"—a vital question, one often discussed by thinking Jews (cf. Luke 10:25). The aorist verb *do* implies that the achievement of some great exploit, which he expected Jesus to point out to him, would assure him of eternal life after what he had already achieved. He asked to know what he should do to secure eternal life, the blessings of the messianic kingdom here and hereafter. In Jewish usage *inherit* carried the sense of "to come into possession of, to obtain." He assumed that he had the necessary ability and willingness to do whatever was yet required. He needed only guidance in its identification. Thompson well notes, "The concept that salvation, or life in its largest religious sense, is something that can be won by 'doing' any one thing, or a number of things, is completely false. The young man was on the wrong road."[23]

"Why callest thou me good?"—the stress falls on the word *good*. Jesus was challenging the inquirer's superficial use of it. His faulty conception of goodness was his basic problem.

"*There is* none good but one, *that is,* God"—God alone is the true standard for understanding what is good or morally beneficial. He alone is absolutely good, and all human goodness, moral and spiritual, is derived from God and must be recognized as wrought by Him. The young man thought of goodness as a personal moral attainment and regarded Jesus simply as one who had excelled in that attainment. He needed to recognize that God alone is beneficially good, the true source of the salvation which he mistakenly sought to attain by his own heroic effort.

---

[23] Ernest Trice Thompson, *The Gospel According to Mark and Its Meaning for Today,* p. 166.

The implications of this statement for Jesus Himself have been differently understood. The view that Jesus was thus denying His own sinlessness and deity is unwarranted. Such a view is "at variance with the entire Synoptics portraiture of Jesus."[24] Some interpreters hold that Jesus did not intend to make any pronouncement about His own nature but was simply interested in getting the man to see his own inadequate conception of goodness. This view has an element of truth but fails to recognize the contrast which the words imply. There was a contrast between the man's view of Him and what He was. Others, like Taylor, hold that the question of Jesus "implies a tacit contrast between the absolute goodness of God and His own goodness as subject to growth and trial in the circumstances of the Incarnation."[25] But Mark's picture of Jesus never hints that His goodness was limited or that it was in need of growth and further development. The asserted contrast between the two types of goodness seems unnecessary. A common view, held by many of the church fathers, is that Jesus was thus indicating His own deity: if the young man called Him "good," and only God is good, did he accept the implication in thus calling Him good? This view seems most consistent with Mark's picture of Christ. Certainly Mark's readers would have no trouble in accepting the implication that Jesus was God.

"Thou knowest the commandments"—the inquirer had framed his question on the basis of law works, and Jesus began with him on that basis. The commandments quoted are all from the second table of the law, those dealing with man's relationship with his fellow men. Jesus quoted in order the sixth, the seventh, the eighth, the ninth, and the fifth commandments. The unexpected command "Defraud not," found only in Mark, is not part of the Decalogue. Alexander holds that it was "probably a summary abbreviation of the tenth commandment, which alone is wanting to complete the second table."[26] Plummer suggests that "it may be added by Christ as a special warning to the rich man."[27] Jesus thus began with him on the level of human relationships. If He could induce in him a realization of his own inadequacy on this level, so much the better.

"Master"—the adjective *good* was now dropped.

"All these have I observed from my youth"—his claim was an expression, not of self-praise, but of personal disappointment. Instead

---

[24] V. Taylor, *The Gospel According to St. Mark,* p. 426.

[25] Ibid., p. 427.

[26] Joseph Addison Alexander, *The Gospel According to Mark,* pp. 279-80.

[27] Plummer, p. 239.

of some difficult task yet to be performed, which he had anticipated, Jesus was asking that which the man had been in the habit of doing from his youth. The term does not reveal anything about his age; a man of thirty years might still be called a youth. He meant that he had observed, or solicitously guarded, the commandments from being broken or dishonored ever since he had become personally responsible for his conduct as a "son of the law." He was sincere in his assertion, but the claim showed that he thought only of compliance with the external form and had no true conception of the inner spiritual nature of the law. In keeping with the Pharisaic emphasis upon the letter of the law, he felt that he had met all its requirements and regarded himself as blameless (cf. Phil. 3:6). Had he truly understood the inner moral demands of the law, he would have been brought to a consciousness of his own moral bankruptcy and been induced to acknowledge his need for saving grace to enter the kingdom. He had lived an outwardly exemplary life, but his quest betrayed the spiritual void in his heart. Jones remarks, "He was like Paul in his Pharisee days, laboriously and punctiliously performing every legal duty, and yet finding out there was no righteousness by the works of the law."[28] According to Matthew, he acknowledged his sense of need by asking, "What lack I yet?" (19:20).

"Then Jesus beholding him loved him"—in response to his reply, Jesus gave the man a searching, penetrating look. His frank, earnest face revealed that he had spoken in sincerity. Only Mark mentions this characteristic look by Jesus. Plummer comments, "It indicates that behind Mark is someone who was present, who was intimate with Christ, and who knew from experience how penetrating a look from Christ could be (Luke xxii, 61)."[29] Also, Mark alone makes reference here to the emotional reaction of Jesus. *Loved him* is probably best rendered "began to love him." Jesus felt strongly drawn to this young man for what he already was, and in love yearned to lead him to the full realization of his quest. *Loved* denotes not mere emotional affection but that high spiritual love which, regardless of the worthiness or unworthiness of the one loved, desires his highest welfare. "In love, Jesus calls; and in calling, he makes a radical demand."[30]

"One thing thou lackest"—in love, Jesus declared His diagnosis of the case. One thing caused his deficiency. That crucial need was not

---

[28] J. D. Jones, p. 350.

[29] Plummer, p. 240.

[30] Lamar Williamson, Jr., *Mark,* Interpretation, p. 183.

an additional personal virtue. "The one thing lacking is the all-important thing, a single-hearted devotion to God, obedience to the first of the Ten Commandments."[31]

The remedy was set forth in a double command. The first duty, set forth in three verbs of command—*Go, sell,* and *give*—prescribed the removal of the hindering cause. His root sin was that his wealth had usurped the place of God in his life. He must tear himself loose from his earthly possessions and his self-righteous achievements so that God could fill the place of supreme worth in his life. This was not a general counsel for all believers but a special measure needed in his case. While Jesus does not always make this demand on people, He always demands that the seeker must give up that which has usurped the place of God in his life. There are other idols in men's hearts besides wealth.

"Thou shalt have treasure in heaven"—Jesus made a stringent demand, yet the resultant compensation far outweighed the sacrifice. The selling of his possessions and giving the money to the poor was not a meritorious act which would *earn* a reward. His willingness to carry out the command would be external evidence that he had removed the idol from his heart and fixed his devotion on God. He would thus gain God's gracious approval and be assured of spiritual riches in future glory.

"Come, . . . follow me"—the second part of the command, relating to His demand on his further life. *Follow* is present tense, "be following me." Jesus invited him to a life of continuing fellowship with Himself. He was the answer to the man's need. To follow Him, to accept Him as Savior and Lord, is the way to eternal life. "Christ is seen putting Himself in the place of God to the soul of a man."[32]

"He was sad at that saying"—an observation preserved only in Mark. An expression of deep gloom clouded the man's face.[33] The word of Jesus to him was hard and caused his eagerness to give way to a feeling of deep sorrow and disappointment.

"Went away grieved"—his outward response and inner feeling. He went away, apparently in silence. His conscience permitted him to make no objection to the demand. *Grieved* renders a present passive participle, "being made sorrowful, aggrieved," and denotes the continual feeling of sorrow caused by the unexpected demand of Jesus.

---

[31] C.E.B. Cranfield, *The Gospel According to Saint Mark,* Cambridge Greek Testament Commentary, p. 330.

[32] G. Campbell Morgan, *The Gospel According to Mark,* p. 235.

[33] In Matt. 16:3, the only other place where this verb appears in the New Testament, it is applied to the gloomy appearance of the stormy sky.

This is the only instance in the Gospels in which Jesus' invitation "Follow Me" failed to win a positive response. Whether his sorrow later led him to repentance and obedience is not known.

"For he had great possessions"—apparently estates and lands. The demand upon him was costly, but the response proved that the diagnosis of Jesus was correct. He preferred his present earthly possessions to future spiritual possessions in heaven. "He wanted God, but not at the cost of his gold; he wanted life, but not at the expense of luxury; he was willing to serve, but not to sacrifice."[34]

5. Discussion About Wealth and Reward (vv. 23-31)

The discussion on wealth and reward, evoked by the departure of the rich young man, is recorded in all the synoptics (Matt. 19:23-20:16; Luke 18:24-30). Matthew preserves the fullest account.

"And Jesus looked round about"—having watched the rich young man depart, Jesus turned to give His disciples a deliberate, sweeping look to see what impression the incident had made on them. "He turns His attention back to the disciples, realizing once again that the future of the Gospel depends upon His teaching and their learning."[35] Only Mark records this look. It again points to an eyewitness behind Mark's account.

"And saith unto his disciples"—having arrested their attention with His look, Jesus drew the lesson for His disciples. The historical present *saith* again vividly takes the reader into the presence of Jesus as He utters His amazing pronouncement.

"How hardly shall they that have riches enter into the kingdom of God"—*How hardly,* "with what difficulty," indicates that wealth does not automatically exclude one from the kingdom, but it does constitute a handicap. In the singular the word rendered "riches" means a thing one uses, and in the plural, as here, money, wealth. It is more general than *possession* in verse 22, which seems primarily to denote lands and houses. Jesus' words are a generalization of the truth so clearly demonstrated in the case of the rich young man. In him wealth revealed its power beyond most other things in life to work a deadly effect upon the will when a seeker is confronted with the demand to choose between it and the kingdom. He had made many noble choices, but when he was confronted with this crucial decision, his wealth showed its strong power to weaken his will to choose the highest good. "Wealth," McKenna remarks, "is a human value with a voracious appetite which

---

[34] W. Graham Scroggie, *The Gospel of Mark,* p. 181.

[35] David L. McKenna, *Mark,* The Communicator's Commentary, p. 211.

binds a person to earth.''[36] Jesus did not envy the rich but rather pitied them. It put them under a terrible handicap in their relationship to the kingdom of God, making it hard for them to submit to His rule in simple trust.

Verse 24 is unique to Mark.

''The disciples were astonished at his words''—were utterly astonished at what He said. Only Mark used this verb in the New Testament, always as the effect of some word (1:27) or action (10:32) of Jesus. They were astounded because they had always thought of wealth as an advantage, not a danger. Brooks remarks, ''The dominant Jewish view was that riches were an indication of divine favor and a reward for piety (Job 1:10; 42:10; Ps. 128:1-2; Isa. 3:10).''[37]

''Jesus answereth again''—made a further pronouncement in response to their amazement, replying to their bewildered thoughts.

''Children''—used only here in the Gospels of the Twelve (''little children'' in John 13:33). Aware that the Twelve, as His spiritual children, were still young and immature, Jesus felt affectionate sympathy toward them.

''How hard is it for them that trust in riches to enter into the kingdom of God!''—the words present a difficult textual problem. Important manuscripts omit the words *for them that trust in riches*. If retained, they provide an explanation for the rich man's difficulty. The words bring into sharp focus the real danger of riches. Not their possession but the trust in them constitutes the danger. The statement implies that this false reliance on wealth is natural and almost always is connected with its possession. If the phrase is omitted, the statement is a generalization concerning the difficulty of entrance for any man. The textual evidence is fairly evenly divided.[38] Advocates for omission hold that the words are a scribal addition to tone down the drastic assertion about the rich. But the words clarify rather than tone down the assertions. Bruce argues for their omission by pointing out that ''it is not merely difficult but impossible for one *trusting* in riches to enter the Kingdom.''[39] Clearly such a trust in riches excludes the rich man, but the words of Jesus indicate how difficult it is to change this attitude in the rich man (cf. v. 27). The generalization—the statement minus

---

[36] McKenna, p. 211.

[37] Brooks, p. 163.

[38] Modern critical editors omit the phrase but recognize that the textual evidence is not strongly decisive. The manuscript evidence is probably stronger for than against omission, but the internal evidence seems to point the other way.

[39] Bruce, 1:411. Bruce's italics.

the disputed phrase—states a vital theological truth which Christ's followers are prone to overlook, but the context argues against the generalization here. The assertion was evoked by the sight of a rich man declining to enter because of his wealth, and verse 25 again centers on the rich man's entrance. The wider breadth of the generalization does not appear until verse 26 and after. Both readings make good sense, but the longer reading seems somewhat more suitable in the context.

"It is easier for a camel to go through the eye of a needle"—a bold comparison that indicates an utter impossibility. The statement has in view the rich man who *trusts* in his riches; otherwise all rich men would be summarily excluded. His trust in his riches, excluding trust in God's grace, effectively keeps him out. *It is easier* points to some work more easily performed than that to which it is compared. The rich man's entrance would be more difficult work than for a camel to go through a needle's eye. The picture is apparently a popular proverb denoting something impossible. The Babylonian Talmud twice mentions an elephant passing through the eye of a needle as an impossibility. Christ's reference to the camel, the largest beast of burden familiar to Palestine, going through the eye of a common sewing needle would be readily recognized as a humorous suggestion of an utter impossibility. The statement was quoted in the Koran, and Bruce notes that "proverbs about the camel and the needle-eye, to express the impossible, are still current among the Arabs."[40] There is no warrant for attempts to tone down the force of the words as they stand.[41]

"They were astonished out of measure"—this strong verb, meaning "to strike out of one's senses," is in the imperfect to denote the protracted feeling of utter bewilderment on the part of the disciples. The adverb *out of measure* stresses that it broke all bounds. They were shocked beyond all measure by His words.

"Who then can be saved?"—literally, "And who is able to be saved?" *And* at the head of the question accepts what has just been

---

[40] Ibid.

[41] Two different efforts to lessen the force of the picture have been made. The hypothetical suggestion, dating from the fifth century, that we should read *kamilos*, "a rope, a ship's cable," rather than *kamelos*, "camel," does not help, since it is still utterly impossible for a cable used on the anchor of a ship to pass through the eye of a needle. In the fifteenth century, it was suggested that the "needle's eye" had reference not to a common needle but to a side gate in the wall of Jerusalem used for foot passengers, through which an unloaded camel could squeeze with difficulty. This suggestion is without historical foundation and negates the force of Christ's comparison. There is no justification for attempts to reduce the size of the camel or to enlarge the orifice.

said and makes a rejoinder, carrying the statement to its conclusion. It is a protest. Their meaning is, "If a rich man can't be saved, then nobody can."

"Jesus looking upon them saith"—both Matthew and Mark record this look. His look riveted their attention to His reply. Jesus did not retreat from His position but revealed that God alone can solve the situation.

"With men *it is* impossible"—*it,* "to be saved," is an impossibility with men, that is, on the human level as a human achievement. This categorical assertion is true for rich and poor alike.

"But not with God"—the strong adversative *but* introduces the only hope. God is able to work in men a supernatural work of transformation.

"For with God all things are possible"—*for* points to the divine ability as the one basis for hope. God's power is unlimited, but He does not do things contrary to His character and purposes. *All things* relates to things necessary for man's salvation. On the basis of the atonement, He can provide the perfect righteousness which man can never attain; through the work of the Holy Spirit, He can bring men to a change of heart, leading unwilling and sinful hearts to accept the divine provision. "Therefore all must depend entirely upon God. Such absolute trust in God makes possible a life of faithful discipleship (v. 28)."[42]

"Peter began to say unto him"—all the synoptics here mention Peter as the spokesman. The absence of any connecting participle is in keeping with Peter's sudden, impulsive outburst. *Began to say* indicates that his comment turned the discussion into a new direction.

"Lo, we have left all, and have followed thee"—the exclamation, *Lo,* draws strong attention to what he is saying, while his emphatic *we* contrasts the Twelve with the rich young ruler. The wording reveals Peter's consciousness of the importance of what the Twelve, unlike the rich young man, have done. *Left all* is aorist and looks back to the definite break that they had made in response to His call; they had abandoned all to follow Him. *Have followed* is perfect tense and stresses that the following then begun still continues. What they had done was a costly thing. Anderson points out, "Peter puts the act of renunciation first (even exaggerating it, *we have left everything,* since his break with home ties was not complete, see 1:29; 3:9; 4:1, 36; cf. 1 C. 9:5), and discipleship second, thus implying from the Marcan viewpoint that he is still among the blind ones who put what men can do

---

[42] Brooks, p. 165.

before what God can give.''[43] Matthew recorded the implied question in Peter's assertion, ''What shall we have therefore?'' (19:27). It reveals that the Twelve were still thinking in terms of material rather than spiritual riches.

''Jesus answered and said''—His answer, directed to the Twelve, reveals His tenderness and wisdom. He gave an answer that related to the Twelve personally, preserved only in Matthew 19:28-29, and then stated the principle of reward in general terms. He did not rebuke Peter but did add a warning of the self-seeking spirit latent in his words.

''Verily I say unto you''—this formula of solemn affirmation calls upon the Twelve to fix their attention on and accept what He now declares.

''There is no man that hath left''—there are no exceptions to the promise here made to the man who actually made the break, ''did leave.'' Jesus knew that the call to follow Him involved the severing of strong ties. His enumeration is remarkably full, ''houses, or brethren, or sisters, or mother, or father, or children, or lands'' (ASV). Luke added, ''or wife.'' The things left fall under the general categories of home, relatives, property. The disjunctive *or* implies that not all have been required to leave all of them. Life is not mentioned since none of them had as yet faced the challenge of martyrdom.

''For my sake, and the gospel's''—the high motives for their action. Their forsaking was prompted by their relationship to Him as well as their adherence to the gospel. The words reveal Christ's high consciousness that He and the gospel were distinct yet inseparable. Morison well said, ''Without Him the gospel would be nothing; without the gospel men would know nothing of Him.''[44] ''For the gospel's sake'' may imply that they had left these things in order to proclaim the gospel, the good news.

''But he shall receive an hundredfold''—there will be no one who has made the sacrifice who will not as a definite act receive sublime compensation, a hundredfold, the highest degree of return. It will be a return in kind, yet different: a spiritual relationship and possessions in exchange for natural connections and material substance. ''A man's Christianity might involve the loss of home and friends and loved ones, but his entry into the Christian Church brought him into a far greater and wider family than ever he had left, a family who were all spiritually kin to him.''[45]

---

[43] Hugh Anderson, *The Gospel of Mark,* p. 251.

[44] James Morison, *A Practical Commentary on the Gospel According to St. Mark,* p. 290.

[45] Barclay, p. 249.

"Now in this time"—sacrifices made for Him will receive a present reward. *Now,* not just in a far-off future. *This time,* or "this season," seems to refer to the time of the first advent, while Christ was here to call His followers. More generally, it would relate to the present age, before the establishment of the kingdom in glory, while sacrifices for Him are still called for.

"With persecutions"—added in Mark alone. The experience of persecutions would accompany the experiences of the rewards here. They are in reality part of the blessings. It has been the common experience that persecutions only sweeten the rich social and religious fellowship enjoyed by the saints.

"In the world to come eternal life"—more literally, "in the coming age," the future messianic age, when the kingdom has been established in glory. But in that age, the further rewards experienced by the saints are no longer connected with persecutions. Then the redeemed will share life in its highest sense through the ages without interruption.

Verse 31 is a wise warning against the self-seeking spirit which lurked behind Peter's comment. The Twelve were warned that their priority in being called did not guarantee their preeminence in the future if they lacked the necessary spirit. The explanatory parable preserved in Matthew 20:1-16 reveals the spirit warned against. The rewards of the kingdom are given not on the grounds of priority in time or self-seeking service or human ideas of merit, but simply on the grounds of confidence in God and love for His kingdom. "It is a warning that the ultimate judgments belong to God who alone knows the motives of men's hearts. It is a warning that the judgments of heaven may well upset the reputations of earth."[46]

6. Third Announcement of the Passion (10:32-34)

The announcement has parallels in Matthew 20:17-19 and Luke 18:31-34. It is Christ's third and last explicit announcement to the Twelve of His coming Passion and is the fullest of the three (cf. 8:31; 9:31).[47] Mark alone gives a vivid account of its historical setting.

"They were in the way going up to Jerusalem"—the first mention of the goal of the journey recorded in this chapter. This scene took place while they were on the open highway, going up to Jerusalem. A journey to Jerusalem was always referred to as going *up,* because of the exalted nature of the holy city in the eyes of the Jews as well as its geographic location. Situated on a high point of the highlands of

---

[46] Ibid., p. 250.

[47] He also referred to His death while descending from the mount of transfiguration with the three disciples (9:12).

Palestine, the city could not be approached from any direction without an ascent.

"Jesus went before them"—mentioned only in Mark. *Them* refers to the Twelve. Jesus did not walk with the disciples as usual but rather walked ahead alone. The imperfect tense, "was going," pictures this as His protracted action. Mark's mention of this fact indicates an unusual activity on Jesus' part.

"They were amazed"—the same verb used in verse 24. The cause of the amazement of the Twelve is not stated, but clearly it was the unusual action of Jesus. In verse 24 the disciples were amazed at Jesus' words; here they are amazed at His action. John's Gospel makes it clear that the raising of Lazarus had brought the hostility of the religious leaders at Jerusalem to a head, and Jesus, to escape their wrath, had withdrawn to Ephraim (John 11:47-57). But now, He was resolutely and energetically leading the way back to Jerusalem; with solemn determination, He was pushing forward in the face of the obvious danger involved. Knowing the danger and struck by their Master's silent preoccupation with His own thoughts as He was walking ahead alone, the Twelve were gripped with a sense of amazement. The nervous disciples apparently were reluctant to follow the lead of Jesus. Manson comments: "They are baffled and bewildered by Him, and yet they cannot desert. There is something touching about this stubborn blind devotion to a leader whom they love but cannot understand."[48]

"They that followed were afraid" (ASV)—the article with the participle, making it substantival, refers to a group distinct from the Twelve. Without the article, the words would refer to the Twelve. This undefined group of followers came behind the Twelve. They were adherents of Jesus who kept close to Him while making their way to Jerusalem for the Passover. They too sensed the atmosphere of tension, and forebodings of evil filled their hearts with fear.

"He took again the twelve"—after having walked ahead alone in silent meditation, Jesus now gathered the Twelve close around Him for a special word to them. The mention of the Twelve implies the presence of a larger group which was not invited to hear His message (cf. Matt. 20:17). "Took again" stands in contrast to His previous "going before." This action underlines the continuing incomprehension of the Twelve and Jesus' yearning to overcome their blindness.

"Began to tell them what things should happen unto him"—sensing the tension that His action had produced, Jesus acted to explain its significance to His disciples. Having dwelt in thought on the things

---

[48] T. W. Manson, as quoted in Thompson, *The Gospel According to Mark,* p. 170.

that lay ahead for Him, He now unfolded them to the disciples. The unwelcome topic of His coming suffering had been dropped for a while, but now He resumed it. He presented to them the most specific description of His coming death and resurrection yet given them.

"Behold, we go up to Jerusalem"—*behold* invited their attention to His words as something important. *We* united the disciples with Him in this fateful journey to Jerusalem; they would be there to witness what would happen to Him. According to Luke, Jesus prefaced His mention of the things ahead with the remark that they were the fulfillment of prophecy (18:31). These coming events Jesus delineated in a series of eight future verbs, implying their certainty and nearness. His coming condemnation will be brought about by a judicial process on the part of the chief priests and the scribes, the Sanhedrin. Since the power of capital punishment had been taken from the Sanhedrin, the condemnation of Him will cause them to deliver Him unto the Gentiles. For Jews to be told by a Jew that he would be delivered to the Gentiles for execution added further terror to the picture. The disciples would readily understand the reference as being to the Roman officials in Jerusalem.

The verbs *mock, scourge, spit upon,* and *kill* graphically depict the treatment He will receive at the hands of the Gentiles. Each element mentioned here found an exact fulfillment in the subsequent narrative of the Passion. Mark's *kill* is less specific than Matthew's *crucify* (20:19), but the execution of a Jew by the Romans would be by crucifixion.

"The third day he shall rise again"—the concluding element in all the announcements. But unlike the others, this is never enlarged upon.

Nineham remarks concerning this announcement, "In its present form it is regarded by almost all commentators as a 'prophecy after the event.' "[49] But there is no reason why the Christ depicted in the Gospels should be regarded as unable to foresee the future and make this explicit prediction of specified events. It is unwarranted to reject this detailed prediction as being the actual words of Jesus. Aside from His messianic character, as an observant man Jesus might have anticipated all of the elements mentioned in connection with an official execution at that time. The events mentioned in verse 34 are not in the order given in the account of the historical fulfillment.

Mark includes nothing of the reaction of the Twelve to this announcement, but Luke again comments on their failure to understand (18:34).

---

[49] Nineham, p. 278.

7. Problem of Position Among the Disciples (vv. 35-45)

This paragraph, verses 35-45, which has a parallel only in Matthew 20:20-28, again demonstrates the failure of the disciples to comprehend the true significance of Christ's announcement of His coming sufferings (vv. 32-34). They were conscious that a crisis was impending, but the only crisis they could conceive of was the open establishment of the messianic kingdom at Jerusalem. After the second announcement (9:31), the disciples disputed among themselves which of them would be the greatest in the kingdom. Following this announcement, two of them sought to secure for themselves favored positions in the kingdom. Their deep-rooted expectation that Jesus would soon unveil His messianic rule blocked any comprehension by the disciples of the natural meaning of Christ's predictions. This paragraph relates the self-seeking request of James and John (vv. 35-40) and the teaching to the Twelve about greatness because of that request (vv. 41-45).

a. Request of James and John (vv. 35-40).

Mark's opening *and* indicates no chronological connection, but Matthew's *then* establishes a close sequence. Rawlinson regards this story as "quite disconnected with the immediate context."[50] Admittedly, the request of the two disciples was most inopportune, but the timing is clear evidence of their misapprehension of what Jesus was seeking to teach them. Yet as Barclay notes, "There is amazing confidence and amazing loyalty there. Misguided James and John might be, but their hearts were in the right place. They never doubted Jesus' ultimate triumph."[51]

"And James and John, the sons of Zebedee, come unto him"—approached Jesus in the absence of the other disciples. The historical present *come* again vividly presents the scene. As members of the inner circle, they had already received favors from Jesus (5:37; 9:2). Now they selfishly wanted Jesus to assure them of positions of privilege in the kingdom. *The sons of Zebedee* identify the two by their father's name (cf. 1:19). Matthew records that "the mother of the sons of Zebedee" came with them and acted as the spokesman. Whether she was the prime mover behind the endeavor, she had the full approval of her sons. If she was the sister of the mother of Jesus, as seems probable, she hoped that family connections would assure the granting of her desire.

---

[50] A.E.J. Rawlinson, *St. Mark,* p. 144.

[51] Barclay, p. 254.

"Master"—the Greek form for the familiar *rabbi* (cf. 9:5). According to Matthew, both her homage and the form of her request indicated that the wife of Zebedee was approaching Jesus as a mighty monarch who was able to grant the requests of His subjects without limitation.

"We would that thou shouldest do for us whatsoever we shall desire"—regarding Jesus as a mighty King, though presently in disguise, they desired His pledge that their undefined request would be granted. Perhaps because of an inner consciousness that their selfish request might properly be refused by Him, they sought to bind Him in advance.

"What would ye that I should do for you?"—Jesus declined to assume the role of a ruling Sovereign, granting their unspoken request as an expression of His sovereign power. Instead, He asked them to state their desire openly. The formulation of their request would reveal what was in their hearts. "The Lord, as usual, allows men to display their own spiritual depth or shallowness by disclosing their aims."[52]

"Grant unto us"—"give to us." What they asked would be a gift from Him, an expression of His favor.

"That we may sit, one on thy right hand, and one on *thy* left hand, in thy glory" (ASV)—placed before the verb, the two place designations, "on thy right hand" and "on thy left hand," are stressed. In a royal court, they were the places of highest honor, the one on the right having the precedence. *On (ek)* is literally "out of" and denotes direction; it views the two places as extending out from the monarch seated on his central throne. Their repeated *one* left it to Jesus to decide which position each was to occupy. To be seated there would indicate that they had been assigned these positions of honor and authority. *In thy glory* points to their anticipation of His splendor in His coming kingdom. A glimpse of that glory they had seen on the mount, and they felt sure that He would soon unveil His glorious rule as Messiah. They thus expressed their firm allegiance to Him, but their request was selfishly motivated. They did not err on the side of modesty. For them the question "who *should be* the greatest" (9:34) had not been settled. Clearly, they did not hold that Jesus had assigned the position of primacy to Peter.

"Ye know not what ye ask"—Matthew's account also indicates that this reply was directed to the two disciples personally. Their mother had only spoken for them. In verse 35, their verb *ask* is in the active voice; Jesus here used the middle which stresses personal interest,

---

[52] R. A. Cole, *The Gospel According to St. Mark*, p. 169.

"calling attention to the self-seeking which inspired the request and was its deepest condemnation."[53] Their ambitious request was foolish because they did not know what was involved in it. They spoke in ignorance.

"Can ye drink of the cup that I drink of?"—in the Old Testament, the cup is a symbol of joy (Pss. 23:5; 116:13) as well as of retribution and suffering (Ps. 75:8; Isa. 51:17-23; Jer. 25:15-28; Zech. 12:2). *Can drink* indicated that to drink of this cup would not be pleasant. Jesus personally knew what it meant. *I* is emphatic, and *drink* is in the present tense, indicating continuing action. The present tense here may mean that He was already drinking the cup but had not yet reached the dregs. Swete thinks that His drinking of the cup "was coextensive with the incarnate life on earth, but the Passion is of course chiefly in view."[54] Cranfield holds that Jesus was "apparently thinking of the cup of God's wrath against sin" which He would drink during the coming Passion.[55] According to this view, the tense is a futuristic present, denoting its future certainty. The use of the present also in the next questions seems to make the futuristic present more probable here.

"And be baptized with the baptism that I am baptized with?"— restating the same question under a different figure. The verb *baptized,* which has the basic meaning "to dip, immerse," was commonly used in a metaphorical sense of being flooded or overwhelmed with calamities. In the first question, *to drink* is active, questioning their willingness to drink voluntarily the cup of suffering; here, *to be baptized* is passive, pointing to the fact that these sufferings come from without, are imposed upon Him. He too is thus being baptized. The passive points to God as the agent laying the sufferings upon Him. Jesus was thinking of His coming sufferings at Jerusalem which would overwhelm His soul and culminate in His death. He was voluntarily facing the sufferings incurred in the establishment of the kingdom. Were they morally qualified to join Him?

"We can"—their eager assertion of their ability reveals their bond of loyalty to Him; they thought they were willing to pay the price involved. But they spoke in rash self-confidence, not understanding the cost. They regarded His questions as a test of their moral courage, little realizing the spiritual power that would be needed.

"Jesus said unto them"—Jesus did not question their own estimate of their ability but told them that what they so readily accepted would

---

[53] Swete, p. 236.

[54] Ibid., pp. 236-37.

[55] Cranfield, p. 337.

have a future fulfillment. They would indeed share the cup and baptism, although obviously their sufferings would not have the redemptive character of His own sufferings. The words of Jesus indicate that James and John would endure great sufferings, but they do not assert their actual martyrdom. James indeed became the first apostle to drink the cup of martyrdom (Acts 12:2), while John, although escaping physical martyrdom, was a living martyr suffering persecution, banishment, and the loneliness of old age, being left behind as the last apostle to stand against the pervading trend toward apostasy.[56]

"But to sit on my right hand and on my left hand is not mine to give"—they had asked that the positions be given to them as a personal favor. Jesus replied that He had no positions to give as a mere personal favor. Their request asked Him to act as an earthly monarch, bestowing personal favors on His favorites according to His own caprice.

"But *it shall be given to them* for whom it is prepared"—positions in the kingdom are for those who are morally qualified for them. They will be granted according to the righteous determination of the Father (Matt. 20:23). They will be given to those for whom "it has been prepared." The perfect tense implies that the matter has already been settled, while the impersonal construction means "God has prepared." Those for whom the positions have been prepared will themselves be prepared for them. They will have a fitness of character to occupy them, achieved through sacrificial service. "He who goes nearest in time to Christ the crucified shall get nearest in eternity to Christ the glorified."[57]

b. Teaching to the Twelve (vv. 41-45).

This lesson concerning greatness is a fuller statement of the teaching Christ had already given while yet in Capernaum (9:35-37). Luke recorded similar teaching given to the Twelve in the upper room during Passion Week (22:24-30).

"When the ten heard *it*"—how they heard of the request of James and John is not indicated. Jones offers the interesting conjecture: "When the other disciples saw James and John on their knees before the Master, they inferred that they were begging for something, and perhaps begging for something to the detriment of others. So when the whole incident was over, they began to cross-examine the two brothers as to the subject of this private interview of theirs, and it was not long

---

[56] On the questionable tradition that John suffered an early martyrdom with James, see V. Taylor, p. 442.

[57] Morison, p. 296.

before they had wormed the ugly secret out of them."[58] *The ten,* an expression found only in connection with this incident, views the rest of the Twelve as united in their reaction. Perhaps Peter was the leader in expressing their feeling.

"They began to be much displeased"—the verb, used of Jesus in verse 14, denotes a strong emotional response ("moved with indignation," ASV). They strongly resented the effort of James and John "to steal a march" on them. When Jesus bestowed special privileges on Peter, James, and John (5:37; 9:2), the others showed no resentment; that was His prerogative. But they were deeply offended when the two brothers privately requested preferential treatment for themselves. *Began* apparently suggests that their strong feeling against James and John was not allowed to continue for long; Jesus acted at once to arrest it. Their reaction was no more praiseworthy than the selfish ambition of the two. All of them would have gladly accepted the positions James and John had the audacity to ask for themselves, but they resented the unfair efforts of James and John to secure those positions. They "betrayed their spiritual shallowness by being indignant at the spiritual shallowness of the two."[59]

"Jesus called them *to him*"—*them* refers directly to the ten, but the two certainly were not excluded from the lesson. Perhaps they were nearby when Jesus called the group to Him for a face-to-face encounter. He acted to meet the threat to the harmony in the apostolic circle. The ten had reason to be offended, but all needed the lesson He wanted to teach.

"Ye know"—Jesus began with their knowledge of greatness as it operated in the Gentile world. The worldly principle of greatness, by contrast, would furnish the basis for His teaching concerning spiritual greatness.

"They which are accounted to rule over the Gentiles"—*Gentiles* might better be rendered "nations"; the reference is to the non-Jewish world. *Accounted* has been taken to mean that their rule was only apparent, for the real rule belongs to God. But the word probably refers to their being recognized as ruling. Impressed by their exercise of power, men acknowledge them as rulers. Jesus was not awed by their worldly power, and saw that their position as rulers depended upon a reputation which might suddenly be destroyed, resulting in their overthrow.

---

[58] J. D. Jones, p. 379.

[59] Cole, p. 170.

"Exercise lordship over them"—practice complete domination over their subjects. The picture touches "on the tender spot of men who have been ground under the heel of Roman oppression."[60] The compound verb, literally "lord it down on them," indicates the imposition of power from above; they use their lordship to their own advantage. It is the picture of more or less oppressed subjects.

"Their great ones exercise authority upon them"—a parallel statement. *Great ones* denotes the Gentile magnates who occupy positions of grandeur. *Exercise authority* is again a compound verb, picturing the imposition of authority from above, exploiting those beneath.

"But it is not so among you" (ASV)—*but* points to the contrast between worldly greatness and the greatness operative in His kingdom. *Is* asserts present reality; the spiritual principle for attaining greatness is already operative "among you," in the sphere of Christ's followers. But it is obvious that they had not yet grasped the principle.

"Whosoever will be great among you"—in speaking of world rulers, Jesus used the plural to denote the class; in speaking of those in His kingdom, He used the individualizing singular, *whosoever*, leaving the desire to be great open to all. *Will be* might be rendered "wishes to be"; it is a matter of individual will. The aspiration to be great is not condemned.

"Shall be your minister"—setting forth the true way to attain greatness. *Minister*, or "helper," denotes one whose activities are directed toward serving others rather than toward furthering his own interests. It views the aspiring man in relation to his helpfulness toward others. Greatness in the kingdom is attained by the measure of beneficent services voluntarily rendered.

"Whosoever of you will be the chiefest, shall be servant of all"—there is a threefold advance here. *The chiefest*, or "first," contemplates the individual who has the holy ambition of attaining to the highest position even among those who are "great." *Servant*, literally, "slave," denotes a lower position than *minister*, implying that such a one foregoes his own rights in order to serve others for Christ's sake. *Of all* enlarges the scope of service to all to whom he may be helpful. Preeminence in Christ's kingdom is attained through primacy in self-sacrificing services voluntarily rendered. "The test was not, What service can I extract? but, What service can I give?"[61]

"For"—giving a reason in justification of the rule just laid down for His followers. Even the messianic King Himself is not excluded

---

[60] McKenna, p. 218.

[61] Barclay, p. 257.

from the principle of greatness just enunciated. He Himself is its highest example. Jesus is the exemplary Servant of God.

"The Son of man came"—this verse contains the clearest statement of the object of Christ's coming found in the Gospels. But this theological declaration was made to enforce a practical truth for everyday conduct. *Came* suggests a voluntary coming. He came of His own free will to carry out the principle of service just set forth.

"Not to be ministered unto, but to minister"—the motive of His life stated negatively and positively. Jesus did receive ministries rendered to Him as voluntary expressions of love (Luke 8:2-3), but that was not His purpose in coming. He did not compel others to serve Him but rather spent Himself in serving others. His total ministry was aimed at helping others. "Jesus did not identify the kind of service he performed but affirmed that his life was characterized by a servant attitude and by actually performing many kinds of service and ministry."[62]

"And to give his life a ransom for many"—His ministry would culminate in His death as the highest point of His service. "The *subjects* of the Kingdom must submit to the *life* of a slave, but the King submits to the *death* of a slave: the higher the position the greater the sacrifice."[63] *To give* again denotes a voluntary act, while the aorist tense designates the full actuality of the self-giving. To give His life, or "his soul," is to give Himself, the supreme gift. A ransom is the price paid to effect the release of prisoners or captives. Jesus viewed men as the captives of sin, wholly unable to free themselves from its power. His death for them would be the means for effecting their release. The preposition rendered *for* (*anti*) has the basic meaning of two equivalents that may be exchanged. It expresses the thought of equivalence and conveys the further thought of *substitution,* its common meaning in the papyruses. Moulton and Milligan point out that in the papyruses "by far the commonest meaning of *anti* is the simple 'instead of.' "[64] This sense is in accord with the substitutionary view of Christ's death. He gave His own life "instead of"—dying as the substitute for—many. *Many* points to the contrasts between the one life of the Redeemer and the many thereby redeemed. It does not imply a contrast to "all" but pictures the great multitude affected by His gracious act.

---

[62] Brooks, p. 171.

[63] A. F. Hort, *The Gospel According to St. Mark,* p. 142. Hort's italics.

[64] James Hope Moulton and George Milligan, *The Vocabulary of the Greek Testament,* p. 46.

8. Healing of the Jericho Beggar (vv. 46-52)

This vivid account, suggesting the reminiscence of an eyewitness, is the last miracle of healing recorded in Mark's Gospel. All the synoptics have the account, but there are divergent details. The critics have appealed to them to prove contradictions in the Bible, while defenders of its accuracy have diligently sought ways of harmonization. The variants clearly show the independence of the Gospel accounts. If all the facts were known, there undoubtedly would be no difficulties of reconciliation.

"They came to Jericho"—*they* denotes Jesus and His disciples. The arrival at Jericho brought them to the last stage in the journey to Jerusalem recorded in this chapter. Leaving Perea, they had crossed the Jordan east of Jericho and were following the usual route to Jerusalem. "Jericho is five miles west of the Jordan, six miles north of the Dead Sea, and fifteen air miles and twenty-one road miles northeast of Jerusalem."[65] This is the only recorded visit to Jericho by Jesus, although no doubt He had passed through the city on His previous trips to Jerusalem. The New Testament Jericho stood some distance south of the site of the Old Testament Jericho. It was a fine city, built by Herod the Great and adorned by his son Archelaus (Matt. 2:22). The mountains of Judea rose abruptly a little to the west.

"As he went out of Jericho"—Matthew also notes that the healing took place as they "departed from Jericho" (20:29), but Luke reports that it was "as he was come nigh unto Jericho" (18:35). Various harmonizations have been suggested. Unlikely are the suggestions that there were two different healings, one before and one after the entry into the city, or that Jesus was first approached as He entered Jericho but that the healing took place when He left, perhaps the next morning. Another suggestion is that the healing took place after Jesus had passed through Jericho but was returning to the city with Zacchaeus. More probable is the suggestion that there were two Jerichos in Jesus' day, one on the old site, the other the Herodian city. There is no direct evidence for the existence of two separate cities at that time, but the suggestion receives some plausibility from the fact that Elisha's Fountain, the main source of water supply for the area, is adjacent to the old site. Numerous dwellings may well have been located there. Still others hold that Luke's language simply means that Jesus was "near"

---

[65] Brooks, p. 172.

or in the vicinity of Jericho when the healing took place.[66] This seems the simplest reconciliation.

"With his disciples and a great number of people"—the crowd was composed of Passover pilgrims who joined Jesus and His disciples for the trip up to Jerusalem. The crowd had apparently been swollen by various accessions from the towns through which they had passed. It indicates that Jesus no longer shunned publicity. The story to be told had a sufficient, or considerable, number of witnesses.

"Bartimaeus, the son of Timaeus"—only Mark preserves the man's name. The remembrance of his name may mean that he was a well-known member of the early church in Jerusalem. *The son of Timaeus* may be regarded as a translation of the Aramaic *Bartimaeus*. But elsewhere Mark always gives his translation after the original (3:17; 5:41; 7:11, 34); here it is not. Apparently the double designation here was not intended as a translation. *Bartimaeus,* a patronymic, was apparently used as the man's personal name, while *the son of Timaeus* indicated his paternal relationship.

"Blind, . . . sat by the highway side begging"—blindness was tragically common, and blind men were proverbially beggars. This beggar had intentionally taken his station on the road leading to Jerusalem in order to attract the attention of the Passover pilgrims. Mark and Luke mention only one man, but Matthew says there were "two blind men." Matthew, centering attention upon the messianic deed, recalls that there were two men healed; their double testimony established an authentic witness to the Son of David. Bartimaeus probably was the leader and, as a member of the church, was later remembered as an example of the healing power of Jesus.

"When he heard that it was Jesus of Nazareth"—may be rendered as direct discourse: "When he heard, 'It is Jesus the Nazarene.' " This rendering would vividly preserve the very words of the informant. The tramp of many feet alerted the beggar that something unusual was happening, and he eagerly inquired of its meaning (Luke 18:36). His informant, who recognized Jesus as the leader of the travelers, told him that Jesus the Nazarene was passing by. "The Nazarene" at times was used as a contemptuous designation, but here it apparently was simply a term of closer identification.

"He began to cry out, and say"—the news at once stirred him to begin a loud clamor for the attention of Jesus. *Cry out* and *say* both

---

[66] The original in Luke could quite literally be rendered "in his being near unto the city." This would agree with either an entrance into or a departure from the city.

express continued action. *Cry out* indicates a loud and urgent cry which might be heard at a distance.

"Jesus, *thou* son of David"—the original order is "Son of David, Jesus." All three synoptics here employ the title *Son of David*. It is the first occurrence of the title in Mark's Gospel, although Matthew recorded its previous use in Galilee (9:27; 12:23) and even by a Canaanitish woman in Phoenicia (15:22). It was a recognized messianic title (cf. Mark 12:35-37) and recalled the divine promises made to King David (2 Sam. 7:8-16). It embodied the nationalistic hopes of Israel as centered in the promised greater Son of David. It acclaimed the royal estate and function of the Messiah and acknowledged the kingly rights of the one so addressed. It was this implication in the use of the title during the triumphal entry that aroused the anger of the Jewish leaders (Luke 19:39-40). Its royal implications thus made it an appropriate title on the lips of those who appealed to Jesus in their distress (Matt. 9:27; 15:22). In making his urgent appeal, the blind beggar knew of no better title to use. Its use was his open confession of Jesus' messiahship. The added name *Jesus* identified the person thus acclaimed. Clearly he had received considerable information. Not long before, Jesus had raised a ferment of excitement by raising Lazarus from the dead, who had been in his grave four days (John 11). This and other accounts of the works of Jesus had quickened a flame of faith in the heart of Bartimaeus. That faith now prompted his persistent outcry to Jesus.

"Have mercy on me"—he appealed to Jesus to extend a definite act of mercy toward him. What that act was to be he left unexpressed. His cry was "an acknowledgment of misery, unworthiness, and help-lessness, as well as of strong confidence in Christ's ability and will-ingness to help him."[67]

"Many charged him that he should hold his peace"—chided him, urging him to keep quiet. Luke notes that the rebuke was given by those who were in the front (18:39). *Many* denotes the number who joined in this effort to silence the man. The reason for their attempt is not indicated. Some think that they tried to silence his use of the title *Son of David,* to avoid a premature disclosure of His messiahship. More probably, they simply regarded his yells as a nuisance, contemptuously feeling that a blind beggar should not be allowed to trouble Jesus.

"He cried the more a great deal"—their rebuke only intensified his cries. His refusal to allow his appeal to be thwarted proved his strong desire for help and his faith in the ability of Jesus to help him.

---

[67] Alexander, p. 295.

His faith was an active faith, a faith that pressed on and persisted until it got an answer.

Verse 49 records that the beggar's cries reached the ears of Jesus. He stood still, made a halt, and ordered those around Him to call the man. His direct command, *Call ye him* (ASV), "was a virtual reproof of the reprovers."[68] His response makes it evident that Jesus made no move to silence the beggar's use of the messianic title. Now that the crisis was at hand, Jesus made no effort to silence this individual acknowledgment of His messianic identity.

"They call the blind man"—some would refer *they* to those who had tried to silence him; others think new voices friendly to Jesus now spoke up. It is best to leave the indefinite *they* undefined as simply meaning members of the crowd. Jesus' words produced a friendly attitude toward the beggar.

"Be of good comfort, rise; he calleth thee"—Mark alone preserves these encouraging words. Two present-tense commands issue the invitation to him to be full of good cheer and to be getting to his feet so that he can hurry to Jesus. *He calleth thee* added motivation. He was assured that his cry for attention had been granted by Jesus.

"He, casting away his garment, rose"—Mark alone preserved these vivid details. Both were acts of faith and eagerness. The garment was the outer cloak. *Casting away* may mean that he threw off this outer mantle in order to avoid being entangled in it as he rushed to Jesus. It may, however, have been spread before him on the ground to receive the alms of the passing pilgrims, and he thrust it aside in his eagerness to get to Jesus. It was an unusual act for a blind man; ordinarily, he would be careful to keep his garment within reach. *Rose,* better "sprang up," a graphic verb found only here in the New Testament, pictures his spirited response.

"Jesus answered and said unto him"—answered either his persistent cries, which had reached His ears, or his eager approach to Jesus. Jesus related to the man in his need.

"What wilt thou that I should do unto thee?"—all three synoptics include this question to the man. Jesus desired to have the man articulate his faith by asking him to make a specific statement of his request.

"Lord"—Mark alone here uses the original Aramaic form of the man's address to Jesus (*rabbouni*). (Matthew and Luke used the Greek equivalent, *kurie,* "Lord.") The term also occurs in John 20:16 as the excited exclamation of Mary Magdalene at the tomb. It is the heightened form of *rabban* and means "my lord, my master." It apparently implies more reverence than the ordinary "rabbi."

---

[68] Ibid., p. 296.

"That I might receive my sight"—an open confession of faith in the ability of Jesus to heal him. The verb may mean to recover sight, but it could also be used of one born blind (John 9:11, 15, 18). Whether this man lost his eyesight or had never had it is not certain.

"Jesus said unto him"—the synoptics again show considerable independence in recording the answer to the man's request. Matthew records that Jesus was moved with compassion and healed him with a touch, while Luke notes that Jesus spoke the word of healing: "Receive thy sight." Mark simply records Jesus' words following the healing command. As Brooks remarks, "Mark emphasized the importance— even the necessity—of faith. This is highlighted by the absence of a description of the healing."[69]

"Go thy way"—dismissing the man as no longer needing His presence. The command left him at liberty to choose his own path, to follow Him if he wished.

"Thy faith hath made thee whole"—more literally, "Thy faith hath saved thee." The man's faith, centering in a Person who had the ability to heal him, was the subjective means of making him permanently whole, bringing him into the state of being "saved." "Saved" here apparently had a double meaning, referring to physical as well as spiritual salvation. Morison remarks, "What was happening in the man's body was really, we may presume (ver. 47, 48), but the outward picture of what had happened in his soul."[70]

"Immediately he received his sight"—all three accounts stress the immediacy of the healing. Luke notes that both the man and the people glorified God for the healing.

"Followed Jesus in the way"—*followed* is imperfect tense, denoting continuing action. Apparently, the man joined the body of travelers and went up to Jerusalem with Jesus. Plumptre suggests that at Jerusalem, the man's "new-found gift of sight qualified him to take his place among the eyewitnesses of the things that were done in the ensuing week."[71]

Barclay aptly summarizes the character of Bartimaeus: "He was a man of gratitude. Having received his sight, he followed Jesus. He did not selfishly go on his way when his need was met. He began with need, went on to gratitude, and finished with loyalty—and that is a perfect summary of the stages of discipleship."[72]

---

[69] Brooks, p. 174.

[70] Morison, p. 301.

[71] E. H. Plumptre, "The Gospel According to St. Mark," in *Ellicott's Commentary on the Whole Bible,* 6:219.

[72] Barclay, p. 262.

10
Ministry in Jerusalem
(Part 1; 11:1-25)

D. Ministry in Jerusalem

Mark devoted the major portion of his Gospel to an account of the ministry of Jesus (1:14–13:37). The last phase of the ministry took place at Jerusalem (11:1–13:37). His record is devoted to several preparatory events (11:1-25), the public ministry in Jerusalem, which consisted almost entirely of encounters with the religious leaders (11:27–12:44), and His eschatological discourse to His disciples (13:1-37).

1. Preparatory Events (11:1-25)

Mark described four events which were preparatory to the public ministry at Jerusalem: the entry into Jerusalem as Messiah and the return to Bethany that evening (vv. 1-11), the cursing of the fig tree the next morning (vv. 12-14), followed by the cleansing of the temple (vv. 15-19), and the lesson from the withered fig tree to the disciples the following morning (vv. 20-25). Brooks notes, "Unlike the previous part of the Gospel, the passion narrative is characterized by specific time references."[1] Mark alone enumerated three successive entries into Jerusalem on three successive days of Passion Week—Sunday, Monday, and Tuesday.

a. Entry into Jerusalem As Messiah (vv. 1-11).

This is the second time that all four Gospels record the same event (Matt. 21:1-11; Luke 19:29-44; John 12:12-19). (The only previous event recorded by all four Gospels was the feeding of the five thousand.) The synoptics agree in following Jesus from Bethany on His

---

[1] James A. Brooks, *Mark,* The New American Commentary, p. 176.

way to Jerusalem, while John's Gospel begins with the crowd's coming out from Jerusalem to meet Jesus. These accounts reveal the deep impression this event made on the apostolic band.

"When they came nigh to Jerusalem"—a general statement, marking the termination of the journey narrated in chapter 10. The repeated historical present tenses in this passage carry the reader along as present at the scene. Mark omitted any reference to Jesus' visit with His friends at Bethany upon arriving from Jericho (John 12:1-11).

"Unto Bethphage and Bethany, at the mount of Olives"—a more precise statement of the neighborhood where the entry began. Bethphage and Bethany were both villages on the slopes of the well-known Mount of Olives just east of Jerusalem. Bethphage, meaning "house of unripe figs," appears in Scripture only in connection with this event. It has completely disappeared, and its location is uncertain. Tradition locates it closer to Jerusalem than Bethany; it apparently was on the southern side of the Mount of Olives. Tradition places Bethany on the eastern slope of the mount, agreeing with the statement in John 11:18 that it was "fifteen furlongs," nearly two miles, from Jerusalem. All the synoptics have this reverse order of the two names. As Jesus left Bethany for Jerusalem, the Mount of Olives loomed before him, hiding the city of Jerusalem.

"He sendeth forth two of his disciples"—Jesus took the initiative in preparing for this entry into Jerusalem. All the synoptics noted that two of His disciples were sent, but they are left unidentified. Peter was probably one of them; the numerous details preserved by Mark suggest that they were derived from the reminiscences of an eyewitness. *Sendeth* denotes that they were dispatched on a specific mission on His behalf.

"Go your way into the village over against you"—apparently Bethphage, but left unnamed since it was visible before them. *Over against you,* "opposite you," may imply that the village lay somewhat off the main road.

"As soon as ye be entered into it"—assuring them that no long search would be required. Jesus foresaw the scene.

"A colt tied"—not further identified in Mark. In classical Greek, the term was used of the young of any animal, generally a horse, but in papyrus usage it generally meant the colt or foal of an ass. Matthew mentioned the mother with the colt; Mark and Luke mentioned only the colt.

"Whereon never man sat"—the colt would not have been used as long as it was running with its mother. Unused animals were regarded as specially suited for sacred purposes (Num. 19:2; Deut. 21:3; 1 Sam. 6:7). This was in keeping with the unique nature of the intended rider.

Gould holds that these words were put into the mouth of Jesus by Mark, who later discovered this fact and regarded it as having undesigned significance.[2] But it is unwarranted thus to take the words out of the mouth of Jesus. His mention of the fact indicated that He regarded the colt as particularly suited for His present purpose.

"Loose him, and bring *him*"—*loose* (aorist) states the one act of untying the colt, and *bring* (present) pictures the longer process of bringing it to Jesus. Matthew indicates that both the mare and her colt were brought. "The unbroken animal would be quieter, if the mother was with him."[3]

"If any man say unto you"—to go and take away another's colt might appear like a high-handed act; Jesus anticipated that they might be challenged.

"Say ye that the Lord hath need of him"—this explanation would remove any objections. It is generally held that by "the Lord," Jesus meant Himself. This meaning is questioned by some, since Mark (and Matthew) does not elsewhere use the term with this meaning. It is doubted that Jesus would thus refer to Himself until after the resurrection. Some have thought it meant Jehovah, as used in the Septuagint. But such a reference directly to God does not seem necessary in the context. The disciples were not told to present any special credentials of a divine commission. Others, like Taylor, hold that the reference is to the owner who is thought of as being with Jesus and thus sending a message that his colt was needed.[4] But this involved conjecture is unlikely. It springs out of the view that the reference cannot be to Jesus Himself. But admittedly, the designation *the Lord* is common for Jesus in Luke and John. In view of what He intended to do, it is not improbable that Jesus would thus refer to Himself. As Anderson remarks, "For Mark Jesus appears as the one with the knowledge and power to make things happen."[5] It is clear that this message would appeal only to someone who was familiar with the claims of Jesus and recognized Him as "the Lord," or "the Master." Jesus and His disciples were well known in the area (John 11), and the owner would readily understand that the reference was to Jesus.

---

[2] Ezra P. Gould, *A Critical and Exegetical Commentary on the Gospel According to St. Mark,* International Critical Commentary, p. 206.

[3] Matthew B. Riddle, "The Gospel According to St. Mark," in *International Revision Commentary on the New Testament,* p. 143.

[4] V. Taylor, *The Gospel According to St. Mark,* p. 455.

[5] Hugh Anderson, *The Gospel of Mark,* New Century Bible, p. 261.

"Straightway he will send him [back, Gr.] hither"—as assurance to the owner that the colt would not be kept longer than necessary. The words are still a part of Jesus' message to the owner. The adverb *back* is well attested and rules out the view that the words are a comment that the owner will immediately send the colt to Jesus. This is the assertion in Matthew (21:3), but Mark's account adds another aspect. *Will send* is a futuristic present tense, conveying a note of certainty.[6]

"Found the colt tied"—the exact fulfillment of the words of Jesus to them must have impressed the two disciples. It seems clear that Mark viewed the event as demonstrating supernatural knowledge on the part of Jesus. It is possible to resort to the view of a previous arrangement with the owner, but the detailed events described rather imply divine foreknowledge. Anderson asserts, "The notion that Jesus had entered into a pre-arrangement with someone in the city and knew that the colt would be ready is quite foreign to the spirit of the story."[7]

"At the door without in the open street" (ASV)—these details imply the recollection of an eyewitness. The door was that of the owner's house; the colt had been tied near the door but outside and had not been taken into the open courtyard where such animals were usually kept. *In the open street,* literally, "on the way around," suggests the winding street that ran around the house. The term (*amphodou*), only here in the New Testament, was used of a section of houses surrounded by a street, and then seems to have been used of any public street. Alexander comments, "The very obscurity of this description serves to show that it is not a subsequent embellishment, but the vivid recollection of an eye-witness, perhaps Peter."[8]

"Certain of them that stood there said unto them"—Luke indicated that they were the owners (19:33). Apparently, the colt had just been tied there, and the owners were still out on the street talking.

"What do ye, loosing the colt?"—a natural question, challenging the action of the disciples. *What do ye* asks what the action really is, while the participial clause, *loosing the colt,* identifies the action outwardly. The question means, "What right do you have to do that?"

"And they let them go"—the answer of the disciples "even as Jesus had commanded" proved satisfactory. The owners knew that

---

[6] Eric F.F. Bishop suggests that probably "Mark rode the colt back to Bethany after the crowds with Jesus had reached the Temple precincts" (*Jesus of Palestine,* p. 212).

[7] Anderson, p. 261.

[8] Joseph Addison Alexander, *The Gospel According to Mark,* p. 299.

they could trust Jesus with the colt. Probably, they were also proud to have the famous Master use their colt.

"Cast their garments on him"—the unridden colt would be without a saddle. Knowing that Jesus intended to ride into Jerusalem, the disciples hastily prepared it for Him. Although *they* is the natural subject of the verb *cast,* it need not be limited to the two disciples. Some of the other disciples may well have joined in throwing their garments, their long outer robes, across the back of the colt as a cushion for Jesus.

"He sat upon him"—Jesus mounted the colt to ride into the city. Luke remarked that the disciples "set Jesus thereon" (19:35). Jesus thus deliberately acted to ride into the city in fulfillment of Zechariah 9:9. Mark and Luke made no reference to the prophecy, but Matthew and John noted the definite fulfillment of it in the manner of Jesus' entry. He thus openly presented Himself as the fulfillment of messianic prophecy. But the very manner of His entry indicated that He presented Himself not as the political Messiah they were eagerly expecting. The ass was the animal of peaceful daily pursuits and was not associated with thoughts of conquest as the horse was. He did not present Himself as the glorious, irresistible ruler that their messianic expectations had conceived. There was a recognition that a messianic sign was being given, but its true significance was not apprehended.

"Many spread their garments in the way"—recognizing the entry as messianic, the crowd eagerly entered into the spirit of the occasion. They spread their outer robes in the dusty road to carpet the way for Him. It was an ancient practice in welcoming a new sovereign (cf. 2 Kings 9:13).

"And others branches, which they had cut from the fields" (ASV)—another method of expressing their welcome. Those who would not or could not use their clothes used this way to express their welcome to the messianic rider. The word rendered "branches" properly denotes a mass of straw, rushes, or leaves strewn over the road to form a carpet of green litter. *Cut from the fields* indicates how the material was obtained. Matthew used a different word which denotes "branches from the trees" (21:8), while John noted that the people coming out from Jerusalem carried "the branches of palm trees" (12:13).

"They that went before, and they that followed"—distinguishing two crowds. Matthew also noted two groups (21:9), while Luke simply spoke of "the whole multitude of the disciples" (19:37). Those who went before would indicate the contingent that came out from Jerusalem to meet Jesus (John 12:12-13); upon meeting the group that was with Jesus, they turned around and led the procession.

"Cried, saying, Hosanna"—the imperfect tense indicates that the cry was repeatedly heard. Luke noted that the cries began "at the descent of the mount of Olives" (19:37), perhaps at a turn in the road where the city of Jerusalem burst into view. The outstanding cry was "Hosanna," mingled with other shouts. Hosanna was originally a prayer, "Save, we pray." The appeal had become a liturgical formula; probably it here was used simply as an acclamation of welcome. But verse 10 favors the meaning as an appeal for divine help to bring about the expected messianic deliverance through Jesus. It was a familiar expression, and Mark did not translate the Aramaic.

The varied exclamations in the four Gospels may be set forth thus:

MATTHEW 21:9	MARK 11:9-10	LUKE 19:38	JOHN 12:13
Hosanna to the Son of David:	Hosanna;		Hosanna:
Blessed *is* he that cometh in the name of the Lord;	Blessed *is* he that cometh in the name of the Lord:	Blessed *be* the King that cometh in the name of the Lord:	Blessed *is* the King of Israel that cometh in the name of the Lord.
	Blessed *be* the kingdom of our father David, that cometh in the name of the Lord:		
Hosanna in the highest.	Hosanna in the highest.		
		Peace in heaven, and glory in the highest.	

"Blessed *is* he that cometh in the name of the Lord"—a quotation from Psalm 118:26, part of the Hallel sung especially at the Passover. In their shouts, the people were using terms that would be much in their minds at the Passover season. This cry is recorded in all four Gospels, although Luke wrote "the king that cometh" (19:38), making clear the royal character of the one being welcomed as blessed, celebrated with praises. *He that cometh* is more literally "the coming one" and was a term with recognized messianic import among the Jews (Matt. 11:3; Luke 7:19; John 3:31; 6:14; 11:27; Heb. 10:37). While not technically a messianic title, it was understood to have messianic implications. While not naming the Messiah, the designation gave expression to the ardent yearning among the Jews for the assured coming of the promised one upon whom all their expectations for the future centered. This coming one they now welcomed in the name of the Lord, the name of Jehovah. He came in the authority denoted by that supreme name.

"Blessed *is* the kingdom that cometh, *the kingdom* of our father David" (ASV)—a cry recorded only in Mark. Matthew noted that He was greeted as "the son of David" (21:9). The cry acknowledged Jesus as bringing in the messianic kingdom, the kingdom promised to David's Son. The cry is not an Old Testament quotation but their own acknowledgment of Jesus as the fulfiller of prophecy. It was a strictly messianic tribute. In the acclamation "the kingdom that cometh," more literally, "the coming kingdom," the present tense participle "represents the coming kingdom as already on its way and drawing nearer. It is no longer in a postponed and indefinite future, but in sight."[9]

"Hosanna in the highest"—not in the highest degree but in the highest places, the very heavens themselves. Hosanna here seems to be a prayer, "May our prayer for salvation be heard in the heaven." Thus Barclay asserts, "When the people shouted *Hosanna,* it was not a cry of praise to Jesus, which it often sounds like when we quote it. It was a cry to God to break in and save his people now that the Messiah had come."[10]

Matthew recorded the impression made on the city (21:10-11); John noted that the scene evoked a feeling of despair among the Pharisees (12:19), while Luke spoke of their vain attempt to have Jesus silence the crowd (19:39-40). Luke completed the picture by preserving the startling lament of Jesus over Jerusalem as He approached the city (19:41-44). Mark omitted all this to fasten his attention on Jesus entering the temple.

"Jesus entered into Jerusalem, and into the temple"—instead of leading the procession through the holy city, Jesus dismounted and walked into the temple; not the sacred sanctuary but the whole temple area with its courts and buildings.

"When he had looked round about upon all things"—peculiar to Mark, apparently another of Peter's reminiscences. This is the last

---

[9] Ernest Trice Thompson, *The Gospel According to Mark and Its Meaning for Today,* p. 178.

[10] William Barclay, *The Gospel of Mark,* Daily Study Bible, p. 268.

mention of these characteristic looks by Jesus in Mark's Gospel.[11] His all-embracing survey of conditions in the temple left nothing unobserved. He acted as one who had the right to inspect conditions in the temple of the Lord. The unholy traffic which He observed was confined to the Court of the Gentiles.

"Now the eventide was come"—the time when He completed His inspection. Because of the lateness of the hour, no further action was taken. Matthew and Luke did not note the time interval between the entry into the temple and its cleansing, but Mark's precise chronology establishes that the cleansing took place the following day. This failure to follow up the messianic acclaim given Him with some definite steps to establish His kingdom must have been a disappointment to His disciples.

"He went out unto Bethany with the twelve"—He apparently left the city to forestall any premature action by the Jewish leaders against Him. Bethany would provide comparative security against sudden arrest. Whether this night was spent in the home of Martha and Mary or out on the quiet slopes of Olivet at Bethany is not certain (cf. Luke 21:37). During Passion Week the Twelve maintained close attendance on Jesus until the desertion of Judas (Mark 14:10) and the subsequent dispersion of the rest in the garden (v. 50).

b. Cursing of the Fig Tree (vv. 12-14).

This singular story also appears in a more compressed form in Matthew 21:18-19. Both give it in the same connection.

"On the morrow"—the day following His entry into Jerusalem as Messiah. Matthew noted that it was "in the morning" (21:18), "early," that is, before 6 A.M.

"When they were come from Bethany"—following the night at Bethany, Jesus returned early to Jerusalem as the scene of His public activities. This was His practice during the first half of Passion Week.

"He was hungry"—the aorist tense is probably ingressive, "He became hungry." The indicative asserts the reality of His hunger; it was not feigned. Morison thinks that it is evidence that Jesus "had not spent the night under the hospitable roof of Martha and Mary" and holds that Jesus probably spent the night in prayer out in the open.[12]

---

[11] W. Graham Scroggie characterizes these various *looks* in Mark's record: "the look of displeasure (iii. 5), of discernment (iii. 34), of discovery (v. 32), of dependence (vi. 41), of depression (vii. 34), of discrimination (viii. 33), [of detection (x. 23),] and of disappointment (xi. 11)." (*The Gospel of Mark*, p. 182).

[12] James Morison, *A Practical Commentary on the Gospel According to St. Mark*, p. 308.

Bruce thinks that He did spend the night in the house of friends but wonders if the sights He had observed in the temple "killed sleep and appetite, so that He left Bethany without taking any food."[13] Brooks offers a natural explanation: "Inasmuch as the first meal of the day was not eaten until midmorning, Jesus was understandably hungry."[14] Mark simply recorded the fact without any explanation. Perhaps Jesus had been so engrossed with what lay ahead of Him in Jerusalem that He had no inclination to eat until the sight of the fig tree in full leaf suddenly made Him conscious of His need for food. Alexander aptly remarks, "That this was a simulated hunger, is not only an unworthy and irreverent but a perfectly gratuitous assumption, as our Lord, by his incarnation, shared in all the innocent infirmities of human nature."[15] The mention of His hunger prepares the way for the story.

"Seeing a fig tree afar off having leaves"—the green foliage caught the eye of Jesus while He was still a long way off. Matthew noted that it was a solitary fig tree standing by the wayside (21:19). Its location implies that it was not private property. Other fig trees in the neighborhood still were without leaves, but this one was in full foliage. It was an exceptional tree, apparently located in a favored spot, so that its development was far ahead of other fig trees. In the fig tree, the fruit appears coincident with, and sometimes even before, the appearance of the leaves. If the leaves alone appear, there will be no fruit that year. The fact that this tree had an abundance of foliage ahead of season held out the promise of a corresponding precocity in regard to its fruit.[16]

"If haply he might find any thing thereon"—*if haply* might more literally be rendered, "if then" or "if consequently." The expression summarizes the circumstances just stated and infers from them the possibility of finding fruit on the tree. Had the tree not been in full foliage, Jesus would not have gone to it with any expectation of finding figs. He approached the tree to see if its promise of fruit was fulfilled. Mark's use of the vivid future, "if he will find," strongly suggests the expectation of finding fruit on it.

---

[13] Alexander Balmain Bruce, "The Synoptic Gospels," *The Expositor's Greek New Testament,* 1:417.

[14] Brooks, p. 182.

[15] Alexander, p. 303.

[16] Bishop relates the unusual experience of finding a fig tree near the wall of Jerusalem on Good Friday, 1936, which "had figs quite large enough to warrant picking." For the next ten years, he found no ripe figs on the tree at that season (*Jesus of Palestine,* p. 217).

"He found nothing but leaves"—actual inspection revealed that there were no figs under the leaves. The tree did not fulfill its promise. This incident has often raised a discussion of the problem of the supernatural knowledge of Jesus. It does not disprove the clear possession of such knowledge on certain occasions, nor does it prove that His action here was a pretense. The fact that He looked for fruit to satisfy His own hunger indicates that Jesus did not use His supernatural knowledge or power to meet His own needs. He accepted the ordinary limitation of human nature and used His supernatural knowledge only where and when it was needed to fulfill His mission. Here He used His divine power, in keeping with His messianic mission, only after the discovery that the tree was without fruit.

"The time of figs was not *yet*"—unique to Mark. The comment is historically correct; the season for ripe figs was in June, more than a month away. This explanatory comment underlines the fact that there was no reason for expecting the tree to have figs beyond the promise of its preseasonal foliage. It stresses the precocity of the tree.

"Jesus answered and said unto it"—Jesus answered the fair and deceptive profession of the tree. What He said to it was spoken in judgment upon its empty profession. Lenski well observes, "It is, of course, unwarranted to say that this lying tree made Jesus angry, and that he vented his anger by cursing it."[17] His words to it were a calm command, not a rash utterance in petulant anger. He condemned it as a vivid illustration of a fair profession without performance.

"No man eat fruit of thee hereafter for ever"—His death sentence upon the tree. His direct address to the tree made it a personification of the evil condemned. His words are in the form of a negative wish, but they have the force of an imperative. Verse 21 shows that the disciples regarded His words as a curse upon the tree. *Hereafter,* or "any longer," implies that the tree had borne figs in former times. *For ever* terminated all further opportunity for it to bear fruit. The drowning of the pigs in the sea (5:11-13) is the only other miracle of destruction.

"His disciples heard *it*"—they were personal witnesses of what was said and done. *Heard* is imperfect tense, "were hearing." The open ended tense implies a sequel. The comment, peculiar to Mark, is in harmony with his recognition of a time interval between the pronouncement and the effect.

This account has evoked much critical discussion. Branscomb bluntly asserts that it "most obviously cannot be taken as sober history," and holds that it was a "pious legend" developed to explain

---

[17] R.C.H. Lenski, *The Interpretation of St. Mark's and St. Luke's Gospels,* p. 300.

the withering of a certain fig tree at Jerusalem.[18] This is an open attack upon the veracity of the Scriptures; for clearly, Mark and Matthew intended to present the account as a historical occurrence. Others suggest that it is simply the parable of the fig tree (Luke 13:6-9), which during the process of transmission, was transformed into an actual deed by Jesus. But the moral of the parable is quite different from this incident. The parable was a warning against unproductiveness; here the tree is judged, not for its lack of fruit, but for its "deceptive show of exceptional producing power."[19] English concludes, "We are justified in taking the story as it stands, and in seeing in its starkness and destructiveness a solemn warning of what was in fact to happen in the destruction of Jerusalem in A.D. 70."[20]

While recording an actual occurrence, clearly Mark and Matthew recognized a symbolic significance behind the action of Jesus. Neither writer explained its significance, which must be deduced from the historical circumstances. The fig tree is an Old Testament type of the nation of Israel (Hos. 9:10; Nah. 3:12; Zech. 3:10). This fig tree with its precocious leaves, making a bold profession of fruitfulness, was an apt symbol of the Jewish nation with its proud boast of being God's favored people. The tree was a fitting symbol of Israel's failure to produce the spiritual fruit that it professed to have. Jesus used the tree to convey to His disciples a lesson of His condemnation of hypocrisy. Gould comments, "Jesus was on the eve of spiritual conflict with a nation whose prime and patent fault was hypocrisy or false pretense, and here he finds a tree guilty of the same thing. It gives him his opportunity, without hurting anybody, to sit in judgment on the fault."[21] The acceptance of such a symbolic significance behind the event seems to offer the most satisfactory explanation of this unusual story. Jesus' response to this display of evil was in harmony with the very nature of God (Rom. 11:22). "A God who winked at and never punished sin would not be a good God."[22]

c. Cleansing of the Temple (vv. 15-19).

This cleansing is recorded by all the synoptics; but unlike Mark, Matthew (21:12-13) and Luke (19:45-46) did not indicate the precise

---

[18] B. Harvie Branscomb, *The Gospel of Mark,* Moffatt New Testament Commentary, pp. 201-2.

[19] Alfred Plummer, *The Gospel According to St. Mark,* Cambridge Greek Testament, pp. 261-62.

[20] Donald English, *The Message of Mark,* The Bible Speaks Today, p. 189.

[21] Gould, pp. 211-12.

[22] J. D. Jones, *Commentary on Mark,* p. 406.

day of the cleansing. John (2:13-22) also recorded a cleansing of the temple but placed it at the beginning of Jesus' public ministry. The critics generally hold it unlikely that Jesus cleansed the temple twice, but they are not agreed whether the chronology of the synoptics or John is correct.[23] But Plummer admits, ''There is no improbability of His having done so both at the beginning and at the end of His ministry.''[24] The denial of two cleansings is an attack upon the veracity of the Gospels. It is entirely credible that Jesus should assert messianic authority over the temple both at the beginning and end of His ministry.

The cleansing told in John's Gospel took place before the opening of the Galilean ministry with which the synoptics begin; the fourth gospel paid particular attention to the opening stages of Jesus' public ministry in Judea. While there are obvious similarities between the two cleansings, there are also definite differences. At the first cleansing, Jesus was at once openly confronted by the religious authorities challenging His action; in the second cleansing, no such confrontation immediately followed. At the first occurrence, Jesus replied with an enigmatic reference to His death; in the second, He quoted Scripture in denunciation of the abuse. In the first, Jesus made His reply to the religious leaders; in the second, He addressed Himself to all those present.

''They come to Jerusalem''—specifically marks the second entry during Passion Week. If, on the preceding day, Jesus had entered as the King of Israel, on this day He entered as God's High Priest, pronouncing His judgment upon the perversion of worship in the temple.

''Jesus went into the temple''—The term ''the temple'' (*to hieron*) denotes the entire temple area on the top of Mount Zion, covering about thirty acres, and surrounded by high walls on all sides. A wide outer space around this entire area was called *the court of the Gentiles,* open to Gentiles and Jews alike. A low inner wall, with signs at its gates declaring that no Gentile was allowed to go beyond, enclosed three further courts: *the court of the women,* beyond which Jewish women might not go; *the court of the Israelites,* into which Jewish men might go, and often the place for Jewish gatherings; and *the court of the Priests,* the innermost court into which only the priests might enter; it led directly into the temple proper (*ho naos*) where sacrifices according to the Mosaic law could be offered. The scene depicted

---

[23] Taylor, pp. 461-62.

[24] Plummer, p. 264.

related only to the court of the Gentiles which had been ''turned into a bazaar for selling sacrificial animals and taxing worshipers.''[25]

''Began to cast out them that sold and bought in the temple''— began the work of the day with this decisive action against the commercial activities carried on in the court. The use of definite articles distinguishes the buyers and the sellers as two distinct groups; both shared in the evil practice. The things bought and sold were things needed by the Jews for their sacrificial offerings at the temple. The sale was carried on under the authorization of the high priest and for the convenience of the Jewish worshipers. Those who came from a distance found it convenient to buy there since it eliminated the trouble of bringing their own animal with them and assured that the animal procured would pass the inspection of the priest. The operation of the sellers furthered the financial interests of the high priestly family. Worshipers either belonged to the hierarchy or paid a considerable fee to the temple authorities for the privilege. By authorizing this market in the court of the Gentiles, the only area open to Gentiles, the priestly authorities revealed their personal greed and showed their traditional contempt for the Gentiles.

The action of Jesus was a rebuke to the mercenary motives of the high priestly authorities and a direct challenge to their authority. His action was in reality a claim to a higher authority than that exercised by the high priest. ''It was in effect,'' Thompson says, ''a second appeal to the nation to repudiate their present rulers and to accept Him as the promised Messiah; a more positive effort than He had made on the previous day in His 'triumphal entry.' ''[26]

''Overthrew the tables of the moneychangers''—every male Jew twenty years or over was required to pay yearly a half shekel toward the cost of the religious services in the temple (cf. Exod. 30:11-16). Foreign coins with their idolatrous images were refused for this purpose. The moneychangers were in the temple court to change the Greek and Roman coins of the pilgrims into the Jewish or Tyrian coinage which alone could be used for the payment. But a fee, sometimes as high as 10 or 12 percent, was charged for making the exchange. The moneychangers sat cross-legged on the court pavement behind their tables, or stool-like benches, on which their coins were stacked. *Overthrew* speaks of vehement action. Wuest notes, ''To have their tables overturned and their money thrown all over the floor on the eve of the Passover, was to deal their business a serious blow at a time when the

---

[25] David L. McKenna, *Mark,* The Communicator's Commentary, p. 230.

[26] Thompson, p. 187.

money traffic was at its height.''[27] It was an expression of "the wrath of the Lamb." Jesus acted in the spirit of Malachi 3:1-3.

"The seats of them that sold doves"—the chairs of those sitting beside their cages of doves. At the first cleansing, the dove-sellers were ordered to move out; now their seats were overturned. Doves or pigeons were so commonly used for sacrifice that separate mention was made of them. Jesus acted to express His indignation against the sellers, not the doves. "Doves were the prescribed offering for the poor who could not afford an animal (Lev. 12:6; 14:22; 15:14, 29; cf. Luke 2:22-24).''[28]

Verse 16 is peculiar to Mark, perhaps because of Peter's recollection. Jesus would not suffer, better, "permit," any individual to carry a vessel through the temple, use the large court of the Gentiles as a shortcut from one part of the city to the other. *Vessel* here applies to any kind of utensil or container used in transporting things. This practice turned the temple court into a common thoroughfare, revealing the irreverence that prevailed toward the temple. Perhaps Jesus was enforcing a regulation that had already been laid down but had been allowed by the priest to become of no effect.[29] The verse implies that for some time, Jesus remained in the court to enforce the regulation. Jones suggests that apparently Jesus stationed His followers at the entrances to the court to enforce the demand.[30]

"And he taught"—the imperfect tense implies a period of teaching. He taught more than is recorded. What is recorded implies that the subject of His instruction was the purpose of the temple and how the divine purpose had been perverted. The bold action of Jesus brought the crowds together, and He used the opportunity to teach them.

"Is it not written"—introducing a quotation from Isaiah 56:7. The perfect tense asserts that what the prophet wrote still stood on record as authoritative. It was an appeal to an authority that no Jew could contradict. Only Mark introduced the quotation in the form of a question.

"My house shall be called a house of prayer for all the nations?" (ASV)—all the synoptics have the quotation, but only Mark preserved

---

[27] Kenneth S. Wuest, *Mark in the Greek New Testament for the English Reader*, p. 221.

[28] Brooks, p. 185.

[29] The Mishnah laid it down that a man was not to make the court opposite the Eastern Gate "a short by-path." (Herbert Danby, trans., *The Mishnah*, p. 10). Josephus asserts that it was unlawful to "carry any vessel into the holy house," but the reference seems to be to the temple proper, rather than the court of the Gentiles (*Against Apion* 2. 8.).

[30] Alexander Jones, *The Gospel According to St. Mark*, p. 177.

the words *for all the nations*. This was significant since this court alone was available to Gentiles for prayer, reverent approach unto Jehovah. For the convenience of the Jewish worshipers, this part, the only place where Gentiles were permitted, had been turned into a common market where barter and greed ruled. It defeated the very purpose of the temple for the Gentile. "With the conversion of the court of the Gentiles into a bazaar with all its noise and commotion and stench, they were deprived of the only place in the temple where they could worship."[31]

"But ye have made it a den of thieves"—*but* introduces the contrast between the divine purpose for the temple and the use the Jews had made of it. His emphatic *ye* is directed to the crowd, but the Jewish leaders are not excluded. All shared in the guilt. The perfect tense, *have made,* asserted the present state of the temple; it was a den of robbers, or "a brigands' cave." The words are an allusion to Jeremiah 7:11. The cave of brigands was not used for robbing but as a refuge for the robbers. The very temple was being used as a shelter to shield and protect their wanton practice of cheating those who had come to make their sacrifices.

"The scribes and chief priests heard *it*"—the tidings of events in the court of the Gentiles reached their ears. The combination (inverted in the original) "the chief priests and the scribes" occurs here for the first time in Mark. They formed the two principal groups in the Sanhedrin. Hereafter, the combination occurs several times in Mark (11:27; 14:1, 43, 53).

"Sought how they might destroy him"—the action of Jesus was an attack on their vested interests, and they reacted in active hostility. *Sought* (imperfect tense) points to their continued deliberation. *How* indicates that the need for His destruction was assumed, the only problem was how, by what means it was to be accomplished. Thompson remarks, "From the human point of view it was the cleansing of the Temple which more than any other act precipitated Jesus' death. He had previously aroused the deadly antagonism of the Pharisees and the Herodians in Galilee; but it was the Sadducees, the priestly aristocrats, who actually encompassed His death."[32]

"For they feared him"—in Mark alone. It explains why they sought to destroy Him indirectly. *Feared* is imperfect tense, "stood in fear of him."

"All the people was astonished at his doctrine"—the multitude was composed of Passover pilgrims from all parts of the world. *Astonished* is the same strong verb used in 1:22 (see comments). The teaching

---

[31] Brooks, p. 186.

[32] Thompson, p. 188.

of Jesus produced the same profound impression on the crowds in Jerusalem that it had in Galilee. His teaching never lost its freshness and power.

Verse 19 summarizes the practice of Jesus during the first three days of Passion Week. *When even was come* is literally "whenever it became late." He was busy in Jerusalem until sunset, when the crowds departed and the city gates were to be closed. Only then did He leave the city.

d. Lesson from the Withered Fig Tree (vv. 20-25).

Only Matthew and Mark recorded the lesson which Jesus drew for the disciples from the withered fig tree. Matthew gave a briefer account (21:19-22) and did not indicate the time interval which Mark explicitly noted. This paragraph opens the account of events on Tuesday of Passion Week.

"In the morning, as they passed by"—as Jesus and His disciples were proceeding along the same road to Jerusalem as the previous morning. Jesus was returning in the morning, "early," to get in a full day at Jerusalem. Luke noted that "all the people came early in the morning to him in the temple, for to hear him" (21:38).

"They saw the fig tree dried up from the roots"—the condition of the tree was observed by all. The morning before, it had been conspicuous for its abundance of green leaves; this morning it was equally conspicuous because of its totally blighted condition. *Dried up,* perfect tense, indicates that it was in a state of being dried up. The blight had begun from the roots, death spreading upward through the entire tree, the destruction now being total and final. Matthew characteristically telescoped the events connected with the fig tree, causing his account to be taken to mean at times that the disciples watched the tree wither before their very eyes. But his statement that "immediately the fig tree withered away" does not assert that the disciples observed it, only that the effect began to operate immediately. Apparently, the preceding morning, the disciples had passed on without paying any further particular attention to the condition of the tree.

"Peter calling to remembrance"—implying an interval between the words of Jesus and the condition now observed. The form of the verb in the original is aorist passive, "was reminded." Peter's thoughts had been elsewhere, but the sight of the dry fig tree in a flash recalled the events of yesterday. Only Mark noted that Peter acted as spokesman to express the surprise of the disciples (Matt. 21:20). Peter at once connected the condition of the tree with the word of Jesus. He recognized that its present condition was no ordinary event.

"Master, behold"—addressing Jesus directly as "rabbi" (cf. 9:5), Peter cried, "behold," or "look." It is not the exclamation "lo," but the aorist imperative singular, bidding Jesus to take a look at the withered tree.

"The fig tree which thou cursedst is withered away"—the stark effect of His words on the tree was obvious to all. It may be noted that the effect went beyond the statement; Jesus had asserted that it would henceforth be fruitless, but now it was totally lifeless. Abbott comments, "But both in nature and in grace fruitlessness always issues in death. It is only by and through fruit-bearing that life is ever perpetuated."[33] Peter's words only stated the facts concerning the tree, but they implied the question How? Matthew indeed recorded that the amazed disciples asked, "How did the fig tree immediately wither away?" (21:20, ASV).

"Jesus answering saith unto them"—Jesus' answer was addressed to the whole group. All were surprised at the manifestation of power which the condition of the tree revealed, and Jesus spoke in reply to their surprise at the miracle. The fact that He had cursed the fruitless tree did not raise a moral problem for the disciples. Concerning the significance of the action, they did not inquire, and He left the point unexplained, allowing later events to make it clear to them.

"Have faith in God"—directing their attention to the source of the power displayed. They are bidden to have a faith that rests *in God.*[34] The present imperative *have* demands that they must go on having such a faith. *Faith,* without an article, stressed the quality of the faith as centered in God. His reply was a gentle rebuke of their lack of faith in the power of His word. The withered fig tree gave them a vivid demonstration of its power. Let them maintain that faith amid what lay ahead.

"Verily I say unto you"—a prefatory formula indicating an important truth (cf. 3:28).

"Whosoever shall say unto this mountain"—a statement of expectancy. Jesus assumes that someone would find it in his heart to make such a statement. Far from condemning it, Jesus pointed out the conditions under which it would receive certain fulfillment. "This mountain" has primary reference to the Mount of Olives, but the whole statement is obviously figurative. Neither Jesus nor His disciples went about uprooting literal mountains. According to Strack and Billerbeck, in rabbinic literature, a rabbi who could remove noted difficulties of

---

[33] Lyman Abbott, "The Gospel According to Mark," in *An Illustrated Commentary on the Gospels,* p. 52.

[34] The genitive in the original, "of God" (*theou*), is objective; it is not a faith which God bestows but a faith of which He is the object.

interpretation was spoken of as "a remover of mountains."[35] The statement of Jesus is a picture of that which is utterly impossible with men, yet can be accomplished through faith in the power of God.

"Be thou removed, and be thou cast into the sea"—the command of faith in the face of an impossible situation. *Be removed* (more literally, "be taken up") and *cast* are aorist imperative, commanding acts that must take place at once. The passive voice implies that God is the agent behind the actions. "The sea" may refer either to the Dead Sea, visible from the Mount of Olives, or to the Mediterranean, but the metaphorical teaching is the complete disappearance of the encountered difficulty. But such a miraculous achievement demands the fulfillment of specific conditions, negative and positive.

"Shall not doubt in his heart"—there must be no conflict between his outward assertion and his inner attitude. *Doubt* pictures the mind in dispute with itself; the doubter wavers between his conflicting thoughts, now thinking that the petition will be granted, now yielding to the thought that it will not be granted.

"But shall believe that those things which he saith shall come to pass"—*believe* denotes his continuing attitude of trust that the petition will be granted. *Those things which he saith,* "what he utters," points to the particular prayer then being uttered. The present tense "comes to pass" (Gr.) indicates his assurance that the answer comes as a matter of course. Jesus set no limits to the possibilities of prayer, but such successful praying must have a true foundation. The one praying can have such confidence only if he is sure that what he is asking is in harmony with the will of God and furthers His purpose. Such confidence is wrought in the heart by the Holy Spirit through the Word.

"Therefore I say unto you"—because of the power of faith united to the omnipotence of God. *You* now applies the previous, general statement to the disciples personally.

"All things whatsoever ye pray and ask for" (ASV)—*pray* and *ask for,* both present tenses, picture the practice. *Pray* suggests reverential communion with God as the giver of the answer, while *ask for,* in the middle voice, points to the personal interest of the petitioner in his request. *All things* sets no limits to the requests, but they must be in harmony with the purpose of God.

"Believe that ye receive *them,* and ye shall have *them*"—applying the sweeping assurance of the previous verse to the disciples. *Receive* is the aorist tense, "did receive," and stresses that faith accepts that

---

[35] H. L. Strack and P. Billerbeck, quoted in C.E.B. Cranfield, *The Gospel According to St. Mark,* Cambridge Greek Testament Commentary, p. 250.

the petition has already been granted (cf. 1 John 5:14-15). Knowing that the petition is in God's will, faith accepts the answer as granted, although the actual bestowal is future, "ye shall have *them.*" "To faith God's promise is as good as His performance, and so the believing soul enjoys the answer before it arrives."[36]

"And when ye stand praying"—introducing another essential condition for effective praying. *When,* or "whenever," sets no time stipulations for the practice of prayer. *Stand* states the usual prayer posture among the Jews (1 Sam. 1:26; 1 Kings 8:14, 22; Neh. 9:4; Matt. 6:5; Luke 18:11, 13), although kneeling or complete prostration was also used in times of exceptional public importance or deep trouble (1 Kings 8:54; Ezra 9:5; Dan. 6:10; Matt. 26:39; Acts 7:60).

"Forgive, if ye have ought against any"—*forgive* (present imperative) asserts the standing duty of a forgiving attitude. Prayer cannot be used in the service of hate. *Forgive* balances *believe* in the preceding teaching; successful praying requires forgiving as well as believing. "God's healing and forgiving power cannot flow into our lives if we refuse to forgive others."[37] The demand for forgiveness is all-inclusive: *ought,* or "anything," whether an actual sin or something that our dislike causes us to hold against him; *any,* whether a believer or a nonbeliever.

"That your Father also which is in heaven may forgive you your trespasses"—the reason that the one who prays must have a forgiving attitude. The divine forgiveness must motivate our willingness to forgive others. Only here in Mark does the expression "your Father which is in heaven" occur. It is generally taken to prove acquaintance with the Lord's Prayer. Jesus' designation of God as "your Father, the one in the heavens," was well known in the early church. *Trespasses* likewise occurs only here in Mark's Gospel. The term means a falling beside and ethically denotes a deviation or misstep by means of which one falls to the side, departing from the path of truth and uprightness. *Your* reminds the disciples that they too need forgiveness.

Verse 26 is omitted by several of the best ancient manuscripts and is generally regarded here as an insertion from Matthew 6:15, where it is unquestionably genuine.

---

[36] Scroggie, p. 205.

[37] Thompson, p. 185.

11
Ministry in Jerusalem
(Part 2; 11:27–12:44)

2. Public Teaching in Jerusalem (11:27–12:44)

The public teaching in Jerusalem which Mark records consisted of Jesus' answers to a series of questions asked by His enemies (11:27–12:34), His counterattack on the Jewish leaders (12:35-40), and His commendation of the widow's giving (12:41-44). During this busy day Jesus acted as a Prophet. In His public teaching His prophetic function was that of forth-teller, generally in narrative form, applying the truth of God to the scene before Him.

a. Questions by the Enemies (11:27–12:34).

The successive questions directed at Jesus during this day suggest that there had been a caucus of the various religious groups in Jerusalem the preceding night for the purpose of devising means whereby they might publicly discredit Him with the people (cf. v. 18). Four different questions, presented by different questioners, raised the problems of His authority (11:27–12:12), the paying of tribute to the Romans (12:13-17), the credibility of the doctrine of the resurrection (12:18-27), and the nature of the first commandment (12:28-34). His reply to all of them demonstrated His perfect mastery of every situation.

1) Question of authority (11:27–12:12). Mark's account of the attack on Jesus by the Sanhedrin concerning His authority falls into two parts: the questioners silenced (11:27-33) and the questioners exposed (12:1-12). All the synoptics record the encounter (Matt. 21:23–22:14; Luke 20:1-19), but Matthew gives the fullest record of the teaching associated with the event.

a) Questioners silenced (11:27-33). "They come again to Jerusalem"—*again* stresses the entry as a recurring event. It was His third and last public entrance into Jerusalem during Passion Week. His activities during this day revealed the unquestionable spiritual barrenness of the fruitless tree of Israel.

"As he was walking in the temple"—apparently in the colonnades of the court of the Gentiles, in either the royal porch on the south side of the court or Solomon's porch (John 10:23; Acts 5:12) on the east side. Mark alone mentions this walking. Matthew and Luke state that Jesus was teaching the people gathered around Him. It was in these colonnades, offering shelter from the wind and the rain, that most of the teaching in the temple area was done.

"There come to him the chief priests, and the scribes, and the elders"—the three groups composing the Sanhedrin (cf. 8:31). The definite article with each group makes them distinct. The three groups are mentioned together again in 14:43, 55; 15:1. The historical present *come* vividly pictures this august group approaching. It need not be assumed that the entire Sanhedrin, composed of seventy-one members, was present or that their questioning of Jesus was intended as a formal examination before them as a court. Those who came were apparently selected representatives, a formal deputation from the Sanhedrin. The Sanhedrin was accepted as the highest religious authority among the Jewish people.

"By what authority doest thou these things?"—the inquiry was legitimate, in keeping with their acknowledged responsibility to supervise the religious life of Israel. *What* means of what sort or kind and directs attention to the nature of the authority which He claimed. That He acted as one possessing authority, the right and power to do things, was unquestionable. But they asked for His credentials authorizing Him to do "these things," skillfully left undefined. The primary reference seems to be to His act of cleansing the temple the preceding day, which was a visual attack upon the character of these temple authorities; but the vagueness of their expression "covers a reference to the whole career of Jesus, which from their point of view had been continually in conflict with lawful authority, in Galilee as well as in Jerusalem."[1]

"Who gave thee this authority,"—their second question, asking for the source of His authority, naturally arose out of the preceding question. They assumed that authoritative action implied previous authorization. It was their open acknowledgement that Jesus did minister as an authoritative religious leader. Since He had never been authorized

---

[1] Henry Barclay Swete, *The Gospel According to Saint Mark,* p. 262.

as a teacher by any rabbi, from whom had He received His authorization? The question was in keeping with their emphasis upon external authority.

"To do these things"—better, "so that you are doing these things." The words, peculiar to Mark, point out the issue. They were concerned about His unauthorized actions. Only His acceptable authorization could justify such activities.

"I will also ask of you one question"—the use of the counterquestion was a common method of reply among the rabbis. Jesus used it not to evade their question but to point the inquiry in the right direction. *One question* is literally "one word," one preliminary matter. *One* is not meant to contrast with their two questions but points to the one simple matter that will give them the true answer.

"And answer me"—He demanded that they first provide the answer to His question since it would furnish the basis of His answer to them.

"And I will tell you by what authority I do these things"—His conditional promise to give a clear answer to their question. In meeting this attack upon His authority, Jesus calmly stood on His own dignity in the presence of His inquisitors. He was not awed by the august group.

"The baptism of John, was *it* from heaven, or of men?"—*the baptism* of John refers to his entire ministry; it was the distinguishing feature of his ministry. Their evaluation of John's authority was the test case which would reveal their qualification to evaluate His own authority. Jesus implied that His authority stemmed from the same source as that of John. In forcing them to make their evaluation of John's authority, Jesus gave them only two alternatives: "from heaven," that is, from God as the supreme authority or "of men," having a human origin as a self-assumed activity. His demand that they make known their judgment concerning John's ministry was in keeping with their position as the religious guides of the people; it was their duty to evaluate new religious movements and inform the people.

"Answer me"—a peremptory challenge, peculiar to Mark. This renewed demand for their answer implied that they would not have the courage to give a frank answer.

"They reasoned with themselves"—felt keenly that Jesus had confronted them with a dilemma that demanded serious consideration. *Reasoned* points to their calculated efforts to come up with a satisfactory reply. *With themselves* seems naturally to imply that whispered deliberation concerning their answer took place among the Sanhedrin members. But Swete thinks that "in the present instance conference was scarcely possible" and holds that "the same thought flashed across the minds of all."[2] This is the force of Matthew's statement that "they reasoned in themselves" (Gr.). Their dilemma may have been clearly reflected on their faces.

"If we shall say"—they tested both possible responses and recognized that neither was acceptable to them.[3] In arriving at their answer, they were controlled not by the criterion "true or false" but by "safe or unsafe."

"From heaven; he will say, Why then did ye not believe him?"— it was well known that the Sanhedrin had sent a committee to investigate the work of John (John 1:19-27). It was equally obvious that they had not believed and supported John's witness. To accept the alternative "from heaven" was to charge themselves with unbelief and failure to obey this heaven-sent messenger. They instantly perceived that Jesus would condemn them for their inconsistency.

"But should we say, From men—" (ASV)—on the basis of the most important manuscripts, *if* is properly omitted here. This broken construction, indicated by the dash, is consistent with Mark's style. *Should we say* is apparently a deliberative question, implying an alternative to which they must give serious consideration. *From men* would deny that John had been divinely commissioned.

"They feared the people"—Mark, unlike Matthew and Luke, states their thoughts in his own words. The Sanhedrin members were afraid to risk the wrath of the excitable Passover crowd. Had they dared, they would have given an answer which they knew was false.

"For all *men* counted John, that he was a prophet indeed"— indicating the justified ground for their fear. The people would have regarded any denial that John was a prophet, God's inspired spokesman, as blasphemy. This conviction concerning John had been deepened by his martyrdom. The popular esteem of John is confirmed by Josephus, who recorded the opinion of the Jews that the misfortunes which befell Herod Antipas were divine punishment for the death of John the Baptist.[4]

"We cannot tell"—a disgraceful answer of expediency, whereby the members of the Sanhedrin automatically disqualified themselves to be the judges concerning Jesus' authority. He had effectively caught them in their own hypocrisy. They could only make themselves appear

---

[2] Ibid., p. 263.

[3] There was a third alternative, "from Satan," but this would have been so unacceptable now that they did not even suggest it. This was an explanation that had been advanced (Matt. 11:18; Luke 7:33).

[4] Josephus *Antiquities* 18. 5. 2.

ridiculous. "The whole story is a vivid example of what happens to men who will not face the truth."[5]

"Neither do I tell you by what authority I do these things"—their failure to answer His question released Him from His promise to answer their question. Because of their dishonesty the answer would have been useless. But His counterquestion had already indicated the answer to them. Had they been willing to face the truth, He would gladly have given them further enlightenment. Their trouble lay not in their dullness of mind but in their stubborn will.

b) Questioners exposed (12:1-12). The manmade chapter break at the end of chapter 11, while convenient for reference, does not here establish a change in the scene. After putting His questioners to silence, Jesus proceeded to expose their true character.

"And he began to speak unto them by parables"—*and* here simply marks the continuation of the scene in 11:27-33. *Them* most naturally denotes the members of the Sanhedrin whom Jesus had just silenced. This is clear from the reference to them at the close of this parabolic lesson (v. 12). Having silenced them, Jesus was not ready to let them leave; He still had an important lesson for them. His question to them, "But what think ye?" (Matt. 21:28), held their attention. The parable here recorded was an appeal to their conscience and a solemn warning to them of the serious consequences of their hostile efforts. Having silenced the attack upon Him by the Jewish leaders, Jesus with His parable carried the war into the camp of the enemies. Luke notes that the parable was addressed to the people but that the Jewish leaders recognized it was aimed at them (20:9, 19). *Began to speak by parables* marks His resumption of the parabolic method called for by the circumstances. Spoken during a time of crisis, His parables during Passion Week have a marked quality of solemnity and pointedness. *Parables* implies that Mark knew of other parables, although he recorded only one.[6] Matthew here records three,[7] of which Mark and Luke give only the second. Some hold that the plural here simply has reference to His parabolic manner of speaking.

"A *certain* man planted a vineyard"—the order in the original places the emphasis on the vineyard planted at great expense, rather

---

[5] William Barclay, *The Gospel of Mark,* The Daily Study Bible, p. 280.

[6] Schuyler English points out that Mark really gives two parables, "(1) The Parable of the Householder Demanding Fruit from the Vineyard (vss. 1-9); and (2) The Parable of the Rejected Stone (vss. 10-11)" (*Studies in the Gospel According to Mark,* p. 398).

[7] The Two Sons (21:28-32), The Wicked Husbandmen (21:33-46), and The Marriage Feast (22:1-14).

than on the man planting it. The man is not further described except as he is revealed by his actions in the parable. A vineyard was a profitable agricultural project in the East. The details of its preparation are drawn from Isaiah 5:1-2, where the vineyard is the well-known figure of Israel. This familiar Old Testament image (Ps. 80:8-16; Jer. 2:21) in this parable made it unmistakably clear to His audience that Jesus was symbolizing the nation Israel. A number of the features of this parable indicate that it has allegorical implications, skillfully designed to picture the leaders of Israel and their treatment of God's messengers.

The three activities of the owner in preparing the vineyard (v. 1) indicate that nothing was left undone to make this vineyard a choice estate. He *set an hedge about it,* not merely to mark its boundaries but to provide protection against marauders and wild animals. Such a hedge or fence might be built of unmortared stone gathered out of the field or be a planted hedge of thorn bushes. He also dug a pit for the winepress, essential equipment for processing the crop. The phrase *a place for the winefat,* one word in the original, occurs only here in the New Testament and refers to the vat located below the winepress to hold the wine. The winepress, generally hewn out of the solid rock, was composed of two vats—an upper, broad, and shallow hollow where the grapes were crushed and the lower, smaller, and deeper vat connected by a channel where the juice was collected. The *tower* was used for shelter and storage as well as an observation post for the watchman. It was often circular in shape, built of stone, with a flat roof, and was as much as fifteen or twenty feet high.

"Let it out to husbandmen''—here the parable diverges from the picture of Isaiah in preparation for Jesus' own teaching. Instead of farming it with his slaves, the owner let out, or leased, the vineyard to husbandmen, tillers or cultivators of the soil, here "vine-growers." Such a lease might be for a year, but often it was a long-term lease, especially when the owner was not living in the neighborhood. On occasion such long leases were "even hereditary, passing from father to son.''[8] The full management of the vineyard was entrusted to the tenants, who paid the owner an agreed portion of the crop.

"And went into another country'' (ASV)—more literally, "went on a journey.'' Luke adds that he was gone "for a long time'' (20:9). The verb does not indicate distance or place, only that he departed from among his own people. He was not so far away as to be out of

---

[8] Alfred Edersheim, *The Life and Times of Jesus the Messiah,* 2:423.

touch with the situation. This departure may symbolize "God's 'withdrawal' from the nation shown in His ceasing to send them prophets, but it is a withdrawal in which He (like the absentee landlord) does not desert them, but only leaves them free to act."[9]

"At the season he sent to the husbandmen a servant"—the owner at the proper season, the time of the vintage, sent to claim the rent. According to Leviticus 19:23-25, it would be in the fifth year. The servant was sent to the husbandmen who were directly obligated to give him of the fruits. The rent was paid in kind. Bishop says, "The owner might have expected them as grapes or in the form of raisins or as wine."[10]

Verses 3-5 picture three servants or slaves sent successively to receive the rent. The treatment given them by the tenants was increasingly violent. The point of the parable lies in this unprincipled, vicious action of the husbandmen. They selfishly failed to execute their contract and resorted to outrageous opposition to the just claims of the owner.

The first servant they beat and sent away empty. The word *beat* originally meant "to skin, flay," but this meaning had been softened, so that in the New Testament and papyrus usage, it meant to beat severely. The servant was dismissed empty, with none of the fruit in his hands.

The second servant was seriously wounded and shamefully treated. The verb rendered "wounded in the head" does not occur elsewhere, but its formation suggests the meaning to strike on the head.[11] This servant was also handled shamefully, dishonored and insulted.

The third servant they killed. The increasing maltreatment accorded the servants sent to them was climaxed in deliberate murder.

"Many others; beating some, and killing some"—a summary statement picturing the amazing forbearance of the owner in view of the varied mistreatment given the succession of servants sent. This highly unusual reaction of the owner effectively displays the enormity of the guilt of the husbandmen. No ordinary individual would allow such a series of violent actions to continue against his servants. But this owner pictures God as the owner of the Israelite vineyard, and His practice toward her religious leaders was without parallel.

---

[9] A. F. Hort, *The Gospel According to St. Mark*, p. 153.

[10] Eric F.F. Bishop, *Jesus of Palestine*, p. 224.

[11] The reading presents a textual difficulty. A variant reading gives "to sum up" (under one head), which here could hardly mean "treated him summarily." A number of manuscripts add "having stoned," apparently in an effort to explain the wounding.

Verses 6-8 picture the owner's supreme test of the husbandmen in the sending of his only son to them.

"Having yet therefore one son, his wellbeloved"—*yet* indicates that after the wounding and killing of all his servants, there remained to the owner one whom he could still send, a beloved son, the object of his father's love. The son is mentioned in contrast to, and as higher than, the servants. It has been pointed out that this feature of the parable is of immense significance as indicating the self-consciousness of Jesus.

"Also last"—peculiar to Mark. Sending him was the highest and last appeal that the owner could make to the husbandmen.

"Saying, They will reverence my son"—expressing the hope and expectation that this appeal would be effective. The parable shows that the owner acted in a vain hope, not as God acts but as He appears to act. The owner hoped that the dignity of the son sent would cause the husbandmen to "turn in upon themselves" in shame and pay his son the respect due him.

"Those husbandmen said among themselves"—*those* has a disparaging tone. By its use the narrator, having already displayed their character in their actions, denoted his abhorrence by placing them at a distance from himself. *Said among themselves* indicates mutual consultation concerning their treatment of the son.

"This is the heir"—acknowledging him as the future owner because of his hereditary right. He presented the unique obstacle to their desire to own the vineyard. The Christian church readily recognized the aptness of the picture as a figure of Christ Himself.

"Come, let us kill him"—their mutual consultation resulted in a call for mutual action against the son. *Come* is the call for action, and *let us kill him* frankly states the action contemplated. Jesus was not making an unfounded charge; John 11:47-53 shows that the Sanhedrin had already decided upon precisely this action.

"And the inheritance shall be ours"—revealing their determining motive. Involved is the false assumption that the owner must be dead because the son had come to claim possession. It was the success of Jesus in winning a following, even though only partial, that stirred the jealousy of the Jewish leaders and led them to the decision that He must die so that they might recover their dwindling power over the people. They were determined to maintain their position and did not hesitate to trample down any who presented a challenge to them.

"Killed *him,* and cast *him* out of the vineyard"—the order of statement is peculiar to Mark. Matthew and Luke gave the reverse order. Mark's order has been taken to mean that the son was killed in the vineyard and then his dead body was cast out and left unburied. But this would be contrary to history, and it is improbable that Mark intended Jesus to teach this. This interpretation assumes that *cast out* refers to his dead body, but Lenski points out that in the New Testament elsewhere, *to cast forth* or *cast out* somebody "is never used with reference to dragging out a dead body but always with reference to expelling a living person."[12] Mark's order points to the expulsion of the son as the climax of the treatment accorded him. To excommunicate an individual was to cut him off from the people of God and their blessings. This was the treatment accorded Jesus by the Sanhedrin when they condemned Him for blasphemy and had Him crucified outside the city as the symbol of His expulsion from the community of Israel.

"What shall therefore the lord of the vineyard do?"—an invitation to His hearers to share in deciding the appropriate action to be taken against these murderous tenants. *Therefore,* in view of what they have done to his servants and his son, what will the owner do? The question implies that it is improbable that he will submit to their outrages and abandon his claim to the vineyard.

"He will come and destroy the husbandmen"—Matthew noted that this answer came from the audience (21:41); swept along by the vivid account, they spontaneously expressed their verdict upon the action. Luke noted that certain ones in the crowd, upon hearing this answer, perceived its implication and replied with an ejaculation of horror, "God forbid" (20:16). Jesus accepted the answer of His hearers and made it His own by stating it Himself. The owner will himself certainly come and will destroy the tenants, put them to death, thus bringing ruination upon them. This is prophetic of the destruction of Jerusalem and the Jewish state.

"Will give the vineyard unto others"—other tenants more worthy, who will render unto the owner "the fruits in their seasons" (Matt. 21:41). The identity of these "others" is indefinite and is not clarified by Jesus' words. This indicates an impending transfer of religious leadership. This prediction was fulfilled in the church, whose spiritual leadership became entrusted mainly to those of Gentile origin. But the operative factor is their faithfulness, not their national origin.

In verses 10-12, Jesus confirms the verdict just announced by citing the scriptural testimony given in Psalm 118:22-23, quoting the Septuagint. The quotation carries the teaching beyond that of the parable and brings out the destiny of the son whose death formed the climax of the parable. Although not a narrative, the teaching here is still

---

[12] R.C.H. Lenski, *The Interpretation of St. Mark's and St. Luke's Gospels,* p. 317.

parabolic, changing the picture from the Lord's vineyard to His building. This change opens the way for Jesus to make a parabolic reference
to His own resurrection and exaltation. Psalm 118:22-23 is quoted in
the New Testament as clearly messianic, finding its fulfillment in Christ
(Acts 4:11; 1 Pet. 2:4, 7; cf. Rom. 9:32-33; Eph. 2:20).

"Have ye not read this scripture?"—the specific passage to be
quoted. It would be quite familiar to His audience. His inquiry raised
the question whether they actually had read with understanding even
such a familiar passage.

"The stone which the builders rejected"—the quotation begins
with the very thought which climaxed His parable—His rejection by
the Jewish leaders. Like the husbandmen rejecting the son, so the
builders rejected the stone. The builders, those recognized as engaged
in building the Lord's spiritual temple, represent the Jewish priests and
religious rulers. In their official activities, they were confronted with a
stone, Christ Himself, which they rejected, subjected to their scrutiny,
and condemned as failing to pass their test.

"Is become the head of the corner"—declaring the divine reversal
of their verdict concerning the stone. The rejected stone became the
head of the corner, architecturally the most important stone in the
structure. The cornerstone is the stone binding together two adjoining
walls, but it is not certain whether the stone is thought of as being
placed at the bottom or at the top of the corner—probably the latter.
Morison holds that the reference is "to a corner stone *in the cornice.*"[13]
Both positions could apply to Christ.

"This was the Lord's doing"—*the Lord's doing* (or literally "from
the Lord"), standing first, stresses the source. *This* is feminine, and the
precise meaning of the statement has been differently understood. The
feminine pronoun may refer to *the head of the corner* (both being
feminine), in which case the meaning is that this cornerstone came
from the Lord. Since the Hebrew used the feminine for abstract ideas,
the feminine can be regarded as the equivalent of the neuter; then the
meaning is that this thing came to pass from the Lord, namely, the
exaltation of the rejected stone, as in the KJV, "This is the Lord's
doing." This is the probable meaning.

"It is marvellous in our eyes"—God's reversal of the action of
the builders is rightly an object of human wonder. In an amazing way,
God overrules the self-willed attempts of sinful men to thwart His
purposes.

---

[13] James Morison, *Practical Commentary on the Gospel According to St. Mark,*
p. 329. Morison's italics.

"They sought to lay hold on him"—*they* again denotes the Sanhedrin members (11:27), since the next clause clearly distinguishes them from the people. Luke notes that "the same hour [they] sought to lay hands on him" (20:19). The imperfect *sought* indicates that they not only desired to do so but actively endeavored to discover means to arrest Jesus and at that very time when He exposed their murderous plot with His picture of the wicked husbandmen.

"But feared the people"—a second mention of their fear (cf. 11:18). They did not dare to take open action against Jesus for fear of arousing the opposition of the multitude. Matthew notes that the common people regarded Jesus as a prophet (21:46), in a manner similar to their regard for John the Baptist.

"They knew that he had spoken the parable against them"—indicating the reason they were so anxious to arrest Jesus. His parable had brought a tremendous indictment against them, and it stimulated their hatred.

"They left him, and went their way"—only in Mark. Baffled and helpless before Him, they left in defeat to continue their plotting in their council chamber.

2) Question of tribute (12:13-17). All the synoptics record this event as the second attempt by the enemies of Jesus during this day to discredit Jesus with their questions (Matt. 22:15-22; Luke 20:20-26). The payment of tribute to the Romans was a burning question at this time as well as in the decades preceding the destruction of Jerusalem. The question aroused the deepest religious and nationalistic feelings of the Jews.

"They send unto him"—the undefined *they* most naturally refers to the baffled Sanhedrin members mentioned in verse 12. In their fierce determination to discredit Jesus with the masses, they lost no time in devising another scheme against Him. Matthew notes that the Pharisees initiated this scheme; once advanced by the Pharisees, the scheme would receive ready approval by the other groups. Since the Sanhedrin members representing that body had been publicly discredited, separate companies of emissaries were now sent against Jesus.

"Certain of the Pharisees and of the Herodians"—a combination mentioned only in Mark (cf. 3:6). *Certain of the Pharisees* indicates selected members of that party. Matthew notes that they were "their disciples," some of their keenest students whom Jesus would not, they believed, immediately identify as avowed enemies. Luke characterized those sent as "spies." Joining with those sent by the Pharisees were certain of the Herodians, apparently political supporters of Herod Antipas. The Pharisees, known for their intense nationalism, keenly objected to all foreign domination and opposed the paying of tribute to the Romans as signifying such subjection. Since the Herodian dynasty was dependent upon, and cultivated the favor of, Rome, the Herodians would favor the payment of the tax as advantageous. The alliance of the two parties was motivated by their common desire to destroy Jesus. "They hated Jesus more than they hated each other."[14]

"To catch him in *his* words"—revealing the sinister motive behind their question. *Catch* carries the figure of catching wild animals with a net or snare. The hunters were out to catch Jesus, literally, "with a word." The primary reference is to their cleverly devised question, but in order to be successful they must elicit from Him some statement which they would be able to use against Him.

"Master"—they were presenting their question to Him as an acknowledged teacher, or rabbi. It was because of His uprightness of character and forthrightness in answering difficult questions that they were coming to Him. Their cunningly arranged preamble was designed not only to disarm suspicion but also to keep Him from giving an answer that would defeat their purpose.

"We know that thou art true"—*we know* was intended to appear as an honest testimony to their appreciation of His integrity of character. They recognized that He was true—wholly truthful, honest, and transparent. Their hypocritical testimony was an unintentional confession of the profound impression that Jesus' character had made on His enemies. Jones notes, "They were only able to attribute these various qualities to Jesus because he verily possessed them. The eulogism was well founded, though the motive that prompted them to make it was as false as could be."[15]

"Carest for no man"—not that He was indifferent to people but that He was independent of their influence. He did not act simply to please people. In answering their question about paying tribute, He would not allow concern for the reactions of either the Romans or the people to keep Him from asserting the truth with fearless impartiality.

"For thou regardest not the person of men"—*for* justifies their expectation of a forthright answer. The form of the original, "thou lookest not unto the face of men" (Rotherham), is Hebraic, meaning that He does not pay attention to the outward appearance of men to be influenced by their position, wealth, or power. They knew that He would be impartial in His answer, showing no favoritism.

"But teachest the way of God in truth"—passing from His character to the truthfulness of His teaching. They recognized His habitual

---

[14] J. D. Jones, *Commentary on Mark,* p. 445.

[15] Ibid., p. 447.

activity of teaching men the way of God, the way that He has laid out for men to walk in. *In truth,* emphatic by position, stresses that His teaching was "upon a basis of truth." What He taught men as the way of God was the very opposite of the way of falsehood. Thus in answering their question, they were sure that He would give them a true answer. Their honeyed words were skillfully designed to throw Jesus off guard concerning their snare.

"Is it lawful to give tribute to Caesar, or not?"—at length their subtle question was stated. *Is it lawful* stresses that the question must be decided in harmony with the demands of the Torah. Does the law permit it or not? (Cf. Deut. 17:14-15.) The question was vital to the Jews, because, as members of the theocracy, for them to give tribute to Caesar would appear disloyal to the divine government. *To give* implies that such payments might be viewed as an unjust obligation, something not required of them by the law. *Tribute,* a loan-word, is a transliteration of the Latin *census.* It denotes here an annual head tax imposed by the Roman emperor, which went directly to the imperial treasury. It had been levied upon the population of Judea since A.D. 6 when Archelaus, the son of Herod the Great (Matt. 2:22), was deposed for his misrule and Idumea, Judea, and Samaria became one Roman province under the rule of procurators, appointed by the emperor. When first levied, it provoked a revolt (Acts 5:37) against the Romans.[16] This tax continued to be extremely unpopular with the masses. *Or not* required that His answer about the legality of the tax be either yes or no. They thus sought to tie Jesus down to these two answers as the only alternatives.

"Shall we give, or shall we not give?"—peculiar to Mark. The verbs are deliberative subjunctives, implying that the questioners were men with a serious problem of conscience; they needed His assistance to solve this problem. Again their question is presented as having only two possible answers. They thus hoped to catch Jesus in their dilemma, assured that either answer could effectively be used against Him in making charges before the authorities (Luke 20:20). If He said yes, He would offend the people and discredit His messianic claims, for they would declare that no one who claimed to be the Messiah could conceivably sanction such subservience to pagans. If He said no, He could be reported to the governor as a rebel against the Roman government. Scroggie comments, "It looked like an absolute trap, one from which there was no escape, but they, and all like them, had something to learn from Jesus."[17]

---

[16] Josephus *Antiquities* 18. 1. 6.

[17] W. Graham Scroggie, *The Gospel of Mark,* p. 215.

"He, knowing their hypocrisy"—their cleverly chosen words did not deceive Jesus for a moment. All the synoptics employ different terms to indicate His reading of their character. Matthew said that He "perceived their wickedness" (22:18) or maliciousness, while Luke noted that He recognized "their craftiness" (20:23), their readiness to stoop to any cunning, deceptive means to attain their end. *Their hypocrisy* stresses that they sought to conceal their sinister purpose under the pretense of being honest inquirers. Their question to Him about the tribute was basically dishonest, since in practice, they had already decided it; both the Pharisees and Herodians paid it as a matter of expediency.

"Why tempt ye me?"—at once, He publicly tore the masks from their faces. Matthew added "*ye* hypocrites" (22:18). Instead of being honest inquirers, they were conscious liars, testing Him for a malicious purpose. They had said that He always spoke the truth, and He immediately confirmed it by revealing the truth about *them*. His question not only exposed them but also aimed at arousing their conscience.

"Bring me a penny, that I may see *it*"—the questioners themselves were required to produce the denarius, "the tribute money" (Matt. 22:19), by which the tax was paid. It was a small silver coin minted by the imperial government and in value was the standard pay for a day's work in the vineyard (Matt. 20:1-2). His request that they bring Him the coin could mean either that He did not have one with Him or that He was following His practice of keeping them on the defensive. It also revealed that they were men who could readily produce the denarius. In daily life, they received and used it. *That I may see it* (only in Mark) meant not that He had never seen a denarius but that He intended to use it as a visual aid in giving His teaching.

"They brought *it*"—apparently, the coin had to be fetched from one of the money-lenders. The resultant interval must have left the crowd in a state of eager anticipation to learn what His answer would be.

"Whose *is* this image and superscription?"—the image was that of either Augustus or Tiberius, his successor; coins of both emperors were in circulation. *Superscription* does not mean that the writing was above the head of the image; the word means "a writing upon." The legend was in raised letters. The legend on a denarius of Tiberius, reigning at the time, read "Tiberius Caesar Augustus, the son of the Divine Augustus," and on the reverse said, "Chief Priest."[18] The Jews

---

[18] In abbreviated Latin, the inscription reads, "*Ti*[berius] *Caesar Divi Aug*[usti] *F*[ilius] *Augustus*," and on the reverse side, "*Pontif*[ex] *Maxim*[us]." See Florence Aiken Banks, *Coins of the Bible,* pp. 87, 98-99.

objected to the coins not only because of the image but also because the legend proclaimed the deity of Tiberius. Having received the coin, Jesus examined it and then held it up as He asked them to identify this image. The question seemed very innocent, and they readily replied, "Caesar's." The title of *Caesar* was taken by each of the Roman emperors, beginning with Augustus. This identification established that Roman coins circulated in Palestine as standard currency among the people. It was commonly accepted that "sovereignty was coterminous with the rights of coinage and the validity of one's money."[19] It demonstrated that Caesar's authority existed among them and therefore implied his right to exact tribute of them. Even had the questioners suspected what Jesus was aiming at, they would not have been able to avoid answering, since the legend on the coin clearly established the point anyway.

"Render to Caesar the things that are Caesar's"—more literally, "The things of Caesar give back to Caesar." That coin represented "the things that are Caesar's," the rights and duties belonging to the realm of human government. In daily life, they reaped the benefits of the controlling government that it represented. They "therefore" (Matt. 22:21) had the duty to render to Caesar, "to pay back" as a debt, the things that belonged to Caesar. Their use of the coin proclaimed their obligation to the government it represented.

"And to God the things that are God's"—*and* sharply reminded them that they also had an abiding obligation to God. Their duty to God did not eliminate their duty to human government. They had formulated their question on the assumption that the two duties were incompatible, but Jesus insisted that there was no necessary conflict between the two. The two spheres of duty were distinct, although their duty toward God was their crowning responsibility. Their dilemma did not hold; it was not either/or but both/and. Jesus' answer characteristically went to the heart of the matter, setting forth the basic principles, but it did not elaborate on the precise relationship of the two spheres.

"They marvelled at him"—all three synoptics mention this response to His reply. The strong compound verb, found only here in the New Testament, conveys the thought of their grudging admiration, and the imperfect tense denotes the continuation of the feeling. They were justly amazed at His answer. He had not only escaped their trap but had also thrown a flood of light on the problem.

---

[19] B. Harvie Branscomb, *The Gospel of Mark,* Moffatt New Testament Commentary, p. 214.

3) Question about the resurrection (12:18-27). The synoptics
agree in presenting this story as the *third* attempt this day to discredit
Jesus before the people by means of a difficult question (Matt. 22:23-
33; Luke 20:27-40). Even the radical critics raise little objection to the
historicity of this event. Taylor asserts that "the story preserves genuine tradition of the most primitive kind" and points out that its contents are typically Jewish and thoroughly lifelike.[20]

"Then come unto him the Sadducees"—the only mention of this
party in Mark.[21] The humiliation of the Pharisees and Herodians in the
previous encounter left the field open to them. The historical present
come pictures them as confidently approaching, assured that their question will confound Jesus. The Sadducees were the aristocratic party
among the Jews, composed mainly of the high priestly and leading lay
families in Jerusalem. They were rich and powerful, noted for their
arrogance and harshness. They were few in number and never gained
the popular esteem which the Pharisees enjoyed.[22] They were little
known outside of Palestine, and the party disappeared with the destruction of Jerusalem.

"Which say there is no resurrection"—*which,* "which are such
as," marks those approaching as belonging to that class of people who
say—who confidently express it as their opinion—that there is no
resurrection. They rejected the possibility of a resurrection. The Sadducees accepted only the written Scriptures as authoritative and rejected the oral traditions of the Pharisees.[23] Because they could not see
the teaching of a resurrection in the Pentateuch, which alone they
regarded as normative for Jewish life and thought, they rejected it as
a Pharisaic innovation. Since the resurrection was the point of their

---

[20] V. Taylor, *The Gospel According to St. Mark,* p. 480.

[21] They are named only 14 times in the New Testament, in contrast to the Pharisees
who are named almost 100 times (only in Phil. 3:5 outside the Gospels and Acts). The
Gospels of Mark and Luke mention the Sadducees only in connection with this incident.
Matthew mentions them on three different occasions (3:7; 16:1, 12; 22:23, 34), five
times naming them with the Pharisees. In Acts, they appear on three separate occasions
(4:1; 5:17; 22:6-8) as the aggressive opponents of the early church. They are not named
in the Fourth Gospel where the religious leaders are referred to as "the Jews." It
should be remembered that whenever the chief priests are mentioned in John's Gospel,
they are practically the same as the Sadducees.

[22] Josephus *Antiquities* 13. 10. 6.

[23] Ibid.

attack, only this denial in their distinctive negative tenets is here mentioned. Josephus said that they "also take away the belief of the immortal duration of the soul, and the punishments and rewards in Hades."[24] According to Acts 23:8, they also denied the existence of angels and spirits.

"They asked him"—their question is stated in verse 23; all that preceded was rhetorical preparation for the question. In verse 19, they laid their scriptural foundation, while in verses 20-22, they narrated the case that prompted their inquiry.

"Master"—merely a formal address. They resorted to no flattery and made no pretense that they had come to learn from Jesus. They felt themselves superior to Him and intended to expose His inadequacy as a teacher in theological matters. They thus hoped to discredit Him before the people and also to demonstrate the superiority of their position to that of the Pharisees.

"Moses wrote unto us"—their quotation is a free rendering of Deuteronomy 25:5-6, the law concerning levirate marriage (marriage to a husband's brother). *Raise up seed unto his brother* indicates that the intention of the Mosaic regulation was to keep the family line from dying out so that the family inheritance would not be broken up, since the firstborn son would be registered as the son of the dead brother. The practice was older than the Mosaic law (cf. Gen. 38:6-10) and existed in many Eastern nations. It seems to have been seldom observed among the Jews after the return from the Babylonian captivity. Plummer points out that this practice "would be of more importance to Sadducees than to others. Those who deny individual immortality find a kind of substitute for it in the continuation of the family."[25]

"There were seven brethren"—literally, "Seven brothers there were," making the number emphatic. According to Matthew, they added "with us" (22:25), as though it were a case from their own observation. The story probably was their fictional invention, but possibly they had heard of this extraordinary affair somewhere and eagerly seized upon it as a favorite weapon to further their views.

In verses 20-21, the case of the first three brothers was graphically narrated. The vividness was intended to enhance the ridiculousness of the resultant implications for the resurrection.

All seven brothers successively fulfilled their duty to marry their brother's wife, but the seven left no seed. This childlessness left none of them with a superior claim to be her husband in the resurrection.

---

[24] Josephus *Wars of the Jews* 2. 8. 14.

[25] Alfred Plummer, *The Gospel According to St. Mark,* in Cambridge Greek Testament, p. 279.

"Last of all the woman died also"—having survived all seven husbands, she too died. This meant that, for them, interest in the case related wholly to the matter of the future life, if such there were.

"In the resurrection therefore, when they shall rise, whose wife shall she be of them?"—here was the problem raised for them by the teaching of the resurrection, that future resurrection which the Pharisees taught and which they knew Jesus accepted. The question confidently assumed that she would be the wife of one of them in the resurrection, but which one? Their assumption was that "the resurrection life was simply a continuation of life down here, . . . that all the relationships of earth would be resumed in heaven. They thought of the life beyond in terms of life in the flesh."[26]

"For the seven had her to wife"—a reminder intended to underline the absurdity of the whole concept of a resurrection. "Not only were seven men supposed who would have equal claims on the same woman, but these seven men were brothers, between whom a wife in common, or a strife for possession of her, would appear more incongruous than if the seven were strangers to each other."[27] It is easy to sense their superior, cynical tone as they stated their question. For the sake of the argument, they were willing to grant the resurrection, but their question clearly revealed how ridiculous the whole idea was. This was probably a stock conundrum which they had repeatedly used to confound their Pharisee opponents in arguments concerning the resurrection.

"Jesus answering said unto them"—there is gentleness in the answer of Jesus. He did not openly denounce these Sadducees as hypocrites; they at least were candid. Jesus quietly assumed that their denial was due to error and proceeded to point it out to them.

"Do ye not therefore err"—*therefore* looks ahead to the double cause which follows. The rendering *ye err* views the verb as passive, "ye are going astray, are being misled," but more probably it is middle, "ye are deceiving yourselves." Their trouble lay with themselves; they were deceiving themselves by the false deduction they were drawing from Deuteronomy 25:5-6. According to Mark, Jesus skillfully put His answer in the form of a question which implies an affirmative answer. It invited them to examine themselves to discover the truth of the question.

"Because ye know not the scriptures, neither the power of God?"—they thought they doubted the resurrection because they were enlightened. Jesus told them that their doubt was due to their double

---

[26] J. D. Jones, p. 455.

[27] J. W. McGarvey, *Matthew and Mark,* pp. 190-91.

ignorance, doubly inexcusable in priests. "Know not the scriptures," the Old Testament writings, is a charge not of ignorance concerning their contents but of failure to understand the true meaning. Had they understood the true nature of the miracle-working God revealed in those Scriptures, they would not have doubted His power to raise the dead. In His answer, Jesus elaborated both points of His charge, beginning with the second first.

"For when they shall rise from the dead"—*for* indicates an explanation of their error. *They* is not to be confined to the persons of their story, but is general. His statement indicates that Jesus had in mind the resurrection of the just. He asserted the reality of the resurrection, but *when*, better "whenever," left the time indefinite.

"They neither marry, nor are given in marriage"—a revelation concerning the future life, of which the Sadducees were totally ignorant. In the resurrection life, *they neither marry* (do not contract marriages as husbands) *nor are given in marriage* (are given, as the act of their parents, to be wives). His questioners had thought of the resurrection life only in terms of present earthly conditions. They had failed to see that God's power could make a new world in which the conditions of life were wholly different. His power in transforming the resurrection body no longer made marriage a necessary part of the future state. "By the power of the resurrection, marriage, sex and family relationships will be transcended by perfect communion with God and among persons."[28] Therefore, their objection to the resurrection had no validity; the difficulty they envisioned did not apply to the resurrection life.

"But are as the angels which are in heaven"—they will not *become* angels but will be *as* angels in heaven, who now have a heavenly existence and are deathless. The distinction between men and angels will remain. This comparison to the angels, found in all the synoptics, was not lost on either the Sadducees or the Pharisees. It was an indirect correction of the Sadducean error which denied the existence of angels.

Verses 26-27 deal with their failure to rightly understand the Scriptures. The Sadducees had appealed to those Scriptures, and Jesus undertook to expose their error on the very basis of those Scriptures. The possibility that God could raise the dead to a new condition of life was confirmed by the holy writings.

"As touching the dead, that they rise"—once more stating the point at issue. *The dead* relates to their bodily condition. *They rise* is

---

[28] David L. McKenna, *Mark,* The Communicator's Commentary, p. 249.

the present tense of doctrinal certainty. Jesus left no doubt concerning the bodily resurrection of those who had died.

"Have ye not read in the book of Moses"—the question implies an affirmative answer. They had read the written account, but had they ever recognized the true deduction to be drawn from it? The book of Moses was the Pentateuch, the law. The natural implication of the designation is that Jesus accepted its Mosaic authorship.

"In *the place concerning* the Bush" (ASV)—a reference to that portion of the Pentateuch recording God's appearance to Moses at the bush (Exod. 3:1–4:17). It illustrates the manner of citing Scripture before there were chapter divisions. Jesus drew His quotation from this part of Scripture because the Sadducees had appealed to it in making their denial of the resurrection. They had drawn a false deduction from those Scriptures; He revealed to them that the true deduction, consistent with the character of God, supported the doctrine of the resurrection.

"I *am* the God of Abraham, and the God of Isaac, and the God of Jacob"—citing the very words of God declaring His covenant relations to these men (Exod. 3:6). The repetition of *God* with each name emphasizes the distinct personal relationship which God established with each of these patriarchs. In harmony with the covenant relationship which they enjoyed, testified to by their circumcision, specific promises were made to each. "As these patriarchs had in their bodies the sign of this covenant, the body is included in whatever promise is involved."[29] In the Hebrew text quoted, no verb appears, as is normal in such statements. The italicized *am* in our text indicates that there is likewise no verb in the text as quoted in Mark. But in the Septuagint the verb *am* is supplied, indicating that the translators took the words of God to Moses not merely as pointing to a relationship in the historical past but as asserting God's abiding relationship to these patriarchs. (The verb *am* appears in the quotation as given in Matt. 22:32). In itself, the original statement might mean no more than that the God who spoke to Moses had in the past revealed Himself as the God of these patriarchs. But on the basis of His understanding of the nature of God, Jesus insisted that the statement had a deeper meaning. God's living relationship with His people is not terminated by their physical death. His living presence and the eternal life He bestows on believers assures that this relationship culminates in the resurrection life.

"He is not the God of the dead, but the God of the living"—stating the true deduction to be drawn from the divine declaration. They had

---

[29] Matthew B. Riddle, "The Gospel According to St. Mark," in *International Revision Commentary on the New Testament*, p. 161.

drawn a wrong deduction because they failed to understand the true nature of God and His relations to men. Jesus held that God's describing Himself to Moses as Abraham's God, Jacob's God, and Isaac's God referred not merely to a past relationship which no longer existed. By His very nature God is the God not of the dead but of the living. In calling these patriarchs into covenant relations with Himself, He had established a relationship with them that was not terminated with physical death. Death did not break the spiritual relationship into which they had been brought. The patriarchs were dead to the visible world, but they were still alive unto God in the invisible world. "Death is a change of relation to the world and to men; it does not change our relation to God."[30] As the unchanging living God, He is the God of the living, of men who are characterized as having life because of their relationship with Him.

Christ's argument clearly established the immortality of the soul, but it has been denied that it establishes the resurrection. Yet the truth of the resurrection follows when it is recognized that Hebrew thought regarded the human being as a unity; his corporeal and incorporeal natures are so perfectly fused that each is incomplete without the other. The Bible recognizes the separation of the soul from the body at death but does not view this as man's final condition. "Even for the righteous the intermediate state is a time of imperfection, first, because the spirit is without a body, which for human beings is an abnormal condition; and, second, because the rewards promised to the saints are not given in their fulness until the second coming of Christ. See Luke 14:14 and 2 Tim. 4:8."[31] They are in a state of incompleteness, awaiting the resurrection of their bodies (2 Cor. 5:1-8). Only when believers receive their resurrection bodies will they be fully like Christ (Phil. 3:21). "Everlasting life will not be realized in a fragmentary existence, as in an arch of being springing for ever but half way up."[32] The redemptive program of God extends even to the body of man, and He will not fail to bring to its full consummation the salvation which He has already begun in His saints. For man's body forever to remain in the grip of death would mean that death had not been conquered. The hope of the resurrection is based on God's faithfulness. Jesus' answer, while teaching the reality of the resurrection, said nothing about the manner of the resurrection or the nature of the resurrection body.

---

[30] Swete, pp. 282-83.

[31] Loraine Boettner, "Intermediate State," in *Baker's Dictionary of Theology*, edited by Everett F. Harrison, p. 291.

[32] Morison, p. 338.

"Ye therefore do greatly err"—an abrupt, forceful conclusion to the whole discussion. It is found only in Mark. Their self-confident assumption that they were discrediting the teaching of the resurrection was an open error. "The Sadducees are reckoning without their God."[33] Their error was great and had far-reaching implications (cf. 1 Cor. 15:13-19). *Err* may again be middle voice, "Ye are greatly deceiving yourselves" in denying the resurrection.

Mark leaves unrecorded the reaction to Jesus' reply to the Sadducees. Luke notes that certain of the scribes openly commended His answer (20:39), glad to get a solution to that vexing problem. Matthew records that the Pharisees, on hearing that Jesus muzzled the Sadducees, gathered together and put forward one of their number to ask Jesus another question upon which they desired His verdict (22:34-35).

4) Question of the first commandment (12:28-34). Only Matthew also gives this incident (22:34-40), but he leaves out the reaction of the questioner to Jesus' answer. Matthew tells the story from the standpoint of the Pharisees as a group, while Mark relates it from the standpoint of the questioner himself. Many critics hold that this event is only a variant of Luke 10:25-28, but they are not agreed about whether Luke or Matthew and Mark preserve the correct chronology.[34] Others, like Cranfield, rightly conclude that Luke's account "is neither parallel to, nor a doublet of, this passage, but refers to a different occasion."[35] He points out that the one significant feature in common in the accounts in Mark and Luke is the union of Deuteronomy 6:5 and Leviticus 19:18, but there are several significant differences which clearly point to two distinct occasions.

"One of the scribes came"—*one* centers the attention on this individual scribe. Matthew identified him as "a lawyer," an expert in the interpretation of the law. He very likely was one of the scribes who had applauded the reply of Jesus to the Sadducees (Luke 20:39). *Came* renders an aorist participle, the first of three used by Mark to describe this individual. It stands at the opening of the sentence to mark his deliberate approach. He had apparently been selected by the Pharisees to present their question. Mark said nothing about his motive in coming, but Matthew noted that he asked his question "tempting him." The sequel shows that he did not ask his question with a malicious motive,

---

[33] C.F.D. Moule, "The Gospel According to Mark," in *Cambridge Bible Commentary, The English Bible*, p. 98.

[34] See Taylor, pp. 484-85.

[35] C.E.B. Cranfield, *The Gospel According to Saint Mark*, Cambridge Greek Testament Commentary, p. 376.

but rather intended to "test" Jesus' skill in answering this much debated question.

"Having heard them reasoning together"—a second participial description, "having heard." It explains his approach. He had been an attentive listener to the discussion between Jesus and the Sadducees.

"Perceiving that he had answered them well"—a third participial description, giving his own reaction. As an open-minded scribe, he recognized that Jesus had given an admirable reply. Personally pleased with what he had heard, he approached Jesus with his own question. It reveals no obvious trickery but is plain and straightforward.

"Which is the first commandment of all?"—more literally, "What sort of commandment is first of all?" He desired to know *what kind* of commandment was to be ranked in the highest place, what quality made a commandment of principal importance.[36] While holding that all commandments were binding, the rabbis attempted to formulate a basic principle from which the rest of the law could be deduced as a corollary.[37] The question of what commandments were "heavy" or "light" was much discussed. The rabbis counted 613 different commandments, 365 negatives and 248 positive. But their comparative importance was much debated. The scribe desired Jesus to indicate a principle of classification.

"The first of all the commandments *is,* Hear, O Israel"—Jesus at once pointed out that the answer to the question of what commandment is *first* is of primary importance; it had already been indicated by their own religious practice in their use of the Shema (Heb. "hear"). The Shema, consisting of Numbers 15:37-41 and of Deuteronomy 6:4-9 and 11:13-21, was recited by every pious Jew in his worship, both morning and evening, as a religious creed or confession of faith. It proclaimed Jehovah's basic demand upon Israel as His chosen people. Jesus quoted the first part of it, Deuteronomy 6:4-5.

"The Lord our God is one Lord"—only Mark included this affirmation of monotheism. *The Lord* is the Septuagint rendering of the Hebrew tetragram *YHWH,* commonly rendered "Jehovah," or Yahweh, the unchanging covenant Lord, while *our* God stresses Israel's distinctive relationship to Him. This Lord is acclaimed as one, stressing

---

[36] Most commentators support this rendering of *poia,* "of what kind." But others think that it is here simply the equivalent of the interrogative *tis,* "what." While the distinction between them is faint or extinct at times, here it has point and should be preserved.

[37] Perhaps the most familiar example is that of Rabbi Hillel (60 B.C.–A.D. 20), "What is hateful to thyself, do not to thy neighbor; this is the whole law, the rest is commentary."

His unity. In the face of prevailing polytheism, this emphasis on monotheism was important for Israel as well as for the Christian church.

"And thou shalt love the Lord thy God"—Israel's obligation to God stemmed from His nature as well as from Israel's distinctive relationship to Him as *thy God*. Their constant duty was to love Him supremely, with a love of intelligence and purpose. Man's supreme duty toward God is moral, not ceremonial.

"With all thy heart, and with all thy soul, and with all thy mind, and with all thy strength"—*with* is literally "out of" and stresses the source of the love. It must arise out of every area of their being— heart, soul, mind, strength—reference to each part extended with the adjective *whole* for equal emphasis. The original Hebrew (Deut. 6:5) enumerated "heart," "soul," and "might," but the Septuagint rendered "heart" by "mind." In His statement, as quoted by Mark, Jesus included both terms, thus strengthening the stress upon the comprehensiveness of the demand. Love to God must possess the whole heart, the seat of personality, the whole soul, the self-conscious life, the whole mind, the rational faculties, and the whole strength, the entire active powers of man. This command, in its various scriptural occurrences, shows interesting variations in form. These variations make it clear that there is no intention to give a psychological analysis of human personality; the accumulation of terms underlines the comprehensiveness of the duty of love. If God is worthy of man's love, He must be loved with all of man's being. (Cf. Deut. 6:5; Matt. 22:37; Mark 12:30, 33; Luke 10:27, for the variations.)

"The second is this" (ASV)—Jesus added a second commandment in order to set forth the complete duty of love. He knew that the godward and manward aspects of love are inseparable (1 John 4:21). According to Matthew, Jesus asserted that this command was "like" the first in its nature, of primary importance.

"Thou shalt love thy neighbor as thyself"—an exact quotation of Leviticus 19:18 from the Septuagint. *Love* is the same word as in the previous command. Here, the difference is in the measure of love for the neighbor; he is to be loved "as thyself." The love for self, the instinctive desire to promote one's own good, is assumed as a reality. Alexander notes, "Self-love, as being an original principle of our nature, and therefore not subject to the caprices of the will, is wisely made the standard of men's love for one another, which would otherwise be ever sinking far below the level of our natural regard for our own welfare."[38] This command demands that he must exercise a love

---

[38] Joseph Addison Alexander, *The Gospel According to Mark,* p. 333.

equal to that which he has for himself toward his neighbor, the "one near to him," the person with whom he comes into contact, whoever he may be. In Leviticus, *neighbor* meant a fellow-Israelite, but in the New Testament, it is given the widest possible extension of meaning (cf. Luke 10:29-37).

"There is none other commandment greater than these"—asserting the unrivaled importance of the two commands just cited. *None other* recognizes the existence of other binding commands, but none of them can be placed on a level of greatness with these two. All other commands will be fulfilled to the measure that these two are fulfilled. The first commandment summarizes the first table of the Decalogue (Exod. 20:2-11), a man's duties to God, while the second summarizes the second table (Exod. 20:12-17), man's duties to his fellow man. Matthew recorded that Jesus went on to say, "On these two commandments hang all the law and the prophets" (22:40). The prophetic as well as the legal Scriptures find their inspiration in love. This double love comprehends all righteousness. Thus the essence of the believer's duty, both godward and manward, is moral and not ceremonial.

Verses 32-34 are peculiar to Mark. The scribe's reaction revealed that he was an open-minded inquirer, ready to accept the truth even from Jesus. He was the most honest questioner during this day, and he alone received a commendation from Jesus.

"Well, Master, thou hast said the truth"—the scribe again regarded the reply of Jesus as admirable and did not hesitate to say so openly. He commended Him as an able Teacher: "Beautifully, Teacher; of a truth you said." Jesus' reply was excellent because He answered "of a truth," had based His answer on truth. Anderson notes, "Only here in the Gospel is a representative of Jewish religious officialdom found agreeing with Jesus."[39]

"There is one God"—introducing the scribe's rehearsal of the answer as his own. He wholeheartedly approved the essential orthodoxy of the reply of Jesus. His omission of the divine name (literally "he is one") is in keeping with the Jewish practice of avoiding any unnecessary usage of that name.

"There is none other but he"—the scribe's interpretative addition to the answer of Jesus. God was one and unique. This was a fundamental plank in the theology of Judaism.

The two commandments were repeated by the scribe as his own (v. 33), but he substituted *understanding* ("intelligence" and "insight") for *soul* and *mind* (ASV). He stated the same thought less

[39] Hugh Anderson, *The Gospel of Mark,* New Century Bible, p. 282.

abstractly. His repeated *to love* kept the two commands as distinct yet recognized them as continuing duties.

"Is more than all whole burnt offerings and sacrifices"—the scribe's bold acknowledgment of the superiority of the moral over the ceremonial. *Whole burnt offerings,* the more specific of the two terms, were sacrifices that were wholly consumed on the altar; *sacrifices* is wider in scope, including all kinds of sacrificial victims or offerings made on the altar. The two terms summarize and include the entire sacrificial system. In saying that these two commandments of love were more (literally "much more") than the ritual offerings, the scribe did not intend to repudiate such offerings but recognized their minor importance in comparison. It was an acceptance of Old Testament prophetic insight (cf. 1 Sam. 15:22; Isa. 1:11-20; Jer. 7:22-23; Hos. 6:6, Mic. 6:6-8).

"When Jesus saw that he answered discreetly"—Jesus observed the intelligence displayed by the scribe in his answer. *Discreetly,* an adverb used only here in the New Testament, pictures him as replying in the manner of one who possessed a mind of his own and really understood what he said. The man had comprehended the significance of Jesus' reply. Many manuscripts here have a personal pronoun, "When Jesus saw him, that he answered discreetly." The evidence is divided, but it is more probable that the pronoun was omitted by the scribes to smooth out the construction than that it was added. The pronoun indicates that Jesus was appraising the man even while He listened to his answer.

"Thou art not far from the kingdom of God"—a compliment as well as an appeal to the scribe. His realization of the primary importance of love had placed him spiritually near the kingdom of God, the reign of God in the lives of His people (cf. 1:15). He had come a long way for a scribe, but *not far from* made clear that he must go further and accept that love in the Person of Him who was "the kingdom incarnate." "Whether or not he ever actually entered it, is written on the yet unread page of its history."[40] Jones remarks, " 'Not far from the Kingdom,' how aptly it describes the condition of many in our own midst."[41]

"No man after that durst ask him *any question*"—the attempt of the enemies to entrap Jesus with their shrewd and cunning questions was abandoned. They realized that all such hostile questions only recoiled on the questioners. Jesus had foiled all their malicious efforts

---

[40] Edersheim, 2:405.

[41] J. D. Jones, p. 470.

to discredit Him. His authority stood unrivaled. "Every man in the immense surrounding crowd felt that there was such a reach of insight in the Lord that it was in vain to dispute with Him."[42]

b. Counterattack by Jesus (12:35-40).

Having brought the enemy attacks to a halt, Jesus now took the offensive against the religious leaders. With His question concerning Messiah's sonship, He exposed the inadequacy of the scribes as teachers (vv. 35-37) and then uttered His solemn condemnation of their conduct (vv. 38-40).

1) Question concerning Messiah's sonship (vv. 35-37). All the synoptics record how Jesus silenced His enemies with His question concerning Messiah's sonship (Matt. 22:41-46; Luke 20:41-44). His own series of questions during this day had begun with a counterquestion which immobilized the representatives of the Sanhedrin (11:29-30). He concluded His questioning with a problem of interpretation which exposed the inadequacy of the scribal interpretation concerning the Messiah.

"Jesus answered and said, while he taught in the temple"—Mark introduces this event with a general statement of the circumstances. Matthew notes that Jesus asked the question while the Pharisees as a group were still before Him and that He addressed them directly, eliciting a reply from them. *Answered* does not indicate a reply to a question directed to Him but denotes His response to the situation before Him. The scribes, against whom the question was aimed, were well represented in that gathering of Pharisees. The incident occurred while He was teaching in the temple, in the spacious court of the Gentiles.

"How say the scribes that [the, Gr.] Christ is the son of David?"— His question was not meant to deny the correctness of this teaching by the scribes but rather to show that it was not the whole truth. *How* raised the question of the consistency of the scribes in maintaining their views. It was the firm teaching of the scribes that the Christ is the son of David. *The Christ* means the expected Messiah. It is a transliteration of the Greek word *christos,* meaning "the anointed one," which is a translation of the Hebrew word for "Messiah." The title "The Anointed One" recalls the fact that in ancient times a man was made king by being anointed with oil. *Is* is the present tense of doctrinal statement and does not imply that the scribes taught that Messiah was already present. The teaching that the Messiah would be the son, the

---

[42] Morison, p. 344.

promised royal heir, of David was strongly attested in the Scriptures (2 Sam. 7:8-29; Pss. 89:3-4; 132:11; Isa. 9:2-7; 11:1; Jer. 23:5-6; Ezek. 34:23-24; 37:24). Any claimant to messiahship who could not establish Davidic descent would have been scornfully rejected. That no questions were raised on this point against Jesus as Messiah proves that His Davidic descent was unassailable. Only two days before, the crowd had acclaimed Him as "the son of David" (Matt. 21:9; Luke 19:38). But the Jewish masses, following the lead of the scribes, understood the term to mean a human being who would be a triumphant warrior-king.

"David himself said by the Holy Ghost"—*David himself* stresses that it was David's own words, when in prophetic vision he spoke in the Holy Spirit, that created the difficulty concerning the scribal teaching. The quotation is from Psalm 110:1. The formula, "by the Holy Ghost," underscored the prophetic nature of Psalm 110:1 as well as its accuracy and truthfulness. The argument is based on the Davidic authorship of the words quoted. The superscription to the psalm, in both the Hebrew and the Septuagint, designates it as "a Psalm of David." Its Davidic authorship was unquestioned by the Jews. However, modern critical scholarship generally rejects the Davidic authorship of the psalm and holds that Jesus as "a child of his own day" ignorantly accepted the erroneous view or used it because it was the unquestioned view. But this critical claim produces a dilemma which Lenski well states:

> Then we have the sad spectacle of the great Jesus by a mistake proving to Jews caught in the same mistake what both of their mistakes disprove instead of proving. But if the scribes and the Jews were mistaken regarding the authorship of this Psalm, if Jesus knew better, then Jesus used the ignorance of the Jews for his purpose, and then he sinks to the level of a tricky modern lawyer capitalizing the ignorance of his opponent in court. In either case Jesus proves his deity by a false proof, once ignorantly, the other time consciously. . . . A mistaken Jesus or a tricky Jesus is not even the model which the critics would make him for us.[43]

"The LORD said unto my Lord"—the Greek, like the English, uses the one word *Lord* to render two different Hebrew words. The first stands for *YHWH,* "Jehovah" (see v. 29), while the second renders the Hebrew *Adonai,* "my Lord" or "my master." The kind of master that is meant is made clear in the whole psalm. The psalm shows that the reference is to one who is more than a mere man. It is clear that

---

[43] Lenski, p. 338.

both names refer to Persons of the Godhead. It is obvious that the scribes accepted the pictures as messianic; otherwise they would immediately have repudiated the argument of Jesus. While there is no evidence for this interpretation in rabbinic literature until two hundred years later, "the silence is due to anti-Christian polemic stimulated by the freedom with which the Psalm was quoted in the primitive Church."[44] Aside from this event, the psalm is quoted directly five times in the New Testament (Acts 2:34-35; Heb. 1:13; 5:6; 7:17, 21), and numerous allusions to the thought contained in it reveal the profound influence it had upon the teaching of the Christian church (cf. 1 Cor. 15:25; Eph. 1:20-22; Phil. 2:9-11; Col. 3:1; Heb. 8:1; 10:12; 12:2; 1 Pet. 3:22). The Christian church accepted the exaltation and enthronement of the risen Christ as the fulfillment of this prophetic invitation to the Messiah by Jehovah: "Sit thou on my right hand," assume the place of honor and authority. *Till I make thine enemies thy footstool* indicates that the enthronement in heaven would follow Messiah's rejection by His enemies. The Jewish leaders had clearly shown themselves the enemies of Jesus through their efforts during the day.

"David therefore himself calleth him Lord"—a restatement of the unassailable fact shown by David's own words. It was a fact which the scribes would not dare to contradict. But it created their problem.

"And whence is he *then* his son?"—*whence* raises the logical question how the scribes, in the face of David's designation of the Messiah as "Lord," can consistently maintain that the Messiah is David's *son*. "How are these two things to be put together, the lower truth with which the scribes were occupied, and the higher one on which the Holy Ghost specially insists?"[45] The purpose of Jesus in raising this question was not merely to confound the scribes but to show that to be accepted as reliable interpreters of their own Scriptures, they must have a higher view of the true nature of the Messiah. Their view that the Messiah was simply a human being, the descendant of David, though a conquering king, did not do justice to the teaching of Scripture. For the Messiah to be David's Lord, He must be more than a man. "Jesus is more than Son of David; He is Son of Man, i.e., the representative of all humanity and not just the Jews, who had to suffer and then be exalted at God's right hand. Still more important He is Son of God!"[46] Christianity saw that the solution lay in the reality of

---

[44] See Taylor, p. 492, following the suggestion of the rabbinic scholars Strack and Billerback.

[45] William Kelly, *An Exposition of the Gospel of Mark,* p. 177.

[46] James A. Brooks, *Mark,* The New American Commentary, p. 201.

the incarnation. While Jesus made no attempt to explain to them that the solution lay in the recognition of the divine-human nature of the Messiah, His question pointed His enemies in that direction. In rejecting His claims to be more than just a man, they were blinding themselves to the true solution to the problem. Their own Scripture condemned their rejection of the view. The question of Caiaphas in 14:61 suggests that the Jewish leaders understood what Jesus intended to teach.

"The common people heard him gladly"—the rendering *common people* does not adequately give the meaning of the original, "the great multitude." The contrast is between the vast Passover crowd and the Jewish leaders, comparatively few in number, who had been trying to entrap Jesus with their questions. The people had been attentive listeners to the discussions. *Gladly* indicates the keen relish and delight with which they received His teaching. They appreciated the intelligence and power of His answers and the freshness of His method in dealing with these problems. *Heard* is imperfect tense, indicating their continued pleasure in the teaching which He was giving. It was a sustained, favorable response.

2) *Condemnation of the scribes (vv. 38-40).* All the synoptics report that Jesus, having exposed the inadequacy of the scribes as interpreters, solemnly pronounced His condemnation upon the scribes themselves. Matthew reported His words at length (23:1-39), but Mark and Luke (20:45-47) gave only representative fragments. Luke recorded similar words of condemnation on a previous occasion (11:37-52). Christ's condemnation made clear His complete break with the religious leaders.

"He said unto them in his doctrine"—*His doctrine* here does not point to the doctrinal content of what He was saying but rather to His activity of imparting vital truths to the people. The imperfect, "was saying," indicates that Mark is giving only specimens of what was said. Mark does not name those addressed, but Matthew and Luke indicate that Jesus spoke to His disciples in the hearing of the multitude. Later Jesus turned directly to the "scribes and Pharisees," as Matthew indicated.

"Beware of the scribes"—stating the standing duty to watch them so as to be on guard against their evil influence. In 8:15, Jesus used the verb to warn against false teaching; here He warns against the teachers themselves.

"Which love to go in long clothing"—giving the reason for this injunction against the scribes. *Which love* renders an articular present participle standing in apposition to *the scribes;* it describes the character of those warned against. It may be understood as a description of the scribes as a class or be taken as restrictive, those among the scribes who have the characteristics depicted. The latter view is more probable. Jesus was setting forth tests whereby His hearers might determine the character of the scribes in whom they would put their trust. Not all scribes could be justly included in this unmodified condemnation. In verses 28-34, Mark had just pictured a scribe whom Jesus could commend. *Love* pictures these scribes as personally wishing to do the things Jesus mentions because they found keen pleasure in activities which called attention to their own importance.

Their ostentatious activities are depicted in verses 38-39. "To go," more literally, "to walk," points to their needless locomotion for the purpose of display. They took pleasure in walking around in long robes, the long flowing *tallith* which was regarded as the sign of piety and scholarship. Whenever they went into the marketplaces, where the throngs congregated, they loved to receive salutations from the people, the deferential greetings given with honorific titles. Bishop says that this "meant kissing on the hand in full view of the public."[47] *The chief seats in the synagogues* refers to the bench at the end of the synagogue before the "ark" or chest where the sacred scrolls were kept. It faced the audience and was reserved for the leaders and people of distinction. It gratified them to receive such deferential recognition at religious services. *The uppermost rooms at feasts* refers to the places on the reclining couches (cf. 2:15) reserved for the most honored guests at the meal; the feasts were evening meals made festive by the invitation of honored guests. The scribal love for display invaded their social contacts.

Verse 40 passes from their ostentatious manners to their corrupt morals. The change of grammatical construction in the original is marked by the colon at the end of verse 39.[48] Two present participles under one article unveil two characteristic features of their unworthiness.

"Which devour widows' houses"—denouncing their covetous acts. The articular participle, "the ones devouring," dramatically pictures their greedy, unscrupulous practice. Having gained the confidence of rich widows, they swallowed widows' houses, enriching themselves, no doubt under legal forms, with their substance. McKenna elaborates,

---

[47] Bishop, p. 226

[48] The two participles are placed in the nominative rather than in the ablative with *apo* to agree with the preceding items. They may be construed as nominative absolutes intended to continue the previous items; but it is simpler to regard them as beginning a new sentence, with the following *these* emphatically picking up these nominatives. This is in harmony with the fact that there is a shift in the charge made.

"As one of their functions, scribes serve as consultants in estate planning for widows. Their role gives them the opportunity to convince lonely and susceptible women that their money and property should either be given to the scribe for his holy work or to the Temple for its holy ministries. In either case the scribe gains personally."[49]

"And for a pretence make long prayers"—more literally, "and in pretence praying long." This adds the charge of hypocrisy. They hid their covetousness under a guise of great personal piety. They gave themselves to long periods of prayer in order to impress people with their devotion to God. Jesus charged that their prayers were a pretense, a false front to disguise their real motive. As a pretended expression of their love for God, their real aim was to win the esteem of their victims.

"These shall receive greater damnation"—*these* emphatically takes up the double description just given. Jesus solemnly asserted that men of this character will receive greater condemnation, a heavier sentence than they would have received had there been no pretense of piety. "This functionally passive construction," Williamson notes, "is a circumlocution for the action of God, who will at the end judge hypocritical religious leaders with special severity."[50] To rob the poor and the bereaved under the guise of personal piety doubles the guilt. The Gospels leave unrecorded the impact of this devastating denunciation, either upon the Jewish leaders themselves or upon the people who heard it.

c. Commendation of the Widow's Giving (12:41-44).

This beautiful narrative, also given in Luke 21:1-4, forms a bright contrast to the avarice of the scribes, justly condemned by Jesus (v. 40). It need not be assumed that this widow was a victim of the greed of the scribes, but the story provides an instructive contrast between their spiritual poverty and her material poverty.

"Jesus sat over against the treasury"—peculiar to Mark. Having finished His public teaching in the court of the Gentiles, Jesus with His disciples passed through one of the nine gates in the dividing wall around the temple proper and entered the court of the women. In this court was the treasury, accessible to Jewish women. In the plural, the term denotes the "treasure chamber" where the temple treasures were kept. In the singular, as here, the meaning is best taken as denoting the thirteen receptacles for receiving religious and charitable contributions.

---

[49] McKenna, pp. 257-58.

[50] Lamar Williamson, Jr., *Mark,* Interpretation, A Bible Commentary for Teaching and Preaching, p. 233.

Called Shôphār chests because of their trumpet-like shape, each bore an inscription indicating what the money would be used for. According to the Mishnah, on six of them was the inscription, "Freewill-offerings."[51]

"Beheld how the people cast money into the treasury"—the imperfect tense, *beheld,* pictures Jesus as continuing to observe closely the stream of people passing by to make their offerings. Because it was the Passover season, the givers would be numerous. *How* suggests that He observed their manner of giving. "The Saviour noticed not merely the fact or acts of contribution, but also the wonderfully diversified modes in which the acts exhibited themselves. Mode is inseparable from act, and, when outward, reveals the inward essence of the act."[52] *Money* is literally "copper," copper coins, but papyrus usage shows that it denoted money generally. While the majority of the givers would have only copper coins to offer, the rich probably made their offerings in silver coins.

"Many that were rich cast in much"—among those making their offerings, Jesus noted not a few rich Jews who gave liberal offerings. That they were rich would be discernible from their conduct and elegant attire. *Much* is literally "many things" or pieces; perhaps they made their offering in many copper coins. Riddle suggests that they may have used many copper coins, "since in the form the gift would seem larger and make more noise. That Pharisaism could do this is certain."[53]

"There came a certain poor widow"—*came,* rendering an aorist participle standing at the beginning of the sentence, draws attention to her approach. Clearly Jesus was seated in a place where He could observe the approach as well as the act of giving of each worshipper. *A certain poor widow,* literally "one widow, poor," vividly identifies her. The numeral *one* may simply be an indefinite pronoun, but it is possible that it was used to stress her solitary approach. She is placed in contrast to the many rich. *Poor* asserts her condition of extreme poverty. She was not merely a peasant with meager means; she was financially destitute like a beggar. The three terms set forth her sad worldly circumstances.

"Threw in two mites, which make a farthing"—the mite (*lepton*) was a Greek copper coin, the smallest coin in use. Mark at once related it to the coinage with which his Roman readers were familiar. The farthing (*kodrantēs,* transliterating the Latin *quadrans*), the smallest

---

[51] Herbert Danby, trans., *The Mishnah,* p. 159.

[52] Morison, p. 351.

[53] Riddle, p. 168.

Roman coin in use, was one-fourth of the copper *as,* of which sixteen were equal to the silver *denarius.* Her gift therefore had the value of one sixty-fourth of a common laborer's daily wage (Matt. 20:2).[54] The inference that less than two *lepta* was not accepted as an offering is based on a rabbinical rule which related to almsgiving; it is not to the point here.

"He called *unto him* his disciples"—mentioned only by Mark. The disciples were not at His side when Jesus observed the widow's giving. Wishing to teach them an important lesson from actual life, Jesus summoned them to His side and directed attention to the woman as she was leaving.

"Verily I say unto you"—this solemn introductory formula stressed the importance of the lesson He had for them. Here it points to the strange and unexpected nature of His lesson. He made an assertion concerning the widow (v. 43) and added the justification (v. 44).

"This poor widow hath cast more in, than all they which have cast into the treasury"—*this* points out to the disciples the receding figure, while His original word order, "the widow, the poor," stresses her poverty-stricken condition. He contrasts her giving with that of all the others "that are casting" in. The present tense recognizes that the offerings are still being made, but He knew that none would exceed that of the woman. *More than all* does not deny the value of their gifts, but insists that they all gave less than the widow. His words may even mean "more than all those put together."

"For"—adding the reason for His paradoxical assertion.

"All *they* did cast in of their abundance"—gave out of their superfluity, from what was in excess of their actual need. *Did cast in* confines His statement to those who had already made their offerings. He had taken note of what they possessed.

"But she of her want did cast in all that she had, *even* all her living"—proportionally she had given the most. In giving her two mites, she had given all that she possessed, all her living, her entire means of subsistence. Because of her gift, she would need to fast until she could earn more. In giving to God her last means of support, she had completely entrusted herself to His care. Although her gift was only two small copper coins, her faith-prompted love made that gift "entirely of gold in the eyes of the Lord."[55] How Jesus knew that she had given her all is not stated, but it is clearly another instance of His

---

[54] If today we figure the daily pay of a common laborer at $40.00, her gift would have a value of less than 65¢.

[55] Lenski, p. 346.

supernatural insight (cf. 2:8). Some have questioned Jesus' ability to know the amount and the motive of each giver. But as Brooks remarks, ''The real question is not whether he had some supernatural knowledge but whether he was in fact Son of God as Mark claims.''[56] He evaluated her gift not by the amount she gave but by what was left after she gave. ''The test of liberality is not what is given, but what is left.''[57]

The presence of Jesus in the temple this day had stirred controversy and had elicited His strong condemnation upon the Jewish leaders. His recognition of the widow's giving enabled Him to leave the temple with a warm word of commendation. Jesus valued the widow's sacrificial giving so much because it was a foregleam of His own giving: ''She gave her entire livelihood; he gave his very life.''[58]

---

[56] Brooks, p. 203.

[57] Kelly, p. 179.

[58] Brooks, p. 204.

12
Ministry in Jerusalem
(Part 3; 13:1-37)

3. Eschatological Discourse to the Disciples (13:1-37)

This chapter contains by far the longest discourse by Jesus on a single theme recorded by Mark. Its inclusion is evidence of Mark's recognition of its significance and abiding value for his readers. This discourse appears at greatest length in Matthew (24:1–25:46), while Luke's account (21:5-36) contains some independent material. Delivered on the Mount of Olives (v. 3), it is commonly known as the Olivet Discourse. It is a prophetic unveiling of the future for His disciples, yet its specific aim is to warn, exhort, and encourage them to faith and obedience. The occasion was His announcement of the coming destruction of the temple (vv. 1-2) and the consequent question by four disciples (vv. 3-4). The discourse (vv. 5-37) was His reply to their question.

As has been true of all prophetic portions of Scripture, the Olivet Discourse has received varied interpretations. It has also been the subject of much critical and skeptical discussion. While radical scholars have charged that the discourse is wholly unauthentic, many scholars adopt a mediating position in holding that in its present form, the discourse contains only fragments of the genuine teaching of Jesus. It is held that the present account was built around a "Little Apocalypse" which some Christian prophet produced and ascribed to Jesus.[1] But the critics' rejection of portions of the discourse as unworthy of Jesus was due mainly to their subjective dislike of the apocalyptic element. Devoid of all documentary evidence, the hypothesis is incapable of proof and not necessary. The discourse contains nothing that is unworthy of

---

[1] See V. Taylor, *The Gospel According to St. Mark,* pp. 498-99, and the literature there cited.

Christ Himself. It lacks the highly figurative language of Jewish apocalyptic writings and has a strong note of moral exhortation, an element almost entirely lacking in apocalyptic works. Cranfield holds that this chapter "does give us substantially our Lord's teaching" and appropriately goes on to ask "whether the disparagement of this chapter by much recent scholarship has not resulted in a serious impoverishment and weakening of the Church's life."[2] There seems to be no sufficient reason for rejecting this chapter as giving the authentic teaching of Jesus. Certainly, Mark presented it as such. The teaching is consistent with his portrait of Jesus the Son of God (1:1) in this Gospel.

a. Prediction About the Temple (vv. 1-2).

"As he went out of the temple"—His public ministry was ended. His entry into the temple that Tuesday morning was mentioned in 11:27; now He was leaving it for the last time. *Temple* again has reference to the entire temple enclosure. *Went out* pictures Him in the act of leaving, apparently leaving by the eastern gate on the way to Bethany.

"One of his disciples saith unto him"—the disciple is not identified, but he acted as the spokesman for the rest of the disciples (Matt. 24:1). The disciple, perhaps Peter, directed the attention of Jesus to the magnificent building. His motive is not indicated, but it seemingly was in response to the words of Jesus in Matthew 23:38 that the temple would be left "desolate."

"See what manner of stones and what buildings *are here!*"—*see* is an imperative, bidding Jesus to take a look at the grand structure. His words express the disciple's own admiration of its magnificence. *What manner of stones* calls attention to the astonishing size of the stones. According to Josephus, part of it was built of strong, white stones each measuring twenty-five cubits long, eight high, and about twelve in breadth (37 1/2' × 12' × 18').[3] Some of these massive stones weighed more than one hundred tons. The plural *buildings* denotes the temple proper as well as the various courts with their chambers and magnificent colonnades, all of which rested on the platform which Herod the Great had constructed for the enlarged temple area. Luke mentioned also the costly votive offerings with which the temple was

---

[2] C.E.B. Cranfield, *The Gospel According to Saint Mark,* Cambridge Greek Testament Commentary, p. 390.

[3] Josephus *Antiquities* 15. 11. 3.

decorated (21:5). The Herodian temple was recognized as one of the architectural wonders of the Roman world.[4]

"Seest thou these great buildings?"—Jesus acknowledged the magnificence of the temple structure; the disciple was justified in viewing it with admiration. The words may be viewed either as a question or an assertion. If they are a question, Jesus asked the disciple, "Is your attention centered on the grand material structure?" If they are an assertion, Jesus acknowledged that the disciple was occupied with the grandeur before him. To view the reply as a question seems preferable. In either case, His words fixed attention on the material temple itself in preparation for His astonishing announcement.

"There shall not be left one stone upon another, that shall not be thrown down"—an explicit announcement of its coming complete ruination. Up to this point during this day, Jesus had acted as God's "forth-teller," applying the truth of God to the scene before Him; with this statement He turned to predictive prophecy, declaring the near future. The use of a double negative in both clauses in the original stresses the unquestioned certainty of the fulfillment of His words. They received very literal, terrible fulfillment in A.D. 70. The temple was actually destroyed by fire, contrary to the order of Titus, who had hoped to spare the edifice; but later, he gave orders to demolish the entire city and temple.[5] Josephus remarks that the temple and the city walls, except for a few towers, were so thoroughly "dug up to the foundation, that there was left nothing to make those that came thither believe it had ever been inhabited."[6] The large platform on which the temple complex was located remains, but nothing of the buildings which had been erected on it.

b. Question by Four Disciples (vv. 3-4).

"As he sat upon the mount of Olives over against the temple"— having made His startling announcement, Jesus walked on in advance, apparently in silent meditation. He climbed the steep path across the Mount of Olives to Bethany; when at the summit, Jesus seated Himself "over against the temple," lying due west across the Kidron Valley. Mark's informant vividly remembered Jesus' posture and the exact spot where He sat. Before them lay a panoramic view of the temple

---

[4] For a description of the Herodian temple, see Josephus *Antiquities* 15. 11. 3-7; Herbert Danby, trans., *The Mishnah,* pp. 589-98; Alfred Edersheim, *The Temple,* chap. 2; W. Shaw Caldecott, *Herod's Temple, Its New Testament Associations and Its Actual Structure,* part 2.

[5] Josephus *Wars of the Jews* 6. 1; 7. 1. 1.

[6] Ibid.

and the city of Jerusalem in all their splendor. The Mount of Olives is almost 150 feet higher than the temple mount. Probably dusk was beginning to settle over the scene as Jesus spoke to His disciples.

"Peter and James and John and Andrew asked him privately"—named only in Mark. This is the only place where Andrew is named with the other three who formed the inner circle among the disciples. According to 1:16-20, these four disciples had been with Jesus the longest. *Asked* in the original is singular, indicating that Mark thought of Peter as the speaker, the others accompanying him as he presented their question. *Privately* is best taken as not intending to exclude the other disciples but all those who were not of the Twelve. Whether all the Twelve were there (cf. Matt. 24:3; Luke 21:7) is not certain. The announcement and its implications were too startling to be discussed openly.

"Tell us"—all the synoptics record a double question. The first inquired about the time, the second about the visible portent signaling the fulfillment.

"When shall these things be?"—*these things* relates to the announced destruction of the temple, but the plural indicates that they realized this catastrophic event would be related to other events. They accepted this fact without question but wanted to know when the event would happen.

"And what *shall be* the sign when all these things shall be fulfilled?"—*and* ties this second question to the first. *These things* again relates to the temple, but the question assumes that the destruction will be part of the complex events culminating in the consummation of the age and the inauguration of the messianic kingdom. His prophecy of the destruction of the temple naturally led them to think of Zechariah 14 and its eschatological portrayal. This implication is more clearly indicated in Matthew's formulation of the question. "When shall these things be, and what is the sign of thy coming and [the] completion of the age?" (Darby). *Completion of the age* is the noun form of the verb in Mark, rendered "shall be fulfilled," denoting that the things mentioned will be brought to their close, or final fulfillment. *All* stands emphatically at the end of the sentence to stress the total consummation of these crisis events. They were eager to know what *sign* or visible portent would enable them to recognize the inauguration of these cataclysmic events. Clearly, they did not foresee the long interval between the two events. The local event became blended into the eschatological. This use of the local event in the foreground as the type of the eschatological event is seen in the Old Testament in Joel's presentation of the Day of the Lord. This prophetic use of the local crisis as a type of the end time teaches us that each age has its own judgment pointing to the certainty of the final judgment.

c. Prophetic Answer to the Disciples (vv. 5-37).

"Jesus answering them began to say"—the formula promises weighty utterances. *Began to say* implies that an extended discourse will follow. Jesus began with wise warnings to His disciples (vv. 5-13), portrayed the end-time crisis culminating in the second advent (vv. 14-27), and concluded with further instructions and warnings to the disciples (vv. 28-37). While its central portion is distinctly eschatological, the discourse begins and ends with moral exhortations, thus underlining the practical nature of biblical prophecy.

1) Warnings to the disciples (vv. 5-13). Before dealing with the eschatological future, Jesus reminded His disciples that their first duty was to be alert to the dangers that would confront them. Two types of danger are pointed out. In connection with the eschatological interests, they must not be deceived by pretenders and catastrophic occurrences (vv. 5-8); neither must they allow persecutions to destroy their personal allegiance to Him (vv. 9-13).

a) Perils from the character of the age (vv. 5-8). "Take heed lest any *man* deceive you"—all three accounts begin with this warning. *Take heed* lays upon them the standing duty to keep their eyes open to the danger of being misled. They must realize that there is the spiritual danger of being misled by religious error. This is the first of four such admonitions during this discourse (vv. 5, 9, 23, 33). Instead of giving them the sign they had requested (v. 4), Jesus began by alerting them to false signs.

"Many shall come in my name, saying, I am *Christ*"—explaining the danger from pretenders. *In my name* is more literally "upon my name"; they will base their claims on the authority of "my name," which may be taken either personally or officially. If it is understood personally, the meaning is "appealing to my authority"; they are false teachers claiming to speak for Him or on the basis of His revelation. More probably, the meaning is official, "claiming for themselves the title of Messiah which rightly is mine"; then they are false messiahs seeking to usurp His office. The latter meaning seems clear from the egotistical claim, "I am *Christ*," or "I myself am Christ." The italic *Christ* indicates that in the original, no word occurs. The emphasis is on their boastful *I*. But Matthew here added "the Christ" (24:5), thus making clear the claim to be the Messiah personally. The first person after the time of Jesus Christ definitely known to have claimed to be the Messiah was Barcochba, the leader of the last great Jewish revolt in A.D. 132. There have been various other claimants since. Feinberg says, "Up to our day [1953] there is a record of some 64 false Messiahs who have tried to lead Israel astray."[7] The number of the pretenders is not yet complete.

"Shall deceive many"—catching people in the snare of their enthusiasm, such pretenders always gain a following, of sorts. Their success makes them dangerous.

"When ye shall hear of wars and rumors of wars"—pointing out a second false basis for assuming that the end is at hand. *Ye* makes the warning personal. The report of wars and rumors of wars, wars actually in progress and widespread expectation of wars, must not be viewed as signaling the immediate end. Wars and threats of wars will characterize the entire age. Now the danger is not the cunning of others but their own misinterpretation of the turbulent affairs of history.

"Be ye not troubled"—the calming admonition. Amid the commotions of wars and tensions, they must arrest the natural feeling of alarm and inner agitation. They must not allow political and social upheavals to upset them emotionally so that they are unfit to carry on their proper work.

"*Such things* must needs be"—more literally, "It must be." These national convulsions have not been preordained by divine decree but arise as the inevitable consequences of human depravity. They are the natural results of human nature separated from God and ruled by self-interest. They are divinely permitted as part of God's eschatological program for this world, which includes judgment as well as salvation.

"But the end *shall* not *be* yet"—these stirring events do not constitute the immediate sign of the consummation of the age. They demonstrate the rotten moral condition of the world, which will certainly lead to judgment, but *not yet,* implying that more suffering is first in store. *The end* is the eschatological goal of history, the final establishment of God's kingdom on earth.

"For nation shall rise against nation, and kingdom against kingdom"—a confirmation of the preceding statement about wars and rumors of wars. "Shall rise" renders an emphatic future passive, "will be roused," and points to the human perversions provoking these tumults. It is a picture of vast conflicts stirred up by racial and political forces.

"There shall be earthquakes in divers places, and there shall be famines"—these facts are tersely stated without any connecting particles, "suiting the abrupt style congenial to the prophetic mood."[8]

---

[7] Charles Lee Feinberg, *Israel in the Last Days: The Olivet Discourse,* p. 8.

[8] Alexander Balmain Bruce, "The Synoptic Gospels," in *The Expositor's Greek Testament,* 1:384.

Since earthquakes are not produced by wars, it is clear that these items introduce a new source of horror and suffering, namely, natural disasters. *In divers places* means that the earthquakes will occur in various places, perhaps in several places at once. Famines have been a tragic feature of human history, and prospects of a worldwide famine are no longer just a visionary danger. These calamities will augment the sufferings produced by human strife and violence, causing believers to conclude that the end must be at hand. The "groaning and travailing" of creation is intimately connected with the sin and strife in the human world (Rom. 8:19-22).

"These *are* the beginnings of sorrows"—Rotherham more literally renders, "A beginning of birth-pangs are these things." *Sorrows* conveys a note of hope; the term was applied to the sharp pangs preceding childbirth. The sufferings will be intensified in the end-time convulsion, but the prospect is not hopeless. They are the "birth-pangs" for the birth of a new age, the messianic kingdom of peace. The earth's regeneration awaits the time when the Son of man shall return to assume His messianic throne (Matt. 19:28).

b) Personal danger amid persecution (vv. 9-13). "Take [ye] heed to yourselves"—peculiar to Mark. *Ye* is emphatic, "Ye on your part." The warning is to His disciples personally, but also to them as representatives of other disciples who later will undergo the same experiences. The previous warning (vv. 5-8) stressed the perils arising from what would happen in the world; this warning directs attention to what would happen to them personally. The exhortation does not urge them to seek their own safety but rather warns them to be alert against thoughtless or unworthy actions amid persecution. In Matthew 10:17-22, much of this warning is given in another context. Such warnings were an integral part of His training of the Twelve. Matthew also gave this warning here in abbreviated form (24:9). McKenna notes, "In His prophecy of the disciples' passion, Jesus brings them into the '. . . fellowship of His sufferings . . .' (Phil. 3:10), a role of highest honor."[9]

"For they shall deliver you up to councils"—justifying the warning. The indefinite *they* denotes their vicious Jewish enemies. *Deliver you up* need not imply treachery but assures that they will be handed over to the authority of the courts. The councils, or "sanhedrins," were local, Jewish disciplinary courts attached to the synagogues.[10] They

---

[9] David L. McKenna, *Mark,* The Communicator's Commentary, p. 265.

[10] According to Josephus, these local courts in every city consisted of seven judges (*Antiquities* 4. 8. 14). *The Mishnah* says that in every city where there were 100 men, the council consisted of twenty-three judges ("Sanhedrin" 1.6).

handled cases of infraction of the law and charges of heresy. Cases that were too difficult were referred to the high Sanhedrin in Jerusalem.

"In the synagogues[11] ye shall be beaten"—*synagogues* denotes the building for Jewish assembly and worship; the local councils held their sessions there. To be haled before these courts was considered a disgrace, and the beatings administered were severe, although limited to thirty-nine stripes (cf. 2 Cor. 11:24).

"Ye shall be brought before rulers and kings for my sake"—the secular powers too would be involved in the actions against them. On the Palestinian level, the governors were the Roman provincial rulers, such as Felix and Festus (Acts 23:24; 24:27), while kings were minor potentates, such as Herod Antipas or Agrippa I (Acts 12:1). But the scene need not be limited to Palestine; *rulers and kings,* used without an article, may well be intended to denote secular authorities generally. *Shall be brought* is passive, "made to stand," placed before judges as offenders and culprits. They will be haled before these authorities "on account of me," because of their loyalty to Him.

"For a testimony against them"—*them* includes all those hearing their defense, Jewish as well as pagan judges. Being brought into court because of their relationship to Christ will give them an opportunity to bear witness concerning Him. Their case will compel these high potentates to investigate the claims of the gospel. If their courageous testimony is rejected by these officials, it will be a testimony against them in the final judgment day.

"And the gospel must first be published among all nations"—*and* connects this universal preaching with what has just been said. Their being haled before these judges will further the worldwide preaching of the good news in Christ (cf. 1:1). *Among all nations* stands emphatically forward, stressing the scope of the intended preaching or public heralding of the message. *Must* indicates a necessity; it is in accord with the divine desire that all men might be saved (1 Tim. 2:1; 2 Pet. 3:9). *First* looks back to the end mentioned in verse 7. "It is part of God's eschatological purpose that before the End all nations shall have an opportunity to accept the gospel."[12] The result of that preaching is not indicated. The promise of a worldwide preaching of

---

[11] Because of the preposition rendered "in" (*eis,* into), some scholars insist that these words should be joined to the preceding, "They will deliver you into councils and into synagogues," making "Ye shall be beaten" a separate statement. But it seems best to preserve the parallelism of our version. The preposition *eis* here is equal to *en,* "in."

[12] Cranfield, p. 399.

the gospel does not assure that there will be a worldwide acceptance of it. A twofold fulfillment of this prediction seems evident. The preaching of the gospel throughout the Roman world is affirmed by Paul (Rom. 1:8; Col. 1:6, 23). But Matthew 23:14 clearly refers to a preaching which relates to the eschatological end.

"When they shall lead *you*"—*lead* pictures them as persons under arrest on the way to be handed over to the judge. *When they shall lead,* better, "whenever they may lead," indicates that this experience may befall them at any time.

"Take no thought beforehand what ye shall speak"—it will be a terrifying experience, but Jesus bids them quell their natural sense of fear. The negative with the compound verb, which occurs only here in the New Testament bids them stop their distracting anxiety concerning what may happen or should be done. "What is prohibited is not thought, but anxious care."[13]

"But whatsoever shall be given you in that hour, that speak ye"— the effective alternative to futile anxiety. The passive *shall be given* points to God as the giver of the appropriate answer, while *whatsoever* leaves open the nature of the thoughts and answers that will be flashed into their minds. *That speak ye* commands obedient utterance of the very thing communicated to them. They must not attempt to mix it with their own ideas as being more appropriate. *In that hour* indicates that the promise is for particular emergencies, when unexpectedly haled into court to defend their faith. It does not refer to those who have the duty to teach or preach at set times and places.

"For it is not ye that speak, but the Holy Ghost"—*for* explains His command. The real speaker will be the Holy Spirit speaking through them. Their calm, self-possessed attitude will allow the Spirit to use them effectively for witness bearing. This is the last of the few references to the Holy Spirit in Mark's Gospel (1:8, 10, 12; 3:29; 12:36). In Luke, Jesus presents Himself as the giver of the inspiration (21:15). History bears ample witness to the fact that Christians on trial for their faith have been amazed themselves at the aptness of the answers that flashed into their minds at the opportune moment.

Verses 12-13 graphically portray the extremes of the hatred to which His disciples will be exposed because of their relationship to Him. Verse 12 shows how that hatred will manifest itself in the most intimate family relationships. All the nouns in the verse are without the article, thus stressing the character of the relationship, brother and brother, father and child, children and parents. The deadly nature of

---

[13] Taylor, p. 508.

the enmity is underlined by the double reference to death in the verse. It will even be that children shall rise up in rebellion against their parents, report them to the authorities as Christians, thus causing them to be put to death. The plural verb *rise up* marks the numerous instances of this unnatural conduct.[14]

"Ye shall be hated of all *men* for my name's sake"—*all men* means the people generally and points to the extended scope of the hatred to which His followers will be subjected. All three synoptics record these words without variation. The periphrastic form of the future *shall be hated* marks the hatred as a continuing process going on and on. *For my name's sake* indicates the reason for the hatred. It will be His name, the revelation of the Person and all that He stands for, that will arouse the enmity. They will be hated, not for their errors or personal faults, but because they are Christians (1 Pet. 4:16).

"He that shall endure unto the end, the same shall be saved"—a cheering promise to the persecuted. It also points out the demand upon them. *Shall endure* stresses their need to maintain steadfastly and bravely their faith and loyalty to Him. "Endurance is one of the key-notes of Christian life and witness in this age."[15] *He that shall endure* renders an aorist participle, "he that has endured"; the tense looks forward to the completed endurance, when his individual probation will have ended. *Unto the end* here apparently does not refer to the eschatological end mentioned in verse 7. *End* does not have an article, and the phrase is used adverbially, "right through to the end, finally." *The same,* "this one," emphatically resumes the subject, indicating that it is the one who has endured to the end who will be saved. "Perseverance to the end, however bitter, is the evidence of genuine faith."[16] *Be saved* means more than deliverance from evil. It denotes salvation in the eschatological sense, when eternal life will be crowned with glorification (Rev. 2:10).

2) Sign of the end and the advent (vv. 14-27). This difficult section, which has received varied interpretations, forms the heart of the Olivet Discourse as recorded in Mark. It naturally divides into two paragraphs. The first states the event which inaugurates the unparalleled

---

[14] Neuter plural Greek nouns generally take a singular verb. When a plural verb is used with a neuter plural subject, as here (*tekna*), the plural individualizes those comprehended in the subject.

[15] C. E. Graham Swift, "Mark," in *The New Bible Commentary, Revised,* p. 879.

[16] Matthew B. Riddle, "The Gospel According to St. Mark," in *International Revision Commentary on the New Testament,* p. 99.

tribulation and offers appropriate guidance to His followers (vv. 14-23); the second pictures the return of the Son of man in glory (vv. 24-27).

I do not believe that the rapture of the church appears in the Olivet Discourse as recorded in Mark's Gospel. The thorny question of the relation of the rapture of the church to the Great Tribulation is therefore not discussed. I believe that the rapture will be before the Great Tribulation pictured by Jesus in this discourse.[17]

a) End-time crisis (vv. 14-23). In verses 14-23, Jesus describes the end-time crisis, the sign that the disciples had asked for (v. 4). They were ardently hoping that their Master would speedily establish His earthly kingdom. Their views of the future were still essentially Jewish, and they conceived of the anticipated messianic kingdom in relation to the people of Israel. As yet, they had no clear concept of the coming church. If Jesus had spoken to them of the rapture in the future, He would only have added confusion to the limited understanding they had of what He had already said.

The sign given either relates to the destruction of Jerusalem in A.D. 70 or gives the sign of the eschatological end. When the disciples presented their question to Jesus, two crisis events, the destruction of Jerusalem and the consummation of the age, seem to have merged to fill the horizon of their thinking concerning the future. And because of the close parallels between the two events, interpreters have always found it difficult to distinguish the two in Jesus' answer. The sign given in Luke 21:20 relates to the historical fall of Jerusalem. But Luke's sign, Jerusalem surrounded by armies, is not the same as that given in the other synoptics, namely, the abomination of desolation in the temple. Luke 21:20-24 records a part of the Olivet Discourse which has no exact parallel in the other two Gospels. It vividly pictures the capture of the city and the resultant condition reaching to the end of the age. The similarity of Luke's picture to that of the other synoptics had generally led to the assumption that they refer to the same event. While the two events have much in common, there are features in Mark's account which clearly look beyond the fall of Jerusalem and relate to

---

[17] The Olivet Discourse as a recorded in Matthew gives Christ's eschatological projections for three groups: Israel, the church, and the Gentile nations. Under this view, the second part of the discourse, which Morgan identifies as 24:25–25:30, by means of parables pictures the church as waiting for the return of her absent Lord. The duties of watching and occupying until the Lord returns are the essential stress in this section. The parabolic portrayal is suited to set forth the church in its eschatological responsibility, and the picture is compatible with the pretribulational view of the rapture of the church.

the eschatological end. This is evident from the close connection which the paragraph has with the second coming described in the following verses (vv. 24-27). Second Thessalonians 2:3-10 supports the view that the abomination of desolation refers to the eschatological Antichrist. The tribulation connected with the destruction of Jerusalem, standing in the foreground of the Olivet Discourse, foreshadows and contains the essential features of the Great Tribulation of the end time.

"When ye shall see the abomination of desolation"—*when ye shall see* looks forward to a definite, observable future event, but the time is left indefinite, "whenever ye may see." The designation *the abomination of desolation* connects with the prophecy of Daniel (9:27; 11:31; 12:11), as Matthew explicitly asserts. *The abomination* denotes an object of disgust, something loathsome and detestable, while the genitive *of desolation* describes the effect produced, causing something to be deserted and left desolate. In the Old Testament, the term *abomination* denoted idolatry or sacrilege (Deut. 29:16-17; 1 Kings 11:6-7; 2 Kings 16:3; 23:13; Ezek. 8:9-17). In 1 Maccabees 1:54 "an abomination of desolation" is used to describe the altar of Zeus erected in the temple at Jerusalem by Antiochus Epiphanes, 167 B.C., defiling the temple and causing it to be left devoid of loyal Jewish worshipers. The expression thus denotes that which, as a symbol of heathenism, is detestable to God and His people. It portrays not the destruction of the temple but rather its profanation.

"Standing where it ought not"—this leaves the place unidentified, but Matthew explicitly said, "in the holy place" (24:15), in the sacred sanctuary itself. McGee well notes "that the Holy Place was given only to the nation Israel. It was a special place in the Temple on earth. The church has no Holy Place."[18] Mark's expression laid stress on the violation involved. *Standing* is a masculine participle, although the noun *abomination* is neuter. The fact that Mark deliberately, though ungrammatically, used the masculine points to the fact that he regarded the abomination as personal ("he" rather than "it").[19] It seems clear that Mark was thinking of the personal Antichrist (2 Thess. 2:3-10; Rev. 13:1-10, 14-15). In time, the scene relates to the prophecy of Daniel's seventieth week (Dan. 9:24-27), when the prince that shall come "shall cause the sacrifice and the oblation to cease" (v. 27). This

---

[18] J. Vernon McGee, *Mark*, p. 147.

[19] R.C.H. Lenski, *The Interpretation of St. Mark's and St. Luke's Gospels*, p. 143.

interpretation of the words of Jesus presupposes the end-time reestablishment of the Jewish temple and worship.[20]

"(Let him that readeth understand)"—the parenthetical command, found also in Matthew, may be regarded as spoken by Jesus Himself or as an addition by the Gospel writers. Under the former view, Jesus is calling attention to the prophecy of Daniel, bidding the reader to understand its fuller significance; under the latter, the Gospel writer calls attention to the importance of what is written. Since the true text in Mark contains no reference to Daniel, the latter view may be preferred.

"Then let them that be in Judaea flee to the mountains"—*then* relates the commanded action to the appearing of the abomination of desolation in the temple. They must then immediately take to flight because of the bitter persecution that will be launched against those who refuse to receive the Antichrist. Instead of expecting immediate divine interposition on their behalf, let them flee to the mountains as offering places of refuge and safety. The personal safety of His followers during the Great Tribulation was a primary concern for Jesus.

Verses 15-16 describe by means of concrete pictures the extreme haste that will then be essential. Verse 15 describes one who is at home at the time. *The housetop,* the flat roof of the Oriental house, was generally reached by an outside stairway (cf. 2:2-4). It was used for various purposes: sleeping (1 Sam. 9:25-26), keeping a watch (Isa. 22:1), worship (Zeph. 1:5; Acts 10:9), proclaiming tidings (Matt. 10:27), and the like. If a man happened to be up there when the crisis broke, he must rush down and flee without even stopping to remove anything out of his house for his flight.

Verse 16 stresses a similar urgency for a man out in the field, where he is without his cloak, the outer garment. Let him not return, either to his house or to the entrance to the field, to take it, even though it would be highly desirable to have it with him during the cold night. "The danger is so great that there is no time for any delay. Life itself is at stake."[21]

"Woe to them that are with child"—an expression of pity, not condemnation. Jesus felt special compassion for expectant and nursing

---

[20] Thomas S. McCall, "How Soon the Tribulation Temple?" *Bibliotheca Sacra,* 128 (1971): 341-52. See Thomas McCall, "Problems in Rebuilding the Tribulation Temple," *Bibliotheca Sacra,* 129 (1972): 75-80. For a thorough recent treatment, see Thomas Ice and Randall Price, *Ready to Rebuild: The Imminent Plan to Rebuild the Last Days Temple,* 1992.

[21] James A. Brooks, *Mark,* The New American Commentary, p. 213.

mothers whose condition would hinder flight. The time would turn the joy of motherhood into a pathetic handicap.

"Pray ye that it be not in the winter" (ASV)—directing that the prospect of difficulty should lead to specific prayer. *That it be not in the winter* states the content of their petition. Mark's indefinite *it* may mean either the time of the manifestation of the abomination or their flight. Matthew referred it specifically to their flight (24:20). If the flight would come in the winter, during the rainy season, the rains and swollen streams would definitely add to the danger, and they would be unable to glean food from the countryside as they fled. Plummer comments, "Here prayer for temporal advantages is clearly sanctioned."[22]

"For in those days shall be affliction"—giving an explanation for the extreme urgency. Those fateful days will have the character of one long tribulation, dire pressure and continuing distress, caused by outward circumstances. It will be so severe as to be without parallel in human history. *Such as there hath not been the like* (ASV) with redundant fullness stresses its fierceness. It will literally be "the tribulation, the great one" (Rev. 7:14, Greek). The perfect tense *hath not been* pictures its unparalleled intensity as an abiding fact. *Neither shall be* emphatically assures that there never will be another like it. Those who restrict the reference to A.D. 70 must confine this tribulation to that siege, but Taylor well observes, "This assertion is much too emphatic for a siege; it is clear that the thought of 19 is eschatological."[23]

"Except that the Lord had shortened those days, no flesh should be saved"—strong proof of the consuming fierceness of those days. *The Lord,* Jehovah God of the Old Covenant, is in sovereign control of the affairs of this world, and He has graciously decreed a limitation on those days. The aorist tense, *had shortened,* puts this action in the past. God has already decreed that those days will be shortened, literally, "amputated" or "mutilated." The strong figurative statement indicates that God has forcefully acted not to permit them to be extended to the full length that human passions would have carried them. *No flesh* denotes human life in its frailty and infirmity. God has curtailed the period to prevent the destruction of the human race.

"For the elect's sake, whom he hath chosen"—God acted on behalf of the elect, the true believers during the great tribulation. Having chosen them for Himself (middle voice), God acted in their true interest.

---

[22] Alfred Plummer, *The Gospel According to St. Mark,* Cambridge Greek Testament, p. 300.

[23] Taylor, p. 514.

"Then if any man shall say to you"—*then* links this warning with the scene of extreme suffering just depicted. *If any man,* whosoever it may be, states the situation conditionally but implies that its fulfillment can be expected. *To you* marks that these messages will be directly aimed at the believers in Christ.

"Lo, here *is* Christ; or, lo, *he is* there; believe *him* not"—the repeated *lo* underlines the excitement with which these professed revelations are made during that time of pressure and fanaticism. A host of pretenders will arise claiming to be the Christ, the expected Messiah. *Believe him not* commands them to go on rejecting all such claims about a hidden Messiah, because, as Matthew's account points out, when the Messiah comes, it will be "as the lightning" which cannot be concealed (24:23-27). They therefore must have an unbelieving attitude toward all such claims. "Incredulity is sometimes a Christian duty."[24]

"For false Christs and false prophets shall rise"—the preceding admonition was conditionally stated; now the explanatory fact is explicitly affirmed. There shall arise, as a future fact, false Christs and false prophets, pseudo-Christs and pseudoprophets. The pseudo-Christ will falsely give himself out as being the personal Messiah, a pretender to the messianic office; the pseudoprophet will falsely claim to speak as God's spokesman, having a message directly from God. The plurals indicate that they will not be isolated cases.

"Shall shew signs and wonders"—a common phrase for miracles. *Signs* denotes things, whether frequent or rare, which have significance as pointing to something outside and beyond themselves; they are finger posts to a higher reality. *Wonders* views these signs with reference to the astonishment that they produce; they are startling, amazement-evoking portents. Whether pretended or real signs and wonders, these deceivers will not hesitate to resort to their use in order to gain their purpose. This element, not mentioned in the warning in verse 6, will greatly increase the danger. It presents a scene similar to 2 Thessalonians 2:3-10.

"To seduce, if *it were* possible, even the elect"—stating their diabolical aim. Their purpose is to lead astray, to divert from the path of truth, the elect, the believers in the true Christ. *If it were possible* implies that they will not succeed.

"Take ye heed"—*Ye* is again emphatic, "ye on your part," regardless of what others may do or say. For the third time, they are

---

[24] Henry Barclay Swete, *The Gospel According to Saint Mark,* p. 309.

urged to be on their guard (cf. vv. 5, 9). The present imperative again makes this a standing duty; let them not neglect to be alert to danger.

"Behold, I have foretold you all things"—*all things* means all things necessary to keep them from being misled. What He has here said will give them needed guidance. His message will stand as an abiding prophetic reminder.

b) Return of the Son of man (vv. 24-27). The paragraph portrays the second advent, forming the climax of the Olivet Discourse in Mark. The picture is presented in language that was familiar to the disciples from the Old Testament prophets. It is a point of perennial debate whether the passage is to be interpreted literally or figuratively. It may be that an insistence upon a strict literalism is open to question; in our atomic age, it would also be unjustified to insist that the language cannot refer to objective phenomena in the cosmic order. Second Peter 3:10 clearly teaches that the end of the age will be marked by a vast change in the cosmic system. The portents in this paragraph may be portrayed in phenomenal language, but behind the figurative terminology, objective crisis events in the physical universe should be recognized. Central to the whole picture is the reality of the objective, personal return of Christ in glory.

"But in those days, after that tribulation"—the adversative *but* here probably is not strongly adversative and serves to indicate a transition to a new phase of the picture of the end time. Bruce remarks that it sets a contrast between "the false Christs who are not to be believed in" and "the coming of the true Christ."[25] The double statement, "in those days, after that tribulation," suggests a close connection with verses 14-23. The implied close connection is explicitly affirmed by Matthew's "immediately" (24:29). The demonstrative pronouns, *those* and *that,* view the unparalleled tribulation just described as still remote at the time of speaking.

"The sun shall be darkened, and the moon shall not give her light"—cosmic signs will herald the consummation of the age. The terminology has generally been regarded as figurative, simply denoting political and international upheavals. But modern scientific developments have shown that the possibility the language may be a sober description of grim reality cannot be ruled out. Taylor comments, "In the light of 5 f. (wars, earthquakes, famines) and 26 (the coming of the Son of Man with clouds) it seems probable that objective phenomena

---

[25] Bruce, 1:431.

are meant.''[26] If interpreted as cosmological catastrophes, the language speaks for itself. McKenna remarks, ''When the sign of His coming is given, it will defy scientists and pseudoscientists, astronomers and astrologers, but there will be no way to misread its purpose.''[27]

''The stars of heaven shall fall''—the periphrastic form of the future tense here (''shall be falling'') stresses the duration, star after star falling. The language portrays a mighty disorganization in the sidereal world.

''The powers that are in heaven shall be shaken''—a further statement of vast convulsions in the heavenly world. In Acts 16:26, the verb *shaken* is used of the effect of an earthquake, so that the convulsion here might be described as an earthquake in the heavens. Some understand *the powers* to mean the impersonal physical forces of nature which control the movements of the heavenly bodies. But others suggestively hold that here, in contrast to the preceding three statements dealing with inanimate objects, the reference is to personal powers or hosts in the heavens. Then the most likely reference is to the mighty shaking effect that these events will have on the kingdom of Satan and his hosts.

''And then shall they see the Son of man''—a simple statement of the event that forms the grand climax of the age. *Then* points to the time when the celestial events just indicated will have taken place. The adverb, denoting succession, need not mean instantaneous succession, but it does imply that no long interval will occur. The subjects of the verb *see* are left unstated but clearly denotes those living on the earth at the time of the second advent in glory. The returning one is identified as the Son of man, which the disciples would immediately understand as meaning Jesus Himself. Throughout His ministry, Jesus had used this title to refer to Himself (cf. 2:10; John 1:51). In using it here, He clearly identified Himself with the ''Son of man'' in the vision of Daniel (7:13). ''The same one who humbly ministered on earth (10:45), the same one who suffered and died (8:31), will return with 'great power and glory.' ''[28]

''Coming in the clouds with great power and glory''—the present participle *coming* vividly portrays Him in the act of returning. His personal return to earth is in clouds, or ''amid clouds.'' Matthew said, ''in the clouds of heaven.'' The reference is apparently not to natural clouds but to that divine splendor which reveals yet conceals Jehovah's

---

[26] Taylor, p. 518.

[27] McKenna, p. 273.

[28] Brooks, p. 215.

presence (Exod. 19:9; Ps. 97:2; Dan. 7:13; Mark 9:7). *With great power and glory* means not only that the returning one possesses power and glory but that He comes accompanied by a visible display of great power and glory, exercising divine authority and clothed with heavenly glory.

"Then shall he send his angels"—*then* points to a further act in the eschatological drama which will follow the return in due time. While *angels* at times may denote human messengers, *the angels* here obviously denotes the angelic beings who are elsewhere pictured as returning with Christ (Matt. 16:27; 25:31; Mark 8:38) and acting as His mighty servants performing His bidding (Matt. 13:31, 39-41).

"Shall gather together his elect from the four winds"—the third mention of the elect (vv. 20, 22). *His elect* asserts His choice and ownership of them; He will act to establish His claim on them. The double compound verb *gather together* conveys the thought that they will be gathered at a central rallying point, namely, around Himself. The precise identity of these elect will depend upon one's eschatological views. Some would interpret the scene here to include believers of all ages, implying the resurrection of the dead; but there is no reference made to a resurrection here, and the further designation "from the four winds," the four cardinal points from which the winds blow, rather suggests people alive in all parts of the world. More consistent is the view that the reference is to the believers who have come through the Great Tribulation. Some would view them as the church emerging from the Great Tribulation, but more probable is the view that they are the distinctly Jewish believers of that period, those who have been won to faith in Christ as Messiah during the Great Tribulation.

"From the uttermost part of the earth to the uttermost part of heaven"—an appositional restatement of the preceding phrase. It places greater emphasis upon the remote parts of the earth's surface from which the elect shall be gathered. The unusual expression is quite literally "from earth's extremity to heaven's extremity." It is apparently a reference to the fact that the visible extremes of earth and sky meet at the horizon; it thus seems to denote space in all directions. It strongly asserts that there will be no spot on the face of the globe where any of the elect will be overlooked. Nothing is said of the fate of those who are not among the elect. It was not our Lord's intention here to give a complete picture of the eschatological program.

3) Concluding instructions (vv. 28-37). Having brought the eschatological picture to its grand climax, Jesus concluded His discourse with some hortatory instructions. He urged His disciples to be alert to the coming from the signs of the time (vv. 28-29), told them that the date of the coming was unrevealed (vv. 30-32), and stressed their need for constant watchfulness (vv. 33-37).

a) The lesson from the fig tree (vv. 28-29). Jesus began this concluding section with this lesson.

"Now learn a parable of the fig tree"—*now* is transitional, marking the turn to the concluding hortatory section. The definite article, *the fig tree,* does not refer to some well-known fig tree but views the tree as representative of its class. A fig tree may have been close at hand. The fig tree was a recognized symbol of Israel (cf. comments on 11:14), but there is no indication that the reference here has an intended symbolic meaning. The reference seems to be to the literal tree; that Luke so understood the reference seems clear from his added "and all the trees" (21:29). The olive and the fig were common trees in Palestine, but since the olive is an evergreen, only the fig tree could be used to teach the intended lesson. *Learn* (ye) is aorist imperative, bidding the disciples to master the moral parable (cf. 4:2) which the tree taught. This command is another instance of Jesus' insistence that the observant believer can learn valuable spiritual lessons from the most familiar material objects.

"When her branch is yet tender, and putteth forth leaves"—the condition of the fig tree conveying the parabolic message. *When,* better, "whenever," refers to a variable point in time to be determined by the condition of the fig tree. The first part of the sign is that the branch, the young shoot, has become tender, succulent because of the flowing sap; this is followed by the sprouting of the leaves. The present tense, *putteth forth,* pictures the branch leafing out as in the very process.[29]

"Ye know that summer is near"—the message conveyed by the condition of the tree. The leafing out of the fig tree was the earliest sign of approaching summer. *Ye know,* "ye recognize," is not to be restricted to the disciples; it was a matter of common knowledge.

"So ye in like manner"—"in the manner just described," points out an analogy between their careful observation in the material realm and their duty of understanding the moral significance of these crucial world events. *Ye* is emphatic, contrasting them to other men who have not the spiritual insight to discern their meaning.

"When ye shall see these things come to pass"—better, "whenever ye may actually see these things taking place." *These things*

---

[29] Depending on the accent placed on the verb, it is either a present subjunctive active, "may be putting forth leaves," or an aorist subjunctive passive, "the leaves may have sprouted." The former is preferable as avoiding a change of subject for the verbs.

cannot include the events of verses 24-27 since they constitute the end itself; the events to be interpreted are the signs pointing to the nearness of the end. The reference is to the events in verses 14-23 which mark the beginning of the end. The present tense *come to pass* views these crucial events as actually beginning to transpire.

"Know that it is nigh, *even* at the doors"—*know* urges them to be realizing what is happening. The events transpiring mean that it is nigh. The verb *is* has no stated subject; it may refer to a person, "he is," or to an event, "it is." The rendering "he is nigh" (ASV) makes it a reference to Christ, viewed as just outside the door. But the impersonal *it is* is more probable as assuming that the unexpressed subject is the end-time crisis which is the point under discussion. Luke interpreted it as "the kingdom of God." The phrase *at the doors* is a common figure to denote nearness. The plural *doors* views the outer entrance to the house as consisting of folding doors. *At,* literally, "upon," pictures the subject so near as in fact already located on the doorstep.

b) Date of the consummation (vv. 30-32). These verses deal with the question of the time of the fulfillment of these events (cf. v. 4) under three aspects: the limited duration for their fulfillment (v. 30), the certainty of the fulfillment (v. 31), and the unrevealed time for the fulfillment (v. 32).

"Verily I say unto you"—marking an important statement demanding serious attention (cf. 3:28).

"This generation shall not pass, till all these things be done"—the double negative makes a strong denial, "In nowise shall this generation pass away" (Rotherham). The terminus is the fulfillment of "all these things." It comprehends the same events as "these things" in verse 29, but now the stress is on the totality of those events. Because of the context, varied meanings have been given to *this generation*. The basic meaning of *generation* (*genea*) is family, descent, those descended from a common ancestor; more generally, "race," those possessing common characteristics. With a time idea, it denotes those living at the same time, contemporaries. In other places where Jesus used the term,[30] it always seems to refer to His contemporaries, but there is always a qualifying criticism of their moral character.[31] It is generally held that

---

[30] Matt. 11:16; 12:39, 41-42, 45; 16:4; 17:17; 23:36; Mark 8:12, 38; 9:19; Luke 7:31; 9:41; 11:29-32, 50-51; 17:25.

[31] Thus we read of "an evil and adulterous generation" (Matt. 12:39), "this evil generation" (Matt. 12:45), a "faithless and perverse generation" (Matt. 17:17). Often the context indicates the point of His condemnation against "this generation" (Matt. 11:16; Mark 8:12).

by *this generation* Jesus meant those living at the time He spoke. That generation certainly saw the fulfillment of His prophecy concerning the destruction of Jerusalem, but this view faces the obvious difficulty that it did not see the fulfillment of the eschatological aspects of the discourse. To avoid the conclusion that the words of Jesus did not prove true, other meanings for *this generation* have been advocated. Lenski stresses the qualitative aspect of the expression to mean "this kind" and holds that "the type of Jews that Jesus contended with" on that very day "will continue to the very Parousia."[32] Thus, the expression is given the force "this *kind of* generation," that is, the evil men who perpetrate the horrors described. Others hold that the reference is to the preservation of the Jewish race as a distinct people until the return of Christ. Bishop Ryle gives this meaning here as "my decided opinion."[33] This view can appeal to the facts of history. English comments, " 'This race (Israel) shall not pass, till all things be done.' The Jewish race is one of the wonder-miracles of mankind. Without a homeland, driven to every quarter, despised, hated and persecuted—yet it has survived. The Jew is never absorbed anywhere."[34] But both of these views eliminate the thought that the words of Jesus assure a definite time-limit for the fulfillment of the things predicted. It seems best to preserve the natural meaning of generation as denoting the people alive at a given time and accept the view that the reference is to that future, turbulent, wicked generation that will see the actual beginning of those eschatological events (vv. 14-23). The assurance is that the end-time crisis will not be of indefinite duration.

"Heaven and earth shall pass away"—a positive assertion of the future disappearance of the present cosmic order. In spite of all their stability, the heaven and the earth as we know them will yet pass away, come to an end of their present state of existence.

"But my words shall not pass away"—the primary reference is to the present discourse, but the unqualified expression *my words* indicates that the claim holds for all of His teachings. His words will never lose their validity. When viewed in relation to the dark outward circumstances when uttered, this calm assertion of perfect assurance is a revelation of His unique self-consciousness. Brooks remarks, "Such a fantastic claim is another indication that for Mark the Son of Man was also the Son of God."[35]

---

[32] Lenski, pp. 363-64.

[33] J. C. Ryle, "Mark" in *Expository Thoughts on the Gospels,* p. 290.

[34] E. Schuyler English, *Studies in the Gospel According to Mark,* p. 434.

[35] Brooks, p. 217.

"But of that day and *that* hour knoweth no man"—while the eschatological revelation is certain of speedy fulfillment, the precise time is hidden from all but the Father. Jesus declared that the chronological point of occurrence of that day and that hour cannot be determined. It is a clear warning against all attempts at date setting, yet it is a warning that has repeatedly been disregarded by misguided souls. "To persist in similar experiments of calculation is but to persist in a waste of ingenuity."[36]

"Not the angels which are in heaven"—although the angels will have a part in the work of the eschatological day (v. 27), the time has not been revealed to them. Their limited knowledge is also indicated in Ephesians 3:10 and 1 Peter 1:12.

"Neither the Son"—a surprising assertion found also in the true text in Matthew (24:36). Since the asserted limitation upon His knowledge in this matter is something that the early church would not have invented, it is generally accepted by even the radical critics that this is an authentic saying of Jesus.[37] This acknowledged limitation upon His knowledge does not deny His deity, although during the Arian controversy, the orthodox church found it embarrassing. It is a mark of His true humanity. Only here in Mark does Jesus use the title "the Son," rather than "the Son of man," of Himself. This title, placing Him alongside the Father, points to His consciousness of His unique nature as the divine Son. Since it is not the prerogative of any man "to know times or seasons, which the Father hath set within his own authority" (Acts 1:7), in His incarnation, Jesus also voluntarily accepted this limitation. Plummer points out that "after the Resurrection Christ does not say that He is ignorant."[38] It was not expedient that His people should know the day and hour of the end, and it was not a part of His revelation to them. God's wisdom graciously withheld any indication of a definite date for the Second Coming, otherwise no believer living before the indicated date could have experienced the purifying hope of His coming (1 John 3:2-3).

Need for watchfulness (vv. 33-37). The announcement of the coming of the end led easily into the need for watchfulness.

"Take ye heed, watch and pray"—the practical duty in view of the uncertainty of the time. *Take ye heed* for the fourth time sounds the call to alertness (vv. 5, 9, 23). The hortatory note runs through the

---

[36] James Morison, *A Practical Commentary on the Gospel According to St. Mark*, p. 374.

[37] D. E. Nineham, *The Gospel of St. Mark*, p. 360.

[38] Plummer, p. 306.

entire discourse. The double present tense command, *watch and pray,* sets forth the proper activity for alert men. *Watch* has the root meaning "to chase sleep," hence, it is a call "to be awake," with the added idea of being on the lookout for danger. *Pray*[39] indicates the constant need to call for divine assistance in confronting spiritual danger. Alexander notes "that neither watchfulness nor caution is sufficient to avert the danger here in question without a special divine interposition, and that this can only be obtained by asking."[40]

Verse 34-37 are peculiar to Mark and enforce the call to watchfulness by means of the parable of the absent householder.

"For the Son of man is as a man taking a far journey"—the sentence is incomplete, for the opening *as* has no corresponding *so.* But the meaning is clear. *Taking a far journey* renders a single adjective meaning "away from home, gone on a journey" (cf. the verb in 12:1).

Two aorist participles further describe the absent householder. *Who left his house* reverts back to the time when he left home. *And gave authority to his servants, and to every man his work* takes another step back to state what he did before leaving. The first phrase indicates the authorization given to his servants collectively to carry on the work of the household during his absence, while the second indicates that he assigned each slave his proper work.

"Commanded the porter to watch"—after the participles, the finite verb, *he commanded,* states the main feature of the parable. The porter was the doorkeeper who guarded the outer gate, thus controlling all access to the entire house. *Watch,* present tense, sets forth his standing duty. It is a different word than that in verse 32 and has the basic meaning "to be aroused from sleep." The two verbs both stress the idea of being awake and watchful.

"Watch ye therefore"—applying the parable to His disciples. "The *therefore* crowds into itself the whole force of the comparison contained in the preceding verse."[41] In applying the lesson, Jesus made no distinction between the porter and the other servants. In their attitudes, all of His disciples must be like the porter.

"For ye know not when the master of the house cometh"—the reason for watchfulness. With admirable skill, the title informally transfers the picture of the absent lord to Jesus Himself.

---

[39] The word has doubtful manuscript authority and is omitted by modern textual critics, although admittedly with great uncertainty. Prayer is an appropriate part of spiritual alertness.

[40] Joseph Addison Alexander, *The Gospel According to Mark,* p. 365.

[41] Morison, p. 375.

"At even, or at midnight, or at the cockcrowing, or in the morning"—popular designation of the four watches of the night (cf. 6:48). Morison points out that the names for the watches are drawn "from their termination, rather than from their beginnings."[42] The third watch derived its name from the familiar crowing of cocks about midway between midnight and sunrise.

"Lest coming suddenly he find you sleeping"—the danger His warnings are intended to avert. *Suddenly* states not the speed but the unexpectedness of the return. "If the suddenness causes disaster, the fault lies with those who have not watched."[43] *You* applies the warning directly to His disciples. The time of our Lord's absence is the world's night, but it is no time for His servants to yield to spiritual sleep, to grow unresponsive to the hope of His return.

"What I say unto you I say unto all, Watch"—what He was telling His disciples while seated on the Mount of Olives was not for them alone. This brief conclusion lays the duty of watchfulness upon His followers in every age and generation. "It gives us the great task of making every day fit for him to see and being at any moment ready to meet him face to face. All life becomes a preparation to meet the King."[44]

---

[42] Ibid.

[43] Plummer, p. 308.

[44] William Barclay, *The Gospel of Mark,* The Daily Study Bible, p. 321.

Part 3
The Self-Sacrifice of the Servant

13

The Self-Sacrifice of the Servant (Part 1; 14:1-52)

Mark's portrayal of the ministry of Jesus (1:14–13:37) made clear to his readers the true nature of the Servant of the Lord as the Son of God (1:1). The ministry of the Servant culminated in and gave meaning to the narrative of the self-sacrifice of the Servant. Mark began his account of the Passion of our Lord with a dual portrait of the foes and friends of Jesus (14:1-11), recorded the Passover observance with His disciples (14:12-25), described the sufferings in Gethsemane and His arrest (14:26-52), recounted some events of His two-part trial (14:53–15:20*a*), narrated His crucifixion (15:20*b*-41), and gave the events relating to the burial of the body of Jesus (15:42-47).

A. Foes and Friends of Jesus (14:1-11)

This preparatory section (14:1-11) skillfully portrays opposing reactions to the Servant of the Lord when He was about ''to give his life a ransom for many'' (10:45). It tells of the plotting of the Sanhedrin (vv. 1-2), the anointing of Jesus during a feast at Bethany (vv. 3-9), and the treachery of Judas (vv. 10-11).

1. Plotting of the Sanhedrin (vv. 1-2)

The synoptics here run parallel, but Matthew's account is the fullest (Matt. 26:1-5; Luke 22:1-2). Matthew records that Jesus reminded His disciples the Passover was coming in two days and explicitly announced His crucifixion. This plain prophecy of His impending crucifixion Matthew placed over against the deliberations of the Sanhedrin concerning His death.

''[Now, Gr.] after two days was *the feast of* the passover, and of unleavened bread''—*now* is transitional, marking the change to the new subject. This is the first explicit indication in Mark that Jesus' visit to Jerusalem was during the Passover season. The double designation *the passover and the unleavened bread* is characteristic of Mark and views this chief Jewish festival from its two aspects. The *Passover* was the solemn, annual, Jewish observance in commemoration of "the passing over" of the houses of the Israelites by the death angel in the destruction of the firstborn in Egypt (Exod. 12:1–13:16). It was celebrated on the fourteenth day of Nisan (March-April), the first month of the Jewish religious year, and continued into the early hours of the fifteenth; the Passover lamb was slain on the afternoon of the fourteenth but was eaten after sundown, which according to Jewish reckoning was the fifteenth. The Passover observance was immediately followed by the Feast of the Unleavened Bread, in commemoration of the Israelites' exit from Egypt (Exod. 23:15), from the fifteenth to the twenty-first. Popular usage merged the two feasts and regarded them as one, since all leaven was removed from Jewish homes before the slaying of the Passover lamb. In keeping with Deuteronomy 16:5-6, the Passover could be observed only in Jerusalem. The term *the passover* was used in three senses, the Passover lamb (14:12; Luke 22:7), the feast at which it was eaten (Matt. 26:19; Mark 14:16; Luke 22:8), and the Paschal festival as a whole (Luke 22:1; Acts 12:4). Here the Passover festival as distinct from the Feast of Unleavened Bread seems to be intended. *After two days* points to the beginning of the festival. If the two days are figured according to the usual inclusive Jewish count, the time was Wednesday of Passion Week; but if two whole days are meant, the time was Nisan 12, Tuesday. Matthew explicitly said that it was when Jesus had finished the Olivet Discourse, which is generally accepted as having been given on Tuesday afternoon. His announcement of His crucifixion in two days was probably made as Jesus and the disciples were nearing Bethany on Tuesday evening.

"The chief priests and the scribes"—the religious leaders of the Jewish nation (cf. 8:31; 11:27). Matthew here mentioned "the chief priests, and the scribes, and the elders of the people" (26:3). It was apparently an unofficial meeting, but all the orders in the Sanhedrin were involved.

"Sought how they might take him by craft, and put *him* to death"—the imperfect *sought,* "were seeking," may be viewed as extending back over the previous days of Passion Week, but more probably the reference is to the continued discussion during this meeting. Their concern, two days before the Passover, was not the removal of some questionable "leaven" but the elimination of a young rabbi who was going beyond accepted bounds and was a real threat to their own authority and prestige. *How* indicates that there was agreement with the previously announced policy of Caiaphas that Jesus must die (John

11:50-52), but there was uncertainty about the means whereby to accomplish it. They recognized that it could be effected only with subtlety, by their use of crafty strategy and deceptive means. This reference to their guileful malice throws a flood of light upon the true character of these Jewish religious leaders.

"But they said, Not on the feast *day*"—*but* (better, "for") marks the explanation why they did not dare to act openly against Jesus. *Said* is again the imperfect, indicating that again and again during this discussion, they voiced the conclusion, *Not on the feast.* If by *feast* they meant the Passover day, they indicated that they must act before that time or wait until the following day. If they meant the whole Passover festival, then they were saying they would have to wait until the people had left. The view that they meant they must act at once and not wait until the Passover is improbable because of the shortness of the time and the fact that most of the pilgrim crowd had already arrived (John 11:55). Their subsequent action makes it clear that they had no aversion to acting against Jesus during the feast when the opportunity presented itself. Quite probable is Jeremias's suggestion that their caution, "not during the feast," simply meant "in the absence of the festival crowd."[1]

"Lest there be an uproar of the people"—the fear that restrained them from taking immediate action. By *the people* they meant the vast Passover crowds from outside of Jerusalem.[2] Since many of the Galileans were sympathetic to Jesus, if not His acknowledged followers, they feared that these Galileans, known for their turbulence, would rise up and create a riot. Swete says that the Greek future indicative "shall be," rather than the subjunctive, "presents the danger as real and imminent, and adds force to the deprecation."[3] Their caution shows how highly the Sanhedrin members estimated the influence of Jesus upon the common people.

---

[1] Joachim Jeremias, *The Eucharistic Words of Jesus,* pp. 72-73. But D. E. Nineham remarks, "Although the Greek word (*heortē*) was occasionally used to mean 'crowd' at a later date, it remains doubtful whether it had this meaning as early as Mark's time" (*The Gospel of St. Mark,* p. 374).

[2] According to Josephus, in A.D. 65, a count by the priests showed 265,000 Passover lambs slain; with a minimum of ten people to a lamb, this means a crowd of about three million. (*Wars of the Jews* 6. 9. 3; cf. also *Wars* 2. 14. 3.) Even if the figures are exaggerated, the crowds must have been immense.

[3] Henry Barclay Swete, *The Gospel According to Saint Mark,* p. 320.

2. Anointing in Bethany (vv. 3-9)

Matthew gave a parallel account (26:6-13), but Luke omitted it, apparently because he recorded an earlier anointing in Galilee (7:36-50).[4] The anointing recorded in John 12:2-8 is clearly the same episode, but John's account had some remarkable divergences from that in the synoptics.

"Being in Bethany"—one of the few specific place designations in Mark. The expression used by Mark does not afford any precise time indication. The accounts in Mark and Matthew do not suggest any chronological dislocation, but John's Gospel records the anointing in connection with the arrival of Jesus at Bethany "six days before the passover" (12:1). John's arrangement suggests that it occurred on Friday or Saturday evening before Palm Sunday, while the synoptic order suggests that it occurred on Tuesday, or possibly Wednesday, evening of Passion Week. Most modern scholars prefer John's chronology as being more precise and hold that the synoptic arrangement is due to a desire to show the close connection between the anointing and the treachery of Judas. Robertson, however, thinks it better to follow the Marcan order and suggests that John mentioned the anointing in connection with Jesus' arrival at Bethany "because it is the last mention of Bethany in his Gospel."[5] Mary's action seems even more intelligible if it occurred on Tuesday evening, after she had been informed by one of the disciples of Jesus' prediction given in Matthew 26:1-2.

"In the house of Simon the leper"—he is not mentioned elsewhere. His actual relationship to Martha and Mary is unknown to us, although various relationships have been conjectured: the father of Martha, Mary, and Lazarus; the deceased husband of Martha; the brother of Lazarus; the owner of the house of which Lazarus was the tenant. John's account does not actually say that the feast took place in the home of Martha; rather, Lazarus appears to be a guest at the feast (John 12:1-8). *Simon* was a common Jewish name, and the leper was apparently a convenient label to distinguish him from others with the same name. The language does not prove that he was actually present; he

---

[4] Attempts to equate the anointing in Luke 7:36-50 with this anointing in Bethany are unjustified. The only points of similarity are the act of anointing and the name Simon. All else is different: the time and place, the character of the women and their motives for anointing Jesus, the reactions of those present at the time, the reply of Jesus to the critics. There, Simon was a central figure in the story; here, he has no part at all. A. T. Robertson remarks, "In view of all these differences it is absurd to represent the two anointings as the same, and outrageous on such slender ground to cast reproach on Mary of Bethany" (*A Harmony of the Gospels for Students of the Life of Christ*, p. 187).

[5] Robertson, p. 152 note.

may have died of leprosy. If he was present as the host, apparently Jesus had healed him some time previously, since as a leper he would have been excluded from society (cf. Mark 1:40). Apparently in gratitude to Jesus, he joined with other friends in Bethany to make this feast for Jesus. His house may have provided the largest room in Bethany.

"As he sat at meat"—more literally, "as he was reclining." This further description of the circumstances makes passing reference to the reclining posture of Jesus during the meal[6] (cf. 2:15).

"There came a woman"—Mary, the sister of Martha and Lazarus (John 12:3). Williamson comments, "The reprehensible roles in Mark 14:1-11 are played by men; the one praiseworthy character is identified only as a woman."[7] The absence of her name in Mark does not prove that he did not know it; the promise in verse 9 implies that her name was known. Perhaps her name was prudently omitted while Mary was still alive. When John wrote, such a consideration was no longer necessary.

"An alabaster cruse[8] of ointment of pure nard very costly" (ASV)—the cruse was a long-necked flask with no handles used for preserving precious perfumes or fragrant oils. Although such flasks might be made of other materials, perfumes were found to be best preserved in vessels made of alabaster, a finely textured, translucent stone. The flask contained "a pound of ointment," twelve ounces of highly aromatic perfume which evaporated rapidly and left a very pleasant odor (John 12:3). The ointment is described as "of pure nard very costly." *Nard* identifies the ointment as derived from nard plants, native to India, and the source of the finest ointments. The meaning of the adjective rendered *pure* is uncertain, but the most probable meaning is "unadulterated."[9] The nard was "trustworthy," or "pure," as opposed to nard adulterated with inferior substances. Such ointment naturally was very costly. Mary's possession of such costly perfume indicates that the Bethany household must have been comparatively wealthy.

---

[6] This reference to His posture is inconsistent with the suggestion that those at the meal "were seated cross-legged on the floor" (Sherman E. Johnson, *A Commentary on the Gospel According to St. Mark,* p. 224).

[7] Lamar Williamson, Jr., *Mark,* Interpretation, A Bible Commentary for Teaching and Preaching, p. 247.

[8] The word rendered "cruse" or "jar" is not in the original but is correctly added from the scene described. The rendering "box" gives an inaccurate implication to the modern reader.

[9] Advocated meanings are (1) genuine or unadulterated; (2) drinkable or liquid; (3) a derivation from some name, either some place name or a word referring to the pistachio

"She brake the box"—peculiar to Mark. *Brake* implies force but does not mean that the whole vessel was shattered. She forcefully snapped the narrow neck of the flask so that she might quickly pour out the entire contents. It expresses the wholeheartedness of her devotion, for she had destined its entire contents for Jesus.

"Poured *it* on his head"—*poured*, literally, "poured down," pictures the stream of liquid flowing from the vessel. Mark and Matthew mentioned His head, while John noted that Mary poured the ointment on His feet and that the precious liquid was so abundant that she wiped His feet with her hair. His recumbent position made the anointing of both head and feet readily possible. Pouring some oil on the head was common treatment of a festive guest (Ps. 23:5; Luke 7:46), but anointing the feet was unusual, an act of special esteem. Scroggie comments, "The story of Mary's graceful act is one of the most beautiful on record; it is a story of loving devotion revealing the acceptable motive, natural modes, and true measure of Christian service."[10]

"And there were some"—*some* veils the identity of the critics. Matthew said they were "the disciples," while John identified Judas as the originator of the criticism. Once expressed, the adverse evaluation of the deed would be readily approved by the others. With their austere background, they could not condone such extravagant use of such costly ointment.

"Had indignation within themselves"—the verb expresses their pained, angry reaction (cf. 10:14). *Within themselves* could mean that the indignation was a strong, inner individual reaction. More probably, it means that by exclamation or gesture they expressed their feelings to each other. The formulated criticism certainly expressed the feeling.

"Why was this waste of the ointment made?"—*this waste* portrays the pouring out of the ointment as a wasteful destruction of it. The perfect tense, "has been made," views the act as completed and now standing as an irreparable loss. *Why* asks what end it has served, implying that the act was unjustified.

"For it might have been sold"—justification for the strong disapproval. *Might have been sold,* "was able to be sold," contemplates its value before it was wasted.

"For more than three hundred pence"—literally, "for over three hundred denarii." *More than* denotes that this evaluation was not excessive. It represented a whole year's work for a common laborer

---

nut, the oil of which was used in making perfumes. The familiar "spikenard" is derived from the *nardi spicati* of the Vulgate. The problem of the meaning is still unsolved.

[10] W. Graham Scroggie, *The Gospel of Mark*, p. 240.

(cf. 6:37). Such a sum used up in one short moment they could view only as a waste. The criticism viewed the act only from the monetary standpoint. Judas could readily evaluate its material worth, but he was unable to comprehend the love that prompted the act.

"And have been given to the poor"—this concern for the poor, a mark of a pious Jew, gave plausibility to the criticism. John's Gospel makes clear that Judas was hiding his avarice under the mask of charity (12:6). Jones remarks, "It is not the concern of the philanthropist you have here, but the rage of a disappointed thief, parading itself as the concern of a philanthropist."[11]

"They murmured against her"—peculiar to Mark. The imperfect tense indicates that the criticism was not confined to a single utterance. The strong verb denotes indignant displeasure (cf. 1:43). Wuest renders it, "They bristled with indignation against her."[12] Their anger was vented against her since none dared to criticize Jesus for receiving it without protest.

"Let her alone"—Jesus acted to protect the woman. His words are a peremptory command demanding immediate compliance. The verb here does not mean "Permit her," but rather that they must stop their attacks. "Jesus alone sees the woman's act of devotion to him for what it is, *a beautiful thing.*"[13]

"Why trouble ye her?"—*why* indicates that their response was unreasonable. They were causing her needless labor or difficulty.

"She hath wrought a good work on me"—His contrasted evaluation of the deed. *A good work,* standing emphatically forward, declares it "a noble deed, beautiful in its insight and courageous faith."[14] It was an act with deep spiritual import, wrought *on me.* Jesus acknowledged that its value was related to His Person; it was an act of devotion to Him. "The Lord's tacit acceptance of supreme devotion as His due is not less remarkable than Mary's readiness to render it."[15]

Verses 7-8 state His vindication of her action.

"For"—it was appropriate because of its timeliness and its secret motive.

---

[11] J. D. Jones, *Commentary on Mark,* p. 509.

[12] Kenneth S. Wuest, *Mark in the Greek New Testament for the English Reader,* p. 256; *Wuest's Expanded Translation of the Greek New Testament,* vol. 1, *The Gospels,* p. 155.

[13] Hugh Anderson, *The Gospel of Mark,* New Century Bible, p. 306.

[14] Thomas M. Lindsay, "The Gospel According to St. Mark," in *Handbooks for Bible Classes,* p. 211.

[15] Swete, p. 324.

"Ye have the poor with you always"—an acknowledged fact of history. *Always* stands first, stressing that charity is not a limited opportunity. *With you* reminds them that they would always have the poor in their midst. This fact does not deny that aggressive social action should be taken against poverty. But 1,900 years of history are in accord with the view of McGee: "The presence of the poor is one of the characters of this age. There will be no elimination of poverty until Jesus comes."[16]

"Whensoever ye will ye may do them good"—only in Mark. If they have the personal concern, they will have constant opportunity to help the poor. A concern for charity must not be used as a pretext for blaming this woman for using her unique opportunity of showing her devotion to Him.

"She hath done what she could"—peculiar to Mark. *What she could,* standing first, stresses the definite opportunity that she had. *Hath done* acknowledges her effective use of it. She saw and embraced the only opportunity that was open to her to serve Him. In the words of Jones: "She spent herself to the uttermost. 'What she could': and I confess that I feel a stab at my conscience as I read the little phrase. How many of us can say that?"[17]

"She is come aforehand to anoint my body for the burying"—that she anointed Him beforehand indicates that she anticipated His speedy death and anointed Him in preparation for it. The burying referred to is not only the entombment but also includes the preparations for burial. She perceived that when the tragedy struck she would be utterly unable to reach Jesus to anoint His body, and so she acted to show her love and sympathy while she could. Her love discerned what the disciples could not see. She had a deeper understanding of His references to His coming death and resurrection than did any of His other followers. This does not mean that she had plumbed the significance of His death, but she "had begun to understand something of the mystery of a Messiah who must die."[18] Mary of Bethany was not among the women who went to the tomb on Sunday morning to anoint the body. Swete points out that "it seems the only anointing which the Lord received was this anticipatory one at Bethany."[19]

"Verily I say unto you"—stressing the certainty of His unparalleled promise to this woman.

---

[16] J. Vernon McGee, *Mark,* p. 153.

[17] Ibid., p. 516.

[18] I. H. Marshall, *St. Mark,* Scripture Union Bible Study Books, p. 51.

[19] Swete, p. 325.

"Whersoever this gospel shall be preached"—in whatever place the gospel may be heralded as a definite act. His statement leaves indefinite the time or place of the proclamation.

"Throughout the whole world"—accepted as certain in the divine purpose.

"*This* also that she hath done shall be spoken of"—along with the good news concerning Himself, which constitutes the gospel, there will also be told the story of this woman's deed. The worldwide preaching of the gospel has secured the fulfillment of the prediction. That fact would be the standing contradiction to their evaluation of her deed.

"For a memorial of her"—as a means of keeping alive a remembrance of her among men. No other human being received such a promise from Jesus. "The Lord erected a memorial for all time to her who had done her best to honor Him."[20]

3. Treachery of Judas (vv. 10-11)

The treacherous action of Judas, told in all the synoptics (Matt. 26:14-16; Luke 22:3-6), stands in contrast to the love and devotion to Jesus demonstrated by Mary of Bethany. Mark's *and* does not show a close connection, but Matthew's *then* points to a time relationship and implies that Judas was stimulated to action by what had just taken place. After his list of the Twelve (3:19), Mark mentions Judas only here and in verse 43.

"One of the twelve"—literally, "the one of the twelve." The use of the definite article with the phrase, found only here in the New Testament, is strange and has caused much discussion.[21] Since "one of the twelve" is a common designation for Judas in the Gospels,[22] the article here probably has a connotation of censure, "that notorious one of the twelve." "His original honor is the special badge of his infamy."[23]

"Went unto the chief priests"—apparently that very night after the company dispersed. Judas realized that in Jerusalem the chief priests were the most influential opponents of Jesus. Apparently, the session in the house of Caiaphas was still in progress (Matt. 26:3-5).

"To betray him unto them"—his deliberate purpose was to hand over Jesus to His implacable enemies. His sinister action was aimed

---

[20] Ibid., p. 326.

[21] The use of the article with *one* is found in the early papyruses (James Hope Moulton and George Milligan, *The Vocabulary of the Greek Testament*, p. 187).

[22] Matt 26:14, 47; Mark 14:10, 43; Luke 22:47; John 6:71.

[23] William Newton Clarke, *Commentary on the Gospel of Mark*, An American Commentary, p. 205.

directly at Jesus. Matthew recorded the very words of his brazen offer to the chief priests (26:15). Mark's objective account indicates no motive. Judas's action is puzzling, and his motives have been differently understood. Some have suggested that Judas was attempting to force Jesus to declare His messiahship openly and compel Him to vindicate it by a miracle. This seems very unlikely. Others think that he was outraged at the rebuke he had received and was out to get revenge. This too seems inadequate. More probable is the explanation that Judas had become a disciple of Jesus with strong political aspirations, but Jesus' failure to set up His kingdom as expected left Judas deeply disappointed. Jesus' persistent indications that He would die disillusioned Judas; and, because of his greed, he determined to make the best of a hopeless situation by betraying Jesus for a price. That Judas was spurred on by feelings of disillusionment, frustration, and defeat seems clear. While the Gospels do not offer an interpretation of the action of Judas, they do point to the presence of avarice (John 12:6) and satanic temptation (Luke 22:3; John 13:2, 27) as motivating forces.

"When they heard *it,* they were glad"—the unexpected offer of Judas was almost too good to believe. They would never have dared even to make such a proposal to one of the Twelve, yet here one of them was voluntarily offering to betray Jesus into their hands. Their reaction to the traitorous proposal is a further revelation of their character.

"Promised to give him money"—Judas had proposed a monetary reward, and they acted on that level, meeting his demand with a monetary promise. Matthew said "they covenanted with him for thirty pieces of silver" (26:15). It has been questioned whether this sum was the total price or only the initial payment, the rest "promised" when the deed was done. Perhaps it was the total price they were willing to pay. Since Judas had compromised himself by making his offer to them, he was obliged to take what they offered.

"He sought how he might conveniently betray him"—*sought,* "began to seek," points to the effort of Judas to carry out his agreement. "The Priests had transferred their anxieties to the traitor; it was for him now to contrive and plot."[24] *How he might betray him* indicates that Judas had the same problem that the Sanhedrin members had debated, how to find a suitable occasion. His task was not merely to tell them where to find Jesus; he had to be the active agent in transferring Him into their hands. *Conveniently,* "opportunely," stresses that the time must be suitable for the traitorous action, "in the absence of

---

[24] Swete, p. 328.

the multitude'' (Luke 22:6). Clearly this was a condition that the high priests had placed on Judas in accepting his offer.

B. Passover Observance (14:12-25)

Mark's account of the last Passover falls into three parts: the extraordinary method used by Jesus to direct two of His disciples to the place where they were to prepare the Passover (vv. 12-16), His announcement of the betrayal during the meal (vv. 17-21), and the institution of the Lord's Supper (vv. 22-25). If the generally accepted chronology of Passion Week is correct, none of the Gospels record any activity by Jesus on Wednesday. The day was probably spent quietly with His disciples and friends at Bethany.

1. Preparation for the Passover (vv. 12-16)

All the synoptics record this episode (Matt. 26:17-19; Luke 22:7-13). Matthew's account is abbreviated.

"The first day of unleavened bread, when they killed the passover''—the double time designation is again according to popular usage. *The first day of unleavened bread,* strictly taken, would be Nisan 15, but the added phrase shows that Nisan 14 was meant (cf. 14:1). The second designation defines the first more exactly. *The Passover* means the Passover lamb, while the imperfect *they killed* points to the customary annual practice.

"His disciples said unto him''—they took the initiative in bringing up the subject. Matthew said that they "came to Jesus," perhaps implying that He had been alone for a while. The time was Thursday forenoon.

"Where wilt thou that we go and prepare''—Clearly "Jesus had been in the habit of observing the Passover, for the disciples did not ask *if* they should prepare, but only *where*.''[25] They accepted that the determination of the place was His, but the task of preparing the Passover was theirs. The work of preparation involved procuring and preparing the lamb, making the necessary room arrangements for the feast, and procuring unleavened cakes, wine, water, bitter herbs, and crushed fruit moistened with vinegar.

"That thou mayest eat the passover''—deferentially they spoke of Him eating, for He would be the host; but it was assumed that they would eat with Him. It was a family feast, but the disciples accepted that they would eat the Passover with Jesus rather than scatter to their respective families. It speaks of the close relationship between Jesus and His disciples.

---

[25] Scroggie, p. 243.

"He sendeth forth two"—Peter and John (Luke 22:8). Although Judas was the treasurer (John 12:6), he was not given the task of purchasing the needed provisions. McKenna notes, "Treachery shadows the final hours. Jesus must protect Himself by limiting His confidence to two disciples who will know the time and place for the Passover feast."[26]

"Go ye into the city"—Jesus was somewhere outside Jerusalem, apparently at Bethany.

"There shall meet you a man bearing a pitcher of water"—after they entered the city, apparently through the eastern gate. *Meet* means to encounter, to come toward, and need not imply a previous arrangement. As they entered the city, their path would cross that of a man bearing a pitcher of water. A man on the street carrying a pitcher, an earthenware vessel used for transporting water, would be an unusual and conspicuous sight. The disciples would have no trouble in identifying him. It was the custom for the women to carry the water jars, while the men carried the water skins. *There shall meet you* declares a future fact. It has been questioned whether Jesus had secretly prearranged the meeting or spoke from supernatural knowledge. As in the case of the colt (11:2-4), it is possible to resort to an explanation of prearrangement, but the narrative leaves the impression of another instance of His foreknowledge. Nineham says, "There can be no doubt that Saint Mark regarded the incident as evidence of supernatural foresight on the part of Jesus," but Nineham questions the historicity of the narrative.[27] Alexander holds that "it can only be regarded as a prophetic sign, like that which Saul received from Samuel (I Sam. 10, 1-8), and this would imply, not a previous agreement, but a supernatural foresight and control of human actions."[28]

"Follow him"—this was essential to finding the place. Unless *meet* is assumed to involve a greeting, the man probably was an unconscious guide to the disciples through the network of narrow streets. The aorist tense indicates nothing of the duration of the following.

"Wheresoever he shall go in"—the identity of the house was thus left wholly indefinite.

"Say ye to the goodman of the house"—the man with the pitcher apparently was a slave; their message was for the master, "the house lord," the head of the household. The conjecture that this was the home

---

[26] David L. McKenna, *Mark,* The Communicator's Commentary, p. 285.

[27] Nineham, p. 376.

[28] Joseph Addison Alexander, *The Gospel of Mark,* p. 377.

of John Mark (cf. Acts 1:13; 12:12) is attractive, but the evidence for it is slender (cf. the young man in Mark 14:51-52).[29]

"The Master saith"—this self-designation implies that Jesus was well known to the householder; no further identification was necessary. Perhaps the man also recognized the spokesmen as disciples of Jesus.

"Where is the guestchamber"—*guestchamber* is rendered "inn" in Luke 2:7. It properly denotes a place where a traveler unloads his beast and halts for the night, commonly an inn; more generally, it meant a place of lodging, a guest room. Morison suggested that the place was "some 'hostelry,' "[30] but more probably it was a private home. The possessive, *my guestchamber* (Gr.), does not claim right of ownership but right of use. Nineham says, "There is perhaps a hint of messianic sovereignty in the word."[31]

"Where I shall eat the passover with my disciples"—they would act as a family group. He wanted to celebrate alone with His disciples.

"He will shew you"—he would be friendly and be ready to give them his personal service, himself conducting them to the place assigned to them.

"A large upper room furnished *and* prepared"—*upper room,* "something raised above the ground," denotes a room upstairs, probably a roof chamber built on the flat housetop. Such rooms were commonly approached by an outside stairway, making it unnecessary to enter the first floor of the house. It would be spacious, accommodating a considerable group. The perfect participle *furnished,* "having been strewn," may mean carpeted, but more probably, furnished with covered couches for reclining at table. The adverb "prepared" or "ready" indicates that the room was already in shape to be used for a passover meal.

"There make ready for us"—the room had been prepared, but their duty was to prepare what was needed for the Passover meal. *For us* joins Jesus with His disciples in a common bond in observing this final Passover. *There* points to the place identified in this remarkable way. It seems obvious that Jesus used this method of keeping Judas from learning where the Passover would be observed so that he could not report it to the chief priests.

"His disciples went forth"—from the place where Jesus and the other disciples remained meanwhile. The historical statement of the

---

[29] Alfred Edersheim, *The Life and Times of Jesus the Messiah,* 2:485.

[30] James Morison, *Practical Commentary on the Gospel According to St. Mark,* p. 387.

[31] Nineham, p. 377.

fulfillment suggests the recollections of Peter behind the account. *As he had said* asserts exact fulfillment, "even as," and reflects the wonder of the disciples as the events unfolded just as Jesus had said.

"They made ready the passover"—clearly indicating that Mark held that Jesus and His disciples ate the regular Passover. This is the consistent picture in the synoptics (Matt. 26:2, 17-19; Mark 14:1, 12-16; Luke 22:1, 7-8, 11-15). But there are certain expressions in the Fourth Gospel (13:1, 27-29; 18:28; 19:24) which chronologically seem to be at variance with the synoptic position. John's account seems to present the position that Jesus did not eat the regular Passover but rather ate an anticipatory meal and actually died at the time that the Passover lamb was slain. There thus seems to be a contradiction between the Passover chronology of the synoptics and that of the Fourth Gospel. Basically, three different views concerning this problem have been adopted. One view is that the two positions cannot be harmonized.[32] Those who maintain this position generally hold that John's account is to be preferred; a few prefer to accept the accuracy of the synoptic account. But neither position is acceptable to those who are convinced of the historical accuracy of the scriptural accounts.

Two other views, either of which can be accepted by the evangelical, have been advanced. One view is that in reality there is no contradiction and that upon closer examination the troublesome passages in John are found to be in agreement with the synoptic assertions.[33] The other view accepts actual disagreement between the statements of John and the position of the synoptics but holds that both can be accepted as reliable because of calendar differences: the synoptics followed one reckoning for the date of the Passover, while John followed another dating.[34] Under this view, the confusion is actually due to the confusion that existed among the Jews during this Passover season about the precise date of the Passover.

The evidence on the problem is confusing, and different conclusions have been drawn accordingly. Because of the present inconclusiveness of the evidence, a dogmatic decision between these two views

---

[32] B. Harvie Branscomb, *The Gospel of Mark,* Moffatt New Testament Commentary, pp. 249-55; Alfred Plummer, *The Gospel According to St. Mark,* Cambridge Greek Testament, pp. 316-17; V. Taylor, *The Gospel According to St. Mark,* pp. 664-67.

[33] Samuel J. Andrews, *The Life of Our Lord upon the Earth,* pp. 542-81; C.E.B. Cranfield, *The Gospel According to Saint Mark,* Cambridge Greek Testament Commentary, pp. 420-22; Norval Geldenhuys, *Commentary on the Gospel of Luke,* New International Commentary on the New Testament, pp. 649-70; Jeremias, pp. 16-84.

[34] Leon Morris, *Commentary on the Gospel According to John,* New International Commentary on the New Testament, pp. 774-86; W. M. Christie, *Palestine Calling,* pp. 129-41.

is precarious. I believe that upon careful study the apparent discrepancies disappear.

2. Announcement of the Betrayal (vv. 17-21)

All four Gospels mention Jesus' announcement of His betrayal during the Passover observance (Matt. 26:21-25; Luke 22:21-23; John 13:21-30). John's account gives important additional information.

"In the evening"—after sunset, the beginning of Nisan 15. The Passover meal, whose origins had nocturnal associations (Exod. 12:8-14), was always eaten at night but had to be concluded by midnight.[35]

"He cometh with the twelve"—the historical present *cometh* vividly takes the reader back to Jesus' last trip from Bethany to Jerusalem. *The twelve* most naturally means that Peter and John had returned to announce that all was ready and to lead the group to the place in Jerusalem. If they did not return, the designation is conventional to denote the Twelve as a distinct body of Jesus' followers. It was not to avoid recognition that Jesus made the trip after sunset. People in Jerusalem would be occupied with their own final preparations for the Passover.

"As they sat and did eat"—circumstances of the scene in the upper room when the announcement of the betrayal was made. *Sat,* literally "were reclining," indicates their recumbent posture on couches around the Passover table. John 13:23-26 gives a fuller picture. The Israelites ate the original Passover in haste, apparently while standing in traveling attire (Exod. 12:11), but now a reclining posture was used to typify their freedom and repose in the land of promise. *Did eat,* or "were eating," indicates that the Passover meal was in progress. Mark's account leaves an interval in the events (cf. Luke 22:14-16, 24-30; John 13:1-20).

"Verily I say unto you"—the startling disclosure was made with full solemnity. John 13:21 indicates that the presence of the traitor troubled Jesus and constrained Him to speak.

"One of you shall betray me, *even* he that eateth with me" (ASV)—*one of you* restricts the betrayer to the assembled group. Previously He had told them in general terms He "would be delivered up" to His enemies; now He announces His betrayal by someone in the room. The added characterization, *he that eateth with me,* is peculiar to Mark, although Luke preserves the thought (22:21). It is not a specific identification, since it applied to all of them. It was a reminder of Psalm 41:9 (the treachery of Ahithophel) and brings out the enormity

---

[35] Herbert Danby, trans., *The Mishnah,* p. 151.

of the crime. It added to the horror of the betrayal, since for Orientals to eat bread with a man absolutely precludes hostile action against him.

"They began to be sorrowful"—this unexpected announcement threw the company into consternation and deep grief.

"To say unto him one by one, *Is* it I?"—no one doubted the truth of His word, and none suspected the identity of the betrayer. None said, "Is it he?" Challenged to question themselves, *one by one* they successively spoke to clear themselves. The form of their question calls for a negative answer—"It is not I, is it?"—and asks for His reassuring denial. Aware of their own weakness, they expressed a feeling of uncertainty about themselves; yet none of the eleven knew of anything in himself that could lead him to such a deed of treachery.

"*It is* one of the twelve"—peculiar to Mark. His reply emphatically restated the charge that the traitor was present, but it did not identify him. It permitted Judas to make a voluntary confession.

"That dippeth with me in the dish"—this does not identify the traitor but implies his nearness to Jesus. *The dish,* or bowl, apparently denotes the side dish which would be used together by only three or four at a table. It contained the sauce of dried fruits, spices, and vinegar, into which pieces of the unleavened bread and the bitter herbs were dipped. The present middle participle, "the one dipping for himself," pictures the traitor as repeatedly during the meal dipping into the same dish with Jesus.

"The Son of man indeed goeth, as it is written of him"—this verse sets the announced betrayal in its larger context. Jesus was not announcing His betrayal as a helpless victim. He accepted His coming suffering as the Son of man in fulfillment of Scripture, but that did not relieve the betrayer of his awful guilt. The statement confirms that Jesus identified his role as the Son of man with the suffering Servant of the Old Testament (cf. 8:31; 9:31; 10:33), a challenging claim since the Old Testament does not directly ascribe suffering to the Son of man. *Goeth* implies a voluntary act of "homegoing" on His part. The figure softens the picture of His violent death. What lay ahead He accepted as the will of God for Him, as set forth in Scripture. His suffering and death would be not the simple result of the action of the traitor but the exact fulfillment of the scriptural record concerning Him (cf. Ps. 22, Isa. 53, and the symbolism of the whole Old Testament sacrificial system).

"But woe to that man"—*but* marks the contrast between Him and the betrayer. *Woe* is not a malediction but the lament of frustrated love. But Alexander holds that both wrath and pity are here appropriate.[36]

---

[36] Alexander, p. 380.

The demonstrative pronoun *that* views the man as already morally distant from the Lord. "Our Lord seems to forget His own woes in pity for this man."[37]

"By whom the Son of man is betrayed"—*by whom* recognizes that Judas is the instrument of Satan (Luke 22:3; John 13:2, 27). The present tense, "is being betrayed," views the betrayal process as already started, while the repetition of the title *the Son of man* stresses anew the high identity of the one being betrayed.

"Good were it for that man if he had never been born"—*good* here has the force of a comparative. Nonexistence would be preferable to the fearful fate awaiting the betrayer. There is a sinning which utterly negates the good of human existence. The original order, "Good for him if he had not been born—that man," places the repeated designation *that man* at the close of the warning with solemn cadence.

Mark's account does not identify the betrayer personally. According to Matthew, when Judas also asked, "Master, is it I?" Jesus replied, apparently in a low voice, that he was the one (26:25). John's account makes it clear that none of the other disciples besides John heard when Jesus made the identification and that when Judas left the room they did not understand the significance of Christ's parting words to Judas (John 13:23-30). It is commonly accepted that Judas left before the institution of the Lord's Supper.[38]

3. Institution of the Lord's Supper (vv. 22-25)

The Fourth Gospel contains no parallel to the synoptic accounts of the institution of the Lord's Supper (Matt. 26:26-29; Luke 22:19-20), but a fourth account is given in 1 Corinthians 11:23-25. Matthew and Mark are closely parallel, while Luke and Paul show interesting similarities.

"As they did eat"—as in verse 18, this remark again indicates a general time setting for this second memorable event in the upper room that night. The present tense again indicates that the meal was still in progress; it was some time later during the protracted Passover meal. In instituting the Lord's Supper, Jesus utilized the things on the table from the Passover meal. The table was not cleared to indicate a new start.

---

[37] Matthew B. Riddle, "The Gospel According to St. Mark," in *International Revision Commentary on the New Testament,* p. 192.

[38] The only reason for placing the departure of Judas *after* the institution of the Lord's Supper is the order in Luke, where this announcement is recorded after the supper. But the other synoptics place the announcement of the betrayal before the supper. Luke's account does not follow a strict chronological order in recording the events in the upper room.

"Jesus took bread, and blessed"—rendering two aorist participles stating two definite preliminary acts. The bread was one of the thin unleavened cakes on the Passover table. Having taken it into His hands, Jesus uttered a benediction, taking the form of a thanksgiving (cf. 6:41). *Blessed* has no expressed object, but Jewish usage in such contexts implies "not so much the hallowing, or consecrating, of the bread, as a solemn blessing or thanking of God over the bread."[39] Luke, as well as Paul, here used the verb *gave thanks*.

"And brake *it*, and gave to them, and said"—the three aorist indicative verbs, stating definite acts, center attention on Christ. The thin cake was readily subdivided by breaking, not cutting. The breaking was for the purpose of distribution and has no symbolic significance (cf. John 19:32-36). Perhaps Jesus broke the bread on a plate which was passed around. *Said* points to His explanation accompanying the distribution.

"Take"—commanding the disciples as a definite act to take of the broken bread. Matthew's added "eat" is implied in Mark. Let them personally appropriate what He offered them.

"This is my body"—these simple words, found in all four accounts, have been the occasion for much ecclesiastical controversy, and views concerning their full meaning are still sharply divided.[40] Claims have often gone beyond the basic teaching of the text. When Jesus said, "This is my body," it seems obvious that the disciples would not understand Him to mean that what He asked them to take was actually His literal body. As men familiar with figurative language, they would readily understand Him in a nonliteral sense. He had repeatedly used figurative language, such as "I am the door" (John 10:7); "Beware ye of the leaven of the Pharisees, which is hypocrisy" (Luke 12:1). Clearly, His statement here is representative. In the original, *bread* is masculine, but *this* is neuter, meaning *this* broken *thing* which represents my body. "The bread which had been given them, after being broken, stood symbolically for His body, or rather the sacrificial giving of Himself for them."[41]

---

[39] Nineham, p. 384.

[40] Four views concerning the elements of the Lord's Supper are held: (1) *transubstantiation*—upon consecration the bread and wine become the real body and blood of Christ; (2) *consubstantiation*—the body and blood of Christ are mysteriously and supernaturally united with the unchanged elements; (3) *spiritual presence*—the natural elements are instrumentally used to convey the spiritual presence of Christ to the partaker through faith; (4) *symbolic*—the elements commemorate the sacrificial work of Christ, and their value to the participant is the spiritual blessing received thereby.

[41] Ernest Trice Thompson, *The Gospel According to Mark*, p. 217.

"And he took the cup, and when he had given thanks"—*and* introduces the second part of the Lord's Supper as instituted by Jesus that night. Two aorist participles again state the preliminary acts. The *Mishnah* prescribed at least four cups of wine at the Passover feast.[42] If Jesus followed the later Passover ritual, this was probably the third cup, known as "the cup of blessing," and concluded the eating of the meal. Luke 22:20 says it was "after supper" (also 1 Cor. 11:25). *Given thanks* is the verb Luke and Paul used in connection with the bread, confirming that the two terms were used quite synonymously (cf. Mark 8:6-7). From this verb, *eucharisteō,* is derived the name "Eucharist," meaning that the Lord's Supper is a feast of thanksgiving.

"He gave it to them"—the one cup was passed around the table.

"They all drank of it"—*all,* standing emphatically at the end, stresses that all participated in the drinking from the cup. Mark's historical statement replaces the command, "Drink ye all of it," in Matthew 26:27. Riddle observes, "Hence as the old covenant forbade the drinking of blood, it could not be commanded here in a literal sense."[43]

"This is my blood of the new testament"—*this,* "this cup" (Luke 22:20), refers to the wine in the cup; the statement again is representative. Two modifiers describe the blood, pointing to two relationships; *my* asserts that it is Christ's own blood, while *of the testament* ("new" probably omitted in the original) designates it as the seal and ratification of the covenant, the new covenant (Luke 22:20; 1 Cor. 11:25), which He is inaugurating. As sacrificial blood established the Mosaic covenant (Exod. 24:8; Lev. 17:11), so His blood established the new covenant (Jer. 31:31-34). God's covenant with Israel was no voluntary agreement between two equals; it was initiated by Jehovah, and He set its terms, while Israel voluntarily agreed to obey its stipulations. Likewise the new covenant was a divine work, its nature and conditions stipulated by God and offered to men on the basis of faith.

"Which is shed for many"—an appositional identification of the blood. *Which is shed* renders a present articular participle, "that [blood] being poured out." The present tense views the pouring out as a certainty. Only that blood in being poured out could ratify the new covenant. *Shed* implies the violent pouring out of His blood in death. This pouring out of His blood was not represented in the symbolic action at the institution of the Lord's Supper. *For many* (Luke, "for you") points to the vast number benefited by that sacrificial pouring

---

[42] Danby, p. 150.

[43] Riddle, p. 194.

out. *For (huper),* "over, in behalf of," implies the vicarious nature of
His death. *Many* is not opposed to "all" but denotes the vast number
in contrast to the one making the sacrifice. The blood of the suffering
Servant of God (Isa. 53:11-12) was shed for many for "remission of
sins" (Matt. 26:28).

"Verily I say unto you"—sealing the authoritative nature of this
important pronouncement.

"I will drink no more of the fruit of the vine"—*the fruit of the
vine,* a periphrastic term, denoting wine as such. The original has an
emphatic triple negative: "No more will I in any wise drink of the fruit
of the vine" (Rotherham). It was His solemn declaration to His disciples that this was His last Passover, His last regular meal in fact.

"Until that day that I drink it new in the kingdom of God"—the
discussion ends with the bright prospect of the future. *Until that day*
looks forward to the future eschatological day when the kingdom will
be established in all its glory. *That,* better, "when" or "whenever,"
leaves the time undetermined but assumes the coming reality. *Drink
. . . in the kingdom* metaphorically describes the kingdom in terms of
a messianic banquet. The present tense *drink* indicates that the feast
will not be a single event but a continuing feast. *New* denotes that the
wine will be new in quality, pointing to the spiritual character of that
feast. *I drink it* assumes that He will be the host at that banquet. It
reflects His messianic consciousness. Thus on the basis of His impending self-sacrifice on the cross, Jesus confidently announced His
messianic triumph in the eschatological kingdom. Even so the believer,
united by faith with the risen Christ, can face the present with its risks
and sufferings in the assurance of sharing that coming glory.

C. Garden of Gethsemane (14:26-52)

Verse 26 is transitional, properly printed as a separate paragraph
in the ASV. It marks the conclusion of the upperroom events and leads
to the scene in the garden. *When they had sung an hymn* probably
means the singing or chanting of Psalms 115-118, the second part of
the Great Hallel, the great song of praise. It marked the conclusion of
the Passover observance. *Went out into the mount of Olives* records the
departure of Jesus with the eleven from the upper room and the city.
They turned their steps *into* or toward the Mount of Olives (cf. 13:3).
The Garden of Gethsemane lay across the brook Kidron (John 18:1),
low on the western slope of the mount of Olives. Mark records the
revelation Jesus made to the disciples on the way to the garden (vv.
26-31), describes the agony in the garden (vv. 32-42), tells of the
betrayal and arrest (vv. 43-50), and concludes the scenes in the garden
with the singular picture of the young man who fled (vv. 51-52).

1. Revelation on the Way to the Garden (vv. 26-31)

Jesus' warning to Peter concerning his denials is recorded in all four Gospels (Matt. 26:31-35; Luke 22:31-34; John 13:36-38). Mark and Matthew agree in placing the warning on the way to Gethsemane, but Luke and John record the warning as given in the upper room. It is often assumed that all four Gospels record the same occurrence and that a slight displacement occurs in two of them.[44] It seems best to accept the view that two different warnings were given, one before and one after they left the upper room.[45] This is quite in harmony with the Gospel accounts as well as with Peter's character. Swete points out that "in Luke and John, Peter only is warned and the other ten do not appear."[46] But in Matthew and Mark, Jesus' warning is directed to all the disciples, and impulsive Peter acts as spokesman in making their protest.

"All ye shall be offended"—Jesus' frequent warnings against offenses (Matt. 24:10; Mark 4:17; 9:42) are now directed toward the disciples themselves. All of them without exception "this night" (Matt. 26:31) *shall be offended,* "caused to stumble," quite literally, "be scandalized." The verb, which has the basic idea of being caught in a trap (cf. 4:17), does not mean that the disciples would feel offense at Jesus personally but that they would be caught and overwhelmed by what would happen to Him that very night. It would stagger their faith and shake their confidence in Him as the Messiah. It would challenge their loyalty to Him.

"For it is written"—His prediction was grounded in Scripture. Jesus had reflected upon the effect of His death on the disciples; that effect He saw clearly portrayed in Zechariah 13:7.

"I will smite the shepherd"—Jesus' change of the original imperative "smite" to *I will smite* is interpretative. The change makes clear that Jesus saw His coming sufferings as not just inflicted by men but in some proper sense, inflicted by God Himself. The Shepherd would not be smitten contrary to divine providence. It indicates that He was thinking of His death in the spirit of Isaiah 53, the picture of the suffering Servant.

---

[44] For the different combinations that have been proposed, see Andrews, pp. 494-96.

[45] For such a harmonization, see Johnston M. Cheney, *The Life of Christ in Stereo: The Four Gospels Combined as One,* pp. 176, 185, 222.

[46] Swete, p. 340.

"And the sheep shall be scattered"—the unexpected smiting of their Shepherd will leave the sheep utterly bewildered, scattering them in all directions. That Scripture was a forewarning to the disciples.

"But after that I am risen"—*but* strongly contrasts the darkness of His death with the light of the resurrection. The passive voice, "am raised up," points to God as the agent; the God who will smite the Shepherd will also raise Him from the dead. Jesus seldom spoke of His coming death without also speaking of His resurrection (8:31; 9:31; 10:34). But these references to His resurrection, never enlarged upon, seemingly made little impression on the minds of the disciples.[47] Jesus had repeatedly told them that He would be raised up on the third day, but now His *after* looks beyond that crucial event to what it will mean for Him and them.

"I will go before you into Galilee"—a continuation of the Shepherd figure. After His resurrection, He will regather and resume the leadership of His sheep. He declares that He will precede them into Galilee for a glad reunion. *Go before* does not mean that He will personally conduct them back to Galilee; for in 16:7, where the promise is recalled, it cannot have that meaning. It is a promise of a postresurrection appearance in Galilee. The reference seems to be to a signal and exceptional meeting in Galilee (cf. Matt. 28:16-20; 1 Cor. 15:6). Such a meeting is not recorded in this Gospel as we have it.

"But Peter said unto him"—Jesus' announcement had been made to the group, but impulsive Peter responded with a quick repudiation.

"Although all shall be offended, yet *will* not I"—Peter did not repudiate the prediction as such, but insisted upon one exception to it. *Although,* "if also," admits the general statement, while *yet,* literally "but," strongly insists upon a contrast between *all* and himself, much to his own credit. His claim contradicted the explicit statement of Jesus. Although there was genuine love for Christ behind his protest, it revealed his sad ignorance of his own weakness. With his boast, Peter arrogantly elevated himself above the other disciples. "This is one of the most unfavorable specimens on record of the dark or weak side of this great apostle's character, because it exhibits, not mere self-sufficiency and overweening self-reliance, but an arrogant estimate of his own strength in comparison with others, particularly with his brethren

---

[47] The argument that v. 28 cannot be original here because "verses 29-31 proceed as if the words of verse 28 had not been uttered" (Frederick C. Grant, in *The Interpreter's Bible* [1951], 9:879) is quite groundless. Peter, stung by the suggestion of disloyalty, heard nothing further; and when Jesus ceased speaking, he uttered his hot protest. Cf. John 13:33-36 for a similar delayed reaction by Peter.

and associates in the apostolic office."[48] Jesus seems to make reference to this claim in John 21:15, "Lovest thou me *more than these?*"

"Verily I say unto thee"—Jesus' reply to Peter was made with a solemn note of certainty. Jesus singled him out to reveal to him that his failure would be greater than that of the rest.

"This day, *even* in this night, before the cock crow twice, thou shalt deny me thrice"—*thou* is emphatic. Peter had singled himself out as one who would remain faithful amid general defection; Jesus singled him out to inform him that he would not only desert but actually deny his Master. The time of his disgraceful action is stated with ascending precision. *This day* denotes the twenty-four hour day begun with sunset; *this night* abbreviates "today," limiting it to the time of darkness; *before the cock crow twice* further limits it to before dawn. The time before Peter's fall was short. Mark alone mentions the cock crowing twice, a detail apparently due to Peter's vivid recollection of the events.[49] *Deny* is a strong compound form, "deny utterly." That very night Peter would deny any personal connection with Jesus. All the Gospels record the fulfillment of this prediction.

"But he spake the more vehemently"—the revelation only evoked further passionate protest. *Spake* (imperfect tense) denotes that he kept on protesting. *The more vehemently,* an adverb found only here in the New Testament, means that he spoke "excessively," beyond all normal bounds.

"If I should die with thee"—Peter's *if* implies expectancy. He is willing to admit that his joint death with Jesus may be necessary. But he will not allow the fear of death to induce him to deny Jesus. His statement of contradiction, using a double negative, is very strong: "I will in no wise deny." It was no doubt sincere; the very thought was revolting to him. He maintained that he would never deny his beloved Master. But "in his vehemence he does not see that he is charging Christ with uttering false predictions."[50]

"Likewise also said they all"—Peter's position was approved and accepted by the other disciples. Come what may, all were sure that they would remain loyal to Jesus. They readily accepted Peter here also as their spokesman. Truly he was "the leader, at least in denying

---

[48] Alexander, p. 384.

[49] In 13:35, "cockcrowing" was identified with the third of the four night watches. Some think that here the reference is to the *gallicinium* (cockcrowing), the bugle call sounded to mark the change of the Roman guard at the Tower of Antonia at the northwestern corner of the temple area. But 14:72 shows that Mark thought of a literal successive cockcrowing.

[50] Plummer, p. 340.

that he could deny.''[51] Brooks well comments, ''That Mark—in this instance the other Gospels as well—did nothing to spare Peter and the other apostles is one indication of the trustworthiness of the accounts.''[52]

2. Agony in the Garden (vv. 32-42)

Christ's agony in Gethsemane is recorded in all the synoptics (Matt. 26:36-46; Luke 22:39-46). The Fourth Gospel mentions His withdrawal to the garden but says nothing of the agony (18:1). Mark's vivid and moving narrative reveals the true humanity of Jesus. Its Petrine origin seems clear.

''They came to a place which was named Gethsemane''—*came,* the historical present, graphically carries the reader back to the scene. (The historical-present tense occurs nine times in this paragraph.) The exact time of the arrival is not certain, perhaps some time before midnight. The word *place,* a diminutive noun (''a little field''), is called a ''garden'' in John. The name *Gethsemane,* mentioned only here (Mark and Matthew), is the Greek form of a Hebrew word probably meaning ''oil press.'' It apparently was an olive orchard enclosed with a stone wall and equipped with an oil press. Quiet and secluded, it was a favorite place with Jesus when He was in Jerusalem (Luke 22:39; John 18:2). That Jesus went there at this time shows that He was not trying to evade Judas. The present Franciscan garden may not be on the site of the original Gethsemane, but the biblical Gethsemane certainly was nearby. Brooks notes, ''Today there is a Latin (Roman Catholic), Armenian, Greek Orthodox, and Russian Orthodox Gethsemane.''[53]

''Sit ye here, while I shall pray''—upon entering the garden with His disciples (John 18:1), Jesus directed them to be seated there ''while I shall pray.'' It may be an injunction He had often given them. It may be rendered ''until I have prayed,'' implying that they were to remain there until such a time as He had finished His praying. Here we have a final instance showing how vital prayer was to Jesus personally.

''He taketh with him Peter and James and John''—the definite article with each name suggests that the three were named individually to accompany Him. The three had been similarly selected previously (5:37; 9:2). Having been chosen to behold His glories on the mount of transfiguration, they are now chosen to witness the opposite extreme, His deepest agony of soul. But His soul also craved the comfort and

---

[51] Clarke, p. 214.

[52] James A. Brooks, *Mark,* The New American Commentary, p. 232.

[53] Brooks, p. 233, footnote 58.

support of their sympathetic companionship in His struggle. But, as Cranfield notes, "the effect of his taking them with him is actually to make more inescapably clear the fact of his aloneness."[54]

"Began to be sore amazed, and to be very heavy"—*began* marks the commencement of a new state of things. As Jesus walked farther into the garden with the three, a strong agitation swept over Him, visible to them before He spoke. Mark used strong terms to describe His feelings. The two infinitives are present tense, stressing the continuation of the emotional experience. *Sore amazed* (cf. 9:15) suggests a feeling of terrified surprise. Jesus had long foreseen His coming death, but now that the shadow of the actual cross fell upon Him, He felt the shuddering horror of the terrible ordeal. "The cause of Jesus' sore-trouble was not physical fear, but the pressure upon His sinless soul of the sin of the world, together with His knowledge of what bearing it involved."[55] It came with stunning effect. *Very heavy* (ASV "sore troubled") denotes His resultant feeling of extreme anxiety, leaving Him emotionally torn and restless.

"My soul is exceeding sorrowful unto death"—He did not conceal His agitation from the three but gave forceful expression to it. His soul, His inner self-conscious being,[56] was *exceeding sorrowful,* engulfed in sorrow (cf. 6:26). *Unto death* indicates that the sorrow was so great that it threatened to crush out His life. It swept Him to the very limits of His endurance. The whole picture denotes an overwhelming agony which is quite beyond human comprehension.

"Tarry ye here, and watch"—the aorist imperative *tarry here* ordered them to stay at the place where they were. He felt that He must be alone with the Father. *Watch,* a present imperative, asked of them an attitude of watchfulness. Matthew notes that He asked them to watch "with me" (26:38). The double command to the three shows His desire for solitude and for sympathy. He desired their understanding sympathy in His struggle. He did not ask them to pray for Him but wanted the comfort of their presence. It was a new form of their relationship to Him, a trust which ought to have made them alert and watchful.

"He went forward a little"—Luke's "about a stone's cast" (22:41) seems to refer to this withdrawal. In facing His struggle, He separated Himself from the three, knowing He must tread the winepress alone (Isa. 63:3).

---

[54] Cranfield, p. 431.

[55] Scroggie, p. 254.

[56] "Mention of His 'soul' is rare, and that fact may warn us not to be curious in attempting to pry into 'the Self-consciousness' of Christ" (Plummer, p. 327).

"Fell on the ground"—revealing the intensity of His agony. *Fell* is imperfect, describing the prostration as a process. First He "kneeled down" (Luke 22:41), then sank to the ground "on his face" (Matt. 26:39).[57]

"And prayed"—the imperfect tense of repeated or continued prayer. Hebrews 5:7 records that His words of prayer were uttered with "strong crying and tears," hence were entirely audible to the three. Luke mentions only one prayer session; Mark notes two, implying a third; Matthew explicitly indicates three prayer sessions.

"That, if it were possible, the hour might pass from him"—Mark's own statement of the sum and substance of the prayers. *The hour,* a familiar Johannine expression (John 7:30; 8:20; 12:23, 27; 13:1; 17:1), means the divinely appointed time of His sacrificial death (cf. Mark 14:41). The hour had been long anticipated; but now that it was upon Him, as a real man He naturally shrank from it. His petition was that if there were a possibility for Him to complete His messianic mission without that sacrificial death, He desired that. His *if* assumes that if there were such a possibility, the Father would let the hour pass away from Him. "His expressed desire to escape is to be strictly understood as a necessary incident of his humanity, and also as a part of his vicarious suffering."[58]

"Abba, Father"—the bilingual form of address, used only here in the Gospels, stresses His filial consciousness even in His agony. He knew God was His Father even when He was being offered the bitter cup. *Abba* is Aramaic, while *Father* is the Greek equivalent. *Abba* was an everyday Jewish family term, used in the intimacy of the family. Among the Jews, it was seldom used with reference to God and then always with modifiers which denoted the distance between man and God. The Gospel writers never employ the term *Abba* in recording the teaching of Jesus concerning the Father, but the Aramaic term was apparently regularly used by Him in His teaching. His use of the term, which may mean "my father" or "our father," thus conveyed a sense of intimacy in relation to God. His use of it for *God* may well have seemed somewhat disrespectful to His hearers, but it served to suggest a closeness with God which was something new to Judaism. The double title *Abba, Father* occurs only three times in the New Testament (Mark 14:36; Rom. 8:15; Gal. 4:6), always in the salutation in prayer to God. Mark's employment of the double title here in the prayer of Jesus has

---

[57] The view of Wuest that Jesus "repeatedly" fell to the ground is improbable (*Mark in the Greek New Testament for the English Reader,* p. 264).

[58] Alexander, p. 387.

been differently explained. Some regard it as Mark's interpretative addition for the benefit of his Greek readers. But Mark gives no indication, as elsewhere, that he was adding a translation. Others hold that the double title was part of the original prayer as used by Jesus; it was preserved in the preaching of Peter as part of his vivid recollection of the scene. Since Jesus was bilingual, in His deep emotion He may well have felt impelled to use both terms. This seems probable. Still others think that Mark's double designation was derived from the common usage of the bilingual Palestinian congregations. Paul's employment of the double title in his epistles makes it clear that the double title had passed into common use among the Greek-speaking churches. It had apparently become a quasi-liturgical formula in addressing God. It probably came into common usage in the churches because Jesus had used it and because it denoted a new intimacy with God which Jesus had revealed and which had become a vital reality in the lives of His followers.

"All things *are* possible unto thee"—in Mark only. His recognition of divine omnipotence encouraged Him to make His request. The scope of *all things* is limited by what is consistent with God's nature (cf. 2 Tim. 2:13).

"Take away this cup from me"—*this cup,* corresponding to *the hour* in verse 35, is used figuratively for its contents. It is the bitter cup of His suffering and death which He must drain to the dregs as the suffering Servant of the Lord. It meant that He, the holy and sinless one, in becoming identified with sinful men as their sin-bearer would be the object of God's holy wrath against sin (2 Cor. 5:21; Gal. 3:13; 1 Pet. 2:24).[59] It was the recoil of His holy nature against taking upon Himself human sin and corruption that produced His agony and caused Him to petition the Father to remove this cup, to let it be carried past untasted.

"Nevertheless not what I will, but what thou wilt"—*nevertheless,* "but," marks the strong contrast between His request as His natural desire and His ruling consideration which must govern the answer. *What thou wilt* is at the very heart of His prayer. He resolutely subordinated His own will to the divine will, refusing to hold to any expression of His will in conflict with the Father's will. Doing the Father's will was His supreme concern during His life (John 5:30; 6:38); it also governed Him as He faced the cross. His complete submission now to the Father's will was the climax of His experience as the incarnate Son

---

[59] For a perceptive interpretation of the garden agony in the light of his own experience, see Robert W. Cummings, *Gethsemane.*

in learning obedience (Heb. 5:7-8). It was thus that He wrought our redemption.

"He cometh, and findeth them sleeping"—He craved the comfort of their fellowship in His agony, but their sleeping revealed that the three disciples had not identified with Him in His suffering. He was thus deprived of the comfort that their sympathetic watchfulness would have given Him.

"Saith unto Peter, Simon, sleepest thou?"—Peter was singled out for the rebuke because that very night Peter had singled himself out as the one most confident of his own sufficiency. The question, "Simon, sleepest thou?" is full of pained reproach. This is the first use of the name Simon in Mark since 3:16. The use of his old name here apparently was intended to remind Peter that he was not living up to the meaning of his new name.

"Couldest not thou watch one hour?"—having professed his readiness to die with Jesus (v. 31), did he not have the strength to be alert and attentive, for even one hour? The time designation need not imply that the prayer session had lasted a whole hour, but it was of considerable duration. As it was protracted, the three had fallen into a drowsy, dozing condition.

"Watch ye and pray, lest ye enter into temptation"—the imperatives are plural, addressed to all three. The present tenses demand continued watchfulness and prayer on their part. An attitude of alertness was important as enabling them to continue in prayer. *Lest ye enter into temptation* may denote the content of their prayer, but more probably, it points out the danger they are to avoid by their watching and praying. In verse 34, Jesus urged their watchfulness in connection with His own sorrow; now they need it for their own safety. Watching and praying will enable them to resist the fierce temptation that will assail them. Outward circumstances will test their confidence in Him as Messiah; their attitude of alertness and prayer will enable them to escape a damaging entrance into the temptation of believing that He is not the Messiah. That temptation they can escape through active compliance with His exhortation.

"The spirit truly *is* ready, but the flesh *is* weak"—a gracious apology for their failure. The use of the differentiating Greek particles *men* and *de,* the spirit on one hand and the flesh on the other, marks the antithesis. Some hold that spirit and flesh here have a nontheological meaning and that the reference is simply to their mind or inner desire and the weary physical body which frustrates their desire. More probably, the two terms have their usual ethical significance. Their higher spiritual nature, already quickened by the Spirit of God, was eager to be loyal to Him, but the flesh, the old nature, was weak and opposed to the desire of the spirit. By calling them to watch and pray, Jesus sought to arouse their higher nature to full activity so that they will not yield to the flesh.

"Again he went away, and prayed"—from the sleeping disciples, who had failed Him, Jesus turned back to the Father who was His only stay in that dread hour. Perhaps their lethargy intensified His feeling of anguish.

"And spake the same words"—*words* is singular, denoting not a verbatim repetition but prayer to the same effect.[60] His first prayer session had not settled the conflict for Him. His conflict has vital significance. "If he had not shrunk from death, it must have been because he was impassive, incapable of suffering, and therefore unfit to become the substitute of sinners doomed to everlasting woe. If he had not humbly consented to endure the will of God for man's sake, the great purpose of his incarnation must have been unaccomplished."[61]

"Found them asleep again, (for their eyes were heavy)"—Jesus found the three more sleepy than before. *Were heavy*, literally "were weighed down," is a figure taken from the effect of drowsiness on the eyelids. They were so sleepy that they could not keep their eyes open. The periphrastic imperfect form of the verb pictures the process; sleep was overcoming their most determined efforts to watch and pray.

"Neither wist they what to answer him"—peculiar to Mark. Jesus' presence, perhaps also His word, reproached the sleeping disciples. But they could find no appropriate excuse for their failure to watch and pray as commanded. "The irresistible lethargy of the disciples was for Peter a shameful memory."[62]

"He cometh the third time"—implying a third prayer session. Maclear writes, "The Temptation of the Garden divides itself, like that of the Wilderness, into three acts, following close one on another."[63]

"Sleep on now, and take *your* rest"—both verbs are present tenses, denoting protracted sleep. The punctuation is uncertain: are His words

---

[60] In Jesus' three prayer sessions recorded in Matthew, there is progress in the petitions. In the first, Jesus prayed the prayer of exploration, probing the possibility of the removal of the cup (26:39); in the second, He offered the prayer of resignation, accepting the inevitability of His drinking the cup (26:42); in the third, He offered the prayer of ratification, voluntarily ratifying His drinking of the cup (26:44). With the third prayer session, the agony passed away but not the drinking of the cup.

[61] Alexander, p. 389.

[62] J. Weiss, quoted in Taylor, p. 556.

[63] G. F. Maclear, *The Gospel According to St. Mark,* Cambridge Bible for Schools and Colleges, p. 163.

a command, an exclamation, or a question? If the words are a command, they apparently have a tone of sorrowful irony. In vain did He ask them to watch and pray; now let them continue to sleep. But others, like Morison, think that Jesus spoke in compassion, directing them to get the needed sleep in the remaining interval before His arrest.[64] It is possible to take the words as an exclamation of surprised reproach, "You are still sleeping and taking your rest!" This seems less probable. Still others hold that the words are best taken as a question, aimed at arousing their conscience: "Are you still sleeping and taking your rest?" (RSV, NASB). Many interpreters prefer the punctuation as a question.

"It is enough"—in Mark only. The significance of the single word in the original has been variously understood.[65] The rendering given is probably correct and announces an end to their sleeping, whether a silent interval between this and the preceding words is assumed or not. Two further assertions indicate the reason for the termination of further sleep. His short, unconnected sentences, as well as His exclamation, indicate the tense sense of crisis.

"The hour is come"—the long-expected crisis hour, leading to the end, has arrived. His messianic ministry has reached its climax.

"Behold, the Son of man is betrayed into the hands of sinners"— *behold* draws attention to the startling fact. The present *is betrayed* views the action as already transpiring, while the passive voice points to Judas as the agent. The definite article used with *sinners,* "the sinners," points either to the general class of men who are His opponents or specifically to the wicked Sanhedrin members who will be His judges. Probably the latter is intended.

"Rise up, let us go"—a call, not to flight, but to meet the approaching enemy. *Rise up* indicates that the disciples were still on the ground. Jesus asked them to accompany Him in going to where the eight were.

"Lo, he that betrayeth me is at hand"—the exclamation again directs attention to the startling fact. The articular present participle, "the one betraying me," does not name Judas but describes him by his present action. *Is at hand,* "has come near," asserts that the betrayer has arrived in fulfillment of His previous predictions.

3. Betrayal and Arrest (vv. 43-50)

An integral part of the Passion narrative, Jesus' betrayal and arrest in Gethsemane is related by all four Gospels (Matt. 26:47-56; Luke

---

[64] Morison, pp. 404-5.

[65] See Cranfield, pp. 435-36, who lists no less than eight different interpretations.

22:47-53; John 18:2-12). The Fourth Gospel provides important supplemental material to the synoptic accounts. Mark's account is clear and concise, centering attention on the action of Judas, resulting in the arrest of Jesus. This is the last mention of Judas in Mark's Gospel.

"Immediately, while he yet spake, cometh Judas"—there was no appreciable interval between the words of Jesus to the three and the arrival of Judas at the garden. None of the Gospels say anything directly about the eight disciples left at the gate. They probably withdrew to join Jesus and the three when Judas with his band entered the garden.

"One of the twelve"—all the synoptics give this apparently superfluous identification. It serves to deepen the sense of horror that one of the twelve was the actual agent in the arrest of Jesus and underlines the exact fulfillment of Jesus' announcement in verses 18-20.

"With him a great multitude with swords and staves"—coming first, Judas was acting as "guide to them that took Jesus" (Acts 1:16). Mark indicates nothing about the composition of the multitude or heterogenous throng beyond a hint from the weapons they carried. Swords, "small swords," were the regular hand weapons of the Roman soldiers, while the staves, "objects made of wood," clubs, were the regular weapons of the temple police. John 18:12 explicitly asserts that Roman soldiers under a commanding officer were present as well as Jewish officers. The words of Jesus in verse 49 imply that the temple police were prominent in the arresting crowd. Luke 22:52 also mentions the presence of some Sanhedrin members.

"From the chief priests and the scribes and the elders"—the definite article with each of the three sections composing the Sanhedrin makes each distinct. In sending this throng to arrest Jesus, they were acting in unity. The cooperation of the Roman troops probably was secured by the high priest through a direct request to the commanding officer at the Tower of Antonia for assistance in apprehending the leader of a dangerous Jewish band. Alexander notes, "This was not a personal but national transaction, being managed both by popular and official agency."[66]

"And he that betrayed him had given them a token"—evidence of the worldly wisdom and efficiency of Judas in carrying through his agreement with the Sanhedrin. The articular present participle is best regarded as characteristic, "the betrayer." The basic meaning of the verb is to hand over (cf. 3:19); it was the agreed function of Judas to deliver Jesus into the hands of His enemies. Judas had taken the initiative in giving those with him a token, "a mutually agreed upon sign."

---

[66] Alexander, p. 392.

"Whomsoever I shall kiss, that same is he"—the nature of the identifying sign. The verb rendered "kiss" commonly has that meaning in classical Greek and in the Septuagint, but only in connection with this event does it have that specific sense in the New Testament. Elsewhere, it has the more general meaning "to love, to have affection for." A kiss on the hand was the common greeting given a rabbi by his young pupil. Bishop says, "The token was surely a kiss on the hand. . . . It cannot have taken the form of an embrace, as all too often depicted."[67] His use of this token implies that Judas hoped thereby to keep his intention concealed from Jesus until the very moment of His arrest. *That same is he,* "he is the one," stressed the certain identification. Judas obviously was concerned that no mistake be made concerning the one arrested.

"Take him, and lead *him* away safely"—the kiss would also be the signal for immediate action on their part. What followed the identification would be their responsibility, yet Judas volunteered further advice. *Take him* denotes an act of mastering or overpowering: to seize by force. *Lead him away safely* reflects the concern of Judas that the whole affair should not end in a fiasco. *Safely* may mean "confidently," without fear of Him, but more probably, in such a way as to prevent any attempt to rescue Him. It seems to indicate a sense of apprehension on the part of Judas. Bruce suggests that Judas may have harbored "a superstitious dread of Christ's preternatural power."[68] But others, like Alexander, think that "he may have apprehended some attempt to rescue him by his disciples, such as actually took place but was instantly arrested."[69]

"As soon as he was come, he goeth straightway to him"—*as soon as he was come,* that is, into the garden, upon recognizing Jesus, *straightway,* without hesitating or faltering, Judas advanced toward Jesus in order to give the agreed signal. Not a moment was lost in bringing about the arrest.

"Saith, Master, master; and kissed him"—Matthew noted that Judas said, "Hail, master." The double greeting "Master, master," literally, *Rabbi, Rabbi,* indicates personal warmth in the greeting of

---

[67] Eric F.F. Bishop, *Jesus of Palestine,* p. 246.

[68] A. B. Bruce, "The Synoptic Gospels," *The Expositor's Greek New Testament,* 1:440-41.

[69] Alexander, p. 392.

Judas.[70] He acted greatly delighted to find Jesus here. Without waiting for a response from Jesus, Judas kissed Him. The aorist tense denotes the definite act; the kiss was not repeated. But the use of the compound form of the verb, intensifying its meaning, indicates that the kiss was given with a decided show of affection: "kissed him fervently."[71] Apparently, the kiss was prolonged with a show of affection so that those with him would have ample time to note Jesus' identity. Whether the kiss came before or after Jesus' self-identification to the crowd, as recorded in John 18:4-9, is not certain.

"They laid their hands on him"—Morison well renders it, "they clapped their hands on Him."[72] As a definite act, hostile hands were thrust out to seize Him. Jesus did not resist the arrest. Mark recorded nothing of the reply which Jesus made to Judas following the kiss (Luke 22:48; Matt. 26:50).

"One of them that stood by"—a vague expression leaving the individual unidentified. Matthew 26:51 indicates that he was one of the Twelve, while John 18:10 names Simon Peter. But Mark's indefinite phrase may well imply that he knew the identity of the individual. The numeral *one* limits the violence to the act of one individual.

"Drew a sword"—according to Luke 22:49, the disciples, upon seeing what would take place, asked Jesus, "Lord, shall we smite with the sword?" But Peter, as one of the two disciples with a sword (Luke 22:38), did not wait for Christ's answer. He could not stand idly by while his beloved Master was being arrested. But McKenna remarks, "As usual, his impulsive love is misdirected. In this context, it is foolish."[73]

"Smote a servant of the high priest"—an identification given in all four Gospels. The Greek definite article *the* preceding *servant* points to his distinctive position. He was neither a Roman soldier nor a temple policeman but the trusted personal slave of the high priest, Caiaphas, who had probably sent him along to keep an eye on Judas and report

---

[70] The double greeting in the KJV follows the reading of the *Textus Receptus* (see Zane C. Hodges, Arthur L. Farstad, *The Greek New Testament According to the Majority Text*, p. 167). The singular *Rabbi* in the ASV follows the critical Greek text (see *The Greek New Testament*, edited by Kurt Aland, Matthew Black, Carlo M. Martini, Bruce M. Metzger, and Allen Wikgren, 3rd ed. p. 187).

[71] Taylor points out that "in recent discussions there is a marked tendency to question the meaning 'to kiss fervently' in Hellenistic Greek" (p. 559). But he and others hold that the use of the compound form strongly supports the emphatic meaning here.

[72] Morison, p. 406.

[73] McKenna, p. 298.

to him the events. John 18:10 gives his name as Malchus. Probably aggressive in the move to effect the arrest of Jesus, he was the first man in reach of Peter's sword.

"Cut off his ear"—Peter undoubtedly intended to sever the man's neck, but, catching the flash of the sword, Malchus ducked his head and the sword just clipped his right ear (Luke 22:50; John 18:10). Since Mark elsewhere does not use the diminutive form for *ear,* its use here may be intended to indicate that only the lobe of the ear was cut off. This would help explain Luke's statement that Jesus healed his ear (22:51).

The aggressive action of Peter reflected self-confidence as well as love for Jesus. It also revealed his rashness: he intended to make good his claim that he would not fail Jesus, but he did not stop to consider the risk to himself or the futility of his action. Mark left unrecorded Jesus' rebuke to Peter (Matt. 26:52) as well as His explanation for the necessity of the arrest (Matt. 26:53; John 18:11).

"Jesus answered and said unto them"—He answered the action of those arresting Him. Following His third prayer session in the garden, the heart of Jesus found peace. "He was the only calm, collected, unruffled person in the Garden!"[74] While quietly submitting to the arrest, He protested its manner. His protest was directed against the religious leaders promoting the arrest.

"Are ye come out, as against a thief"—Jesus resented the fact that they acted as though He were a formidable public enemy who must be subdued with armed force. *Thief* means a highwayman, a bandit, one who would be armed and resist arrest. Their nocturnal action against Him is inconsistent with His well-known position as a religious teacher.

"I was daily with you in the temple teaching"—*daily,* day after day that week, He appeared openly in the temple, the most public place in Jerusalem. *With you* reminded them that He had met them face to face while teaching. *Was* acknowledges that those conditions are now a thing of the past. The nocturnal arrest indicates that they had a secret reason for not acting against Him openly. Their whole manner of arresting Him was ridiculous.

"But the scriptures must be fulfilled"—the sentence in the original is incomplete. The suggested thought apparently is, "You did not arrest me then, in order that the scriptures might be fulfilled."[75] Their action in arresting Him represented Him as a malefactor, thus presaging the

---

[74] J. D. Jones, p. 573.

[75] The view that the clause is imperatival, "But let the scriptures be fulfilled" (RSV), seems less in keeping with the context.

fulfillment of Isaiah 53:7-9, 12. *But* points to the contrast between what might have been expected and their actual course of action in fulfillment of prophecy.

"And they all forsook him, and fled"—*they* means the disciples, not the foes of Jesus. Mark, centering his thought on the disciples, did not state the thought transition. When His words and action made it clear that Jesus would offer no resistance to His arrest, their faith in Him as Messiah collapsed. "All their hopes crashed in this dark hour, and their faith was demoralised, but in reality their love remained. But there is the tragic fact—*they fled*."[76] To stay with Him now would only involve them in His unexpected fate. Thus was fulfilled Jesus' prediction that all would be offended in Him (v. 27). *All,* standing emphatically at the end of the sentence, stresses His complete forsakenness. Not even Peter proved the exception that he had claimed he would be.

4. Young Man Who Fled (vv. 51-52)

This strange episode is given in Mark alone. It reads like a personal reminiscence, but Mark cannot have drawn it from Peter's oral accounts, since it occurred after the disciples fled. Various conjectures about the identity of this youth have been advanced, none of which can be proved. Many modern scholars accept as the most probable conjecture that it was Mark himself.[77] If the last Passover was at his mother's house, and if Judas first led the band there looking for Jesus, Mark would have heard the tumult, suspected what was taking place, and hurried to follow the band.

"Followed him"—recording the literal fact that he was following Jesus after His arrest. He was interested in Jesus Himself. Morison suggests that this incident took place not in the garden but on the street as Jesus was being led into Jerusalem.[78] The verb does not necessarily mean that he was one of the disciples of Jesus.[79]

"Having a linen cloth cast about *his* naked *body*"—the linen cloth was either a loose, sleeping garment or simply a linen sheet which he had hastily wrapped around himself. The term used denotes only the

---

[76] Scroggie, p. 257.

[77] See, for example, Scroggie, p. 258; Barclay, pp. 347-48; J. D. Jones, pp. 575-81.

[78] Morison, p. 406.

[79] S. E. Johnson holds that the statement by Papias (in my Introduction) that Mark "neither heard the Lord nor followed him" discredits the view that the young man was Mark (p. 238). But the statement of Papias most naturally means simply that Mark was not personally associated with Jesus' public ministry and was not one of His acknowledged followers during His ministry.

material, not its shape. Since linen was expensive, it implies that he was a member of a well-to-do family. Clearly, he had been aroused out of bed and had left without taking time to dress.

"The young men laid hold on him"—*the young men* ("they"; the subject is not stated in the original) must refer to some of the band leading Jesus away. His presence, and especially his strange attire, attracted attention and revealed that he was sympathetic to their prisoner.

"He left the linen cloth, and fled from them naked"—in the endeavor to capture him, hands fastened on the linen cloth, but the young man readily disengaged himself and left it in their hands as he fled. *Naked* here is probably literal, although the term was sometimes used of a person wearing only an undergarment.

14

The Self-Sacrifice of the Servant
(Part 2; 14:53–15:47)

D. Trials of Jesus (14:53–15:20*a*)

All the Gospels make it clear that the trial of Jesus fell into two general parts. He was tried first by the ecclesiastical authorities and then by the political authorities. A comparison of the different accounts indicates that both parts comprised three stages. None of the Gospels record all of the different stages. Mark describes the appearance of Jesus before the Sanhedrin at night (14:53-65), narrates the denials of Peter (14:66-72), recounts the trial before Pilate (15:1-15), and concludes his narrative of the trials with the mockery of Jesus by the Roman soldiers (15:16-20).

1. "Trial" Before the Sanhedrin (14:53-65)

The appearance of Jesus before the Jewish authorities was in three stages. He was subjected to a preliminary questioning by Annas (John 18:12-14, 19-24), arraigned before Caiaphas and the Sanhedrin at a night session (Matt. 26:57-68; Mark 14:53-65), and formally condemned by the Sanhedrin in a brief meeting after dawn (Matt. 27:1; Mark 15:1; Luke 22:66-71).

"They led Jesus away to the high priest"—the band that arrested Jesus, having bound Him for greater security (John 18:12), led Him off to the high priest, Caiaphas (Matt. 26:57; John 18:24), who had ordered His arrest. Caiaphas, not named in Mark, was the official high priest during A.D. 18-36. Annas, who had been high priest during A.D. 6-15, was the father-in-law of Caiaphas, and the two worked in close cooperation. Both apparently resided in the same palace. Here we have the beginning of the condemnation announced by Jesus in 8:31.

"With him were assembled all the chief priests and the elders and the scribes"—the historical present *were assembled* dramatically presents this nocturnal flocking together of the Sanhedrin members. When it was certain that Jesus had been arrested, the high priest hurriedly sent messengers to summon the members for a meeting. *With him* means that the members filed in with the high priest when they were ready to proceed. Jesus had been detained before Annas until the members had arrived (John 18:12-13). Mark's mention of the three orders composing the Sanhedrin indicates again that the entire Sanhedrin was involved in the procedure. The stated order of the constituent parts may vary (cf. 8:31; 11:27; 14:43; 15:1). *All the chief priests,* the whole hierarchy, indicates that they were out in force and were the leaders in the action.

"Peter followed him afar off"—after the flight in panic at the arrest, Peter had regained sufficient composure to follow Jesus afar off, drawn by love but keeping at a safe distance because of fear. He was concerned "to see the end" (Matt. 26:58).

"Even into the palace of the high priest"—the accumulation of Greek particles rendered "even into" denotes that his actual entry was an unexpected act. How Peter was able to enter the court, the quadrangle around which the various chambers of the high priest's residence were situated, is explained in John 18:15-18. Access to the court and house could be gained only through the gate or "porch" (Mark 14:68) opening onto the street. Peter's first denial occurred as he was admitted (John 18:17).

"He sat with the servants"—when the arresting band reached the house of Caiaphas, the Roman soldiers went on to their barracks,[1] while the Jewish temple police took Jesus inside. The word *servants* originally meant "under-rowers in a galley"; in general usage it denotes subordinates acting under the direction of another, "attendants." The temple police acted under the authority of the high priest. They remained out in the court while Jesus was before the Sanhedrin. Peter joined them. The open-ended imperfect, "was sitting," prepares the mind for what will follow because of his position there.

"Warmed himself at the fire"—spring nights in Jerusalem, 2,500 feet above sea level, could be cold. To warm themselves, the officers had kindled a charcoal fire in a brazier (John 18:18). Feeling cold, Peter too warmed himself at the fire—more literally, "toward the light," facing it. The blaze from the fire illuminated his face, before long leading to his identification.

"The chief priests and all the council"—the double designation again means the whole Sanhedrin but makes prominent the priestly

---

[1] Uncircumcised Roman soldiers would have been unwelcome in the house of the Jewish high priest.

leadership. Their obviously hostile attitude is consistent with Mark's picture in 14:1-2, 10-11. Thompson remarks, "Nominally they were His judges; actually they were His prosecutors."[2]

"Sought for witness against Jesus to put him to death"—*sought,* "were seeking," pictures continued effort to find witness against Jesus, incriminating evidence to support a foregone conclusion. Their predetermined aim was to impose on Him the highest possible penalty. The whole procedure had the character of a grand-jury investigation rather than of a formal trial. It is fairly clear that it was an unofficial, even illegal, meeting dominated by the priestly faction. The high priest's residence was not the proper place for a formal meeting, nor could a verdict of capital punishment be pronounced at night. But what was done at this night session was in reality a trial, since the outcome of the session determined the nature of their pretense at a formal trial after dawn (15:1).

"And found none"—the imperfect tense again underlines their continued failure to attain their purpose.

"For many bare false witness against him"—*for* explains the failure. There was no lack of witnesses. Many came forward, apparently at the invitation of the Sanhedrin, to testify against Jesus. No witnesses favorable to Him were presented. Those appearing consciously bore false, or lying, testimony.

"Their witness agreed not together"—literally, "the testimonies were not equal," did not tally, or match. The law required exact agreement of two witnesses (Deut. 17:6; 19:15). These garrulous witnesses did not establish a consistent charge. "It is harder to agree on a consistent lie than to tell the simple truth."[3]

"There arose certain"—Matthew more definitely said "two" (26:60). At length, it seemed that their purpose had been attained when two witnesses came who testified concerning the same matter. Mark alone added that their testimony also was false.

"We heard him say"—their emphatic *we* stressed that they were ear-witnesses to the charge being made. They spoke from personal knowledge, assuring that their testimony was reliable.

"I will destroy this temple that is made with hands, and within three days I will build another made without hands."—*I will destroy* presents this as the emphatic personal claim of Jesus. *Temple* is not *hieron,* the entire temple complex, the term always previously used

---

[2] Ernest Trice Thompson, *The Gospel According to Mark and Its Meaning for Today,* p. 223.

[3] R. A. Cole, *The Gospel According to St. Mark,* p. 226.

by Mark,[4] but *naos,* the sacred sanctuary itself. The demonstrative *this* indicates that Jesus boldly made the claim in the very presence of the sacred temple. The appositional description *made with hands,* carefully built by skilled labor, underlines that the material temple in Jerusalem is meant. In three days, "through an interval of three days," the destroyed temple would be replaced by Him with one made without hands. *I will build* is placed emphatically at the end, asserting the future fact.

The nearest approach to such a statement by Jesus is in John 2:19. His arresting words, made to the Jewish religious leaders three years before, were not understood by them, but they were not forgotten. They then misinterpreted Him as referring to the literal temple, and the same misrepresentation is now spoken by these witnesses. It is obvious that these witnesses garbled His words with malicious intent. It is possible that their charge was based on a blend of His figurative statement about His death and resurrection as given in John 2:19-22 and His prediction of the literal destruction of the temple in Mark 13:2. That He would replace the present temple with one of a different kind implied an overthrow of the divinely instituted form of worship and therefore involved Him in open disloyalty to the sacred institution. Also, the claim that He would quickly rebuild the temple without hands was a usurpation of supernatural power and authority, hence blasphemous.

"Neither so did their witness agree together"—only in Mark. *Neither so* indicates that this was the nearest approach to a consistent testimony that night. It also reflects the disappointment of the Sanhedrin that this last hope likewise failed. Just how the two testimonies were discordant is not indicated.

"The high priest stood up in the midst"—the continued failure to establish a charge against Jesus had produced a tense situation. When it seemed that the case was lost, Caiaphas suddenly acted to save the situation. Arising, he stepped "into the midst," close to where Jesus stood facing the semicircle of the Sanhedrin members.

"Answerest thou nothing? What *is it which* these witness against thee?"—by his double question,[5] the belligerent high priest sought to goad Jesus into saying something that could be used against Him. His

---

[4] 11:11, 15, 16, 27; 12:35; 13:1, 3; 14:49. *Naos* is used only here, 15:29, and 15:38 in Mark.

[5] Some regard his words as forming a single question, "Are you answering nothing to what these are witnessing against you?" (the Vulgate, some copies of the Old Latin, the Bohairic and Georgian versions, Luther, the NEB, and the Nestle Greek text). But the double question is more in keeping with Mark's language and better reflects the exasperated spirit of the high priest.

first question has an intensive force because of the original double negative. In view of these witnesses against Him, how can He remain silent, treating them with contempt? The second question indicates that the testimony is of such a nature as to demand an explanation from Him. What is the meaning of all these charges against Him?

"But he held his peace, and answered nothing"—Mark's characteristic double statement is not idle repetition. It serves to bring out the full force of Jesus' continued silence. In majestic silence, Jesus refused to dignify the self-refuting testimony by any explanation of His own. "The silence of Jesus fulfilled Ps. 38:13-14 and especially Isa. 53:7."[6] His resolute silence loudly declared to the Sanhedrin His disdain for their lying efforts to establish a charge against Him. Even the high priest could not twist His silence to mean a tacit admission of guilt.

"Again the high priest asked him, and said unto him"—*again* denotes a new strategy on the part of the high priest. He abandoned all further attempts to use witnesses against Jesus and directed his question to Him personally, going at once to the very heart of the issue. The historical present *said* dramatically portrays the crucial scene.

"Art thou the Christ, the Son of the Blessed?"—the emphatic *thou* has a contemptuous tone. Matthew records that the answer was required of Jesus under oath (26:63). *The Christ* recalls His claim to be the promised Messiah, while *the Son of the Blessed* points to His claim to deity. The second title, used only here in the New Testament in this absolute sense, was a typical Jewish circumlocution to avoid use of the name of God (cf. Matt. 26:63, "the Son of God"). The two titles are not synonymous and unite two aspects of the claim of Jesus. In Jewish thought, they were not always associated in the person of the Messiah. How far the combination was accepted in the first century is not clear. But it is clear from the Gospels that Jesus united both ideas in Himself. While Jesus avoided the use of the term *Messiah,* apparently because of its political and materialistic implications in Jewish thought, He did not repudiate the title (John 4:25-26). But it was His claim to be "the son of God," variously expressed, that always aroused the fierce opposition of the Jewish leaders (John 5:19-47; 8:16-19, 53-58; 10:29-39). It seems clear that the high priest now deliberately combined the two designations to attain his own purpose.

"Jesus said, I am"—a clear and unqualified affirmation that He is both the Messiah and the Son of God. Having been put under oath to tell the truth, He made a plain avowal of His true nature and status,

---

[6] James A. Brooks, *Mark,* The New American Commentary, p. 242.

even though He knew it would seal His death. To have remained silent now would have been in effect an abdication of His messianic ministry.

"Ye shall see the Son of man sitting on the right hand of power, and coming in the clouds of heaven"—a confirmation and explanation of the assertion just made. *Ye shall see* indicates that the facts He is asserting had meaning for them personally. His reference to Himself as the Son of man is a reminder of Daniel 7:13, while His position as seated at the right hand of Power, another conventional substitute for the use of the divine name, indicates the fulfillment of the messianic picture in Psalm 110:1. *Coming in the clouds of heaven* is best understood as an assertion of His eschatological return as the Judge (cf. 13:24, 26). While some object to the eschatological interpretation, holding that the coming in Daniel 7:13 is a coming *to* God rather than a coming from God to earth, the order of the two parts of His statement supports the eschatological view. Following His exaltation at the right hand of God, He will come again as Judge. It is a reminder to the members of the Sanhedrin that His own position and that of His judges would then be reversed. It is a last ineffectual appeal to their conscience. Morison comments, "How august the self consciousness of our Lord, to realize all this, at the very moment when He was standing like a felon at the high priest's bar."[7] Scroggie aptly remarks, "Either Jesus was what He said He was, or He was the greatest impostor that ever lived, and was guilty, as was said, of blasphemy."[8]

"The high priest rent his clothes"—a contrived expression of horror at the blasphemous answer. The reaction was hypocritical, for the answer was exactly what he had expected and wanted. His reaction was in conformity with what was ritually expected of the high priest in the presence of blasphemy. *Clothes* renders a plural term meaning inner garments as contrasted to the outer cloak; it may imply that the high priest, like rich people generally, wore two tunics. Bishop says, "The implication of the plural is that due to the coldness of the night he was wearing several garments. This is still a common practice."[9] But since Matthew uses the term meaning the outer garments, in the plural, clothing generally, this general meaning, "clothes," seems preferable.

"What need we any further witnesses?"—an expression of relief, terminating an embarrassing situation. Since the prisoner had incriminated Himself, witnesses against Him were no longer needed.

---

[7] James Morison, *Practical Commentary on the Gospel According to St. Mark,* p. 413.

[8] W. Graham Scroggie, *The Gospel of Mark,* pp. 260-61.

[9] Eric F.F. Bishop, *Jesus of Palestine,* p. 247.

"Ye have heard the blasphemy"—*Have heard* is aorist, "heard" as a definite occurrence. Refusing to accept the validity of Christ's claim, the high priest promptly stamped it as blasphemy. The words of Jesus were not blasphemy according to the strict interpretation of Leviticus 24:10-23, but the use of the term in Mark 2:7 and 3:28-29 shows that it was commonly used with a wider and more inclusive denotation. Caiaphas regarded the words as blasphemy because Jesus claimed the position and power of deity.

"What think ye?"—a call to register their reaction by vote. No suggestion was made that the claim should be further investigated.

"They all condemned him to be guilty of death"—a ratification of their foregone conclusion. Their unanimous vote was that Jesus was worthy of death, "deserving death," as His proper punishment. Mark's expression may indicate that this was their judicial opinion, rather than a formal sentence. Because of the circumstances of the session, it would need to be confirmed in a formal meeting.

"Some began to spit on him"—*some,* standing in contrast to the preceding *all,* clearly seems to mean that certain Sanhedrin members thus expressed their hatred of Jesus. This seems confirmed by the reference to the officers at the end of the verse. *Began* marks a definite change in the scene. Having decided His fate, all restraint in their actions toward Jesus broke down. The activities engaged in are stated by four present infinitives, denoting that they continued for some time. *To spit* on His face (Matt. 26:67) is an act which is still universally regarded as the strongest and grossest form of personal insult (Num. 12:14; Deut 25:9).

"To cover his face, and to buffet him, and to say unto him, Prophesy"—throwing a cloth over His head, they proceeded to buffet Him, to hit Him with clenched fists, and then jeeringly asked Him to use His prophetic powers to tell them who had struck the blow (Matt. 26:68). These acts of brutality were intended as a brilliant demonstration of the absurdity of His messianic and prophetic claims. They succeeded only in demonstrating the awful depravity of the human heart.

"The officers received him with blows of their hands" (ASV)— tiring of their hate-prompted actions against Jesus, the Sanhedrin members turned Him over to the officers (cf. v. 54) for safekeeping until He would again be called for. Imitating their superiors, they added their own insults "with blows of their hands." The word may denote blows with a rod or with the hand, but New Testament usage suggests the latter meaning. During all this brutality, no word of protest came from the lips of Jesus (1 Pet. 2:21-23).

2. Three Denials by Peter (14:66-72)

All four Gospels candidly record three denials by Peter (Matt. 26:69-75; Luke 22:55-62; John 18:15-18, 25-27), but the details vary considerably. Efforts to arrange all the Gospels into one consistent narrative have produced varied combinations.[10] In the synoptics, the three denials are told together, but in the Fourth Gospel, they are related to the course of events that evening. In view of the difference in the accounts, it seems clear that, aside from the initial denial when Peter was admitted into the court (John 18:16-17), his denials sprang from episodes of recognition and challenge by various individuals. On each occasion, Peter was challenged to declare his true relationship to Jesus, but each time, he failed to give brave witness to his Lord and basely denied Him. The account in Mark is extraordinarily vivid, doubtless derived directly from Peter.

"As Peter was beneath in the palace"—the word *palace* here more likely carries the meaning "courtyard." This circumstantial comment resumes the account of Peter in verse 54. *Beneath* indicates that the apartments around the courtyard were on a higher level than the open court. The rooms were approached by steps. It need not mean that the trial of Jesus took place in an upstairs apartment.

"There cometh one of the maids of the high priest"—the maid, a female slave in the household of the high priest, approached Peter sitting by the fire. She may have been the person who admitted Peter. Suspicion and curiosity may have caused her to come into the courtyard for a closer look at him. Brooks notes, "A certain amount of escalation is in the charges and denials."[11]

"When she saw Peter warming himself, she looked upon him"— *saw* and *looked upon* are two aorist participles, but the double usage is not superfluous. One glance at him established that Peter was a stranger; but upon giving him a penetrating look (cf. 10:21), she recalled having previously seen him in the company of Jesus.

"Thou also wast with the Nazarene, *even* Jesus" (ASV)—the maid's *thou* is emphatic; she confronted Peter directly. Here *also* implies that she knew of another disciple present, no doubt John (cf. John 18:15). The emphatically placed designation *the Nazarene* carries a contemptuous note, probably reproducing the expression as she had heard it used by her superiors. Him she further identified as Jesus,

---

[10] See J. M. Cheney for a harmonization of the denials based on the view that there were two separate warnings to Peter and that both found distinct fulfillment in his varied denials (*The Life of Christ in Stereo,* pp. 190-92, 222-24).

[11] Brooks, p. 246.

literally, "the Jesus," the one now on trial before the members of the Sanhedrin. Her charge correctly defined Peter's relationship to Jesus and challenged him to admit it.

"But he denied"—Matthew records, "before *them* all" (26:70). The unexpectedness, as well as the publicity, of the exposure filled Peter with sudden panic. Instead of making a bold confession, he played the coward.

"I know not, neither understand I what thou sayest"—the redundancy reflects Peter's agitation. His two verbs make his denial as emphatic as possible. He denied all knowledge, and even understanding, of what the maid was saying. His *thou* is also emphatic: she had singled him out; he directly denied her claim.[12] It was an indirect denial of Christ through a claim of ignorance and personal inability to understand the charge.

"He went out into the porch"—the exposure at the fire left Peter feeling uncomfortable. Assuming that he would be safer in the shadows, he withdrew to the porch, "the fore-court," the covered archway opening onto the street. The term is used only here in the New Testament.

"And the cock crew"[13]—the audible sound reached Peter's ears, but his agitated mind did not heed it. His conscience remained unreached.

"[The] maid saw him"—the definite article most naturally means the same maid who had challenged him by the fire. Either she returned to her post as doorkeeper, or she maliciously followed Peter into the porch, motivated by a sense of self-importance.

"Began to say to them that stood by, This is *one* of them"—the loquacious maid again, as previously out in the court, directed the

---

[12] Some propose to punctuate Peter's words as two sentences, making an assertion and a question: "I neither know nor understand. What are you saying?" This is improbable, since the last thing Peter was likely to do was to ask her for a fuller explanation of what she meant.

[13] The words are omitted by many of the ancient manuscripts, and their authenticity is uncertain. They are omitted in the critical texts of Westcott and Hort as well as Nestle. The text of the United Bible Societies puts them in brackets as questionable. Many commentators accept the omission. But Taylor points out that "the authorities for omission are mainly Alexandrian with partial Western support, and seems to reflect desire to cancel the Markan allusions to two cockcrowings in favour of the one mentioned in Matthew, Luke, and John. It is possible also that the correctors asked themselves how it was that, if Peter heard a cock crowing, he did not at once repent" (*The Gospel According to St. Mark,* p. 574). C.E.B. Cranfield suggests that the words were omitted "perhaps in order to make the denial seem a little less shameful" (*The Gospel According to Saint Mark,* Cambridge Greek Testament Commentary, p. 447).

attention of others to Peter. Her assertion, "This is *one* of them," suggests that the presence of some disciples of Jesus had become a subject of discussion by those in the court. She insisted that Peter was certainly one of the disciples of Jesus. Since Matthew mentions "another *maid*" (26:71) and Luke mentions "another [man]" (22:58), it is clear that several joined in challenging Peter this time.

"He denied it again"—*denied* is imperfect, suggesting repeated expressions of denial to the different ones challenging him. *Again* notes that it was a shameful repetition. This time it was a denial of Jesus by claiming he was not one of His followers. He thus separated himself from Jesus as well as His disciples.

"And a little after"—Luke remarks that "about one hour" passed between the second and third denials which he recorded (22:59). Mark and Matthew are less specific concerning the time.

"They that stood by"—Peter's identity had by now become a matter of general discussion. Having been accosted in the porch, Peter returned to the court and sought to lose himself in the crowd. But with their curiosity aroused concerning his identity as a disciple of Jesus, they confronted Peter again with their assertion.

"Surely thou art *one* of them: for thou art a Galilaean"—*surely* insists that in spite of his denials, Peter actually is "of them," the circle of Jesus' disciples. His identity was established by the well-known leader he followed. His denials have not allayed but strengthened their suspicion of his true identity. *For thou art a Galilaean* leaves untranslated the conjunction *kai,* "also," in the original. They assert that in addition to other considerations, he is also Galilean. Matthew records their assertion that Peter's speech made clear his Galilean origin (26:73).[14] According to John, a relative of Malchus provided further circumstantial evidence by recalling that he had seen Peter in the garden with Jesus (18:26).

"He began to curse and to swear"—the two verbs portray Peter's frantic efforts to shake off the identification. *Began* implies that his verbal efforts were continued for some time. The meaning is not that Peter lapsed into an old habit of using foul language. *To curse,* "to anathematize," means to place oneself or another under a curse. Peter was calling down the curse of God upon himself if he were not telling the truth. Such conditional curses were well known to the Jews (cf.

---

[14] "His *speech* (talk or dialect) *resembled* (that of Galilee), probably in accent and pronunciation in confounding the gutterals and the two last letters of the Hebrew alphabet" (Joseph Addison Alexander, *The Gospel According to Mark,* p. 406).

Acts 23:12, 14, 21). *To swear* means "to take an oath" for confirmation, as is done in court. The verb is used of God in Acts 2:30 to confirm that He will fulfill His promise.

"I know not this man of whom ye speak"—his denial of his relationship with Jesus has grown into a direct denial of Jesus Himself. In saying "this man of whom ye speak," Peter claimed that he knew of Him only from their mention of Him. While invoking the witness of God to the truthfulness of his claim, Peter combined a breach of promise, conscious falsehood, and personal disloyalty to Jesus in this third denial. As Salmond puts it, "Peter plunges, desperate and reckless, into this last depth of falsehood and disloyalty."[15] This moral tragedy in the court below paralleled the moral perversity demonstrated up in the council chamber.

"And the second time the cock crew"—this immediate crowing is mentioned in all four Gospels. Luke adds, "while he yet spake" (22:60). Mark alone says that it was the second time (cf. v. 68).

"Peter called to mind the word"—this time, the sound of the crowing cock registered forcefully on Peter's mind. It stirred a vivid recollection of the specific utterance Jesus had spoken to him in warning that very night (v. 30), here reproduced with slight verbal variations. Luke alone records that also at this very time, Jesus "turned, and looked upon Peter" (22:61). The remembrance of the Lord's warning and His sad look of love broke the tension of Peter's fear and awakened his conscience, opening the door to true repentance.

"When he thought thereon, he wept"—*when he thought thereon* represents a single compound participle in the original, the precise meaning of which has puzzled interpreters from earliest times. Plummer concludes that "we must be content to share the ignorance of all the ages as to what Mark meant by *epibalōn*."[16] Various suggestions have been made. Its literal meaning is "having thrown upon," but no object is expressed. Some would supply "his mind," as above. Others think the meaning is that he threw his cloak over his head, or threw himself on the ground, or rushed out. Moulton, calling attention to the use of this very form in a Ptolemaic papyrus, suggests that Mark means "he set to," and holds that the aorist participle with the imperfect verb "expresses with peculiar vividness both the initial paroxysm and its long continuance."[17] This seems the most probable view. Thus, Peter

---

[15] S.D.F. Salmond, "St. Mark," in *The Century Bible,* p. 342.

[16] Alfred Plummer, *The Gospel According to St. Mark,* Cambridge Greek Testament, p. 342.

[17] J. H. Moulton, *A Grammar of New Testament Greek,* 1:131-32.

fell to weeping with vehemence; with an awakened mind and a broken heart Peter continued to sob for a long time. McGee aptly remarks, "Peter could repent of his sin, and that is the real test of a genuine believer."[18]

Following these demands, Peter dropped completely out of the picture until after the crucifixion. The terrible shame of his base denials, with their public implications, were wiped out only by the risen Christ appearing to Peter (Luke 24:34; John 21:15-23; 1 Cor. 15:5).

3. Trial Before Pilate (15:1-15)

With this paragraph, Mark turned to the political phase of the trial of Jesus. His narrative of this part of the trial is the briefest in the four Gospels (Matt. 27:1-26; Luke 22:66–23:25; John 18:28–19:16). Mark's brief and simple account omits much that is given in the other Gospels. This section of his Gospel does not seem to be based on the narrative of an eyewitness and lacks his usual eyewitness touches. Clarke saw in this fact "a very interesting confirmation of the opinion that Peter's influence was the leading one in the preparation of this book."[19]

"Straightway in the morning"—immediately after daybreak, "as soon as it was day" (Luke 22:66). This would be between 5 and 6 A.M.[20] Although the Sanhedrin had settled upon the condemnation of Jesus during the night session, to give a plausible legality to the proceedings, a formal meeting was called when morning came. A legal sentence could be pronounced only in the daytime. *Straightway* points out that action was taken as soon as possible, but after the night meeting probably no long wait was necessary.

"The chief priests held a consultation"—the noun rendered "consultation" may mean a discussion to determine a plan of action or a council meeting. The latter view harmonizes with Luke 22:66-71, which describes a morning meeting.[21] Probably, the meeting was held in the regular council chamber. This is Mark's only hint of such a morning meeting of the Sanhedrin.

---

[18] J. Vernon McGee, *Mark,* p. 168.

[19] William Newton Clarke, *Commentary on the Gospel of Mark,* An American Commentary, p. 56.

[20] W. M. Christie holds that the date was "the 7th April, 30 A.D. The sun rose at 5:40 A.M. that morning" (*Palestine Calling,* p. 189).

[21] An alternative reading, accepted in the Nestle text, may be translated "prepared their decision." It probably arose from a scribal understanding that Mark spoke of only a night meeting of the Sanhedrin. This reading eliminates the reference to a second meeting.

"With the elders and scribes and the whole council"—the characteristic Marcan fullness points out the fact that the whole Sanhedrin was involved. The three constituent parts named made up the whole council. But Mark's unusual construction here names the chief priests as the leaders in this action, while the other two groups, united under one article after the preposition *with,* are pictured as the willing followers.

"Bound Jesus, and carried *him* away"—Mark's first mention of Jesus being bound. The cords placed on Him in the garden (John 18:12) apparently had been removed after Jesus was safely inside the court of the high priest. Perhaps the bonds were intended to suggest to Pilate that they considered Jesus a dangerous individual. But in leading Him off to Pilate, they would think it prudent to fetter Him to forestall any attempt at escape. *Carried him away* depicts His forcible transference. At this point, Matthew introduces his account of the remorse and suicide of Judas (27:3-10).

"Delivered *him* to Pilate"—a literal fulfillment of Jesus' prediction in 10:33. This is the first mention of Pilate in Mark's Gospel, but he felt no need to add any further identification. His readers would know the historical facts. When, in A.D. 6, Archelaus (Matt. 2:22) was banished by the emperor Augustus, Judea was annexed to the Roman province of Syria and governed by a procurator directly appointed by the emperor.[22] Pontius Pilate, the fifth in order of these procurators, held office A.D. 26-36. He usually resided at Caesarea by the sea but found it expedient to be in Jerusalem during the Passover season. It is not certain where he stayed when in Jerusalem, whether in Herod's palace or at the Antonia. He may have lodged at Herod's palace but came to the Tower of Antonia, just north of the temple, for the trial. Jesus was led inside; but when the scrupulous Sanhedrinists refused to enter, Pilate came out to them (John 18:28-29).

"Pilate asked him"—Mark's abbreviated account at once goes to the heart of the charges made against Jesus by the chief priests. From John's Gospel it is clear that when the hierarchy first handed Jesus over to Pilate, they hoped to get the governor simply to confirm their death sentence against Jesus (John 18:29-32). When Pilate insisted upon hearing the case himself, three charges were lodged against Jesus (Luke 23:2), only one of which Pilate took seriously, namely, that Jesus claimed to be "a King." The charge reveals that the crafty Jewish

---

[22] "The province of Judea included Idumea to the south and Samaria to the north. The remainder of Palestine was still client kingdoms, Galilee and Perea under Herod Antipas and northeastern Palestine under Philip (cf. Luke 3:1)" (Brooks, p. 248, note 81).

leaders had turned Jesus' acknowledgment that He was the Messiah
into a political claim. His "royal pretension" to the throne of Israel
merited death because it was treason against Caesar, the one unpardonable sin for imperial Rome. The charge of blasphemy (Mark 14:64)
had been turned into treason.

"Art thou the King of the Jews?"—All four Gospels have the
identical question. The pronoun *thou* is emphatic and carries an obvious
tone of disdain or surprise. It appeared ridiculous to Pilate that the
disheveled prisoner before him should claim to be the King of the Jews.
This is the first occurrence of the term "King of the Jews" in Mark,
but it occurs six times in chapter 15 (2, 9, 12, 18, 26, 32; in 32 the
synonymous expression "King of Israel" is used).

"Thou sayest *it*"—Jesus' answer has been differently understood.
The words have been taken as a denial, as being noncommittal, or as
a firm acknowledgment. A denial is inconsistent with the facts. If
understood as a Hebrew idiom, it was the regular way of affirming the
contents of a question. But the Greek may well be taken as a qualified
assent. Christ's *thou* is also emphatic and may be intended to mean,
"Yes, but not with your exact meaning." It implied that His answer
was open for further discussion. He could not deny that He was "the
King of the Jews" but not in the political sense as Pilate thought. John
18:33-37 gives a fuller account of the interview, indicating that Jesus
did explain to Pilate the true nature of His kingdom. Convinced that
Jesus was no threat to the Roman government, Pilate brought Jesus out
and announced that he found "in him no fault" (John 18:38).

"The chief priests accused him of many things"—the verdict of
Pilate evoked a flood of vicious charges against Jesus from the chief
priests. *Many things* may denote intensity, "much," as frequently in
Mark (1:45; 3:12; 5:10, 23, 43; 9:26; 12:41), but more probably the
term here refers to the multiplicity of the charges made. Besides the
three already made (Luke 23:2), various other charges were now hurled
at Jesus.

"Pilate asked him again, saying, Answerest thou nothing?"—when
the torrent of accusations subsided, Jesus remained silent.[23] Since Pilate
had just announced that he found Jesus innocent, Jesus calmly refused
to dignify these false charges by replying to them. But this failure to
reply was incomprehensible to Pilate. *Asked* is imperfect tense, apparently indicating that during the silence Pilate repeated his question.

---

[23] The last part of verse 3, "but he answered nothing," is generally omitted by the
textual critics as lacking manuscript authority and may have been imported from Matt.
27:12. But Taylor thinks it more probable that the words were original but were omitted
by scribes to avoid repetition (*The Gospel According to St. Mark*, p. 579).

"Behold how many things they witness against thee"—Pilate implied that Jesus could not afford to allow these charges to go unanswered. But the Roman governor did not understand the character of Jesus which made it morally impossible to stoop to self-defense in the face of such slanders, even though His silence placed His life in jeopardy.

"Jesus yet answered nothing"—Mark's double negative (*ouketi ouden*) underscores the absolute silence of Jesus. Having previously revealed to Pilate His true character and position, Jesus refused to give any further reply to the false charges but let the facts of His life speak in refutation. "He knew that the lines of communication were broken. The hatred of the Jews was an iron curtain which no words could penetrate. The cowardice of Pilate in face of the mob was a barrier no words could pierce."[24]

"So that Pilate marvelled"—the silence of Jesus impressed Pilate with the fact that this was no ordinary prisoner. It was an amazing spectacle, since Pilate expected the usual voluble protestations of innocence. Pilate *marvelled,* continued to feel wonder and astonishment at the refusal of Jesus to bring any pressure to bear on the governor in His own behalf. He recognized it as a difficult thing to do, and he somehow admired Jesus for it. It did not lead Pilate to conclude that Jesus was guilty as charged.

Luke at this point tells how the mention of Galilee caused Pilate to transfer the case to Herod Antipas (23:5-12). When Jesus refused to entertain the corrupt ruler (cf. Mark 6:14-29) with miracles, Antipas returned the prisoner to the court of original jurisdiction.

"Now at *that* feast"—*now* is explanatory, introducing background information for the concluding phase of the trial before Pilate. *Feast* in the original has no article, pointing to the character of the time, "at feast time" (Rotherham); but as Swete points out, "the Passover was so clearly in view that *heortē* [feast] required no definition."[25] The custom mentioned was limited to the yearly Passover festival.

"He released unto them one prisoner, whomsoever they desired"—both verbs are imperfect tense, denoting customary action. It was the custom of Pilate to release one prisoner at the season, and the people made it a practice to request a specific individual. *Whomsoever they desired* indicates that the prized point in the custom lay in the selection of the prisoner by the Jews themselves. It was a definite favor to the

[24] William Barclay, *The Gospel of Mark,* p. 355.

[25] Henry Barclay Swete, *The Gospel According to Saint Mark,* p. 369.

people, since under dictatorial governments, patriotic and heroic men at times suffer along with criminals as prisoners.

How far back the custom extended is not known. *As he had ever done unto them* (v. 8) indicates that the custom had been faithfully observed by Pilate. There is no definite reference to it outside the Gospels, but it is in harmony with the known policy of the Romans to show a conciliatory attitude toward subject peoples. A partial parallel has been cited in Livy's account (5. 13) of the *lectisternium,* the feast of the gods, when chains were removed from the limbs of prisoners. A closer parallel is found in a papyrus, dating about A.D. 85, in which a certain prisoner was released by the governor of Egypt because the people begged that he should not be scourged.[26] "Amnesties at festival times are known in many parts of the world and in various periods."[27]

"And there was *one* named Barabbas"—*and* again introduces a further explanatory statement. Verse 6 sets forth the custom that came into operation during the trial; here information is given concerning the "notable prisoner" (Matt. 27:16) who became involved. Mark's phrase "*one* named Barabbas," the one called Barabbas, is somewhat unusual and may imply that he was a well-known individual. *Barabbas,* meaning son of Abba, or son of his father, was probably a patronymic,[28] although it was the proper name of several noted rabbis in the Talmud. The view that it means son of a rabbi, the son of some noted religious teacher, is less probable.

"*Which lay* bound with them that had made insurrection"—an indication of the character of Barabbas. Luke notes that the insurrection was "made in the city" (23:19). John further identifies Barabbas as "a robber" (18:40), a brigand. Barabbas was probably a Zealot, one of those fierce and uncompromising patriots whose fanatical agitation against the Romans contributed much to the outbreak of the war that

---

[26] For details, see Adolf Deissmann, *Light from the Ancient East,* pp. 266-67.

[27] Sherman E. Johnson, *A Commentary on the Gospel According to St. Mark,* p. 249.

[28] A number of scholars hold that there is a strong probability that Barabbas's name was "Jesus," based on the fact that this name occurs in Matt. 27:16-17 as an inferior variant reading. Although Origen rejected the reading on theological grounds, he said that it was found in many old copies. C.E.B. Cranfield even suggests that the unusual reading "*one* named Barabbas" in Mark probably indicates that the name originally also appeared in Mark, but that "Jesus" was "omitted for the sake of reverence" (*The Gospel According to Saint Mark,* p. 450). The name was common enough at the time, but the evidence for its authenticity as the name of Barabbas is weak, even though the resulting coincidence is intriguing. But the assumption of Rawlinson that "the Barabbas episode . . . arose as the result of a strangely dramatic historical coincidence" (*St. Mark,* p. 227) that both men bore the name of "Jesus" is unwarranted.

led to the ultimate destruction of Jerusalem in A.D. 70. Apprehended and sentenced by the Romans, he was now securely in chains, awaiting execution. "Jesus, on the other hand," Thompson notes, "had revealed Himself—in this particular emergency, at least—as a pacifist, as a man who refused to allow His followers to strike a single blow on His behalf."[29]

"Who had committed murder in the insurrection"—*who* (*hoitines*), "who are such as," characterizes them. "They were such desperate characters that they had gone to the length of murder."[30] *The insurrection* may mean that the insurrection led by Barabbas was well known, but Bruce objects to this implication and holds that the definite article simply refers back to "the insurrection implied in their being insurrectionists."[31] This is more probable since nothing further is known of this uprising.

"The multitude went up and began to ask him" (ASV)—the composition of this multitude is not indicated. The term, quite general in Mark, distinguishes the common people from the Sanhedrin members. They had gathered before the procurator's tribunal upon learning of the trial. That they were the same crowd that welcomed Jesus on Palm Sunday (Mark 11:8-11) is not probable, although some of them probably were present. The suggestion that the reference is to a distinct group of partisans of Barabbas who had now arrived to seek the release of Barabbas is not indicated. Yet some interpreters feel that the contrast between the acclaim given Jesus on Palm Sunday and the rejection of Him now implies two different crowds. Thus Barclay suggests, "It may well be that this was a crowd which had assembled with the deliberate intention of demanding the release of Barabbas. They were in fact *a mob of Barabbas's supporters. . . .* To the chief priests this was a heaven-sent opportunity."[32] Mark's words stress that the people assembled took the initiative in urging Pilate to observe the usual custom. Swete notes that the multitude seems "to have been animated by the desire of claiming a right, rather than by any special goodwill towards Jesus."[33] *Went up* suggests that Pilate was seated on his elevated judge's seat when they approached. *Began to ask* implies a certain

---

[29] Thompson, p. 229.

[30] Swete, pp. 370-71.

[31] A. B. Bruce, "The Synoptic Gospels," *The Expositor's Greek New Testament,* 1:447.

[32] Barclay, p. 357. Italics in original.

[33] Swete, p. 371.

amount of formality in urging their request. The present middle infinitive implies a personal interest in their repeated request.

"Pilate answered them"—Pilate responded to the request in the hope of using the people to secure the release of Jesus. According to Matthew (27:17), he nominated Jesus and Barabbas for them to choose from. By his selection he intended to make the outcome sure in advance. But for Pilate to put Jesus, as yet uncondemned, on a level with the condemned Barabbas was an injustice to Jesus.

"Will ye that I release unto you the King of the Jews?"—Pilate's question, as given in Mark's abbreviated account, makes it clear that he wanted to release Jesus and asked the people if that was their wish. To Pilate, the charge that Jesus was the King of the Jews seemed absurd, and he used the title with half-concealed sarcasm; but if Jesus was the kind of king they wanted, he was ready to let them have Him.

"For he knew that the chief priests had delivered him for envy"— *for* introduces the explanation that the charge of the chief priests did not deceive Pilate. He readily recognized that their animosity against Jesus stemmed from envy or jealousy, because He was too influential with the common people. "This is the *jealousy* or party-spirit, rather than personal *envy*, which the governor correctly saw to be the motive of their whole proceeding against Christ."[34] So Pilate jumped at the opportunity to pit the interest of the common people in Jesus against the Jewish leaders.

"But the chief priests moved the people"—the interval between the presentation of the choice and the call for their vote was probably due to the urgent message from his wife which Pilate received at this point (Matt. 27:19). Matthew noted that "the elders" joined the chief priests in using their influence to determine the vote (27:20). What arguments they used are not indicated, but the people were psychologically prepared to respond to them. *Moved,* literally, "shook up," metaphorically pictures the impact produced.

"That he should rather release Barabbas"—the stated goal of the priestly efforts. *Rather* underlines that Barabbas was preferable to Jesus. The people were receptive because it was a deep shock to them to see the one they had expected to overthrow the Romans and establish the messianic kingdom standing before the Roman governor a helpless prisoner. No true Messiah, they felt, would endure such indignities. Disappointed in His failure to act as they had anticipated, they turned fiercely against Him. If He were such a helpless "King of the Jews," they wanted nothing of Him. Barabbas at least had tried to do what

---

[34] Alexander, p. 413.

they believed Jesus might have done but refused to do. For a later Spirit-inspired evaluation of this choice of a murderer instead of the Lord of life see Acts 3:13-15.

"Pilate answered and said again unto them"—*again* points to Pilate's further effort following his disappointment with the vote of the multitude. He next tested the popular feeling of the multitude toward Jesus personally.

"What will ye then that I shall do *unto him* whom ye call the King of the Jews?"—*then,* or "therefore," inquired about their wish concerning Jesus, since they had asked for Barabbas. His question implies that he was willing also to release Jesus if that was their wish. What did they want done with *"him* whom ye call the King of the Jews?" Pilate's use of the title is sarcastic and throws the responsibility for it back on the people. He does not accept the title, but surely they will not want a Roman ruler to condemn the very one to whom they have given this high title.

"They cried out again, Crucify him"—*again* implies their previous shout for Barabbas, which Mark did not record. Infuriated by what they considered Pilate's insult, they "all" (Matthew) joined in shouting "Crucify him." Since Pilate had placed Jesus on a level with Barabbas, let Jesus now take his place. They demanded that Pilate issue the order to crucify Jesus.

"Why, what evil hath he done?"—literally, "For what evil did he do?" Pilate's "for" implies a negation of their surprising demand. He recognized the unjustness of the demand and belatedly sought to reason with the excited crowd. He invited them to produce evidence of any evil or injurious deed Jesus did to justify their demand.

"They cried out the more exceedingly"—the only answer of the crowd was a louder and fiercer demand for the crucifixion of Jesus. They knew the power of public pressure through clamor and shouting. "Jesus was falsely accused by the Jews and condemned by Pilate for the very thing of which Barabbas was actually guilty."[35]

"Pilate, willing to content the people"—literally, "wishing to do the sufficient thing for the people." The expression, found only here in the New Testament, is a rendering of the Latin *satisfacere,* "to satisfy, appease." Pilate no longer was concerned simply to dispense justice but was motivated by other considerations. He now deliberately resolved to satisfy the demands of the people lest they accuse him to emperor Tiberius and his own position be jeopardized. Pilate had been a rapacious governor (cf. Luke 13:1-2) and had repeatedly been at

---

[35] Brooks, p. 252.

loggerheads with his subjects, resulting in complaints against him. He knew he could not afford to be accused again to the emperor.

"Released Barabbas unto them, and delivered Jesus"—the two sides of his act of capitulation. Barabbas had his fetters removed and was released to the people. Jesus was handed over to the Roman centurion who supervised the crucifixion. Mark's abbreviated account again stated only the essential facts. John's more detailed account (19:1-15) indicates that Pilate sought to avoid crucifying Jesus by having Him scourged, hoping to move the people to pity so that they would be satisfied with this terrible punishment. But this attempt also failed, for they refused to accept anything less than His execution. When Pilate sought to clear himself of responsibility for the death by washing his hands, the people assumed the responsibility (Matt. 27:24-25).

"When he had scourged *him*"—the single aorist participle in the original refers back to a scourging administered before Pilate issued his order to crucify Jesus. None of the Gospels supply details of the scourging, which was a brutal affair. Stripped of clothes, the victim was forced to bend over a low pillar, while a short-handled whip with several leather thongs studded with sharp objects was used to lash and lacerate the back. Roman law laid no limits on the number of blows to be administered. Such scourgings were sometimes fatal. This scourging fulfilled Jesus' own prophecy in 10:34.

4. Mockery by the Soldiers (15:16-20a)

Mark's account of the mockery by Pilate's soldiers is vivid and detailed, his historical-present tenses adding to the dramatic scene. Luke, who recounted the mockery before Herod (23:8-12), did not refer to this mockery, but Matthew 27:27-30 is a close parallel. According to John's account (19:1-16), the mockery was in connection with the scourging, as part of Pilate's last futile effort to avoid crucifying Jesus. Such mockery was not an ordinary part of scourging. Lenski asserts that it was "so exceptional that nothing like it has ever been found."[36] The partial parallels that have been gathered show only that the coarse mockery of the soldiers is readily conceivable.

"And the soldiers led him away"—*and* indicates that something further is being added to the picture of the trial before Pilate. The soldiers, whose presence is here first mentioned by Mark, were under Pilate's command (Matt. 27:27). They were part of the guard Pilate had brought with him from Caesarea. They were non-Jewish, recruited from Palestine and other parts of the empire. *Led away* implies that

---

[36] R.C.H. Lenski, *The Interpretation of St. Mark's and St. Luke's Gospels*, p. 429.

the scourging had taken place elsewhere than in the court. Whether Jesus was scourged outside and publicly or in some other part of the building is not certain.

"Into the hall, called Praetorium"—as in 14:54, 66, *the hall* means the open courtyard and not the surrounding building itself.[37] The view that the term means "palace, not 'courtyard,' "[38] is due to Mark's addition "which is the Praetorium," apparently equating the two. *Praetorium,* a Latin loan-word used only here in Mark, originally meant "the praetor's tent in camp with its surrounding" and then came to mean "the governor's official residence."[39] The latter is always its meaning in the Gospels and Acts (Matt. 27:27; John 18:28, 33; 19:9; Acts 23:35). Mark's comment is a "loose conversational statement."[40] Views differ as to whether the reference here is to Herod's palace or the fortress Antonia; archaeologists generally support the latter view.

"They call together the whole band"—all the members of the band who would be available and not on duty elsewhere. *Band* is the Greek translation for the Latin "cohort," normally composed of six hundred men, the tenth part of a legion. Arndt and Gingrich think that this is always its meaning in the New Testament, although Moulton and Milligan state that the term was also applied to "maniple," a body of two hundred soldiers.[41] At any rate, a large number of soldiers participated in the mockery. Having participated in the arrest of Jesus that night (John 18:12), the band would be interested in the case. This is the third instance of Jesus being mocked before His crucifixion: first before Caiaphas (Mark 14:65), then before Herod (Luke 23:11), and now by the soldiers of Pilate.

"They clothed him with purple"—their first step in their mock coronation of Jesus as King of the Jews. Purple denoted initially the purple dye and then the cloth or garment of that color. The garment thrown over His shoulders was apparently a discarded scarlet cloak worn by Roman soldiers. Matthew termed it "a scarlet robe" (27:28). Alexander states that the term was used "to designate a great variety of shades from bright red to deep blue."[42]

---

[37] "So far as we have observed, there is nothing in the *Koine* to support the contention that in the NT *aulē* [court] ever means the house itself." James Hope Moulton and George Milligan, *The Vocabulary of the Greek Testament,* p. 92.

[38] Johnson, p. 251.

[39] W. F. Arndt and F. Wilbur Gingrich, *A Greek-English Lexicon of the New Testament and Other Early Christian Literature,* p. 704.

[40] Plummer, p. 349.

[41] Arndt and Gingrich, p. 768; Moulton and Milligan, p. 582.

[42] Alexander, p. 418.

"Platted a crown of thorns, and put it about his *head*"—a further step in His mock arrayal as king. His head was encircled with a crown made of twigs from a thorn bush twisted together to form a rough wreath. The precise species of the thorn cannot be determined. The use of such a crown was intended to make the "king" look ridiculous and to add pain to the insult. Matthew added that they put a reed into His hand as His scepter. Although the Gospels do not mention it, they probably seated Jesus on a stool representing the royal throne.

"And began to salute him"—verses 18-19 describe their mock homage to the king thus crowned, mingled with brutal insults. *Salute* is the usual term for personal greetings.

"Hail, King of the Jews!"—a mocking play on the familiar greeting given the emperor, *Ave Caesar, victor, imperator.* The imperative *Hail,* basically meaning "Rejoice," was a sarcastic acknowledgment of His royal dignity, while *King of the Jews* was heavy with contempt. Before the Sanhedrin, His prophetic powers were derided (14:65); here, His kingly claims are ridiculed.

In verse 19, all the verbs are imperfect, denoting that the actions continued for some time. Snatching out of His hand the reed they had put there, they "smote him on the head," repeatedly struck Him to symbolize that His royal power was futile. *Did spit upon him* portrays how they added the grossest personal insult to their mock homage. John (19:3) says they also struck Him with their hands. *Bowing* their *knees worshipped him* marks their mock homage as in studied imitation of Oriental obeisance to royalty. The phrase *bowing* their *knees,* literally "placing the knees," is used elsewhere in the New Testament of posture in prayer,[43] leading Taylor to observe that "a mockery in terms of Caesar worship, or Oriental ideas of kingship, is probably meant."[44]

It seems obvious that the mockery of the soldiers was not motivated by animosity against Jesus personally, since no doubt most of them had no previous contact with Him. Having heard the charge that the prisoner claimed to be the King of the Jews, they were led by their sense of loyalty to the emperor to ridicule such a claim. They held in utter scorn all Jewish hopes for a king of their own. They used the occasion to vent their anti-Jewish feelings against this Jewish pretender.

"When they had mocked him"—the aorist tense marks the completion of the brutal, insulting activity. How long it lasted is not known, but apparently it was terminated when Pilate called a halt or they tired

---

[43] Luke 22:41; Acts 7:60; 9:40; 20:36; 21:5.

[44] Taylor, p. 586.

of their coarse sport. The silence of Jesus during these wanton insults is remarkable. It deeply impressed the early believers (1 Pet. 2:23).

"They took off the purple from him, and put his own clothes on him"—the mock raiment was removed after Pilate's last futile attempt to get the Jews to accept the punishment inflicted as sufficient (John 19:6-16). Nothing is said about the thorn crown being removed. However, Plummer points out that "in the most ancient representations of the crucifixion the Saviour does not wear a crown of thorns."[45]

E. Account of the Crucifixion (15:20*b*-41)

When Pilate yielded to the demands of the crowd and ordered the crucifixion of Jesus, the centurion entrusted with the execution of the order at once prepared to carry it out. No law demanded any delay between the sentence and the execution. Mark's account is remarkably impersonal, sober, and restrained. It does not have the personal details of an eyewitness account. Yet his frequent use of the historical present, "together with the use of short sentences connected by *and,* gives the original a sort of breathless vividness."[46] Mark mentions the road to Golgotha (15:20*b*-22), tells of the crucifixion and the first three hours on the cross (vv. 23-32), describes events in connection with the last three hours and death (vv. 33-39), and makes reference to the women at the cross (vv. 40-41).

1. Road to Golgotha (vv. 20b-22)

All the synoptics refer to Simon of Cyrene being compelled to bear the cross for Jesus (Matt. 27:31-33; Luke 23:26-33), but Luke alone records Jesus' words to the women who bewailed Him. John's brief reference adds new information (19:16-17).

"[They] lead him out to crucify him"—*they* is not further defined; clearly, it does not mean all the soldiers who participated in the mockery. The change to the historical present, as well as the changed behavior, indicates that the reference is to the centurion with his assistants assigned to carry out Pilate's orders. *Lead him out* means not merely from the praetorium but outside the city to the place of execution. "That they may crucify him" (Rotherham) gives a literal statement of their purpose. John's statement that Jesus "went out bearing the cross for himself" (19:17) marks the commencement of this movement to Golgotha. It was the practice to compel the one to be crucified to bear his own cross to the place of crucifixion. He carried not the entire cross

---

[45] Plummer, p. 350.

[46] D. E. Nineham, *The Gospel of St. Mark,* p. 421.

but the *patibulum,* or transverse beam, which would weigh more than a hundred pounds.

"They compel one Simon a Cyrenian, who passed by, coming out of the country"—the Fourth Gospel does not mention this event, but the terminology leaves room for it. The synoptics do not mention that Jesus started toward Golgotha with His own cross, but the action here recorded clearly implies a change in the situation which necessitated it. *Compel,* rendering a term of Persian origin but long known in the Roman world, denotes a requisitioned service, exacted under imperial authority (cf. Matt. 5:41). Because of all that Jesus had suffered since His arrest, His strength gave out after He had carried the cross to the city gate. Seeing that even their lashes could not revive His exhausted strength, the soldiers wantonly seized upon a man conveniently near to carry the cross for Jesus. No Roman soldier would demean himself to carry it for Him, nor did anyone else volunteer to do so. Mark's indefinite designation, *who passed by,* implies that the man was chosen at random and had no personal connection with Jesus.

All the synoptics identify him thus by name and origin, implying that his identity was well remembered in the early church. The name *Simon,* one of the few proper names outside of the Twelve in Mark's Gospel, implies that he was a Jew. He was *a Cyrenian,* a native of Cyrene on the northern coast of Africa opposite the Greek peninsula. It does not support the suggestion that he was an African Negro. The city had a large Jewish colony. Jews from there had a synagogue in Jerusalem (Acts 6:9), and people from there were present at Pentecost (Acts 2:10). Whether Simon was resident in Jerusalem or had come to attend the Passover is not certain. *Coming out of the country* does not assert that he had been working; the time of the day is against that suggestion. *Country,* or field, is here used as opposed to city. He was entering the city when he encountered the procession coming out. Apparently, he was not aware of all the tumultuous events that had just taken place.

"The father of Alexander and Rufus"—only in Mark. The identification, not necessary for the story, implies that his sons had become persons of some distinction in the church. The reference would be of interest to Mark's readers. Apparently, they were members of the church at Rome. Efforts to identify them further are precarious. Alexander cannot be identified with anyone else with that name in the New Testament. Rufus, a rare name in the East, may be the individual mentioned in Romans 16:13. McKenna remarks, "One thing is sure.

When the Roman Christians read Mark's Gospel, they find encouragement to bear and to share the weight of the cross they are compelled to carry."[47]

"To bear his cross"—Mark's wording is reminiscent of Jesus' words in 8:34. Simon was compelled to do literally what all of Jesus' followers must do spiritually (Luke 23:26).

"They bring him"—*bring* basically means to bear, carry, and may imply that Jesus was so exhausted that the soldiers had to support and partially carry Him to the place of crucifixion. But, probably, the verb here simply means to conduct or lead.

"Unto the place Golgotha"—literally, "upon the Golgotha place." The preposition *upon* denotes not direction but rather attainment of a position upon. It is consistent with the view that Golgotha was a knoll, a place that could be seen from afar (Matt. 27:55). But nowhere is it stated that it was a hill or mount. *Golgatha* is the Aramaic form of the Hebrew word meaning skull.

"Being interpreted, The place of a skull"—Mark again translates the term for his readers, "Skull's place." Our familiar English term *Calvary* is derived from the Vulgate rendering, *calvaria*, "a skull." The name cannot mean that skulls were lying there; unburied skulls would not be tolerated by the Jews, and the singular number is against it. Jerome mentioned in an ancient legend that the name was derived from the fact that Adam's skull lay there. Most probably, the name was derived from the shape of the place; the roundness and smoothness of the knoll bore the resemblance of a human skull. Both the way leading there and its exact location are uncertain. The stations of the modern *Via Dolorosa* are of medieval origin. Scripture indicates that the place was outside but near the city (John 19:20; Heb. 13:12). John mentioned that there was a garden cemetery at the place (19:41). Two Jerusalem localities today are claimed for the original site, the Church of the Holy Sepulchre and "Gordon's Calvary," a short distance beyond the northern wall. The latter identification is of modern origin. The tradition connecting the place with the site of the Church of the Holy Sepulchre reaches back at least to the fourth century. The church is now within the city walls, but recent archaeological excavations seem to confirm that the place was then outside the north wall of the city. "Its immediate vicinity is now known to have been a cemetery in Jesus' day."[48]

---

[47] David L. McKenna, *Mark,* The Communicator's Commentary, p. 312.

[48] Robert Houston Smith, "The Tomb of Jesus," *The Biblical Archaeologist,* Sept. 1967, pp. 82-83.

2. Crucifixion and First Three Hours (vv. 23-32)

Parallel accounts occur in Matthew 27:34-38, Luke 23:33-43, and John 19:18-27. Matthew's account is closely parallel to that of Mark, while Luke and John both add new material.

"They gave him to drink wine mingled with myrrh"—the undefined *they* in its context naturally means the soldiers. Their offer of wine to the one to be crucified was apparently not a Roman custom. Rabbinic writings indicate that the drink was provided as a charitable act by rich women in Jerusalem, done in accordance with Proverbs 31:6-7. "Wine having been myrrhed" means that the addition of myrrh had made the wine taste bitter, giving it the taste of "gall" (Matt. 27:34). It was intended to deaden the sense of pain. Lenski holds that the offer of the drink was not intended as an act of mercy on the part of the soldiers but "was done to make their labor of crucifying easier."[49]

"But he received *it* not"—the aorist tense records His definite refusal to drink, even though He was repeatedly urged to do so. Matthew noted that He tasted it (27:34). Its bitter taste at once told Him its nature, and He refused it, determined to meet His suffering and death in the full possession of His faculties. It meant that in His self-giving, there was to be no self-sparing. He was determined to drink the bitter cup of His vicarious sufferings consciously to the very last. He would voluntarily drink the cup that the Father had given Him.

"And they crucify him" (ASV)—stating the horrible fact in the simplest words. All the Gospels state the historical fact, but none has a single word of description of the physical agonies involved. They throw a veil over His physical sufferings. "It was one of the most horrifying forms of execution ever devised."[50] Nor do any of them give an explicit interpretation of the cross as an atonement for sin. Mark alone uses the historical present tense, but he too hastens on with his narrative.

Crosses were of various forms, but the fact that His superscription was placed "over his head" (Matt. 27:37) indicates that Jesus' cross was the familiar Latin cross. The exact procedure varied with circumstances, and the precise steps in Jesus' crucifixion are not certain. Some think that the whole cross was laid on the ground, Jesus was stretched upon it, and nails were driven through His hands and feet (cf. Luke 24:39), following which the raised cross was dropped into a hole

---

[49] Lenski, p. 434.

[50] Brooks, pp. 255-56.

prepared for it.[51] Others think that He was probably nailed to the crossbar lying on the ground and then elevated and placed with His back against the upright already fixed in the ground, the crossbar being inserted in a notch in the upright.[52] In either case, the crucified one would not be raised more than two feet above the ground, left in the very midst of the crowd around him.

"They parted his garments"—the middle voice indicates that the soldiers acted in their own interest. *Garments* is here used generally to include all His clothes, which passed to the quaternion of soldiers (John 19:23) who carried out the crucifixion. Apparently, there were four soldiers for each man crucified. "A Jew," Barclay notes, "wore *five* articles of clothing—the inner robe, the outer robe, the sandals, the girdle and the turban. When the four lesser things had been assigned, that left the great outer robe."[53] There is no indication that Roman respect for Jewish scruples left the crucified even a loincloth.

"Casting lots upon them, what every man should take"—John, who was present, gave a more precise account (19:23-24). The lot was apparently cast with dice brought along to pass the long hours of guard duty around the cross (Matt. 27:54). *What every man should take,* "who what should take," is a double indirect interrogative; it blends two distinct questions, both answered by the outcome of the lot. Their action was an unconscious fulfillment of Psalm 22:18.

"It was the third hour"—that is, 9:00 A.M. according to Jewish reckoning. This precise statement of time, found only in Mark, has raised much discussion concerning its reconciliation with John's statement that it was "about the sixth hour" (19:14) when Pilate made his last vain effort to rescue Jesus. Several proposed harmonizations have been suggested. Swete concludes that "the problem cannot be said to have been solved yet."[54] The most probable solution is the view that John, writing in Asia Minor, used the Roman official mode of computation, reckoning from midnight, so that the sixth hour would be 6 A.M.[55] The interval was filled with the mockery and preparations for the crucifixion. Perhaps during this time, Pilate also made his decision concerning the other two men.

---

[51] For a vivid description of the physical sufferings of crucifixion, assuming this procedure, see Frederic W. Farrar, *The Life of Christ,* chapter 61.

[52] For a presentation of this view, see Pierre Barbet, *A Doctor at Calvary,* chapter 2.

[53] Barclay, p. 362. Italics in original.

[54] Swete, p. 381.

[55] A. T. Robertson, *A Harmony of the Gospels for Students of the Life of Christ,* pp. 284-87.

''And they crucified him''—*and* couples the fact of the crucifixion with the time already stated. Mark's coordinated construction has the force of a temporal conjunction, *when.*

''The superscription of his accusation was written over''—the writing, fastened over His head at the time of crucifixion, set forth the official charge on which Jesus had been condemned. *Superscription,* used by all the synoptics, denotes that the accusation had been written upon something, apparently a white tablet, not engraved. John's word *title* was the technical term for this record.

''THE KING OF THE JEWS''—all the Gospels agree that Jesus was officially crucified as the King of the Jews, but no two Gospels agree in the exact wording they use (cf. Matt. 27:37; Luke 23:38; John 19:19). The minor variations may well be due to the fact that the superscription appeared in three languages (John 19:20). The aim of the Gospel writers was to convey the nature of the charge, and all have the same import. The very nature of the accusation recorded was intended by Pilate as a thrust at the Jews, a fact which the chief priests keenly felt (John 19:21-22). It insultingly declared that Jesus belonged to the Jews as their king and because of that very fact He had been crucified. While Pilate clearly intended the superscription as an insult to the Jews, he thereby unwittingly proclaimed Jesus' true identity.

''With him they crucify two thieves''—Luke first mentions these two as Jesus' companions on the road to Golgotha (23:32). *Thieves,* better ''brigands,'' indicates that they were men of the character of Barabbas (John 18:40). They may have been associates, but the Gospels do not state the connection. Plummer remarks, ''They had probably been condemned at the same time as Jesus, for they know how His case differs from theirs (Luke xxiii. 40, 41, 42).''[56]

''The one on his right hand, and the other on his left''—This spatial detail is mentioned in all four Gospels. Apparently done at Pilate's orders, it was a caricature of Jesus' central position as king. Intended as a further insult to the Jews, it was an unconscious fulfillment of Isaiah 53:12.

Verse 28 is omitted in the oldest manuscripts; modern textual critics agree that the verse was interpolated from Luke 22:37, where it is unquestionably genuine. As Plummer remarks, ''It is not Mark's habit to point out the fulfillment of Scripture.''[57]

''They that passed by railed on him''—introducing a fourth outburst of insult and mockery endured by Jesus. He had already been

[56] Plummer, p. 354.

[57] Ibid., p. 355.

insulted following the night trial before the Sanhedrin (14:65; Luke 22:63-65), by Antipas and his soldiers (Luke 23:11), and by the Roman soldiers (15:17-19). Now, various groups joined in mocking the crucified King. Mark first mentioned those that passed by, apparently Jews from the city who had come to see the execution. Repeatedly they "railed on him," more literally "were blaspheming him." In its lower sense, the verb denotes reviling, defamation, but in the higher sense, it means blaspheming Deity. The latter certainly actually took place here, God blasphemed in His Son.

"Wagging their heads"—a familiar Old Testament gesture of scorn and derision (2 Kings 19:21; Ps. 109:25; Lam. 2:15).

"Ah!"—an exclamation of applauding admiration or of surprise, found only here in the New Testament. Its use here is ironic. Their identification of Jesus as the destroyer and builder of the temple is a taunt based on the charge against Him made before the Sanhedrin (14:58).

"Save thyself, and come down from the cross"—His descent from the cross should be His means of saving Himself. *Save* is used with a purely physical connotation: "Deliver Yourself from your awful suffering and sure death." The taunt is based on the stark contrast between His large claims of power and His obvious helplessness. "What they taunt him for not doing, saving himself, is precisely so because he is doing what they ridicule, saving others. He could not do both."[58]

"Likewise also the chief priests"—the dignified Sanhedrin members in like manner descended to participation in the crude public mockery. Plummer comments, "Judges capable of striking and spitting at their Prisoner (xiv. 65) would be equally capable of making derisive remarks in His hearing."[59]

"Mocking said among themselves with the scribes"—it was below their dignity to speak to the one on the cross directly, but repeatedly, they passed their jeers about Jesus in His hearing while conversing among themselves. *With* indicates that "the scribes and elders" (Matt. 27:41) were the willing subordinates of the chief priests; they were of one heart with them. The derision was the public act of all three divisions of the Sanhedrin.

"He saved others; himself he cannot save"—a taunt of His supposed loss of power when He needed it most to help Himself. *Saved* is used in two senses: "He saved others from disease, he cannot save

---

[58] Donald English, *The Message of Mark*, pp. 233-34.

[59] Plummer, p. 355.

Himself from dying.''[60] Their mockery acknowledged the reality of His miracles, which they were never able to deny, although they did try to discredit their source (3:22). They could only conceive of a power that would act in self-interest. If His power had deserted Him now, it proved that it was not of God; otherwise would God not deliver Him now (Matt. 27:43)? Yet in their spiritual blindness, they expressed a sublime spiritual truth. If the Servant of the Lord was to make atonement for sins, He must use His power to sacrifice Himself and thus appear to be utterly helpless. ''Had He been a self-saviour He could never have been the world's Saviour. Sacrifice is at the heart of all salvation, and to live one must die.''[61]

''Let Christ the King of Israel''—making a mockery of His messianic claims (14:62). Pilate's superscription identified Jesus as ''the King of the Jews''; but the Jewish leaders, in speaking among themselves, scornfully designated Him the King of Israel. They derided His claim to be the King of the chosen people of God.

''Descend now from the cross, that we may see and believe''— *now* challenged Him to use His power that very moment to substantiate His messianic claim by a miraculous descent from the cross. Now was the opportune moment for Him to act and win their acceptance of Him! Their implication that such a visual demonstration would win their faith is discredited by the fact that they would not believe the greater miracle of His bodily resurrection. Their failure to believe lay in their stubborn will, not in the lack of convincing evidence. ''If in the end he had come down from the cross, it would have meant that there was a limit to God's love, that there was something which that love was not prepared to suffer for men.''[62]

''They that were crucified with him reviled him''—''the co-crucified'' also joined the mockery. The imperfect tense verb *reviled,* ''heaped insults upon,'' implies repeated expression of insult. Luke alone (23:39-43) related that one of them reproved his companion for his mockery and implored Jesus to remember him. Probably both initially joined in the reproach, but one of them soon came to a better mind as he compared the unjust fate of Jesus with their own deserved punishment. Less probable is the view that only one, acting as the representative, reviled Jesus.

---

[60] Swete, p. 383.

[61] Scroggie, p. 273.

[62] Barclay, pp. 362-63.

3. Last Three Hours and Death (vv. 33-39)

All the synoptics mark the distinctiveness of the last three hours that Jesus suffered on the cross and relate events connected with His death (Matt. 27:45-54; Luke 23:44-48). John's brief account (19:28-30), which does not mention the darkness, gives some independent material.

"When the sixth hour was come"—at midday, when the sun was at its zenith. All the synoptics mark the hour, although Luke's statement is less precise: "about the sixth hour." This precise designation divided the time that Jesus suffered on the cross into two distinct periods of three hours each.

"There was darkness over the whole land until the ninth hour"— asserting the unique feature of this period and its duration. "A darkness came" states the historical fact, while the aorist tense seems to indicate that it came quite suddenly. This unusual darkness settled over, "upon," the whole land, either the entire land of Israel or the whole earth, the Greek word allowing either interpretation. The former view is generally accepted here, although Salmond points out that the usual biblical significance of the expression points to the latter view. [63] Luke's statement "the sun's light failing" (23:45) does not assert an eclipse (astronomically impossible at full moon) but does suggest that the cause lay in the sun itself rather than in an atmospheric obstruction to its rays. Whatever its cause, it is clear that the synoptics regarded it as a supernatural occurrence, though none of them noted its significance. It clearly seems to signify God's judgment, for darkness and judgment are often associated in Scripture (Isa. 5:30; 9:19; Joel 2:31; 3:14-15; Amos 8:9-10).

"At the ninth hour"—there had been much activity around the cross during the first three hours, but the Gospels record not a single event until the ninth hour. With the darkness, there fell an awed hush upon the scene.

"Jesus cried with a loud voice"—the strong cry of Jesus suddenly broke the long silence. He spoke not with the feeble voice of one exhausted but with a strong voice of deep emotion.

"Eloi, Eloi, lama sabachthani?"—the only one of the seven statements from the cross preserved in two Gospels (Matthew and Mark). Both quote the original and add the translation. Mark's quotation "is a Hebrew-tinged Aramaic version of Ps. xxii. 1."[64] It is generally

---

[63] Salmond, p. 354.

[64] Cranfield, p. 458.

agreed that Matthew gives the Hebrew while Mark here uses the Aramaic. From the reaction to His cry, it seems most probable that Jesus used the words of the original Hebrew.

"My God, my God, why hast thou forsaken me?"—the repeated *my God* denotes intensity of feeling, while the double pronoun stresses His clinging trust; even when He felt Himself deserted, He claimed God as His God. *Forsaken* is aorist tense: "Why did You forsake Me?" It looks back to the time when He entered upon the awful experience out of which He was now emerging. The verb pictures someone being abandoned in adverse circumstances. *Why,* or "for what end," implies an effort to understand what has happened. Coming at the close of the three hours of darkness during which Jesus suffered in silence, this cry reveals the unfathomable depths of His suffering. It confronts us with the mystery of the atonement, beyond human ability to understand fully or explain. The darkness served to emphasize the uniqueness and unexampled intensity of those sufferings. This cry must be understood in the light of 14:36. The cup from which He shrank in the garden but willingly accepted He has now been made to drink in all its fearful fullness. "The cry of dereliction reflects the awfulness of fulfilling that task, described elsewhere in Scripture so graphically (Rom. 3:21-26; 2 Cor. 5:18-19, 21; 1 Pet. 1:18-20)."[65] The barrier which He felt between Himself and God was the barrier of the world's sin laid on Him. As the world's sin-bearer (John 1:29; 2 Cor. 5:21), He endured the divine wrath against sin. "The burden of the world's sin, his complete self-identification with sinners, involved not merely a felt, but a real, abandonment by his Father."[66] The true nature of the punishment of sin is eternal separation from God (2 Thess. 1:9), and Jesus endured the wrath of God against sin in being forsaken by Him. This does not mean that Jesus personally was the object of divine displeasure, but "in the sphere of the Divine moral government He was, as the world's Representative and Substitute, 'left' alone with the world's sin, 'bearing' it."[67]

"Some of them that stood by, when they heard *it,* said"—the reference seems to be to the Jewish bystanders, since the Roman soldiers would not likely understand His cry as a call for Elijah. Apparently, the unusual darkness had constrained them to remain to see what the outcome of this unusual affair would be. The loudness of the cry

---

[65] English, p. 234.

[66] Cranfield, p. 458.

[67] Morison, p. 435.

assured that His words were clearly heard, and no Jew would fail to understand their meaning.

"Behold, he calleth Elias"—the assertion is intelligible only as a piece of mockery. It reveals their continued animosity toward Jesus. Their prefatory interjection, *Behold,* sarcastically calls attention to what they claim is taking place. Jesus' cry, "My God, my God" (*ēli, ēli,* Matthew), is asserted to be a call for Elijah (*ēlias*). Earle thinks they mean, "This poor deluded 'Messiah' thinks Elijah will come to his rescue."[68]

Verse 36 records another event at the ninth hour, following in close succession. John's account, which is fuller than those in Matthew and Mark, indicates that this action was prompted by Jesus' further word, "I thirst." The one who ran to provide a drink for Jesus must have been one of the Roman soldiers who had brought with him some vinegar, or sour wine, for his own refreshment while on duty at the scene. It was the drink used by the common soldier and the field laborer (Ruth 2:14). It is not the same wine that was offered Jesus at the beginning. During the first three hours, the soldiers had joined in the mockery by approaching Jesus and offering Him vinegar (Luke 23:36).

Mark uses three aorist participles to record the preliminary actions of the soldier. He ran to "a vessel full of vinegar" (John 19:29), filled a sponge (mentioned in the New Testament only in connection with this incident), and then put it on a reed, literally "having placed it around a reed," so that it covered and surrounded the tip of the reed. Holding the sponge to Jesus' lips, he thus gave Him to drink. *Drink,* in the imperfect tense, denotes that he continued to hold it there while Jesus continued to suck some of the wine from the sponge. McGee notes: "He took this in order to fulfill the prophecy: 'They gave me also gall for my meat; and in my thirst they gave me vinegar to drink' (Psalm 69:21)."[69]

"Saying, Let alone; let us see whether Elias will come to take him down"—Mark gave these words as spoken by the soldier, while Matthew said that "the rest," those standing by, said, "Let be; let us see whether Elias will come to save him" (27:49). In Matthew, "Let be" is singular, indicating that it was addressed to an individual, while in Mark the term is plural. In Matthew, the meaning apparently is "Leave off" or "Let Him alone," while in Mark it means "Don't stop me; let me alone." The remonstrance of the bystanders was apparently made

---

[68] Ralph Earle, "The Gospel According to St. Mark," in *The Evangelical Commentary on the Bible,* p. 185.

[69] McGee, p. 178.

while the soldier was giving Jesus the drink. While not allowing them to stop him, the soldier also gave expression to the heartless taunt of the spectators. Gould suggests that the soldier meant, "Let me give Him this, and so prolong His life, and then we shall get an opportunity to see whether Elijah comes to help Him or not."[70]

"Jesus cried with a loud voice"—all the synoptics recorded this loud shout. It was unusual for one whose natural forces had been weakened by long agony, and it impressed the spectators. It was Jesus' second loud cry (cf. v. 34), as Matthew noted by his use of "again." This shout obviously was the triumphant cry given by John, "It is finished" (19:30). His words of self-committal, recorded by Luke (23:46), were apparently next uttered in a calm and trustful manner.

"And gave up the ghost"—literally "and breathed out," or "expired." The aorist tense suggests that the end came suddenly. None of the Gospel authors say that Jesus "died." They knew that it was no ordinary death. John alone adds the detail that "he bowed his head," while his expression "gave up the ghost" (19:30) implies that His end came voluntarily. "He refused to use His will and miraculous power to fend off that death by any supernatural means and hence 'yielded up His spirit,' dying as the result of physical causes which He did not attempt to overcome miraculously."[71] His comparatively early death was not due to His physical sufferings alone, and it is a mistake to center major attention on the physical agonies of our Lord. Clarke asserts, "He died of his agony, the inward woe and struggle of his soul—this is to say, he died directly in consequence of his agony respecting sin."[72]

"The veil of the temple was rent in twain from the top to the bottom"—this effect is mentioned in all the synoptics. Luke records it as occurring just before Jesus' death, the other writers as happening immediately after it, implying that the two events took place at the same time, so that either order could be used. *The veil* of the sanctuary denotes the inner veil or curtain which hung between the holy and the holy of holies. The aorist tense records the rending as a single occurrence. It was torn into two separate parts, from the top to the bottom, severed by a mighty stroke from above. It was clearly a supernatural act. The earthquake did not cause it (Matt. 27:51), for then it would have been torn in several directions; furthermore, a quake sufficient to

---

[70] Ezra P. Gould, *A Critical and Exegetical Commentary on the Gospel According to St. Mark,* International Critical Commentary, p. 295.

[71] R. C. Foster, *Studies in the Life of Christ: The Final Week,* p. 231.

[72] Clarke, p. 246.

rend so heavy a curtain would certainly also have severely damaged the temple structure. None of the Gospel writers offer any explanation of this startling event, but its spiritual significance is given in Hebrews 6:19-20; 10:19-22. The assertion of Taylor that the story "appears to be a legendary addition doctrinal in origin" is unwarranted skepticism.[73] The time was three o'clock in the afternoon, the very time that the priests in the temple were busy with their activities of the evening sacrifice. The sudden rending of that veil must have profoundly shaken them, and the patching up of that veil could not have been kept from public knowledge.

"The centurion, which stood over against him"—the Roman officer who supervised the crucifixion and was directly accountable to Pilate (cf. v. 44). The word *centurion* (*kenturiōn*) is a transliteration of the Latin *centurio,* a commander over a hundred soldiers. Only Mark uses this Latinism (vv. 39, 44, 45); elsewhere in the New Testament, the equivalent Greek form is always used.[74] *Stood over against him* describes the centurion as standing opposite the cross of Jesus but facing Him where he would have a full view of all that happened. Matthew notes that there were other soldiers standing guard with him (27:54). As the one responsible for what happened, the centurion had kept a close watch; this had been especially necessary during the darkness, and nothing had escaped him.

"Saw that he so cried out, and gave up the ghost"—Mark's account stresses that the centurion was deeply impressed by the manner of Jesus' death. Matthew notes that he was also awed by the events that accompanied His death.

"Truly this man was the Son of God"—his *truly* marked the centurion's expression as his firm conviction concerning Jesus. *This man* emphatically designates Jesus, while *was* denotes that he felt it was now all over for this remarkable man whom he acknowledged as the Son of God, or better "God's Son." No doubt, he had heard the charge of the Jewish leaders that Jesus "made himself Son of God" (John 19:7, Darby), and certainly he had heard their use of that title in mockery around the cross (Matt. 27:40). He too may have learned that Jesus had demonstrated supernatural powers. Having observed His behavior throughout and heard how Jesus addressed God as His Father, the centurion felt that the claim to be God's Son could not be a lie. It is obvious that the centurion did not use the term in the full Christian

---

[73] Taylor, p. 596.

[74] It had two forms. *Hekatontarchos* is used 16 times in Matthew, Luke, and Acts, and *hekatontarchēs* occurs 5 times in Acts alone.

sense, but clearly Mark regarded the confession as giving expression, whether consciously or unconsciously, to the truth that lay at the very heart of the Christian gospel (cf. 1:1). For him, it formed the true climax to the earthly life of Jesus, the unique Servant of the Lord.

4. Women Watching from Afar (vv. 40-41)

All the synoptics mention these women as witnesses of the crucifixion scene (Matt. 27:55-56; Luke 23:49). Luke here mentions no names but speaks of "all his acquaintance" before mentioning these women. The masculine term indicates that these "acquaintances" were men.

"There were also women looking on afar off"—*also* points to a second group of witnesses. The Roman soldiers had witnessed the events as part of their duty; these witnesses were there because of personal interest and strong affection. John earlier mentioned all the women named here as standing "by the cross" (19:25-27). When John took the mother of Jesus to his own home, the others apparently withdrew to watch from afar, where they would be sufficiently removed from the mocking crowd and yet able to observe all that occurred. *Looking on* carries the picture of a spectator attentively viewing a scene with interest for the purpose of observing details. While the facts of a crucifixion were public knowledge, these women could offer personal, confirmatory evidence.

"Mary Magdalene"—the articular adjective, "the Magdalene," distinguished her from other Marys among the women followers of Jesus; she was from Magdala on the western shore of the Sea of Galilee, about 3 miles north of Tiberias.[75] Whereas she is here first mentioned in Mark, the earliest reference to her is in Luke 8:2, where it is recorded that Jesus freed her of a severe case of demon possession. Except in John 19:25, Mary Magdalene is always named first in these lists of women. Apparently her dynamic personality gave her a position of leadership among the women comparable to that of Peter among the Twelve. Plummer rightly stamps as "a monstrous error" the attempt to identify her with the sinful woman in Luke 7:37-50.[76]

"Mary the mother of James the less and of Joses"—she is distinguished from the other Marys by the names of her sons.[77] In Matthew

---

[75] R. Earle, "Magdalene," in *The Zondervan Pictorial Encyclopedia of the Bible*, Merrill C. Tenney, gen. ed., 4:30.

[76] Plummer, p. 361.

[77] In 15:47 she is called "Mary of Joses" and in 16:1 "Mary of James." The original in 15:40 does not have a word for "mother," being simply "Mary of James the less and Joses." Normally the expression might mean that she was their daughter, which is obviously impossible.

27:61, she is simply called "the other Mary." James the less and Joses were probably well known in the early church. *The less* apparently served to distinguish this James from other men of that name by a reference to his stature, although, not as probably, the reference could be to his age or importance. The view that they are the brothers of Jesus mentioned in 6:3 is improbable; in that case, Mark's indirect identification of the mother of Jesus is strange indeed.

"Salome"—her name appears only in Mark's Gospel (15:40; 16:1). A comparison with Matthew 20:20 and 27:56 indicates that she was "the mother of Zebedee's children." From a comparison with John 19:25, it is commonly held that she was also the sister of Jesus' mother.

"Who also, when he was in Galilee"—*who* limits the reference to the three women just named. It clearly distinguishes them from the "daughters of Jerusalem" who bewailed Jesus (Luke 23:27-28). Their connection with Jesus extended back to His great Galilean ministry.

"Followed him, and ministered unto him"—both verbs are imperfect, picturing their habitual practice, as recorded in Luke 8:2-3. These women followed Jesus from place to place, not merely as His devout hearers but also in order to minister to His needs from their own material means. "During the whole period of His public ministry Jesus was entirely dependent upon the kindness of His friends for sustenance and support."[78]

"Many other women which came up with him unto Jerusalem"— Mark takes notice here of the presence of numerous other women followers who had not been His habitual attendants. All of them had come to Jerusalem for the Passover, but *with him* points to their personal attachment to Jesus. Like the men, they undoubtedly had expected that Jesus would reveal Himself at Jerusalem as the expected Messiah and take steps to establish His kingdom.

F. Burial of the Body (15:42-47)

This paragraph (15:42-47) has a corresponding section in all the other Gospels (Matt. 27:57-61; Luke 23:50-56; John 19:38-42). The burial of Jesus was an important part of the preaching of the early church (1 Cor. 15:3-4). It forms the connecting link between Jesus' actual death and His glorious resurrection.

"Now when the even was come"—Jesus died shortly after 3:00 P.M. *Even* here means the first evening, from midafternoon to sunset, and not the second evening, from sunset to dark, since Jesus was buried

---

[78] J. D. Jones, *Commentary on Mark,* p. 644.

before sundown. It was probably about 4:00 P.M. when Joseph secured permission to remove the body.

"Because it was the preparation"—explaining the urgent need for action to get the body of Jesus buried. *Preparation,* "a making ready," is used in the New Testament as the technical name for Friday, the day of preparation for the Sabbath. Since no work was to be done on the Sabbath, the preceding day was customarily used to prepare all that would be needed during the Sabbath day. The burial had to be completed before the Sabbath began, for no Jew would think of doing it during that day. A further motive was the law in Deuteronomy 21:23 that dead bodies should not remain hanging on a tree overnight. Only the Fourth Gospel records the steps the Jewish leaders took to assure the removal of the bodies before sundown (John 19:31-37).

"That is, the day before the sabbath"—Mark's explanation for his non-Jewish readers. The phrase "that is, pro-sabbath," marks the characteristic feature of the day as preceding the Sabbath. "For the sake of clarity, Mark uses two technical terms here, both of which unmistakably designate what we call 'Friday.' "[79] It confirms that Jesus died on Friday, quite irrespective of the problem of the precise day on which the Passover fell that year.

"Joseph of Arimathaea"—the articular designation, "the one from Arimathaea," distinguishes him from other men called Joseph by indicating his place of origin. *From* implies that he no longer resided at Arimathaea but was a settled resident in Jerusalem, where he had provided a place of burial for himself (Matt. 27:60). The location of Arimathaea is uncertain.

"An honourable counsellor"—the phrase denotes his social prominence. *Honorable* renders an adjective meaning "presentable," or "prominent," and asserts his social position, carrying with it the implication of wealth. Matthew says he was "a rich man." *Counsellor,* "a member of a council," further identifies him as a member of the Sanhedrin (Luke 23:51).

"Which also waited for the kingdom of God"—asserting his characteristic religious attitude. The phrase marks him as a spiritually minded individual, possessing an eager anticipation for the fulfillment of the messianic hope. He had probably long cherished the hope, but the hope was quickened by the appearing of Jesus. John's Gospel reveals that he was a secret disciple of Jesus but that fear kept him from making any public confession of his hope (19:38). Luke notes that "the same had not consented to the counsel and deed of them" (Luke 23:51).

---

[79] Samuel Bacchiocchi, *The Time of the Crucifixion and the Resurrection,* p. 39.

"Came, and went in boldly unto Pilate"—speaking of Joseph's courageous initiative. *Came* does not mean that he now first came to Jerusalem from Arimathaea but that he now stepped forward to prevent the body of Jesus from being profaned by being thrown rudely into a common grave with the two criminals. He apparently knew that Pilate's order to hasten the death of the crucified meant that the bodies would be dumped into a common grave. The action of Joseph is a remarkable instance of God's ability to raise up the needed help from an unexpected source. *Boldly,* an aorist participle, is perhaps best rendered "having dared" or "become bold." The comment is peculiar to Mark. "Through these momentous months his love had been subjected to his fear, but now, in this hour of crisis, love rises triumphant over fear."[80] It took courage to face Pilate, who would likely be in a bad mood toward all Sanhedrin members because they had forced him to crucify Jesus. Joseph also knew that to identify himself with the cause of Jesus would bring upon him the hostility of his colleagues. Probably *boldly* was meant to mark a contrast between his former timidity and this decisive act, marking a change from secret to open discipleship. His action took all the more courage when the cause of Jesus seemed to be hopelessly lost. In approaching Pilate he disregarded ceremonial defilement (cf. John 18:28), since success in his decision to secure and bury the body of Jesus would make him ceremonially unclean anyhow.

"Pilate marvelled if he were already dead"—peculiar to Mark. He marveled not at Joseph's request but at Jesus' early death. *If* means that he did not yet accept as beyond doubt Joseph's report that Jesus had already passed into the state of death (perfect tense). Often death came as long as two or three days after crucifixion. In his question to the centurion Pilate used the aorist tense, asking if the death as an observable event had occurred some time previously.

"When he knew *it* of the centurion"—to assure himself of the speedy demise of Jesus, Pilate called in the centurion for a report. Whether the centurion was still at Golgotha or had returned to headquarters is not indicated. Pilate accepted his report as trustworthy, for the centurion had seen too many people die to be mistaken on the point. Thus the actual death of Jesus was confirmed by official Roman testimony. "This was significant in rebutting a heresy suggesting that he only 'appeared' to die."[81]

"He gave the body to Joseph"—*gave,* or "gave as a gift," suggests that Pilate freely agreed to the request without demanding a fee.

---

[80] Scroggie, p. 277.

[81] English, p. 237.

It was common procedure to relinquish for burial, on request, the dead bodies of those crucified. Only here is the ignoble term "corpse," or "carcass," used of the body of Jesus. Perhaps the terminology reflects Pilate's contempt. Nineham thinks the term reflects "something of St. Mark's stark insistence on the reality of Jesus' death."[82]

"He bought fine linen"—only Mark mentions Joseph's purchase of the linen sheet on his way back to Golgotha. Taylor points to this purchase as support for his view that the crucifixion took place the day before the Passover.[83] But Brooks insists that "the purchase of the linen cloth probably has no significance for dating the crucifixion." He remarks that "probably things that were necessary for burial could be purchased at any time."[84]

"And took him down"—the procedure in removing the body from the cross is not certain, but clearly Joseph had assistance. The Fourth Gospel records that Nicodemus, his fellow counselor, joined him (19:39-40). The contribution which each made to the burial shows that they acted by mutual prearrangement.

"Wrapped him in the linen"—the linen sheet was not merely folded around the body; at least in part, the body was wrapped or bound in linen cloth, with spices freely used between the folds, and then bound with strips of cloth, "as the manner of the Jews is to bury" (John 19:40).

"Laid him in a sepulchre which was hewn out of a rock"—the tomb, near the place of crucifixion (John 19:42), had been cut out horizontally into the side of a rock cliff. Such carefully hewn tombs were common around Jerusalem and generally belonged to well-to-do families. It was Joseph's own tomb (Matt. 27:60) and had never yet been used (Luke 23:53). Jesus' burial in a rich man's tomb was a fulfillment of Isaiah 53:9.

"Rolled a stone unto the door of the sepulchre"—the stone was not a rough boulder but a large, circular, flat stone, fitted with a groove, which could be rolled back to open the tomb when necessary. The stone was rolled over the rectangular entrance to keep out marauding men and beasts. "We may be grateful," English remarks, "that the gospel story includes men like Joseph (and Nicodemus)—not easily persuaded, not naturally given to public demonstration of their loyalties, but in the crisis ready to rise to the occasion as disciples."[85]

---

[82] Nineham, p. 435.

[83] Taylor, p. 601.

[84] Brooks, p. 266.

[85] English, p. 238.

"Mary Magdalene and Mary *the mother* of Joses"—only two of the women mentioned in verse 40 remained. If Salome was the sister of our Lord's mother (cf. v. 40), she had gone to comfort her mourning sister.

"Beheld where he was laid"—Matthew notes that they were "sitting over against the sepulchre" (27:61). The imperfect tense *beheld* stresses that they continued to observe with keen interest all that took place as well as the exact place where the body was laid. Out of love these two women "constituted themselves a party of observation."[86] They apparently remained seated there in silent contemplation even after the tomb was closed. The others, Luke records, "returned, and prepared spices and ointments" (23:56).

---

[86] Gould, p. 298.

Part 4

The Resurrection
of the Servant

15

The Resurrection of the Servant
(16:1-20)

The narrative of Jesus' resurrection forms the grand climax of the story of Jesus Christ in all four Gospels. It is the keystone to the Christian message: without His resurrection, there never would have been any preaching of the good news of salvation in Him. "Every sermon in the book of Acts is a message on the resurrection—every speaker got to this subject. The early Church dwelt upon it constantly."[1]

The Gospel accounts of the resurrection are told with the same dignity and restraint that characterize their narratives of Jesus' crucifixion and death. None of them report all the events, and it is not easy to combine their narratives into one continuous story.[2] But the fragmentary character of the narratives does not imply that they are unreliable. Such differences as exist are "not the fault of the historians, but the natural effect of the events themselves, as impressed upon the sense and the memory of different witnesses."[3]

The last chapter of Mark, devoted to Christ's final victory, falls naturally into two parts. The first part (vv. 1-8) vividly portrays the visit of the women to the empty tomb, while the remainder of the chapter (vv. 9-20) consists of a summary of Jesus' various postresurrection appearances and His ascension.

---

[1] J. Vernon McGee, *Mark,* p. 183.

[2] For a careful study of the postresurrection appearances and the problems of harmonization, see Samuel J. Andrews, *The Life of Our Lord upon the Earth* (1862; reprint ed., 1954), pp. 589-639.

[3] Joseph Addison Alexander, *The Gospel According to Mark,* p. 432.

A. Women Coming to the Empty Tomb (16:1-8)

In all the Gospels, the first incident in the resurrection accounts is the coming of the women to the tomb of Jesus early on the first day of the week (Matt. 28:1-8; Luke 24:1-8; John 20: 1-2). The synoptics have their own differences but are clearly parallel. The narrative in the Fourth Gospel mentions only the coming of Mary Magdalene and the resultant visit of Peter and John to the tomb (20:1-10). "Mark showed that identifiable persons witnessed the crucifixion, the burial, and the empty tomb."[4]

"When the sabbath was past"—the compound verb conveys the thought of an intervening period of time. The women felt that the intervening Sabbath agonizingly frustrated the service which they were eager to perform.

"Mary Magdalene, and Mary the *mother* of James, and Salome"— all three witnessed the crucifixion (15:40), and the first two observed the burial (15:47). In recording the events of early Sunday morning, John spoke only of Mary Magdalene (20:1), Matthew named only two women (28:1), while Luke added the name of Joanna and indicated that there were "other women with them" (24:10). Just how many women were involved is not known, but it is clear that no men came with them. As a reward of their faithfulness, the women were the first to receive intimations of Jesus' resurrection.

"Had bought sweet spices"—their purchase was made Saturday evening after sunset, when the shops opened for a few hours of brisk trade. According to Luke 23:56, some of the women from Galilee "prepared spices and ointments" on Friday evening before sundown. Apparently their evaluation of the supply available prompted further purchases on Saturday evening. *Spices* is a comprehensive term for sweet-smelling substances, here "aromatic oils."

"That they might come and anoint him"—anointing was not the same as embalming, which was not a common Jewish practice. The purpose of the women apparently was to add externally their fragrant ointments as an expression of their love, which they would have done earlier had the Sabbath not intervened. That they still desired to do so after the body had already been in the grave two nights and a day is unusual. "Love often prompts people to do what from a practical point of view is useless."[5] Their purpose is unmistakable evidence that they

---

[4] James A. Brooks, *Mark,* The New American Commentary, p. 268.

[5] C.E.B. Cranfield, *The Gospel According to Saint Mark,* Cambridge Greek Testament Commentary, p. 464.

regarded the death of Jesus as real and final. They had no expectations of His resurrection. Significantly, nothing further is heard of their spices. They were not needed.

''Very early in the morning the first *day* of the week''—the time of day indicates their eagerness to carry out their purpose as soon as possible. All the Gospels stress the earliness of the hour. The expression seemingly denotes a time before sunrise. Whether the women lodged in Bethany or Jerusalem is not known.

''They came unto the sepulchre at the rising of the sun''—''are coming upon the tomb'' vividly pictures their arriving at the spot where the tomb was located. *At the rising of the sun* precisely marks the time as just after sunrise. This time indication has been considered inconsistent with the previous time note. These two references to time occur in one sentence; Mark clearly did not regard them as discordant. Probably, his compressed sentence refers to two facts: the women started just before daybreak but arrived at the tomb when the sun had just risen. Others think that more probably the two statements simply mean that the women came as early in the morning as possible. Jones says, ''The work of anointing needed light, it was useless to arrive before sunrise; hence Mark's 'very early' means at the earliest useful moment.''[6] Then the second designation defines the first.

''They said among themselves''—marking their conversation as they were approaching the tomb. They suddenly remembered the stone which some of them had seen placed before the door (15:46-47), and it became the object of their definite concern.

''Who shall roll away the stone''—a vividly remembered anxiety, recorded in Mark only. Engrossed with their purpose, they had not thought of asking some men to come with them to remove the stone. They now wondered whether they might find some workmen to remove the stone. Obviously the women did not know about the sealing of the tomb and the guards stationed there (Matt. 27:62-66).

''When they looked, they saw that the stone was rolled away''—*when they looked [up]* implies their downcast eyes and anxious consultation; it may suggest that the tomb was at a slight elevation. *Was rolled away* records that the stone had been removed and remained so. The tomb stood open, inviting entry. The stone was rolled back not to let the risen Christ out, but to let the people in to see that He was not there. Mark does not pause to indicate how the stone was rolled back (cf. Matt. 28:2-4).

---

[6] Alexander Jones, *The Gospel According to St. Mark,* p. 245.

"For it was very great"—the phrase is commonly taken as explaining the question in verse 3 but artlessly delayed by Mark until the complete story of the stone was given. But perhaps Mark meant that the stone was so great that the women, from where they were, at once saw what had happened. The open tomb would suggest that violent hands had wrenched the stone away to get access to the body. According to John's account, this was the immediate conclusion of Mary Magdalene (20:2-16).

"Entering into the sepulchre"—preliminary to their startling discovery, they entered the vestibule of the tomb. It was a spacious excavation, intended as a family sepulcher.

"They saw a young man sitting on the right side"—clearly Mark regarded this "young man" as an angelic being, but he is described as he appeared to the women. "The bloom and beauty of youth are never effaced from angelic natures."[7] *The right side* marks his position in relation to the women as they entered. The burial area was to the right of the vestibule.

"Clothed in a long white garment"—the youth was noted as "having thrown around him a white stole." The stole was a long, flowing robe worn by priests and other persons of distinction. *White* asserts not merely its color but its unearthly effulgence. No human youth wore such a robe. Luke spoke of the women's seeing two angels after observing with perplexity that the body was not there (24:3-4). Perhaps Mark was content simply to speak of the angel who acted as spokesman.

"They were affrighted"—the strong compound verb, used only by Mark in the New Testament, expresses a strong feeling of awe and agitation in response to the highly extraordinary. The aorist tense indicates that they were gripped and overwhelmed with wonder.

"He saith unto them, Be not affrighted"—*saith,* the last occurrence of the historic present tense in Mark, dramatically pictures the angel making his unique announcement. It was no apparition they saw, but a being who understood their feelings and at once spoke to calm them, "Stop being amazed."

"Ye seek Jesus of Nazareth, which was crucified"—the angel also knew the purpose of their coming. The original order, "Jesus ye are seeking, the Nazarene, the one having been crucified," stresses that their search centered on a specific person. The double identification serves to portray the extreme humiliation that had befallen Jesus. The

---

[7] James Morison, *Practical Commentary on the Gospel According to St. Mark,* p. 444.

career of the despised Nazarene had ended in the abiding fact of His crucifixion. Because of that end, they had expected to find His body in the tomb. But their search revealed their failure to remember His teaching (Luke 24:5-8). Less probable is the view that the angel's words are to be taken interrogatively, "Are you looking for Jesus?" This would imply that their search was useless labor.

"He is risen; he is not here"—the announcement of the glorious fact with the explanatory result. Thus the first announcement of Jesus' resurrection was made by a heavenly messenger. The aorist tense, *he is risen,* states the reality as a past event. The passive verb may be intransitive in force, "He arose," or carry the passive sense, "He was raised." The verb form is used with either connotation, and both are true. His resurrection explains why they cannot find His dead body in the tomb. The living one is not to be found among the dead. His actual resurrection is nowhere described, and no human eye saw it. The angel with his message provided the needed connecting link between the resurrection event and the condition in the tomb.

"Behold, the place where they laid him"—with his exclamation *Behold,* the angel directed attention to the shelf or niche carved out of the soft rock where the body had been laid. What they saw there was proof that He was no longer dead (cf. John 20:6-7). "Christ in the totality of His personality—soul and body—had risen again."[8] The condition of the grave clothes was the first ground for certainty concerning Jesus' resurrection. The empty tomb has ever since been an apt symbol of Christianity.

"But go your way, tell his disciples and Peter"—the strong adversative, *but,* recalled them from their wonder and awe to the task that the resurrection of Jesus placed upon them. *Go your way,* "be going," is a command to the women. Their knowledge of the truth called for action. "God does not disclose the Resurrection fact except to enlist people in a task."[9] Their faithfulness had qualified them to be the first recipients of the good news, and it laid on them the duty of being its first messengers to His disciples. The addition "and Peter," appearing in Mark only, has poignant force if Mark's Gospel drew from Peter's preaching. Peter was thus singled out, not because of his prominence among the disciples (then he would more likely have been named before the others rather than after them) but as a message of assurance that he was still considered as included in the circle of the

---

[8] J. D. Jones, *Commentary on Mark,* p. 667.

[9] Paul S. Minear, *The Gospel According to Mark,* The Layman's Bible Commentary, p. 134.

disciples, his denials notwithstanding. "It was characteristic of Jesus that he thought, not of the wrong Peter had done him but of the remorse he was undergoing. Jesus was far more eager to comfort the penitent sinner than to punish the sin."[10] In recounting the facts of the resurrection, Peter would not fail to mention this token of Christ's grace to him personally.

"He goeth before you into Galilee"—a reminder to the disciples of the appointment made with them before His arrest (Matt. 26:32; Mark 14:28). In their confusion and sorrow, they had forgotten all about His promise. *Goeth before you* does not mean that He will personally lead them back to Galilee but that He will go there ahead of them. Because of their lack of faith, the disciples did not immediately act on these words. The appearances to them in the vicinity of Jerusalem were necessary to convince them of the reality of His resurrection. The angel's consistent use of *ye* throughout his message to the women implies that the announcement was not confined to the eleven disciples. All the references point to one special, prearranged appearance in Galilee to which all His followers were invited (Matt. 28:16-20; Luke 24:9; 1 Cor. 15:6).

"There shall ye see him"—a clear promise of a resurrection appearance in Galilee. It does not exclude the Jerusalem appearances. (The attempt to turn this into an eschatological appearance, teaching that the *parousia* would occur in Galilee, is not supported by the context.)

"As he said unto you"—added only in Mark. *As,* better "even as," assures them that His promise will have an exact fulfillment. Their acceptance of the announcement of His resurrection hangs upon their acceptance of the veracity of His word. According to Luke (24:5-7), the angels reminded the women of Jesus' teaching of His death and resurrection while yet in Galilee; the fulfillment of His word concerning His death should have assured them that His promise of His resurrection would also be fulfilled.

"They went out quickly, and fled from the sepulchre"—their immediate reaction. Understandably, they fled in a tumult of excitement.

"For trembling and astonishment had come upon them" (ASV)—a description of their emotional condition. *Had come upon* is imperfect tense, "was holding them." It marks their continuing excitement, causing their bodies to tremble. As they gained control of themselves and they began to realize the profound reality that had been declared to

---

[10] William Barclay, *The Gospel of Mark,* p. 369.

them, they felt "great joy" (Matt. 28:8) and astonishment, or "ecstasy." They felt an utter amazement which swept them quite beyond their normal selves.

"Neither said they anything to any *man;* for they were afraid"— the strong double-negative assertion, *neither said they anything to any man,* is peculiar to Mark. It cannot mean that they never delivered the message as directed (cf. Luke 24:9; Matt. 28:8). Mark's statement stresses that the stupendous events so unexpectedly encountered left them with mingled and confused emotions. *Were afraid* is imperfect tense, marking the duration of the feeling. The verb may denote alarm and fright, especially if the verse is regarded as an incomplete sentence. More probably the meaning here is reverential awe at the amazing message disclosed to them. It was an awesome message which they did not dare to break to others; only after they had found those to whom they were to give the message did they find themselves able to speak of it.

B. Longer Ending of Mark (16:9-20)

"The Longer Ending of Mark," the current common designation for these concluding verses (16:9-20), at once points to the textual uncertainty concerning the ending of this Gospel. No other Gospel reveals such variations in the manuscripts concerning its ending or is beset with a similar divergence of scholarly views attempting to explain the existing phenomena. These last twelve verses constitute one of the major textual problems of the New Testament.

The overwhelming majority of the existing Greek manuscripts contain the full twelve verses. They are found in the Greek lectionaries appointed to be read at Easter time and on Ascension Day. The ending is also found in numerous copies of the Old Latin, in the Vulgate, and in other ancient versions. The earliest Christian writers show acquaintance with these verses. They were used by Tatian in compiling his *Diatessaron* (ca. 175), and Irenaeus (ca. 180) quoted verse 19 as being found at the end of Mark.

Over against this voluminous evidence stands strong evidence pointing in the opposite direction. The great uncial manuscripts ℵ and *B,* both dating from the fourth century, end with verse 8. Contrary to his usual practice, the scribe of *B* left a blank column after concluding Mark with the words *according to Mark.* This probably means that he knew of a longer ending but that his copy ended with verse 8. Cursive 2386, of the twelfth century, also ends with verse 8. The longer ending is likewise absent in the Siniatic Old Syriac and in most copies of the Armenian and the Ethiopic versions. A number of cursives have verses 9-20 but add a mark or note of uncertainty concerning them. Four uncial manuscripts, dating from the sixth century or later,[11] as well as manuscripts in the Sahidic, Ethiopic, Harclean Syriac, and the earliest Bohairic copies have two endings. A shorter ending, following verse 8, reads:

> But they reported briefly to Peter and those with him all that they had been told. And after this, Jesus himself sent out by means of them, from east to west, the sacred and imperishable proclamation of eternal salvation (RSV).

This shorter ending is followed by verses 9-20. There can be no doubt that this shorter ending is a scribal addition prompted by an abrupt ending at verse 8. It was a scribal attempt to complete an unfinished account.

Eusebius of Caesarea (ca. 265-340) is the first Christian writer to express doubts concerning the long ending. In dealing with a harmonization of the resurrection accounts in Matthew and Mark, he remarked that ''nearly all the copies of the Gospel according to Mark'' end with verse 8. Jerome, writing from Bethlehem in A.D. 406 or 407, made almost the same statement. Victor of Antioch (fifth century), the first known commentator on Mark, repeated the statement of Eusebius, yet he added comments on the longer ending because he found them in very many copies. An Armenian manuscript of the Gospels written in A.D. 986 contains a note that Mark 16:9-20 was ''of the presbyter Ariston.'' While this statement of authorship is much too late to be of any authority, it does bear witness to the view that these verses were not from the hand of Mark.

Thus, the external evidence is sharply divided. It is generally accepted today that the suspicion thrown on these verses by the external evidence is strongly confirmed by the internal evidence. Hort summarizes this unfavorable evidence: ''It does not join to the end of 8, the change of subject being extremely abrupt. The style is wholly unlike Mark; we have here not a narrative, but a summary or epitome of events after the Resurrection, covering in a few lines a considerable period; and the writer shews a strong desire to 'point a moral', which is not in the least characteristic of Mark.''[12] Harrison further points to transcriptional probability as favoring an abrupt end at verse 8. If verses 9-20 were part of the original, it is difficult to see why the scribes should have omitted them, but if the copies ended abruptly at verse 8,

---

[11] The uncials are *L*, Ψ, 099, 0112. Minuscule 579 of the thirteenth century also has two endings.

[12] A. F. Hort, *The Gospel According to St. Mark,* p. 199.

"it is easy to see that there was a felt need for supplementation."[13] Swete states his evaluation of the phenomena: "When we add to these defects in the external evidence the internal characteristics which distinguish those verses from the rest of the Gospel, it is impossible to resist the conclusion that they belong to another work."[14] Warfield, a staunch conservative likewise concludes, "The combined force of external and internal evidence excludes this section from a place in Mark's Gospel quite independently of the critic's ability to account for the unfinished look of Mark's Gospel as it is left or for the origin of this section itself."[15]

Yet not all students of the problem have reached this same conclusion after studying the phenomena. Although the view labors under serious difficulties, the position that 16:9-20 is a part of the original Gospel of Mark has had its staunch defenders.[16] Some scholars today still feel that it is a live option. They hold that the unfavorable force of the external evidence is blunted by the fact that the early church fathers, who lived one hundred and fifty years before ℵ and *B* were written, quoted it as Scripture.[17] Irenaeus reflects no evidence that its authenticity was questioned. Morison points out that the sweeping statement of Eusebius was motivated by harmonizing interests and that the evidence was not as strong as he presented it.[18] Hills suggests that those texts which omitted these verses probably were influenced from, or had their origin in, Alexandria where "a type of textual criticism flourished which concentrated on the problem of removing spurious additions from literary texts."[19] Proponents admit that there is a marked difference in style and manner of presentation between these verses and the remainder of the Gospel but hold that they are not irreconcilable with their Marcan authorship. They hold that the summary character of its contents is consistent with the writer's special purpose of pointing out the successive steps by which the unwillingness of the apostles to

---

[13] Everett F. Harrison, *Introduction to the New Testament*, pp. 87-88.

[14] Henry Barclay Swete, *The Gospel According to Saint Mark*, p. cxiii.

[15] B. B. Warfield, *An Introduction to the Textual Criticism of the New Testament*, p. 203.

[16] John W. Burgon, *The Last Twelve Verses of the Gospel According to S. Mark;* Morison, pp. 446-49; Samuel Zwemer, *Into All the World*, chapter 5; R.C.H. Lenski, *The Interpretation of St. Mark's and St. Luke's Gospels*, pp. 463-79; Edward F. Hills, *The King James Version Defended!* pp. 102-13.

[17] Hills, p. 109.

[18] Morison, pp. 468-69.

[19] Hills, p. 113.

accept the fact of the resurrection was subdued and they were prepared for the reception and execution of the Great Commission. Proponents point out that these verses do contain some material not in the other Gospels and the fact that there are some apparent discrepancies favors the Marcan authorship, for a later compiler would avoid such differences. Concerning the summary character of the section, Lenski insists that "Mark uses similar and even greater brevity elsewhere" and points to 1:12-13, 14-15.[20] Thus, equally conscientious students differ widely in their evaluation of the actual phenomena. J. D. Jones well concludes: "By whomsoever they were written, these verses were attached to the Gospel from its very earliest days. In the second century they were already recognized as part of the Gospel; and even if they are not Mark's own workmanship, they do not on that account lose their authority and force. We may confidently accept the passage as an 'exceedingly ancient and authentic record of the words and deeds narrated in it.' "[21]

Aware of these divergent views, we turn to our study of this passage, seeking to understand what it says. This "long ending" may be divided into three parts. It presents a summary account of resurrection appearances (vv. 9-14), records the commission of Christ to His followers (vv. 15-18), and closes with His ascension and the preaching of the gospel (vv. 19-20).

1. Appearings of Jesus (vv. 9-14)

Verses 9-14 give a summary report of three different appearances of the risen Christ. Emphasis is laid upon the fact that reports of His resurrection were met with unbelief.

"Now when *Jesus* was risen early the first *day* of the week"—the opening particle *now* is continuative in force, but the account does not follow out the story of the previous verses. Instead of completing the story of the women fleeing from the tomb, it refers to another visit that morning, namely, the return of Mary Magdalene to the tomb and Jesus' appearing to her there (John 20:11-18). *Was risen* leaves the subject unidentified (the italicized *Jesus* was added by the KJV revisers), as though named in what just preceded. This fact is pointed to as evidence that this section comes from a different hand, but advocates of the Marcan origin reply that such an artless writer as Mark did not feel it necessary to name Jesus since "throughout the whole preceding context" he had been "thinking of the risen Saviour."[22]

---

[20] Lenski, p. 467.

[21] J. D. Jones, p. 680.

[22] Morison, p. 450.

"He appeared first to Mary Magdalene"—the verb means that Jesus showed Himself or made Himself visible to her. "So far as we know, none could see Him in this new condition of being but those to whom He was pleased to manifest Himself."[23] *First* may carry an absolute sense or a relative sense in relation to the appearances recorded in this section. If the latter is meant, then the appearance recorded in Matthew 28:9-10 may have taken place earlier.

"Out of whom he had cast seven devils"—since this is the fourth mention of Mary Magdalene (15:40, 47; 16:1), it is indeed strange that this experience was not mentioned earlier. It would have been more natural at 15:40. This naturally seems to suggest that the passage is not from Mark, but proponents of his authorship insist that the mention here is natural as explaining why Christ first appeared to her. *Out of whom he had cast* points to the Person of her Benefactor. "Her faithfulness as one of the women who did not abandon Jesus is rewarded."[24] The perfect tense *had cast* underlines the permanent result of His action.

"She went and told them that had been with him"—*she* is the demonstrative pronoun, "that one," but it is generally agreed that the pronoun here is not emphatic but simply recalls the main subject. Although this is good Greek, it is not in Mark's style. The common verb *went* (*poreuomai*) has not previously appeared in this Gospel. Since Mark had ample opportunity to use the term before, Gould holds that its three occurrences here (vv. 10, 12, 13) are strong evidence of the non-Marcan origin of this passage.[25] Proponents ask why a man must lose his claim to authorship just because he has not used a certain word before. The periphrastic designation *them that had been with him* occurs nowhere else in the Gospels, but it is in harmony with Mark's statement that Jesus appointed twelve "that they should be with him" (3:14; cf. also 5:18). Alexander holds that the term is "suggestive of the fact that they had formerly been with him, but had since forsaken him, and been far from him, at the very time when their presence and attentions seemed to be most needed."[26] The term is elastic and need not be confined to the chosen twelve. (Cf. Acts 1:21.)

"As they mourned and wept"—not derived from the other Gospels. The present participles describe their continuing emotional despondency. They believed that with the death of Jesus, everything was

---

[23] Andrews, p. 590.

[24] David L. McKenna, *Mark,* The Communicator's Commentary, p. 326.

[25] Ezra P. Gould, *A Critical and Exegetical Commentary on the Gospel According to St. Mark,* International Critical Commentary, p. 306.

[26] Alexander, pp. 438-39.

irreparably lost. It was an unconscious fulfillment of John 16:20. Their sorrow stands in contrast to the joy of the people in Jerusalem on that very day observing the Feast of First Fruits (Lev. 23:4-11).

"That he was alive, and had been seen of her, believed not"— Mary reported not only that Jesus was alive but that He had been seen by her. The verb rendered "had been seen," which occurs nowhere else in Mark, indicates that she had attentively viewed Him. She was sure that it was no apparition she had seen. *Believed not* means that they refused to believe her report. They regarded it as the unreliable claim of an overwrought woman who was the victim of some hallucination or optical illusion. Thomas was not the only skeptic who insisted upon having reliable evidence before accepting the claim that Jesus was alive (John 20:24-25). This reaction to Mary's report is not recorded in John's Gospel (20:18); but in Luke, Mary Magdalene is named with the "other *women*" whose "words seemed to them as idle tales, and they believed them not" (24:11).

Verses 12-13 are a two-sentence summary of the story of the Emmaus disciples told in Luke 24:13-35. *Two of them* asserts that they were in the group to whom Mary reported: while not of the eleven, they belonged to "them that had been with him" (v. 10); they had been His close associates. *In another form* could mean in a form different from that in which He had appeared to Mary Magdalene, but more probably the meaning is that He appeared to them in a form which they did not recognize as being Jesus. It is thus in harmony with Luke's statement that their failure to recognize Jesus lay in themselves.

"Neither believed they them"—when reporting back to the group, these two men did not fare any better than Mary Magdalene and the other women. "To reject the woman's testimony is understandable because of Jewish custom, but to scoff at two fellow disciples whose unanimous word is a credible testimony by Jewish Law means that the disciples need to see for themselves before they will believe."[27] This reaction does not appear to be in harmony with Luke 24:34, which says that when the Emmaus disciples returned to Jerusalem they were greeted with the announcement, "The Lord is risen indeed, and hath appeared to Simon." But the remainder of Luke's account shows that the group was still far from being truly convinced that Jesus really was alive. It was not until after Jesus appeared to them and gave them visual demonstration of His identity that they became fully convinced of the reality of His resurrection. Luke's remark that when Jesus suddenly appeared they "supposed that they had seen a spirit" (24:37) suggests

---

[27] McKenna, p. 327.

that they tended to regard all these resurrection appearances as phantom appearances. Perhaps it was due to their inability to understand how He could show Himself now here and now there in one form and then in another.

"Afterward he appeared unto the eleven"—*afterward* is an indefinite designation of time, simply denoting a time subsequent to the appearances just mentioned. "The eleven" here appears to be a reference to the group of Jesus' disciples as such, not to the actual number present. Apparently the reference is to the appearance recorded in Luke 24:36-43 and John 20:19-29. Thomas was absent (John 20:24).

"As they sat at meat"—this is not stated in the other accounts but is implied in Luke 24:41-43.

"Upbraided them with their unbelief and hardness of heart"—the strong verb *upbraided,* "reproached or censured," is not used elsewhere of Jesus in the resurrection accounts. Apparently, this drastic treatment was necessary to shake them out of their unbelief or lack of faith in His resurrection; it was a matter of supreme concern to Him. They were guilty of hardness of heart, obstinacy, and stubbornness, refusing to bow in faith to the evidence before them.

"Because they believed not them which had seen him after he was risen"—stating the reason for His upbraiding. They refused to receive the testimony of eyewitnesses. Plummer remarks, "The Apostles may have been allowed to hear of the Resurrection before seeing the risen Christ in order that they might know from personal experience what it was to have to depend upon the testimony of others, as would be the case with their converts."[28]

2. Commission to His Followers (vv. 15-18)

If these verses are placed in the same paragraph with verse 14, the transition is very abrupt indeed. *And* does not demand any close connection; it simply serves to introduce additional matter. The introductory formula, "And he said unto them," implies a break. What is here recorded is best understood as belonging to a later occasion. Just when and where this commission was given is not known.

"Go ye into all the world"—literally, "having gone into all the world." The aorist participle simply states the preliminary duty. This duty to go forth is worldwide in its scope, inclusive of *all the world.* The adjective *all* is the strengthened form (*hapas*), "the whole, all together," indicating that no part is to be omitted.

[28] Alfred Plummer, *The Gospel According to St. Mark,* Cambridge Greek Testament, p. 372.

"Preach the gospel to every creature"—*preach,* an aorist imperative, is a peremptory command, asserting a binding duty. The verb means to proclaim as a herald. It is the same term used of the preaching of John the Baptist (1:4) and of Jesus Himself (1:14). *The gospel* to be preached is the message of the risen Christ. "The story of Christ, living, dying, rising again is Gospel to all who hear it. It is a faith which is confirmed by all the facts."[29] *Every creature* again stresses the universality of their proclamation. *Creature,* or "creation," here means all mankind, man viewed as the crown and masterpiece of creation. Taylor claims that this cannot be "an actual saying of Jesus; otherwise, the controversy culminating in the Council of Jerusalem (Acts xv.) would not have been possible."[30] But this misconceives the nature of the controversy between Paul and the Judaizers. The question never was whether they were to evangelize the Gentiles but on what terms the Gentiles were to be admitted into the church. Cranfield further observes that such a claim "does not take seriously enough the perverseness and disobedience which have from the beginning been an element in the life of the Church."[31]

"He that believeth and is baptized shall be saved"—passing from the duty to preach the gospel to the result of that preaching. The singular number points to the individual response to the gospel. The aorist participles, "he who believed and was baptized," point to actions viewed as past in relation to the time of the verb "shall be saved." They are united under one article, connecting the inward reception of the gospel by faith and the outward testimony to that faith in baptism. *Shall be saved*—that is, from his sins—states the assured result of faith and confession. The passive voice points to the salvation as God's act.

"He that believeth not shall be damned"—stating the opposite side. There will be others who after having heard the message will respond in disbelief, deliberately refusing to receive it. There was no need to say anything about baptism, since their definite refusal of the message would involve a refusal to make a confession of faith in baptism. Such unbelief carries a serious penalty: "shall be damned," shall have an adverse verdict pronounced against them by the divine Judge. This is the austere side of the gospel and is a part of the full message to be preached.

---

[29] J. D. Jones, p. 704.

[30] V. Taylor, *The Gospel According to St. Mark,* p. 612.

[31] Cranfield, p. 473.

"These signs shall follow them that believe"—*these* looks forward to the five kinds of signs enumerated as specimens. These signs are promised to accompany, to attend closely, "them that believe," those who as a definite act of faith embraced the gospel. The promise points to faith as the initial and fundamental feature of the Christian life. It is not limited to the preachers but includes their converts. No *all* is added. The promise is not that each individual believer will experience such signs in his own life. The promise is to the church collectively. Jesus referred to these miraculous occurrences as signs, events pointing to something beyond and higher than themselves. These signs were the authenticating credentials of the apostolic message, exhibiting the presence of the living Christ working with and through His messengers. They served to accredit not the faith of the individual but the validity of the faith he represented. "The infant Church needed them, the adult Church is not without them"[32] McGee notes, "They disappeared even in the early church, but they do manifest themselves on some primitive mission frontiers even today."[33]

"In my name"—this qualifying phrase stands emphatically at the head of this list of signs. The power will not be their own, nor is it to be exercised for their own aggrandizement. The signs will be granted as they invoke Christ's power as His representatives.

"Cast out devils"—an experience already familiar to them. The Twelve (6:13) as well as the seventy (Luke 10:17-19) had already exercised the gift to exorcise demons. The ability continued in the apostolic church (Acts 8:7; 16:18; 19:15-16). It proclaimed Christ's victory over the realm of Satan. This miracle is "placed in the first rank among the miracles of Jesus and his apostles, as extending to another world and to another race of spiritual beings."[34]

"Speak with new tongues"—this can mean only languages not before known to the speakers. The promise was fulfilled at Pentecost and in the later experiences of the church (Acts 2:4-11; 10:46; 19:6; 1 Cor. 12:10; 14:1-28).

"Take up serpents"—Paul's experience at Melita when he unintentionally picked up a serpent (Acts 28:3-4) is the only New Testament instance of this type of miracle. Clearly, Christ's promise of immunity points to an occasion when His disciples shall be compelled by their persecutors to go through such an ordeal. There is no evidence that voluntary snake-handling was a practice in the early church. Thompson

---

[32] Alexander Jones, p. 249.

[33] McGee, p. 187.

[34] Alexander, p. 442.

asserts, "Modern cultists who handle rattlesnakes and copperheads thinking that the Scripture has promised them immunity are badly mistaken."[35]

"And if they drink any deadly thing, it shall not hurt them"—*and* combines this miracle with the preceding, indicating that in both supernatural protection was in view. The double negative in the original, simply rendered *not,* strengthens the assurance. The New Testament records no instance of such an experience, but Eusebius preserves the testimony of Papias that Justus Barsabas had such an experience.[36] Bruce declares that these two miracles "introduce us into the twilight of apocryphal story."[37] Authenticated instances of such miracles are rare in the history of the church, but is it fair to stamp such experiences "apocryphal" whenever the living Christ has reportedly given His servants such a manifestation of His protecting power?

"Shall lay hands on the sick"—healing the sick, "the strengthless," those made weak by sickness, is a well-known miraculous gift in the New Testament (1 Cor. 12:30). Only in Acts 28:8 is there mention of the laying on of hands for the purpose of healing. It is interesting that the anointing with oil is not mentioned here (cf. Mark 6:13; James 5:14).

3. Ascension of the Lord Jesus (vv. 19-20)

This closing picture is in two parts, describing the ascension of the Lord Jesus and the subsequent activities of His followers. The use, in the original, of *men,* "on the one hand" (v. 19), and *de,* "on the other hand" (v. 20), clearly marks the distinction between the exalted Lord and the mission of His servants.

"After the Lord had spoken unto them"—the time and place are left indefinite. *After* looks back to the communications just recorded; how long after is left undetermined. The aorist tense *spoken* implies that His postresurrection communications to them had been completed. The designation "the Lord," here "does not mean that something had happened which has 'ennobled' Christ; but that something has happened which enabled the disciples to see the glory that had been His all along. That something was the Resurrection."[38]

---

[35] Ernest Trice Thompson, *The Gospel According to Mark and Its Meaning for Today,* p. 244.

[36] Eusebius *Ecclesiastical History* 3. 39.

[37] A. B. Bruce, "The Synoptic Gospels," *The Expositor's Greek New Testament,* 1:465-66.

[38] J. D. Jones, p. 711.

"Was received up into heaven, and sat on the right hand of God"—the first part of the double statement was visually observed by His followers (Luke 24:50-51; Acts 1:9), but the second part, also here recorded as a historical fact, was not a matter of their actual observation. Morison calls it "the language of spiritual insight and inspiration."[39] Their unquestioned acceptance of His heavenly enthronement was based directly on the prophetic declaration in Psalm 110:1. On the day of Pentecost, Peter pointed to the occurrences of that day as proof of Jesus' exaltation at the right hand of God (Acts 2:33-35). The reality of His heavenly exaltation was confirmed by the vision granted to Stephen (Acts 7:56).

"They went forth, and preached every where"—summarily recording the prompt and widespread activity of the early church. *Went forth* does not make clear their point of departure. The aorist participle simply records the fact as preliminary to their work of heralding the gospel everywhere, in every place where the doors were opened to them.

"The Lord working with *them*"—the present participle denotes the Lord's continued cooperation with His messengers. The verb, also used by Paul in 2 Corinthians 6:1, denotes "the gracious use of human instrumental agency in executing the divine plan."[40] Their activity was empowered by Him; He did through them that which they could not do themselves.

"Confirming the word with signs following"—the present tenses again picture the repeated activities. The mention of the signs as "confirming," establishing and authenticating, "the word," the gospel message, indicates that their preaching of that message was their central activity. "Their work was done in a blessed partnership."[41]

Opponents of the Marcan authorship of these verses point out that in this last verse three verbs appear, *working with, confirming,* and *followed,* which do not occur elsewhere in this Gospel. Gould remarks that "they belong to the vocabulary of the Pauline Epistles."[42] Lenski replies, "All the words are simple, the very ones that are proper for the thought, and no law exists that in a small book like Mark's every word has to be used at least twice in order to be used at all."[43]

---

[39] Morison, p. 462.

[40] Alexander, p. 444.

[41] J. D. Jones, p. 720.

[42] Gould, p. 308.

[43] Lenski, p. 478.

The felt difficulties concerning the longer ending of Mark are not of modern origin, but the developments of modern textual criticism have brought them into sharper focus. We have seen that these difficulties have received different evaluations with regard to their significance for the Marcan authorship. While a few scholars still believe that the evidence is not inconsistent with Mark's authorship, the majority of modern scholars are convinced that the combined external and internal evidence shuts out that conclusion.

No one today suggests that the shorter ending, found in a few manuscripts, has any claim to recognition as the authentic ending.[44] The acceptance of the conclusion that the longer ending was not written by Mark leaves open two alternative positions.

First, the original Gospel of Mark, terminating with verse 8, is incomplete. This view had evoked a variety of hypotheses seeking to explain the incompleteness. The suggestion that the original ending was later intentionally removed is difficult to take seriously. It involves the inconceivable position that these mutilated copies completely displaced the older copies with the original ending. More plausible is the generally accepted view that the original ending has been *accidentally* lost. According to this view, the scroll containing Mark's Gospel lost its last page, leaving it incomplete. But the ending of the manuscript in the scroll would ordinarily be on the inside and less likely to be damaged than the beginning. Also, if the ending was accidentally lost, it must have happened very early; otherwise the lost ending could have been recovered from other copies. The early interest in Mark's Gospel makes it highly improbable that only one mutilated copy survived. Another conjecture is that Mark stopped with verse 8, intending to complete the story, but something happened to him so that the work was never finished. In the very nature of the case, such a conjecture cannot be confirmed, but it is the most plausible suggestion if the incompleteness of Mark is assumed.

A second possibility is that Mark intended to conclude with verse 8. According to this view, the Gospel of Mark has been entirely preserved as written. Modern scholars are increasingly inclining toward the abrupt ending.[45] It is maintained that this theory best accounts for

---

[44] The printing of this ending in the RSV as an alternative ending without indicating that it has very meager textual support cannot be approved. To place it thus alongside the longer ending as a possible alternative is to do injustice to the evidence for the longer ending.

[45] See the references in Werner Georg Kümmel, *Introduction to the New Testament*, pp. 71-72. For a full presentation of the view, see Ned Bernard Stonehouse, *The Witness of Matthew and Mark to Christ* (2nd ed.), chapter 4.

the confusion that exists concerning the ending of Mark. The abrupt ending, which leaves the initial impression of incompleteness, explains the origin of both the longer and the shorter endings as scribal attempts to provide an acceptable conclusion. It also explains the widespread phenomenon of the manuscripts terminating with verse 8. It is further asserted that this abrupt ending is in keeping with Mark's abrupt style throughout. Stylistic evidence for the possibility that the book could have ended with "for" (*gar*) has received at least partial verification. It is further held that the real point in this abrupt conclusion lies not in verse 8 but rather in verse 7, where the reality of Jesus' resurrection in accordance with His word is declared. This provides striking testimony to the fact that the resurrection of Christ is a matter of faith which must be accepted on the basis of God's Word. The brief ending thus leaves the women in awed, silent reflection upon the marvel of His resurrection which has been declared to them.

The serious objection to the view that the Gospel ended with intentional abruptness at verse 8 is the feeling that it is highly improbable Mark would end his story without any personal appearances of the risen Christ. References to such appearances cannot be regarded as unimportant for a complete Gospel. The resurrection appearances formed an important part of early gospel preaching (1 Cor. 15:5-8). So abrupt an ending leaves unfulfilled the promise of His appearing to His disciples given in verse 7. The existence of two different endings in the manuscripts bears strong testimony to the common feeling throughout the course of Christian history that to end at verse 8 is to leave the story incomplete.

None of the views proposed to explain the complex phenomena concerning the end of Mark are without difficulties. While no one can maintain that the longer ending can no longer be regarded as a possible option, that view is beset with grave difficulties. That the true ending has been lost involves conjectures which cannot be verified. The view that Mark actually ended with verse 8, is not without its difficulties, but is worthy of serious consideration as a possible solution.

BIBLIOGRAPHY

Biblical Texts

Greek

Aland, Kurt; Black, Matthew; Metzger, Bruce M.; and Wikgren, Allen, eds. *The Greek New Testament*. London: United Bible Soc., 1966.

Aland, Kurt; Black, Matthew; Martini, Carlo M.; Metzger, Bruce M.; and Wikgren, Allen, eds. *The Greek New Testament*. 3rd ed. London: United Bible Soc., 1975.

Hodges, Zane C., and Farstad, Arthur L., eds. *The Greek New Testament According to the Majority Text*. Nashville: Thomas Nelson Publishers, 1982.

Nestle, Erwin, and Aland, Kurt. *Novum Testamentum Graece*. 24th ed. New York: American Bible Soc., n.d.

Scrivener, F. H. *Hē Kainē Diathēkē. Novum Testamentum. Textus Stephanici A.D. 1550*. London: Cantabrigiae, Deighton, Bell et Soc, 1867. (The Textus Receptus).

Westcott, Brooke Foss, and Hort, Fenton John Anthony. *The New Testament in the Original Greek*. 2nd ed. 1907. Reprint. New York: Macmillan, 1935.

English Versions

Beck, William F. *The New Testament in the Language of Today*. St. Louis: Concordia, 1964.

Darby, J. N. *The "Holy Scriptures": A New Translation from the Original Languages*. Reprint. Kingston-on-Thames, Eng.: Stow Hill, 1949.

Goodspeed, Edgar J. *The New Testament, An American Translation*. 1923. Reprint. Chicago: University of Chicago Press, 1951.

King James Version. *The Holy Bible Containing the Old and New Testaments*. Nashville: Holman Bible Publishers, 1979.

Moffatt, James. *The New Testament: A New Translation.* Rev. ed. New York: George H. Doran, n.d.

New American Standard Bible. Carol Stream, Ill.: Creation House, 1971.

New English Bible, New Testament. Oxford and Cambridge: University Press, 1961.

New Testament in Today's English Version. New York: American Bible Soc., 1966.

Norlie, Olaf M. *Norlie's Simplified New Testament in Plain English— For Today's Reader.* Grand Rapids: Zondervan, 1961.

Revised Standard Version. *The Holy Bible, Containing the Old and New Testaments.* Philadelphia: A. J. Holman, 1962.

Rotherham, Joseph Bryant. *The Emphasized New Testament.* Reprint. Grand Rapids: Kregel, 1959.

Weymouth, Richard Francis. *The New Testament in Modern Speech.* Revised by James Alexander Robertson. 5th ed. New York: Harper, 1929.

Williams, Charles B. *The New Testament: A Private Translation in the Language of the People.* Reprint. Chicago: Moody, n.d.

Wuest, Kenneth S. *The Gospels.* Wuest's Expanded Translation of the Greek New Testatment, vol. 1. Grand Rapids: Eerdmans, 1956.

German Version

Luther, Martin. *Die Bibel, oder die ganze Heilige Schrift des Alten and Neuen Testaments.* Stuttgart: Wurttembergische Bibleanstalt, 1897.

Books on the Gospel of Mark

Abbott, Lyman. ''The Gospel According to Mark.'' In *An Illustrated Commentary on the Gospels.* New York: A. S. Barnes, 1906.

Alexander, Joseph Addison. *The Gospel According to Mark.* 1881. Reprint. London: Banner of Truth, 1960.

Anderson, Hugh. *The Gospel of Mark.* New Century Bible. London: Marshall, Morgan & Scott. 1976.

Barclay, William. *The Gospel of Mark.* Rev. ed. The Daily Study Bible. Philadelphia: Westminster Press, 1975.

Barnhouse, Donald Grey. *Mark, The Servant Gospel.* Edited by Susan T. Lutz. Wheaton, Ill.: Victor Books, 1988.

Blunt, A.W.F. *The Gospel According to Saint Mark.* The Clarendon Bible. Oxford: Clarendon, 1929.

Branscomb, B. Harvie. *The Gospel of Mark.* Moffatt New Testament Commentary. London: Hodder & Stoughton, 1937.

Brooks, James A. *Mark.* The New American Commentary. Nashville: Broadman Press, 1991.

Bruce, Alexander Balmain. "The Synoptic Gospels." In *The Expositor's Greek Testament.* Vol. 1. Reprint. Grand Rapids: Eerdmans, n.d.

Clarke, W. N. *Commentary on the Gospel of Mark.* An American Commentary. 1881. Reprint. Philadelphia: American Baptist Publications Society, n.d.

Cole, R. A. *The Gospel According to St. Mark.* Tyndale New Testament Commentaries. Grand Rapids: Eerdmans, 1961.

Cranfield, C.E.B. *The Gospel According to Saint Mark.* Cambridge Greek Testament Commentary. Cambridge: University Press, 1966.

Earle, Ralph. *The Gospel According to Mark.* The Evangelical Commentary. Grand Rapids: Zondervan, 1957.

English, Donald. *The Message of Mark: The Mystery of Faith.* The Bible Speaks Today. Downers Grove, Ill.: InterVarsity Press, 1992.

English, E. Schuyler. *Studies in the Gospel According to Mark.* New York: Our Hope, 1943.

Gould, Ezra P. *A Critical and Exegetical Commentary on the Gospel According to St. Mark.* International Critical Commentary. Edinburgh: T. & T. Clark, 1896.

Grant, Frederick C., and Luccock, Halford E. "The Gospel According to St. Mark." In *The Interpreter's Bible.* Vol. 7. New York: Abingdon-Cokesbury, 1951.

Guelish, Robert A. *Mark 1–8:26.* Word Biblical Commentary. Dallas: Word Books, 1989.

Gutzke, Manford George. *Go Gospel: Daily Devotions and Bible Studies in the Gospel of Mark.* Glendale, Calif.: Gospel Light, Regal Books, 1968.

———. *Plain Talk on Mark.* Grand Rapids: Zondervan, 1975.

Harrisville, Roy A. *The Miracle of Mark: A Study in the Gospel.* Minneapolis: Augsburg Publishing House, 1967.

Hort, A. F. *The Gospel According to St. Mark.* 1902. Reprint. Cambridge: University Press, 1928.

Hurtado, Larry W. *Mark.* A Good News Commentary. San Francisco: Harper & Row, Publishers, 1983.

Jamieson, Robert; Fausset, A. R.; and Brown, David. *New Testament.* A Commentary, Critical and Explanatory, on the Old and New Testaments, vol. 2. Hartford: S. S. Scranton, n.d.

Johnson, Sherman E. *A Commentary on the Gospel According to St. Mark.* Black's New Testament Commentaries. London: Adam & Charles Black, 1960.

Jones, Alexander. *The Gospel According to St. Mark: A Text and Commentary for Students.* New York: Sheed & Ward, 1963.

Jones, J. D. *Commentary on Mark.* 1914. Reprint. Grand Rapids: Kregel Publications, 1992.

Kelly, William. *An Exposition of the Gospel of Mark.* Reprint. London: C. A. Hammond, 1934.

Lenski, R.C.H. *The Interpretation of St. Mark's and St. Luke's Gospels.* Columbus, Ohio: Lutheran Book Concern, 1934.

Lindsay, Thomas M. *The Gospel According to St. Mark.* Handbooks for Bible Classes. Edinburgh: T. & T. Clark, 1883.

McGee, J. Vernon. *Mark.* Pasadena: Thru the Bible Books, 1975.

McKenna, David L. *Mark.* The Communicator's Commentary. Dallas: Word Books, 1982.

Maclaren, Alexander. "St. Mark." In *Expositions of Holy Scripture.* Vol. 8. Reprint. Grand Rapids: Eerdmans, 1944.

Maclear, G. F. *The Gospel According to St. Mark.* Cambridge Bible for Schools and Colleges. Cambridge: University Press, 1890.

McGarvey, J. W. *Matthew and Mark.* The New Testament Commentary. 1875. Reprint. Delight, Ark.: Gospel Light, n.d.

Marshall, I. H. *St. Mark.* Scripture Union Bible Study Books. London: Scripture Union, 1967.

Martindale, C. C. *The Gospel According to Saint Mark.* Stonyhurst Scripture Manuals. London: Longmans, Green & Co., 1955.

Meyer, Heinrich August Wilhelm. *Critical and Exegetical Hand-Book to the Gospels of Mark and Luke.* Meyer's Critical and Exegetical Commentary on the New Testament. Translated, revised, and edited by William P. Dickson. New York: Funk & Wagnalls, 1884.

Minear, Paul S. *The Gospel According to Mark.* The Layman's Bible Commentary. Richmond, Va.: Knox, 1962.

Morgan, G. Campbell. *The Gospel According to Mark.* New York: Revell, 1927.

Morison, James. *A Practical Commentary on the Gospel According to St. Mark.* 8th ed. London: Hodder & Stoughton, 1896.

Moule, C.F.D. *The Gospel According to Mark.* The Cambridge Bible Commentary. Cambridge: University Press, 1965.

Nineham, D. E. *The Gospel of St. Mark.* Pelican Gospel Commentaries. Baltimore: Penguin Books, 1967.

Plummer, A. *The Gospel According to St. Mark.* Cambridge Greek Testament. 1914. Reprint. Cambridge: University Press, 1938.

Plumptre, E. H. "The Gospel According to St. Mark." In *Ellicott's Commentary on the Whole Bible.* Vol. 6. Reprint. Grand Rapids: Zondervan, 1954.

Rawlinson, A.E.J. *St. Mark.* Westminster Commentaries. London: Methuen, 1925.

Riddle, Matthew B. *The Gospel According to Mark.* The International Revision Commentary on the New Testament. New York: Scribner, 1881.

Robertson, A. T. *Studies in Mark's Gospel.* Revised and edited by Heber F. Peacock. Nashville: Broadman, 1958.

Ryle, J. C. *Expository Thoughts on the Gospels.* 1866. Reprint (6 vols. in 4). Grand Rapids: Zondervan, 1956.

Salmond, S.D.E. *St. Mark.* The Century Bible. Edinburgh: T. C. & E. C. Jack, n.d.

Scroggie, W. Graham. *The Gospel of Mark.* Study Hour Commentaries. Grand Rapids: Zondervan, 1976.

Sloyan, Gerard S. *The Gospel of St. Mark.* New Testament Reading Guide. Collegeville, Minn.: Liturgical Press, 1960.

Swete, Henry Barclay. *The Gospel According to St. Mark: The Greek Text with Introduction, Notes, and Indices.* 1898. Reprint. London: Macmillan, 1905.

Swift, C. E. Graham. "Mark." In *The New Bible Commentary, Revised.* Edited by D. Guthrie and J. A. Motyer. Downers Grove, Ill.: InterVarsity, 1970.

Taylor, Vincent. *The Gospel According to St. Mark, the Greek Text with Introduction, Notes, and Indexes.* New York: St. Martin's, 1966.

Thompson, Ernest Trice. *The Gospel According to Mark and Its Meaning for Today.* Rev. ed. Richmond, Va.: John Knox Press, 1962.

Williams, George. *The Student's Commentary on the Holy Scriptures.* 5th ed. London: Oliphants, 1949.

Williamson, Lamar, Jr. *Mark.* Interpretation: A Bible Commentary for Teaching and Preaching. Atlanta: John Knox Press, 1983.

Wuest, Kenneth S. *Mark in the Greek New Testament for the English Reader.* Grand Rapids: Eerdmans, 1950.

Other Books

Adams, J. McKee. *Biblical Backgrounds.* Revised by Joseph A. Callaway. Nashville: Broadman, 1965.

Alexander, William Menzies. *Demonic Possessions in the New Testament: Its Relations Historical, Medical, and Theological.* Edinburgh: T. & T. Clark, 1902.

Andrews, Samuel J. *The Life of Our Lord upon the Earth.* 1862. Reprint. Grand Rapids: Zondervan, 1954.

Arndt, William F., and Gingrich F. Wilbur. *A Greek-English Lexicon of the New Testament and Other Early Christian Literature.* Chicago: University of Chicago Press, 1957.

Avi-Yonah, Michael. *The Holy Land, from the Persian to the Arab Conquests.* Grand Rapids: Baker, 1966.

Bacchiocchi, Samuele. *The Time of the Crucifixion and the Resurrection.* Enlarged ed. Berrien Springs, Mich.: Biblical Perspectives, 1991.

Banks, Florence Aiken. *Coins of Bible Days.* New York: Macmillan, 1955.

Barbet, Pierre. *A Doctor at Calvary: The Passion of Our Lord Jesus Christ as Described by a Surgeon.* New York: P. J. Kennedy, 1953.

Barclay, William. *The Master's Men.* New York: Abingdon, 1959.

Bigg, Charles. *A Critical and Exegetical Commentary on the Epistles of St. Peter and St. Jude.* International Critical Commentary. 1901. Reprint. Edinburgh: T. & T. Clark, 1910.

Bishop, Eric F.F. *Jesus of Palestine: The Local Background of the Gospel Documents.* London: Lutterworth, 1955.

Burgon, John W. *The Last Twelve Verses of the Gospel According to S. Mark.* 1871. Reprint. Sovereign Grace Book Club, 1959.

Caldecott, W. Shaw. *Herod's Temple: Its New Testament Associations and Its Actual Structure.* London: Charles H. Kelly, n.d.

Cheney, Johnston M. *The Life of Christ in Stereo: The Four Gospels Combined as One.* Edited by Stanley A. Ellisen. Portland, Oreg.: Western Baptist, 1969.

Christie, W. M. *Palestine Calling.* London: Pickering & Inglis, n.d.

Cummings, Robert W. *Gethsemane.* Springfield, Mo.: Gospel Publishing, 1944.

Danby, Herbert, trans. *The Mishnah.* 1933. Reprint. Oxford: University Press, 1964.

Deissmann, Adolf. *Light from the Ancient East.* Translated by Lionel R.M. Strachan. London: Hodder & Stoughton, 1910.

Edersheim, Alfred. *The Life and Times of Jesus the Messiah.* New York: Longmans, Green, 1901.

———. *The Temple: Its Ministry and Services as They Were at the Time of Jesus Christ.* Reprint. Grand Rapids: Eerdmans, 1950.

Emerson, James G., Jr. *Divorce, the Church, and Remarriage.* Philadelphia: Westminster Press, 1961.

Farrar, Fredric W. *The Life of Christ.* New York: N. Tibbals, 1876.

Feinberg, Charles Lee. *Israel in the Last Days: The Olivet Discourse.* Altadena, Calif.: Emeth, 1953.

Foster, R. C. *Studies in the Life of Christ: The Final Week.* Grand Rapids: Baker, 1962.

Geldenhuys, Norval. *Commentary on the Gospel of Luke.* The New International Commentary on the New Testament. Grand Rapids: Eerdmans, 1950.

Guthrie, Donald. *New Testament Introduction.* Rev. ed. Downers Grove, Ill.: InterVarsity, 1971.

Harrison, Everett F. *Introduction to the New Testament.* Rev. ed. Grand Rapids: Eerdmans, 1971.

Hiebert, D. Edmond. *An Introduction to the Non-Pauline Epistles.* Chicago: Moody, 1962.

―――. *In Paul's Shadow: Friends & Foes of the Great Apostle.* Greenville, S.C.: Bob Jones University Press, 1992.

Hills, Edward F. *The King James Version Defended!* Des Moines, Iowa: Christian Research, 1956.

Howard, W. F. *Christianity According to St. John.* Philadelphia, Westminster Press, 1946.

Ice, Thomas, and Price, Randall. *Ready to Rebuild: The Imminent Plan to Rebuild the Last Days Temple.* Eugene, Oreg.: Harvest House Publishers, 1992.

Jeremias, Joachim. *The Eucharistic Words of Jesus.* New York: Scribner, 1966.

Josephus, Flavius. *The Life and Works of Flavius Josephus.* Translated by William Whiston. Philadelphia: John C. Winston, n.d.

Kelly, J.N.D. *A Commentary on the Epistles of Peter and of Jude.* Harper's New Testament Commentaries. New York: Harper & Row, 1969.

Kümmel, Werner Georg. *Introduction to the New Testament.* Revised, edited, and translated by A. J. Mattill, Jr. Nashville: Abingdon, 1966.

McBirnie, William S. *The Search for the Twelve Apostles.* Wheaton, Ill.: Tyndale, 1973.

McClain, Alva J. *The Greatness of the Kingdom.* Chicago: Moody, 1959.

Mansfield, M. Robert. *"Spirit and Gospel" in Mark.* Peabody, Mass.: Hendrickson Publishers, 1987.

Manson, T. W. *Studies in the Gospels and Epistles.* Edited by Matthew Black. Philadelphia: Westminster Press, 1962.

Metzger, Bruce M. *A Textual Commentary on the Greek New Testament: A Companion Volume to the United Bible Societies' Greek New Testament (Third Edition).* London: United Bible Societies, 1971.

Moldenke, Harold N., and Moldenke, Alma L. *Plants of the Bible.* New York: Ronald, 1952.

Morgan, G. Campbell. *The Gospel According to Matthew.* New York: Revell, 1929.

Morris, Leon. *The Gospel According to John.* The New International Commentary on the New Testament. Grand Rapids: Eerdmans, 1971.

Moulton, James Hope. *Prolegomena.* A Grammar of New Testament Greek, vol. 1. Edinburgh: T. & T. Clark, 1908.

Moulton, James Hope, and Milligan, George. *The Vocabulary of the Greek Testament Illustrated from the Papyri and Other Non-Literary Sources.* Reprint. London: Hodder & Stoughton, 1952.

Murray, John. *Divorce.* Philadelphia: Presbyterian & Reformed, 1961.

Nevius, John L. *Demon Possessions and Allied Themes: Being an Inductive Study of Phenomena of Our Own Times.* New York: Revell, 1892.

Pentecost, J. Dwight. *Things to Come.* Findlay, Ohio: Dunham, 1958.

Price, Walter K. *Jesus' Prophetic Sermon: The Olivet Key to Israel, the Church, and the Nations.* Chicago: Moody, 1972.

Robertson, A. T. *A Grammar of the Greek New Testament in the Light of Historical Research.* 5th ed. New York: Richard R. Smith, 1923.

————. *A Harmony of the Gospels for Students of the Life of Christ.* New York: Harper, 1922.

Ropes, James Hardy. *A Critical and Exegetical Commentary on the Epistle of St. James.* International Critical Commentary. New York: Scribner, 1916.

Scott, Ernest Findlay. *The Literature of the New Testament.* 1932. Reprint. New York: Columbia University. 1948.

Sloan, W. W. *A Survey of the New Testament.* New York: Philosophical Library, 1961.

Stauffer, Ethelbert. *Jesus and His Story.* Translated by Richard and Clara Winston. New York: Alfred A. Knopf, 1960.

Stonehouse, Ned Bernard. *The Witness of Matthew and Mark to Christ.* 2nd ed. Grand Rapids: Eerdmans, 1958.

Unger, Merrill F. *Biblical Demonology: A Study of the Spiritual Forces Behind the Present World Unrest.* Wheaton, Ill.: Van Kampen, 1952.

————. *Demons in the World Today.* Wheaton, Ill.: Tyndale, 1971.

Warfield, Benjamin B. *An Introduction to the Textual Criticism of the New Testament.* London: Hodder & Stoughton, 1899.

————. *The Lord of Glory: A Study of the Designations of Our Lord in the New Testament with Special Reference to His Deity.* Reprint. Grand Rapids: Zondervan, n.d.

Wenham, John. *Redating Matthew, Mark and Luke: A Fresh Assault on the Synoptic Problem.* Downers Grove, Ill.: InterVarsity Press. 1992.

Wikenhauser, Alfred. *New Testament Introduction.* New York: Herder, 1963.

Wuest, Kenneth S. *Studies in the Vocabulary of the Greek New Testament for the English Reader.* Grand Rapids: Eerdmans, 1945.

Zwemer, Samuel M. *"Into All the World."* Grand Rapids: Zondervan, 1943.

Dictionary and Encyclopedia Articles

Boettner, Loraine. "Intermediate State." *Baker's Dictionary of Theology,* edited by Everett F. Harrison. Grand Rapids: Baker, 1960.

Bruce, F. F. "Messiah." *The New Bible Dictionary.* Edited by J. D. Douglas. Grand Rapids: Eerdmans, 1962.

Earle, R. "Magdalene." *The Zondervan Pictorial Encyclopedia of the Bible.* Edited by Merrill C. Tenney. Grand Rapids: Zondervan, 1975.

Foerster, Werner. *"daimōn, daimonion."* *Theological Dictionary of the New Testament.* Edited by Gerhard Kittel. Grand Rapids: Eerdmans, 1964.

Gould, George P. "Son of Man." *A Dictionary of Christ and the Gospels.* Edited by James Hastings. Edinburgh: T. & T. Clark, 1909.

Harrop, J. H. "Publican." *The New Bible Dictionary.* Edited by J. D. Douglas. Grand Rapids: Eerdmans, 1962.

Hillyer, Norman. "Salt." *The New International Dictionary of the New Testament Theology.* Edited by Colin Brown. Grand Rapids: Zondervan, 1978.

Ladd, George E. "Kingdom of God." *Zondervan Pictorial Bible Dictionary.* Edited by Merrill C. Tenney. Grand Rapids: Zondervan, 1963.

Michel, Otto. *"tēlonēs."* *Theological Dictionary of the New Testament.* Edited by Gerhard Friedrich. Grand Rapids: Eerdmans, 1972.

Richardson, Alan. "Kingdom of God." *A Theological Word Book of the Bible.* Edited by Alan Richardson. New York: Macmillan, 1951.

Ridderbos, H. "Kingdom of God, Kingdom of Heaven." *The New Bible Dictionary.* Edited by J. D. Douglas. Grand Rapids: Eerdmans, 1962.

Schaeder, H. H. *"Nazarēnos, Nazōraios."* *Theological Dictionary of the New Testament.* Edited by Gerhard Kittel. Grand Rapids: Eerdmans, 1967.

Schrenk, Gottlob. *"eudokeō, eudokia."* *Theological Dictionary of the New Testament.* Edited by Gerhard Kittel. Grand Rapids: Eerdmans, 1964.

Stalker, James. "The Son of Man." *The International Standard Bible Encyclopedia.* Edited by James Orr. Grand Rapids: Eerdmans, 1939.

Wallace, David H. "Messiah," *Baker's Dictionary of Theology.* Edited by Everett F. Harrison. Grand Rapids: Baker, 1960.

Wright, D. F. "Papias." *The New International Dictionary of the Christian Church.* Edited by J. D. Douglas. Grand Rapids: Zondervan, 1974.

Wright, J. S. "Possession." *The New Bible Dictionary.* Edited by J. D. Douglas. Grand Rapids: Eerdmans, 1962.

Periodical Articles

Conley, Drew. "The Christology of the Gospel of Mark: Portrait of the Suffering Sovereign." *Biblical Viewpoint* 25 (April 1991): 59-67.

McCall, Thomas S. "How Soon the Tribulation Temple?" *Bibliotheca Sacra* vol. 128, no. 512 (Oct.-Dec. 1971): 341-51.

————. "Problems in Rebuilding the Tribulation Temple," *Bibliotheca Sacra* vol. 129, no. 513 (Jan.-Mar. 1972): 75-80.

Rowley, H. H. "The Herodians in the Gospels." *Journal of Theological Studies* 41 (1940): 14-27.

Smith, Robert Houston. "The Tomb of Jesus." *The Biblical Archaeologist* vol. 30, no. 3 (Sept. 1967): 74-90.

Scripture Index

---

† The boldface page numbers represent the main discussion of that passage. The passages are taken from the smallest subdivision of the text in the overall outline of the book.

Subject Index